ALIGNED WITH
**you
science™**
INDUSTRY CERTIFICATIONS

Managing Your
Personal Finances

8th Edition

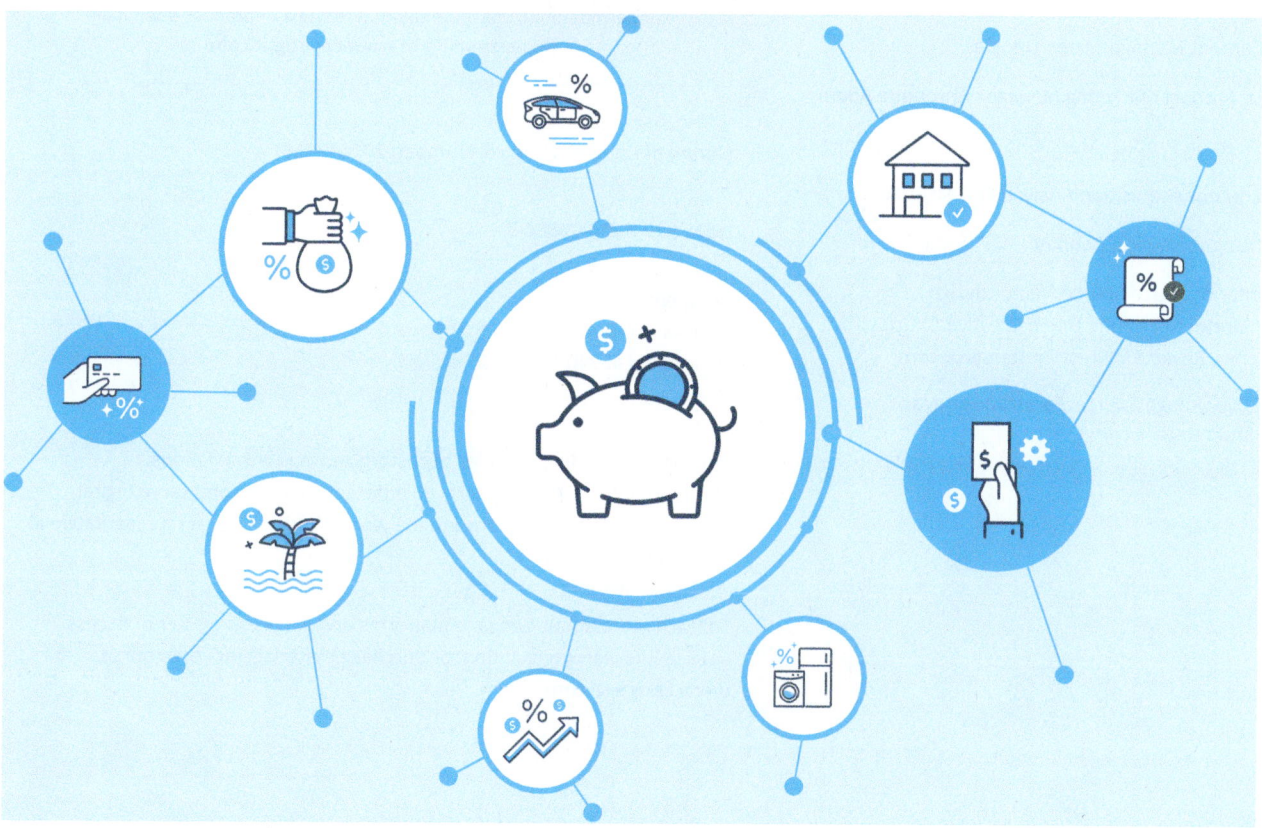

Tamra S. Connor
Ben Owen

✴ **Cengage**

Australia • Brazil • Canada • Mexico • Singapore • United Kingdom • United States

Managing Your Personal Finances,

Eighth Edition

Tamra S. Connor

SVP, Product Management: Cheryl Costantini

VP, Product Management: Audrey Turjanica

Portfolio Product Director: Jason Fremder

Portfolio Product Manager: Lina Hasiba

Associate Portfolio Product Manager: Nick Perry

Product Assistant: Eduarda David

Sr. Learning Designer: Jennifer Starr

Development Editor: Janet Witalec

Content Manager: Jalen Douglas

Sr. Product Marketing Manager: Antonette Adams

Director, Product Marketing: Adam Bolingbroke

Content Acquisition Analyst: Erin McCullough

Designer: Felicia Bennett

Interior Image Source: Vector.design /Shutterstock.com, Helen Creative/Shutterstock .com, Boyko.Pictures/Shutterstock.com

Cover Image Source: Farah Sadikhova /Shutterstock.com

For product information and technology assistance, contact us at
Cengage Customer & Sales Support, 1-800-354-9706
or support.cengage.com.

For permission to use material from this text or product, submit all requests online at **www.copyright.com**.

Library of Congress Control Number: 2024939661

ISBN: 979-8-214-06884-8

Cengage
5191 Natorp Boulevard
Mason, OH 45040
USA

Cengage is a leading provider of customized learning solutions. Our employees reside in nearly 40 different countries and serve digital learners in 165 countries around the world. Find your local representative at **www.cengage.com**.

To learn more about Cengage platforms and services, register or access your online learning solution, or purchase materials for your course, visit **www.cengage.com**.

Printed in the United States of America
Print Number: 03   Print Year: 2025

Dedication

To my amazing husband, Tim, this book is for you, the one who willingly sacrificed weekend adventures so I could work on this project. Your unwavering support is a testament to dedication and love. And let's not forget your humor and occasional nagging, which have kept me both smiling and motivated (sometimes through gritted teeth).

To my dear parents, Johnny and Brenda, your sacrifices and love have shaped me into who I am today.

To my children, Justin and Jessica, thank you for the moments that made me proud and the occasional ones that had me questioning my parenting skills. You keep life interesting in the most entertaining ways!

Last but certainly not least, to my lively, hilarious, and utterly lovable grandchildren, Kaidon, Coltn, Lane, Gage, Levi, and Emerie, you are my greatest treasure, and I am endlessly grateful for the laughter and love you bring into my life.

Brief Contents

Contents

Managing Your Personal Finances, 8e

Managing Your Personal Finances, 8e, prepares students for life's financial responsibilities by emphasizing the skills and knowledge they need to succeed in their roles as citizens, family members, consumers, and participants in the business world. Students will discover new ways to develop financial decision-making skills, set financial and life goals, develop strategies for managing resources, maximize their earning potential, learn skills for the wise use of credit, and gain insight into the different ways of investing money. They will also explore possible career pathways and connect what they are learning to their own long-term goals. Financial well-being and security is emphasized throughout the chapters. The lessons include current trends and issues that are immediately relevant to students, employability skills that support career success, and authentic examples that demonstrate to students how to secure their financial future. Also included are many opportunities for practical application of concepts presented in the chapters, such as chapter- and unit-level projects and additional activities to prepare students for career and technical student organization (CTSO) competitive events related to personal financial literacy. The 8th Edition provides current coverage of timely topics, including social media, health care, postsecondary education options and costs, and identity theft, to increase student awareness of these critical areas related to personal finance. It also aligns to the Jump$tart® National Standards for Personal Financial Education and YouScience® (Precision Exams) Certification Standards for General Financial Literacy and Personal Financial Responsibility.

New To This Edition

Managing Your Personal Finances, 8e, was extensively revised, updated, and reorganized to better align to teacher and student needs. The 8th Edition focuses on financial well-being through real-world and collaborative lessons and activities and offers current and relevant content to enhance the learning experience.

- Technical content was thoroughly revised to reflect the latest practices, information, and issues in personal finance, and to provide relevancy for high school students, including topics such as career exploration and planning, personal decision making and goal setting, long-term financial planning, financial independence, and investing for the future.

- A new chapter focusing on postsecondary education was added to allow students to explore the many options available after high school, understand the factors to consider when making postsecondary education decisions, calculate the costs associated with these opportunities, and explore financial aid and cost-saving options for college or career training.
- Chapter and unit features were re-envisioned to engage students and provide authentic and relevant information and insights to promote personal growth and long-term career and financial success, including both new and newly revised features such as *Consider This, Connections to Your World, Sharpen Your Personal Finance Skills, Sharpen Your Employability Skills, Career Exploration, Unit Projects*, and the *Winning Edge.*
- Assessments were also re-envisioned to build student knowledge and skills through thoughtfully scaffolded questions and activities that progress from lessons to chapters and then culminate in unit projects. Intentionally aligned to the learning objectives, these assessments feature opportunities for students to evaluate their own learning and build employability skills through recall, application, collaboration, and reflection.
- All-new *Unit Profiles* reflect a unique and diverse set of notable individuals who, through dedication and perseverance, have achieved financial success and made significant contributions to their communities.
- Technical content was updated to align to the latest standards, including Jump$tart® and YouScience® Industry Certification Standards for Personal Financial Responsibility and General Financial Literacy.

Transform Your Course with

Measurable Outcomes

> ### Learning Objectives
>
> By the end of this lesson, you should be able to:
>
> LO 12.2.1 Explain the costs associated with postsecondary educational opportunities.
>
> LO 12.2.2 Discuss financial aid and cost-saving options for college or career training.
>
> LO 12.2.3 Complete a Free Application for Federal Student Aid (FAFSA).

Validated Learning Objectives align with content throughout every chapter, providing a clear pathway for learning. Learning objectives are identified at the point of introduction, at all major headings, and in the end-of-lesson and end-of-chapter activities and assessments, making it easier for students to stay on track. Clear, relevant learning objectives provide a strong framework for mastering key concepts and help students focus on what is important so you can better measure outcomes.

Jump$tart® National Standards for Personal Financial Education Aligning to the 2021 Jump$tart® National Standards for Personal Financial Education for Grade 12, and building upon learning in earlier grades, this edition of *Managing Your Personal Finances* ensures that all students have equitable opportunities to deepen their knowledge and skills in financial literacy.

YouScience® Industry Certification Standards (Precision Exams by YouScience®) This edition of *Managing Your Personal Finances* prepares students for careers under the national Finances Career Cluster and fully aligns to the **General Financial Literacy (4501)** and **Personal Financial Responsibility (1002)** industry certifications. These certifications are backed by national industries, offer knowledge standards, and focus on preparing students for the workforce. Visit the accompanying Companion Site for correlations to these industry exams.

Transform Your Course with

Engaging and Relevant Content

Unit 2: Profile

Thasunda Brown Duckett

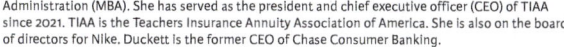

Thasunda Brown Duckett was born in July 1973 in Rochester, New York, and moved to Texas as a child, graduating from Sam Houston High School. She attended the University of Houston and earned a bachelor's degree in finance and marketing. She then attended Baylor University, earning a Master of Business Administration (MBA). She has served as the president and chief executive officer (CEO) of TIAA since 2021. TIAA is the Teachers Insurance Annuity Association of America. She is also on the board of directors for Nike. Duckett is the former CEO of Chase Consumer Banking.

Duckett is the fourth Black woman to be CEO of a Fortune 500 company. The mission of TIAA is financial inclusion and opportunity, which are values she follows in her own life. TIAA provides investment opportunities for millions of Americans who work in the educational sector. Since becoming the CEO, Duckett has expanded the opportunity for retirement savings for all Americans. Duckett serves on the President's Board of Advisors on HBCUs (Historically Black Colleges and Universities). The board advises the president of the United States on federally sponsored programs and how to strengthen HBCUs through the private sector.

She created the Otis and Rosie Brown Foundation. The foundation honors her parents and "recognizes and rewards people who use ordinary means to empower and uplift their communities in extraordinary ways." In 2023, Forbes named Duckett the 34th most powerful woman in the world. She states on her LinkedIn profile that she is "passionate about helping communities of color close achievement gaps in wealth creation, educational outcomes and career success."

Connect and Reflect

Duckett has made a career out of following her passion. Explore how your passions may impact your financial future:

1. What is your passion? Do you have more than one? Brainstorm ways your passion(s) can contribute to your potential career.
2. What type of lifestyle would your potential career allow you? ... adjustments to meet your needs and wants?

Unit Profiles

This feature highlights financially successful individuals who have made a difference in their field, revealing to students how an individual can achieve success through the application of the career and financial concepts presented in the chapters.

Consider This ...

Adohi and Sequoia are finishing their junior year of high school. Both have taken part in career exploration activities and a variety of career and technical education classes while in high school to help them determine a career of interest.

"I really liked my classes this year. They helped me decide that I want to become an electrician or pursue a career in business," Adohi told his friend Sequoia. "That's great," Sequoia replied. "How does that impact your plans after high school?"

"Well, I'm not quite sure. If I want to become an electrician, I need to go to a technical school and complete an apprenticeship. If I decide to pursue business, I need to start taking college classes. I heard that financing trade school is different than college, but I'm not exactly sure how. I think I need to find ways to explore the careers more this year and find someone who can help me better understand what the path and costs for each looks like," stated Adohi. "That sounds like a great plan. They both seem like great careers. Finding more information sooner rather than later would give you a better idea of the advantages and disadvantages of each and help you decide," replied Sequoia.

Connections to Your World
Online Car Shopping

In recent years, many people have begun exploring options to purchase cars online. Buying a car online has especially been embraced by individuals between the ages of 18 and 24 years. There are many different online options for purchasing vehicles; CarGurus, CarMax, and Carvana are all examples of online car shopping websites. As Rya begins her search for a car, she is considering using an online automobile retailer. She has worked with her credit union and knows that she can get an interest rate of 5 percent, maybe better, for her loan. She has also learned that there will be additional cost for...

Connections to Your World

Integrated throughout the chapters, these features align with the topics discussed in lessons and focus on financial issues and situations that are immediately relevant to students.

Consider This ...

Included in each chapter, this feature tells the story of a fictional young person facing a financial decision related to the content in the chapter's lessons. Follow-up questions encourage students to reflect on and think critically about the situation and connect what they are learning to the real world.

Building Career Skills for Financial Success

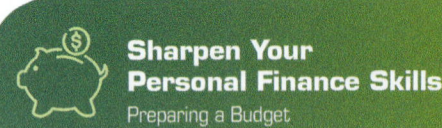

Sharpen Your Personal Finance Skills
Preparing a Budget

Preparing a budget is essential to ensure financial well-being. When you first prepare a budget, it can be a challenging process. You must make sure you include everything, accurately estimate income and expenses, and are realistic about spending habits. This process becomes more complicated when another person is involved. You will likely have to create a budget with another person in the future. Whether that person is roommate or a spouse or partner, it is impor...

Sharpen Your Personal Finance Skills
These features provide students the opportunity to practice and apply core personal finance skills to specific and relevant financial situations.

Sharpen Your Employability Skills
Communication

Take a moment to think of all the ways you interact with others during a normal school day. These interactions require communication skills. As you continue to work toward achieving your career goals, the frequency and impact of communication will increase. The Perkins Collaborative Resource Network states that communication skills "enable employees to successfully perform work tasks by communicating effectively with others in multiple formats." Communication skills are essential for everyone regardless of their career path; more than 80 percent of all work activities involve communication. The forms of communication (verbal, nonverbal, written, and digital) will be explored in greater detail later in this chapter and throughout the remainder of the book.

Sharpen Your Employability Skills
Designed to support students as they prepare for and/or enter the workplace, these features illustrate how developing essential employability skills and career aptitude relates to long-term financial success.

Unit 6: Career Exploration

Reflecting on Your Career of Interest
Once you begin planning for and working toward a career of interest, it is important to periodically reflect on the steps you are taking to prepare yourself and to assess how well the chosen career aligns with your goals.

Reflect and Revisit
Based on the career exploration research and activities you completed in previous units, reflect on your findings to determine how well your chosen careers aligns with your personal interests, skills, and ability to provide your desired standard of living after high school. Write a short reflection essay or create a presentation that addresses, at a minimum, the following

Career Exploration
Included at the end of each unit, this activity provides students with insight into the 16 career and technical education (CTE) Career Clusters and allows them opportunities to explore, develop, and revisit their own personal career plan.

Winning Edge
This feature highlights competitive events held by DECA in personal financial literacy and includes practice role-play activities that prepare students for these competitions.

Unit 4: Winning Edge

Personal Financial Literacy
The Personal Financial Literacy Event measures your personal finance knowledge. Students must be able to apply reliable information and systematic decision making to personal financial decisions. The Personal Financial Literacy Event consists of a financial literacy exam and a role-play scenario with a business executive. Finalists will compete in a second role-play event. Participants will have 10 minutes to review the scenario and develop a professional approach to solving the problem. Participants will have 10 minutes to present their action plan to the judge. After the participant's explanation, the judge can ask questions about the scenario.

Transform Your Course with

Comprehensive Assessment Options

The **Essential Question** at the beginning of each lesson focuses students on the overarching theme of the lesson. The question is revisited in the Lesson Review and includes a summary answer highlighting key takeaways. **Checkpoint** questions throughout lessons also help measure students' recall of the material.

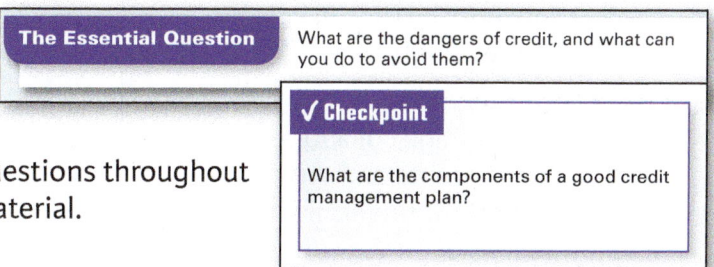

The Essential Question What are the dangers of credit, and what can you do to avoid them?

✓ Checkpoint

What are the components of a good credit management plan?

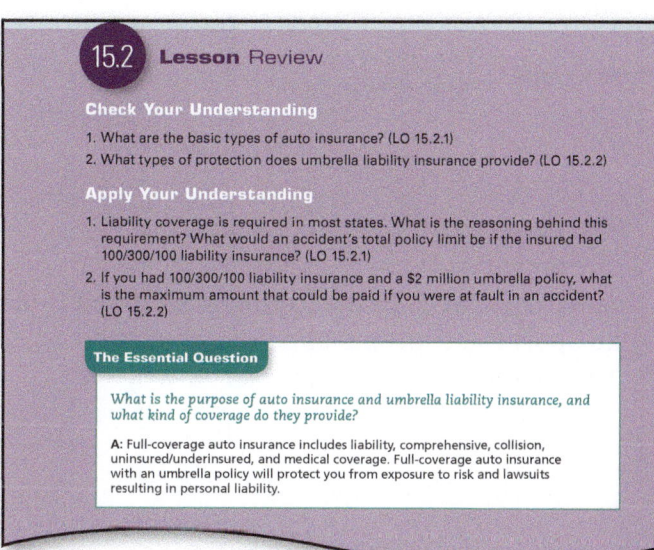

15.2 Lesson Review

Check Your Understanding

1. What are the basic types of auto insurance? (LO 15.2.1)
2. What types of protection does umbrella liability insurance provide? (LO 15.2.2)

Apply Your Understanding

1. Liability coverage is required in most states. What is the reasoning behind this requirement? What would an accident's total policy limit be if the insured had 100/300/100 liability insurance? (LO 15.2.1)
2. If you had 100/300/100 liability insurance and a $2 million umbrella policy, what is the maximum amount that could be paid if you were at fault in an accident? (LO 15.2.2)

The Essential Question

What is the purpose of auto insurance and umbrella liability insurance, and what kind of coverage do they provide?

A: Full-coverage auto insurance includes liability, comprehensive, collision, uninsured/underinsured, and medical coverage. Full-coverage auto insurance with an umbrella policy will protect you from exposure to risk and lawsuits resulting in personal liability.

Lesson Review

At the end of each lesson are assessments and activities that focus on the key concepts presented in the lesson. These include:

- **Check Your Understanding** questions evaluate if students have learned and understood the key concepts.

- **Apply Your Understanding** activities evaluate if students can apply the key concepts in context of a specific financial situation.

Chapter Review

At the end of each chapter are assessments and activities that focus on the key concepts presented in each lesson in the chapter. These include:

- **Check Your Knowledge** questions evaluate if students learned the key concepts and retained them across lessons.

- **Apply Your Knowledge** activities evaluate if students can connect the key concepts learned in each lesson in a meaningful way.

- **Share Your Knowledge** group activities encourage collaboration among students and serve to develop important financial and employability skills.

- **Connect and Reflect** activities encourage students to reflect on what they are learning in context of their current life and future goals.

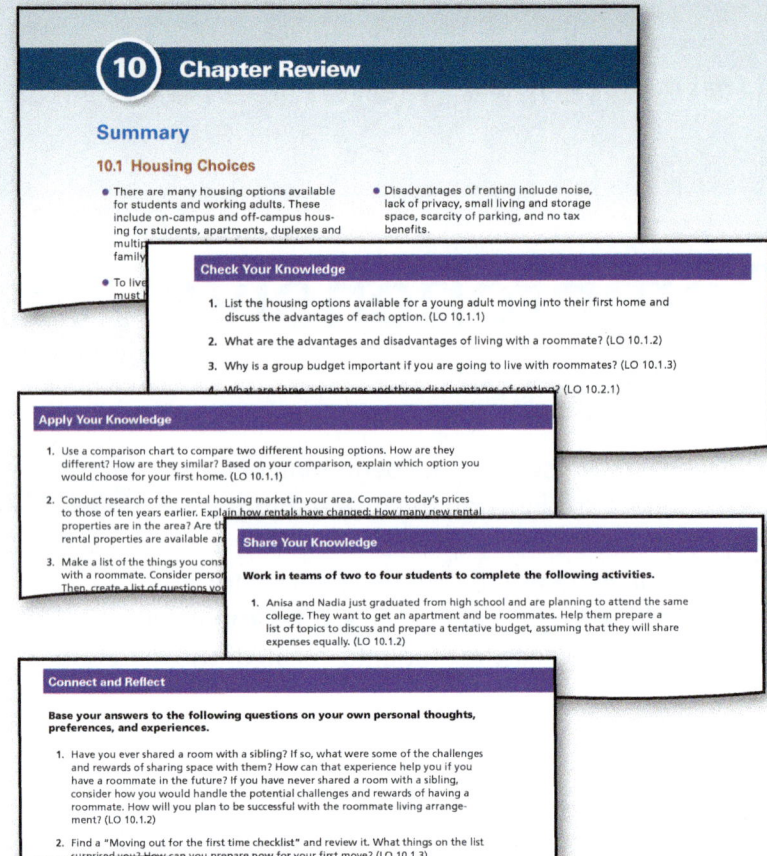

Chapter and Unit Projects Appearing at the end of each chapter and each unit is a summative activity that prompts students to apply the concepts and skills presented in that section.

Cengage Testing by Cognero is a flexible online system that allows instructors to author, edit, and manage test bank content from multiple Cengage solutions, create multiple test versions in an instant, and deliver tests from their learning management system or classroom. Continue on to learn more about our digital solutions.

Transform Your Course with

Solutions That Enhance Teaching and Learning

MindTap for *Managing Your Personal Finances*, 8e

The MindTap for *Managing Your Personal Finances*, 8e, features an integrated course offering a complete digital experience for the student and teacher. This MindTap is highly customizable and combines the enhanced ebook along with interactivities, auto-graded quizzing, and additional activities to enable students to directly analyze and apply what they are learning and allow teachers to measure skills and outcomes with ease.

- A Guide: Relevant interactivities combined with prescribed readings, featured multimedia, and quizzing to evaluate progress will guide students from basic knowledge and comprehension to analysis and application.

- Personalized Teaching: Teachers can control course content—hiding content, rearranging existing content, or adding and creating their own content to meet the needs of their specific program.

- Promote Better Outcomes: Through relevant and engaging content, assignments, and activities, students can build the confidence they need to ultimately lead them to success. Likewise, teachers can view analytics and reports that provide a snapshot of class progress, time in course, engagement, and completion rates.

The enhanced ebook includes highlighting and note-taking features, read-speaker, both English and Spanish definitions at point of reference, and hyperlinked figures and tables to increase comprehension.

Student Workbook

The *Student Workbook to accompany Managing Your Personal Finances*, 8e, supports classroom learning. Featuring a series of questions and activities, each chapter includes questions that evaluate student knowledge of financial concepts presented in each lesson, along with a set of exploratory and/or practice activities that enable students to practice these concepts through practical, real-world application. For this edition, the workbook has been thoroughly revised to reflect new content in the student edition, and questions have been intentionally scaffolded and refined to offer opportunities for students to build their confidence as they learn key concepts.

Companion Site

The companion site offers online access to tools and content for teaching and learning.

- The **Teacher Resource Guide** includes important resources for the teacher such as lesson plans that outline key topics in each lesson and align to the learning objectives; student edition narrative content and the accompanying PowerPoint® slides; additional activities to engage students; and insight into how to differentiate learning, enrich the learning experience, and encourage further exploration among students.

- **Solution and Answer Guides** are provided for both the student edition and the accompanying student workbook, consisting of solutions and answers to all the activities and assessments appearing in these two offerings.

- **PowerPoint® presentations** align to the learning objectives and lesson plans and include photographs and illustrations to visually reinforce the key points in each chapter.

- **Worksheets** that support the projects in the student edition are also available to be downloaded from the Companion Site.

- **Testing powered by Cognero** offers a bank of auto-graded questions for teachers to evaluate student comprehension. Questions align to learning objectives and narrative content in the student edition and include a variety of question types. Cognero is a flexible online system that allows instructors to author, edit, and manage test bank content from a learning management system or the classroom.

- **Jump$tart® Correlation** aligns the content in *Managing Your Personal Finances, 8e*, to the **National Standards for Personal Financial Education**.

- **YouScience® Correlations** align the content in *Managing Your Personal Finances, 8e*, to the **General Financial Literacy** and **Personal Financial Literacy** exams.

- The **Transition Guide** outlines the revisions and enhancements that occurred between the seventh and eighth editions.

- The **MindTap Educator Guide** describes the assets that are available in the accompanying MindTap, including the intent, the relevancy to the student, and estimated seat time for completion.

- The **Guide to Teaching Online** offers practical technological and pedagogical advice to teachers who choose to teach online in an asynchronous mode or utilize a combination of synchronous and asynchronous methodologies.

About the Author

TAMRA CONNOR (née Tamra Davis) is an innovative and creative education specialist whose career has spanned almost four decades. Raised in rural Oklahoma, she was the first in her family to attend university. Tamra earned a bachelor's degree in business administration from Oklahoma State University, majoring in business education. She returned to her home high school as a business teacher to begin her teaching career. She continued her education, earning a Master of Science in Business Education from the prestigious College of Business at Oklahoma State. After teaching high school for 11 years, she began teaching at a local community college while working toward her PhD in occupational education from Oklahoma State. She joined the faculty at Illinois State University in 2011, where she had the privilege of teaching future business teachers. Tamra is an accomplished researcher, teacher, and administrator. She is the Associate Dean for Accreditation and Operations in the College of Business at Illinois State. She has taught thousands of students throughout her career, many of whom are currently teaching across the United States. In addition to teaching, she has owned several businesses and served as an educational consultant. She is active in many professional associations and has served in multiple leadership roles. Outside of her work, Tamra enjoys writing, capturing light through photography, and traveling.

Tamra S. Connor

About the Contributing Author

BEN OWEN is a versatile professional with a unique blend of business acumen and a passion for education. Graduating with a bachelor's degree in organizational management from Northern Illinois University, he later pursued and earned his Master of Business Administration from Bradley University. Ben's career in the business industry spanned almost 5 years, during which he held various roles in operations management and human resources. Ben's trajectory shifted when he was invited to work with local students on workforce preparation, which ignited his passion for education. This led him to pursue a bachelor's degree in business education from Illinois State University, which set the stage for a full-time transition into education. Ben's journey in education commenced as a high school business and technology teacher, and since then, he has assumed diverse roles, including positions in Multi-Tiered System of Supports (MTSS), building administration, as a CTE Educator in partnership with the Illinois State Board of Education, and as an executive board member of the Illinois Association for Career and Technical Education. Ben has also earned a master's degree in education leadership. Presently, Ben serves as an administrator for college and career readiness in a district serving nearly 21,000 students in grades K–12, where he continues to make a significant impact on the future of education and workforce preparedness.

Acknowledgments

The authors and Cengage wish to thank the individuals who provided feedback and assistance during the preparation of this edition. Reviewers who contributed their expertise include:

Marsha Iverson
Associate Professor and Program Director
Hofstra University School of Education
Personal Finance Specialist for the New York City
Public Schools

James Russell Smith, Jr.
Senior Director, Teaching and Learning
Wake Technical Community College

1 Unit

Managing Careers and Money

Source: Hxdbzxy/Shutterstock.com

1 Career Exploration and Planning and the Changing Work Environment

2 Pay, Benefits, and Work

3 Taxes

4 Banking and Investing

Unit 1 covers career exploration and prepares you for financial security by laying the foundation for future success. When selecting a career path, it is important to understand how to set education and career goals, develop effective career planning techniques, prepare for an ever-changing work environment, and understand the career outlook for your chosen field. Once you have a job and begin to earn income, learning how to prepare a budget and calculate net worth will allow you to make good financial decisions and achieve your financial goals. It is also important to learn how to evaluate and manage your paycheck; the benefits you may receive; the taxes you pay; and the banking services you will need, including how to manage your accounts and the savings options available to you. The skills learned in Unit 1 will allow you to set goals, develop a career and financial plan, and learn the basics of money management, giving you the foundation to develop more advanced decision-making and problem-solving skills that will be required as you manage your personal finances.

Source: DFree/Shutterstock.com

Tim Cook

Timothy Cook was born in Mobile, Alabama, on November 1, 1960. He grew up in Robertsdale, Alabama, where his father was a shipyard worker, and his mother worked in a pharmacy. He went to Auburn University for his undergraduate degree in industrial engineering and earned his master of business administration (MBA) at Duke University.

Cook became the chief executive officer (CEO) of Apple, Inc. in 2011. He had been the chief operating officer (COO) under Steve Jobs, Apple cofounder. Cook advocates for political reform related to international and domestic surveillance, cybersecurity, American manufacturing, and environmental preservation. He is also a savvy businessperson. Between 2011 and 2020, he doubled Apple's revenues and profit. Under his tenure, Apple has grown in value from just under $350 billion to almost $2 trillion. Cook also serves on the board of directors for Nike and the National Football Foundation as well as the board of trustees for Duke University. Cook was the first CEO of a Fortune 500 company to publicly announce that he is gay, writing in an essay for *Bloomberg Businessweek* that "while I have never denied my sexuality, I haven't publicly acknowledged it either, until now: I'm proud to be gay."

Cook began his career at Apple in 1998 after meeting Steve Jobs. He considered Jobs a creative genius, and working with him at Apple was a once-in-a-lifetime opportunity. Cook found ways to keep costs under control and help generate huge profits as leader of Apple. In 2021, Cook was named to the *Time* 100, a list of the 100 most influential people in the world. He has received numerous awards during his career, including the Human Rights Campaign's Visibility Award and the Courage Against Hate Award from the Anti-Defamation League. Before joining the team at Apple, Inc., Cook worked at Compaq and IBM. He plans to leave his fortune to charity.

Cook has a unique leadership style. He begins his day with email at 4:30 a.m. and has held Sunday-night staff meetings to prepare for the week ahead. He shared his leadership philosophy, which is focused on people, strategy, and execution: "If you get those three right, the world is a great place."

Connect and Reflect

Cook is known for his democratic leadership style that is focused on cooperation. He has also emphasized workplace skills such as curiosity, creativity, and collaboration. Explore how these skills are important in a changing work environment:

1. In your own words, what do you think Cook meant when he said that if you get people, strategy, and execution right, the world is a great place?

2. Why do you think Cook places such importance on collaboration?

3. What workplace skills do you think are most important, now and in the future? Explain.

4. How can you incorporate the development of these skills into your career planning?

1 Chapter

Career Exploration and Planning and the Changing Work Environment

1.1 Career Exploration and Planning

The Essential Question

What factors are important to consider when exploring and planning for a career?

Learning Objectives

By the end of this lesson, you should be able to:

LO 1.1.1 Describe effective career exploration and planning techniques for an employee.

LO 1.1.2 Explain the importance of career exploration and planning for self-employment.

Key Terms

- goal
- short-term goal
- intermediate-term goal
- long-term goal
- experience
- self-employment
- entrepreneur
- side business
- lifestyle business
- venture business
- business plan

Consider This ...

"I'm trying to get my first job and have no idea where to start," Emy told her friend Carlos. "I remembered you've been working at your job for over a year and was hoping you could give me some tips."

"I'd be happy to help," said Carlos. "One thing I learned is that it is so important to have quality application materials and be prepared for an interview. You can really stand out by doing these things."

"Thanks, Carlos! That's great advice," Emy replied. "Is there anything else you would suggest?"

"There is one other thing to consider," Carlos stated. "Explore things you may be interested in now. Try to find a job that will allow you to develop skills that align with your career goals. Even if the job you have now does not turn into a lifelong career, you can use this opportunity to develop valuable skills that will help you in the future."

Read and Reflect

1. Do you agree that the advice that Carlos gave Emy is helpful?
2. Is there any other advice you would give Emy?

Employee Career Planning

Planning for your future career is an important task. Consider the total time spent working: 8 hours a day; 5 days a week; over 2,000 hours each year, not including any overtime. If you work an average career span of 45 years (from age 22 to age 67), you will spend approximately 100,000 hours or more on the job! Because your work will likely take so much of your time, you will need to plan your career carefully.

Steps in Career Planning

Effective career planning involves careful investigation and analysis—a process that you should start now and revisit throughout your work life. The steps in career planning involve self-analysis, research, action planning, and periodic re-evaluation.

Self-Analysis

Using resources available from schools, employment offices, testing services, and the internet, explore personal factors that relate to your career choice.

1. Determine your wants and needs.
2. Determine your values and desired lifestyle.
3. Assess your aptitudes and interests, then determine how they match job skills.
4. Analyze your personal qualities and the kinds of jobs that best suit your personality.

Research

Based on a good self-analysis, determine the careers that best suit your interests and aptitudes and that will help you meet your lifestyle goals.

Why is self-analysis a necessary component of career planning?

Source: iStock.com/dusanpetkovic

1. Seek information from a variety of sources that are available from libraries, career counseling centers, and employment offices.
2. Compare your interests, aptitudes, and personal qualities to job descriptions and requirements.
3. Talk to people in the fields of work you find interesting. These informal discussions reveal positive and negative features of a career that you might not have anticipated.
4. Observe occupations, learn about jobs and companies, and seek part-time work to get direct experience. Sometimes following someone throughout their workday will give you real insight into a career's daily activities and requirements.
5. Intern or volunteer at a business that interests you.

Action Planning

After doing job research, develop a plan of action that will eventually bring you to your career goals.

1. Use good job-search techniques. Get organized, plan, follow through, and be persistent.
2. Develop necessary skills by taking courses (traditional or online) and gaining exposure to the field in which you want to pursue a career.

3. Seek a part-time or volunteer job to gain experience in your area of choice.
4. Evaluate your choices over time. People change and so do jobs. If you discover you are following the wrong career path, make a change by learning new skills and developing new talents.

Re-Evaluation

Because the world changes rapidly, we all need to prepare ourselves to meet the challenges ahead. You may wish to prepare for career changes to take advantage of new opportunities. About every 5 years, think about what you will be doing and where you would like to be in the next 5 years.

The Importance of Goals

A **goal** is a desired end toward which efforts are directed. Goals provide a sense of direction and purpose in life. There are three types of goals: short term, intermediate, and long term.

- A **short-term goal** is one you expect to reach in a few days or weeks. A short-term goal could be to achieve at least a B on next week's math test. You know you must plan study time to meet your goal.
- An **intermediate-term goal** is something you wish to accomplish in the next few months or in the next year. Some examples are graduating from high school, going on a vacation, and finding summer employment. These goals take longer to achieve and require more planning.
- A **long-term goal** is what you wish to achieve in the next year or longer. It could involve completing post-secondary education or college, starting your career, getting married, or starting a family. Many people find it helpful to write down long-term goals and revisit them frequently to evaluate their progress.

If goals are to be meaningful, they should be well-defined and realistic. They should also be written down to become a part of your life. If you are like most people, your goals will change every few years, either because you have accomplished them or because your values have changed. You may decide to take a different path. Many people find a checklist a handy way to help them reach their goals. **Figure 1.1** shows a typical goals checklist. Use it as a guide to create your own goals checklist.

When developing your short-term, intermediate-term, and long-term goals, it is advantageous to create SMART goals, which focus on five critical components that increase your chances of success. These goals, when carefully crafted, are **S**pecific, **M**easurable, **A**ttainable, **R**elevant, and **T**ime-bound.

The Roles of Experience and Education

In today's highly competitive job market, experience and education play key roles in protecting and enhancing your employability. For many careers, applicants will need a college or technical degree and skills before being considered for employment.

Experience

Experience is the knowledge and skills acquired from working in a career field. As you gain experience in a field, you become more valuable to an employer. Most employers give wage increases that reflect the increased value of an employee's experience. However, when you change career fields, you no longer have the advantage of experience. You may need to accept a lower wage as you work to gain experience in your new career field.

Figure 1.1   Goals Checklist

GOALS CHECKLIST

Week of _____

Accomplished

Short-term goals (today/this week):

1. *Buy birthday gift for mom*   _____

2. *Get haircut (Saturday)*   _____

3. *See counselor about chemistry class*   _____

Intermediate-term goals (next month/year)

1. *Get a C or better in chemistry*   _____

2. *Prepare for SAT (test in May)*   _____

3. *Finish class project (due December 14)*   _____

Long-term goals (future)

1. *Graduate from college*   _____

2. *Buy a car*   _____

3. *Get a full-time job*   _____

Education

A post-secondary or college degree may make you more attractive to employers. Post-secondary education can be obtained through a trade school, community college, or 4-year college or university degree. A degree, certificate, or industry credential focused on the area in which you will work is even more critical. A recent study shows that some degrees will give you a very limited match to available jobs. For example, college degrees in anthropology, history, or the humanities may interest you, but jobs in these areas may not be in demand or pay well.

As your level of education increases, your earnings usually increase with it. Many young people today are delaying entering the workforce to stay in college longer and obtain an advanced degree. An advanced degree is a specialized, intensive program (taken after obtaining a bachelor's degree) that prepares students for higher-level work responsibilities with more challenges and often higher pay. An advanced degree may include a master's degree, a doctorate in a specialized field, or a professional degree. Many medical fields require a professional degree.

The Need for a Plan B

Many people find it to their advantage to be prepared for the worst while they are hoping for the best. Job security is a thing of the past in many jobs and industries. Thus, workers need to look out for themselves so they do not end up unemployed and lacking the skills or qualifications needed for other jobs.

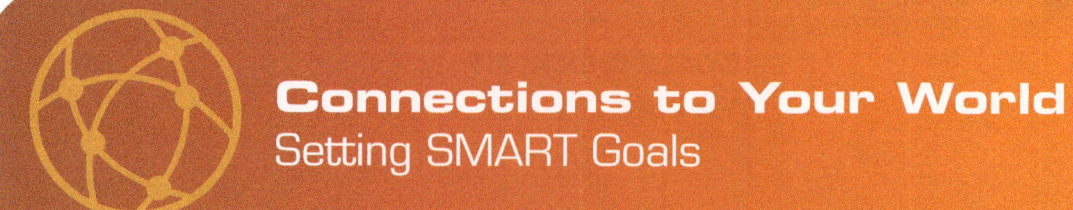
Goal setting is important to help you successfully plan and prepare for a career; it also helps you accomplish other things you want in life. A SMART goal is a specific type of goal that ensures necessary components are present to increase the likelihood of meeting your goal. The five components of a SMART goal help ensure that the goal is specific, measurable, achievable, relevant, and time-bound. You can find a brief description of each component of a SMART goal below:

SMART Goal Component	What Does This Mean?
Specific	The outcome of the goal is clearly outlined.
Measurable	The goal is quantifiable. Progress and result can be tracked against desired outcome.
Attainable	The goal must be realistic. You must have the ability to obtain the desired outcome.
Relevant	For personal goals, the goal must be important to you. For business goals, the goal must align with what the company is trying to accomplish.
Time-bound	The goal should a clear timeframe for completion.

You can read more about SMART goals and see examples by visiting the Forbes Advisor website at: https://www.forbes.com/advisor/business/smart-goals/

Think Critically

1. Think about a goal that you may have achieved in the past. Did your goal contain one or more of the five components of SMART goals? If so, do you believe that they contributed to your success in reaching the goal? Why or why not?

2. Think about a goal that you may have set for yourself that you did *not* achieve. Based on the SMART goal format, is there anything you could have done differently to help you achieve your goal?

Plan B is the label used to describe what you would do if your job ended. For example, you might do the following:

- Get a part-time job. In addition to your full-time job, take a part-time job where you can learn new skills, add value, and do something you enjoy.
- Work a hobby. Learn how to do something well—to the point that you could make a living doing it if your full-time job ended.
- Develop networking contacts. Networks are informal groups of people with common interests. Keep in touch with people who would know about openings in a field where you are qualified and would like to work.
- Learn new skills. In addition to your current job skills, lifelong learning opportunities will allow you to develop new job proficiencies to qualify for advancement at your current employer or some other employer. These added skills will give you opportunities to change jobs if needed.
- Be aware. Know what's happening with your company and your industry. As changes occur, look for ways to adapt or move on.

> ✓ **Checkpoint**
>
> How do experience and education impact your career planning goals?

LO 1.1.2   Self-Employment

Working for yourself is called **self-employment**. A person who takes the risks of being self-employed and owning a business is called an **entrepreneur**. Small businesses contribute billions of dollars to the U.S. economy annually and employ more workers than the country's large corporations combined. Owning a business can be challenging, but it can be very rewarding as well.

Advantages of Self-Employment

A significant advantage of being the owner is that you make decisions about how the business is run. The owner can say what the business will and will not do, including the choice of products and services that will be offered. This also includes the hours of operation, the customer base the business will serve, and the prices it will charge. Small business owners also keep the profits of the business in the form of income that represents revenues earned by the business minus the expenses of doing business.

Disadvantages of Self-Employment

If the business fails, money invested in the business is lost. Most money invested in a small business comes from the owner and/or the owner's family and friends.

Owning a small business is risky because it can be challenging to obtain credit. In many cases, the owner must use their personal credit, including credit cards, a home equity line of credit (HELOC), or personal or business loans to start and keep the business running. Credit cards and HELOC loans have higher interest rates because there is more risk to the lenders.

With most small businesses, especially during the first few years, the owner works

Why do you think some people prefer to work for themselves?

long hours and does many different tasks to ensure the business succeeds. Most of the profits are put back into the business rather than the owner's pocket. And because money is tight, the owner cannot always hire others to do the work.

Types of Small Businesses

There are three basic types of small businesses. A **side business** is where the owner pursues their passion, hobby, or secondary occupation, while working full-time for an employer. The side business consumes the owner's personal or spare time. It does not grow into a business that can be sold; most often, it is run from the owner's home. Business activities are conducted "on the side."

A **lifestyle business** is one that provides a good income for the owner and allows them more freedom to meet personal needs. The business is typically a full-time job for the owner, but they intend to keep the business small. The business exists for the owner's lifetime and usually has no resale value. For example, a dentist may elect to be a one-dentist office and provide services for their patients. When the dentist retires, the business closes.

Other business owners want their businesses to grow into large companies with unlimited growth potential—this type of business is called a **venture business**. As it grows, the business will eventually become a corporation with many employees. For example, Phil Knight started a business designing athletic shoes in his garage in Eugene, Oregon. When his business grew, it became a publicly held corporation known as Nike. Unlike other small business owners, a venture business owner has an "exit plan" so that others can continue operating the business when they decide to leave. The business owner becomes one of the many stockholders and steps down from running the business.

Getting Started in Business

Certain cultures encourage entrepreneurship more than others. Also, people whose parents owned a small business are more likely to start a business than those whose parents worked for someone else. Often, entrepreneurs work for other businesses to gain needed knowledge and experience. Many business owners seek formal and/or informal education about running a business before starting their own company.

If you want to run your own business, you should spend time preparing yourself

© Monkey Business Images/Shutterstock.com

to be successful. A good place to start is to talk with the advisers at a Small Business Development Center (SBDC). These centers are in cities across the country and are sponsored and funded by the U.S. Small Business Administration (SBA). Visit the SBA's website to learn about its services. Another good resource is SCORE, a foundation that works with the SBA and offers accessible business mentoring services from both active and retired business executives from a wide array of backgrounds.

Business Planning

Before starting a business, many small business owners conduct planning to assess the viability of the business or to help attract investors to fund the business. A traditional **business plan** is an extensive document that outlines the path a business intends to take to earn and grow revenues. In recent years, it has become more common to move away from a traditional business plan and utilize more streamlined planning tools that focus on high-level, essential components. The Small Business Association (SBA) refers to this as a lean startup plan. Lean startup plans and other streamlined planning tools,

Why do entrepreneurs need to keep good records to be successful business owners?

Source: iStock.com/Paul Bradbury

such as the Business Model Canvas, can be more easily updated as things change to ensure they provide an accurate snapshot of business operations or plans at any given point in time. The Small Business Association website offers templates, resources, and guidance for writing both a traditional business plan and a lean startup plan.

Is Entrepreneurship Right for You?

How can you decide whether being an entrepreneur is the right choice for you? Your answers to the following questions will give you a better idea of whether you should consider self-employment.

1. Are you self-motivated? Business owners must do what needs to be done without being told or reminded. They enjoy making their own decisions.
2. Do you like people? A friendly disposition goes a long way in winning over customers. You should be able to get along with others.
3. Are you a leader? Entrepreneurs can get others to follow their lead. They are confident and persuasive.
4. Do you take responsibility? Entrepreneurs take charge and follow through.
5. Are you organized? Business owners must have a good plan before they get started.
6. Do you work hard? To be a successful business owner, you must lead by example. Business owners work long, hard hours. They do not expect others to do what they themselves are unwilling to do.
7. Do you make decisions easily and quickly? Decisions sometimes must be made on the spot without complete or up-to-date information.
8. Are you trustworthy? Others must trust you and accept that you are knowledgeable. Long-term relationships are built on honesty.

9. Are you persistent? Business owners persevere, even when the going gets tough. They meet goals without giving excuses.
10. Do you keep good records? Entrepreneurs must account for their expenses and revenues and pay taxes based on this data. They should understand profitability and cost analyses.

If you have a good business idea, start the process early. Get your thoughts and plans on paper, get advice from those you trust, and work toward your dream of owning your own business. A small business owner is a risk-taker. You must be willing to take financial and personal risks. It will not be easy, but the payoff can be very rewarding!

✓ **Checkpoint**

Why is career planning important for people who want to be entrepreneurs or self-employed?

Check Your Understanding

1. Goals can be short-term, intermediate-term, or long-term goals. What do each of these terms mean, and why are they important in career exploration and planning? (LO 1.1.1)

2. What is a SMART goal, and why would you write a SMART goal for each of the terms above? (LO 1.1.1)

3. What is meant by a Plan B? Why is it important? (LO 1.1.1)

4. What are the three types of small businesses? Describe each of them. (LO 1.1.2)

5. What are the advantages and disadvantages of self-employment? (LO 1.1.2)

Apply Your Understanding

1. Develop a career plan for a career path you might wish to explore after high school. (LO 1.1.1)

2. If you are considering becoming an entrepreneur (owning your own business), what steps would you take before you make that commitment? Outline how you would develop your business idea. Would you want a side business, a lifestyle business, or a venture business? Explain. (LO 1.1.2)

The Essential Question

What factors are important to consider when exploring and planning for a career?

A: To prepare for a career, begin by exploring careers that meet your personal values, goals, and aptitudes, then develop a career plan, set goals, continue your education or training, and develop a Plan B. As an entrepreneur, make sure self-employment is right for you; start small and get advice from trusted consultants, such as the Small Business Association (SBA).

The Essential Question   How can you be successful in an ever-changing work environment?

Learning Objectives

By the end of this lesson, you should be able to:

LO 1.2.1   Identify ways you can be prepared for a changing work environment.

LO 1.2.2   Explain the benefits of diverse work schedule models.

LO 1.2.3   Describe the importance of unions and professional work associations in the workplace.

Key Terms

- life-work balance
- lifelong learning
- professional development
- upgrading
- retraining
- self-assessment inventory
- remote work
- flextime
- compressed workweek
- job rotation
- job sharing
- union
- bargaining
- seniority
- right-to-work laws
- lobbying

Consider This ...

On her way to work, Emy stopped at the local coffee shop for coffee. As she was waiting for her order, she heard her friend Carlos say, "Hey, Emy! How's the new job going?"

Emy replied, "It's going great! I'm learning a lot, and I'm almost done with my training, which means I'll have more flexibility with my schedule soon. Once I am done with training, I can work remotely 2 to 3 days a week if I want to. So now, I'm trying to decide how to structure my schedule."

"That's great that you have the flexibility," Carlos replied. "I don't think that I would be as productive if I worked remotely, but I know it works great for some people."

Read and Reflect

1. Why are more companies allowing employees to work remotely or have flexible schedules?

2. What are potential benefits and challenges of working remotely?

LO 1.2.1 Coping with Change

With rapidly advancing technologies, change is certain. You have three options when it comes to change: You can accept it, reject it, or ignore it. If you accept change, you can help shape it. If you reject change, you may not be able to control the outcome, and the change may happen regardless of your decision. If you ignore change, you will be left behind. You will end up frustrated, unemployed, or both by rejecting or ignoring change. You can be aware of changes by staying informed, becoming a lifelong learner, and taking classes to stay up to date. By completing a self-assessment, you can make an action plan that will enable you to cope with and reduce the stress of uncertainty.

Stay Informed

Staying current with the latest technologies and advancements is a long-term commitment. You should stay aware of new and emerging trends, whether they will impact you directly or not. The more you know about what is happening, the more you benefit. For example, electronic medical records (EMR) have become the norm in recent years. The benefit of EMR is that you should receive better, more efficient care. However, your privacy can be compromised more quickly, meaning sensitive information about you can be exposed through an information breach. By being aware of this, you can take steps to help prevent the misuse of your data.

Various resources report national and international trends related to technology, politics, the economy, climate, and jobs. Information is available online and in the news about any topic, allowing you to stay current with what is happening in the United States and worldwide. You can also attend conferences, expos, and other events that discuss emerging trends and cutting-edge technology. Participate and be active in the changes. Casting your vote and being politically active may help preserve your rights.

Be a Lifelong Learner

Today's younger workers want to explore careers and work in companies where they can find fair compensation while maintaining a positive **life–work balance** where the employee places as much emphasis on personal life goals as they do on career goals. They prefer to explore careers instead of climbing the corporate ladder as their parents often did. Hopping from one job to another is more accepted now than in the past. The knowledge and skills required in the workplace change over time, and job hopping helps today's workers learn new skills and develop additional talents. **Lifelong learning** means seeking new knowledge, skills, and experiences to add to your professional and personal growth. You can join professional associations and service organizations that will inform you of what is new in specific job areas. You can attend workshops and seminars to learn about current trends. Attending these events will help make you a more knowledgeable and engaging person and increase your opportunities to interact with others in your profession. Lifelong learning is essential to successful career management and can affect your lifetime income.

Updating Your Skills Through Professional Development

Sometimes technology brings change that requires new skills—skills you cannot learn by yourself. When this happens, it is time to actively seek new knowledge by learning new skills through formal classroom education, seminars, and online learning modules. Collectively, updating your skills is called **professional development** in the business world.

Upgrading means advancing to a higher skill level to increase your usefulness to an employer. Many jobs, especially those affected by technological improvements, require regular employee upgrading.

Retraining involves learning new and different skills so that an employee can retain the same level of employability. Community college and career-technical training are geared as much toward retraining displaced employees as toward preparing employees for entry-level positions. There are numerous sources of retraining:

- Many companies offer technical courses to retrain their employees. Those who volunteer and are eager to learn will position themselves for advancement.
- Training is available through technical schools, career and technical centers, job placement services, business colleges, and community colleges. Many employers reimburse employees for the cost of classes related to their jobs.
- Online learning is one of the most popular ways to upgrade your skills. Employer-sponsored training is often free for employees.

Complete a Self-Assessment

As you go through life, your needs and values will change. Looking inward to

Why do employees need to update their skills through professional development?

iStock.com/skynesher

define what is important to you and then using this knowledge to plan your future is essential. You should consider what you like doing, what you do well, and what skills and knowledge you want to enhance. For example, you might want to strengthen your understanding of the latest technologies. By learning how to use the newest form of social media, you can communicate with others more effectively. Being more tech-savvy can also help you perform better on the job.

You can find many self-assessment questionnaires at online career sites or by searching with the keyword *self-assessment*.

A **self-assessment inventory** lists your strong points and areas of needed growth and development. It will also include your plan for improvement. As you improve your weak points, they become strengths in your inventory.

Ask another person to assess your strengths and weaknesses objectively. A different point of view helps clarify your self-assessment. Also, many high schools, colleges, and technical training institutes assist with self-assessment inventories.

✓ Checkpoint

What are ways you can cope with change in the workplace?

LO 1.2.2 The Changing Work Environment

The digital age has brought new opportunities and challenges for employers and the employees they hire. As needs have evolved, many new work models have been developed to reduce employee burnout, increase safety, and lower costs for employers. The COVID pandemic accelerated the pace of change in working environments, primarily introducing remote or work-from-home policies in business.

Companies have developed alternative working times and conditions as they explore new work models for increasing efficiency and effectiveness. Many businesses have realized that the standard workweek (8 hours a day, 5 days a week) no longer meets their needs to provide quality customer service and products. Newer work models allow more flexibility for both the employer and the employee.

Remote Work and Work-from-Home

Advances in technology have made it possible for many employees to work from home. **Remote work** is a working model that allows employees to work offsite and remain in contact with their employers through technology. Often these employees can complete work tasks using cloud computing and video conferencing. Work can be deposited in an internet cloud site and accessed by both the employer and the remote employee, regardless of location. This technology eliminates the need for storage on a hard drive, desktop, or other location that cannot be accessed remotely.

Some remote workers travel extensively and require flexibility. Employees who work from home must be responsible for managing their schedules and submitting work promptly. Companies that allow work from home have procedures and policies that employees must follow.

Flexible Schedules and Compressed Workweeks

Flextime is a work schedule that allows employees to choose their working hours within a defined time limit. While all employees generally are needed during core periods, such as times of high customer volume, employees on flextime can choose their other work hours to meet their needs. For example, an employee with young children might choose to start work at 10 a.m. after the children are in school instead of at the standard starting time of 9 a.m. Assuming that the core hours are between 10 a.m. and 3 p.m., employees could arrange their workdays to arrive and depart outside the peak times. Flexible schedules may also include a mixture of work-from-home and working in person.

A **compressed workweek** is a work schedule that fits the standard 40-hour workweek into less than 5 days. The typical compressed workweek is 10 hours a day for 4 days, followed by 3 days off. In some employment fields, such as the medical professions, doctors, nurses, and other staff work three 12-hour shifts per week and are paid for 40 hours. A compressed workweek gives employees more time to get their job done. Some types of work are better suited to this type of schedule than others.

Flextime and compressed workweeks are good for business because employees are responsible for working their standard hours regardless of when they arrive or leave the job. Employees are satisfied and motivated because they can fulfill their needs, such as attending doctor's appointments. Flextime and compressed schedules reduce the stress caused by trying to balance work time and personal time.

Job Rotation

Job rotation is a job design in which employees are trained to do more than one specialized task. They regularly rotate from one task to another. This approach gives employees more variety in what they do daily, often making work more satisfying. A significant advantage for employers and employees is that information and ideas are freely exchanged, thus improving efficiency. When more than one employee is skilled at a particular job, others can keep the work flowing if a colleague is absent.

Job Sharing

Job sharing is a job design in which two people share one full-time position. They split the salary and benefits according to each person's contributions. Job sharing is desirable to people who want part-time work while raising children or handling other family responsibilities. By allowing employees to meet their personal needs, job sharing reduces absenteeism and lowers fatigue, thus improving productivity. It also gives the employer more than one person skilled in a particular job or task.

Permanent Part-Time

Today's labor force comprises more people who desire to work only part-time. Working part-time generally means working 16 to 25 hours a week. Companies can reduce absenteeism and fatigue while saving money on salaries and benefits by hiring part-time employees. Part-time employees may receive some employment benefits, but their health insurance needs are typically met through some other source. The part-time employee has the flexibility to meet personal needs while maintaining job security and employment skills. Parents with small children, older employees, and others find that permanent part-time work fits their lifestyles well.

✓ **Checkpoint**

How have different work models affected the workplace?

Professional Work Associations

Many jobs in the private and public sectors involve union membership and/or participation in professional organizations as employment requirements. A **union** is a group of people who work in the same or similar occupations and who are organized to benefit the employees in those occupations.

The Purpose of Unions

Unions have four significant functions:

- Engage in collective bargaining
- Support political candidates and positions that benefit members
- Provide support services for members
- Recruit new members

Unions support their members by lawfully representing these members' interests. For example, if a member is mistreated by their supervisor, the union assists in resolving the issue. The union collects dues from the employees to provide such services.

The primary function of unions is collective or group bargaining. **Bargaining** is the process of negotiating an employment contract for union members. Terms of the employment contract set working conditions, wages, overtime rates, hours of work, and benefits. The employment contract also addresses other issues, such as how layoffs or downsizing of employees will be handled.

Procedures must be followed so that employees' rights are protected. A grievance is a formal complaint brought by an employee (or by the union on behalf of the employee) that states how the employer has violated the employment contract.

Employment contracts often provide for seniority rights. **Seniority** refers to the length of time a person has held a job. It is used to determine promotions, transfers, and vacation time. Generally, more seniority means more job security. If layoffs are necessary, the most recent hires are the first to lose their jobs.

When the union and the employer cannot agree on the terms of a new contract or when a grievance cannot be resolved, the dispute can be mediated. Mediation is using a neutral third party (mediator) to help the two parties reach an agreement. It is voluntary, and both parties must fully agree to try to resolve the problem. When mediation fails, the union contract usually provides for arbitration. Arbitration is a formal process whereby an arbitrator (a neutral third party with expertise in legal issues) makes a formal decision with the same effect as a court order.

Sometimes contract negotiations fail, and the parties cannot reach an agreement. When this occurs, the union may strike or refuse to work until an agreement is reached. Before this can happen, strikes require a vote by union members.

Why do workers need a union to represent them in contract negotiations?

Source: iStock.com//monkeybusinessimages

Union Leadership and Structure

Unions are self-governing organizations. They are organized around employees and their needs for representation. Union leaders work full-time in their positions. They often have lawyers on their staff and hire experts such as economists to advise them on contract issues and economic needs. Dues collected from members are used to pay union staff members' salaries and provide the budget to pay for other experts, services, and union activities.

Craft Unions

Membership in a craft union is limited to those who practice a specific craft or trade. For example, bricklayers, carpenters, and framers each have their union and receive work assignments through the union. Major craft unions exist in the building, printing, and maritime trades. Railroad employees also belong to a craft union.

Industrial Unions

Members of an industrial union are skilled, semiskilled, or unskilled employees in a particular industry, no matter their skill or trade. This gives workers in the same sector more leverage in bargaining employment contracts. These unions include the AFL-CIO, Teamsters, and United Auto Workers. Most of this country's primary manufacturing industries (steel, automobiles, rubber, glass, machinery, and mining) are unionized.

Retail Workers and Healthcare Industry Workers

Members of a retail union include people employed in grocery stores, pharmacies, chain drug stores, and department stores. Service employee unions often represent healthcare employees who bargain with hospitals, clinics, and other healthcare providers.

Public Employee Unions

City, county, state, and federal employees often belong to public employee unions. Members include firefighters, police officers, teachers, clerks, office staff, inspectors, and other support positions.

Right-to-Work Laws

Some states have **right-to-work laws** in place. These laws vary by state; however, they all have the same effect. States with right-to-work laws prohibit unions from requiring employees to become union members. The companies are considered open shops, a place of employment where the workers are not required to join or financially support a union.

Professional Associations

A professional association consists of people in a particular occupation who require considerable training and specialized skills. These organizations also collect dues from members and provide support services. Notable professional organizations include the following:

- American Bar Association (for lawyers)
- American Medical Association (for doctors)
- National Education Association (for educators)

In some cases, membership in professional organizations is required to maintain certifications and meet educational requirements. For example, the Institute of Management Accountants (IMA) administers a national exam for the certified management accountant (CMA) certification. Still, individual state Boards of Accountancy rather than the American Institute of Certified Public Accountants (AICPA) administer the certified public accountant (CPA) exam. The IMA and the AICPA provide most other functions of a professional organization, and membership is required.

Professional organizations provide the following types of services for members:

- Establish and maintain professional standards
- Set and enforce ethical practices by members
- Discipline, sanction, and suspend members for unethical or illegal activities
- Supervise and enforce educational updating of skills and certification requirements of members
- Administer exams, accreditations, and admission requirements
- Publish professional journals to keep members up to date
- Maintain contact with members and keep them apprised of current practices, new research, and emerging trends in the field
- Provide pension, retirement, and insurance benefits for members
- Participate in political action activities to promote and protect the interests of their members

Taking political action often involves lobbying. **Lobbying** is an organized activity by lobbyists (paid activists) to influence public officials to pass laws and make decisions that benefit a profession. Lobbying efforts can be extensive and have powerful effects on laws that are passed (or rejected) by members of state and federal legislative bodies.

✓ Checkpoint

How do unions and professional organizations protect the interests of their members?

Check Your Understanding

1. How can you be a lifelong learner? (LO 1.2.1)

2. Describe various work models that offer employees flexibility. (LO 1.2.2)

3. What is the primary function of unions? (LO 1.2.3)

Apply Your Understanding

1. Visit www.16personalities.com and complete the self-assessment. Write a reflection about what you learned from the assessment and develop a plan of action to improve in an area highlighted by the self-assessment. (LO 1.2.1)

2. Compare two types of diverse work schedules by creating a Venn diagram that shows the similarities and differences between them. (LO 1.2.2)

3. Visit the website of a union or professional association. Create a slide deck that describes the organization's benefits to its members. (LO 1.2.3)

The Essential Question

How can you be successful in an ever-changing work environment?

A: To be successful, updating your skills and being a lifelong learner are essential in an ever-changing work environment.

The Essential Question   What factors impact career outlook, and how do you successfully apply and interview for a job?

Learning Objectives

By the end of this lesson, you should be able to:

LO 1.3.1   Discuss factors that impact career outlook.

LO 1.3.2   Explain the job-seeking process.

Key Terms

- downsizing
- job creation
- professional jobs
- service jobs
- trade jobs
- job application
- resume
- references
- cover letter
- letter of recommendation
- job interview
- follow-up

LO 1.3.1   The Impact of Consumer Demand on Career Opportunities

Consumer demand determines the jobs needed to produce the products and services people want. To stay in business, companies must offer products and services that meet customers' diverse and changing needs. Some careers will be sustainable far into the future, whereas others will not survive. In addition, rapidly evolving technology and an expanding global economy have created new and challenging pathways for career development.

The Effects of Technology and the Economy on Career Choice

No matter your career path, technology and the world economy will affect how you work. They will also affect your job choices and how you prepare for your future.

Technology

The internet, as well as new technological improvements and innovations, has dramatically affected the job market. The internet has opened worldwide markets and has created global competition for businesses of all sizes. As a result, today's employers look different from past employers as they explore various ways to meet changing demands. For example, many companies exist only in cyberspace and have no brick-and-mortar buildings.

Source: iStock.com//maginima

What effect has technology had on the job market?

Technology has eliminated or reduced the need for many jobs. For example, travel agents are no longer needed to make most plane and hotel reservations. In years to come, new technologies will continue to make some careers obsolete because the work can be done more efficiently with robots, websites, or artificial intelligence. For example, the chat feature on many websites is now generated using AI technology, not human workers.

However, today's technology also opens up many career options. For example, more web designers, web content developers, and others working in computer-related fields are needed to maintain online businesses.

Connections to Your World
Outsourcing

Take a few minutes to look at items in your classroom or around your house; you can look at clothing, shoes, towels, classroom supplies, or any other readily available items. As you look at the items, note where the items were produced. You can tell where an item was produced by looking for the words "Made in ..." followed by a country. This is commonly found on the item's tag or on the bottom of the item. It is very likely that some, or even many, of the items you reviewed indicate that they were made in another country. Why is it that so many items are made outside of the United States?

To cut costs, many American businesses are hiring firms outside the United States to handle work that domestic or U.S.-based employees used to do, from managing customer service call centers to manufacturing products to be sold. This strategy is known as outsourcing. Companies pay for work to be done in other countries because labor costs are often cheaper. Companies argue that they must control costs and provide shareholder value in the form of higher profits. On the other hand, workers argue that good jobs are being lost to foreign workers and Americans are unable to find jobs to pay the high cost of living in America. In addition, many argue that the quality of products is often sacrificed when production is outsourced.

Work as a Team
Working in small groups of three to four students, discuss the following questions.
1. What are the pros and cons of outsourcing?
2. How does the state of the economy play a role in this issue?
3. Do you think increasing the minimum wage in the United States impacts outsourcing?
4. Outsourcing is one factor that may impact career outlook in different industries. What other factors may impact career outlook?

Also, people find it possible to work from home while interacting with colleagues worldwide. And online job postings allow individuals to easily apply for jobs in other states or countries.

As you consider your career, you may be unable to visualize how it will change over time. Instead, you will need to rely on research by others to assess a career's potential.

Economy

Economic factors can also affect jobs. During an economic downturn, jobs—and entire industries—may downsize. **Downsizing** is an economic event where jobs are eliminated because company revenues are falling while costs are rising. People are spending less, so fewer products are needed. Jobs that are downsized often re-emerge with new and different skill sets. Some are never replaced as businesses learn to operate more efficiently.

Job creation occurs when the economy grows (consumer demand is increasing) and new workers are hired. High demand for new workers affects the labor supply by reducing the number of available workers. As a result, companies may start offering higher wages to persuade job seekers to work for them. Many of the jobs created may be temporary jobs, often in the service industries. When creating jobs, it's important to consider whether they will be sustainable over time or eliminated in the next economic downturn.

Careers of the Future

Many of today's growing occupations focus on collecting, using, and distributing information. Computers and the internet are tools for gathering, transmitting, and storing data. As a result, the skills required to succeed in today's jobs change rapidly.

One of the highest-paying career groups is classified as **professional jobs**. Workers in professional jobs are considered knowledge workers. Examples of professionals include doctors, lawyers, app developers, AI programmers, database administrators, and engineers. These types of jobs involve creating, processing, storing, retrieving, and transmitting information. As technology continues to evolve, new professional careers will emerge, and other careers will grow. For example, because identity theft is becoming more common, retailers are hiring information security analysts to ensure their customers' privacy and security.

Service jobs are those in which you perform a task or a service for a person or business. Service jobs are a large and increasing sector of the job market. Over the last 50 years, the nation has shifted from an economy that creates goods to an economy that provides services. Service employees often use highly sophisticated information storage and retrieval devices, such as point-of-sale computers and optical scanners linked to inventory management and customer databases. Also, new service industries related to health care have been created to support the aging population in the United States. For example, home health care is a growing service field that has created other jobs, such as delivery services for healthcare equipment and products. Jobs in entertainment, food service, and personal services such as house cleaning, dog walking, and in-home childcare are growing. Unfortunately, many service jobs need to pay better. Higher-tech service jobs are more likely to provide more significant earnings potential. Demand for skilled workers in the trades is also growing. **Trade jobs** require advanced training and skills usually gained through means other than a 4-year degree. Examples include jobs in cosmetology, HVAC, plumbing, carpentry, and welding. Such jobs often pay high wages and provide opportunities for people to own businesses in these fields.

Job Descriptions and Career Outlook

General research into careers before choosing your career path is essential. This will help you identify dead-end jobs and learn whether the career of your choice will pay you an adequate salary. Several U.S. government publications, available online and in most libraries, provide detailed job descriptions:

- *Dictionary of Occupational Titles (DOT)*, available online as *0*NET* (https://www .onetonline.org/)
- *Occupational Outlook Handbook (OOH)* (www.bls.gov/ooh)
- *Monthly Labor Review* (www.bls.gov/mlr)

0*NET is the *DOT* in the form of an online searchable database. It describes occupations in terms of the skills and knowledge required, work tasks performed, and tools and technology used. You can search the database for occupations by entering keywords or by selecting from a list of job families.

The *Occupational Outlook Handbook* provides in-depth job descriptions and information about job opportunities nationwide. The A–Z index arranges careers alphabetically. You can learn whether a career is growing, stagnant, or declining by reading about the job outlook.

Additional statistics and graphic information are available in the *Monthly Labor Review*. In addition, articles in this publication provide current information about specific occupation clusters (groups of similar occupations) across the nation.

Online career sites also provide career advice and information about different jobs.

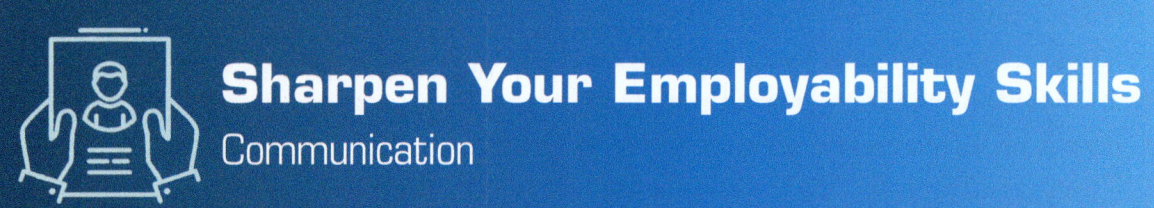

Sharpen Your Employability Skills
Communication

Take a moment to think of all the ways you interact with others during a normal school day. These interactions require communication skills. As you continue to work toward achieving your career goals, the frequency and impact of communication will increase. The Perkins Collaborative Resource Network states that communication skills "enable employees to successfully perform work tasks by communicating effectively with others in multiple formats." Communication skills are essential for everyone regardless of their career path; more than 80 percent of all work activities involve communication. The forms of communication (verbal, nonverbal, written, and digital) will be explored in greater detail later in this chapter and throughout the remainder of the book.

✓ **Checkpoint**

How would you learn more about careers of the future?

LO 1.3.2 Applying and Interviewing

The job-seeking process involves multiple steps. Preparing an application and interviewing for a job are not always easy, yet they are vital steps in landing a job.

The Job Application

Your formal job application process is likely to begin with filling out an online **job application**, which is a form that asks questions to be sure you are qualified for a job opening. In addition, most employers today require you to fill out a job application online. When completing a job application, follow these steps:

- Answer every question. When you cannot answer a question, write "N/A" (for "not applicable") to show that you have not skipped the question.
- Be truthful. Give complete answers. Do not abbreviate if there is any chance the abbreviation could be misread or misunderstood.
- Be prepared. Have all the information that might be requested on the application form, such as telephone numbers, email addresses, and dates.
- Proofread carefully. Check the document for accurate grammar and spelling.

The Resume

You will likely be asked to include a resume with your application. A **resume** describes your work experience, education, abilities, interests, and other information that may interest an employer. The resume tells the employer neatly and concisely who you are and what you can do, and it highlights key skills and interests. Always have an up-to-date resume ready for potential employers. **Figure 1.2** shows a commonly used resume style. Resumes should emphasize your best qualifications and do it in an easy-to-read, attractive, and convincing manner.

Resume Guidelines

There are no set rules for preparing a resume. You should choose the style that best presents you to an employer. However, here are some helpful guidelines:

- Early in your career, keep your resume to one page by carefully arranging the information you choose to include. Employers are busy people. They want a quick overview—not a lot of words to read. If you do not have enough information to fill a page, center what you have vertically on the page to make it attractive. After you have more education and work experience to summarize, your resume may extend to a second page. Resumes for professional applicants with extensive work experience may run several pages.
- Include all information pertinent to the job for which you are applying. An employer wants to know that you are interested in the specific job opening. Rather than preparing a "generic" resume to fit all possible openings, use keywords from a job posting to show that your skills match the job posting.
- Carefully choose fonts, bold, italic, spacing, and other tools to arrange your information in a way that is attractive yet professional looking and easy to read. Place the most important items in the upper third of the page.

Figure 1.2 Resume

Sample Resume

EMY B. DAVIS

8800 South West Street   EmerieDavis0324@gmail.com
Mannford, Oklahoma   www.linkedin.com/in/emerie-davis
(918) 555-5555   www.emeriedavis.com

Education

Small Town High School, Mannford, OK

Senior
- **GPA:** 3.6
- **Relevant Coursework:** Accounting 1 and 2; Agriculture 1, 2, 3, and 4; Agribusiness
- **Honors:** Member of the National Honors Society and FFA Academic Scholars
- **Clubs:** FBLA, FFA, Varsity Softball

Major Achievements

FBLA

President   *20__ — Present*
- Plan and lead weekly meetings
- Mentor younger students to prepare for state competition
- Placed first in leadership and accounting state competitions

FFA

Chapter Vice-President   *20__ — Present*
- Work with the Chapter President to plan weekly meetings
- Mentor younger students with SAE
- Participated in the state fair and placed 'Best in Class' with show calf

Work Experience

The Mason Jar

Bookkeeper   *May 20__ — Present*
- Prepare financial statements for a family-owned restaurant
- Prepare daily bank deposits
- Reconcile monthly bank statements

OKY Horse Rescue

Volunteer   *June 20__ — Present*
- Provide weekly care for rehabilitated horses
- Assist with the rescue's biannual horse show

Additional Skills

- Proficient in QuickBooks
- Proficient in Word, Excel, and PowerPoint
- Leadership and Mentoring

- Proofread thoroughly. Do not rely solely on your word processor's spell-check. Your resume must have zero errors.
- For hard copies, use a high-resolution printer and good-quality 8½ × 11-inch paper. Avoid bright colors, odd sizes, and stained or discolored paper.

Parts of a Resume

A simple resume should include personal contact information; education; experience; additional qualifications; special items of interest (if applicable); and references, which are often provided as a separate document. You may arrange your resume according to personal preference. However, you should show your most favorable section first. For example, if your work experience relates to the open position more closely than your education does, list experience first.

Personal Information

This information appears first on the resume and includes your name and contact information. Typically, your contact information should be your mobile phone number and email address. Make sure to have a professional voice mail message as well as a professional email address. Do not give information such as age, gender, marital status, number of dependents, or ethnic background.

Education

List all high school and post-secondary school institutions you have attended, starting with the most recent. You may include areas of study, activities, honors, specific courses that are applicable to the job opening, or other facts that you think will create a favorable impression. For example, extracurricular activities tell an employer that you are a well-rounded person, offices held in school organizations show that you have leadership skills, and volunteer activities show your civic engagement.

Experience

List paid and unpaid jobs that you have held, including assisting at school functions, working as a teacher's aide, and any part- or full-time summer or vacation jobs (such as camp counselor). Using bullet points makes your resume easier for a potential employer to read quickly. Include information such as name and address of employer, job title, work duties, employment dates or length of time employed, and specific achievements while with this employer. Emphasize tasks you performed that relate to the open position.

Additional Qualifications

You may have additional skills to bring to an employer's attention. For example, you may list special equipment you can operate, the software you can use, or foreign languages you know. You can also list awards you have received. All these things give an employer a complete picture of you and the skills you can bring to the business.

References

Some potential employers will require references. **References** are people who have known you for at least a year and can provide information about your skills, character, and achievements. References should be adults, over age 18, and not related to you. The best types of references include teachers, advisers, current and former employers, counselors, coaches, and adults in business. Be sure to ask permission before listing people on your resume. If you choose not to list references on your resume, state "references available upon request." Then prepare a list of your references' names, phone numbers, and email addresses.

Searchable Resumes

Most job applications are completed online, and you will upload your resume to the job application site. Some employers use special software to search for keywords and phrases that match the skills required in their job descriptions. They can scan paper copies as well as electronic resumes. The scan determines which resumes will be considered further and which will not.

To create a resume that can be scanned by the software, describe your qualifications using keywords from your field. For example, a publisher looking for an editor might scan for words such as *English*, *journalism degree*, *writing*, or *editing*. Use a standard font, such as Times New Roman, Arial, or Calibri; font size of 10 to 12 points for the body of the resume; and headings that are 14-point bold or caps.

Cover Letters

A **cover letter** is also known as a letter of application and is a one-page formal business letter that describes your interest in and qualifications for the position. The cover letter may be requested as part of the job application process. If you are asked to provide a cover letter, it should be written as a formal business letter. Include your contact information in the letter. In the first sentence, indicate the position you are applying for and how you learned about the position. Follow with information that tells the potential employer why you are the best candidate for the position by referring to the skills you have related to the job description. Do not repeat your resume.

Instead, highlight or expand upon information in your resume that is directly related to the job.

In the second paragraph, describe your employability skills like communication, leadership, time management, and organizational skills. The final paragraph should include when you are available to begin the job, how you can be contacted, and a thank you for considering your application.

Letter of Recommendation

A **letter of recommendation** attests to your character, abilities, and experience. It is written by someone who can be relied upon to give an honest report of your skills and abilities. It is helpful to give those writing a reference letter a copy of your current resume or a short summary of your accomplishments and background. The letter should be on letterhead. A sample reference letter is shown in **Figure 1.3**. Note that "To Whom It May Concern" is an acceptable salutation in this case, since copies may be provided to multiple prospective employers.

Make copies of your reference letters to give to potential employers along with your resume and keep the original for your files because you may need to make additional copies for future job applications.

The Job Interview

A **job interview** is a face-to-face meeting, which can take place in-person or via an online meeting tool such as Zoom, with a potential employer to discuss a job opening. During the interview, the employer will have your completed application, resume, and reference letter(s). The interviewer may ask you for more information on any of these documents or about any other job-related matters. Therefore, you should spend at least

Figure 1.3　Letter of Recommendation

FARWEST TRUCK CENTER
402 First Street, NW
Eugene, OR 97402-2143

June 4, 20--

Re: Emy Davis

To Whom It May Concern

I have known Emy for the past three years. She was an employee in our customer service division. Emy began work here as an intern. She was an excellent employee, so at the end of her internship we hired her on a temporary basis. That temporary job lasted three years until Emy moved away.

Emy proved to be energetic and competent. She learned quickly and was a valuable member of our team. She took great pride in her work. She was able to work well independently and as a team member.

Without reservation, I can recommend Emy to you as a potential employee. I would gladly hire her again if she were to move back to our area.

If you have any further questions, please do not hesitate to call me.

Sincerely

Harry Chen

Harry Chen
Manager

as much time preparing for the interview as you did creating your resume and cover letter. It is possible that you may encounter an interview situation where you are asked to interact with a computer program to assess employability skills and personal values. You may also be asked to provide a recorded verbal response to predetermined questions.

Preparing for the Interview

Review your resume so that all your qualifications will be fresh in your mind. Prepare a list of likely questions and rehearse how you will answer them. Be prepared to answer open-ended questions, which are designed to encourage full, meaningful answers (rather than "yes" or "no" answers). These questions may include "Tell me about yourself," "Why do you want to work for us?" or "What would you like to be doing in five years?" Your responses show how well you organize your thoughts, speak, and think under pressure. Emphasize your skills, achievements, and career plans. Avoid speaking negatively about others.

Sharpen Your Employability Skills
Verbal and Nonverbal Communication

Verbal communication skills are a main component of communicating clearly, effectively, and with reason. Verbal communication is used when we speak publicly, listen actively, convey an idea, and express information. Strong verbal communication skills involve speaking slowly and clearly, listening carefully to another person's positions and reactions, asking questions to clarify what was said, and responding appropriately. Information must be exchanged clearly to solve problems. Communicating in a manner that is respectful and courteous is expected. Saying "please" and "thank you" is always good business etiquette.

Body language, or nonverbal communication, can be just as important as verbal communication. Making eye contact with coworkers, employers, and customers is one way to indicate that you pay attention and listen. Smiling and displaying other pleasant facial expressions are often perceived as friendliness and acceptance. Nodding while the other person is speaking conveys an understanding. The way you dress can also relay a message to others. Even your behavior during an interaction, such as a meeting, can make a lasting impression. It is important to understand that nonverbal communication may look different for different individuals. For many, cultural beliefs and other personal differences will shape their nonverbal communication. For example, some cultures view direct eye contact as a sign of disrespect. So, if someone does not display nonverbal communication in the same manner as you, it does not necessarily mean that the person is not paying attention, is being unfriendly, or is disrespectful.

Think Critically

1. Describe a situation in which you communicated well with a classmate or other person. What verbal and nonverbal communication skills did you use?
2. Describe effective verbal and nonverbal communication skills to use during an interview.

It is also important to learn something about your potential employer before the interview. You want to be able to speak intelligently about the company. Do some company research ahead of time, where you find out what the company makes or sells, its history, and its future prospects. This kind of information can be obtained from several sources such as Indeed and Glass Door websites:

- The company's website contains its products, history, financial performance, and other data.
- A contact you have with someone who works for the company can provide first-hand knowledge.

- Annual reports (often available on the company website) describe the company and its financial resources.
- Articles in current magazines and newspapers, including online publications, may discuss the company's economic health or plans for expansion.

Think of questions you might ask the interviewer about the company and the open position. Ask questions about the job. One good question is to ask about a typical day of someone in the role. Questions about the specific job duties and expectations for success will provide you with important information to determine if the job is a right fit for you. You may also want to ask about performance evaluations and how well the team works together. You are interviewing the company just as much as they are interviewing you.

Making a Good Impression

The interview is an essential moment in your life. Prepare for it carefully to make a good impression.

- Arrive on time. Better yet, arrive 10 minutes early to check your appearance and compose yourself. Never be late.
- Dress appropriately. Be neat and clean. Be conservative in dress, hairstyle, jewelry, perfume, cologne, makeup, and appearance. It is better to be overdressed than to appear too casually dressed.
- Go alone. Do not bring along a friend or relative.
- Be prepared. Bring copies of your resume, cover letter, and reference letter(s). Bring a pad of paper, a pen, and any necessary information. Use a padfolio or other item to keep your papers organized.
- Appear self-confident. Being nervous is normal, but do not let your emotions control you. Present the appearance of being relaxed and comfortable by maintaining

good eye contact and occasionally smiling. Do not chew gum, fidget, play with your pen/pencil, or display other nervous habits. Allow the interviewer to lead the discussion.
- Think before you speak. Take a moment to organize your thoughts before speaking. Do not fear the silent pause; the interviewer will not be annoyed. Be polite, accurate, and honest. Use proper grammar. Avoid slang and informal speech. Say "yes" rather than "yeah." Speak slowly and clearly.
- Emphasize your strong points. Talk about your favorite school subjects, grades, attendance, skills, experience, activities, and goals in a positive manner. Avoid negative comments.
- Be enthusiastic. Act interested in the company and the job. Show that you are energetic and ready to work. Let the interviewer know you are excited about the company, the job, and your future.
- Look for cues. Nonverbal cues from the interviewer will tell you when to say less or more. Watch and listen carefully, and then respond appropriately. It is acceptable to ask the interviewer to repeat a question. This can give you a few seconds to think about how to respond. You can also begin your answer by repeating the question you were asked. For example, if you are asked to "Tell us about a time that you displayed leadership," you can respond with "A time that I displayed leadership was …"

How can you make a good impression in a job interview?

Source: iStock.com/VioletaStoimenova

When the interview is over, thank the interviewer for their time. Say you will check back later. Then do so. Exit with a smile and a positive comment, such as "I look forward to hearing from you."

The Follow-Up

After the interview, the employer will have various candidates to consider. Your follow-up may help you stand out from the crowd. **Follow-up** is contact with the employer after the interview but before hiring occurs. It reminds the employer who you are, which could improve your chance of getting the job.

Thank-You Email

A thank-you email is one form of follow-up. The email shows appreciation to the employer for taking the time to speak with

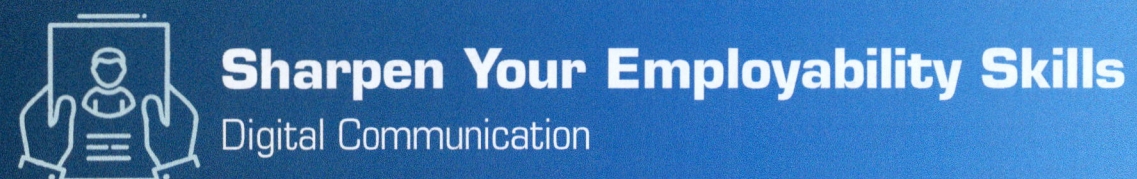

Sharpen Your Employability Skills
Digital Communication

Many businesses now use digital communication as part of their daily operations; the increased use of digital communication in the workplace reinforces the need to develop strong digital communication skills. Digital communication skills allow you to use your understanding of email, video conferencing, social media, and other digital media to convey work that is clear, direct, professional, and grammatically correct. Much of communication today is electronic because it is quick and convenient.

Email is one of the most commonly used forms of digital communication. It is important for you to understand and utilize appropriate and professional email etiquette. In school, you likely use email to communicate with teachers and other adults. In the workplace, it is common to use email to communicate with supervisors, coworkers, and customers. When composing an email, the message should be professional, well written, clear, and concise, and it should provide relevant information. A poorly crafted or unprofessional email can easily misconstrue the intended tone and purpose. When this occurs, it may result in unintended emotions for the recipient and could potentially damage a relationship.

Think Critically

1. Much of the process of applying for and interviewing for a job will be in-person. How can digital communication skills be utilized during the process to make you stand out as a candidate?
2. If an email is not professionally crafted, how might it cause negative emotions for the person receiving it?
3. What advice would you give to a friend who needs to send important information through email communication?
4. Are there situations when email may not be the right method of communication? Why?

Figure 1.4   Thank-You Email

Dear Mr. Phillips

Thank you for the time you spent with me during our interview yesterday.
I enjoyed meeting you and members of your staff.

I am very excited about the prospect of working for your company. The tour guide
position is exactly what I was hoping for. As you recall, I have experience and
background that make it possible for me to "hit the ground running." I am attaching
another reference who can attest to my ability to learn quickly and fit in well.

If there is any other information I could provide, please feel free to contact me at
(971) 555-3344. I look forward to hearing from you.

Sincerely

Emy B. Davis

Emy B. Davis

you. It also brings you to the forefront of the interviewer's mind, providing a reminder of your qualifications and interest in the company.

When writing a thank-you email, address the interviewer by name. If more than one person interviewed you during your visit, write a brief email to each person. Keep it simple, and make sure the email is error-free. This final opportunity to represent yourself to the potential employer may make the difference in getting the job.

Figure 1.4 is a sample follow-up thank-you email. The first paragraph thanks the interviewer. The second paragraph reminds the interviewer of your interest and desire to work for the company. The final paragraph closes on a positive note.

✓ Checkpoint

What are the steps involved in successfully applying and interviewing for a job?

1.3 Lesson Review

Check Your Understanding

1. How does technology impact jobs? (LO 1.3.1)
2. How does the economy impact available jobs? (LO 1.3.1)
3. What sources are available to help you research job descriptions, job skills, and job outlooks? (LO 1.3.1)
4. What kind of information is found on a resume? (LO 1.3.2)
5. What is the purpose of a cover letter? (LO 1.3.2)
6. How can you make a good impression during the job application process? (LO 1.3.2)

Apply Your Understanding

1. Consider a career that interests you. What factors should you consider if you want to find an entry-level job in that career field? (LO 1.3.1)
2. Find a job opening on an employment site or company website. What kinds of education and experience is the employer seeking? Prepare a resume that you think would help get you an interview for that job. (LO 1.3.2)

The Essential Question

What factors impact career outlook, and how do you successfully apply and interview for a job?

A: Consumer demand, technological innovations, economic factors, job type, and growing occupations impact career outlook. General research into careers before choosing your career path is essential. The job-seeking process involves multiple steps, possibly including preparing a job application, writing a resume and cover letter, obtaining letters of recommendations, preparing for a job interview, and following up after the interview.

Summary

1.1 Career Exploration and Planning

- Career exploration and planning is needed in today's rapidly changing world. Steps include self-analysis, research, action planning, and re-evaluation.

- Goals provide a sense of direction in life and in career planning. There are three types of goals: short term, intermediate term, and long term.

- A short-term goal is one you expect to reach in a few days or weeks, an intermediate-term goal is something you want to accomplish in the next few months or in the next year, and a long-term goal is what you wish to achieve in the next year or longer.

- Goals should also be SMART: Specific, Measurable, Attainable, Relevant, and Time-bound.

- Experience and education play key roles in protecting and enhancing employability.

- Experience is the knowledge and skills acquired from working in a career field.

- Post-secondary education can be obtained through a trade school, community college, or 4-year college.

- Degrees, certificates, and industry credentials can impact job opportunities and earning potential.

- In the event of unemployment, it is always best to be prepared by having a Plan B.

- There are advantages and disadvantages to self-employment. An advantage is that you can make your own decisions about how the business is run. A disadvantage is that starting a business can be risky.

- There are three basic types of entrepreneurial businesses: a side business, a lifestyle business, and a venture business.

- Resources for those interested in starting their own business include Small Business Development Centers (SBDCs); the U.S. Small Business Administration (SBA); and SCORE, a foundation that works with the SBA.

- It is sometimes necessary to create a business plan before starting a small business. A traditional business plan is a document that outlines how the potential business will earn and grow revenues.

- In recent years, more streamlined planning tools like a lean startup plan have been used. These tools can be more easily updated as things change.

- The SBA and other organizations offer resources for guidance when creating traditional business plans and lean startup plans.

- Questions you should ask yourself when deciding to become an entrepreneur include are you self-motivated, are you a leader, and do you take responsibility?

1.2 Being Successful in the Workplace

- The digital age has created new opportunities and challenges for employers and employees.

- Seeking new knowledge, skills, and experiences to add to your professional and personal growth and to adapt to an ever-changing work environment is called lifelong learning.

- Updating your skills is called professional development.

- Upgrading means advancing to a higher skill level to increase your usefulness.

- Retraining involves learning new and different skills. Sources of retraining include technical schools, career and technical centers, community colleges, and online learning. Companies also often offer resources to retrain their employees.

- Completing a self-assessment is another way to identify areas of needed growth and development.

- There are several working models in today's job market, including the standard workweek, remote work, flexible schedules and compressed workweeks, job rotation, job sharing, and permanent part-time.

- Many jobs in private and public sectors involve union membership and/or participation in professional organizations.

- Unions have four main functions: collective bargaining, supporting political candidates and positions that benefit members, providing support for members, and recruiting new members.

- Unions are self-governing organizations that collect dues from members. There are different types of unions, including craft unions, industrial unions, retail unions, service employee unions, and public employee unions.

- Professional associations provide services to professional workers who are members of the association. These organizations also collect dues from members and provide support services.

- Examples of professional organizations include the American Bar Association (for lawyers) and the National Education Association (for educators).

- Some professional organizations require members to maintain certifications and meet education requirements.

- Professional organization services can include establishing and maintaining professional standards, administering exams and accreditations, publishing journals, and providing retirement and insurance benefits to members.

1.3 Career Outlook and the Job-Seeking Process

- Consumer demand determines the jobs needed to produce goods and services.

- Some careers will last far into the future, while others will not survive.

- Rapidly evolving technology and an expanding global economy are factors that impact career opportunities and choices.

- Economic factors also impact the job market, possibly leading to downsizing during economic slowdowns and job creation when the economy is growing.

- Many careers of the future will focus on collecting, using, and distributing information.

- Given changing technology and other advancements, the skills required to succeed in today's job market can change rapidly.

- Professional jobs are one of the highest-paying career groups. Workers in this group are considered knowledge workers and include lawyers, programmers, and engineers.

- Service jobs are those in which workers perform a task or service for a person or a business. It is a large and increasing sector of the job market, but many service jobs do not pay well.

- Trade jobs include careers in areas such as plumbing, carpentry, and welding. They often pay high wages and provide opportunities for people to own businesses in these fields.

- Research on jobs and career outlook can be conducted at several U.S. government websites as well as at online career sites.

- The job-seeking process involves multiple steps, including completing a job application, creating and submitting a resume and cover letter, preparing for and participating in a job interview, and following up.

- The process has changed because of technology; most steps are now completed online.

- A resume concisely summarizes your work experience, education and training, and skills and abilities.

- A cover letter is a formal business letter that describes your interest in and qualifications for a position. It may be requested as part of the job application process.

- Letters of recommendation may also be requested. They are written by individuals who can be relied upon to give an honest report of your skills and abilities.

- The job interview requires preparation, including preparing a list of likely questions, researching your potential employer, and thinking of questions to ask the interviewer.

- Making a good impression during an interview is important. You should be on time, dress appropriately, be prepared, and show confidence.

- After an interview, a follow-up thank-you email reminds the interviewer of your qualifications and interest in the job.

Check Your Knowledge

1. How does a self-analysis help you with career exploration and planning? (LO 1.1.1)

2. Explain how experience and education enhance your ability to get promotions and better job opportunities. (LO 1.1.1)

3. List the four major steps in career planning. (LO 1.1.1)

4. What are some disadvantages to self-employment or owning your own business? (LO 1.1.2)

5. How do upgrading and retraining help you cope with change? (LO 1.2.1)

6. Describe two nontraditional work models. (LO 1.2.2)

7. List three different kinds of unions and their purpose. (LO 1.2.3)

8. How does the economy affect jobs that are created or eliminated? (LO 1.3.1)

9. How does technology affect careers and income? (LO 1.3.1)

10. Name five jobs in the professional sector that are directly related to technology. Explain how these jobs are related to technology. (LO 1.3.1)

11. What information should be included on a resume? (LO 1.3.2)

12. Why is it important to do company research before a job interview? (LO 1.3.2)

13. Why would you follow up after a job interview? What might this follow-up involve? (LO 1.3.2)

1. Write one short-term, one intermediate-term, and one long-term goal related to your career plan. Explain why each goal is a SMART goal. (LO 1.1.1)

2. Based upon your self-assessment, what technology skills do you need to improve? Where would you receive training to improve your skills? Create an action plan to improve your technology skills. (LO 1.2.1)

3. Do you think the COVID pandemic has permanently altered the working model for some industries? Explain your answer. (LO 1.2.2)

4. Using the two nontraditional work models you described above, identify the benefits and challenges of each from both the employee's and the employer's viewpoint. (LO 1.2.2)

5. Search the term *passive income* online. What does the term mean? How could you incorporate earning passive income into your long-term career plan? (LO 1.2.2)

6. Conduct online job research about three potential careers you might like to pursue. Use the *Occupational Outlook Handbook*'s A–Z index. Create a table listing the pros and cons of each potential career choice. Include the median annual wage for each of them and any other pertinent information you learn. (LO 1.3.1)

Share Your Knowledge

Work in teams of two to four students to complete the following activities.

1. Working with your team, develop a presentation about the steps in career planning to share with younger students. Include specific examples of how a middle school student can start developing their personal career plan. (LO 1.1.1)

2. Using online research tools, collaborate with a partner to learn about generative AI programs. Create a project, such as a poster or newsletter, to share the ethical implications of using generative AI to complete work assignments. (LO 1.3.1)

3. Select a job posting that interests you. Create a resume and cover letter for the job. Working with a partner or in a small group, exchange documents. Evaluate your partner's resume and cover letter, offering suggestions for improvement. (LO 1.3.2)

Base your answers to the following questions on your own personal thoughts, preferences, and experiences.

1. Selecting a future career is often difficult for a young adult. What advice would you give to a friend whose parents or guardians are pushing them to consider a career in a field that your friend hates? (LO 1.1.1)

2. Owning your own business is often a goal for many people. Do you have the characteristics to be an entrepreneur? Using the questions in the section on self-employment in this chapter, write a response to each question. Discuss your responses with a trusted mentor, then create a career plan using the information you learned about yourself. (LO 1.1.2)

3. What does the term *lifelong learning* mean to you? How can you update your job skills as part of a personal lifelong learning plan? (LO 1.2.1)

Chapter Project

Emy wants to own her own business in the future. She is interested in working with animals but does not want to be a veterinarian. Emy wants to create a career plan that includes long-term goals to help her decide what type of business she could start and the education she will need to succeed. She has asked you for help. Create a career plan for something you want to do after school. Include your lifestyle preferences, the type of career you want, and the education or training you may need to enter this career. Using SMART goals, write short-term goals to meet during this school year, intermediate-term goals to meet within the next three years, and long-term goals so that you can share your plan with Emy.

Chapter 2

Pay, Benefits, and Work

What components make up an employee's total compensation?

Learning Objectives

By the end of this lesson, you should be able to:

LO 2.1.1 Differentiate between gross pay and net pay and how each is calculated.

LO 2.1.2 Identify employment benefits and incentives available to workers in multiple industries.

Key Terms

- gross pay
- minimum wage
- independent contractors
- gig worker
- wage
- overtime
- salary
- deductions
- Social Security
- Medicare
- withholding allowances
- net pay
- benefits
- incentives
- vested
- incentive pay
- profit sharing
- bonus
- Section 125 plans

Consider This ...

Sofia was just hired for her first job as a cashier at a local store. She will work 15 hours per week, which allows her to participate in school athletics and after-school clubs. Her pay rate is $12.50 per hour, and she is paid weekly. After her first week of work, Sofia is excited to receive her first paycheck. However, when she receives her check, she is surprised that it is less than the $187.50 she expected. Her check is for $144.87. She double-checks her math (15 hours × $12.50/hour) and is confused why her check is less than she thought it would be.

Read and Reflect

1. Why is Sofia's check less than she was expecting?

2. What advice would you give to a friend who is trying to estimate their take-home pay?

LO 2.1.1 Gross Pay

When you work for an employer, you agree to perform certain tasks in exchange for payment. **Gross pay** is the total amount you earn before deductions are subtracted. Gross pay is determined by either an hourly wage or a monthly salary. For example, you may receive minimum wage when you first enter the workforce. The **minimum wage** is a base-level hourly wage that employers are required to pay for some employees. As you progress in your career, your hourly wage should increase. Additionally, professionals like teachers, engineers, software developers, and others receive a fixed monthly salary. Some people do not work for an employer. Instead, they work for themselves and contract with businesses. They are known as **independent contractors**. Independent contractors do not have payroll taxes deducted and are not covered by the same employment rules as employees. Gig workers are considered independent contractors. A **gig worker** works a temporary or on-demand job, typically in a service industry. Many young people work for Uber, DoorDash, or other delivery services in the gig economy. Others may design websites, provide care, act as a personal shopper, or provide consulting services.

Minimum Wage

The federal minimum wage provisions are part of the Fair Labor Standards Act (FLSA), and the federal minimum wage is currently $7.25 per hour. The federal minimum wage has not been increased since 2009. Young workers under age 20 may be paid less than the minimum wage during their first 90 days of employment. Other exceptions apply to the federal minimum wage for students who participate in on-the-job training, full-time students, or people with disabilities. Because the federal minimum wage has not kept pace with inflation, more than 30 states have a required minimum wage higher than the federal minimum wage. Alabama, Louisiana, Mississippi, South Carolina, and Tennessee have not adopted a state minimum wage. Workers in these states will receive the federal minimum wage if the employer is subject to the FLSA. Georgia and Wyoming have adopted a state minimum wage of less than $7.25. However, employers who are subject to FLSA must pay the federal minimum wage. Because individual laws can change, workers need to research their state's employee compensation legislation to understand minimum wage requirements in their state.

Hourly Wages

A fixed hourly rate earned by employees is a **wage**. Your wage rate is multiplied by the number of hours you worked; typically, those hours are recorded in an electronic time system.

If you work for $12 an hour and agree that you will work 30 hours a week, your gross pay from wages would be $360 per week ($12 × 30 hours). The regular rate of pay times the regular hours worked is your gross pay for the week.

Hourly Rate × Hours Worked = Gross Pay

$12 × 30 hours = $360

Overtime

Overtime is time worked beyond your regular hours. When working overtime, you work more hours than the standard agreed-upon workday or workweek. In most states, working 40 hours in a five-day period is considered a standard workweek, and working more hours beyond that is considered overtime.

The typical wage rate for overtime pay is 1.5 times your regular rate. So, if your regular hourly rate is $12 an hour, your overtime rate is $18 an hour ($12 × 1.5). A person who works 48 hours in a 5-day period would receive 40 hours of regular pay and 8 hours of overtime pay. Gross pay would be computed as follows:

40 hours × $12/hour (regular pay)	$480.00
8 hours × $18/hour (overtime pay)	+144.00
Gross Pay	$624.00

Salary

You may work for a fixed amount rather than an hourly rate. A **salary** is a fixed amount of gross pay. Salaried employees often receive additional pay for overtime work only if it is agreed upon between the employee and employer.

A salary stated as a yearly amount is divided into regular pay periods. If you work for $52,000 a year and there are 12 monthly pay periods, you will receive $4,333.34 per month ($52,000 ÷ 12). Some employers pay biweekly, or every two weeks, so there are 26 pay periods (52 weeks ÷ 2). In this case, you would receive gross pay of $2,000 per paycheck ($52,000 ÷ 26). Another common pay period is semimonthly, or twice a month. Instead of 12 monthly paychecks, you would receive 24 paychecks, and your gross pay would be $2,166.67 each pay period ($52,000 ÷ 24).

Most salaried employees are considered exempt employees and do not receive overtime. A salaried employee will receive the same pay regardless of the number of hours worked. If a salaried employee

is paid overtime based on their employment contract, it is typically based on their hourly pay rate. There are 52 weeks in a year. If a person is paid $52,000 annually, their earnings would be $1,000 per week. Based on a normal work week of 40 hours, the hourly rate would be $25.00 per hour ($1,000/40). The overtime rate would be $37.50 ($25 × 1.5).

Deductions

Amounts subtracted from gross pay are called **deductions**. Some deductions, such as income tax, **Social Security** tax (FICA), and **Medicare** tax, are required by law. Social Security is a federal insurance program that benefits people who are retired or disabled. Medicare is federal health insurance for people age 65 and older. **Withholding allowances** are reductions in the amount of tax withheld from your paycheck and are based on your income tax filing status. The number of allowances is reported on Form W-4, which you will complete when you start a new job. The form includes a simple worksheet to help you calculate your allowances. A W-4 is shown in **Figure 2.1**.

Other deductions are optional. For example, you may have your employer deduct a regular amount each pay period to pay for your health insurance premiums, retirement, or life insurance.

Figure 2.2 is a paycheck that shows an employee's gross pay and deductions. Required deductions include federal income tax, state income tax, Social Security tax, and Medicare tax. Optional deductions may not be withheld without the employee's written consent, except in the case of a court order. Child support payments or wage

Sharpen Your Employability Skills
Multiplying Decimals

Multiplication is a skill that you will use throughout your life. Oftentimes, multiplication will include decimals. Decimals are commonly used in multiplication in situations that include money. Below is a quick refresher on how to multiply when decimals are involved.

Step 1: Ignore the decimals.

Step 2: Multiply the two numbers as if they were whole numbers.

Step 3: Add the number of digits to the right of the decimal in the numbers being multiplied. For example, if you are multiplying 10.5 by 6.75, there are three numbers total to the right of the decimal points.

Step 4: Starting at the end of the product, move left one digit for each decimal counted, and place the decimal in the appropriate place. For example, if you are multiplying 10.5 by 6.75, you would have a calculated value of 70875, so when you account for the decimals, you would have a value of 70.875.

Try It Out!

Sofia makes $12.50 an hour and is expected to work 15.25 hours next week. What would her gross pay be? We can find gross pay by multiplying hourly wage by hours worked:

12.50 × 15.25 = ?

Answer

```
      1250
×     1525
   1906250
```

Since there are four numbers to the right of the decimal in the original numbers (two numbers in $12.50 and two in 15.25), we count four numbers in, beginning at the right, to place our decimal: 1906250 = $190.6250, which rounds to $190.63.

---

garnishments for unpaid debts are examples of optional deductions imposed by a court.

Employers must keep detailed records of wages, salaries, hours worked, rates of pay, and deductions. With each paycheck, even if it is deposited electronically, the employee must receive an earnings statement, sometimes called a pay stub, or a detailed list of pay (regular and overtime) and deductions (required and optional).

Net Pay

The amount left after all deductions are taken is your **net pay**. It is the amount of the paycheck. This is your take-home pay, and in most cases, it is about 65 to 70 percent of your gross

Figure 2.1   Form W-4

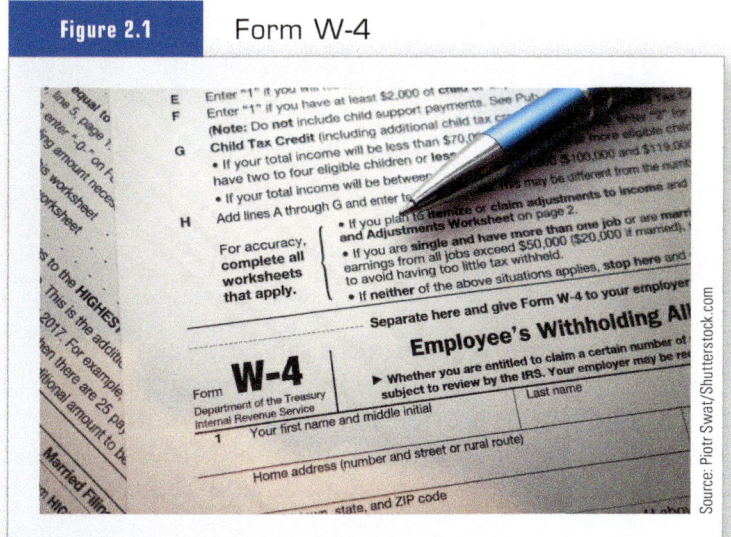

Source: Piotr Swat/Shutterstock.com

pay. So, what is left for you to spend is considerably less than your gross pay. Stated mathematically, net pay is calculated as follows:

Regular Pay (Wages or Salary) +
               Overtime Pay = Gross Pay

Gross Pay − Deductions (Required
            and Optional) = Net Pay

Figure 2.2 shows an employee earnings statement. It lists semimonthly gross pay, deductions, and net pay. The amounts withheld for federal and state income tax are determined from withholding tables or formulas. Employers use specialized software to help calculate the amount of income taxes to withhold from

your paycheck. As an employee, you can estimate your federal and state income taxes using a free online calculator.

The Social Security deduction is withheld at the standard rate of 6.2 percent of the first $168,600 for 2024. Medicare tax is withheld at 1.45 percent of all pay earned. Since 2013, an additional tax of 0.45 percent has been assessed on earned income exceeding $125,000 for each married individual filing separately; $200,000 for individuals filing as single; and $250,000 for married couples filing jointly. Employers must contribute matching amounts to each employee's Social Security and Medicare accounts.

Many states also have a state income tax. As of 2024, Alaska, Florida, Nevada, New Hampshire, South Dakota, Tennessee, Texas, Washington, and Wyoming did not have a state income tax for earned income, although New Hampshire and Tennessee do tax dividend and interest income. All other states deduct state income taxes. Each state calculates state income taxes differently. Some counties and cities also charge a local income tax.

In **Figure 2.3**, Sofia's pay period is June 1–15. This is a semimonthly pay period. Sofia is single and claims no allowances on her W-4. She worked 60 hours during the pay period and earned $12.50 per hour. We will calculate her gross and net pay.

Gross Pay:

Hours Worked × Hourly Wage
60 × $12.50 = $750.00

To calculate net pay, we must calculate the required and optional deductions. The employee withholding sheet in Figure 2.3 can be used to keep track of your calculations.

Figure 2.2   Paycheck with Earnings Statement

...nings Information	Current		M /02
...mal Gross	4,389.30		
...uctions	0.00		
...itions	0.00	Year to Date	
...rtime	0.00		
EARNINGS TOTAL	4,389.30	5,277.30	
...-Taxable Gross	351.14	418.18	
...able Gross	3,971.12	4,859.12	

...atutory & Other Deductions	Current	Year to Date
...eral Withholding	311.17	311.17
...itional Federal Withholding	0.00	*****
...te Withholding	135.96	135.96
...itional State Withholding	0.00	*****
...SDI	62.67	55.06
...dicare	0.00	75.55
...dicare Buyout	0.00	0.00
...ate Disability Insurance	351.14	351.14
...RS	0.00	0.00
...RS	0.00	0.00
...ernate Retirement	67.04	0.00

Source: Josh randall/Shutterstock.com

Connections to Your World
Taxes and Net Pay

It is important to understand how taxes impact the amount of pay you take home (net pay) from your earned wages. As you saw at the beginning of the chapter with Sofia, many young adults are shocked and disappointed when they receive their first paycheck, since it is often less than anticipated. To estimate the amount of taxes that will be taken out of your paycheck, you can use an online paycheck calculator.

Many factors, such as pay frequency, where you live, and the number of allowances you claim, will impact how much is withheld in taxes. It is important to ensure that enough taxes are withheld so that you do not owe money to the government when you file your taxes.

Use the paycheck calculator found at https://smartasset.com/taxes/paycheck-calculator (or another you find online) to see what Sofia's paycheck would look like if she worked where you live. As a reminder, Sofia works 15 hours per week, makes $12.50 per hour, and is paid weekly. For this example, Sofia claims zero allowances to ensure that she has enough taxes withheld from her paychecks. Be sure to accurately enter the information in the paycheck calculator to get the best estimate.

Now, use the paycheck estimator to see what the take-home pay would be for the following jobs if the people worked where you live.

Job	Pay Type	Pay Frequency	Pay Rate
Teacher	Salary	Every two weeks (biweekly)	$46,760/year
Auto mechanic	Hourly	Weekly	$22.50/hour 40 hours/week
Web developer	Salary	Monthly	$80,000/year

Using a paycheck calculator will allow you to consider taxes and help you better understand the amount of money you will receive in each check. This is important to ensure that you are budgeting properly; budgeting will be discussed in greater detail later in this chapter. You can use a paycheck calculator for jobs you are considering now or to explore what net pay may look like for future careers you have an interest in.

Figure 2.3   Employee Withholding Sheet

EMPLOYEE WITHHOLDING SHEET

Name: Sofia Urdaniz Garcia

Pay Period: Semimonthly

Marital Status: Single

Social Security Number: on file

Number of Allowances: 0

Pay Date: June 22, 202X

Gross Pay:	$750.00
Overtime:	0.00
Total:	$750.00
Required Deductions:	
Federal income tax (use tax tables):	$ 51.00
State income tax for Illinois (4.95%):	37.13
Social Security Tax (6.2%):	46.50
Medicare Tax (1.45%):	10.88
Other Deductions:	
Insurance Premiums:	0.00
Union Dues:	0.00
Retirement Account:	0.00
Charitable Contributions:	0.00
Total Deductions:	145.51
Net Pay:	$604.49

Federal Income Tax

Use **Figure 2.4** to determine Sofia's federal income tax. Find the gross pay amount by using the first two columns. $750 is in the wage range of $730 to $780. Now look at the column for 0 allowances. The amount in that column is her federal income tax. For Sofia, the amount is $51 for this pay period.

State income tax in Illinois is 4.95% of gross wages. Multiply $750 by 4.95%. Her state income tax is $37.125, which is rounded to the nearest penny $37.13.

Social Security tax is 6.2% of gross wages. Multiply $750 by 6.2%. Her Social Security tax is $46.50.

Medicare tax is 1.45% of gross wages. Multiply $750 by 1.45%. Her Medicare tax

is $10.875 which is rounded to the nearest penny, $10.88.

Sofia does not have any optional deductions. Her net pay is calculated by subtracting the deductions from gross pay. The calculation is:

$$\$750 - (51 + 37.13 + 46.50 + 10.88) = \$604.49$$

On pay day, the employee may receive a paper check that needs to be deposited into a bank or cashed, or the employee may receive their pay via direct deposit. With either form of payment, the employee will receive an earnings statement that shows their gross pay, deductions, and net pay for the current pay period and for the year-to-date as shown in **Figure 2.5**.

Figure 2.4 Federal Tax Withholding Table—Semimonthly Payroll

2024 Wage Bracket Method Tables for Manual Payroll Systems With Forms W-4 From 2019 or Earlier
SEMIMONTHLY Payroll Period

If the Wage Amount (line 1a) is		SINGLE Persons										
		And the number of allowances is:										
At least	But less than	0	1	2	3	4	5	6	7	8	9	10
		The Tentative Withholding Amount is:										
$0	$250	$0	$0	$0	$0	$0	$0	$0	$0	$0	$0	$0
$250	$260	$1	$0	$0	$0	$0	$0	$0	$0	$0	$0	$0
$260	$270	$2	$0	$0	$0	$0	$0	$0	$0	$0	$0	$0
$270	$280	$3	$0	$0	$0	$0	$0	$0	$0	$0	$0	$0
$280	$290	$4	$0	$0	$0	$0	$0	$0	$0	$0	$0	$0
$290	$300	$5	$0	$0	$0	$0	$0	$0	$0	$0	$0	$0
$300	$310	$6	$0	$0	$0	$0	$0	$0	$0	$0	$0	$0
$310	$320	$7	$0	$0	$0	$0	$0	$0	$0	$0	$0	$0
$320	$330	$8	$0	$0	$0	$0	$0	$0	$0	$0	$0	$0
$330	$340	$9	$0	$0	$0	$0	$0	$0	$0	$0	$0	$0
$340	$350	$10	$0	$0	$0	$0	$0	$0	$0	$0	$0	$0
$350	$360	$11	$0	$0	$0	$0	$0	$0	$0	$0	$0	$0
$360	$370	$12	$0	$0	$0	$0	$0	$0	$0	$0	$0	$0
$370	$380	$13	$0	$0	$0	$0	$0	$0	$0	$0	$0	$0
$380	$390	$14	$0	$0	$0	$0	$0	$0	$0	$0	$0	$0
$390	$400	$15	$0	$0	$0	$0	$0	$0	$0	$0	$0	$0
$400	$410	$16	$0	$0	$0	$0	$0	$0	$0	$0	$0	$0
$410	$420	$17	$0	$0	$0	$0	$0	$0	$0	$0	$0	$0
$420	$430	$18	$0	$0	$0	$0	$0	$0	$0	$0	$0	$0
$430	$440	$19	$1	$0	$0	$0	$0	$0	$0	$0	$0	$0
$440	$450	$20	$2	$0	$0	$0	$0	$0	$0	$0	$0	$0
$450	$460	$21	$3	$0	$0	$0	$0	$0	$0	$0	$0	$0
$460	$470	$22	$4	$0	$0	$0	$0	$0	$0	$0	$0	$0
$470	$480	$23	$5	$0	$0	$0	$0	$0	$0	$0	$0	$0
$480	$490	$24	$6	$0	$0	$0	$0	$0	$0	$0	$0	$0
$490	$500	$25	$7	$0	$0	$0	$0	$0	$0	$0	$0	$0
$500	$510	$26	$8	$0	$0	$0	$0	$0	$0	$0	$0	$0
$510	$520	$27	$9	$0	$0	$0	$0	$0	$0	$0	$0	$0
$520	$530	$28	$10	$0	$0	$0	$0	$0	$0	$0	$0	$0
$530	$540	$29	$11	$0	$0	$0	$0	$0	$0	$0	$0	$0
$540	$550	$30	$12	$0	$0	$0	$0	$0	$0	$0	$0	$0
$550	$560	$31	$13	$0	$0	$0	$0	$0	$0	$0	$0	$0
$560	$570	$32	$14	$0	$0	$0	$0	$0	$0	$0	$0	$0
$570	$580	$33	$15	$0	$0	$0	$0	$0	$0	$0	$0	$0
$580	$590	$34	$16	$0	$0	$0	$0	$0	$0	$0	$0	$0
$590	$600	$35	$17	$0	$0	$0	$0	$0	$0	$0	$0	$0
$600	$610	$36	$18	$0	$0	$0	$0	$0	$0	$0	$0	$0
$610	$620	$37	$19	$1	$0	$0	$0	$0	$0	$0	$0	$0
$620	$630	$38	$20	$2	$0	$0	$0	$0	$0	$0	$0	$0
$630	$640	$39	$21	$3	$0	$0	$0	$0	$0	$0	$0	$0
$640	$650	$40	$22	$4	$0	$0	$0	$0	$0	$0	$0	$0
$650	$660	$41	$23	$5	$0	$0	$0	$0	$0	$0	$0	$0
$660	$670	$42	$24	$6	$0	$0	$0	$0	$0	$0	$0	$0
$670	$680	$43	$25	$7	$0	$0	$0	$0	$0	$0	$0	$0
$680	$690	$44	$26	$8	$0	$0	$0	$0	$0	$0	$0	$0
$690	$700	$45	$27	$9	$0	$0	$0	$0	$0	$0	$0	$0
$700	$710	$46	$28	$10	$0	$0	$0	$0	$0	$0	$0	$0
$710	$720	$47	$29	$11	$0	$0	$0	$0	$0	$0	$0	$0
$720	$730	$48	$30	$12	$0	$0	$0	$0	$0	$0	$0	$0
$730	$780	$51	$33	$15	$0	$0	$0	$0	$0	$0	$0	$0
$780	$830	$57	$38	$20	$2	$0	$0	$0	$0	$0	$0	$0
$830	$880	$63	$43	$25	$7	$0	$0	$0	$0	$0	$0	$0

Source: Department of the Treasury Internal Revenue Service, (Circular E), Employer's Tax Guide, For use in 2024. www.irs.gov/pub/irs-pdf/p15.pdf

Figure 2.5   Employee Earnings Statement

Earning Statement

Sofia Urdaniz Garcia
6574 Mulberry Lane, Peoria, IL 61614

The Red Door Eatery
1865 N. Lincoln, Peoria, IL 61614

Even if you get direct deposit, make sure your Payroll Dept has your **current address**. They will need this to send your W-2, which is necessary to file your tax return.

Pay Periods is the start and end date of the time the paycheck covers.

Pay Period: June 1 - June 15
Pay Date: June 22

Pay Date is the actual day that payment is issued to you.

Earning	Rate	Hours	This Period	Year to Date
Regular	12.50	60.00	750.00	1,500.00
Other		0.00	0.00	0.00
	Gross Pay		$750.00	$1,500.00

Earnings includes your pay rates, how many hours worked and your **Gross Pay**, which is the total you make before taxes are deducted.

Deductions or taxes show what is subtracted (withheld) from your total pay. In some cases, you may see Voluntary Deductions like 401k contributions, insurance payments and more.

Deductions		This Period	Year to Date
Federal Income Tax This Period		$51.00	$102.00
State Income Tax This Period		$37.13	$74.26
Medicare		$10.88	$21.76
SSTax		$46.50	$93.00
	Total	**Deductions**	**Net Pay**
Current	$750.00	$145.51	$604.49
YTD	$1,500.00	$291.02	$1,208.98

Net Pay is the final amount after all of the deductions are applied.

Source: iStock.com//NicoElNino

Why should you learn about employee benefits before starting a new job?

LO 2.1.2   Benefits and Incentives

Employers often offer benefits only to full-time, permanent employees; in some industries, such as service industries, full-time employees are not offered benefits. Employee **benefits** are compensation or perks that are provided to the employee in addition to their salary or wages. Most employers do not offer benefits such as sick pay, holiday pay, or vacation pay to part-time employees. Gig workers and other independent contractors work for themselves without access to employer benefits. Many employers in professional industries offer benefits, which are forms of employer compensation and pay. Common benefits provided wholly or in part by employers include health insurance, retirement savings plans, paid sick leave and vacations, and profit sharing. Some benefits are required by law, such as unemployment compensation, workers' compensation, and matching Social Security and Medicare taxes, for all employees, regardless of part-time or full-time status. Gig workers, who profit from their businesses, are required to contribute to Social Security and Medicare as both an employer and an employee.

Incentives can be monetary or nonmonetary rewards used to motivate employees to work harder. The three most common types of incentives are additional compensation, recognition, and rewards. For example, salespeople can earn higher commissions for making more sales. This would be a compensation incentive.

Sick Pay and Bereavement Pay

Although not required by law, some businesses provide paid sick days each year to their full-time employees. Some employers allow unused sick pay to accumulate and carry over to the next year. This gives an employee additional sick days if they have a serious injury or illness. Employees typically are allowed to use sick leave to stay home to care for a sick child or to help an elderly parent who may be ill. Bereavement pay is sometimes available to employees who have had a death in their family. Typically, the employee is allowed three to five days to deal with their loss and attend memorial services.

Paid Vacations and Holidays

Full-time, permanent employees usually have a set amount of paid vacation time. This means they will be paid as usual while on vacation. Vacation pay allows employees to rest and recharge, which helps prevent fatigue and increases employee morale and productivity. According to the U.S. Bureau of Labor Statistics, the average paid vacation is approximately two weeks of vacation leave per year.

Workers who are paid by a federal, state, or local government work in the public sector. Companies in the public sector may offer holiday pay, as required by federal or state law, to their full-time employees. Many companies in the private sector offer holiday pay as well. The average worker in the United States receives eight paid holidays per year, and the paid holidays in the United States typically include New Year's Day, Martin Luther King, Jr. (MLK) Day, Memorial Day, Independence Day, Labor Day, Thanksgiving Day, and Christmas Day. If state law requires employers to observe the holiday, paid time off may also be offered for state holidays. Some employers now offer floating holiday pay. A floating holiday is a paid day off that the employee can take as a substitute for a public holiday. For example, an employee may choose to work on Christmas and then take a day off to celebrate Hanukkah or Kwanza. Although not required by law, full-time employees who work on holidays may be paid overtime or double-time rates.

Health and Life Insurance

Employers with more than 50 employees are required by law to offer health insurance. Health insurance is covered in more detail in a later chapter. Most plans today are covered partly by the employer and partly by employee contributions. Typically, employers will pay most, if not all, of the health insurance premiums for employees, while employees must pay for coverage for their dependents, such as a spouse and children. Some employers also offer dental and vision insurance.

Employers may also provide life insurance, typically up to the amount of an employee's annual pay. Employees may be able to buy additional life insurance at the group rates. Insurance rates through an employer are often lower than individual policy premiums, especially for older employees. Any additional coverage selected by the employee can be paid through payroll deductions. It is important to know that life insurance usually ends when an employee leaves the company or retires.

Pension and Retirement Plans

Although less frequently offered than in the past, some employers provide employer-paid pension plans for their employees. When the employee retires, they receive a monthly check, which is taxable income. The employee becomes **vested** or entitled to the full retirement amount after a specified period, such as five years. The more common practice today is for companies to offer employer-sponsored retirement savings plans, such as a 401(k) account for private employers or a 403(b) account for government and nonprofit employees. Money that is voluntarily withheld from employees' earnings goes into these accounts. Employers sometimes match employee contributions, but this is not required. For example, a company may match an employee's contribution up to 3 percent. This means that for every dollar you place into your 401(k), your employer may match that dollar up to 3 percent of your annual wages. If you make $50,000 and invest $1,500 of your salary, your employer will also contribute $1,500 to your retirement account.

Incentives

Incentive pay is a form of compensation that encourages employees to strive for higher performance levels. The theory behind incentives is that employees will be more motivated to work for the company's benefit when they can share in its success. This long-term strategy has proven to benefit both the employer and the employee. Companies offer many kinds of incentives to their employees. Incentives can take several forms. The most common type of incentive pay is a cash bonus based on job performance. Salespeople can earn a commission or bonus if they reach higher sales levels in a pay period. Profit sharing and stock options are also types of incentive pay and are usually offered by larger corporations. Noncash incentives can include a company car, gifts, and a health club membership.

Profit Sharing

Profit sharing is a plan that allows employees to share a portion of the company's profits at the end of the corporate year. The more profits the company makes, the more it shares with its employees. This

How do companies benefit by offering incentives or other benefits to their employees?

type of plan may be offered to key executives; management-level and higher-level employees; or in some cases, all employees. Profits can be measured in terms of sales, income, or stock price increases.

Leaves of Absence

Some employers allow employees to leave their jobs temporarily (usually without pay) for certain reasons, such as having children, completing their education, or caring for elderly or sick family members. The Family and Medical Leave Act (FMLA) of 1993 allows eligible employees to take unpaid, job-protected leave for specified family and medical reasons. Private employers with 50 or more workers are typically required to offer employees FMLA. Government agencies are also required to offer FMLA to employees.

Expense Accounts

An expense account is typically provided for management-level employees who must travel or perform out-of-office tasks during their work. They may be given a mileage allowance or, in some cases, a company vehicle to travel to conferences, meetings, or other events. Using a company credit card, they can pay for hotel rooms, meals, registration fees, car rentals, and other work-related expenses. These employees typically submit an expense report, receipts, and documentation to support the amounts spent.

Some employers allow expense reimbursement. Employees who travel on company business keep track of the expenses they pay for themselves and submit an expense report for reimbursement when they return. Reimbursements for these types of expenses are not taxable income.

Employee Discounts and Extras

Many companies offer extras to their employees to improve morale. Employee discounts allow employees to buy the company's products or services at a reduced price. Social and recreational programs, free parking, tuition reimbursement, wellness programs, and mental health counseling provide employees with extras they value as part of their nontaxable compensation plans. Since the COVID pandemic, more companies have offered flexible work hours or work-from-home options to recruit or retain employees. Companies may also offer a sign-on bonus to entice well-qualified workers to take a job with them.

Childcare is a major issue for working parents. Some companies provide on-site childcare facilities or assist with childcare costs. In years to come, federal laws may include more employer childcare incentives for working parents. Some companies are pet-friendly and allow employees to bring their pets to work. Companies like Amazon, Ben & Jerry's, Google, and even the U.S. Congress allow dogs at the office. A recent study found that employees' stress levels declined throughout the day when dog owners were allowed to bring their pets to work.

Bonuses and Stock Options

Larger corporations and employers may provide bonuses and stock options to management and executive employees. A **bonus** is incentive pay based on the quality of work done, years of service, or a company's sales and profits. Holiday bonuses often are based on years of service. If a company achieves its target goals for the year, bonuses may be awarded to thank employees for their work.

Although not common in most industries, some corporations offer stock options that allow employees to buy shares of company stock at reduced prices (lower than market value).

Evaluating Employee Benefits and Incentives

Many of these optional benefits and incentives are of great value to employees. They are not taxable to employees (except bonuses and other benefits paid in cash), yet they provide valuable coverage and advantages. Generally, large companies provide more extensive optional benefits and incentives than smaller companies.

In recent years, employee benefits have become more flexible to meet the changing needs of the workforce. Section 125 plans are also called flexible benefits plans. A **Section 125 plan** must meet the regulations of the Internal Revenue Code Section 125. They are programs that allow employees to customize benefit plans to meet their specific needs with flexible plan options on a pretax basis. Benefits that are part of Section 125 allow the employee to deduct the costs of the benefits from taxable income, which reduces the income taxes the employee owes on their salary or wages. Some of the benefits an employee can select include health savings accounts (HSA), health flexible spending accounts (FSA), premium-only health insurance (POP), and dependent care assistance plans (DCAP). Offering flexibility in

Connections to Your World
Employee Benefits

Different companies offer different benefits. In addition, part-time employees typically receive fewer benefits than full-time employees, if part-time employees receive any benefits at all. The benefits you will need will change throughout your life and depend on what you value as an individual.

Think Critically

1. What employee benefits are commonly offered to part-time employees? What benefits are typically offered only to full-time employees? Why do you think full-time and part-time employees have different benefits available to them?

2. What employee benefits would be important to you right now? Why?

3. Once you are established in a career, how would your opinion of employee benefits change? What benefits would be most important to you when you are working full-time after completing college or some other education or training?

What employee benefits are important to you?

the selection of benefits is highly valued by employees. For example, a married employee with children might opt for increased life and health insurance, while a single employee may choose a 401(k) contribution.

Benefit packages typically cost about 30 percent or more of payroll costs. So, if an employee earns $40,000 a year, the value of the benefit package is about $12,000 ($40,000 × 30%). The employer matches Social Security and Medicare deductions in addition to paying a portion of health insurance premiums, sick pay, vacation pay, profit sharing, and all the other perks used to attract and keep qualified employees. When evaluating benefit packages, you should ask these questions:

- Does the benefit package meet my essential insurance needs?
- How much of the benefit package is nontaxable?
- What options are available for retirement plans?
- Does the benefit package allow sufficient flexibility so I can care for my family members and myself in the event of illness or major events?

✔ Checkpoint

What benefits and incentives are typically offered to workers?

Check Your Understanding

1. What is included in gross pay? List some required and optional deductions from gross pay. (LO 2.1.1)

2. List benefits provided to most full-time, permanent employees. (LO 2.1.2)

Apply Your Understanding

1. If your annual pay is $36,010, what is your biweekly pay based on 26 biweekly paychecks? What is your hourly pay rate if you work 40 hours per week? What is your overtime rate? (LO 2.1.1)

2. Assuming you contribute up to 5 percent of your gross pay of $30,000 into a 401(k) and your employer matches your contribution up to 1 percent of your salary, what total amount would be contributed to your account each year? (LO 2.1.2)

The Essential Question

What components make up an employee's total compensation?

A: An employee's total compensation package includes wages or salary (Gross Pay – Deductions = Net Pay), benefits, and incentives.

The Essential Question | How does budgeting help you achieve your financial goals?

Learning Objectives

By the end of this lesson, you should be able to:

LO 2.2.1 Prepare a personal budget using sound financial planning principles.

LO 2.2.2 Prepare a net worth statement and a personal property inventory as part of an effective record-keeping strategy.

Key Terms

- disposable income
- financial plan
- budget
- fixed expenses
- 50-30-20 budget plan
- variable expenses
- cash surplus
- cash deficit
- assets
- wealth
- liabilities
- net worth

Consider This ...

Since Sofia has started a part-time job, she no longer receives a weekly allowance from her parents. She pays for all her own clothes, gas, insurance, and entertainment. Last year, she was able to save over $600.

"How do you do it?" asked her friend Ana. "I work just as much as you do, my parents pay for my clothes and most of my expenses, and I still don't have any money left over for entertainment. I didn't save a dime last year!"

"I have a budget," said Sofia. "Every time I get paid, I put money aside for savings. I created a budget and plan for my expenses; I know how much I spend on everything I buy. Keeping a good record of income and expenses helps me with this, so I don't overspend and run out of money. I can't always buy everything I want, but I do know how much I can spend, which helps me stretch my money and to save.

Read and Reflect

1. What expenses should a typical teenager include as they create a budget?
2. How does budgeting help you be more financially responsible?

Financial Planning

Do you have unlimited resources to buy all the things you want? Some people do, but if you are like most Americans, you will have to plan and work hard to achieve financial success. Planning, budgeting, and keeping good records provide the road map that leads to financial security.

Get Started

Everyone should plan no matter their income. There are two elements to consider: your income and your expenses. Your gross income is important, but it does not represent money over which you have control. Your **disposable income** is the money you have left to spend or save after taxes and other required and optional deductions are taken. If you spend all your income, there will not be money to set aside for the future. You need a financial plan to use your income to your best advantage.

All money you receive is spent, saved, or invested. You may spend it on things you need or want, save it for future needs, or invest it to earn more money. A **financial plan** is a set of goals for spending, saving, and investing the money you receive. As part of your financial plan, you should set short-term, intermediate-term, and long-term goals. Financial planning helps you do the following:

- Avoid money worries by planning your savings, spending, and borrowing so you can live within your income
- List and evaluate your choices (what you want to achieve and what is important to you); consider your short-term, intermediate-term, and long-term goals
- Assign a dollar amount to your goals
- Prioritize your choices so your money goes as far as possible

Why is it important to plan for the future?

Source: iStock.com/JLco - Julia Amaral

- Avoid careless and wasteful spending
- Organize your financial resources and sources of income to achieve your financial goals

The first step in budgeting is understanding your financial resources—the sources and amounts of money you expect to receive—and your obligations. Before preparing a budget, you may wish to keep track of money coming in and going out for a month or two. This will give you a clearer idea of what you can expect. Many people use spreadsheets, online budget trackers, or banking apps to track their spending. If you primarily use your debit card for purchases, reviewing your spending over time can be accomplished by reviewing your bank statement for one or two months. You should keep receipts for cash purchases when you are tracking expenses. This record forms the basis for understanding what is happening in your current financial picture.

Visualize Your Future

Once you have a good idea of what comes in and how it goes out, you can start thinking about any changes you would like to make. For many people, just keeping track of what you receive and how you spend it makes a difference. When people see how much they spend on something, they may realize that changes are needed to manage their money more effectively. How you spend should reveal your values, choices, obligations, and priorities. By preparing a budget, you will help make your financial planning visions a reality. It is important to recognize that you should factor in short-term, intermediate-term, and long-term goals you want to achieve as part of your financial planning. For example, short-term goals may include creating a monthly budget to evaluate your spending and savings. An intermediate-term goal could be saving to buy a car or creating an emergency fund. Long-term goals may include planning for a particular career or beginning to invest for retirement.

Prepare a Budget

The next step toward achieving your financial goals is to prepare a budget. A **budget** is a spending and saving plan based on your expected income and expenses. In a budget, money from earnings, gifts, and borrowing must equal money going out through spending and savings. The budget must be balanced. A budget helps you plan your spending and saving, so you should not have to borrow money or use credit to meet your daily needs.

Steps in Preparing a Budget

The steps in preparing a budget are as follows:

1. Estimate your total expected income for a certain time period. Include all the money you expect to receive. Use a weekly, biweekly, or monthly budget—whichever best matches how often you expect to receive money.

2. Estimate your expenses, or money you will need for day-to-day purchases—for example, lunches, fees, personal care items, cell phone service, a car payment, and clothing.

3. Decide how much of your income you want to save, or set aside, to meet your short-term, intermediate-term, and/or long-term goals. Most experts advise saving at least 10 percent of your disposable income each pay period. By saving, you will have money to pay for future needs, both expected and unexpected.

4. Balance your budget. If your expenses plus savings exceed your income, adjust your budget to make them balanced. To do this, you may have to delay buying some items you want but don't need. Or you may decide to save a little less this month. If you can't cut your expenses, you must increase your income.

Figure 2.6 shows a high school student's budget for one month. This student expects to receive $420 and plans to use the money for certain needs and wants. She also wants

Figure 2.6	Simple Budget

Sofia Urdaniz Garcia
Budget for September

Income:

Part-time job (10 hours per week)	$420
Allowance from parents	$100
Monetary gifts	$100
Total income	$620

Expenses:

Daily lunches at school	$120
Supplies for a school project	$ 50
New fall jacket	$100
New video game	$ 75
Eating out with friends	$150
Total expenses	$495
Savings:	$125

to put some money into savings for the future. Notice that total income equals total savings plus expenses. A balanced budget is one where total income equals total savings and expenses. When you spend no more than what you take in, your budget remains in balance.

Budget Line Items

Some people create a monthly budget by taking an annual budget and dividing it into 12 months. This can be helpful for people who do not have a regular monthly income. Line items in a budget represent each item of income and spending that is anticipated during the month or year. Some line items occur only once a year. Other line items may occur monthly, such as rent or insurance.

There are two types of expenses. **Fixed expenses** are costs that do not change from month to month. You are obligated to pay them regardless of income changes. For example, people must pay rent or a house payment, a car loan, and insurance premiums when they are due. Most financial experts recommend a 50-30-20 budget plan. The **50-30-20 budget plan** is based on net pay. The plan is to spend 50 percent of your net pay on needs, 30 percent on what you want, and 20 percent on savings and retirement. However, this standard is difficult to achieve for young people just starting life on their own or those with limited incomes. **Variable expenses** are costs that vary in amount and type, depending on your choices. For example, your grocery bill can be larger or smaller, depending on what you choose to buy. Other examples of variable expenses are costs for eating out, going to movies, and buying clothes.

Figure 2.7 shows a monthly budget for a married couple. Qiang and Xia Xiao both work and have no children. They estimate their income by adding the net pay from both paychecks. They also expect income from savings and investments.

Qiang and Xia subtract estimated expenses from income, leaving a **cash surplus** where their income exceeds expenses. They apply the cash surplus to savings, approximately 16 percent of their monthly income ($815 ÷ $5,085). This enables them to set aside money for emergencies, short-term savings, and long-term investing.

When estimated expenses are greater than estimated income, the result is a **cash deficit**. When faced with a cash deficit, you must borrow money, bring in more income by working overtime, or cut your expenses. Managing a budget, or budgeting, is not always easy. It often means adjusting variable and fixed expenses so that needs and priorities can be met.

Balancing Your Budget

You can do three basic things when your budget is not balanced. You can cut your expenses, borrow money or dip into savings, or increase your income. Dipping into savings is not a good thing because it reduces your ability to meet emergency needs in the future. It is not always easy to increase income, such as working overtime or getting another job.

Sometimes balancing your budget is as easy as turning off the lights when you leave home or turning down the thermostat from 70 to 68 degrees during the winter. But often, it is more serious than that. Food and gas prices can rise 10 to 15 percent or more, leaving you without enough income to cover

Figure 2.7   Budget for a Couple

Qiang and Xia's Budget

Income	Monthly	Yearly
Salary (Qiang's take-home pay)	$2,375	$28,500
Salary (Xia's take-home pay)	2,700	32,400
Interest on savings	10	120
Total Income	5,085	61,020
Fixed Expenses		
Rent	1,000	12,000
Utilities	275	3,300
Car payment	450	5,400
Car insurance (Health Insurance is withheld from paychecks)	200	2,400
Total fixed expenses	1,925	23,100
Variable Expenses		
Cell phone plan	90	1,080
Gasoline	200	2,400
Car repairs and maintenance	100	1,200
Streaming and internet	175	2,100
Groceries	750	9,000
Personal care items	250	3,000
Insurance deductibles and copays	80	960
Recreation and entertainment	400	4,800
Gifts, donations, miscellaneous	300	3,600
Total variable expenses	2,345	28,140
Total fixed and variable expenses	4,270	51,240
Cash surplus (income – expenses)	815	9,780
Savings (allocations of cash surplus)		
Emergency fund	200	2,400
Short-term savings	115	1,380
Long-term savings	500	6,000
Total savings	815	9,780
Total expenses plus savings	5,085	61,020

rising costs. When this happens, more serious action is required.

Fixed costs are difficult to change in the short run. For example, if you move to a location with lower rent, you will find your costs go up for a month or two. You must pay moving costs, new deposits, installation and startup fees, and other expenses related to moving. In the long run, however, you can reduce your fixed costs. As

Sharpen Your Personal Finance Skills
Preparing a Budget

Preparing a budget is essential to ensure financial well-being. When you first prepare a budget, it can be a challenging process. You must make sure you include everything, accurately estimate income and expenses, and are realistic about spending habits. This process becomes more complicated when another person is involved. You will likely have to create a budget with another person in the future. Whether that person is roommate or a spouse or partner, it is important to ensure transparency; the budget must address needs and concerns and be agreed upon by everyone involved.

Communication will be key to successfully developing a budget with another person. Examples of interpersonal skills include active listening, speaking clearly and with purpose, contributing fairly to the task, discussing options, and showing respect for others. Prepare a list of questions that would be important to discuss with a roommate when setting up a budget.

another example, you can reduce car insurance premiums by shopping around and switching insurance carriers every few years, but to do this, you need a good driving record. When you purchase a car, you should consider the payment, fuel economy, and insurance costs associated with the type of car you purchase.

Variable costs are easier to change in the short run. You can eat out less, spend less on clothing and entertainment, and save on gas by combining trips, avoiding trips, and carpooling. Many variable costs reflect current trends and values. For example, you may spend more on communicating (your cell phone and internet bills) than on groceries. Consider less expensive options to save money on these variable costs.

✓ **Checkpoint**

What four steps are necessary for preparing a budget?

LO 2.2.2 Keeping Good Records

Planning for your future also includes keeping track of your progress. As you achieve goals, you can track what you have accomplished and what remains to be done. This helps you focus on your goals. Keeping good personal records makes long-range planning easier. It also helps when you prepare tax returns, credit applications, and other financial forms. You should keep five types of records: income and expense records, your net worth statement, a personal property inventory, tax records, and other miscellaneous documents.

Income and Expense Records

Your W-2 forms show money earned and deductions from your paycheck. They also reveal taxes withheld, including Social Security and Medicare. When collecting benefits such as Social Security, you may need these forms to verify your proof of earnings. Banks and investment companies provide statements through their websites or apps. You should download and save year-end statements from banks and investment companies showing interest and dividend earnings.

Expense items such as receipts for charitable contributions, medical bills, or work-related costs should also be downloaded from the appropriate website or app and saved. These receipts and statements will serve as proof of income and expenses and help you plan your budget.

Net Worth Statement

A net worth statement, such as the one shown in **Figure 2.8**, shows a person's net worth based on their assets and liabilities.

Assets are items of value that a person owns. The number of assets usually grows over your lifetime as you buy property, make investments, and save money. **Wealth** is the accumulation of assets. Wealth allows you to be financially secure, help others, and achieve your goals.

Liabilities are money or debts owed to others. For example, if you borrow money so you can buy a car, your car loan is a liability, or debt you owe. A person should plan to repay their debts because there are consequences if debts are not paid. Short-term liabilities must be paid off soon, usually within a year or less. This might include money borrowed from a family member or a friend. Long-term liabilities are paid off over several years, such as a large furniture purchase.

The difference is called **net worth** when you subtract your liabilities from your assets. As your net worth increases, your wealth is also growing. Over time your assets increase while your liabilities decrease because you pay off your debts. When assets are greater than liabilities, you are said to be solvent, or in a favorable financial position. When liabilities exceed assets, you are said to be insolvent,

Figure 2.8	Net Worth Statement

Net Worth Statement
Sofia Urdaniz Garcia
January 1, 20—

Assets		Liabilities	
Checking account	$ 500	Loan on car	$1,800
Savings account	900	Loan from parents	300
Car value	3,000		
Personal property (inventory attached)	5,000	Total liabilities	$2,100
		Net Worth	
		Assets – Liabilities	7,300
Total assets	$9,400	Total	$9,400

What assets do you own or would you like to own in the future?

or in a poor financial position. Many people are temporarily insolvent. For example, if you attend college, your expenses will likely exceed your income, and your debts may be greater than your assets.

The net worth statement will provide the necessary information for applying for credit. The bank or other lender will want to know that you can repay your debt. A person who has too much debt is a high risk. Lenders are reluctant to make loans to those who are insolvent or already have a lot of debt.

Personal Property Inventory

Personal property is anything of value that you own, except real estate. It includes such things as cars, clothing, furniture, appliances, electronics, and other valuable items. A personal property inventory is a list of the valuable items you own, along with their purchase prices and estimated current values.

A personal property inventory is useful in case of fire, theft, or property damage. The inventory will help you list lost items and their value when you make an insurance claim through homeowners or renters insurance, which will be covered in a later chapter. As a further safeguard, you can take pictures of the items of value and store them electronically or keep them in a secure place.

A personal property inventory also helps you see what you have to show for the money you have spent. As you buy new items and dispose of others, you should revise the inventory and keep it current.

Figure 2.9 is a personal property inventory. In most cases, the approximate current value is less than the purchase price (except for collectibles). Personal property is a depreciating asset, meaning it decreases in value over time. If the property is lost or stolen, you will receive the current approximate value, not the current market value.

Tax Records

All taxpayers should keep copies of their tax records for at least three years after they file their tax return. Tax records include a signed copy of the tax return, W-2 forms, and other receipts verifying the income and expenses listed on each return. Keep your tax records in a safe place in case of an audit. The Internal Revenue Service (IRS) has the legal right to audit your tax returns and supporting records for three years from the filing date or longer if fraud or intentional wrongdoing can be proved.

Other Records

Many consumers use mobile apps to keep track of their credit card accounts. They can manage the account from the app and lock the card if it is lost or stolen. They can also access the monthly statements through the app, if needed. As a part of your financial plan, it is a good idea to reflect on the number of credit accounts you have, the balances for each, the interest rates charged, and the monthly payments required. It is important to use credit wisely. Overusing your credit can affect your ability to plan for your financial future.

Figure 2.9   Personal Property Inventory

Personal Property Inventory
Sofia Urdaniz Garcia
January 1, 20—

Item	Purchase Date	Purchase Price	Approximate Current Value
Samsung 65" Class LS03B Smart TV	3/26/2023	$1,700.00	$995.00
Sony PlayStation 5 Video Game Console	Gift 12/2022	$500.00	$450.00
Furniture			
Bedroom set with full-size bed, dresser, and nightstands	9/1/2021	$1,500.00	$1,200.00
Sofa and recliner	2019	$750.00	$250.00
Small kitchen appliances	various	$500.00	$100.00
Clothing	various	$2,500.00	$250.00
Polygon Siskiu D5 Mountain Bike	5/15/2024	$950.00	$900.00
Laptop with docking station and two monitors	8/15/2024	$1,675.00	$1,250.00
Total Value		$10,075.00	$5,395.00

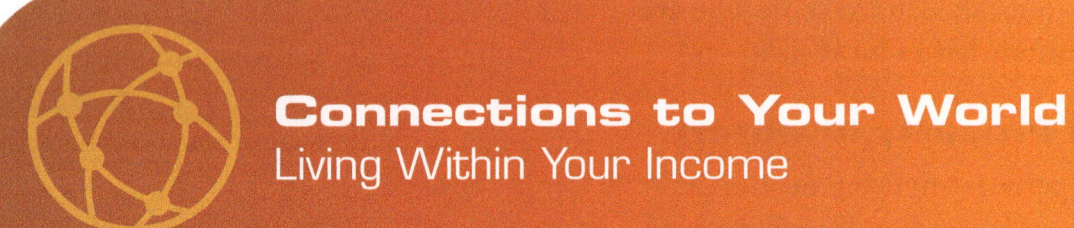

Connections to Your World
Living Within Your Income

To be financially responsible, you must recognize that you are accountable for your own financial future.

A balanced personal budget is the first step to financial security. Living within your income means that you spend less than you make and that you plan savings for future as well as current needs. Keeping a log, or transaction register, of all income and expenses helps with the budgeting process. This is commonly done in a spreadsheet or with an app on your cell phone. Transaction registers and saving are explored in greater detail in a later chapter.

Setting financial goals is the next step to securing your financial future. You cannot achieve future financial goals if you are not paying your current bills on time. Using the SMART goal process, which is discussed in the previous chapter, helps with setting and meeting financial goals.

(continues)

(continued)

When you are looking to make a purchase, ask yourself the following questions:

- Do I need it?
- Why am I buying it?
- How else could I spend the same money?
- How will buying it affect my financial goals?

Many people have a limit on how much money they will spend. Whatever your limit, before spending a large sum or accepting a loan that will take a big bite from your future earnings, think through the decision carefully.

Living within your income is an important part of being happy. Regardless of your income, careful planning and budgeting can enhance your lifestyle and secure your future.

Think Critically

1. Make a list of things you would like to have, along with the purchase price of each. Read this list a week from now. Do you still want the same things? If so, what do you plan to do to buy one or more of them?
2. Do you know people who live within their income? If so, ask one of them to share how they do it. Based on the advice you receive, create a list of budgeting tips.
3. Do you know people who live beyond their income? What do you observe about their stress, financial stability, and financial goals?

You may also choose to keep other records, including car titles, insurance policies, birth and marriage certificates, wills, and passports. These documents are sometimes needed for certain financial transactions. The original documents should be placed in a safe place (such as a safe deposit box), and photocopies or digital pictures should be kept on your smartphone kept for easy reference. If you keep these at home, ensure they are in a secure location that is safe from intrusion, fire, and theft.

✓ Checkpoint

How can keeping good records help you with financial planning?

2.2 Lesson Review

Check Your Understanding

1. What is the first step in budgeting? (LO 2.2.1)

2. How are fixed expenses different from variable expenses? (LO 2.2.1)

3. Why would you prepare a net worth statement? (LO 2.2.2)

Apply Your Understanding

1. Using Figure 2.6 as a model, prepare a simple budget for yourself. Try to use the 50-30-20 budget plan. If your budget does not balance, make adjustments until it does. How much will you set aside for savings? (LO 2.2.1)

2. Prepare a personal property inventory of your assets. Explain why having a personal property inventory as part of your financial plan is important. (LO 2.2.2)

The Essential Question

How does budgeting help you achieve your financial goals?

A: Budgeting is a financial plan by which you can assign dollar amounts to your goals and prioritize them, allowing you to take action.

Summary

2.1 Gross Pay, Net Pay, and Benefits

- Gross pay includes your regular pay plus any overtime earned during the pay period before taxes, benefits, and other deductions are subtracted.

- The federal minimum wage is set by the Fair Labor Standards Act (FLSA). The federal minimum wage in 2023 was $7.25 per hour, but some states may have laws for higher or lower wages than the federal minimum wage depending on compensation legislation in their state.

- Hourly wages are a fixed amount for each hour worked.

- Overtime is paid if a person works more hours than the agreed-upon standard work period.

- A salary is an agreed-upon amount per year. Most salaried employees are not paid overtime.

- Deductions (both required and optional) are subtracted from gross pay to determine net (take-home) pay.

- Net pay is the amount left after you have paid taxes, benefits, and other deductions.

- Benefits, in addition to pay, may include paid time off for vacations and holidays, sick pay, bereavement pay, group health and life insurance coverage, and retirement plans. Benefits are usually offered only to full-time, permanent employees.

- Incentives encourage employees to strive for higher performance levels. Examples of employment incentives include profit sharing, leaves of absence, expense accounts, employee discounts, bonuses, and stock option plans.

- Employees become vested in pension plans and other employer-funded retirement plans after a specified number of years with the company.

- Section 125 plans allow employees to choose benefits that best meet their needs.

- Employees should evaluate the benefits offered by various employers to determine whether they meet their needs, especially health insurance and retirement plans.

2.2 Budgeting and Planning

- Financial planning provides a road map to financial security.

- A financial plan is a set of goals for spending, saving, and investing money you receive.

- Everyone should plan no matter their income.

- Two main elements to consider when planning include your income and expenses.

- Disposable income is the money you have left to spend after taxes and other required and optional deductions.

- A financial plan should include short-term, intermediate-term, and long-term goals.

- A budget is a spending and saving plan based on expected income and expenses.

- To prepare a budget, you should estimate your income and expenses and set short-term, intermediate-term, and long-term financial goals.

- If expenses plus savings exceed income, adjust your spending or saving to balance your budget or find a new source of income.

- Fixed expenses are costs that do not change monthly, while variable expenses change depending on choices made.

- Types of personal records to keep include income and expense records, a net worth statement, a personal property inventory, and tax records.

- Net worth is the difference between assets (items of value owned) and liabilities (money owed).

Check Your Knowledge

1. Explain how to calculate net pay. (LO 2.1.1)

2. Why would an employer offer incentive pay? (LO 2.1.2)

3. What are common benefits that employers offer to full-time employees? (LO 2.1.2)

4. Define the 50-30-20 budget plan. (LO 2.2.1)

5. What is the purpose of a statement of net worth? (LO 2.2.2)

6. How do you calculate net worth? (LO 2.2.2)

Apply Your Knowledge

1. What is the gross pay for an hourly employee who earns $12 an hour and worked 56 hours last week, assuming the standard workweek is 40 hours? (LO 2.1.1)

2. Calculate the net pay for the following situations. You will need to use Figure 2.5 to find the federal income tax. Use the formulas provided to calculate the Illinois state income tax, the Social Security tax, and the Medicare tax.

   - A single person, one allowance, who made $564 and has $76 withheld each pay period for health insurance, pre-tax

   - A single person, no allowances, who made $682 and has no additional deductions

   - A single person, three allowances, who made $843 and has 10% of their gross pay withheld for retirement, pre-tax (LO 2.1.1)

3. Visit the Social Security Administration online at www.ssa.gov. What are the maximum taxable earnings amounts and the tax rates for Social Security and Medicare for the current year? Why do these amounts change each year? (LO 2.1.1)

4. Prepare an employee withholding sheet like the one shown in Figure 2.3 using the following information: Charlie Suarez (Social Security number 999-00-9962) is paid weekly; he is single and has one allowance. He works in Oregon. He worked 40 hours at his regular rate of $15 per hour plus 6 overtime hours last week. In addition to required deductions, he had $22 for insurance, $12 for union dues, and $10 for charitable contributions withheld. (LO 2.1.1)

5. Employee benefits are an important form of compensation and, in some cases, are more important to workers than the amount of net pay. Conduct online research to determine which benefits are most important to employees and create a slide deck or poster of your top-10 list. Be prepared to explain your list and share why each benefit may be so important to employees. (LO 2.1.2)

6. What choices do you have when balancing your budget? If you had to reduce your spending to balance your budget, which would you try to reduce first: fixed or variable expenses? Why? (LO 2.2.1)

7. Using Figure 2.8 as a model, prepare a net worth statement. List your assets and liabilities and then compute your net worth. How can you use this information? (LO 2.2.2)

Share Your Knowledge

Work in teams of two to four students to complete the following activities.

1. Alexi works for an annual salary of $36,000 and gets 12 monthly paychecks. As a salaried employee, she is not given any overtime pay, but she works more than 60 hours each week.

   - Do you think she should be entitled to overtime pay? Discuss and then explain your answer.

   - Is it ethical for an employer to require a salaried employee to work more than a standard workweek all the time? Discuss and then explain your answer.

   - Compute Alexi's overtime rate. How much additional pay would she earn each week if she were paid for her overtime hours? How much more would she earn over the course of one year? If you were Alexi, what would you do? (LO 2.1.1)

2. You live in an apartment with two roommates. What kinds of expenses would you share with others? What kinds of expenses would be each person's responsibility? Prepare a summary of a group budget that ensures everyone's needs and priorities are being met. (LO 2.2.1)

Connect and Reflect

Base your answers to the following questions on your own personal thoughts, preferences, and experiences.

1. Many part-time and gig workers do not receive benefits such as sick pay, holiday pay, or vacations. If companies follow all minimum federal, state, and local requirements, the businesses have the right to dictate terms of benefit packages. Why do you think so many young workers take jobs that do not provide benefits? (LO 2.1.2)

2. Which benefits and incentives do you consider the most important to you at this point in your life? How do you think that will change over time? (LO 2.1.2)

3. Why is it important for you to have a balanced budget? What can you to do ensure your budget will balance? (LO 2.2.1)

Chapter Project

Working as a team of three to four students, prepare a monthly and yearly budget for Harald and Ella O'Brien, using Figure 2.7 as a model. Their monthly income and expenses are as follows:

Harald's net pay, $3,675; Ella's net pay, $3,785; interest on savings, $50; rent, $1,150; utilities, $300; gasoline, $250; insurance, $150; groceries, $800; clothing, $100; car payment, $610; car maintenance, $50; cell phone, $120; streaming and internet, $175; gifts, donations, and miscellaneous, $500; personal care items, $250; insurance deductibles and copays, $100; entertainment and recreation, $800.

Calculate their monthly cash surplus and distribute it as follows: retirement fund, $1,200, then evenly distribute the remaining cash surplus between their emergency fund and short-term savings.

Think Critically

1. Determine if Harald and Ella's budget meets the 50-30-20 budget plan. If not, how would you adjust their budget to meet the accepted guidelines?

2. Are Harald and Ella saving enough to build an emergency fund equal to 3 months' net pay within the next year? If not, how much more should they be saving in an emergency fund to reach their goal of 3 months' net pay in their emergency fund?

3. If you were Harald and Ella, what would you change about their budget? Would you try to reduce expenses? Would you increase savings? Explain your answer.

3 Chapter

Taxes

3.1 Our Tax System

What types of taxes does the government levy against individuals?

Learning Objectives

By the end of this lesson, you should be able to:

LO 3.1.1 Explain the purpose of different types of taxes.

LO 3.1.2 Explain how the U.S. tax system works.

Key Terms

- tax
- revenue
- progressive tax
- regressive tax
- proportional tax
- tax bracket
- voluntary compliance
- tax evasion
- audit

Consider This ...

Asa just finished his first full year of full-time employment after graduating from high school. When he started, he filled out a Form W-4, a form to let your employer know how much money to withhold from each paycheck for federal taxes. On his W-4, Asa declared zero withholding, which means Asa would have the maximum amount of taxes taken out of his check each pay period. He chose zero withholding to ensure he does not have to pay taxes when he files his tax return. Because of Asa's total earnings and the amount of taxes he paid over the year, he is expecting a tax refund.

When Asa received his Form W-2 listing his taxable income and tax withholdings, he compared it to his pay stubs and verified its accuracy. Now, he is ready to prepare his federal and state tax returns. He does so by going to the Internal Revenue Service (IRS) website along with his state's Department of Revenue website. He downloads the appropriate tax return forms, including Form 1040, which all taxpayers must complete, and files them electronically.

"I chose to have my tax refund directly deposited into my checking account this year. According to the IRS website, my tax refund should be deposited in my account within a couple of weeks," Asa tells his friend Davu.

"It's great that you are getting a tax refund," replies Davu. "I don't know a lot about taxes or how taxes are withheld from my check. I'm not sure if I should pay more taxes during each pay period or claim allowances to net more in each paycheck."

(continues)

(continued)

Read and Reflect

1. What are the pros and cons of choosing zero withholding to have the maximum taxes taken out of each paycheck? What are the pros and cons of having less taxes taken out of each paycheck?

2. What advice would you give to Davu if you were Asa?

LO 3.1.1 Types of Taxes

To support the activities of the government in a market economy, taxes are collected from individuals and businesses. A **tax** is a payment imposed on a taxpayer by a governmental unit. Incoming taxes are a source of income, also known as **revenue**, for the government. Taxes make up approximately 95 percent of the federal government's revenue. The government can spend revenue collected according to priorities set by Congress, as established by the U.S. Constitution.

The largest source of revenue for federal government spending is the personal income tax. Other taxes are also levied and provide additional revenue to federal governmental units, including Social Security and Medicare taxes, unemployment insurance, sales taxes, inheritance and estate taxes, gift taxes, import duties, and payroll taxes.

A commonly accepted principle of tax fairness is that individuals with higher incomes should pay more taxes than those with lower incomes. This theory is called the ability-to-pay principle. Some believe this principle is unfair because it penalizes those who earn more money by making them pay higher taxes. Others counter that part of the government's role is to redistribute money from those with much to those with little. Social responsibility dictates that we care for those who need help.

Do you think the ability-to-pay principle is a fair way to determine how much in taxes you owe? Why or why not?

Source: iStock.com/AndreyPopov

Some states and local governments also collect income taxes to fund the state government. There are three classifications for state income taxes: no income tax, a flat tax, or a progressive tax. Currently, eight states do not collect personal income taxes. They include Alaska, Florida, Nevada, South Dakota, Tennessee, Texas, Washington, and Wyoming. These states tend to have higher property, sales, and fuel taxes.

Progressive Taxes

A **progressive tax** takes a larger share of one's income as the amount of income grows. Revenue from a progressive tax is based on the ability-to-pay principle. The federal income tax is an example of a progressive tax. The more you earn, the more you pay. Someone with a low income may pay 12 percent of income as taxes, while someone with a higher income might pay 32 percent or more.

Regressive Taxes

A **regressive tax** takes a smaller share of one's income as the amount of income grows. A sales tax is an example of a regressive tax. It is regressive because lower-income people pay a higher percentage of their income on sales taxes than those with higher incomes. Assuming you purchase a $40,000 car and pay a 5 percent sales tax ($2,000), here is how the percentage of income affects low- and high-income earners:

Earnings: $150,000 per year
$2,000 ÷ 150,000 = 1.3% of income

Earnings: $40,000 per year
$2,000 ÷ 40,000 = 5% of income

Thus, a person earning $150,000 spends 1.3 percent of their income on sales tax, while a person earning $40,000 spends 5 percent on sales tax.

Almost all consumption or use taxes, taxes on goods and service, are regressive. State and local governments may limit the impact of regressive taxes through variable sales tax rates. Some state and local governments will have lower or no taxes on necessities, such as food and medications, which make up a large share of overall consumption for lower-income consumers. In most states, online purchases are now subject to sales taxes. The general rule for online sales is that sales taxes will be collected if the business has a physical presence in the state, such as a store, headquarters, or warehouse.

An excise tax is a form of consumption tax. An excise tax is imposed on specific goods and services, such as gasoline, cigarettes, alcoholic beverages, air travel, and cell phone service. Excise taxes are also considered regressive taxes.

Proportional Taxes

A **proportional tax**, also known as a flat tax, is one for which the rate stays the same regardless of income. The real property tax is an example of a proportional tax. All people who own property worth $100,000 in a community will pay the same tax amount, regardless of income. All people will pay the same rate whether they own property worth $50,000 or $500,000. However, those who own property with a lower value will pay proportionally less in property taxes than those who own property with a higher value.

Property taxes typically fund local education, city/county libraries, parks, police, fire, and health departments. Most of the services funded by property taxes provide for the general welfare of all citizens.

Other Taxes

Thousands of governmental units (federal, state, and local) can levy and collect taxes. In addition to income, sales, and property taxes, you will find capital gains taxes, value-added taxes, tariffs, license and registration fees, user fees, and tolls. A luxury tax is imposed on items like yachts and private planes. All these taxes are collected to fund government spending. A special type of excise tax is often levied on goods that are considered to be harmful to the public, such as alcohol, tobacco, soft drinks, fast foods, gambling, and single-use plastics.

The Federal Insurance Contributions Act (FICA) is a U.S. federal payroll tax. The tax rate is 6.2 percent of your gross wages for Social Security tax and 1.45 percent for Medicare tax. The amount of tax collected for Social Security is capped each year. Social Security taxes were collected on earnings up to $160,200 in 2023. If you earned more than $160,200 in 2023, your maximum Social Security tax was $9,932.40 (160,200 × 0.062). Medicare taxes are collected on all gross income. There is no earnings cap for Medicare. Instead, you will pay an additional 0.9 percent in Medicare taxes if you have a high income. You are considered a high-income earner if you make more than $200,000 in a year as a single person or $250,000 per year as a married couple. Social Security taxes provide benefits for retirees, the disabled, and children. Medicare taxes are used to provide healthcare benefits for people over age 65.

> ### ✓ Checkpoint
>
> Identify which level of government (federal, state, or local) levies income, payroll, property, and sales taxes.

LO 3.1.2 How the Tax System Works

Our tax system is very complex. Both individuals and businesses pay income taxes and must file income tax returns yearly. The Internal Revenue Service (IRS) is a federal government agency that administers the tax laws of the United States. The IRS collects federal taxes from individual and corporate taxpayers.

The IRS

The Internal Revenue Service is an agency within the U.S. Treasury Department. It is headquartered in Washington, D.C., and has regional offices nationwide. The main functions of the IRS are to collect income taxes and to enforce tax laws.

The IRS provides services to taxpayers. In local offices, IRS employees help taxpayers find information and forms. The IRS website offers essential information, instructions, and assistance in understanding tax laws. You can even file your tax return electronically at the IRS website. If you receive a refund, you can have the refund deposited directly into your bank account.

The Power to Tax

The power to levy federal taxes rests with the U.S. Congress. The U.S. Constitution provides that "all bills for raising revenue shall originate in the House of Representatives." Proposals to increase or decrease taxes or tax rates may come from the president, the Department of the Treasury, or a member of Congress representing a geographic area. The House Ways and Means Committee studies the proposals and makes recommendations to the full House of Representatives. Revenue bills must pass a vote in both the House and the Senate and then be signed into law by the president.

Paying Your Fair Share

The federal income tax system is progressive. This means that tax rates increase as taxable income increases. A tax rate is applied to an income range or **tax bracket**. Tax brackets are also called marginal rates because they apply to the next dollar you earn. Each year, the IRS updates the tax brackets for inflation. For example, in 2023, your tax bracket was 10 percent if you earned up to $11,000, but it became 12 percent when you earned one dollar more than $11,000. In a recent year, there were seven IRS tax brackets for individuals, as shown in **Figure 3.1.**

Figure 3.1   IRS Tax Brackets for Individuals

2023 Tax Table: Single Filers

Tax rate	Taxable income bracket	Tax owed
10%	$0 to $11,000	10% of taxable income
12%	$11,001 to $44,725	$1,100 plus 12% of the amount over $11,000
22%	$44,726 to $95,375	$5,147 plus 22% of the amount over $44,725
24%	$95,376 to $182,100	$16,290 plus 24% of the amount over $95,375
32%	$182,101 to $231,250	$37,104 plus 32% of the amount over $182,100
35%	$231,251 to $578,125	$52,832 plus 35% of the amount over $231,250
37%	$578,126 or more	$174,238.25 plus 37% of the amount over $578,125

Source: www.irs.gov

The U.S. Congress raises taxes when more revenue is needed, such as when there is a large national debt. When the federal government spends more than it receives in revenue, it has a deficit. An accumulation of deficits makes up the national debt. Sometimes Congress approves tax decreases, often when there is a tax surplus (more taxes are collected than money spent). Or if the economy needs stimulating, Congress may approve a tax decrease. Most tax increases and decreases are temporary until the economy stabilizes.

Our income tax system, both federal and state, is based on **voluntary compliance**, which means all citizens prepare and file tax returns on their own. Responsibility for filing a tax return and paying taxes rests with the individual. Failure to do so can result in a penalty, which usually includes interest on taxes owed plus a fine. Willful failure to pay taxes is **tax evasion**, a serious crime punishable by fine or imprisonment, or both. This is not the same as tax avoidance, taking all available deductions to reduce taxes.

An IRS Audit

The IRS audits millions of taxpayers each year. An **audit** is an examination of income tax returns. It questions the validity of information on a tax return and requires a response from the taxpayer. Taxpayers can represent themselves or authorize someone else to take their place or attend the audit,

Now that Asa has a full-time job, he is beginning to consider purchasing a house. When he talks with his parents, they tell him to make sure that he considers property taxes in the cost of buying a house. After looking at the cost of property taxes on a couple of houses he likes, Asa went back to his parents for additional information.

"I never thought about property taxes before you mentioned it. I saw property taxes will add to the cost of a house I want, but I still don't understand why I have to pay property taxes."

Asa's parents replied, "Property taxes are used for a lot of things in our community; they help with road repairs, funding police and fire departments, and so much more. Oh, and property taxes also help fund our public schools."

According to the National Center for Education Statistics, the national average for public school funding from property taxes is 37%, and in some states it is as high as 62%. This funding from property taxes, also known as local funding, results from taxes paid by property owners who live within the school districts. With this funding, schools find it easier to provide students with materials and resources for learning, cover operational costs, and pay the salaries of teachers and other staff. School funding, including that from tax dollars, is often a hot topic of discussion among community members and different stakeholder groups. It is usually the responsibility of the school district's Board of Education to ensure that tax funds are being used responsibly and appropriately.

Think Critically

1. How would you communicate the importance of local tax revenue to a friend who was questioning why they must pay taxes?

2. Why is local tax revenue such an important component of school budgets? How do students benefit from these local tax funds?

3. While the community funds schools, community members are not necessarily involved in directly choosing how those funds are spent in the school district. What concerns may community members have about tax dollars and school budgets?

4. Some community members may feel that they should not have to fund schools since they no longer have school-age children. How do you respond to complaints that property taxes for homes without school-aged children are unfair?

such as a lawyer, accountant, family member, or someone licensed to prepare tax returns. Most audits occur because numbers do not match (the W-2 does not agree with the income reported) or there are math errors.

The most common is a correspondence audit, where the taxpayer receives a letter requesting proof of items reported or deducted. An office audit requires the taxpayer to appear in person to answer questions and provide records to justify items on the tax return. A field audit is like an office audit, except the auditor visits the taxpayer's home or business to examine records or assets and ask specific questions. Once the IRS auditor has decided on taxes owed, errors, and other items of dispute, the taxpayer can appeal that decision to a court of law.

✓ Checkpoint

What does it mean to "pay your fair share" when discussing income taxes in the United States?

3.1 Lesson Review

Check Your Understanding

1. List three types of taxes levied in the United States. Give examples. (LO 3.1.1)
2. What is the IRS, and what is it empowered to do? (LO 3.1.2)
3. What is the purpose of an IRS audit? (LO 3.1.2)

Apply Your Understanding

1. Consider the taxes you and your family pay in a year, including income, sales, and gasoline taxes. Create a chart of the taxes paid. Identify if each tax is progressive, regressive, proportional, or other. (LO 3.1.1)
2. Using Figure 3.1, calculate the amount of income tax you would owe to the federal government if you earned $65,000 in income. (LO 3.1.2)

The Essential Question

What types of taxes does the government levy against individuals?

A: Progressive, regressive, proportional, and other taxes and fees are levied against individuals.

The Essential Question What kinds of income and deductions may be reported on a tax return?

Learning Objectives

By the end of this lesson, you should be able to:

LO 3.2.1 Define basic tax terminology.
LO 3.2.2 Prepare tax form 1040.

Key Terms

- filing status
- exemption
- gross income
- adjusted gross income
- standard deduction
- itemized deductions
- tax liability
- taxable income
- tax credit
- exempt status
- estimated tax

LO 3.2.1 Tax Terminology

U.S. citizens must file tax returns each year and pay their taxes. When preparing tax returns, there are many dos and don'ts to follow. We will start with the basic tax terms you will need to know.

Why is marital status important when filing an income tax return?

Source: Buccina Studios/Getty Images

Filing Status

Filing status describes your tax-filing group based on your marital status as of the last day of the tax year. Married taxpayers can choose to file jointly (with lower tax rates), or they may choose to file separately. Single taxpayers and those who are married but filing separately pay higher taxes than others.

When filing taxes, you must choose one of the following as your filing status:

- Single person (not married)
- Married person filing a joint return (even though only one spouse may have earned income)
- Married person filing a separate return
- Head of household (you may qualify as a head of household whether you are married or single if you provide a home for a dependent)
- Qualifying widow(er)

The IRS website (www.irs.gov) contains a more detailed description of these classifications.

You may also get advice about which filing status is right for you from a tax accountant or by answering questions within tax software that you can use to create your tax return.

Exemptions

When computing taxes, an **exemption** is an amount you may subtract from your income for each person who depends on your income to live. Each exemption reduces your taxable income and your total tax. As a taxpayer, you are automatically allowed one exemption for yourself unless someone else (such as a parent) claims you as a dependent on their return. If you file a joint return, you can take an exemption for yourself and your spouse.

You also are allowed exemptions for dependents. A dependent is a person who lives with you and for whom you pay more than half of their living expenses. Dependents can include children, a spouse, elderly parents, or disabled relatives living with and dependent on the taxpayer.

Gross Income

Gross income is all the taxable income you receive during the year. Earned income refers to money you earn from working. Unearned income refers to money you receive from a passive activity (not from working). Some forms of payment are not subject to income taxes. Examples are shown in **Figure 3.2.** Scholarships and grants are a form of unearned income. They may be taxable for amounts used for expenses other than tuition and books. Employer-paid tuition is often taxable. Gifts can be taxable if they exceed the maximum gift limit. In 2023, the maximum gift limit was $17,000 to an individual. The person making the gift is responsible for paying the gift tax.

You are also taxed on other forms of income, including winnings from gambling, bartering income, pensions and annuities, Social Security benefits, self-employment income, rental income, royalties, estate and trust income, and income on the sale of property.

Figure 3.2   Forms of Income

Earned Income	Unearned Income	Nontaxable Income
Wages	Capital gains	Child support
Salaries	Interest	Gifts under $17,000 (2023 amount)
Tips	Dividends	Inheritances
Business income	Alimony	Life insurance benefits
	Social Security	Veteran's benefits
	Unemployment compensation	Workers' Compensation benefits
	Scholarships/Grants	
	Prizes/Awards	

Wages, Salaries, and Tips

This category of earnings appears on your Form W-2, which is a summary of the income you earned and the taxes withheld by the employer during the year. It contains all income you receive through employment, including bonuses and noncash benefits or income, such as use of a company car. If you receive tips on your job, you must report your tips to your employer. These earnings must be reported as income and are included with your wages on Form W-2.

Interest Income

Interest income includes the income someone receives from bank accounts or from lending money to someone else. You should receive a Form 1099-INT for each investment that earned interest during the year. The form reports the amount of interest you earned from the investment.

Dividend Income

Dividends are money, stock, or other property corporations pay stockholders in return for their investment. You will receive a Form 1099-DIV for each stock investment, listing the dividend income.

Unemployment Compensation

If you receive any unemployment compensation during the year, you will receive a Form 1099-G, which shows the total you received. You must enter this amount as income on the tax return. Several factors are considered to determine if unemployment compensation is taxable.

Social Security Benefits

If you receive Social Security payments during the year, as much as 50 to 85 percent of this money is taxable if your total income exceeds the income limit set each year. In 2023, individuals who made between $25,000 and $34,000 had to pay income taxes on 50 percent of their Social Security income. Those earning over $34,000 paid income taxes on 80 percent of their Social Security income. You will receive a Form SSA-1099, which lists the total you received for the year.

Alimony and Child Support

Money paid to support a former spouse is called separate maintenance or alimony. In 2019, the Tax Cuts and Jobs Act (TCJA) went into effect and changed the rules related to spousal support. The person receiving spousal support is not required to report the alimony as taxable income. The spouse who is paying the alimony is required to pay the income taxes. Money paid to support dependent children is called child support. This income is not taxable for the person receiving it, nor is it deductible for the person paying it.

Adjusted Gross Income

The law allows you to subtract some types of spending from gross income. You can adjust your income by subtracting contributions to individual retirement accounts (IRAs), some student loan interest, and tuition and fees. These adjustments are subtracted from gross income to determine **adjusted gross income** and will reduce income that is subject to tax.

Taxable Income

In a previous chapter, you learned that deductions are amounts subtracted from your gross pay to determine your net pay. You will be eligible to take the **standard deduction** if you do not have many deductions. The standard deduction is determined annually by

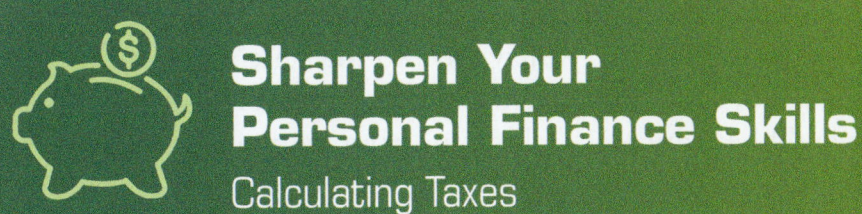

Sharpen Your Personal Finance Skills
Calculating Taxes

Take a closer look at Asa's income and federal tax withholding information to see what his federal tax refund should be. Asa's Form W-2 indicated that he earned $31,200 in taxable income and paid $5,096 in federal taxes. Using the tax tables on the IRS website, calculate the amount of taxes that Asa is liable for based on his income. Find his expected tax refund by subtracting his tax liability from the taxes he paid ($5,096). Remember, income tax calculations are marginal; even though Asa would fall into the 12% tax bracket, you cannot simply multiply his income by 12%, as that will incorrectly inflate his tax liability.

Answer:

Based on the 2023 tax table for single filers included in the chapter, Asa's tax liability would be:

$$\$1,100 + (\$31,200 - \$11,000) \times 0.12 = \$3,524$$

To calculate Asa's tax refund, you would take the amount of taxes he paid ($5,096) less his tax liability ($3,524) and find that his expected federal tax refund is $1,572.

the federal government. You will subtract the standard deduction amount from adjusted gross income, which changes yearly. However, it is possible that you qualify for many deductions. If so, you can itemize deductions. **Itemized deductions** are expenses you can subtract from adjusted gross income to determine your taxable income. Your taxable income determines your **tax liability**, which is the total tax you owe on a year's income. You can claim only the standard deduction or itemized deductions, not both. The Tax Cuts and Jobs Act of 2017 limited the amount taxpayers can deduct for state and local taxes and nearly doubled the standard deduction for taxpayers. In most cases,

you should itemize deductions only if the amount of your deduction is higher than the standard deduction.

To itemize deductions, you must use Schedule A. The list of expenses that can be itemized is long and can be found on the IRS website. Some common expenses you may deduct include some medical and dental expenses, mortgage interest, charitable contributions, and state or local taxes.

After the standard deduction (or itemized deductions) are subtracted from adjusted gross income, you arrive at your **taxable income**, which is the income on which you will pay tax. You can then determine your tax by looking up your taxable income in a tax table.

Tax credits may also be available to you. A **tax credit** is a reduction of taxes owed. Thus, if your tax (from the tax table) is $800 and you have a tax credit of $100, then the amount of taxes you owe would be reduced to $700. Because it directly reduces taxes, a tax credit is better than a deduction. The five largest tax credits are the Earned Income Tax Credit, the American Opportunity Tax Credit, the Lifetime Learning Credit, the Child and Dependent Care Credit, and the Savers Tax Credit.

✓ Checkpoint

Why is it important to understand the terms related to taxes?

LO 3.2.2 Preparing a Tax Return

Once you have gathered your income and expense records, you can start working on your tax return. There are several ways you can complete your tax return. You can complete and submit your taxes for free on the IRS website or you can use tax software. Tax software asks questions that you can answer, and the software will complete the return for you. You can submit your taxes to the IRS from the software. If you are a gig worker, own a business, or have investments, you may want to have a tax professional complete your return for you. If you overpaid income taxes throughout the year, you will receive a tax refund that can be directly deposited into your checking or savings account. If you did not pay enough taxes throughout the year, you will owe taxes. You can use a debit or credit card to make a payment if you owe taxes. In addition to a federal tax return, you may have to file state and local income tax returns. Save copies of your tax returns and all supporting evidence (receipts), Forms W-2, Forms 1099, and other tax forms for seven years. In the event you are audited, you are expected to have your records for three previous tax years or, if the IRS believes fraud is involved, seven years.

Who Must File and When?

You must file a tax return if you earned enough income to owe taxes. Because the gross income requirement is adjusted yearly, you can check the IRS website to see if you must file. If you did not earn enough to owe taxes, but taxes were withheld from your paychecks, you should file a return to claim a refund.

Exempt status is available to those who know they will not earn enough in one year to owe income tax. To claim exempt status, just write the word "exempt" on your Form W-4 (Employee's Withholding Allowance Certificate). Your employer will still withhold Social Security and Medicare taxes but will not withhold income taxes. If you are exempt, you do not have to file a tax return.

If you must file a tax return, the deadline is April 15 of each year. If that date falls on a weekend or holiday, your tax return is due on the next weekday. Penalties and interest charges are assessed if you file late.

Estimated Tax

If you received income for which taxes were not withheld, you may need to submit estimated tax payments during the tax year. **Estimated tax** is the amount of tax you estimate you will owe on income received without withholdings. For example, if you are in the 10 percent tax bracket and you received $5,000 in income for which no income taxes were withheld, you should send estimated taxes of $500 ($5,000 × 10%) to the IRS so you will not owe interest on that amount.

People who are self-employed, independent contractors, and business owners must pay estimated taxes quarterly (January 15, April 15, June 15, and September 15) based on estimated income for the quarter and for the year. Just like taxes that are withheld, estimated taxes are compared to your tax liability to see if more tax is owed or if a refund is due. Tax forms for paying estimated tax can be found on the IRS website.

Which Form to Use?

All taxpayers must use a Form 1040 when filing their individual tax return. There are many other supporting forms that may be required to support line items on the basic form.

In general, if your deductions add up to more than the standard deduction, your total tax will be lower if you use Form 1040 and itemize your deductions.

Where to Begin?

During the year, save all receipts and proof of payment for things that could be itemized deductions. You will need these receipts to prove the accuracy of your tax return if you are audited. Save all employee withholding records, such as your pay stubs. By January 31 you should receive a Form W-2 from each of your employers. Compare it with your records to check for accuracy. Any discrepancies between Form W-2 and your

Why would a taxpayer choose to itemize deductions?

Source: iStock.com//Hoxton/Tom Merton

records should be reported immediately to the employer and corrected.

Gather all other necessary information, including tax form instructions and last year's tax return as a model for preparing this year's return. Once you have gathered all your information, you can prepare your tax return.

Even if you hire a professional tax preparer, you are responsible for supplying accurate and complete information. Hiring a tax preparer will not guarantee that you are paying the correct amount. You must check the form before you sign it. If you discover an error after the return has been filed, you may file an amended return (Form 1040X) to make corrections.

Tax Preparation Software

Most professional tax preparers use a tax preparation computer program. You can also use tax preparation software to do your own taxes. Good software provides all the necessary forms and guides you through the process of filling out the forms. Most tax software also provides tips and additional information to help you identify all the deductions and credits you are allowed. Search the internet to find information about different brands of tax software. Software producers usually provide a feature tour at their website.

Form 1040

Completing a Form 1040 is not hard, but it does require you to pay close attention to detail and answer each question on the form correctly.

To complete the form, you need to have access to the form or use tax software. The IRS offers a PDF version of Form 1040 that you can complete manually. There is also a Free File Fillable Form available at the IRS website during the tax season (mid-January through mid-October). To complete the form, follow the general steps below.

Step 1: Fill in Your Basic Information

This includes your name, address, filing status, and the names of your spouse and dependent children.

Step 2: Report Your Income

Income can be from several sources, including:

- Wages reported on a W-2
- Interest and dividends reported on a 1099-INT or 1099-DIV
- Gig worker income reported on a 1099-NEC
- Miscellaneous income reported on a 1099-MISC
- Retirement income from IRAs, 401(k)s, pensions, and Social Security

Connections to Your World
Factors That Impact Tax Rates

There are several factors that impact the amount of taxes a person pays. Your tax rate may be different than a family member or friend based on these factors. After researching the reasons tax rates differ, discuss the following questions with classmates.

Think Critically

1. Which factors are most likely to impact the taxes you owe now? How do you think this will change at different stages of your life?
2. What are the two factors that you think may change and impact your tax liability the most in the next 10 years?

It is possible that you may be in a situation where you have other income such as from a business you own, rental property, farming, unemployment, and others. If this is the case, you will need to complete additional forms, and you may want to consult with a tax professional.

Step 3: Claim Your Deductions

This is choosing to use the standard deduction or itemizing deductions.

Step 4: Calculate Your Tax

The instructions for Form 1040 include tables for help with the tax calculations. If you are using tax software the calculation is done for you.

Step 5: Claim Tax Credits

If you have dependents, you may be able to claim the child tax credit. Many tax credits require you to complete an additional form.

Step 6: Calculate Your Refund or Amount Owed

Step 7: Sign and Submit the Document

If you are using tax software, you can submit electronically. If your income is less than $50,000, you can submit on the IRS website using their free submission tool. You can also mail the printed copy of the Form 1040 to the address provided in the instructions.

Example Form 1040

Figure 3.3 shows Form W-2 for Asa Ito. **Figure 3.4** shows his completed Form 1040 tax return. Asa is single. His wages are found on the W-2. Follow along on Asa's Form 1040 as you read the detailed instructions.

Step 1: Enter Name, Address, and Social Security Number, and Other Basic Information

You can download the form from the IRS website and fill in this information using

---

Figure 3.3   W-2 for Asa Ito

22222	**a** Employee's social security number 999-00-3894	OMB No. 1545-0008		
b Employer identification number (EIN) 93-899348488			**1** Wages, tips, other compensation $36,750.00	**2** Federal income tax withheld $3,398.00
c Employer's name, address, and ZIP code Blanton School District T-31 23855 SW 85th Portland, TX 78734			**3** Social security wages $36,750.00	**4** Social security tax withheld $2,279.00
			5 Medicare wages and tips $36,750.00	**6** Medicare tax withheld $534.00
			7 Social security tips	**8** Allocated tips
d Control number			**9** Advance EIC payment	**10** Dependent care benefits
e Employee's first name and initial Last name Suff. Asa Ito 285 SW 28th Street, #8 Portland, TX 78734			**11** Nonqualified plans	**12a**
			13 Statutory employee ☐ Retirement plan ☐ Third-party sick pay ☐	**12b**
			14 Other	**12c**
				12d
f Employee's address and ZIP code				

15 State Employer's state ID number TX 2384762	**16** State wages, tips, etc. $36,750.00	**17** State income tax $0.00	**18** Local wages, tips, etc.	**19** Local income tax	**20** Locality name

Form **W-2** Wage and Tax Statement   20--   Department of the Treasury—Internal Revenue Service

Source: Base art is W-2 from www.irs.gov; fictional copy added

Figure 3.4 1040 Tax Return for Asa Ito

Form **1040**
Department of the Treasury—Internal Revenue Service
U.S. Individual Income Tax Return 20**23** OMB No. 1545-0074 IRS Use Only—Do not write or staple in this space.

For the year Jan. 1–Dec. 31, 2023, or other tax year beginning _____, 2023, ending _____, 20 _____ See separate instructions.

Your first name and middle initial	Last name	Your social security number
Asa	Ito	9 9 9 0 0 3 8 9 4

If joint return, spouse's first name and middle initial | Last name | Spouse's social security number

Home address (number and street). If you have a P.O. box, see instructions. | Apt. no. | **Presidential Election Campaign**
285 SW 28th Street | #8 | Check here if you, or your spouse if filing jointly, want $3 to go to this fund. Checking a box below will not change your tax or refund.

City, town, or post office. If you have a foreign address, also complete spaces below.	State	ZIP code
Portland	TX	78734

Foreign country name | Foreign province/state/county | Foreign postal code | ☐ You ☐ Spouse

Filing Status
Check only one box.

☑ Single
☐ Married filing jointly (even if only one had income)
☐ Married filing separately (MFS)
☐ Head of household (HOH)
☐ Qualifying surviving spouse (QSS)

If you checked the MFS box, enter the name of your spouse. If you checked the HOH or QSS box, enter the child's name if the qualifying person is a child but not your dependent: _____

Digital Assets
At any time during 2023, did you: (a) receive (as a reward, award, or payment for property or services); or (b) sell, exchange, or otherwise dispose of a digital asset (or a financial interest in a digital asset)? (See instructions.) ☐ Yes ☑ No

Standard Deduction
Someone can claim: ☐ You as a dependent ☐ Your spouse as a dependent
☐ Spouse itemizes on a separate return or you were a dual-status alien

Age/Blindness You: ☐ Were born before January 2, 1959 ☐ Are blind **Spouse:** ☐ Was born before January 2, 1959 ☐ Is blind

Dependents (see instructions):

(1) First name Last name	(2) Social security number	(3) Relationship to you	(4) Check the box if qualifies for (see instructions):	
			Child tax credit	Credit for other dependents
			☐	☐
			☐	☐
			☐	☐
			☐	☐

If more than four dependents, see instructions and check here . . ☐

Income

Attach Form(s) W-2 here. Also attach Forms W-2G and 1099-R if tax was withheld.

If you did not get a Form W-2, see instructions.

1a	Total amount from Form(s) W-2, box 1 (see instructions) **1a**	36,750
b	Household employee wages not reported on Form(s) W-2 . . . . **1b**	
c	Tip income not reported on line 1a (see instructions) **1c**	
d	Medicaid waiver payments not reported on Form(s) W-2 (see instructions) **1d**	
e	Taxable dependent care benefits from Form 2441, line 26 . . . . **1e**	
f	Employer-provided adoption benefits from Form 8839, line 29 . . . . . **1f**	
g	Wages from Form 8919, line 6 . . . . **1g**	
h	Other earned income (see instructions) **1h**	
i	Nontaxable combat pay election (see instructions) **1i**	
z	Add lines 1a through 1h **1z**	36,750

Attach Sch. B if required.

2a	Tax-exempt interest . . .	**2a**		b	Taxable interest	**2b**	
3a	Qualified dividends . . .	**3a**		b	Ordinary dividends	**3b**	
4a	IRA distributions . . .	**4a**		b	Taxable amount	**4b**	
5a	Pensions and annuities . .	**5a**		b	Taxable amount	**5b**	
6a	Social security benefits . .	**6a**		b	Taxable amount	**6b**	

Standard Deduction for—
• Single or Married filing separately, $13,850
• Married filing jointly or Qualifying surviving spouse, $27,700
• Head of household, $20,800
• If you checked any box under Standard Deduction, see instructions.

c	If you elect to use the lump-sum election method, check here (see instructions) . . . . . ☐		
7	Capital gain or (loss). Attach Schedule D if required. If not required, check here . . . . . ☐	**7**	
8	Additional income from Schedule 1, line 10	**8**	
9	Add lines 1z, 2b, 3b, 4b, 5b, 6b, 7, and 8. This is your **total income**	**9**	36,750
10	Adjustments to income from Schedule 1, line 26	**10**	
11	Subtract line 10 from line 9. This is your **adjusted gross income**	**11**	36,750
12	**Standard deduction or itemized deductions** (from Schedule A)	**12**	13,850
13	Qualified business income deduction from Form 8995 or Form 8995-A	**13**	
14	Add lines 12 and 13	**14**	13,850
15	Subtract line 14 from line 11. If zero or less, enter -0-. This is your **taxable income**	**15**	22,900

For Disclosure, Privacy Act, and Paperwork Reduction Act Notice, see separate instructions. Cat. No. 11320B Form **1040** (2023)

(continues)

Figure 3.4 (continued)

Form 1040 (2023)   Page **2**

Tax and Credits	16	**Tax** (see instructions). Check if any from Form(s): **1** ☐ 8814 **2** ☐ 4972 **3** ☐		16	2,531
	17	Amount from Schedule 2, line 3		17	
	18	Add lines 16 and 17		18	
	19	Child tax credit or credit for other dependents from Schedule 8812		19	
	20	Amount from Schedule 3, line 8		20	
	21	Add lines 19 and 20		21	
	22	Subtract line 21 from line 18. If zero or less, enter -0-		22	
	23	Other taxes, including self-employment tax, from Schedule 2, line 21		23	
	24	Add lines 22 and 23. This is your **total tax**		24	2,531

Payments	25	Federal income tax withheld from:			
	a	Form(s) W-2	25a	3,398	
	b	Form(s) 1099	25b		
	c	Other forms (see instructions)	25c		
	d	Add lines 25a through 25c		25d	3,398
If you have a qualifying child, attach Sch. EIC.	26	2023 estimated tax payments and amount applied from 2022 return		26	0
	27	Earned income credit (EIC)	27	0	
	28	Additional child tax credit from Schedule 8812	28	0	
	29	American opportunity credit from Form 8863, line 8	29	0	
	30	Reserved for future use	30		
	31	Amount from Schedule 3, line 15	31	0	
	32	Add lines 27, 28, 29, and 31. These are your **total other payments and refundable credits**		32	0
	33	Add lines 25d, 26, and 32. These are your **total payments**		33	3,398

Refund	34	If line 33 is more than line 24, subtract line 24 from line 33. This is the amount you **overpaid**		34	867
	35a	Amount of line 34 you want **refunded to you**. If Form 8888 is attached, check here ☐		35a	
Direct deposit? See instructions.	b	Routing number x x x x x x x x x **c** Type: ☑ Checking ☐ Savings			
	d	Account number x x x x x x x x x x x x x x x x x x			
	36	Amount of line 34 you want **applied to your 2024 estimated tax**	36	0	

Amount You Owe	37	Subtract line 33 from line 24. This is the **amount you owe**. For details on how to pay, go to *www.irs.gov/Payments* or see instructions		37	
	38	Estimated tax penalty (see instructions)	38		

Third Party Designee	Do you want to allow another person to discuss this return with the IRS? See instructions	☐ **Yes.** Complete below. ☐ **No**
	Designee's name	Phone no. Personal identification number (PIN) ☐☐☐☐☐

Sign Here	Under penalties of perjury, I declare that I have examined this return and accompanying schedules and statements, and to the best of my knowledge and belief, they are true, correct, and complete. Declaration of preparer (other than taxpayer) is based on all information of which preparer has any knowledge.

	Your signature	Date Your occupation	If the IRS sent you an Identity Protection PIN, enter it here (see inst.)
Joint return? See instructions. Keep a copy for your records.	Spouse's signature. If a joint return, **both** must sign.	Date Spouse's occupation	If the IRS sent your spouse an Identity Protection PIN, enter it here (see inst.)
	Phone no.	Email address	

Paid Preparer Use Only	Preparer's name	Preparer's signature	Date	PTIN	Check if: ☐ Self-employed
	Firm's name			Phone no.	
	Firm's address			Firm's EIN	

Go to *www.irs.gov/Form1040* for instructions and the latest information.   Form **1040** (2023)

your computer or print a copy and fill it in by hand. This example is based on the 2023 tax year. The forms are updated each year to represent the most recent tax code.

- Fill in your name, address, and Social Security number.

- Check the "Yes" box if you want $3 to go to the Presidential Election Campaign Fund. This is a fund established by Congress so that taxpayers can share in the costs of election campaigns. The $3 contribution will not increase your tax or reduce your refund.

- Check the appropriate box if you have a digital asset (cryptocurrency). Asa did not receive any digital assets this year.
- Check the box if someone can claim you as a dependent. Asa is an adult, so he did not check the box. Asa is single. The question about a spouse does not apply.
- Asa is not blind, and he was born after 1959, so he did not check the box.
- Asa does not have any dependents.

Step 2: Report Income

- First, enter your total wages, salaries, and tips, as shown on your W-2 form(s). On Asa's Form W-2, you can see that he earned $36,750. He entered this amount on line 1a.
- If you have other types of income, you will enter the amounts in the appropriate lines numbered 1b through 1i. Asa did not have any other income to report.
- Add the amounts on line 1a to 1i and enter the amount on line 1z. Asa entered 36,750.
- If you have interest, dividends, retirement distributions, pension, or Social Security income, you will report those amounts on lines 2b through 6b. Asa did not have any other type of income.
- If you have capital gains or losses, you will include them on line 7.
- Line 8 asks for any other type of income. Asa did not have any other income.
- On line 9, add lines 1z, 2b, 3b, 4b, 5b, 6b, 7, and 8. Enter the total on line 9. Asa entered 36,750.
- If you completed Schedule 1, you would enter the amount found on line 10. Asa did not complete Schedule 1 because he had no adjustments to his income.
- For line 11, subtract line 10 from line 9. Enter the amount on line 11. Asa entered 36,750.
- Asa did not itemize his deductions, so he will enter the amount for a standard deduction. Since he is single, he entered 13,850.

- Asa did not have a business, so he entered 0 on line 13.
- For line 14, add lines 12 and 13. Asa entered 13,850.
- Line 15 is used to find your taxable income. Subtract line 14 from line 11. Asa entered 22,900. This is his taxable income.

Step 3: Compute Tax

On line 16, enter the total federal tax due. To figure tax owed, look up your taxable income (line 15) in the tax table from the instruction booklet on the IRS website (https://www.irs.gov/pub/irs-pdf/i1040gi.pdf). It will look similar to the one in **Figure 3.5**. In the tax table in the instruction booklet, Asa found that his taxable income of $22,900 fell within the range of $22,900 to 22,950. In that row, he located his total tax liability of $2,531 in the "Single" column and recorded it on line 16. Asa had no tax credits, so he followed the instructions and entered the values as directed on lines 17–24.

Step 4: Calculate Payments

Line 25a is where you enter the amount of federal income tax withheld. You find this amount in Box 2 of the Form W-2. Asa entered $3,398. Asa had no additional income. He entered the total tax payments he made on line 25d. Asa did not have any estimated payments, so he entered 0 on line 26. He did not qualify for any tax credits, so he entered 0 on the appropriate lines. Line 33 is his total payment for taxes during the year. Asa entered $3,398.

Step 5: Calculate Refund or Amount Owed

If the amount of federal taxes withheld (the amount you already paid) is larger than your total tax (from the tax table), you will receive

Figure 3.5 Part of 1040 Tax Table

2023 Tax Table

See the instructions for line 16 to see if you must use the Tax Table below to figure your tax.

Example. A married couple are filing a joint return. Their taxable income on Form 1040, line 15, is $25,300. First, they find the $25,300-25,350 taxable income line. Next, they find the column for married filing jointly and read down the column. The amount shown where the taxable income line and filing status column meet is $2,599. This is the tax amount they should enter in the entry space on Form 1040, line 16.

Sample Table

At Least	But Less Than	Single	Married filing jointly*	Married filing separately	Head of a household
			Your tax is—		
25,200	25,250	2,807	2,587	2,807	2,713
25,250	25,300	2,813	2,593	2,813	2,719
25,300	25,350	2,819	(2,599)	2,819	2,725
25,350	25,400	2,825	2,605	2,825	2,731

21,000

At least	But less than	Single	Married filing jointly*	Married filing separately	Head of a household
21,000	21,050	2,303	2,103	2,303	2,209
21,050	21,100	2,309	2,108	2,309	2,215
21,100	21,150	2,315	2,113	2,315	2,221
21,150	21,200	2,321	2,118	2,321	2,227
21,200	21,250	2,327	2,123	2,327	2,233
21,250	21,300	2,333	2,128	2,333	2,239
21,300	21,350	2,339	2,133	2,339	2,245
21,350	21,400	2,345	2,138	2,345	2,251
21,400	21,450	2,351	2,143	2,351	2,257
21,450	21,500	2,357	2,148	2,357	2,263
21,500	21,550	2,363	2,153	2,363	2,269
21,550	21,600	2,369	2,158	2,369	2,275
21,600	21,650	2,375	2,163	2,375	2,281
21,650	21,700	2,381	2,168	2,381	2,287
21,700	21,750	2,387	2,173	2,387	2,293
21,750	21,800	2,393	2,178	2,393	2,299
21,800	21,850	2,399	2,183	2,399	2,305
21,850	21,900	2,405	2,188	2,405	2,311
21,900	21,950	2,411	2,193	2,411	2,317
21,950	22,000	2,417	2,198	2,417	2,323

22,000

At least	But less than	Single	Married filing jointly*	Married filing separately	Head of a household
22,000	22,050	2,423	2,203	2,423	2,329
22,050	22,100	2,429	2,209	2,429	2,335
22,100	22,150	2,435	2,215	2,435	2,341
22,150	22,200	2,441	2,221	2,441	2,347
22,200	22,250	2,447	2,227	2,447	2,353
22,250	22,300	2,453	2,233	2,453	2,359
22,300	22,350	2,459	2,239	2,459	2,365
22,350	22,400	2,465	2,245	2,465	2,371
22,400	22,450	2,471	2,251	2,471	2,377
22,450	22,500	2,477	2,257	2,477	2,383
22,500	22,550	2,483	2,263	2,483	2,389
22,550	22,600	2,489	2,269	2,489	2,395
22,600	22,650	2,495	2,275	2,495	2,401
22,650	22,700	2,501	2,281	2,501	2,407
22,700	22,750	2,507	2,287	2,507	2,413
22,750	22,800	2,513	2,293	2,513	2,419
22,800	22,850	2,519	2,299	2,519	2,425
22,850	22,900	2,525	2,305	2,525	2,431
22,900	22,950	2,531	2,311	2,531	2,437
22,950	23,000	2,537	2,317	2,537	2,443

23,000

At least	But less than	Single	Married filing jointly*	Married filing separately	Head of a household
23,000	23,050	2,543	2,323	2,543	2,449
23,050	23,100	2,549	2,329	2,549	2,455
23,100	23,150	2,555	2,335	2,555	2,461
23,150	23,200	2,561	2,341	2,561	2,467
23,200	23,250	2,567	2,347	2,567	2,473
23,250	23,300	2,573	2,353	2,573	2,479
23,300	23,350	2,579	2,359	2,579	2,485
23,350	23,400	2,585	2,365	2,585	2,491
23,400	23,450	2,591	2,371	2,591	2,497
23,450	23,500	2,597	2,377	2,597	2,503
23,500	23,550	2,603	2,383	2,603	2,509
23,550	23,600	2,609	2,389	2,609	2,515
23,600	23,650	2,615	2,395	2,615	2,521
23,650	23,700	2,621	2,401	2,621	2,527
23,700	23,750	2,627	2,407	2,627	2,533
23,750	23,800	2,633	2,413	2,633	2,539
23,800	23,850	2,639	2,419	2,639	2,545
23,850	23,900	2,645	2,425	2,645	2,551
23,900	23,950	2,651	2,431	2,651	2,557
23,950	24,000	2,657	2,437	2,657	2,563

24,000

At least	But less than	Single	Married filing jointly*	Married filing separately	Head of a household
24,000	24,050	2,663	2,443	2,663	2,569
24,050	24,100	2,669	2,449	2,669	2,575
24,100	24,150	2,675	2,455	2,675	2,581
24,150	24,200	2,681	2,461	2,681	2,587
24,200	24,250	2,687	2,467	2,687	2,593
24,250	24,300	2,693	2,473	2,693	2,599
24,300	24,350	2,699	2,479	2,699	2,605
24,350	24,400	2,705	2,485	2,705	2,611
24,400	24,450	2,711	2,491	2,711	2,617
24,450	24,500	2,717	2,497	2,717	2,623
24,500	24,550	2,723	2,503	2,723	2,629
24,550	24,600	2,729	2,509	2,729	2,635
24,600	24,650	2,735	2,515	2,735	2,641
24,650	24,700	2,741	2,521	2,741	2,647
24,700	24,750	2,747	2,527	2,747	2,653
24,750	24,800	2,753	2,533	2,753	2,659
24,800	24,850	2,759	2,539	2,759	2,665
24,850	24,900	2,765	2,545	2,765	2,671
24,900	24,950	2,771	2,551	2,771	2,677
24,950	25,000	2,777	2,557	2,777	2,683

25,000

At least	But less than	Single	Married filing jointly*	Married filing separately	Head of a household
25,000	25,050	2,783	2,563	2,783	2,689
25,050	25,100	2,789	2,569	2,789	2,695
25,100	25,150	2,795	2,575	2,795	2,701
25,150	25,200	2,801	2,581	2,801	2,707
25,200	25,250	2,807	2,587	2,807	2,713
25,250	25,300	2,813	2,593	2,813	2,719
25,300	25,350	2,819	2,599	2,819	2,725
25,350	25,400	2,825	2,605	2,825	2,731
25,400	25,450	2,831	2,611	2,831	2,737
25,450	25,500	2,837	2,617	2,837	2,743
25,500	25,550	2,843	2,623	2,843	2,749
25,550	25,600	2,849	2,629	2,849	2,755
25,600	25,650	2,855	2,635	2,855	2,761
25,650	25,700	2,861	2,641	2,861	2,767
25,700	25,750	2,867	2,647	2,867	2,773
25,750	25,800	2,873	2,653	2,873	2,779
25,800	25,850	2,879	2,659	2,879	2,785
25,850	25,900	2,885	2,665	2,885	2,791
25,900	25,950	2,891	2,671	2,891	2,797
25,950	26,000	2,897	2,677	2,897	2,803

26,000

At least	But less than	Single	Married filing jointly*	Married filing separately	Head of a household
26,000	26,050	2,903	2,683	2,903	2,809
26,050	26,100	2,909	2,689	2,909	2,815
26,100	26,150	2,915	2,695	2,915	2,821
26,150	26,200	2,921	2,701	2,921	2,827
26,200	26,250	2,927	2,707	2,927	2,833
26,250	26,300	2,933	2,713	2,933	2,839
26,300	26,350	2,939	2,719	2,939	2,845
26,350	26,400	2,945	2,725	2,945	2,851
26,400	26,450	2,951	2,731	2,951	2,857
26,450	26,500	2,957	2,737	2,957	2,863
26,500	26,550	2,963	2,743	2,963	2,869
26,550	26,600	2,969	2,749	2,969	2,875
26,600	26,650	2,975	2,755	2,975	2,881
26,650	26,700	2,981	2,761	2,981	2,887
26,700	26,750	2,987	2,767	2,987	2,893
26,750	26,800	2,993	2,773	2,993	2,899
26,800	26,850	2,999	2,779	2,999	2,905
26,850	26,900	3,005	2,785	3,005	2,911
26,900	26,950	3,011	2,791	3,011	2,917
26,950	27,000	3,017	2,797	3,017	2,923

27,000

At least	But less than	Single	Married filing jointly*	Married filing separately	Head of a household
27,000	27,050	3,023	2,803	3,023	2,929
27,050	27,100	3,029	2,809	3,029	2,935
27,100	27,150	3,035	2,815	3,035	2,941
27,150	27,200	3,041	2,821	3,041	2,947
27,200	27,250	3,047	2,827	3,047	2,953
27,250	27,300	3,053	2,833	3,053	2,959
27,300	27,350	3,059	2,839	3,059	2,965
27,350	27,400	3,065	2,845	3,065	2,971
27,400	27,450	3,071	2,851	3,071	2,977
27,450	27,500	3,077	2,857	3,077	2,983
27,500	27,550	3,083	2,863	3,083	2,989
27,550	27,600	3,089	2,869	3,089	2,995
27,600	27,650	3,095	2,875	3,095	3,001
27,650	27,700	3,101	2,881	3,101	3,007
27,700	27,750	3,107	2,887	3,107	3,013
27,750	27,800	3,113	2,893	3,113	3,019
27,800	27,850	3,119	2,899	3,119	3,025
27,850	27,900	3,125	2,905	3,125	3,031
27,900	27,950	3,131	2,911	3,131	3,037
27,950	28,000	3,137	2,917	3,137	3,043

28,000

At least	But less than	Single	Married filing jointly*	Married filing separately	Head of a household
28,000	28,050	3,143	2,923	3,143	3,049
28,050	28,100	3,149	2,929	3,149	3,055
28,100	28,150	3,155	2,935	3,155	3,061
28,150	28,200	3,161	2,941	3,161	3,067
28,200	28,250	3,167	2,947	3,167	3,073
28,250	28,300	3,173	2,953	3,173	3,079
28,300	28,350	3,179	2,959	3,179	3,085
28,350	28,400	3,185	2,965	3,185	3,091
28,400	28,450	3,191	2,971	3,191	3,097
28,450	28,500	3,197	2,977	3,197	3,103
28,500	28,550	3,203	2,983	3,203	3,109
28,550	28,600	3,209	2,989	3,209	3,115
28,600	28,650	3,215	2,995	3,215	3,121
28,650	28,700	3,221	3,001	3,221	3,127
28,700	28,750	3,227	3,007	3,227	3,133
28,750	28,800	3,233	3,013	3,233	3,139
28,800	28,850	3,239	3,019	3,239	3,145
28,850	28,900	3,245	3,025	3,245	3,151
28,900	28,950	3,251	3,031	3,251	3,157
28,950	29,000	3,257	3,037	3,257	3,163

29,000

At least	But less than	Single	Married filing jointly*	Married filing separately	Head of a household
29,000	29,050	3,263	3,043	3,263	3,169
29,050	29,100	3,269	3,049	3,269	3,175
29,100	29,150	3,275	3,055	3,275	3,181
29,150	29,200	3,281	3,061	3,281	3,187
29,200	29,250	3,287	3,067	3,287	3,193
29,250	29,300	3,293	3,073	3,293	3,199
29,300	29,350	3,299	3,079	3,299	3,205
29,350	29,400	3,305	3,085	3,305	3,211
29,400	29,450	3,311	3,091	3,311	3,217
29,450	29,500	3,317	3,097	3,317	3,223
29,500	29,550	3,323	3,103	3,323	3,229
29,550	29,600	3,329	3,109	3,329	3,235
29,600	29,650	3,335	3,115	3,335	3,241
29,650	29,700	3,341	3,121	3,341	3,247
29,700	29,750	3,347	3,127	3,347	3,253
29,750	29,800	3,353	3,133	3,353	3,259
29,800	29,850	3,359	3,139	3,359	3,265
29,850	29,900	3,365	3,145	3,365	3,271
29,900	29,950	3,371	3,151	3,371	3,277
29,950	30,000	3,377	3,157	3,377	3,283

Source: www.irs.gov

a refund. If you owe more tax than was withheld, you must pay the difference. Write your check to the U.S. Treasury and enclose it with your return. Or if you file electronically, you can use a debit or credit card to pay the tax owed.

When Asa subtracted his total tax of $2,531 from his taxes withheld $3,398, the difference was $867, which he recorded on line 34. He wanted his refund deposited electronically into his checking account, so he entered the routing number (the first nine numbers printed on the bottom of his checks) and account number (the last seven numbers on the bottom of his checks) in the Refund section of his tax form and checked the box for account type: Checking. Asa did not want to apply any of his refund to his 2024 estimated taxes, so he entered 0 on line 36.

Step 6: Sign the Return

Sign and date your tax return. Make sure your W-2 form(s) and check (if you owe taxes) are included with the completed return, and mail them to the regional IRS office designated for your area. Or, if you file electronically, be sure to print a hard copy of the return for your files. You can also save the file electronically on your travel or thumb drive.

> **✓ Checkpoint**
>
> Why is it important to accurately complete a Form 1040 each year?

3.1 **Lesson** Review

Check Your Understanding

1. How is gross income different from taxable income? (LO 3.2.1)

2. How are deductions different from tax credits? (LO 3.2.1)

3. What information should you collect before filling out your tax return? (LO 3.2.2)

Apply Your Understanding

1. How does your filing status affect the amount of taxes you owe? Conduct research to determine who pays more taxes, a single person or a married couple filing jointly. Based on the tax table in Figure 3.5, who pays more taxes—someone single or married filing jointly? (LO 3.2.1)

2. Using the most recent instruction booklet for Form 1040 on the IRS website, calculate the income tax owed if the taxable income is $31,286 for a single person and a married couple filing jointly. (LO 3.2.2)

The Essential Question

What kinds of income and deductions may be reported on a tax return?

A: Taxable income includes wages, salaries, tips, and other forms of earned and unearned income. Deductions include mortgage interest, property and state income taxes, medical expenses, and charitable contributions.

Summary

3.1 Our Tax System

- Market economies collect taxes from individuals and businesses to support the activities of government.

- A tax is a payment imposed on a taxpayer by a governmental unit. Incoming taxes are a source of income or revenue for the government.

- The U.S. government collects revenue from citizens and businesses to spend as specified by Congress.

- The largest source of revenue for federal spending is the personal income tax.

- Other taxes are also levied, including Social Security and Medicare taxes, sales taxes, inheritance and estate taxes, gift taxes, import duties, and payroll taxes.

- A commonly accepted principle of tax fairness is that individuals with higher incomes should pay more taxes than those with lower incomes. This is called the ability-to-pay principle.

- As income grows, progressive taxes take a larger share of income and regressive taxes take a smaller share. The federal income tax is an example of a progressive tax. A sales tax is an example of a regressive tax.

- A proportional or flat tax is one for which the rate stays the same regardless of income. Real estate property tax is an example of a proportional tax.

- States, counties, and cities also collect revenue through taxes and fees.

- The IRS is the government agency responsible for collecting taxes, enforcing tax laws, and supplying information to help taxpayers prepare their tax returns.

- The federal income tax system is progressive. Different tax rates apply to different income ranges, or tax brackets.

- Our income tax system is based on voluntary compliance, which means all citizens must prepare and file tax returns on their own.

- Willful failure to pay taxes is tax evasion and is a serious crime punishable by a fine, imprisonment, or both.

- An audit is an examination of income tax returns by the IRS. The IRS audits millions of taxpayers every year.

- Most audits occur because numbers to not match or there are math errors.

3.2 Filing a Tax Return

- U.S. citizens must file tax returns each year and pay their taxes.

- Basic tax terminology includes filing status, exemptions, gross income, and taxable income.

- Filing status is your tax-filing group based on your marital status.

- Exemptions are the amount you may subtract from your income for each person who depends on your income to live. Dependents can include children, elderly parents, and others.

- Gross income consists of taxable income received from all sources.

- Gross income less certain allowable adjustments is called adjusted gross income.

- To determine taxable income, subtract adjustments and deductions from gross income.

- Tax deductions reduce taxable income, while tax credits are subtracted directly from taxes owed.

- You may take a standard deduction or itemize deductions if they will exceed the standard deduction. The standard deduction is determined by the federal government each year.

- There are different ways to complete a tax return, including using a free form on the IRS website or tax preparation software.

- All taxpayers must use a Form 1040 when filing their individual tax return. Some taxpayers may need to complete supporting forms depending on their individual circumstances.

- Tax Day is typically April 15 or the next business day if the 15th is on the weekend or a holiday. This is the filing deadline for most individuals.

- The taxpayer will need basic information such as name, address, and Social Security number to complete a Form 1040. In addition, documentation for reported income (wages, interest, dividends, and more) will be required.

- If the amount of taxes withheld from your paychecks exceeds the total taxes you owe, you will receive a refund. If the amount withheld is less than you owe, you must pay the difference when you file your tax return.

Check Your Knowledge

1. Why are taxes collected from individuals and businesses? (LO 3.1.1)

2. Why are regressive taxes considered unfair to lower-income taxpayers? (LO 3.1.1)

3. How is tax avoidance different from tax evasion? (LO 3.1.2)

4. How do new federal tax laws get passed? (LO 3.1.2)

5. How do deductions affect the amount of tax you will pay? (LO 3.2.1)

6. What is meant by noncash income? Is it taxable? (LO 3.2.1)

7. What types of adjustments can you claim to reduce your adjusted gross income? (LO 3.2.1)

8. How is tax liability different from taxable income? (LO 3.2.1)

9. What are deductible expenses for taxpayers who itemize? (LO 3.2.1)

10. What information is required to complete a Form 1040? (LO 3.2.2)

Apply Your Knowledge

1. Compare your state's tax system with that of other states. Which states are considered the worst (in terms of high taxes)? Which states are considered the best (in terms of low taxes)? Create a table or a graphic of your findings. (LO 3.1.1)

2. Create a poster or other creative project that explains how the U.S. tax system works. (LO 3.1.2)

3. Which would reduce tax liability more—a $300 deduction or a $300 tax credit? Explain. (LO 3.2.1)

4. Download a copy of Form 1040 for the year 2023 (https://www.irs.gov/pub/irs-pdf/f1040.pdf) and the 2023 tax tables (https://www.irs.gov/pub/irs-pdf/i1040tt.pdf) from the IRS website. Using the tax form and information from the tax tables, calculate the tax liability for Joon Lee and the refund or money he owes. Joon is single and claims the standard deduction. He had taxable income of $21,134 and taxes withheld of $1,916. (LO 3.2.2)

5. Using the tax form and tax tables you downloaded from the IRS website in the previous question, prepare a tax return for Tomeka Hunt. Tomeka's information is as follows:

   ▪ Tomeka is a part-time engineer who lives at 54 Center Street, San Francisco, CA 96214-3627. Tomeka's Social Security number is 999-00-9892. She wants $3 to go to the Presidential Election Campaign Fund. She is single and claims the standard deduction. Tomeka's salary is $32,880. She earned interest of $155 on her investments. No one else claims her as a dependent, and she had $2,825 in federal taxes withheld. (LO 3.2.2)

Share Your Knowledge

Work in teams of two to four students to complete the following activities.

1. Explore proportional, progressive, and regressive taxes and their impact on individuals. As a team, prepare a letter to your local House of Representatives member sharing what you have learned about taxes and suggest ways to improve the tax system. (LO 3.1.1)

2. Some people feel that the IRS is too powerful. Find a classmate with a view that is in opposition to yours. Take turns trying to convince your classmate that your viewpoint is correct. Listen actively and respectfully as they attempt to convince you that they are correct. Create a summary of what you learned by listening to an opposing viewpoint. Include if you changed your perspective on this issue. (LO 3.1.2)

3. Exchange the Form 1040 you completed for Tomeka in the previous activity with a classmate. Conduct an audit of their completed form, highlighting any errors you find. Meet with your classmate to discuss the errors you found and determine how to correct them. (LO 3.2.2)

Connect and Reflect

Base your answers to the following questions on your own personal thoughts, preferences, and experiences.

1. Some people believe that this country's income tax rates are too high. Others feel that the tax burden is not spread equitably among taxpayers, with some paying much more than others without justification. What do you think about the progressive tax system in this country? How do you think it will affect you in the future? (LO 3.1.2)

2. In what ways can you minimize your tax burden over your lifetime? How can you engage in tax avoidance without entering into tax evasion? (LO 3.2.1)

3. What steps would you take to estimate your taxes for a tax year? If you believe you will owe more taxes than you are having withheld, what can you do? Why is it important to do this type of tax planning? (LO. 3.2.2)

Chapter Project

Voluntary compliance is an important part of our tax system. When everyone contributes their fair share, the country can meet its obligations to its citizens. However, a group of people called tax protestors believe that the U.S. Constitution does not require them to pay federal income taxes and that tax payment is voluntary. Research tax protestors. Write a paper, create a poster, or prepare a slide deck about tax resisters and those who refuse to pay taxes. Is their argument rational? On what is it based? What is your position on this issue?

Chapter 4

Banking and Investing

The Essential Question   How can you maximize your services and minimize your fees at a financial institution?

Learning Objectives

By the end of this lesson, you should be able to:

LO 4.1.1   Describe banking services available at most financial institutions.

LO 4.1.2   Explain fees charged by financial institutions for their services.

Key Terms

- Federal Deposit Insurance Corporation (FDIC) insurance
- credit union
- certified check
- payee
- payor
- cashier's check
- debit card
- overdraft protection
- electronic funds transfer (EFT)
- stop-payment order
- safe deposit box
- notary public
- bank fees
- nonsufficient funds (NSF) fee
- Truth in Savings Act (TISA)
- automated teller machine (ATM) fee

Consider This ...

DeAndre recently started working his first part-time job. When he was hired, his employer encouraged him to sign up for direct deposit, but he chose to receive paper checks since he did not have a checking account. DeAndre received his first check and was excited to cash it; he has received two additional checks that are sitting on his desk at home.

DeAndre's friend Isaac asked him to go to lunch, and DeAndre replied, "I would love to, but I don't have any cash with me. It's hard to make it to the bank to cash my checks with school and practice."

"Why don't you open a checking account so you can have direct deposit and a debit card?" Isaac asks. "Once you have an account, you'll have access to your money the day you are paid and can use your debit card whenever you need. There are a lot of other great services that banks provide to make financial planning and saving easier too."

(continues)

(continued)

Read and Reflect

1. What services can a bank offer young adults?
2. How can opening a checking account benefit you as you begin working and planning for the future?

LO 4.1.1 Banking Services

A full-service bank is a for-profit company that offers many different types of services, from savings and checking accounts to credit cards, safe deposit boxes, loans, and online banking. Other services may include bank by phone, certified checks, cashier's checks, money orders, and debit cards. Most banks offer **Federal Deposit Insurance Corporation (FDIC) insurance**. The standard insurance amount is $250,000 per depositor, per banking institution, for each account type. Many people may have access to a **credit union**. A credit union operates like a bank; however, it is a nonprofit company owned by people with accounts there. The account holders are called members. The National Credit Union Administration (NCUA) insures deposits at credit unions and is similar to the FDIC.

Guaranteed-Payment Checks

A **certified check** is a personal check a bank has certified. Certified checks are written from a personal or business account and delivered to the **payee**. A payee is the person who receives the check. The **payor** is the person or business writing the check. For example, if you buy a used car from someone, the owner of the car would be the payee in the transaction since they are the one receiving the payment; in this case,

Why would you need a certified or cashier's check?

Source: iStock.com//skynesher

the owner of the vehicle, the payee, might want a certified check before allowing you to take the car. To have a check certified, you must go to the bank in person. A bank employee will immediately deduct the amount from your checking account and will provide you with a check that has the word *Certified* stamped on it. The bank deducts the check amount from your account for the specific check payment. Most financial institutions charge the account holder for this service. Typically, the fee ranges from $10 to $20 per check.

A **cashier's check**, also called a bank draft, is a check written by a bank on its own funds. You can pay for a cashier's check through a withdrawal from your savings or checking account, or in cash. After receiving your payment, the teller makes out the cashier's check to the payee, and a bank officer signs it.

Cashier's checks are generally used when the payee requires a guaranteed payment, but cash is not desirable. A cashier's check can also be used for transactions in which you wish to remain anonymous. As with certified checks, many banks charge a fee for issuing cashier's checks.

Money Orders

Some banks sell money orders to people who do not wish to use cash or do not have a checking account. A money order is like a cashier's check. There is a charge for purchasing a money order. It can cost from 50 cents to $5 or more, depending on the money order amount. You can also purchase money orders through the post office and local merchants.

Debit Cards

A **debit card** is a bank card that deducts money from a checking account to pay for purchases. When a debit card is used, the purchase amount is quickly deducted from the customer's checking account and paid to the merchant. The debit card transaction is like writing a check to pay for purchases. The issuing bank may charge an annual fee for the card or a fee for each transaction. A debit card is not the same as a credit card because the funds are quickly withdrawn from your checking or savings account. Some businesses, like a gas station or hotel, will do an initial authorization for a debit card purchase. The gas station may place up to a $100 hold on your account, which will later be updated for the actual purchase amount within 24 to 48 hours. While the initial authorization is pending, you will not have access to those funds for other purchases.

Debit cards can also be used for cash withdrawals at ATMs. Debit cards with a Visa or MasterCard logo can be used for purchases wherever credit cards are accepted. Usually, there is a daily limit on how much can be withdrawn from an account using a debit card. This is to protect consumers from fraud if they lose their cards.

Bank Credit Cards

You can apply to a full-service bank for a bank credit card, such as a Visa or MasterCard. If you meet the requirements and are issued a card, you can use it instead of cash at any business that accepts credit cards. Banks often offer special credit card perks to their best customers whose accounts are in good standing. For example, a bank's best customers may be offered lower interest rates and no annual fees on their credit cards.

Banks offering national credit cards usually charge both an annual fee for use of the card and interest on the unpaid account balance. The topics of credit and credit cards will be discussed in more detail in a later unit.

Overdraft Protection

Overdraft protection is a service that your bank or credit union will offer you. If you accept **overdraft protection**, the bank will pay for transactions even if your checking account does not have enough money to cover transactions. It does this by moving funds from your savings account or a line of credit into your checking account. Typically, there will be a maximum overdraft amount that allows you to cover checks or withdrawals up to the limit. Protection may be offered in the form of an instant loan with high interest rates. Other banks may charge a flat fee. Banks may charge transfer fees for this type of protection. If you do not have overdraft protection, your debit card may be declined when you attempt to purchase or withdraw cash from an ATM.

Automated Teller Machines (ATMs)

Many banks provide ATMs for their customers. At an ATM, you can make cash withdrawals, using your debit card from your checking or savings account. Using a Visa or MasterCard, you can receive a cash advance electronically. Many banks also allow you to make cash or check deposits at an ATM. To use 24-hour ATMs, you must have a card that is electronically coded. You also must know your personal identification number (PIN), which usually is a combination of numbers and letters. For safety, memorize your PIN.

Online and Telephone Banking

Most financial institutions offer online and telephone banking services. These services allow you to access your accounts from a computer or telephone, transfer money from one account to another, and pay bills by authorizing the bank to disburse money. You can find out your current balance, what checks have cleared, and which deposits have been entered. Online and telephone banking enable you to access your account 24, hours daily.

Most banks also allow and encourage electronic transfers of money. An **electronic funds transfer (EFT)** uses a computer-based system that enables you to move money from one account to another without writing a check or exchanging cash. This can be done by telephone, by computer, or in person. Money is available immediately, so you do not need to wait for a check to clear. Electronic transfers can also be made between banking institutions, and funds are available immediately.

Stop-Payment Orders

A **stop-payment order** asks the bank to not honor a specific check. The usual reason for stopping payment is the check is lost or stolen. By issuing a stop-payment order, the payor can safely write a new check, knowing that the original check cannot be cashed if it is found and presented to the bank. Most banks charge a fee for stopping payment on a check. The stop-payment order is usually good for only 6 months. After that, the check may no longer be honored because checks over 6 months old generally are not valid for cashing or depositing.

You can also request a debit card stop payment for scheduled payments. You must submit a request, often in writing, to the bank at least 3 days before the scheduled payment is to be withdrawn from your account. Once the payment is in process, it cannot be stopped.

Safe Deposit Boxes

Financial institutions often offer customers a **safe deposit box** to store valuable items or documents. They charge a yearly fee based on the size of the box. Annual rental fees may range from $50 to $350 or more. The customer is given one or two keys for the box. The bank will also have a key. The customer's and bank's keys must both be used to open the box. Documents commonly kept in a safe deposit box are birth certificates, marriage and death certificates, deeds and mortgages, and other documents that cannot be easily replaced. Jewelry, coin collections, and other small valuables may also be stored in a safe deposit box. Keeping important documents and other items in a safe deposit box ensures that they will not be stolen, lost, or destroyed. Documents that can be easily replaced with a duplicate need not be stored there.

You will fill out a signature card when you rent a safe deposit box. Then, when you enter your safe deposit box, you must sign a form so that your signature can be compared to the one on file. This procedure prevents unlawful entry to your box by an unauthorized person.

Loans and Trusts

Financial institutions also make loans to finance the purchase of cars, homes, vacations, home improvements, and other items. Banks can also provide financial management advice related to retirement and estate planning. You will learn more about estate planning and trusts in a later chapter.

Notary Public Services

A **notary public** verifies a person's identity, witnesses the person's signature on a legal document, and then notarizes the signature as valid. Financial institutions typically have at least one person on their staff, a notary public. This person provides notary services for account holders, usually without charge. For noncustomers, however, there is typically a small fee of $10 or less.

Financial Services

Some banks offer financial services to their depositors, such as purchasing or selling savings bonds and investment brokerage services. You may buy and sell stocks and bonds through the brokerage service. The purchases and sales are cleared through your

checking or savings accounts with the bank. Brokerage services will be discussed in a future chapter.

LO 4.1.2 Banking Fees

Banking fees cover the operating costs of banks and credit unions. Customers pay the **bank fees** for using banking services. For example, when a bank grants you a loan, it charges you a loan origination fee. If you lose your debit card, the bank may charge you a fee to replace the card. If you attempt to spend more than is available in your account, the bank may charge you a **nonsufficient fund (NSF) fee**. Other fees charged by banks may include monthly service, overdraft, and ATM fees.

Banks also charge noncustomers for services such as check cashing. If you want to cash a check at a bank where you do not have an account, the bank may charge you a fee or refuse to cash the check. Nondepositors pay for other services that may be free to depositors, such as cashier's checks, and notary services.

The **Truth in Savings Act (TISA)** is a federal law passed in 1991 and is part of the FDIC Improvement Act of 1991. The purpose of TISA is to promote competition between banks and credit unions by mandating the disclosure of information related

Why is it important to know the fees your bank charges for its accounts and services?

Source: hedgehog94/Shutterstock.com

to interest rates, fees, and other items associated with banking accounts.

An **automated teller machine (ATM) fee** is typically charged by an ATM that does not belong to your bank or credit union. For example, if you do not have an account at Wells Fargo and you use a Wells Fargo ATM, Wells Fargo will charge you a fee. In some cases, your bank will also charge you an ATM fee for using another bank's ATM.

The best way to avoid fees is to choose the right account. For example, if you need to process many transactions each month, sign up for an account that does not charge a per-transaction fee. Shop around and find the account that is right for you. Be aware of the rules of your account so that you do not violate them, resulting in high fees. If your account requires a minimum balance, plan enough cushion so your balance will not drop below that amount. Most banks and credit unions offer free accounts to students.

✓ Checkpoint

Why do banks or credit unions charge service fees?

4.1 Lesson Review

Check Your Understanding

1. List five banking services that are found at full-service banks or credit unions. (LO 4.1.1)

2. List bank fees charged to customers and noncustomers for services provided. (LO 4.1.2)

Apply Your Understanding

1. When transferring a title (such as when selling a car) many sellers require that buyers use a cashier's check. Why? (LO 4.1.1)

2. Checking accounts have many good features, such as overdraft protection. List banking services that appeal to you and indicate whether each is of high, medium, or low value. Would you be willing to pay a monthly service fee to have the service? (LO 4.1.2)

The Essential Question

How can you maximize your services and minimize your fees at a financial institution?

A: Choose accounts that have the right features and be aware of all fees that could be imposed, such as ATM fees, so that you can avoid them.

The Essential Question

What is the purpose of a checking account, and why is it important to reconcile bank accounts?

Learning Objectives

By the end of this lesson, you should be able to:

LO 4.2.1 Describe the purpose of a checking account.

LO 4.2.2 Explain how to use and reconcile a bank account.

LO 4.2.3 Describe the types of checking accounts.

Key Terms

- checking account
- signature form
- demand deposit
- Automated Clearing House (ACH)
- overdraft
- routing number
- account number
- bank reconciliation
- endorsement
- beneficiary
- standard account
- money market account
- share account

LO 4.2.1 Checking Account Basics

Financial institutions such as banks and credit unions offer several services. The first service you will likely want is a checking account. A **checking account** allows you to write checks or transfer money electronically to make payments.

Opening a Checking Account

To open a checking account, you usually go to the bank in person. Most banks will not allow anyone under 18 to open a bank account without a parent or guardian; however, some banks will allow a 16-year-old to open an account.

To open an account, you must have several documents with you:

- A valid, government-issued photo ID, such as a driver's license, state-issued photo ID, or passport

- Birthdate (usually on the photo ID)
- Social Security number or taxpayer identification number
- A minimum amount to deposit to open the account

Information obtained from the new account holder, such as their street address and Social Security number, is entered into the form electronically by the bank's account manager. The form is then signed and becomes an official document, called a signature form. A **signature form** provides an official signature that the financial institution can use to compare to the signature you write on your checks or when signing electronically on debit and credit card transactions. The form helps the bank verify your identity.

Why Use Checks?

A check is a written order to a bank to pay the amount stated to the person or business named on it. A checking account is known as a **demand deposit** because the money may be withdrawn at any time—that is, on demand. Only the account owner can write checks on the account. Although no longer the primary way money is transferred between people, understanding how to write and cash a check remains an important skill. Checks are traceable transactions. This means that if you are paying something important, such as rent or income taxes, a check can provide written proof that the transaction was completed. Some businesses will also send you a check as payment. Family members may give you a check for a special occasion. You will need to know how to deposit the check into your account.

Checks move through the banking system using an electronic process. The paper check is converted to an electronic withdrawal by taking the routing and account numbers from the check and entering them in the Automated Clearing House (ACH) system to transfer the funds from your bank to the receiving financial institution. The **Automated Clearing House** is an electronic network used to securely accept deposits and distribute payments. If you receive your paycheck as a direct deposit, the check has gone through the ACH system. Banks no longer return checks to depositors; canceled checks can be viewed online and printed when needed to verify payment in cases of a dispute with a vendor.

You must also maintain enough money in your account to pay all the checks you write. A check written for more money than your account contains is called an **overdraft**. A bank that does not honor a check returns it to the payee's bank indicating nonsufficient funds (NSF). When this occurs, the check has bounced. Your bank will charge you a fee of $25 or more for each NSF check processed.

Why would you need to write a check in today's environment?

> ✓ **Checkpoint**
>
> What is the purpose of a checking account?

LO 4.2.2 ## Using Your Checking Account

Checking accounts can help you manage your personal finances, but only if you use them correctly. Careless or improper use of a checking account can result in financial loss. Here are some tips on using a checking account.

Parts of a Check

A check consists of the following parts. Look at the lettered elements of the check in **Figure 4.1** as you read the following explanations.

A   Check number. Checks are numbered sequentially for easy identification.
B   ABA number. The American Bankers Association (ABA) number appears as a fraction in the upper right-hand corner of the check. The top half of the fraction identifies the location and district of the

Figure 4.1   Parts of a Check

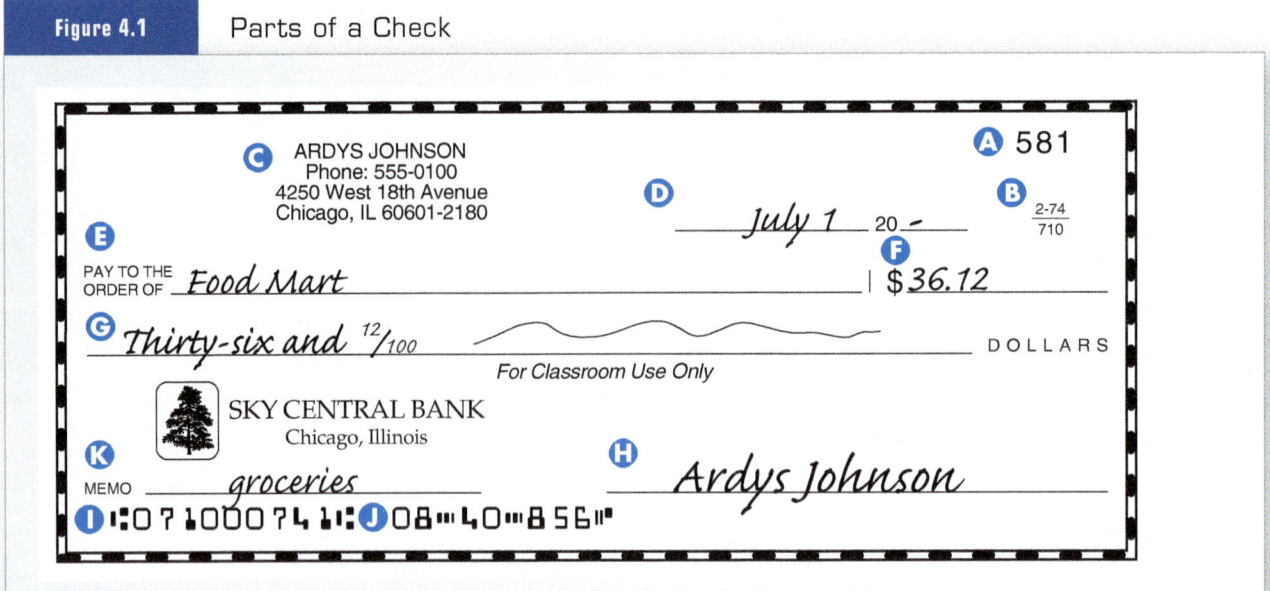

bank. The bottom half identifies the specific area and bank for the account.

C   Name and address of payor. The payor is the person who wrote the check. Ardys is the payor of this check. The account holder's name, address, and phone number are printed on the check.

D   Date. Enter the date the check is written. Checks written with a future date will not be held by the bank to be honored later.

E   Payee. The payee is the person or company to whom the check is payable. Food Mart is the payee in Figure 4.1.

F   Numeric amount. Write the amount neatly and close to the dollar sign, with dollars and cents clearly separated.

G   Written amount. The written amount shows the amount being paid in words. The word *dollars* is usually printed at the end of the line. Use the word *and* to separate dollar amounts from cents.

H   Signature. Sign the check on the signature line the same way as your name appears on the signature card.

I   Routing number. The **routing number** is a unique nine-digit number that is the address of your financial institution. You must provide the routing number for direct deposit or automatic payments.

J   Account number. The **account number** is a 5- to 17-digit number used to identify your personal account.

K   Memo. The memo line appears at the bottom left of the check. There may be identifying information you wish to fill in here.

Financial institutions sell checks to customers. They may provide checks of basic design free to account holders who maintain certain types of accounts. You can also choose to buy checks with special designs or colors, either from your bank or from a check-printing company.

Writing Checks

When writing checks, be sure to do the following:

- Always use a pen, preferably one with dark ink that does not skip or blot.
- Write legibly. Keep numbers and letters clear and distinct, without extra space before, between, or after them.
- Sign your name as it appears preprinted on the check and signature card.
- Avoid mistakes. If you make a mistake, write "VOID" across the face of the check to cancel it and then write a new check.
- Be certain you have deposited adequate funds in your account to cover each check you write.

Paying Bills Online

Instead of writing checks to pay bills, you can pay bills online. It is safer than sending checks through the mail and faster because money leaves your account right away. It is also convenient and saves both postage and the cost of checks.

To pay bills online, you have two choices. First, you can register at the website of the business to which you will be making payments. This choice is often the most convenient and easiest to manage. You can make single payments online or sign up for automatic payments. If using automatic payments, you should always have enough in your account to pay the bill. To set up an automatic payment, you will have to provide the routing number of your financial institution and your checking account number.

Second, you can pay bills from your own bank. To do this, you must first register at your bank's website. During that process, you establish your personal identification number (PIN) or password to enter your account. Screen prompts will lead you to the bank's online bill payment page, such as the one shown in **Figure 4.2**.

After you set up your list of payees, you can pay bills each month by simply selecting the payee from the list and entering the payment amount. The bank will remove the money from your checking account and send it to the payee's account.

Some banks charge a monthly fee for online bill payment privileges. Some limit

Figure 4.2   Online Bill Payment Page

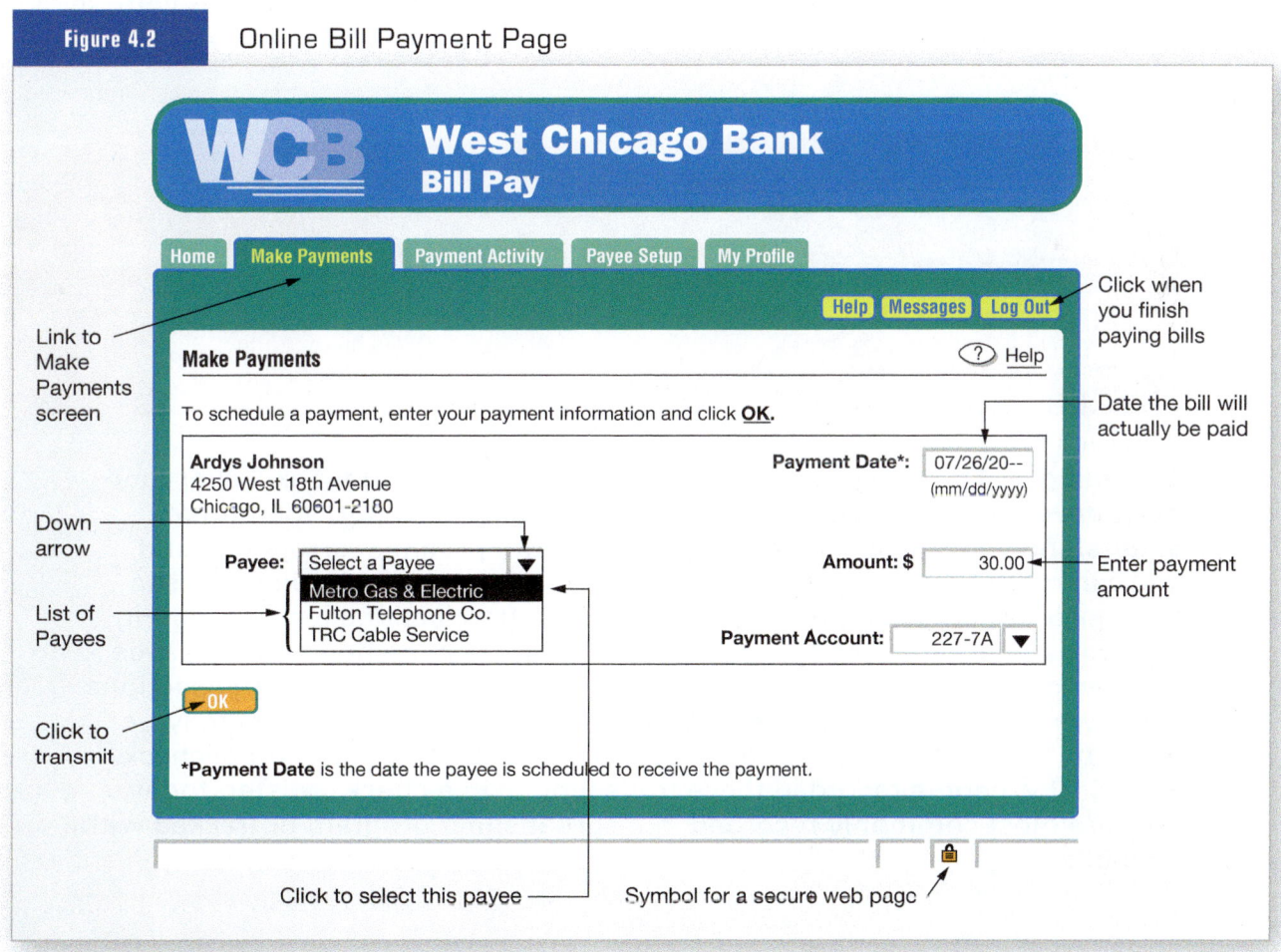

Figure 4.3   Deposit Slip

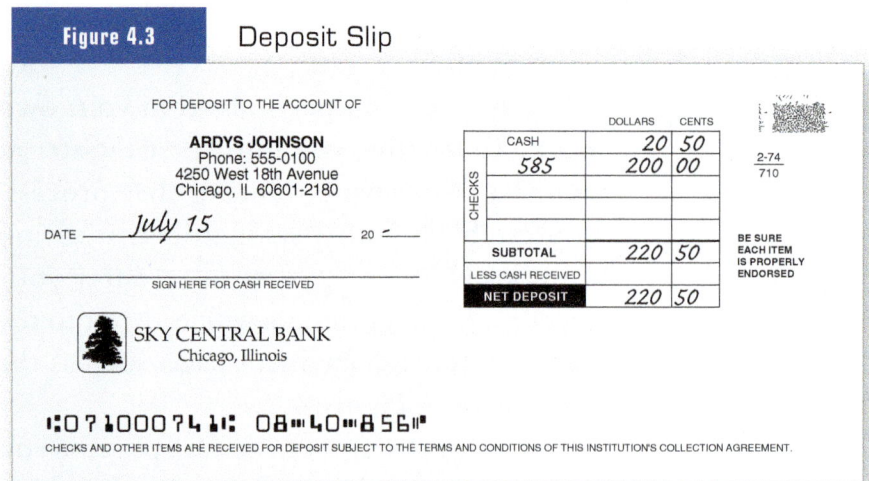

the bank when you make an in-person deposit. Online and ATM deposits are more popular ways to deposit money into your bank account, and they generally do not require a deposit slip because you verify your identity with your debit card or through the mobile app. **Figure 4.3** illustrates a deposit slip.

the number of bills you can pay online each month. Consider the fees and restrictions for online banking when you choose a bank.

Making Deposits

You should complete a deposit slip if you are depositing in person at the financial institution. You will receive a receipt from

Reconciling Your Account

Keeping track of your checking account deposits and withdrawals is an important part of a sound financial plan. The process of matching your checkbook register with the bank statement is known as **bank reconciliation**. Reconciling your spending with your bank balance will help you

Connections to Your World
Recording Account Transactions

Recording and tracking account transactions is an important skill everyone must develop. By tracking the transactions in your account, you better understand your financial standing, can identify potential errors or fraud, and can more accurately develop and follow a budget. Recording transactions includes recording both debit and credit transactions for an account, typically a checking account. Debit transactions occur when money leaves your account, for example, when you pay for something. Credit transactions occur when money is deposited into your account; these deposits may be made by you or through your employer directly depositing your paycheck. Historically, people recorded these transactions in a check register; today, they are most commonly recorded in a spreadsheet program or tracked with a mobile app.

(continues)

(continued)

Try It Out!

Now that you understand how a transaction register works and the benefits of using a transaction register, it is time for you to log transactions. For the next week, log all transactions that you make. It is important you log all of them. You can create a paper and pencil log, use a spreadsheet program, or try a mobile app. Choose the method that works best for you.

One benefit to using a spreadsheet is that you can use formulas so that the spreadsheet program completes the calculations for you; once you enter the initial formulas, you can use the fill handle to copy formulas to other cells that need to calculate. Using formulas for calculations reduces the chance of human error and makes the process more efficient. The images below show what a transaction register may look like if created using spreadsheet software. The first image is in normal view and the second is in formula view.

Note: The same process can be used for income and expenditure tracking when budgeting.

	A	B	C	D	E	F	G	H	I
1	Transaction ID	Date	Description of Transaction	Payment/Debit (−)	Deposit/Credit (+)	Balance			Transaction ID Key
2		9/3/20xx	Starting balance			$ 100.00		DEP	Deposit
3	PUR	9/5/20xx	Gas for car	$ 37.50		$ 62.50		WD	Withdrawal
4	DEP	9/7/20xx	Paycheck		$ 124.88	$ 187.38		PUR	Purchase
5	PUR	9/8/20xx	Lunch at ABC Grill	$ 22.50		$ 164.88		PMT	Bill Payment
6	PMT	9/8/20xx	Cell phone bill	$ 75.00		$ 89.88			
7	DEP	9/11/20xx	Money from mowing lawns		$ 60.00	$ 149.88			
8	PUR	9/12/20xx	Coffee	$ 6.45		$ 143.43			
9	PUR	9/13/20xx		$ 9.88		$ 133.55			
10	DEP	9/15/20xx	Paycheck		$ 112.18	$ 245.73			
11	PUR	9/18/20xx	Clothes	$ 55.00		$ 190.73			
12	DEP	9/20/20xx	Birthday money		$ 50.00	$ 240.73			
13									

	A	B	C	D	E	F	G	H	I
1	Transaction ID	Date	Description of Transaction	Payment/Debit (−)	Deposit/Credit (+)	Balance			Transaction ID Key
2		9/3/20xx	Starting balance			100		DEP	Deposit
3	PUR	9/5/20xx	Gas for car	37.5		=F2−D3+E3		WD	Withdrawal
4	DEP	9/7/20xx	Paycheck		124.88	=F3−D4+E4		PUR	Purchase
5	PUR	9/8/20xx	Lunch at ABC Grill	22.5		=F4−D5+E5		PMT	Bill Payment
6	PMT	9/8/20xx	Cell phone bill	75		=F5−D6+E6			
7	DEP	9/11/20xx	Money from mowing lawns		60	=F6−D7+E7			
8	PUR	9/12/20xx	Coffee	6.45		=F7−D8+E8			
9	PUR	9/13/20xx		9.88		=F8−D9+E9			
10	DEP	9/15/20xx	Paycheck		112.18	=F9−D10+E10			
11	PUR	9/18/20xx	Clothes	55		=F10−D11+E11			
12	DEP	9/20/20xx	Birthday money		50	=F11−D12+E12			
13									

Think Critically

1. Why is recording transactions in a register so important?
2. How can recording transactions in a register or while budgeting help identify spending habits?

avoid overdrafts and can help you maintain your budget. When you track your income and expenses, you will begin to see the pattern of your spending habits, and you can detect problems sooner. Financial institutions that offer checking accounts provide each customer with a monthly statement, usually accessed online. This statement lists checks received and processed by the bank, online payments, and all other withdrawals, deposits, service charges, and interest. While banks no longer return canceled checks with your statement, you can view them online at the bank's website if you wrote any checks during the month. Bank reconciliation forms are also available online at your bank's website.

Endorsing Checks

When you receive a check that must be cashed, it will need to be endorsed. An **endorsement** is a security step to help the bank verify that you are the proper recipient of the funds and authorizes the bank to deposit the money into your account or to give you cash. When two or more people are named as payees, all must endorse the check if the word *and* separates the names. If the names are separated by the word *or*, only one person must endorse it. To endorse a check, the payee named on the check signs the top part of the back of the check in ink. There are two major types of endorsements.

Blank Endorsement

A blank endorsement is the signature of the payee written exactly as their name appears on the front of the check, as shown below on the left. If Donald's name had been written incorrectly on the face of the check, he

would correct the mistake by endorsing the check with the misspelled version first and then with the correct version of his name, as shown below on the right.

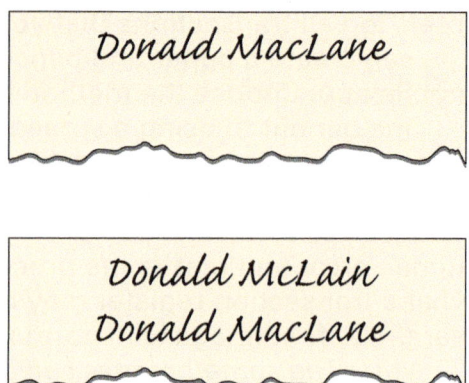

Restrictive Endorsement

A restrictive endorsement restricts or limits the use of a check. For example, a check endorsed with the words *For Deposit Only* above the payee's signature can be deposited only to the account specified. The restrictive endorsement is safer than the blank endorsement for use in mobile deposits, mailing deposits, and night deposit systems, and in other circumstances that may result in loss of a check. If a check with a restrictive endorsement is lost, the finder cannot cash it.

If you are depositing a check through your bank's online app, the restrictive endorsement would read *For Online Deposit Only*. Or you should follow the instructions from the banking app if different wording is needed. To deposit a check using the online app, you will take a picture of both sides of the check and upload them. When depositing a check using the online app, keep the check safe until your bank has approved the deposit. Once approved, you can safely shred the endorsed check.

For Deposit Only
United California Bank
Acct. #8-2011-4
Donald MacLane

✓ **Checkpoint**

Why is it important to reconcile your bank account(s)?

LO 4.2.3 Types of Checking Accounts

Financial institutions offer many types of checking accounts. You should carefully study your options because a wise choice can save you money. Most banks still offer free checking (no service fees) accounts. These accounts do not pay interest and may come with certain conditions. For example, you may be required to maintain a certain balance or limit your use of bank teller services. Free checking may also be available to senior citizens, students, non-profit groups, and others during special bank promotions.

Bank Accounts

Bank accounts can be either individual or joint. An individual can open a bank account, and they will be the only owner of the account. Two or more people can open a joint account. Joint account holders have equal access to the funds in the account and share the responsibility for any fees or charges against the account. Anyone under age 18 will need an adult to be a co-owner of a bank account. Once you are over age 18, you can convert your account to an individual account because you are legally an adult and no longer need to have a parent or guardian on the account. Joint accounts are also known as a survivorship account because any person who signs on the account has the right to the entire amount deposited. If one person using the account dies, the other person becomes the sole owner of the funds in the account.

Individuals can identify a beneficiary for their bank accounts. A **beneficiary** is someone who will inherit the money after the death of the account holder. A bank account with a named beneficiary is called a payable-on-death (POD) account.

Standard Accounts

A **standard account** usually has no or a small monthly service fee. To avoid a monthly service fee, you may be required to maintain an average minimum balance in the account. These accounts may or may not pay interest. Some banks offer reduced interest rates on credit card balances to customers who also have checking, savings, and other accounts at their bank.

Money Market Accounts

Most financial institutions offer checking accounts that earn interest. A **money market account** is an interest-bearing checking account that pays a higher interest rate but usually has more restrictions. With a money market account, your account balance usually must stay within the minimum average set by the bank during any month. The minimum may be $1,000 or more. Interest rates rise and fall with economic conditions. When overall interest rates drop, you may receive less than 1 percent annually in interest.

Share Accounts

Most credit unions offer share accounts. A **share account** is a savings account representing ownership interest. A share draft account is a checking account with low (or no) average daily balance requirements and, generally, no service fees. If you are eligible for credit union membership, this type of account may be the least expensive and most convenient option. It offers most, if not all, of the services of a checking account in a bank.

✓ **Checkpoint**

Describe the different types of bank accounts available to consumers.

4.2 **Lesson** Review

Check Your Understanding

1. What does a bank do when you "bounce" a check? (LO 4.2.1)

2. How does reconciling your bank account help you avoid overdrafts? (LO 4.2.2)

3. When should you use a restrictive endorsement? (LO 4.2.2)

4. How is an individual account different from a joint account? (LO 4.2.3)

Apply Your Understanding

1. Find an overdraft policy statement from a bank or credit union online. Read the statement and then, in writing, explain it in simple terms. Share your explanation with a friend. Did they understand? Why or why not? (LO 4.2.1)

2. Create an infographic or process flowchart that explains the steps in reconciliation. Be prepared to use what you created to explain the importance of reconciliation to a classmate. (LO 4.2.2)

The Essential Question

What is the purpose of a checking account, and why is it important to reconcile bank accounts?

A: Checking accounts allow account holders to write checks or transfer money electronically to make payments. Tracking checking account deposits and withdrawals helps avoid overdrafts and is part of a sound financial plan.

4.3 | Saving Money

The Essential Question | How does saving money contribute to financial planning?

Learning Objectives

By the end of this lesson, you should be able to:

LO 4.3.1 Discuss why it is important to save money for the future.

LO 4.3.2 Explain how money grows through compounding.

LO 4.3.3 List the various places where you can save money.

Key Terms

- 529 college savings plan
- principal
- interest
- compound interest
- yield
- annual percentage yield (APY)

Consider This ...

"Hey Isaac, thanks for suggesting that I open a checking account so I have easy access to my paychecks and can use my debit card to make purchases," DeAndre stated. "Since I have been working for a few months now and have a checking account, I think I want to explore other options my bank offers to help me start saving."

"That's a great idea," Isaac replied. "Now's a great time to start saving for you future and for any unexpected expenses that may come up."

"Let's discuss saving options over lunch," suggested DeAndre. "I'll buy since I can use my debit card!"

Read and Reflect

1. Why is it important for a teenager to begin saving now?

2. What strategies can you use to help you meet your savings goals?

Why You Should Save

The best reason to save money is to provide for future needs, both expected and unexpected. Creating a consistent saving habit will provide you with funds that will allow you to meet those unexpected needs. Saving regularly will also help you meet your short-term, intermediate-term, and long-term needs.

Short-Term Needs

Often you will have short-term needs, which are expenses beyond your regular monthly items. Unless you have extra cash income during the month, you will have to pay for these needs from your savings. Some short-term needs are predictable; others you cannot foresee. Examples of short-term needs include the following:

- Emergencies—short-term unemployment, sickness, accident, or a death in the family
- Vacations—short weekend trips or longer excursions
- Social events—weddings, family gatherings, or other potentially costly special occasions
- Repairs—cars, appliances, plumbing, and other items that need routine or unplanned repairs
- Major purchases—a car, major appliances, furniture, or other items that have limited lives and eventually have to be replaced

Intermediate-Term Needs

Some intermediate-term needs can also be predictable. Major purchases like remodeling a kitchen or bathroom in 3 years may be a goal. Another goal could be to relocate after completing postsecondary education. You may also have plans to move into a larger home or save to start a family. Each of these activities can cost several thousand

Why should a couple consider future family plans as part of their overall financial plan?

Source: iStock.com//enigma_images

dollars. Setting a saving goal to plan for these needs can be a beneficial part of your financial plan.

Long-Term Needs

While you need savings to meet emergencies, short-term and intermediate-term needs, you must also provide for long-term needs. Long-term needs are expenses that are costly and require years of planning and saving. These include predictable costs such as home ownership, education, and retirement. Saving money now will enable you to make larger purchases in the future. It will also allow you to invest and accumulate enough money for a secure retirement.

Home Ownership

Many people want to own their own house. At the time of purchase, you will likely have to pay a large sum of cash, or a down payment. The amount needed is often 10 to 20 percent of the purchase price. The balance will be paid with a mortgage (a home loan), for which you will make monthly payments. The larger the down payment you make, the smaller your monthly mortgage payments will be. You will learn more about mortgages in a future chapter.

Education

Many young people desire to complete some form of postsecondary education or training. Saving for future education is a long-term saving goal. Education is a long-term investment that may provide you with higher income potential. Some couples may begin an educational savings plan when their children are born. A common form of educational savings plan is a **529 college savings plan**. A 529 college savings plan is a state-sponsored investment plan that can be used only for educational expenses. The funds in the 529 college savings plan can be

Connections to Your World
Preparing for a Career after High School

In past decades, many people believed that a college education was the best way to prepare individuals for their future; it was thought that a college education would provide benefits that could not be obtained through other means. Potential benefits included higher earning potential and increased likelihood of advancement through a career. In recent years, there has been a shift to ensuring that all students are prepared for their future; this means that college is now one of many viable options to prepare for a career after high school. College can be expensive and is a large time commitment; and, in some fields, there may be better ways to prepare someone for the work they will be doing.

It is important for students to understand options as they prepare for their desired career. In many cases, this will be college, but it may also be trade school, certificate programs, apprenticeships, or other postsecondary education. All these options have associated costs; it is important to understand the potential costs and plan for your future. In 2023, a public university's average tuition, room, and board cost was nearly $26,000 per year. With the cost of college being so high, it is important to start planning early.

Think Critically

1. Do you feel there is long-term value to receiving a college education? How does this differ from person to person?

2. Is a college education more beneficial for some careers than others? Identify some careers where college may not be the best approach. Explain.

3. What options, other than college, do individuals have to help prepare them for a successful career? How does their cost compare to the cost of attending college?

4. Think of a career you would like to have after college. What is the best way to provide you the skills and knowledge to be successful in that career?

withdrawn to pay for educational expenses, tax-free. If there are no savings (or not enough) to pay for education, it is usually financed through a variety of other sources, such as work, scholarships, and financial aid. Financing postsecondary education will be discussed in greater detail in a future chapter.

Investing

After you have saved enough to cover daily expenses and emergencies, you can afford to invest your extra savings. Investing in stocks, bonds, mutual funds, real estate, and other investments can help your money grow faster than it would if left in a regular savings account. Because investments are often risky, you should make them in addition to—not instead of—regular savings. Types of investments are described in later chapters.

Retirement

The Social Security system was never designed to be the only source of income in retirement. Social Security is meant to supplement an individual's own savings. To have a financially secure retirement, you must begin to save regularly as early in life as you can.

Peace of Mind

Probably the best reason to save is the peace of mind that comes from knowing that when needs arise, you will have adequate money to pay for the expenses. Financial institutions, such as banks and credit unions, allow consumers to feel secure about their savings. These institutions help keep the customers' money safe from theft or loss if large sums of cash are kept at home or in a wallet. Banks also pay interest on savings. As discussed in a previous chapter on budgeting, you should try to follow the 50-30-20 rule of budging, where 20 percent of your disposable income

is placed into savings or investing accounts. The amount of money you can save depends upon several factors:

- The amount of your discretionary or disposable income—what you have left over after paying for all of your needs
- The importance you attach to savings
- Your anticipated needs and wants
- Your willingness to give up present spending to provide for your future

✓ **Checkpoint**

What short-term, intermediate-term, and long-term needs can be met by saving?

LO 4.3.2 How Money Grows

The amount of money you deposit into a savings account is called the **principal**. It is the base on which your savings will grow. For the use of your money, the financial institution pays you money called interest. **Interest** represents earnings on your deposit.

As principal and interest grow, more interest accumulates. This is known as **compound interest**, or interest paid on the original principal plus accumulated interest. **Figure 4.4** illustrates how interest is compounded annually. Notice how interest earned each year increases because the saver is earning interest on the previous year's interest as well as on the initial deposit.

The more often interest is compounded, the greater your interest earnings will be. **Figure 4.5** illustrates what happens when an annual 6 percent interest is compounded quarterly (every 3 months) and added to

Figure 4.4 — Interest Compounded Annually

Year	Beginning Balance	Interest Earned (6%)	Ending Balance
1	$100.00	$6.00	$106.00
2	$106.00	$6.36	$112.36
3	$112.36	$6.74	$119.10

the principal before more interest is calculated. If you compare the ending balances in Figure 4.4 and Figure 4.5, you will notice that you earn more interest with quarterly compounding than with annual compounding.

Earnings on savings can be measured by the rate of return or yield. **Yield** is the percentage of increase in the value of your savings due to earned interest. Because financial institutions compound interest in many ways, comparing yields can be difficult. To solve this problem, the law requires all financial institutions to tell consumers the **annual percentage yield (APY)**, which is the actual interest rate an account pays, stated on a yearly basis with the compounding included.

✓ Checkpoint

How does compounding help your money to grow faster?

LO 4.3.3 Where to Save

You have many options for where to save your money. For short-term and intermediate-term savings needs, opening a savings account through your bank or credit union may be the most convenient. For long-term savings goals, you may want to work with an investment company.

What are some of your options if you want to open a savings account?

Figure 4.5 — Interest Compounded Quarterly

Quarterly Compounding Annual Interest Rate = 6%

Year	Beginning Balance	Rate	Quarterly Interest 1	2	3	4	Ending Balance
1	$100.00	.015	$1.50	$1.52	$1.55	$1.57	$106.14
2	$106.14	.015	$1.59	$1.62	$1.64	$1.66	$112.65
3	$112.65	.015	$1.69	$1.72	$1.74	$1.77	$119.57

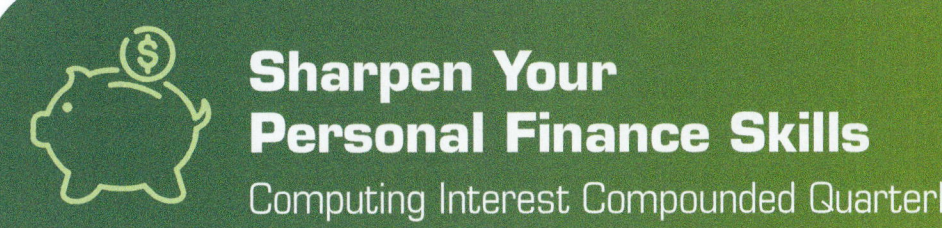

Sharpen Your Personal Finance Skills

Computing Interest Compounded Quarterly

Compound interest means earning interest on principal, and then allowing the interest to remain on deposit so you earn interest on both your principal and your previous interest. To compute interest compounded quarterly, divide the annual interest rate by 4 to get the quarterly rate. For monthly compounding, divide the annual interest rate by 12. For interest compounded every 6 months (a half year), divide the annual rate by 2.

Example

Suppose you deposit $100 in a savings account that will pay you 6 percent per year, compounded quarterly. This means that for each quarter, you will receive one-fourth of the yearly interest. Six percent divided by 4 is 1.5 percent (or 0.015) each quarter. At the end of the first quarter, you earn $1.50 in interest, using the following computation:

$$\$100.00 \times 0.015 = \$1.50$$

At the beginning of the second quarter, you now have $101.50 in your account ($100.00 + $1.50). At the end of the second quarter, you earn interest as follows:

$$\$101.50 \times 0.015 = \$1.52$$

At the beginning of the third quarter, you have $103.02 ($101.50 + $1.52). At the end of the third quarter, you earn interest as follows:

$$\$103.02 \times 0.015 = \$1.55$$

At the beginning of the fourth quarter, you have $104.57 ($103.02 + $1.55). At the end of the fourth quarter (the end of the first year), you earn interest as follows:

$$\$104.57 \times 0.015 = \$1.57$$

Your balance at the end of the first year is $106.14 ($104.57 + $1.57). You earned a total of $6.14 in interest for the year. At the end of year 3, your balance is $119.57. That is total interest of $19.57 on your original deposit of $100.

It is important to understand the concept of compounding interest and the calculations used to determine compounding interest given an interest rate and specified amount of time. Once you understand the concept, you can use spreadsheet software to calculate compound interest. Using spreadsheet software saves time and reduces the chance of human error in calculations.

To do this, you first create a template in a spreadsheet program. This includes applying currency and percentage number formats to cells as appropriate. Once you have a template, you can enter formulas and adjust numbers to calculate for different scenarios. Below is the example from above calculated using a spreadsheet.

(continues)

(continued)

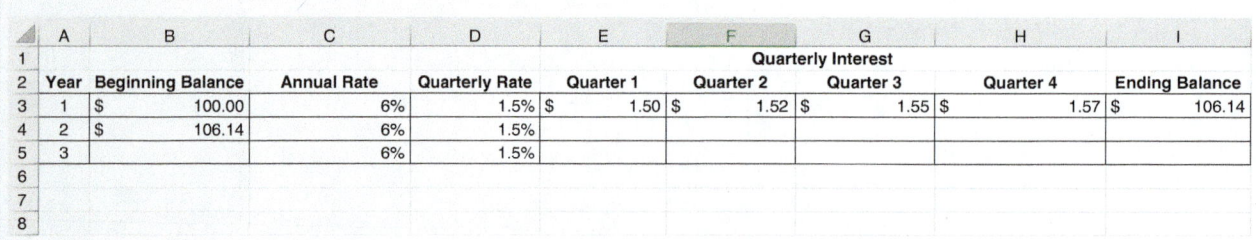

	A	B	C	D	E	F	G	H	I
1							Quarterly Interest		
2	Year	Beginning Balance	Annual Rate	Quarterly Rate	Quarter 1	Quarter 2	Quarter 3	Quarter 4	Ending Balance
3	1	$ 100.00	6%	1.5%	$ 1.50	$ 1.52	$ 1.55	$ 1.57	$ 106.14
4	2	$ 106.14	6%	1.5%					
5	3		6%	1.5%					
6									
7									
8									

When using spreadsheets, you should use formulas to make the process more efficient, reduce the chance of human error, and ensure that all related values are updated changes are made. The formulas below were used to complete the calculations for year one. Note that you should begin year 2 with a formula. Using formulas for all values ensures that if one value is updated, all others update accordingly.

	A	B	C	D	E	F	G	H	I
1							Quarterly Interest		
2	Year	Beginning Balance	Annual Rate	Quarterly Rate	Quarter 1	Quarter 2	Quarter 3	Quarter 4	Ending Balance
3	1	100	0.06	=C3/4	=B3*D3	=(B3+E3)*D3	=(B3+E3+F3)*D3	=(B3+E3+F3+G3)*D3	=B3+SUM(E3:H3)
4	2	=I3	0.06	=C4/4					
5	3		0.06	=C5/4					
6									

Once you have your formulas entered for the first year, you can use the fill handle to copy the formulas to remaining years. Below you will see the calculations and formulas for all 3 years from the example. Note that there is a $0.01 difference between the manual calculation and the spreadsheet calculation; this is the result of rounding when we complete the calculations manually.

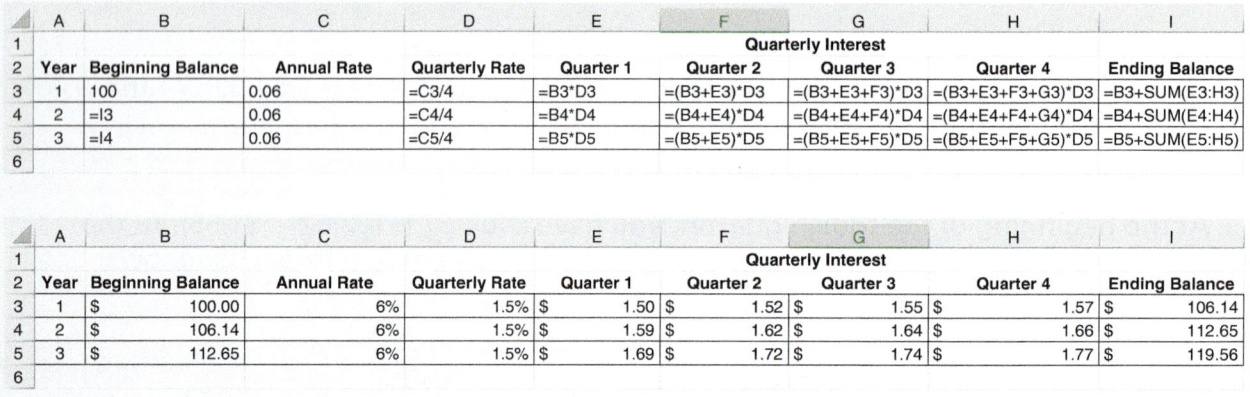

	A	B	C	D	E	F	G	H	I
1							Quarterly Interest		
2	Year	Beginning Balance	Annual Rate	Quarterly Rate	Quarter 1	Quarter 2	Quarter 3	Quarter 4	Ending Balance
3	1	100	0.06	=C3/4	=B3*D3	=(B3+E3)*D3	=(B3+E3+F3)*D3	=(B3+E3+F3+G3)*D3	=B3+SUM(E3:H3)
4	2	=I3	0.06	=C4/4	=B4*D4	=(B4+E4)*D4	=(B4+E4+F4)*D4	=(B4+E4+F4+G4)*D4	=B4+SUM(E4:H4)
5	3	=I4	0.06	=C5/4	=B5*D5	=(B5+E5)*D5	=(B5+E5+F5)*D5	=(B5+E5+F5+G5)*D5	=B5+SUM(E5:H5)
6									

	A	B	C	D	E	F	G	H	I
1							Quarterly Interest		
2	Year	Beginning Balance	Annual Rate	Quarterly Rate	Quarter 1	Quarter 2	Quarter 3	Quarter 4	Ending Balance
3	1	$ 100.00	6%	1.5%	$ 1.50	$ 1.52	$ 1.55	$ 1.57	$ 106.14
4	2	$ 106.14	6%	1.5%	$ 1.59	$ 1.62	$ 1.64	$ 1.66	$ 112.65
5	3	$ 112.65	6%	1.5%	$ 1.69	$ 1.72	$ 1.74	$ 1.77	$ 119.56
6									

Try It Out!

Based on the previous example, use a spreadsheet to compute your quarterly interest for 3 years if you deposit $500 at 8 percent, compounded quarterly.

Most financial institutions have greatly expanded their services in recent years, so the differences between a bank, a credit union, and an investment company may be minimal. Interest rates vary among savings institutions and among the various types of accounts offered. You will have to study your options and determine which type of institution and account is the best deal for you.

Commercial Banks

Commercial banks, also known as full-service financial institutions, provide the widest variety of financial services. Some of these services include safe deposit boxes, 24-hour ATM networks, money transfer services, and loan and investment services. Commercial banks also offer many kinds of savings and checking accounts. Having checking and savings accounts at the same bank makes it easy for people to transfer funds and make deposits and withdrawals. By linking checking and savings accounts, customers can avoid certain service fees. Almost all commercial banks are insured by the Federal Deposit Insurance Corporation (FDIC). The insurance protects each depositor from loss due to bank failure, up to $250,000 per account.

Credit Unions

Credit unions are not-for-profit organizations established by groups of people, such as employees in similar occupations who pool their money. To use a credit union, you must be a member of the group. Potential members must meet membership requirements that vary depending on the credit union's objective. For example, a corporation's credit union may accept only employees and their immediate family members. A credit union for teachers, on the other hand, may accept any teacher who works for a certain school district. A few credit unions have more relaxed requirements and may simply request that members live in a certain city or area.

Credit unions are owned by their members, who save their money in the form of shares, or part ownership in the credit union. From funds accumulated by these shares, the credit union makes loans to its members, generally at lower interest rates. Savings and checking accounts at a credit union are usually called share accounts. Credit unions generally offer higher interest rates on savings accounts than commercial banks do.

Credit unions also offer other financial services to members, such as individual retirement accounts (IRAs), certificate of deposits (CDs), and investment planning. Through membership in the National Credit Union Administration (NCUA), depositors' accounts are insured up to $250,000.

Investment or Brokerage Firms

Investment or brokerage firms buy and sell different types of securities. Securities are stocks and bonds issued by corporations or by the government. Stocks represent equity, or ownership. Bonds represent debt, or a loan. In other words, when you buy stock, you become an owner of the company. When you buy a bond, you are loaning money to the company or to the government. Investors buy and sell securities through a stockbroker

Why would you want your checking and savings accounts at the same bank?

Source: Andrey_Popov/Shutterstock.com

Why might you choose to have an online savings account?

who works for the firm. As you will learn in a later chapter, you can buy stocks, bonds, and mutual funds directly or through brokerage firms. Discount brokerage firms offer broker services for reduced fees. They also offer checking and savings account options. Accounts in brokerage firms are usually not insured.

Online Accounts

Credit card companies and financial services companies offer online accounts that can work in tandem with your credit card. These often are savings accounts that generally pay higher, or market, rates of interest. You can expect to receive a lower interest rate with your credit card agreement if you have an online savings account. However, these accounts can be risky. If the account provider is not a financial institution, these accounts are not insured. Generally, the higher the amount of interest you can earn, the higher the risk associated with the account.

✓ Checkpoint

Where can you open savings accounts to meet your short-term, intermediate-term, and long-term goals?

4.3 Lesson Review

Check Your Understanding

1. Why is it important to start saving early in life to meet your short-term, intermediate-term, and long-term needs? (LO 4.3.1)

2. Explain the concept of compounding and how your money grows. (LO 4.3.2)

3. List the various places where you can have a savings account. (LO 4.3.3)

Apply Your Understanding

1. Define the term *financial peace of mind*. What does it mean to you? How can you achieve financial peace of mind? (LO 4.3.1)

2. Using the simple interest formula, calculate how much you would have saved at the end of one year if you deposited $100 per month at 6 percent APR, compounded monthly. (LO 4.3.2)

3. Use a comparison chart or a Venn diagram to compare a bank to a credit union. Based on your findings, which type of financial institution would you prefer? (LO 4.3.3)

The Essential Question

How does saving money contribute to financial planning?

A: Saving provides you with money to meet your short-term, intermediate-term, and long-term needs, thus giving you financial peace of mind.

4.4 Saving Options

What factors should you consider when choosing among savings options?

Learning Objectives

By the end of this lesson, you should be able to:

LO 4.4.1 Describe the purpose and features of different savings options.

LO 4.4.2 Discuss factors that influence selection of a savings plan.

LO 4.4.3 Describe ways to save regularly.

Key Terms

- liquidity
- certificate of deposit (CD)
- maturity date
- early withdrawal penalty
- maturity amount
- money market account
- safety of principal
- direct deposit
- automatic deduction
- payroll savings plan

LO 4.4.1 Savings Account Choices

Once you have decided to establish a savings plan, you need to know about the different savings options available to you. You may want to deposit money in several types of accounts, because each can contribute to your overall plan in different ways.

Regular Savings Account

A regular savings account has a major advantage—high liquidity. **Liquidity** is a measure of how quickly you can get your cash without loss of value. A regular savings account is very liquid because you can withdraw your money at any time without penalty. The trade-off for high liquidity, however, is a lower interest rate. A regular savings account generally pays the least amount of interest of all savings options.

Once you have opened the account, you may make withdrawals and deposits. Some financial institutions charge service fees when you make more than a maximum number of withdrawals in a certain period. Other institutions charge a monthly fee if your balance falls below a set minimum. In most cases, you will receive a debit or ATM card that goes with the account so

Why is a regular savings account said to be liquid?

Source: iStock.com//CatLane

that you can make withdrawals and deposits at ATMs. If you have a smartphone, you can deposit checks or transfer funds electronically. You can also check your balance and transfer money between your checking and savings accounts online and by phone.

Certificate of Deposit

A **certificate of deposit (CD)** is a deposit that earns a fixed interest rate for a specified length of time—for example, 5 percent for 6 months. A CD requires a minimum deposit. The interest rate on a CD is usually higher than on a regular savings account because a CD is less liquid.

Unlike a regular savings account, you must leave the money on a CD for a certain amount of time. A CD has a set **maturity date**, which is the date on which an investment becomes due for payment. If you take out any part of your money early, you will pay an **early withdrawal penalty**. This penalty could be anywhere from 90 days' interest to the loss of part of your principal, depending on the terms of your CD.

Typically, within a stated number of days after the maturity date, your certificate will renew automatically. When a CD is renewed, it is extended for another 6 months or whatever the original time period was. You may prefer to redeem it for cash or purchase a new certificate for a different amount of time. The **maturity amount** is how much you will receive (principal plus accrued interest from date of deposit) if you choose to redeem your CD. As another option, you may receive a check periodically for the interest earned or have the interest deposited in a separate regular checking or savings account.

Money Market Account

A **money market account** is a type of savings account that offers a more competitive interest rate than a regular savings account. Brokerage firms as well as banks and other financial institutions offer money market accounts.

There are two different kinds of money market accounts: money market deposit accounts and money market funds. A money market deposit account is like a regular savings account, but it offers a higher interest rate in exchange for larger-than-normal deposits. In addition, the interest rate may increase as your balance increases. The FDIC insures these accounts.

A money market fund is a type of mutual fund that invests in low-risk securities. You will learn more about mutual funds in a future chapter. Money market funds are not FDIC insured but are generally considered safe because they invest in short-term government securities. The chance of losing the principal amount you deposited is very low. On average, money market funds will pay a higher interest rate than money market deposit accounts.

Unlike CDs, there is no penalty for taking money out of money market accounts. As a result, these accounts are quite liquid. However, you usually are limited to a certain number of withdrawals each month. In addition, money market accounts require minimum opening deposits and minimum balances.

✓ Checkpoint

What are the advantages and disadvantages of different savings options?

Selecting a Savings Plan

There are important factors to consider when selecting a savings account and a savings institution. All savings or investment options involve a trade-off between liquidity or safety and yield. The safer or more liquid an investment, the less earning potential it is likely to have. Use the following criteria when judging which savings options best meet your needs: liquidity, safety, convenience, interest-earning potential (yield), and fees and restrictions.

Liquidity

Liquidity is how quickly you can turn savings into cash when you want it. The need for liquidity will vary, based on your age, health, family situation, and overall wealth. For example, if you have little money left over after paying your bills, you may need to keep this money liquid so you can get it quickly, without penalty, if you face some emergency. In this case, a regular savings or money market account would be best for you. CDs impose a penalty if you withdraw early, so you should choose this option when you do not expect to need the money before the maturity date.

Safety

You want your money to be safe from loss. **Safety of principal** means that you are guaranteed not to lose your savings deposit, even if the bank or other financial institution fails and goes out of business. Most financial institutions are insured by either the FDIC or NCUA. Accounts protected by insurance are safe up to $250,000. You should be sure the financial institution of your choice has federal insurance to protect your deposit. Deposits in banks, no matter what type, are almost always safer than investments in the stock market.

Convenience

People often choose their financial institution because of the convenience of its location. Many banks have several branches within a limited geographic area, which makes banking convenient. Some banks even have locations in grocery stores and residential areas. A very large bank may have branches in other states, giving you banking privileges while out of town.

In addition to location, people also choose their financial institution because of the convenient services offered, such as drive-thru windows with expanded hours, number of ATMs nearby, and online and mobile banking.

Because interest rates on various savings accounts and CDs may vary only slightly and service fees can be very similar within a community, selection of a bank may depend on location and types of services offered.

Interest-Earning Potential (Yield)

You want to earn as much interest as you can on your deposit while maintaining the degree of liquidity, safety, and convenience

Source: Bob Daemmrich/Alamy Stock Photo

Would convenience be a factor for you when choosing a savings institution?

you want. Shop around for the best APY in your area for the type of account you want. Usually, the more liquid your deposit, the less interest it will earn. A regular savings account usually earns a low rate of interest because you can maintain a low minimum balance and withdraw money as needed. CDs tie up your money for some length of time. In exchange for your commitment to leave this money with the bank for this time period, you will usually earn higher interest.

Fees and Restrictions

Different accounts and institutions have different rules. Before you open an account, be sure to understand the withdrawal restrictions, minimum balances, service charges, fees, and any other requirements. For example, some accounts charge a fee for using a human teller rather than completing transactions through an ATM. CDs may incur a penalty if you withdraw money before maturity. Fees for use of an ATM can vary as well. Some banks may charge nothing to use their ATMs but charge a hefty fee for using another bank's ATM.

> **✓ Checkpoint**
>
> What are five things to consider when selecting a savings plan?

LO 4.4.3 ## Saving Regularly

Saving money for future use is important for every individual. It is important not only to save money but also to save on a regular basis. In addition to meeting all your financial goals, saving regularly will also give you financial peace of mind. Over time, and with compounding interest, your savings can grow into a substantial sum. **Figure 4.6** illustrates the effect of compounding when you make regular deposits and earn interest on interest.

Obviously, no savings plan is effective unless you are able to set aside money. There are ways to make regular saving easier. Pay yourself first by using direct deposit or automatic deductions and payroll savings plans. Even saving spare coins and cash on a regular basis can add up.

Direct Deposit

Both employers and financial institutions offer direct deposit. With **direct deposit**, your net pay is deposited electronically into your bank account. The advantage of this service is that your money is available in your account faster. You do not have to make a special trip to the bank to deposit your paycheck. Instead, your employer provides you with an earnings statement notifying you of the amount deposited directly into your account. You can also split your automatic deposit between accounts, with some going

Figure 4.6	Compounding with Additional Deposits			
Year	**Beginning Balance**	**Deposits**	**Interest Earned (5%)**	**Ending Balance**
1	$ 0.00	$100.00	$ 5.00	$105.00
2	$105.00	$100.00	$10.25	$215.25
3	$215.25	$100.00	$15.76	$331.01
4	$331.01	$100.00	$21.55	$452.56

into savings and some going into checking to cover your bills. This way, you are truly paying yourself first.

Automatic Deductions

An **automatic deduction** represents money you have authorized your bank or another organization to move from one account to another regularly. For example, you can automatically move money from your checking account to your savings account.

With a **payroll savings plan**, you authorize your employer to make automatic deductions from your paycheck each pay period. For example, this money may be deposited into a savings account or a retirement account, or it may be used to buy government savings bonds.

Saving Coins and Cash

Some people find it convenient to set aside their spare change and money left over each day or week. They may put it into a piggy bank, a jar, or another storage container. Once a month or several times a year, they take the cash out and have it counted and deposited in their savings accounts. Setting aside small amounts of change on a daily or weekly basis will lead to large sums over time. It is surprising how pennies can add up to make dollars!

✓ **Checkpoint**

Describe the various ways to save regularly.

Connections to Your World
Mindful Spending

Money can be a stressor for most people. Sometimes they are worried that they do not have enough to cover bills; other times, stress is the result of unexpected expenses. Saving money now is one way you can feel more confident about your finances and reduce the chance of money-related stress in the future.

Saving occurs when you intentionally set aside part of your earnings for future use. What if you do not have much money left after your bills and normal purchases? This is an opportunity to utilize a transaction register to evaluate your spending habits. For example, if someone spends $5 on a cup of coffee three times a week, this costs $780 over the course of the year. Reducing the number of times that coffee is purchased or finding a cheaper alternative, such as making coffee at home, frees up money that can be saved.

Think Critically

1. Do you sometimes buy things that you later wish you had not? If you had the money back, what would you do instead?
2. Reflect on your transaction register or on your spending habits. What changes could you make that would allow you to save more now?

4.4 Lesson Review

Check Your Understanding

1. How is a savings account more liquid than a CD? (LO 4.4.1)

2. To earn a higher interest rate, what trade-off will you likely have to make? Why? (LO 4.4.2)

3. Why is an automatic deduction from your paycheck into a savings account a good way to build savings? (LO 4.4.3)

Apply Your Understanding

1. Create a comparison chart for the various savings options. Include information about ease of accessing your savings and the interest rate difference as well as any potential risks. (LO 4.4.1)

2. Set an intermediate-term savings goal. Determine which type of savings plan would work best for your goal. Explain your choice. (LO 4.4.2)

3. Outline three strategies to help you meet the following goals: a short-term goal of saving $1,000 for an emergency fund within the next twelve months; an intermediate-term goal of saving $2,000 within two years for a down payment on a car; and a long-term goal of saving $5,000 to be used for your housing after graduating from trade school in 5 years. (LO 4.4.3)

The Essential Question

What factors should you consider when choosing among savings options?

A: You should consider the best options to meet your savings goals and to minimize risk.

Summary

4.1 Bank Services

- A full-service bank is a for-profit company that offers many kinds of services, including savings and checking accounts, credit cards, safe deposit boxes, loans, and online banking.

- Most bank deposits are insured by the FDIC (Federal Deposit Insurance Corporation).

- Credit unions operate like a bank, but they are nonprofit companies owned by people with accounts there.

- Credit union deposits are insured by the NCUA (National Credit Union Administration).

- Certified checks and cashier's checks are guaranteed by a bank to be paid.

- Some banks sell money orders to people who do not wish to use cash or do not have a checking account. Money orders are like cashier's checks.

- Automated teller machine (ATM) transactions allow immediate deductions from a checking account.

- Banks often offer special credit card perks to their best customers whose accounts are in good standing.

- With overdraft protection, checks are covered even if there are insufficient funds in a checking account.

- Online and telephone banking enables account holders to make electronic transfers and access their accounts 24 hours a day.

- A stop-payment order is a request that the bank not honor a specific check.

- Financial institutions offer safe deposit boxes for customers to store valuable items or documents.

- Banking fees cover the operating costs of banks and credit unions. Examples include fees for granting you a loan or replacing a lost debit card.

- Most institutions also charge a nonsufficient fund (NSF) fee when you attempt to spend more than what is available in your account.

- The Truth in Savings Act (TISA) is a federal law that mandates the disclosure of information related to rates, fees, and other items associated with banking accounts.

- To avoid high bank fees, choose the type of account that best fits your needs and follow the account rules.

4.2 Checking Accounts

- One of the first banking services a person will need is a checking account.

- It allows you to write checks or electronically transfer money to make payments.

- To open a checking account, bring the required documents to the bank or credit union, sign a form, and deposit money into the account.

- A canceled check is a check that has been cleared or processed by a bank or credit union and deducted from your account.

- Checks move through the banking system using an electronic process.

- The Automated Clearing House (ACH) system is an electronic network used to securely accept deposits and distribute payments.

- You must maintain enough money in your checking account to cover all payments you make.

- It is called an overdraft if you write a check or make a withdrawal for more money than your account contains.

- Checking accounts can help you manage your personal finances only if you use them correctly. You should understand the parts of a check, as well as how to write a check and pay bills online, make deposits, and reconcile your account.

- Reconciling an account means keeping track of deposits and withdrawals. Account owners should reconcile their accounts monthly and correct any errors.

- A blank or restrictive endorsement is needed to cash a check. Endorsements are a way to help financial institutions verify the proper recipient of funds and authorize the deposit into your account or to give out cash.

- There are different types of bank accounts. Banks offer individual accounts, joint accounts, standard accounts, and money market accounts. Credit unions offer share and share draft accounts.

4.3 Saving Money

- Savings provide money for short-term, intermediate-term, and long-term needs.

- Examples of short-term and intermediate-term needs include emergencies, vacations, social events, repairs, and major purchases.

- Long-term needs are expenses that are costly and require years of planning and saving, such as home ownership, education, and retirement.

- The best reason to start saving is to provide for future financial peace of mind.

- Compounding, or interest earned on principal and previous interest, makes money grow faster.

- You have many options for where to save your money.

- For short-term and intermediate-term savings needs, opening a savings account through your bank our credit union may be the best option.

- For long-term savings needs, you may want to work with an investment company.

- To compare accounts with different compounding methods, review the stated annual percentage yields (APY).

- Commercial banks, credit unions, investment or brokerage firms, and online companies offer savings accounts.

4.4 Saving Options

- Savings account options include regular savings accounts, certificates of deposit (CDs), and money market accounts.

- Among the savings options, regular savings accounts usually pay the lowest interest but offer the highest liquidity and safety.

- CDs have a set maturity date and are less liquid, but they pay a higher rate of return than regular savings accounts.

- Money market accounts pay more interest when economic conditions are good (and growing).

- The criteria used in judging which savings options best meet your needs include liquidity, safety of principal, convenience, interest-earning potential (yield), and fees and restrictions.

- Saving regularly helps you meet your financial goals more quickly.

- Direct deposit, automatic deductions, payroll savings plans, and saving spare change and cash are ways to make regular saving easier.

1. List banking services that are available at most financial institutions. (LO 4.1.1)

2. Explain why overdraft protection is important for a checking account. (LO 4.1.1)

3. Describe three fees that are charged by financial institutions for their services. (LO 4.1.2)

4. What is the purpose of a checking account? How could a high school student benefit from having a checking account? (LO 4.2.1)

5. What is the purpose of reconciling a bank account? (LO 4.2.2)

6. Write a short description of the different types of checking accounts. (LO 4.2.3)

7. Why is it important to save for intermediate-term needs? (LO 4.3.1)

8. Why does compounding help your money grow faster? (LO 4.3.2)

9. Describe three different types of savings options. (LO 4.3.3)

10. Describe the purpose of one short-term savings option, one intermediate-term savings option, and one long-term savings option. (LO 4.4.1)

11. Define liquidity. Why is it important to understand liquidity when selecting a savings plan? (LO 4.4.2)

12. Why should you consider discretionary income when developing a savings plan? (LO 4.4.3)

Apply Your Knowledge

1. You know you had $30 left in your checking account after buying fuel, but you were charged a nonsufficient funds fee (NSF) after purchasing a $40 meal at a local restaurant on your way home. Why were you charged this fee? (LO 4.1.2)

2. Determine your ending reconciled checkbook balance when all the following six conditions exist:

    (1) Your ending checkbook balance is $311.40 before the monthly account fee (service charge) is deducted.

    (2) You made a math error, resulting in $30.00 less showing in your account than should be.

    (3) The monthly account fee is $6.00.

(4) The ending bank balance is $402.00.

(5) Outstanding deposits total $100.00.

(6) Outstanding checks total $166.60. (LO 4.2.2)

3. You want to buy a used car so that you can get a part-time job next summer. Write a short-term goal to save $1,000 over the next year. You can earn $12.50 an hour babysitting your neighbor's child 3 days a week after school for 2 hours. Develop a savings plan that will allow you to save $100 per month. What type of account would you use for your savings? Explain your answer. (LO 4.3.1)

Share Your Knowledge

Work in teams of two to four students to complete the following activities.

1. Many people believe that bank fees are too high and banks do not pay depositors enough interest for the use of their money. Do you agree? Explain. Find a classmate with a different opinion. Share your thoughts with each other. Compare your viewpoint for areas where you agree and disagree. Together, write a short paragraph summarizing the differences in your viewpoints and what you learned from each other. (LO 4.1.2)

2. Plan a trip after high school graduation. Set a budget for the trip, then discuss various savings options that work for each team member. Create a savings plan that will allow you to save your share of the expenses. Compare your plan to the plans of the other teams. (LO 4.3.1)

3. Search online for a savings calculator. Plug in different numbers and note the results. For example, enter a savings amount compounded annually, then quarterly, then monthly. Note the differences that occur because of the different compounding methods. Then try different savings amounts using the same compounding method. How does saving just a little more each month affect your total savings in 10 years? Then try different interest rates with the same savings amounts and compounding method. Summarize your team's conclusions by creating a slide deck, poster, video, or blog post to share with the class. (LO 4.3.2)

Connect and Reflect

Base your answers to the following questions on your own personal thoughts, preferences, and experiences.

1. Many people do not reconcile their banking accounts. If you have a bank account, do you reconcile? Explain why or why not. (LO 4.2.2)

2. The cost of living is one of the biggest factors in why people do not save money for the future. Explain why saving even just a small amount each paycheck is an important step in meeting your future financial goals. (LO 4.3.1)

3. Why is it important for young people to start saving early rather than delay it until they are older? How much are you currently able to save each week or month? How much do you plan to save in the future? (LO 4.3.3)

Chapter Project

Complete a mini-practice set for your financial accounts for one month. Using directions and data provided on the Companion Site, prepare checks and deposit slips, record transactions in an electronic register, and reconcile your accounts.

Career Clusters

It is important for students to begin career exploration early so that they can discover possible career paths and better understand the skills, education and training, and qualifications required for different jobs. In addition, career exploration allows students to better understand the earning potential of various careers. It is important for students to ensure that their career goals align with future financial goals. By considering the earning potential of various careers, students can better assess how a career of interest aligns with their desired standard of living.

Advance CTE has developed a National Career Cluster Framework made up of 16 career clusters representing 79 career pathways. The framework helps students better plan for and navigate life after high school by exploring a wide range of careers and industries grouped by similar skills and job tasks. By exploring the 16 career clusters, students will better understand protentional career opportunities so they can make more informed decisions and align their experiences while in high school to future goals. The 16 career clusters and pathways can be found on the Advance CTE website (https://careertech.org/what-we-do/career-clusters/).

It's time for you to begin exploring! Complete the Advance CTE Career Clusters Interest Survey (https://careertech.org/resource/career-clusters-student-interest-survey/) to help identify career clusters that align with your interests, personal qualities, and hobbies. Identify your top three clusters of interest and then research different career opportunities and pathways within each of the three clusters. Gather information about each cluster and identify sample careers. Compile your findings in a table that allows you to compare opportunities within different clusters.

Connect and Reflect

1. Each career cluster can provide a variety of opportunities and career pathways. Which pathway within each of the three clusters best aligns with your interests and personal qualities? Explain.

2. Beginning in Unit 2, you will take a deeper dive into a career cluster of interest. Based on your exploration findings, choose a career cluster from your top three that you would like to explore in greater depth.

Unit 1: Project

This project is designed to help you begin your financial journey by following Emy's path of career exploration and learning how to manage income, a personal budget, banking services, and taxes.

Emy listened to Carlos's advice and found a part-time job at a local restaurant the summer before her junior year in high school. She intended to stay at this job until she graduated. However, while working for the Mason Jar, she learned she did not like working as a server, but she enjoyed her time as a bookkeeper and helping the owners manage their banking accounts. Emy decided to set several career and financial goals for herself.

Emy's short-term career goal was to complete the small business management program at the local Career and Technical Center high school program to learn more about owning and operating a business. Emy set an intermediate-term career goal to complete a career exploration summer program between her junior and senior years of high school. She also set a long-term financial goal. She aimed to save $5,000 for her educational expenses over the next 2 years.

Emy decided to attend the state university, where she studied business teacher education to help others learn about business. She began teaching at the local high school after she graduated. She teaches entrepreneurship, digital marketing, personal finance, and accounting. Emy loves her job and is excited that she can help her students learn to be successful in business and life.

This is Emy's first year teaching. She is paid monthly. Emy found an apartment near where she teaches in Oklahoma, and she needs to calculate and analyze her net pay, set up her budget, open bank accounts, and prepare to file her taxes as an independent adult.

Complete the following tasks as if you were Emy:

1. Complete a Form W-4.
2. Review a pay stub.
3. Create a monthly budget.
4. Reconcile bank statements.

Completing a Form W-4

Before Emy starts her job as a business education teacher, she must complete a Form W-4. This form will ensure her employer is withholding the correct federal income tax from each paycheck. Complete the Form W-4 for Emy included on the Companion Site and then answer the following questions.

Think Critically

1. Read the instructions for step 2 on the Form W-4. Why do you think having more than one job or being married can impact the amount of withholding you might be required to pay?

2. Visit the website provided in step 2a. Find the section that explains "Why check your withholding" and read it. What is the advantage of checking your tax withholding?

Reviewing a Pay Stub

Emy received her first pay stub. She makes $42,540 for a 10-month contract. Emy has a choice of being paid just for the 10 months she works, or she can choose to be paid over 12 months. To help with budgeting, Emy decided to be paid over 12 months.

Calculate Emy's gross monthly income using details found on the Companion Site and then answer the following questions.

Think Critically

1. Why does a pay stub include the pay period and a pay date?

2. Why are all the deductions listed on a pay stub?

3. Why is tax withholding necessary, and how does it benefit the employee and the government?

Creating a Monthly Budget

Creating a monthly budget is an important part of financial management because it provides a roadmap for financial planning. Review the information in the unit chapters for additional information about budgeting and then use the information provided on the Companion Site to create a monthly budget for Emy and to answer the following question.

Think Critically

1. How do personal budgets help individuals set clear financial goals, prioritize spending, and allocate resources to meet short-term, intermediate-term, and long-term goals?

Reconciling Bank Statements

Now that Emy has regular income from her teaching job, she needs to better understand how financial statements are used to assess and monitor financial well-being. Using information provided on the Companion Site, reconcile Emy's bank statement to ensure accuracy of deposits, withdrawals, and transfer activities and then answer the following questions.

Think Critically

1. What advice would you give Emy about the difference between what she spent and her budgeted amount? Why?

2. In your opinion, should Emy make any adjustments to her budget? Explain.

Personal Financial Literacy

The Personal Financial Literacy Event measures your personal finance knowledge. Students must be able to apply reliable information and systematic decision-making to personal financial decisions. The Personal Financial Literacy Event consists of a financial literacy exam and a role-play scenario with a business executive. Finalists will compete in a second role-play event. Participants will have 10 minutes to review the scenario and develop a professional approach to solving the problem. Participants will have 10 minutes to present their action plan to the judge. After the participant's explanation, the judge can ask questions about the scenario.

Go to DECA.org/compete for more detailed information.

Performance Indicators

- Differentiate between gross, net, and taxable income.
- Identify common types of payroll deductions.
- Explain how taxes impact take-home pay.

Try It Out!

You are to assume the role of a financial planner who has volunteered at the local high school to help students who have part-time jobs with basic financial literacy, including understanding their pay stubs and developing a budget. DeAndre, one of the students (the judge), thinks there is an error on his paycheck. DeAndre has his pay stub with him. He works 24 hours a week and is paid $12.00 per hour. DeAndre was expecting his check to be $288. Instead, his check is only $243.

You must explain to DeAndre the common types of payroll deductions, how taxes impact a paycheck, and the difference between gross and net income. Create a short presentation to explain these concepts to DeAndre.

Be prepared to answer the following questions from DeAndre.

1. How are Social Security taxes computed? What would his Social Security taxes be on this paycheck?
2. How are Medicare taxes computed? What would his Medicare taxes be on this paycheck?
3. Why does he have to pay federal income taxes?
4. DeAndre indicated that he has the option of contributing to a retirement account. What advice would you give him (as a high school student) about saving for retirement?

www.deca.org/compete

Managing Credit

Source: sirtravelalot/Shutterstock.com

Unit 2 introduces you to credit and the skills needed to use credit wisely. Today, credit is a "way of life," and learning to manage it wisely is important, especially since millions of Americans are overextended with credit and file for bankruptcy each year. Successful credit management begins with an understanding of how credit has changed over time. From there, knowing the advantages and disadvantages of credit will help you learn about different types of credit, how to build a good credit history, and the importance of knowing your credit score and how to improve it. Learning how to calculate interest and finance charges and identify the dangers of credit and how to avoid them are also key skills. When used properly, credit can help you leverage your financial goals and meet them faster. Used improperly, credit can lead to severe consequences such as bankruptcy and foreclosure.

Thasunda Brown Duckett

Source: U.S. Department of Education

Thasunda Brown Duckett was born in July 1973 in Rochester, New York, and moved to Texas as a child, graduating from Sam Houston High School. She attended the University of Houston and earned a bachelor's degree in finance and marketing. She then attended Baylor University, earning a Master of Business Administration (MBA). She has served as the president and chief executive officer (CEO) of TIAA since 2021. TIAA is the Teachers Insurance Annuity Association of America. She is also on the board of directors for Nike. Duckett is the former CEO of Chase Consumer Banking.

Duckett is the fourth Black woman to be CEO of a Fortune 500 company. The mission of TIAA is financial inclusion and opportunity, which are values she follows in her own life. TIAA provides investment opportunities for millions of Americans who work in the educational sector. Since becoming the CEO, Duckett has expanded the opportunity for retirement savings for all Americans. Duckett serves on the President's Board of Advisors on HBCUs (Historically Black Colleges and Universities). The board advises the president of the United States on federally sponsored programs and how to strengthen HBCUs through the private sector.

She created the Otis and Rosie Brown Foundation. The foundation honors her parents and "recognizes and rewards people who use ordinary means to empower and uplift their communities in extraordinary ways." In 2023, Forbes named Duckett the 34th most powerful woman in the world. She states on her LinkedIn profile that she is "passionate about helping communities of color close achievement gaps in wealth creation, educational outcomes and career success."

Connect and Reflect

Duckett has made a career out of following her passion. Explore how your passions may impact your financial future:

1. What is your passion? Do you have more than one? Brainstorm ways your passion(s) can contribute to your potential career.

2. What type of lifestyle would your potential career allow you? Would you need to make any adjustments to meet your needs and wants?

3. Identify three short-term and three long-term goals that will support your pursuit of your potential career.

5 Chapter

Credit in America

5.1 Credit: What and Why

The Essential Question

How has the use of credit changed over time, and what are the advantages and disadvantages of using credit?

Learning Objectives

By the end of this lesson, you should be able to:

LO 5.1.1 Discuss the history of credit and the role of credit in the U.S. economy.

LO 5.1.2 Explain the advantages and disadvantages of using credit.

Key Terms

- credit
- financing
- debtor
- creditor
- promissory note
- capital
- collateral
- finance charge
- minimum payment
- line of credit
- deferred billing

Consider This ...

It was two days before the spring festival, and Jazmin still hadn't purchased the supplies she needed to make her costume. She had been saving for four months and was still $50 short of her goal.

"I'll just have to borrow the rest and pay it back later," she told her friends. "Otherwise, I won't be able to get the costume finished, and I'll let down the team. I really wanted to pay cash and not go into debt, but in this case, it can't be helped. I probably should have used credit a little sooner to get the materials I needed. Now I'll have to work all night to get this costume completed. I learned an important lesson. There's a time and a place for using credit."

Read and Reflect

1. What options does Jazmin have to access the money she needs?
2. What would you recommend Jazmin consider prior to borrowing the needed money?

LO 5.1.1 The Need for Credit

When you borrow money or use a charge account to pay for purchases, you are taking advantage of the most used method of purchase in the United States: credit. **Credit** is using someone else's money and agreeing to pay it back later.

The need for credit arose in the United States when the country grew from a bartering and trading society to a currency exchange economy. During the 1800s, the Industrial Revolution started a new economy. Items were manufactured in mass for sale to others. People no longer produced everything exclusively for their personal use. They could buy the things they previously had to make for themselves with their earnings. Soon, the need developed for sources of credit to help families meet their financial needs.

Early Forms of Credit

One of the earliest forms of credit in the United States was having a charge account with a local retailer, usually a general store. The account was called a store credit or book credit. As the name suggests, the records

How were some of the earliest forms of credit used?

Source: VisionsofAmerica/Joe Sohm/Getty Images

were kept in a ledger or book. Wage earners or farmers would pick up supplies and put the amount due "on the account." When the borrowers received a paycheck or sold a harvested crop, they would pay their account in total, and the charging process would begin again. The stores rarely charged interest.

This early form of credit was a convenience store owners provided for customers they knew well and trusted. Because of the more personal nature of the business relationship, repayment schedules tended to vary according to when the consumer had funds available. Retailers often extended credit to help a trustworthy, longtime customer during hard times, even though payments were sporadic. It was one of the advantages of this local, more personal system.

In the 19th century, Americans rarely borrowed money for something unnecessary. Instead, they would borrow money only when necessary for things that would increase the value of their property or have productive uses, such as buying a sewing machine, improving fences, building barns, or planting crops. The Singer Sewing Machine Company was among the first to offer an installment plan. However, installment plans became more mainstream in the early 1900s when the General Motors Acceptance Corporation (GMAC) allowed middle-class workers to purchase a car using credit.

During the 20th century, many forms of credit developed—notably the credit card—to meet changing consumer needs and wants. As the use of credit expanded, individual purchasing power also increased. Because credit increased people's ability to buy more goods and services, people bought luxuries and necessities, and the average American's standard of living rose. Both businesses and consumers benefited from credit.

Credit Today

Today, credit is the American way of life. No longer is credit saved for emergencies. Merchants encourage consumers to use credit to buy many different goods and services. Goods are either nondurable and will be used in less than a year, or durable, lasting longer than a year. Goods are tangible products you can touch and see, such as cars, clothing, or food. Services include things that others do for you, like receiving a haircut or having your oil changed in your car, or services that are things you cannot see or feel, such as mobile phone service or internet access. Together, goods and services are called products.

Banks, stores, and credit card companies offer credit in the form of cards, loans, and lines of credit. Both short-term and long-term financing is available. **Financing** is when a consumer borrows money from a bank, store, or credit card company to make a purchase today. When you borrow money, you must repay the amount you borrowed plus interest. Credit cards are the most profitable sector of the American banking system. Everything from airline tickets to cosmetics to groceries can be purchased with a credit card. Some transactions, such as reserving a hotel room, renting a car, or making an online purchase, are challenging to make without a credit card.

Over time, "How can I get credit?" has turned into "How can I wisely manage credit?" Today, millions of Americans are overextended with credit. They have adopted a lifestyle that is dependent on the use of credit to make ends meet. The average American has over $6,000 in credit card debt, and nearly 40 percent carry credit card debt from month to month. Some people live beyond their means and abuse

How is credit used today?

credit. They can barely make the minimum payment on outstanding debt and resort to tactics such as using one credit card to pay the payment on another credit card. In the 1990s, record numbers of people declared bankruptcy, and overuse of credit cards was one of the main reasons.

The Use of Credit

A **debtor** is a person who borrows money from others. This money, called debt, must be repaid. A **creditor** is a person or business that loans money to others. Creditors charge money for this service in the form of interest and fees. A debtor must be qualified to receive credit. When you agree to a credit contract, you will sign the contract, which is also called a promissory note. A **promissory note** is a written agreement between two parties, the debtor and the creditor, to pay back a loan.

Qualifying for Credit

To qualify for credit, you must be able to repay the loan. Before you apply for credit, consider your income, financial position, and collateral.

- Income. You need to have a job and earn an income to make loan payments. Income can also come from other sources, such as interest, dividends, alimony, royalties, and so on. You should compare your cash inflow or income to your cash outflow or expenses. When your earnings exceed your expenses, you have the capacity to take on debt.

- Financial position. Your financial position is based on capital. **Capital** is the value of property you possess (such as bank accounts, investments, real estate, and other assets) after deducting your debts. Having capital means that you have accumulated assets, which indicates responsibility.

- Collateral. To borrow large amounts of money, you may need to provide collateral. **Collateral** is property pledged to assure repayment of a loan. For example, when you buy a car on credit, the car serves as collateral. If you do not make your loan payments, the creditor can seize the pledged property, or repossess it, and sell it to help repay the loan.

Making Payments

Once you have completed a credit purchase, you owe money to the creditor. The principal (amount borrowed) plus interest for the time you have the loan is called the balance due. You generally will make monthly payments until you repay the balance due in full. The **finance charge** is the total dollar amount of all interest and fees you pay for the use of credit. It is the price you pay for the privilege of using someone else's money to buy goods and services now.

Credit cards or store account statements usually specify a **minimum payment**. This is the least amount you may pay that month under your credit agreement, though you may pay more to reduce your debt faster. All credit card payments have a specific

Connections to Your World
Building Credit

According to Forbes, only 9 percent of all purchases made in the United States are paid for using cash. How are the rest paid for? Approximately 54 percent of purchases are made with debit cards, while 36 percent are made with credit cards. The use of credit is common in many parts of the world, including the United States. Building credit at a young age is important. Forbes outlines that 73 percent of Americans will have a credit card by the age of 25, making credit cards the most common first credit experience for many. Starting to build credit now is important.

Think Critically

1. We will all need credit at some point in our lives. How do you believe you will use credit during the different stages of your life? Consider what kinds of purchases you will need to make.
2. Why is it important for you to start building credit now?
3. What are ways you can start building credit?
4. What should you consider as you get your first credit card?

due date. Typically, you will be given 10 to 25 days from receiving a bill to pay. If you do not pay within the allowed time, you will likely be charged a late fee of as much as $35 to $50, which is added to the balance due. Your interest rate may also go up because of late payments.

For particularly expensive purchases, you may have to sign a loan agreement in which you agree to make regular payments for a set period. You will have repaid the entire debt at the end of that time. This is a type of secured loan because the goods you purchased with the loan serve as collateral for the money loaned.

✓ Checkpoint

How has the role of credit changed over time?

LO 5.1.2 **Advantages and Disadvantages of Credit**

Credit can be good when used wisely; however, many people get into trouble by not using credit carefully. Like most things in life, using credit has advantages and disadvantages.

Advantages of Credit

When used correctly, credit has several advantages:

- Purchasing power. Credit can greatly expand your purchasing power and raise your standard of living. For example, most people cannot purchase expensive items, such as a car or house, simply by saving money and paying cash. Credit allows you to purchase these items and then pay for them over time. As a result, you can enjoy these items earlier in your life. In addition to things you want, credit also allows you to purchase things that you need. For example, the cost of education is continuously rising, and many Americans will need to obtain a loan to pay for college or trade school. You will learn more about how to finance postsecondary education in a future chapter.

- Security. Using a credit card is safer than carrying a large amount of cash. If you lose cash, there is no way to replace it. If you lose a credit card, you can contact the company by phone or use an app on your phone to report your lost or stolen card. The company will freeze your account, and you will not be held responsible for fraudulent charges.

- Establishing good credit. Having a good credit history is important, not only when applying for credit cards but also when applying for loans, rental housing, some car or homeowners insurance, and employment. Making timely payments will help you build a good credit history and qualify for loans and lower interest rates.

- Emergencies. Credit can also provide emergency funds. A sudden need for cash can be solved by a **line of credit**, a preestablished amount that can be borrowed on demand with no collateral. To establish a line of credit, you must go to a lender, such as a bank, and apply for it. The lender examines your income and financial position and approves an amount that it believes you can repay.

- Benefits. Credit customers often receive special benefits. Regular charge customers of a department store, for example, receive advance notices of sales and special offers, such as deferred billing, not available to the public. Credit cards also often include rewards or rebates based on purchases. These rewards can be a percentage of dollar purchases or gift items of value.

- **Deferred billing** is a payment method that allows customers to purchase a product or service and delay their payments for a predetermined period of time. For example, merchandise purchased in October might not be billed until January, with no payment due until February.
- Leverage. Consumers also have more leverage when using credit rather than cash or other methods of purchase. With credit, the money remains to be paid, giving the consumer more power in the event of a dispute. With a debit card, check, or cash, money has already been paid for the purchase, which may make it more difficult to settle a dispute and get a refund.

Connections to Your World
Credit Card Traps

Credit offers may sound good, but you must read the terms and conditions carefully. There are many traps to avoid. What may appear to be a great deal can be a very expensive lesson that hurts your credit rating. Watch for the following signs that the credit offer is not as good as it sounds:

- Low introductory rate. Interest rate offers may be as low as 0 percent for a given period, such as 6 or 12 months. The fine print may include provisions that if you are late in making a payment by even one day the rate will rise to 25 to 30 percent or more! This introductory rate may be subject to change without notice.
- Fixed percentage rate. The offer may say the interest rate is fixed, meaning it will not increase. But the fine print may indicate that the fixed rate is subject to change without notice and that it can be "adjusted" (raised) at the creditor's option.
- Closed account rate. You may see terms that say "closed account rate." This is the rate you will be assessed if you close your account. These rates are often very high. This tactic is used by credit card issuers to keep you from closing your account when they raise your interest rate. Without this clause, consumers could reject a change in terms regarding interest rates, close the account, and continue making payments based on the original agreement until the balance is paid off.
- Late fees. Most credit card issuers charge a late fee if you do not pay the minimum payment amount by the specified due date. You may also discover that the issuer will raise your interest rate if you are repeatedly late with your payments. Late payments can impact your credit score by making you appear to be a higher risk. This could also lead to other creditors raising your interest rates.

(continues)

(continued)

- Over-the-limit fees. Card issuers may charge you a fee for exceeding your credit limit. This fee is added to your balance, meaning it will take even more money to pay the account down (remember, interest charges increase your balance daily). The fine print may also indicate that your interest rate will increase if you exceed the limit.
- Transaction fees. Some credit card companies allow you to transfer balances from other credit cards. They may also provide access checks so that you can borrow money without preapproval. There are often transaction fees for these types of borrowing, commonly ranging from 3 to 10 percent of the transaction amount. The transaction fees may also be in addition to flat fees, such as $30 for the transaction.

To avoid being taken advantage of, read credit offers carefully and compare them to offers by known lenders, such as your credit union or bank. Ask questions and be sure you understand the terms and conditions.

Think Critically

1. Look for a credit card offer in the mail or online. Then read the terms and conditions. Make a list of all the potential "traps" you find.
2. Discuss credit offers with your parents or other adults and ask about their experience with credit offers. What did you learn?

Disadvantages of Credit

Although credit has several advantages, you should not lose sight of its disadvantages:

- Fees and finance charges. Merchants must pay fees, which are usually a percentage of credit card sales, to credit card companies. Merchants often pass this cost on to customers in the form of higher prices. In addition, an item purchased on credit and paid for over time costs more because of the finance charge. For example, a finance charge of 18 percent a year is 1½ percent a month. The finance charge on a $1,000 balance would be $15 a month. The larger your balance and the longer you take to pay it off, the greater the finance charge.
- Reduction of future buying power. When you use credit, you tie up future income. You have committed to making payments.

Part of everything you earn in the future will go toward what you bought in the past. This may result in funds not being available when you need to purchase other products. This situation can put a strain on your budget.

Source: iStock.com/praetorianphoto

How does credit lead to overspending?

- Overspending. Buying on credit can lead to overspending. Because no cash leaves your bank account, you may not realize how much you are really spending. Using credit too much can result in debts so high that you can never pay them off, which could lead to bankruptcy. Failure to fulfill financial agreements will result in a poor credit record.
- Identity theft. Having a credit card means that you run the risk that your account information could be stolen, allowing someone else to make purchases on your credit card without your knowledge. You will learn more about identity theft and how to protect yourself from identity theft later in this unit.

✓ **Checkpoint**

What are the most critical advantages and disadvantages of using credit?

Check Your Understanding

1. Compare this country's early use of credit to its use today. (LO 5.1.1)
2. How does credit affect your purchasing power? (LO 5.1.2)
3. How can using credit lead to overspending? (LO 5.1.2)

Apply Your Understanding

1. Research the history of credit in the United States. Work with a partner or group to create a way to share this information with other students or an outside group. (LO 5.1.1)
2. Create a poster, blog post, podcast, or other product that explains the advantages and disadvantages of using a credit card. (LO 5.1.2)

The Essential Question

How has the use of credit changed over time, and what are the advantages and disadvantages of using credit today?

A: Credit in the United States started slowly, with charge accounts at general stores. Today, credit is available in multiple forms, increasing standards of living and convenience but often leading to overspending and abuse of credit.

5.2 Credit: Types and Sources

The Essential Question What kinds of credit are available to consumers and where can they be found?

Learning Objectives

By the end of this lesson, you should be able to:

LO 5.2.1 Explain the types of credit available to consumers.

LO 5.2.2 Compare and contrast sources of credit.

Key Terms

- open-end credit
- unsecured credit
- annual percentage rate (APR)
- fixed rate
- variable rate
- grace period
- installment credit
- service credit
- finance company
- usury law
- loan shark
- pawnbroker (or pawnshop)
- peer-to-peer lending
- predatory lender

Consider This ...

Jazmin's friend, Justin, has been working at his job for 6 months now. After the conversation with Jazmin in which she shared her plan to use credit to buy the supplies needed for her costume, Justin realized he has no credit established. Justin calls Jazmin for advice.

"Hey Jazmin, our conversation the other day really got me thinking. I realized that I have no credit. What are some ways that I can start building credit?"

Read and Reflect

1. What advice should Jazmin give Justin to help him start building credit? Remember, you are not establishing credit when you borrow money from parents, friends, or other private lenders.

2. What might be the best way to establish credit as a teenager without incurring high borrowing costs?

LO 5.2.1   Types of Credit

You likely will use several forms of credit throughout your life. Different types of credit are designed to meet different consumer needs.

Open-End Credit

Credit card accounts are an open-ended form of credit. **Open-end credit** enables a borrower to use credit up to a stated limit. As payments are made, the limit allows for more use of credit. The borrower usually has a choice of repaying the entire balance within 10 to 25 days or repaying it over time while making at least the minimum payment. Open-end credit can be used repeatedly if the balance owed does not exceed the credit limit.

Credit Cards

In a credit card agreement, the cardholder is obligated to pay the balance in full by the due date. It is typical to have up to 3 weeks to pay your credit card payment after receiving the billing statement. If the bill is not paid on time, late fees and other penalties may apply, depending on the card agreement. Finance charges are added to the outstanding balance if the bill is not paid in full.

Revolving Accounts

With a revolving account, the consumer can pay the balance in full by the due date or make payments at least as high as the stated minimum. The minimum payment is based on the amount of the balance due. If the balance is not paid in full, interest is charged.

Most all-purpose credit cards, such as Visa, MasterCard, American Express, Discover, and store accounts, are revolving credit

What are the advantages and disadvantages of a credit card?

agreements. Credit card accounts are also known as unsecured credit. An **unsecured credit** account does not require collateral from the consumer. Retail store cards, such as department store and gasoline company cards, are also based on revolving credit.

Credit Card Agreements

Credit card companies record transactions on your account and send you a bill at the end of each billing cycle. If you pay off the balance in full each month, a finance charge can likely be avoided. But remember, a credit card is a form of borrowing that usually involves interest and other charges. Before selecting a credit card, compare the

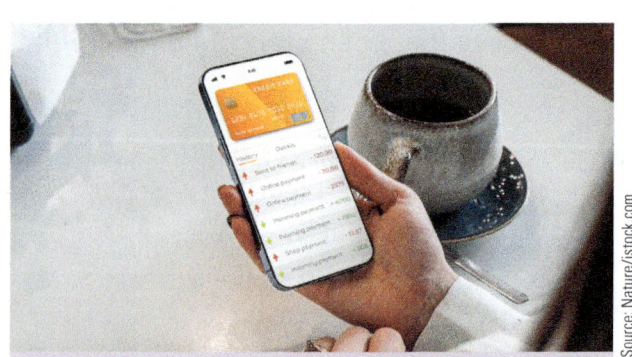

What are the various ways to access your credit card statement?

following terms that will affect the overall cost of the credit you will be using.

- Annual percentage rate. The **annual percentage rate (APR)** is the cost of credit expressed as a yearly percentage. The Truth in Lending Act (TILA) requires lenders to include all loan costs in the APR. The APR must be disclosed to you when you open the account and noted on each monthly bill you receive. Usually, the APR is a variable rate, and it can be very high on credit cards. Unlike a **fixed rate** which does not change, a **variable rate** will change in response to economic conditions. If inflation is rising, the variable rate will also go up. Sometimes credit cards offer an introductory rate, which is often lower than the actual rate. It is important to carefully read the Truth in Lending disclosure statement. The TILA standard format allows you to compare the credit terms to help consumers determine if the loan terms are acceptable.

- Grace period. The **grace period** is a timeframe within which you may pay your current balance fully and incur no finance charge. The grace period runs from the end of a billing cycle to the next payment due date. Under the Credit Card Accountability Responsibility and Disclosure Act of 2009 (Credit CARD Act of 2009), if your credit card balance has a grace period, your statement must be mailed or delivered to you at least 21 days before the finance charge would be added to your balance. If no grace period is specified, the card issuer will impose a finance charge from the date you use your credit card.

- Annual fees. Many credit card issuers charge an annual fee. The fee can range from $40 to up to $100 or more, and you must pay it even if you never use the card. The annual fee is usually charged in the anniversary month of when you opened the account. Most cards with an annual fee offer better reward opportunities than cards without an annual fee.

- Transaction fees. If you use a credit card check for a cash advance or to request a balance transfer, you may be charged a transaction fee. These fees may run from 3 to 10 percent of the transaction amount.

- Penalty fees. If you exceed your credit limit or make a late payment, you will likely be charged a penalty fee. Under the Credit CARD Act of 2009, limits on the amount of late fees that can be charged must be reasonable and proportional.

- Method of calculating the finance charge. If you pay for purchases over time, knowing how the card issuer will calculate your finance charge is important. The method used can make a difference—sometimes a big difference—in how much finance charge you will pay. Examples of these methods will be covered later in this unit.

Installment Credit

Consumers often use installment credit to pay for very expensive items, such as cars, major appliances, or real estate. **Installment credit**, or closed-end credit, is a loan for a specific amount that must be repaid in full, including all finance charges, by a specified due date. Installment credit agreements do not allow continuous borrowing or varying payment amounts. The borrower takes out an installment loan for a particular amount and then repays it with fixed or installments, including principal and interest. Installment loans have a fixed interest rate.

The contract for installment credit states, among other things, the amount loaned, the total finance charge, and the amount of each payment. Sometimes a down payment is required. The product purchased with the loan becomes collateral to assure repayment.

Service Credit

Almost everyone uses some type of service credit. **Service credit** involves providing a service for which you will pay later. Your telephone and utility services are provided for a month in advance; then you are billed. Many businesses extend service credit, including doctors, lawyers, hospitals, dry cleaners, and repair shops. Individual businesses set the credit terms. Some of these creditors do not impose finance charges on unpaid account balances, but they do expect regular payments to be made until the bill is paid in full. Others, such as utility and telephone companies, expect payment in full by a specified due date. However, utility companies usually offer a budget plan, which allows you to average your bills to get lower monthly payments.

> ✓ **Checkpoint**
>
> List the various types of credit available to consumers.

LO 5.2.2 Sources of Credit

The extension of credit is a service to consumers. It is not free; consumers must pay for it the same way they would pay for any other purchased service. As with other things you buy, it pays to shop around for the best deal.

Credit Card Companies

You may receive credit card offers directly from credit card issuers, such as Visa, MasterCard, American Express, and Discover. You can also get credit cards through your financial institution or other organizations. These companies offer many types of credit cards, including all-purpose and affinity cards.

All-purpose cards are credit cards that are generally accepted nationwide, and even internationally, to pay for just about anything, from clothes at department stores to meals at restaurants. With an all-purpose credit card, you have an automatic line of credit up to the limit set by the card issuer. Some cards even allow you to take a cash advance, which is money borrowed against your line of credit. You can access this money at an ATM, at a customer service desk at your bank, or by writing an access check against the credit card account. Access checks, which the credit card company supplies, look just like regular checks and are treated by the credit card company as a purchase. You must pay back the cash advance in the same way that you pay for credit card purchases. There is often a transaction fee for this service in addition to interest charges, which may or may not be the same interest rate applied to purchases made with the card. If you do not use the access checks that are often mailed to your home address, you should destroy them to prevent identity theft.

Affinity cards are credit cards associated with specific organizations, such as professional associations and educational institutions. Although these cards may show the organization's name, they are issued and serviced by a credit card company. Generally, an affinity credit card is cosponsored by the organization it is associated with, and the organization receives a percentage of the sales or profits generated by the card. Rates, fees, and benefits of affinity cards vary widely and may make these cards more expensive to use than similar, nonaffiliated cards.

Retail Stores

Retail and online stores sell goods directly to consumers. Examples include department stores, discount stores, and specialty stores. Some retail store credit cards can be used only at the store, while many retail stores, such as Amazon, Kohl's, Ulta, and Walmart, offer their own store credit cards and, for people with good credit ratings, cards that can be accepted anywhere credit cards are accepted. Store credit customers may receive discounts, advance notice of sales, and other privileges not offered to cash customers or customers using all-purpose credit cards.

Most retail stores also accept credit cards issued by major credit card companies. Accepting credit cards helps retail stores attract customers, because people like to shop where they can buy on credit.

Cobranded Credit Cards

Cobranded credit cards are issued by a financial institution, such as Chase or Citibank, in partnership with a company. Typical cobranded cards include airlines, hotels, and corporations. Cobranded cards are popular with consumers because of the discounts, rewards, and benefits the cardholder may receive. For the consumer, there is no difference between a regular credit card and a cobranded credit card. All can be used anywhere the credit cards are accepted, and payment terms are the same.

The advantages of using cobranded credit cards include:

- Rewards and discounts that are exclusive to the brand
- Preferential treatment at the brand
- Elite status for reaching certain milestones; these can include upgrades, free items, and bonus points toward the next milestone

The disadvantages of using cobranded credit cards include:

- Rewards that may be limited to the specific brand; for example, airline reward miles can only be used for that specific airline
- Temptation to overuse the card to reach the next milestone or a higher reward
- Companies that may devalue the reward over time

Banks and Credit Unions

In addition to offering credit cards, commercial banks and credit unions make closed-end loans to individuals and companies. They loan money to consumers for specific purchases, such as a home, car, or vacation. Interest on closed-end loans tends to be lower than on credit cards, usually because there is collateral used as security on the loans.

Credit unions make loans to their members only. Interest rates are sometimes lower than those charged by banks because credit unions are nonprofit and are organized for the benefit of members. Credit unions may be more willing to make loans because the members who are borrowing also have a stake in the success of the credit union. Most applications for credit begin with an online form through the bank or credit union website or on the app.

Source: glegorly/istock.com

What types of credit do banks and credit unions offer?

Finance Companies

In many cases, people who are turned down by banks and credit unions can get loans at finance companies. A **finance company** is an organization that makes high-risk consumer loans. These high-risk loans usually are accompanied by high interest rates. The rates depend on whether the state has a usury law. A **usury law** is a state law that sets a maximum interest rate that may be charged for consumer loans. In states where usury laws exist, finance companies charge the maximum rate allowed. Where no usury laws exist, finance companies charge as much as the customer is willing to pay. When an emergency or other extreme need arises, consumers may be willing to pay these higher rates to get the money they need.

There are two types of finance companies: (1) consumer finance companies and (2) sales finance companies. Both types of finance companies borrow money from banks and lend it to consumers at higher rates.

- A consumer finance company makes most of its loans to consumers who are buying durable goods. Durable goods are items expected to last several years, such as furniture, appliances, and electronics. There are many consumer finance companies. The smart consumer will shop around for the best possible rates and terms.
- A sales finance company makes loans to consumers through authorized representatives, such as car dealerships. Most car dealerships work with a bank for financing new and used cars.

Finance companies are second only to banks in the volume of credit extended. The growth of finance companies is partially the result of efforts to eliminate loan sharks. A **loan shark** is an unlicensed lender who charges illegally high interest rates.

Finance companies take more risks than banks; therefore, they must be more careful to protect their loans. If you do not make your payments when due, you can expect a call from someone at the finance company who will ask for an explanation as to why you did not make your payment. The company will stay in constant contact with you until you make your payments as agreed. The higher interest rates charged by finance companies serve as a form of protection. The high income earned from interest makes up for the percentage of loans that become uncollectible.

Pawnbrokers

A **pawnbroker** (or **pawnshop**) is a legal business that makes high-interest loans based on the value of personal possessions pledged as collateral. Easily salable possessions (such as jewelry, electronics, and tools) are usually acceptable collateral. The customer brings in an item of value to be appraised. The pawnbroker then makes a loan for considerably less than the item's appraised value. Some pawnshops give only 10 to 25 percent of the value of the item. Most of them give at most 50 or 60 percent.

For example, if you have a ring appraised at $500, you could potentially borrow between $50 and $300 with the ring as collateral. You would turn the ring over to the pawnbroker

What types of possessions do pawnbrokers usually accept as collateral?

and receive a receipt and a specified length of time—from 2 weeks to 6 months—to reclaim the ring by paying back the loan plus interest. If the loan is not paid within the specified time, the pawned item will be offered for sale by the pawnbroker.

Private Lenders

One of the most common sources of cash loans is the private lender. Private lenders might include parents, other relatives, friends, and so on. Private lenders may or may not charge interest or require collateral. Those who loan money to friends and relatives should take special steps to protect their interests. For example, rather than loaning cash to someone based on oral promises, you should get the agreement in writing with a formally signed note or another document to prove the debt.

Another type of private lending is peer-to-peer (P2P) lending. **Peer-to-peer lending**, or social lending, allows individuals to obtain loans from other individuals without using a financial institution. To participate in P2P lending, you must create an account on one of the P2P lending sites. P2P lending has the potential for high returns on your investment; however, before deciding to participate in P2P lending, do your research and make an informed decision.

Other Sources of Credit

Other sources of credit include the following:

- Life insurance policies
- Borrowing against a deposit
- Borrowing against an asset
- Lines of credit

Life insurance policies that build cash value can be used to borrow money. The loan does not have to be repaid; however, the loan amount will reduce the value of the policy. For example, if you borrow $15,000 from a $100,000 life insurance policy and do not pay it back, then the final payout on your life insurance policy will be $85,000 instead of the original $100,000. If you do decide to pay back the loan, you will have to pay interest on the principal. You will learn more about life insurance policies in a future chapter.

If you have a certificate of deposit (CD) or retirement account with a financial institution, you might be able to borrow money against it. A loan against this type of account usually has a good interest rate because of the collateral providing safety. In addition, borrowing against such a deposit allows you to avoid the penalties for early withdrawal. However, you should consider the drawbacks to this type of loan. If you do not repay the loan, the bank or other lender can collect the account balance. Also, you are slowing down the growth of your savings plan by withdrawing money from it. Thus, this type of loan should be considered a last resort.

You may also borrow against personal assets, such as jewelry, collectibles, or your car. For example, if you own a vehicle free and clear (no loan against it), you can take the title to your credit union or bank and ask for a loan. They will use the car title as collateral for the loan. Usually, the car must be newer—five years old or less—for this type of loan.

If you are a good customer of your bank or financial institution, you can set up a line of credit. With a line of credit (LOC), you have a preestablished amount that can be borrowed on demand without collateral. If you own your home, you may be able to receive a home equity line of credit, known as a HELOC. A HELOC acts as a second mortgage on your home. For both a LOC and a HELOC, sometimes the interest rate is fixed; other times it is a rate that changes with the economy, going up as interest rates in general

Connections to Your World
Predatory Lenders

Think back to Jazmin's situation from the start of the chapter; she needed money quickly so she could purchase the items she needed for her costume. You can likely think of a time when you were short funds to purchase something wanted or needed. When this happens, it is important to assess whether the item is needed now or if the purchase can wait until you have the funds in cash. If the item is needed now, you must explore options that allow you to borrow the needed money.

When exploring options, you may see companies that advertise things like "payday advance" or "quick access to cash." When you need funds quickly, it can be tempting to take advantage of these offers. Often, companies that advertise with these strategies are predatory lenders. Before borrowing money from these lenders, it is important to understand the terms of the loan and the risks associated with utilizing this type of loan.

Think Critically

1. Payday loan services and other predatory lenders typically charge very high interest rates. Why would someone utilize payday lenders with such high rates?
2. What should be considered before someone utilizes a payday loan service to cash advance their paycheck?
3. How can using services from a predatory lender, such as cash advancing a paycheck, create a cycle of debt that is hard for an individual to break?
4. What alternatives would you suggest to someone considering using services from predatory lenders?

increase. This form of credit is very convenient because you don't have to arrange a new loan each time you want to borrow money.

Predatory Lenders

A **predatory lender** is one that may take advantage of an emergency. Typically, consumers with little or no credit history who do not qualify for a standard loan may feel forced to use a predatory lender. However, anyone can become a victim of a predatory lender by not reading all the terms carefully when obtaining a loan. Common names for predatory lenders include payday loans, check-cashing services, and car title loans.

✓ Checkpoint

Why might it be more advantageous to borrow money from a credit union than to use other sources of credit?

Check Your Understanding

1. What is a revolving credit account? Give an example. (LO 5.2.1)

2. List five sources of credit and give one advantage and disadvantage of each. (LO 5.2.2)

Apply Your Understanding

1. Using a comparison chart, select three different types of credit and explain the similarities and differences between each. Then, create a blog post, podcast, or other media product to share the information. (LO 5.2.1)

2. Find a peer-to-peer lending site. Read the information about being a peer lender. Would you consider becoming a peer lender? Explain your answer. (LO 5.2.2)

The Essential Question

What kinds of credit are available to consumers and where can they be found?

A: Open-end credit, installment credit, and service credit are available from credit card companies, retail stores, cobranded credit cards, banks and credit unions, finance companies, pawnbrokers, private lenders, predatory lenders, and utility companies.

Summary

5.1 Credit: What and Why

- Borrowing money or using a credit account is one of the most common purchasing methods in the United States.

- Credit is using someone else's money and agreeing to pay it back later.

- Credit began as the United States grew from a bartering society to a currency exchange economy with mass-manufactured products available to consumers.

- Today, credit is a way of life. Merchants encourage consumers to use credit, and banks, stores, and credit card companies offer credit in the form of cards, loans, and lines of credit.

- Credit cards are the most profitable sector of the American banking system, but many Americans are overextended with credit.

- The person who borrows money is called the debtor; the person or business that loans money is called the creditor.

- Creditors charge money for this service in the form of interests and fees.

- Before applying for credit, you should consider your ability to repay debt based on your income, financial position, and collateral.

- Once you make purchases with credit, you will owe the principal (amount borrowed) plus interest for the time you have the loan. Most credit card companies require a minimum payment that is paid monthly.

- Advantages of credit are expanded purchasing power, the security of not having to carry a large amount of cash, the ability to build a good credit record, having a source of emergency funds, deferred billing, and leverage.

- Disadvantages of credit are fees and finance charges, the decreased ability to spend in the future, the tendency to overspend, and the risk of identity theft.

5.2 Credit: Types and Sources

- Different types of credit are designed to meet different consumer needs.

- Open-end credit allows you to borrow again and again, up to a set limit. As payments are made, the limit allows for more use of credit.

- With revolving credit, the consumer can pay the balance in full by the due date or make payments at least as high as the stated minimum, which is based on the amount of the balance due. If the balance is not paid in full, interest is charged.

- Most all-purpose credit cards, such as Visa and Mastercard, are revolving credit agreements.

- It is important to pay attention to the terms and conditions found in credit card agreements.

- The annual percentage rate (APR) is the cost of credit expressed as a yearly percentage.

- The Truth in Lending Act (TILA) requires lenders to include all loan costs in the APR.

- Usually, the APR is a variable rate and can change in response to economic conditions. The APR on credit cards can be very high. A fixed rate does not change.

- With a grace period, you can avoid finance charges so long as you pay your balance in full every month by the due date.

- Some credit card issuers charge an annual fee, transaction fees, and penalty fees.

- It is important to know how the credit card issuer calculates finance charges, since this can make a big difference in the amount of finance charges you pay.

- Installment or closed-end credit is a loan for a specific amount that must be repaid in full by a specified due date. Lenders generally require fixed payments, or installments.

- Many service providers, such as your utility company, provide service credit, allowing you to pay for services a month or more after their use.

- Sources of credit include credit card companies, retail stores, co-branded credit cards, banks and credit unions, finance companies, pawnbrokers, private lenders, and predatory lenders.

- Predatory lenders may take advantage of consumers with little or no credit history who do not qualify for a standard loan. Common names for predatory lenders include payday loans, check-cashing services, and car title loans.

Check Your Understanding

1. Why has the use of credit in the United States grown over the years? (LO.5.1.1)

2. What do you consider to be the two greatest advantages of using credit? Explain your answer. (LO 5.1.2)

3. What do you consider to be the two greatest disadvantages of using credit? Explain your answer. (LO 5.1.2)

4. What is the difference between open-ended and installment credit? (LO 5.2.1)

5. What is the purpose of service credit? (LO 5.2.1)

6. Explain the danger of using a predatory lender. (LO 5.2.2)

Apply Your Understanding

1. Give an example of a situation in which you would use collateral when making a purchase on credit. What would be the advantage to using collateral with an installment loan over making the purchase with your credit card? (LO 5.2.1)

2. Look at the two Truth-in-Lending Disclosures provided on the Companion Site. Examine both carefully. Which loan would be the most advantageous to the borrower? Explain your answer. (LO 5.2.1)

3. Does your state have a usury law? Identify the maximum finance rate that your state allows. Then identify the maximum rates allowed by neighboring states. Create a chart that shows the various maximum rates. Explain the importance of understanding how finance rates impact consumers. (LO 5.2.2)

4. How are consumer finance companies different from sales finance companies? Why do finance companies charge high interest rates? Why do you think consumers use finance companies for loans? (LO 5.2.2)

Share Your Knowledge

Work in teams of two to four students to complete the following activities.

1. The wide use of credit can lead to abuses. Some people take out more credit than they can repay. Then they are unable to pay back what they have borrowed. When merchants get stuck with unpaid balances, they pass along that cost to other customers in the form of higher prices. Thus, we all pay for people who overuse credit. Is it ethical for people to overextend their credit, knowing or suspecting that they will not be able to repay it? What can we all do to keep the cost of products and services at reasonable levels? (LO 5.1.1)

2. Explain how technology makes it possible for consumers to better manage their credit accounts, including loans, credit card accounts, and student loans. (LO 5.2.1)

3. Create a blog post, podcast, or video to describe the dangers of predatory lenders to teenagers. (LO 5.2.2)

Connect and Reflect

Base your answers to the following questions on your own personal thoughts, preferences, and experiences.

1. Have you ever borrowed money from a friend or relative? If so, what were the terms of your agreement? Were they fair to both you and the person you borrowed the money from? How did borrowing money from them help you meet an obligation or goal? (LO 5.1.1)

2. As a teenager, you do not have a credit history. Why is it important for your future financial planning to have access to credit and to start building a good credit history as a young adult? (LO 5.1.2)

3. You want to buy a new car but only have enough money to make a down payment. What are your options to finance the balance of the $10,000 loan? Explain. (LO 5.2.2)

Chapter Project

You have been asked to prepare a 30-minute presentation on the dangers of predatory lenders. Working with a small group, prepare a presentation that describes and compares the various types of predatory lenders. Incorporate the dangers to consumers that predatory lenders present. Your presentation should include appropriate graphics and links to your sources.

6 Chapter

Credit Records and Laws

The Essential Question   Why is your credit history important, and how do you build a good credit history?

Learning Objectives

By the end of this lesson, you should be able to:

LO 6.1.1   Discuss the purpose of credit reports.
LO 6.1.2   Describe the concept of creditworthiness.
LO 6.1.3   Explain how to get started using credit.

Key Terms

- credit history
- credit bureau
- subscribers
- credit report
- credit freeze
- creditworthy
- character
- capacity
- capital
- conditions
- collateral
- secured credit card
- cosigner

Consider This ...

Ashwin is a high school student who works part time during the school year and nearly full-time during the summer. By working, he has been able to build a savings account. Ashwin has just turned 16 and is learning to drive.

"I'd like to buy my own car," he told his friend Ami. "That way I can drive myself to work. If I had my own car, I could work more shifts because I wouldn't have to rely on family and friends to get me there. I'd also have a way to get to more school activities. Even though I've been saving, I don't have enough to pay cash for a car, so I'll have to get a loan. My mom says I'll establish credit by getting a loan, but because I don't have any credit yet, she'll have to cosign for me."

Read and Reflect

1. What should Ashwin consider as he looks to take out a loan for a car?

2. What are potential advantages and disadvantages of Ashwin taking out a loan? Would you recommend that he take out the loan?

3. What risk does Ashwin's mom take by cosigning a loan for him?

LO 6.1.1 Credit History

Before granting credit, a creditor will check your past credit performance: Did you pay your bills on time? How much total credit did you receive? How much do you owe now, and how large are your payments? Your **credit history** is the complete record of your borrowing and repayment performance. This record will answer these questions and help the creditor determine your ability to pay new debts.

Credit Bureaus

Every credit user has a credit history on file at a credit bureau. A **credit bureau** is a business that gathers, stores, and sells credit information to other businesses. Maintaining credit files is big business. Credit bureaus assemble and distribute detailed credit information concerning 340 million consumers.

There are more than 1,000 local and regional credit bureaus around the country. Typically, these smaller local and regional bureaus are affiliated with one of the following three nationwide credit bureaus:

- Equifax (www.equifax.com)
- Experian (www.experian.com)
- TransUnion (www.transunion.com)

In addition to the three main credit bureaus, Innovis (www.innovis.com) is another credit bureau that is growing in the United States. Innovis will run a credit check and provide a credit report; however, the company works directly with businesses to authenticate consumer credit data. The businesses use the authenticated data to provide preapproved credit and insurance offers, among other things. Innovis does not calculate the credit score of consumers.

What is the purpose of a credit bureau?

Source: DNY59/istock.com

Credit bureaus gather information from businesses, called **subscribers**, who pay a monthly fee to the credit bureau for access to this information. Each subscriber supplies information about its customers' accounts—names, addresses, credit balances, on-time payment records, and other credit information—about once a month.

Credit bureaus also gather information from multiple sources. For example, the credit bureau will search public records for information to add to a file. The credit bureau will then compile the information into a credit report.

Credit Reports

A **credit report** is a written statement of a consumer's credit history (**Figure 6.1**). When someone applies to a business for credit, the business asks the credit bureau for the applicant's credit report. The business will use the information in the credit report as the basis for granting or denying credit. Usually, banks, retail businesses, employers, landlords, and insurance companies have an interest in credit reports. Before entering into a financial agreement with someone, they want evidence that the person is financially responsible.

Figure 6.1   Credit Report

Source: scyther5/istock.com

Each credit bureau may arrange the credit reports differently, but they all contain the following information:

- Summary of information. The first section is a summary of negative and positive items. It tells the subscribers what to look for as they go through the information that follows. Negative items could harm your ability to get credit. Any negative information stays on your report for 7 years or until the statute of limitations runs out, whichever is longer. Accounts in good standing are favorable to your credit.
- Public record information. This section lists information found in public records. You would expect to find any lawsuits, judgments, bankruptcy filings, property purchase and sale, marriage, divorce, adoption, and other public information available to anyone who searches public records.
- Credit information. This section lists credit accounts that have been reported to credit bureaus, including those with department stores, credit card companies, and other loans. It reports details such as each account's high balance since its opening and the current payment status.
- Account detail. This section shows the monthly balances of accounts. It also lists the credit limits that have been reported.
- Requests for credit history. This section lists every business that has sought information from your credit file. It includes requests by potential employers, creditors, insurance companies, and others, along with requests you may have made to inspect your credit records.
- Personal information. This section lists the personal information that you have given when applying for credit or that is available through public records. It includes your name and previous names, Social Security number, current and previous addresses, date of birth, driver's license number, telephone number, spouse's name, and employers and salary.

Credit reports may contain errors. For example, a clerical error in entering a name or address, an inaccurate Social Security number, or loan payments applied to the wrong account can cause errors. You will learn more about how to resolve errors in a credit report in a future section. That is why you should review your credit report at least once a year. Consumers may request one free credit report every 12 months from each of the three major credit bureaus. AnnualCreditReport.com (www.annualcreditreport.com), created by the three major credit bureaus, is a centralized service for requesting your free annual credit reports. Although many TV ads, e-mail offers, and online search results offer free credit reports, AnnualCreditReport.com is the only authorized source for a truly free credit report. Other offers include a free credit report when you sign up for a credit monitoring or credit protection service. If you are denied credit, you can also get a free credit report within 60 days of the credit denial. If you need to obtain a credit report at any other time, the credit bureau will charge a small fee. Because the three credit bureaus share information, an error in one system can be replicated in the other two systems. One way to monitor your credit more frequently is to request your credit reports at different times of the year. For example, request a report from Experian in February, TransUnion in June, and Equifax in October. Mobile apps also allow users to view a credit report online anytime. Most credit card companies will provide access to your credit score through the credit card mobile app.

Credit Protection Services

In addition to checking your credit reports regularly, there are other ways to protect your credit files, including credit guard and freezing services.

Connections to Your World
Credit Bureaus

As you begin to establish credit, it is important to understand the roles and responsibilities of different individuals and organizations. Because credit bureaus gather, store, and sell credit information to other businesses, there are sometimes concerns about consumer privacy and the power credit bureaus hold. Some people believe that credit bureaus are too powerful and do not adequately safeguard consumer information. Information may be gathered and shared without the knowledge or consent of consumers. Credit bureaus often sell consumer information and provide lists of consumers who meet certain criteria. This information is used by businesses to send out unsolicited credit offers.

Consumer privacy advocates believe that consumers should have more control over the private and personal information that is contained in credit files. Rather than being allowed to "opt out" of having information supplied at will, they believe that credit bureaus should have to get consumers' written permission (or allow them to opt in) before they can sell and distribute information about them. Credit bureaus disagree and believe that the information is their property and that of their subscribers. They believe they should have free access to it and have the right to share it to generate business profits.

Think Critically

1. What concerns, if any, do you have as you begin building credit?
2. Do you think credit bureaus are too powerful? Why or why not?
3. If it were an option, would you "opt in" to have your information shared with other businesses? How might the credit offers you receive be beneficial? How might they create issues with your credit?

Credit Guard

Credit guard services are available to consumers who wish to hire a company to monitor their credit files at the three major credit bureaus. With this service, you are notified whenever anyone accesses your credit file for any reason. The fee charged for this service ranges from $15 a month to $50 a month, depending on the degree of protection provided. For example, you can supply a list of your credit cards, and if one or more is lost or stolen, the service will have it canceled and notify the credit bureaus on your behalf.

Credit Freeze

As a result of increasing credit card fraud and identity theft, many states have passed laws allowing consumers to freeze their credit reports and files. A **credit freeze** is a consumer request that requires the credit bureaus to deny all access to a consumer's credit information or files. Thus, new credit applications are blocked, and the credit bureau cannot provide loan solicitation information. Consumers who choose a credit freeze can unfreeze their credit files when they wish to obtain new credit and refreeze them when they are ready. Credit bureaus can charge a fee (such as $15) for each activity. Consumers may also freeze individual credit card accounts through the financial institution's mobile app.

> ### ✓ Checkpoint
>
> What is the purpose of a credit report, and why is it important to review your credit report annually?

LO 6.1.2 Creditworthiness

Before potential creditors grant credit to you, they must determine whether you are a good risk—that you are **creditworthy**. To determine this, most lenders utilize some variation of the five "Cs" of credit: character, capacity, capital, conditions, and collateral.

Character: Are You Responsible?

Character is a responsible attitude toward honoring obligations, often judged on evidence in the person's credit history. If you pay your bills on time, your credit history will show it.

In addition to your credit history, creditors also use stability as a measure of character. For example, a person who has held four different jobs over the past year or has gaps in employment might not be considered a good credit risk.

Capacity: Can You Repay Your Debts?

Capacity is the ability to repay a loan with present income. Before lending you money, creditors want to ensure that your current income is sufficient to cover your current monthly expenses plus the payments on the new loan. Capacity is measured as a percentage of take-home pay. For example, payments on your credit card and other forms of revolving credit should not exceed 20 percent of your take-home pay. So, if your take-home pay is $2,000 monthly, your revolving credit amounts should be less than $400 monthly.

Capital: Do You Have Sufficient Assets?

Capital is the value of financial assets in bank accounts, investments, and property you possess after deducting your debts. In other words, when you add up all that you own (assets) and subtract all that you owe (liabilities), the difference (net worth or capital) should be sufficient to ensure payment of your debt. Having capital tells creditors that you are in the process of building wealth and providing for your future financial security. Sometimes when your balance sheet is healthy, creditors will overlook other requirements. You are a solid low-risk borrower if you have financial assets.

Conditions: What Else Is Going On?

External conditions may affect your ability to repay a debt. **Conditions** refer to the overall economic climate and external environment. For example, if the economy is slowing and people in your area are losing their jobs, creditors may be less willing to give you a loan. If you lose your job, you may not be able to meet your payments. Therefore, creditors want to know the answers to questions such as the following: How secure is your job? How secure is the firm for which you work? How is the employment situation in your geographic location and in your occupation?

Collateral: Is the Debt Secured?

Collateral is property pledged to assure loan repayment, such as a house, car, or furniture being purchased. Collateral protects creditors and lowers their risk, making them more willing to lend to you. If you do not repay your debt as agreed, the creditor can seize the pledged property and sell it to repay the debt. For example, if you stop making your monthly house payments, the creditor can take possession of the home through a foreclosure process and sell it to get back the principal it lent you.

It is important to build a good credit history. Consumers with good credit qualify for lower interest rates on loans and may pay

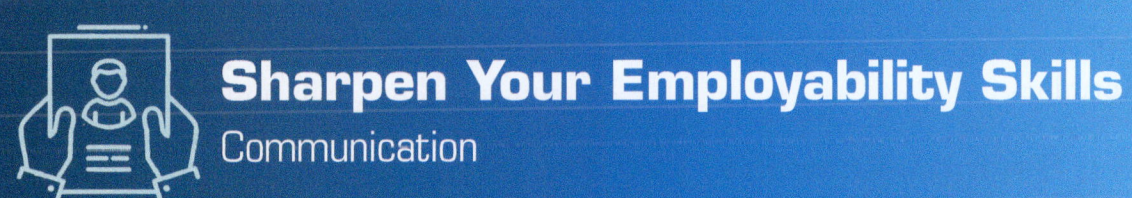

Sharpen Your Employability Skills
Communication

It can be hard getting started with credit. Most credit card companies do not want to take risks on new cardholders. They are looking for responsible people who will take their credit very seriously. There are several actions a young person can take to help them build credit. Make a list of recommendations that you would share with a friend who is just getting started with their credit journey. What should they do or consider? What should they avoid? What are important action steps?

lower fees when setting up loans. Additionally, consumers with good credit may receive lower insurance premiums for auto and home policies. A good credit score may reduce your deposit if you are searching for an apartment. When you open utility accounts, internet services, or cell phone services, you may be allowed to waive the deposit for service, or the deposit may be less. Consumers with poor credit scores will pay higher interest, fees, and deposits on the same items.

> ### ✓ Checkpoint
>
> What are the five "Cs" that determine creditworthiness?

LO 6.1.3 Getting Started with Credit

Establishing a good credit record is a slow process. It can take several years of responsible money management to prove your creditworthiness. But everyone must start somewhere, and here are several effective ways to get you started on the road to creditworthiness.

Open a Savings Account

Opening a savings account is an effective way to start proving your creditworthiness. Start at a financial institution that will not charge you a monthly fee when your savings account balance is small. Some credit unions and banks allow minors to establish accounts with small balances and waive normal fees charged to other depositors. Keep your account growing through regular savings by depositing a small amount of money each month or pay period.

Open a Checking Account

Open a checking account, preferably at the same financial institution where you have your savings account. This will provide a convenient payment method when you have credit accounts and serve as a record-keeping system for your budget. Choose the checking plan that is the least expensive and most convenient for you. Then carefully manage your checking account. Do not make payments or withdraw cash at an ATM when your account contains insufficient funds to cover the transaction. Overdrawing your account will tarnish your creditworthiness. Monitor your account balances carefully by either recording transactions in a check register or using a mobile app from your financial institution.

Open a Secured Credit Card

A secured credit card is like a debit card that allows you to build your credit. Anyone, even someone with no credit history, can open a secured credit card. To open a secured credit card, you must deposit funds equal to your credit limit with the financial institution. This may be between $500 and $1,000 for most young adults. You can then use the credit card anywhere credit cards are accepted. At the end of the month, you should pay the full credit card balance; otherwise, you will be charged interest on the unpaid balance. By making your payments on time and keeping the balance low, you will begin to build a good credit history. If you do not make your payments on time, you will damage your credit history because secured credit cards become part of your credit report. Once you have built a good credit history, you may request to transition the account into a standard credit card account.

Become an Authorized User on Someone Else's Credit Card

If you are not old enough to have your own credit card, your parent or guardian, if willing, can add you as an authorized user on one of their credit card accounts. This allows you to benefit from the positive credit history they have built. The primary owner of the account is responsible for making the payments on time and using the account responsibly.

Get a Credit-Builder Loan

Another option to prove your creditworthiness is to take out a small credit-builder loan from the credit union or other financial institution where you have your savings and checking accounts. Use the money to buy something you really need. Then pay back the loan as agreed. Make early payments if possible. Again, you may need to rely on your parents or another adult with a good credit record to cosign your first loan. A **cosigner** is someone who will take full responsibility for paying back a loan, along with you. The cosigner is obligated to pay any missed payments or the full amount of the loan if you do not pay.

Parents or guardians may also add you to an account or loan or other obligation, such as a car loan. This way, the payment is also recorded as part of the minor's credit history.

Apply for a Credit Card

Once you have an established credit history with credit references, you should be eligible for a major credit card, such as a Visa or MasterCard. It is often easier and usually safer to apply for a card with your credit union or bank. Because you have a savings and checking account with them, they already know you. Plus, you will be less likely to be required to pay high-interest rates or fees than if you apply to a credit card company online or respond to an unsolicited credit card offer. Banks may give you a smaller credit limit to start, but your credit limit will be raised over time if you manage your account wisely.

Regardless of where you apply for your first credit card, be sure to read the terms and conditions of the card carefully before selecting one. This will tell you about the card's various fees, charges, interest rates, and benefits. Some credit cards may look like a great deal until you read the fine print.

Once you have your first credit card and make the payments on time, you will find it easier to obtain additional credit. It is good to have credit available if you need it, but do not take out too much credit.

Finally, follow these rules related to credit.

- Rule 1: Always make your payments on time. Payment history is the biggest factor in your credit score; even one missed payment can cause a large drop in your credit score. One way to always make your payment on time is to set up an automatic payment.
- Rule 2: Keep your use of credit low. Aim always to use less than 30 percent of your available credit limit. This means that if you have a credit limit of $1,000, you should keep your balance under $300.

Connections to Your World
Cosigning for a Loan

You have worked hard to establish your credit. Your credit score is solid. A younger friend who is just starting to establish asks you to cosign on a loan for a car.

Think Critically

1. What would you do? What things would you consider as you make your decision?
2. If you do cosign, what are your responsibilities as a cosigner?
3. Would your answer change if it were a younger sibling who asked you to cosign? Why or why not?

■ Rule 3: Only use your credit card for something you can afford to pay in full when the statement arrives. If you cannot pay in full, you should aim to make more than the minimum payment, since the minimum payment covers only interest and a small amount of principal. Since the average credit card interest rate is over 20 percent, this means you will pay a large finance charge or interest on any outstanding balance on the credit card, putting you into more debt each month.

> ✓ **Checkpoint**
>
> How can you get started using credit?

6.1 Lesson Review

Check Your Understanding

1. How do credit bureaus gather information for your credit file? (LO 6.1.1)
2. What does "creditworthiness" mean? (LO 6.1.2)
3. Describe the five "Cs" of creditworthiness. (LO 6.1.2)
4. What actions can you take to begin building your credit history? (LO 6.1.3)

Apply Your Understanding

1. With your parent or guardian's permission, request a copy of your credit report through the website AnnualCreditReport.com. Once you receive the report, review it with a trusted adult. Explain your findings. (LO 6.1.1)
2. As a teenager, you would like to get started in establishing a good credit history. Based on your personal situation and the stores and banks in your area, prepare a plan that you might follow in getting started using credit. (LO 6.1.3)

The Essential Question

Why is your credit history important, and how do you build a good credit history?

A: Your credit history helps creditors decide your creditworthiness. To get started with credit, begin by opening a savings account. Then, after accumulating some savings, open a checking account and a credit card account.

6.2 Evaluating Credit and Credit Laws

The Essential Question — Why are your credit score and credit rating important, and why are credit laws needed?

Learning Objectives

By the end of this lesson, you should be able to:

LO 6.2.1 Explain how credit scores are used to evaluate credit.

LO 6.2.2 Discuss major credit laws and their impact on consumers.

Key Terms

- credit score
- FICO score
- credit inquiry
- rate shopping
- billing statement
- discrimination
- debt collector

Consider This ...

Ashwin has begun his journey to build credit. He obtained a loan to purchase a car and has opened some credit cards. He knows that it will take time to build credit but wants to monitor his credit score to make sure it is moving in the right direction. Ashwin regularly checks his credit score using Credit Karma. He reviews notes from Credit Karma about things that may negatively impact his credit and recommendations on how to improve credit.

Read and Reflect

1. Why is it important to monitor your credit score?

2. What factors impact your credit score?

3. Since Ashwin now has credit cards, what laws are in place to help protect him as a consumer?

Credit Scores

Credit bureaus evaluate consumers based on information contained in their credit reports. This information is used to assign credit scores to consumers. Credit scores make it easier to interpret a consumer's credit report.

Credit Scores

Credit bureaus use a point system to compute credit scores for consumers. In a point system, the credit bureau assigns points based on factors such as current debt, number of late payments, number and types of open accounts, amount of income, and so on. When your points are added, they result in a **credit score** that tells potential creditors the likelihood that you will repay debt as agreed. The higher your score, the greater your chance of being a good credit risk. Business subscribers then use these scores as part of their decision to grant or deny credit.

The most used credit scoring model, used by over 90 percent of creditors, is a FICO score. A **FICO score** is the credit score created by the Fair Isaac Corporation. Each consumer has three FICO scores— one for each of the three major credit bureaus. Because a consumer's credit report may contain different information at each bureau, FICO scores can vary depending on which bureau provides the score. As information changes, your scores change as well.

Calculating Your FICO Score

To calculate a FICO score, you must have at least one account open for 6 months or more. FICO scores are calculated from several different pieces of data in your credit report. This data is grouped into five categories: payment history, amounts owed, length of credit history, credit mix, and new credit.

- Payment history accounts for 35 percent of your credit score and is based on how you pay your debts; the presence of bankruptcy, liens (financial claims against property), or collections; and whether accounts are past due or paid as agreed.
- Amounts owed is 30 percent of your credit score and is based on how many credit accounts have balances, the amounts owed on those accounts, and the proportion of the credit line used.
- Length of credit history accounts for 15 percent of your credit score and is based on the oldest account opened and the average age of all accounts. Accounts that have been open for a long period of time positively impact your score.
- The credit mix of your accounts is 10 percent of your credit score. Credit mix is determined by the type of credit accounts, such as credit cards, retail accounts, installment loans, and mortgages. It is not necessary to have an open credit account in all categories; however, you should have a mixture of different types of credit.
- New credit is how many new accounts you have requested recently. New credit is 10 percent of your overall credit score and is based on the number of recently opened accounts and the number of recent credit inquiries (discussed below).

Consumers cannot calculate their own credit score; however, if you have a credit card from a major financial instruction such as Chase Bank or Citibank, they will provide you with an up-to-date FICO score through their mobile app. The highest FICO score a person can receive is 850; the lowest is 300. You may also create an account at

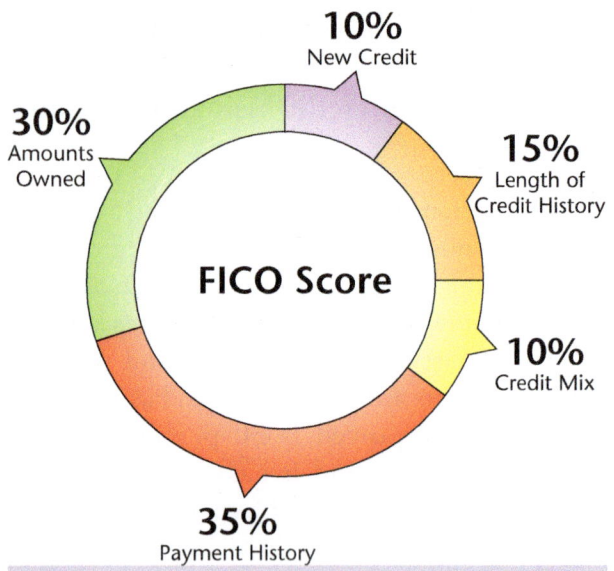

10%
New Credit

30%
Amounts Owned

15%
Length of Credit History

FICO Score

10%
Credit Mix

35%
Payment History

Why is it important to understand how credit scores are calculated?

the myFICO website (www.myfico.com). Another way to monitor your credit score is through a free monitoring service such as Credit Karma or Credit Sesame. Both have mobile apps and websites.

Credit Inquiries

A **credit inquiry** is a request by a business with a permissible purpose to check your credit. Businesses can inquire without your permission or knowledge, but usually, these requests do not count toward your credit score. For example, before a credit card company sends you a preapproved credit offer, it will pull your credit information. A personal credit inquiry made by you to obtain your credit report does not affect your score.

When you apply for a loan or other credit, you authorize the lender to check your credit. These inquiries, which are prompted by your own actions, will affect your FICO score. One exception occurs when you are rate shopping for an auto or mortgage loan. **Rate shopping** involves looking for the best

interest rate on an auto or mortgage loan. This may cause multiple lenders to request your credit report. To compensate for this, your FICO score does not include inquiries made within a short period of time—usually 30 days. Therefore, if you find an auto or mortgage loan within the 30-day period, the inquiries will have little or no effect on your score while rate shopping.

The impact of credit inquiries varies based on a person's credit history. In general, they have a small impact on your FICO score. However, if you have few accounts or a short credit history, inquiries could cause your FICO score to drop quickly. Too many inquiries could mean you are attempting to take on too much debt.

Improving Your FICO Score

Raising your FICO score takes time and patience. There is no quick way to fix a credit score, but following the tips below can help:

- Pay your bills on time. Delinquent payments, even if only a few days late, can have a negative impact on your FICO score.
- Improve your payment history. If you have missed payments, get current and stay current. The longer you pay your bills on time after being late, the more your FICO score will increase.
- Keep balances low on credit cards and revolving credit. High outstanding debt can negatively affect a credit score.
- Pay off your debt rather than move it around. If you pay off one credit card bill by using another credit card, you are simply moving your debt, not reducing it.
- Open accounts slowly—not several at a time. Some experts suggest that too many open accounts, even unused, can hurt your credit score because of the potential for obtaining more available credit than you are able to handle.

The Meaning of Credit Scores

Credit scores are divided into categories by each of the credit bureaus. Experian uses the categories of Exceptional, Very Good, Good, Fair, and Poor. Consumers in the Exceptional, Very Good, and Good categories have the best chances of being approved for mortgages and other large loans, and these consumers will receive the best interest rates for the loan.

Credit scores affect loan terms, such as the interest rate, that you will be offered.

For example, if you have an excellent credit rating, you may be offered a loan at a low interest rate, which means your monthly payments would be lower. However, if your credit rating is only fair, you may be offered the same loan at a higher interest rate, meaning your monthly payments would be higher. The difference may not seem like much in the short term, but when you add up the difference between the payment amounts over the life of the loan, you could be paying thousands of dollars more!

Sharpen Your Employability Skills
Thinking Critically about Establishing Credit

As outlined in the "Consider This ..." at the start of the chapter, Ashwin is looking for ways to establish credit. Review the scenarios below that could likely be part of Ashwin's journey to build credit.

Scenario 1: Ashwin does not have established credit. When he makes purchases, he pays cash for items or uses his debit card. He borrowed $5,000 from his parents to buy the car he was considering in the scenario at the beginning of the chapter; he makes payments of $150/month to his parents. Ashwin has no credit cards and no loans through a bank or lender.

Scenario 2: Ashwin has established credit but is not happy with his credit score of 600. He recently began opening accounts to build credit; in the past 6 months, he opened four new credit cards. He makes most of his payments on time but occasionally misses a payment due date. Ashwin missed one payment and did not notice for 2 months. He carries balances on some of his cards. For example, he is carrying a balance of $820 on a card that has a limit of $1,000.

Think Critically

1. What recommendations would you make for Ashwin to improve his credit score in each of the scenarios above?

2. There are several factors that Ashwin, who is currently 16 years old, should consider as he starts to build credit. Make a list of things Ashwin should consider as he looks to build or improve his credit.

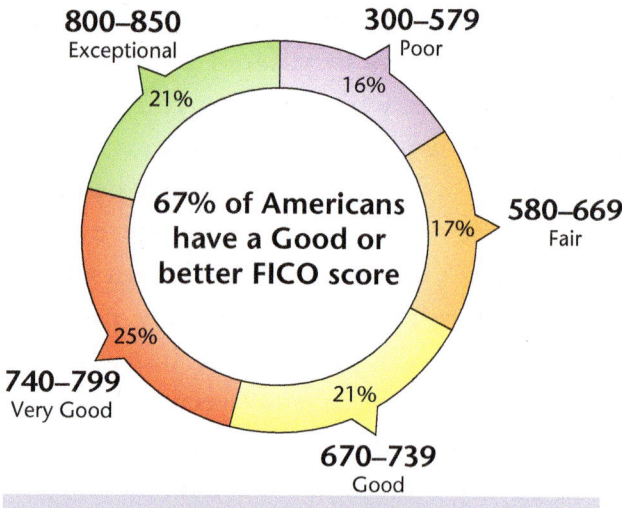

800–850
Exceptional

300–579
Poor

21%

16%

67% of Americans have a Good or better FICO score

17%

580–669
Fair

25%

740–799
Very Good

21%

670–739
Good

How do credit scores impact the terms of a loan?

For example: Two families are searching for a home and the mortgage needed to buy the home is $175,000. Baz and Anita have credit scores of 785 and 750. Evander and Duska have credit scores of 685 and 700. Baz and Anita have Very Good credit scores, almost into the Exceptional category. They can receive a mortgage rate of 5.75 percent APR. Evander and Duska have Good credit scores; however, they are near the bottom of the category. Their interest rate is going to be 7.75 percent APR. The difference in the monthly payments is $230 per month. That is $230 less in disposable income for Evander and Duska each month for the next 30 years. Over the life of the mortgage, they will pay almost $83,000 more in interest than Baz and Anita.

	Baz and Anita	Evander and Duska
Mortgage Amount	$175,000	$175,000
Annual Percentage Rate	5.75%	7.75%
Length of Mortgage	30 years	30 years
Payment for Principal and Interest	$1,020/month	$1,250/month

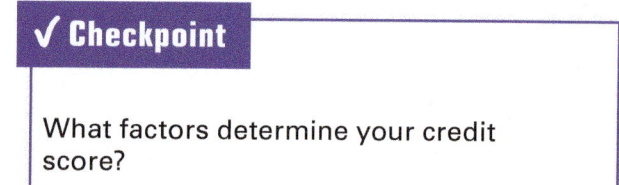

✓ **Checkpoint**

What factors determine your credit score?

LO 6.2.2 Credit Laws

The government has passed several laws to protect consumers from unfair credit practices. Together, these laws set a standard for how individuals are to be treated in their daily credit dealings. Several of these laws are summarized below.

Consumer Credit Protection Act

The Consumer Credit Protection Act of 1968, also known as the Truth in Lending Act, requires lenders to fully inform consumers about all costs of a credit purchase before an agreement is signed. Lenders must disclose the finance charge, which is the total dollar amount of all costs of the credit, including interest, service fees, and any other costs. Lenders must also state the annual percentage rate (APR), which is the yearly percentage of interest charges that must be calculated the same way by all lenders. In addition, the law requires a grace period of three business days in which purchasers can change their mind about a credit agreement. The law also limits the consumer's liability to $50 after the consumer reports a credit card lost or stolen. There is no liability if the card is reported lost prior to its fraudulent use.

Fair Credit Reporting Act

The Fair Credit Reporting Act of 1970 regulates the collection, dissemination, and use of consumer credit information. This act gives you the right to know what is in your credit report and entitles you to a free copy every 12 months from each of the three major credit bureaus. The act also gives you the right to know who has received your credit report in the last year (or two years for employment purposes). A credit bureau may not provide your credit report to an employer unless you give that employer written permission to request your credit report. You may see your credit report from the credit bureau used by the creditor at no charge within 60 days of a credit denial. In addition, the act gives you the right to dispute inaccurate or incomplete information in your report. The credit bureau must correct or delete any inaccurate or incomplete information in your report within 30 days. If potentially damaging information in the file is essentially correct, you can write a statement giving your side of the story and your statement must be added to the file.

Fair Credit Billing Act

Under the Fair Credit Billing Act, enacted in 1974, creditors must resolve billing errors within a specified period. A **billing statement** is an itemized bill showing charges, credits, and payments posted to your account during the billing period. Suppose your monthly statement showed a purchase you did not make. Perhaps you were billed for merchandise you ordered but did not receive. Creditors are required to have a written policy for correcting such errors.

If you believe your statement contains an error, contact the creditor and give a complete explanation of why you believe there is an error. You may contact the creditor via telephone, letter, or their mobile app. Be specific about the amount in dispute and provide any details relevant to the disputed amount. Include your account number and contact information if you are contacting the credit company by phone or mail.

Your complaint must be filed within 60 days of receiving the statement. The creditor must acknowledge the complaint within 30 days. The creditor must either correct the error or show why the bill is correct within 90 days. You are not liable for the amount in dispute while the error is being investigated. However, you must still make payments on all other amounts. You may be asked to provide documentation of why the amount is in error.

Equal Credit Opportunity Act

The Equal Credit Opportunity Act, also enacted in 1974, was designed to prevent discrimination in the evaluation of creditworthiness. **Discrimination** is the act of treating people differently based on prejudice rather than individual merit. There are many legitimate reasons for denying an applicant credit. Some reasons, however, are considered discriminatory. The act specifies the following:

- Credit may not be denied solely because you are a woman, single, married, divorced, separated, or widowed.
- Credit may not be denied specifically because of religion, national origin, race, color, or age (except as age may affect your ability to perform or your ability to enter

contracts; for example, minors cannot be held liable for their contracts because they are not considered competent parties).

- Credit may not be denied because you receive public assistance (welfare), unemployment, Social Security, or retirement benefits.
- Credit applications may be oral or written. However, a creditor is prohibited from asking certain questions, such as: Do you plan to have children? What is your ethnic origin? What church do you attend?
- A creditor may not discourage you, in writing or orally, from applying for credit for any reason prohibited by the act (such as being divorced).

In addition to these prohibitions, the act states that creditors must notify you of whether your credit application is accepted or rejected within 30 days of submission. If you are denied credit, the denial must be in writing and must list a specific reason for the denial.

The act also requires that companies reporting to credit bureaus must make their reports in the names of both the husband and wife if both use an account or are responsible for repaying the debt. In this way, both spouses establish their own credit histories.

Fair Debt Collection Practices Act

The Fair Debt Collection Practices Act of 1978 was designed to eliminate abusive collection practices by debt collectors. A **debt collector** is a person or company hired by a creditor to collect the overdue balance on an account. The fee charged by debt collectors is often half of the amount collected. The law prohibits use of threats, obscenities, and false and misleading statements to intimidate the consumer into paying. It also restricts the time and frequency of collection practices, such as telephone calls, and restricts contacts at places of employment. Debt collectors are required to verify the accuracy of the bill and give the consumer the opportunity to clarify and dispute it.

Credit Card Accountability Responsibility and Disclosure Act

The Credit Card Accountability Responsibility and Disclosure Act (Credit CARD Act) was passed by Congress in 2009 and was enacted to provide more consumer credit protections. The act provided many new provisions regarding interest rates. Credit card issuers were required to give a 45-day written notice of any interest rate increase. In addition, credit card issuers were prohibited from raising interest rates for the first year of a new account except for promotional rates, which must remain in effect for at least 6 months.

The act also placed new provisions on fees. Credit card issuers could no longer charge late fees greater than a minimum payment, and cardholders could no longer face fees if they went over their credit limit unless they gave the creditor permission to authorize over-the-limit transactions.

The act also created new disclosures that must be provided to consumers. Monthly credit card bills must include information on how long it will take you to pay off your balance if you make only minimum payments. The act also required consistency in payment dates and times. Credit card issuers are required to mail statements at least 21 days before payments are due, and monthly due dates must be the same date each month. The act also prohibited double-cycle billing, also known as two-cycle

Why do you think the Credit CARD Act has special credit provisions for those under the age of 21?

billing, or the practice of applying a finance charge on both the current balance and the previous month's balance.

Young consumers received additional protection under the act. Credit card issuers must verify proof of income or otherwise require a cosigner before issuing a credit card to someone under age 21. Also, credit card issuers cannot raise the credit limit for cardholders under age 21 who have a cosigner, unless the cosigner has given written permission to do so. The act also forced all credit card companies to discontinue marketing to college students unless the student opts in to receive the marketing. For many years, credit card companies would target college students by offering free merchandise such as t-shirts, food, coolers, and other prizes for completing a credit card application.

Dodd-Frank Wall Street Reform and Consumer Protection Act

The Dodd-Frank Wall Street Reform and Consumer Protection Act, commonly called the Dodd-Frank Act, was enacted in 2010. The Dodd-Frank Act created the

Connections to Your World
Credit and Economic Downturns

When the Great Recession hit in 2007, many people were caught off guard with a lot of debt. Prior to the Great Recession, many people had mortgaged their homes to the limit, taking out second mortgages in order to cash out their equity. Credit accounts and balances were at an all-time high as consumers bought goods and services. For many families, a second or third job became a reality to pay the high bills that went along with the high levels of debt they had accumulated.

With the economic downturn, many jobs were lost and people with lots of debt were unable to pay their bills. Credit card companies were also impacted as collections dropped and delinquencies rose. To increase profitability and reduce risk, they took immediate and harsh actions. Unfortunately, their actions resulted in further hardships for many Americans.

(continues)

(continued)

Citibank closed millions of consumer credit accounts. These included both new (those less than 2 years old) and long-standing accounts. Regardless of payment records or how well consumers had managed their accounts, many accounts were closed. Visa, MasterCard, and American Express all lowered credit limits and closed accounts as well. Fixed interest rates became variable and were raised substantially following a 30-day written notice. Consumers had no choice but to accept the higher rates or face having their account closed if they opted out.

Other creditors raised minimum payment requirements. If they had formerly required 1 percent of the balance to be paid monthly, they increased it to 2 to 5 percent. This means a minimum payment of $100 a month could have easily increased to $300 or more a month. With lower wages and lost jobs, it was impossible for many Americans to make these higher payments. As a result of these actions, credit scores and ratings dropped significantly, and many turned away from credit and started using debit cards instead.

People found the practices of credit card companies to be both unethical and illogical. With the passage of the Credit CARD Act of 2009, the government tried to tame some of the abusive and deceptive tactics. However, credit card companies continued to find new ways to increase their profitability. Today, credit card use is on the rise again, but hopefully, consumers will be better prepared during the next economic downturn.

Think Critically

1. How can you protect yourself from the tactics credit card companies use to increase their profitability?
2. What recommendations would you make to someone who utilizes credit to ensure they are prepared if an economic downtown occurs?
3. Research the Credit CARD Act of 2009. What benefits does this act provide consumers? Based on your findings, do you think this government action was necessary? Explain.

Consumer Financial Protection Bureau. The bureau's mission is to make markets for consumer financial products and services work for Americans, whether they are applying for a mortgage, choosing among credit cards, or using any other consumer financial products. At the bureau's website, you can file complaints if you have issues with financial products or services, get questions answered, and access information to compare credit products and providers. This agency was designed to help consumers navigate complicated credit and financial markets and to ensure fair practices among all consumers.

✓ Checkpoint

How have credit laws evolved over the past 50 years?

6.2 Lesson Review

Check Your Understanding

1. What are some things you can do to improve your credit score? (LO 6.2.1)

2. What is the purpose of rate shopping? (LO 6.2.1)

3. Choose one of the credit laws discussed in this chapter and explain how it protects consumers. (LO 6.2.2)

Apply Your Understanding

1. Some think that financial institutions harm lower income consumers by charging them higher interest rates. Why do you think financial institutions charge higher rates to some consumers? (LO 6.2.1)

2. Research the Credit CARD Act provision related to people under age 21. What criteria are used to determine if a young adult meets the requirements to obtain a credit card without a cosigner? Do you think this law is beneficial in protecting young adults? Explain your answer. (LO 6.2.2)

The Essential Question

Why are your credit score and credit rating important, and why are credit laws needed?

A: Your credit score and credit rating play a huge role in determining whether creditors grant or deny you credit. Credit laws help protect consumers from unfair credit practices.

Summary

6.1 Establishing Credit

- Your credit history is a complete record of your experience with credit.

- Credit bureaus collect information about consumers and prepare credit reports based on the information they collect.

- There are three nationwide credit bureaus: Equifax, Experian, and TransUnion.

- Credit reports provide information about individual consumers, including public record information, credit information, account details, and personal information. Creditors use a consumer's credit report to decide whether to grant credit.

- It is important to review your credit reports regularly.

- Credit guard and credit freezing services are other ways to protect your credit files.

- Creditors judge your creditworthiness based on the five "Cs" of credit: character, capacity, capital, conditions, and collateral.

- Building good credit is an important step in a financial plan.

- Consumers with good credit will qualify for lower interest rates on loans and credit cards. Good credit can also reduce insurance premiums.

- You may need a cosigner to get started with credit. A cosigner guarantees that payments will be made as agreed.

- To start building a good credit history, follow these steps: open a savings account, open a checking account, open a secured credit card or become an authorized user on another person's account, get a credit-builder loan, and apply for a credit card.

- Once you have your first credit card, you should always make payments on time, keep your use of credit low, and only use your credit card for something you can afford to pay in full.

6.2 Evaluating Credit and Credit Laws

- Many credit bureaus rate consumers' creditworthiness on a point system, assigning points based on debt, payment history, number and types of open accounts, income, and other factors. Assigned points are totaled to determine your credit score.

- A credit score indicates to potential creditors the likelihood you will repay debt as agreed.

- A FICO score is the credit score created by the Fair Isaac Corporation and can vary depending on which credit bureau provides the score.

- To calculate a FICO score, you must have at least one account open for six months or more. FICO scores are calculated using data from five categories: payment history, amount owed, length of credit history, credit mix, and new credit.

- When you apply for credit, the company will inquire about your credit history from one or more of the credit bureaus. This is called a credit inquiry.

- Paying your bills on time, improving your payment history, keeping balances low on credit cards, paying off debt, and opening accounts slowly can help improve your FICO score.

- There are several laws in place to protect consumers from harm.

- The Consumer Credit Protection Act (also known as the Truth in Lending Act) requires lenders to fully disclose all costs of credit, including the finance charge and annual percentage rate (APR).

- The Fair Credit Reporting Act gives you the right to view your credit report and to dispute inaccurate or incomplete information.

- The Fair Credit Billing Act requires creditors to resolve billing errors within a specified time period.

- The Equal Credit Opportunity Act prohibits discrimination in judgment of creditworthiness.

- The Fair Debt Collection Practices Act prohibits abusive collection practices by debt collectors.

- The Credit Card Accountability Responsibility and Disclosure Act (Credit CARD Act) was enacted to provide more consumer credit protections, including new provisions regarding interest rates.

- The Dodd-Frank Act created the Consumer Financial Protection Bureau (CFPB). Consumers can file complaints with the CFPB if they have issues with financial products or services, get questions answered, and access information to compare credit products and providers.

Check Your Knowledge

1. How do creditors use the consumer's credit report? (LO 6.1.1)

2. How can you increase your creditworthiness? (LO 6.1.2)

3. Why is it important to begin building good credit early and then maintaining good credit throughout your life? (LO 6.1.3)

4. What are the five main things that impact a credit score? (LO 6.2.1)

5. List three of the most important laws related to credit in the United States. Explain the purpose of each. (LO 6.2.2)

Apply Your Knowledge

1. Visit the website of one of the three major credit bureaus. Summarize what the bureau includes in its credit reports and outline the procedure you would have to follow to get a copy of your own report. (LO 6.1.1)

2. Are credit guard companies a good deal for consumers? Why or why not? Why would a person choose to freeze their credit? (LO 6.1.1)

3. Conduct an online search for a sample credit report. Analyze the report and use the five "Cs" of credit to determine if the person has good credit. Explain your answer. (LO 6.1.1)

4. What kinds of credit do you think you will be using in 5 years? How will you establish a good credit score to be eligible for increasing credit limits and privileges? (LO 6.1.2)

5. Jazmin wants to sign up for a credit card, but she is too young and needs a cosigner. She is asking you why she needs someone to cosign for her. Explain the purpose of a cosigner and why a young person would need to have one. (LO 6.1.3 and LO 6.2.2)

6. Duska is struggling to pay her credit card payment on time. She does not think one late payment is that big of a deal. Explain to Duska why on-time payments is the biggest factor in calculating a credit score and what one late payment can do to her credit. (LO 6.2.1)

7. Describe what you must do if you believe a billing statement you receive from a creditor contains an error. Describe the process for error correction, including your responsibilities and time limits and the responsibilities and time limits of your creditor. (LO 6.2.2)

8. Assume you have a well-established credit history and have filled out an application for credit at a local department store. The store has notified you that it cannot give you credit because you have a poor credit rating. You have not missed any payments or made any late payments, and you have paid off previous debts as agreed. What are your rights, and what are some things you should do? What responsibilities does the credit bureau have to you? (LO 6.2.2)

Share Your Knowledge

Work in teams of two to four students to complete the following activities.

1. Conduct research about credit bureaus—what they are, when they began, how they are regulated, and the opposition to their practices by consumer privacy advocates. Cite your sources and give direct quotes where possible. Give a historical perspective on the need for credit bureaus by creating a final product that could be a written report, graphical representation, presentation, or other creative output to demonstrate your knowledge. (LO 6.1.1)

2. Prepare a poster about the five "Cs" of creditworthiness. Include a definition of each item, a positive and negative example for each, and an explanation of why the trait is important to determine creditworthiness. (LO 6.1.2)

3. Develop a timeline of the credit laws in the United States in a graphical format. Include a brief description of each law, why it was enacted, and how it protects consumers. (LO 6.2.2)

Connect and Reflect

Base your answers to the following questions on your own personal thoughts, preferences, and experiences.

1. Why would you, as a high school student, want to obtain a copy of your credit report? What would be the purpose of reviewing your credit report before you become an adult? What would you do if you found that your credit report was incorrect? (LO 6.1.1)

2. After reviewing your personal credit report, evaluate your creditworthiness based on the five "Cs" of credit: character, capacity, capital, conditions, and collateral. What do you conclude? (LO 6.1.2)

3. Do you think it is fair that young consumers must now have either a job or a cosigner to obtain credit? Explain your answer. (LO 6.2.2)

Chapter Project

Research one of the consumer credit laws discussed in this chapter. Read the full narrative of the law. Write a report, prepare a poster, or record a video detailing the year the law was passed, why it was deemed necessary at that time in history, who was involved in writing the law, who was president at that time, and any other information you can find pertinent to that law. Conclude with your opinion on whether the law is still needed today. Explain why or why not.

Chapter 7

Costs of Credit

7.1 Using Credit Wisely

The Essential Question   What is involved in using credit wisely?

Learning Objectives

By the end of this lesson, you should be able to:

LO 7.1.1 Describe the responsibilities of consumer credit.

LO 7.1.2 Discuss how to protect your credit accounts from fraud.

LO 7.1.3 Explain how to minimize credit costs.

Key Terms

- comparison shopping
- impulse buying
- judgment
- garnishment
- opt out
- encryption
- phishing
- unused credit
- rewards program
- rebate program

Consider This ...

Sasha has been working hard to ensure that she understands the true cost of using credit and is using credit wisely.

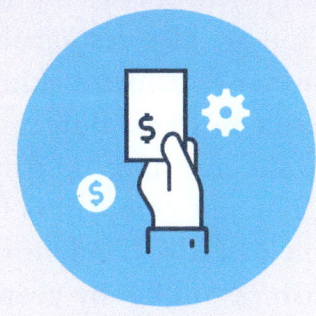

"Last fall, I saw a big sale on clothes and decided to charge a bunch on my credit cards," Sasha told her friend Angelo. "At the time, I thought it was foolish to pass up the 30 percent off, so I purchased way more clothes than I had the money for. It took me 6 months to pay off the balance on my credit card, and any money I saved from the sale was lost to interest charges."

"Wow, that's crazy," Angelo replied. "I would have never thought that interest could add up like that. I'm just starting to build my credit and opened my first credit card this month. What other advice would you have for me as I start?"

"I learned the hard way that all credit isn't created equal," Sasha replied. "Some credit cards have annual fees and others charge very high interest rates. Make sure the credit accounts you have meet your needs and that you understand the terms. Consider the annual fees, interest rates, and the kinds of rewards that different accounts offer."

Read and Reflect

1. When Sasha saw the clothing sale, she used her credit unwisely by charging beyond her means. What could have Sasha done differently in this situation?

2. What other advice would you give Angelo as he starts his credit journey?

Responsibilities of Credit

The freedom of accessing credit brings the responsibility to manage it carefully. Please take this responsibility seriously to avoid having your credit limited or, in some cases, withdrawn. Because using credit is essential to your financial future, you should know your responsibilities to yourself and creditors. In return, creditors have responsibilities to you, their customer.

Responsibilities to Yourself

As a credit user or debtor, you are responsible for using credit wisely and not getting into debt beyond an amount you can comfortably repay. Never having enough money and constantly scrambling to make your next payment is a stressful way to live.

You are also responsible for researching businesses before making credit purchases. Better Business Bureaus and Chambers of Commerce have information about businesses and complaints filed against them. You can also find information about a business online by visiting the company's website, reading consumer reviews and complaints about the company and its products or services, or seeking information from government consumer protection agencies. If you are unfamiliar with a business or it does not have a brick-and-mortar location, do your research before doing business with it.

You owe it to yourself to comparison shop. **Comparison shopping** involves checking several places to be sure you are getting the best price for equal quality. Comparison shopping will also help you avoid impulse buying. **Impulse buying** occurs when you

Why should you check out businesses before making credit purchases?

buy something without thinking about it and making a conscious decision. It is important to take the time to evaluate all options before buying. Be sure you are buying for the right reasons—because you need the product or service. Tying up future income should be done carefully to maximize your purchasing power and quality of life.

Finally, as a credit user, you should have the right attitude about using credit. Enter into each transaction in good faith, fully expecting to meet your obligations and uphold your good credit reputation.

Responsibilities to Creditors

When you open an account, you enter into a relationship with a retail store, bank, or credit card company. You are pledging your honesty and sincerity in the use of credit.

You are responsible for reading and understanding the terms of your credit agreement, including the finance charge, fees, and any other provisions of the agreement. In addition, you are responsible for limiting your spending to amounts you can repay according to the credit agreement terms. By signing a credit application, you agree to make all payments promptly, on or before the due date. If an emergency prevents you from making a payment, you should contact the creditor to arrange to pay later.

If you cannot make payments as agreed, a creditor can take you to court and win a judgment against you. A **judgment** is a court order allowing creditors to collect the debts you have agreed to pay. Once a credit card company has a judgment against you, there are several methods by which it can attempt to collect the judgment. It may take your assets to repay the debt, levy (freeze) your bank account, or take part of your paycheck to pay the debt you owe. **Garnishment** is a legal process that allows part of your paycheck to be withheld for debt payment. Your employer sends the amount directly to the creditor. You wish to avoid this as it hurts your credit score and will make it very difficult for you to get credit in the future.

You must contact the creditor immediately if you find an error on your billing statement or discover that the merchandise you bought needs to be repaired or has a defect that cannot be remedied. You generally can dispute charges for unsatisfactory goods or services (including issues about the quality of an item) if you made a good-faith effort to resolve the dispute with the seller, if the charge is for more than $50, or if you made the purchase in your home state or within 100 miles of your current billing address.

If your credit card is lost, stolen, or used without your permission, you must report it to your creditor immediately. Most credit card companies have apps or websites that make reporting a lost card easy. If a thief uses your card before you report it missing, you may owe up to $50 for any unauthorized charges. If the thief uses your card number but not your card, you are not responsible for the unauthorized charges.

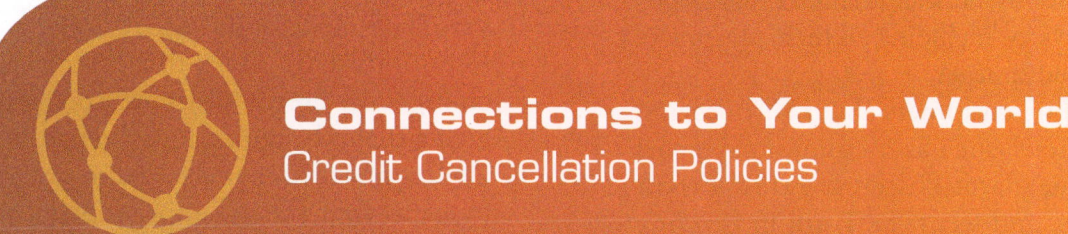

Connections to Your World
Credit Cancellation Policies

The Credit Card Accountability Responsibility and Disclosure (CARD) Act of 2009 helped to increase consumer credit protection by enacting new provisions on interest rate hikes and fees. One area that the act does not address is credit cancellation policies. Credit card issuers can cancel your account without warning if they choose—and it is perfectly legal for them to do so. Even if you have a zero balance in your account and have never been late with a payment, an issuer can cancel your account at any time. The most common reason credit card issuers give for doing this is that you are not using the account often enough.

Many of these customers claim that this practice by credit card issuers is unfair. They feel that because they have been good customers, credit card

(continues)

(continued)

issuers should not be allowed to close their accounts without notice. Credit card issuers counter that getting rid of inactive accounts with large, open lines of credit cuts down on the bank's credit risk and increases their profits by giving that line of credit to someone who will use the card frequently and incur interest charges.

Think Critically

1. Do you agree or disagree with this practice? Why?
2. How might having your account closed by a credit issuer impact your credit score?
3. How can you responsibly use your credit cards to build credit, avoid paying interest, and reduce the chance of a credit card issuer canceling your account due to lack of activity?

Creditors' Responsibilities to You

Creditors also have responsibilities to consumers. These responsibilities include the following:

- Assisting consumers in making wise purchases by honestly representing goods and services, including all their advantages and disadvantages.
- Informing customers about all rules and regulations, such as minimum payments and due dates, interest rates, credit policies, and fees. The Truth in Lending Act requires credit card issuers to disclose this information to consumers prior to entering into a credit agreement.
- Cooperating with credit bureaus by providing accurate, up-to-date information on account holders.
- Making credit card statements available to customers, promptly acknowledging complaints, and fixing billing errors when they occur.
- Establishing and adhering to sound lending and credit policies that do not overburden or deceive customers. This includes setting reasonable guidelines for credit use to avoid extending additional credit to customers who cannot afford it.
- Using reasonable methods of contacting customers who fail to meet their obligations and assisting them whenever possible with payment schedules and other means for solving credit problems.
- Keeping credit users informed when changes in credit policies occur and giving them the opportunity to **opt out**, or elect not to accept changes to policies, by canceling the account. Opting out is a reasonable action when creditors alter their credit policies significantly, such as by drastically raising their interest rates or raising minimum payments excessively.

✓ Checkpoint

What responsibilities do you have when using credit? What responsibilities do creditors have to consumers?

Protecting Yourself from Fraud

Credit card fraud takes place every day in a variety of ways. The most common type of fraud is the illegal use of a lost or stolen credit card or of credit card information intercepted online or hacked from an unsecured website.

Safeguarding Your Cards

It is your responsibility to help protect your cards and credit accounts from unauthorized use. While the credit card holder's liability is limited to $50, the merchant is not protected from loss. Consequently, merchants often raise their overall prices to cover such losses. Use the following commonsense tips to safeguard your card:

- Sign and activate your cards as soon as you receive them.
- Carry only the cards you need.
- Use the website and/or mobile app to monitor your credit cards.
- Set up alerts through the credit card company's website or mobile app to receive suspicious activity alerts.
- Notify creditors immediately by phone or via the mobile app or website if your card is lost or stolen and follow up with a secure email so that you have written evidence of the notification. You should also freeze the account as soon as you discover the card is missing.
- Keep your card in view during transactions and get it back as soon as you can to avoid giving others the opportunity to steal your credit card information either manually or by swiping it on an electronic reader.
- Keep your sales receipts and promptly verify all charges on your credit card statements, using the procedure printed on your statement to question charges that you think are in error.

- Shred old receipts no longer needed that contain account information.
- Do not lend your card to anyone or leave it lying around your home or office.
- Destroy expired cards by cutting them up.
- Destroy any unwanted credit card offers to prevent others from trying to obtain credit in your name.
- Do not give credit card numbers and expiration dates by phone or online to people or businesses you do not know.
- Do not give any personal information to someone who calls you asking for the information. Instead, hang up and call the customer service number on the card to verify the request or report the call as fraud if the request was not valid.

Protecting Your Accounts Online

Making purchases on the internet has opened new avenues for criminals to steal credit card information for illegal use. Software makers and online organizations are fighting back by continuously developing new ways to offer secure electronic transmission of customer information. In addition, there are some steps you can take to help protect your credit card and personal information when making online transactions.

- Deal only with companies online that you know and trust.
- Verify website security. If you are going to shop online, limit yourself to secure websites. You can tell if a site is secure by the URL. A secure website starts with https:// rather than http://. Secure websites will also have a small lock icon in the address bar or somewhere in the browser window. This icon means that the information you enter will be encrypted among other security measures. **Encryption** is a code that protects your account name,

number, and other information by making it unreadable to others. If you do not see the secure site icon, it is not safe to enter your information.

- Many sites attempt to offer assurance by displaying the logo of a nonprofit group, such as the Better Business Bureau (BBB) or TRUSTe. Sites that follow the privacy principles set forth by these organizations are allowed to display their logo. However, oversight of these logos is not fully developed yet, so not all merchants displaying these logos are legitimate.

- Read the company's privacy policy. Legitimate online merchants clearly state their privacy policy, which explains how they use the information you provide and protect your privacy. Review the policy to make sure you are comfortable with it before dealing with that company.

- Do not store your information on the merchant's site. Many online merchants offer you the ability to save your credit card information on their servers to speed up the shopping process for future transactions. Although it is faster to do so, there are some risks to maintaining your personal information elsewhere. For example, if a company that you are shopping with has a data breach, your personal information could be at risk.

- Be alert for phishing scams. **Phishing** (pronounced "fishing") is a scam that uses online pop-up or e-mail messages to deceive you into disclosing personal information. Phishers send e-mail messages or direct you to websites that appear to belong to legitimate businesses but are actually spoofed websites. The messages may ask you to verify private information, such as bank account numbers, passwords, or credit card numbers. The perpetrators then use your private information to commit fraud. Delete any messages that ask you to confirm or provide personal information. Legitimate companies do not ask for this information via e-mail.

✓ **Checkpoint**

What can you do to safeguard your credit cards from unauthorized use?

LO 7.1.3 Avoiding Unnecessary Credit Costs

Credit can be helpful if you use it wisely. Before deciding whether to borrow money, ask yourself these three critical questions: Do I need credit? Can I afford credit? Can I qualify for credit? If you can answer "yes" to these questions, then follow these guidelines to minimize the cost of credit.

- Make more than the minimum payment. Minimum payments will result in maximum cost and will keep you in debt for a long time. For example, if you owe $5,000 on a credit card at 18 percent APR, make no further purchases, and pay only the minimum payment (often 2 percent or less of the balance owed), it will take you 33 years to pay off the debt, and you will end up paying total interest of nearly $12,000 on a loan of $5,000.

- Do not increase spending when your income increases. Instead of spending the income, use it to pay off credit card debt or put it in your savings account.

- Accept only the amount of credit you need. Although having credit available when you need it may be comforting, unused credit can count against you. **Unused credit** is the remaining credit available to you on current accounts; it is your credit limit minus the amount you already owe. For example, if the limit on your credit card is $2,000 and you owe $1,200, your unused credit is $800. Other creditors may be reluctant to lend you money because you could access the other $800 at any time, thereby increasing your debt and reducing your ability to repay their loan. Keeping your credit card usage to less than 30 percent of your available credit limit is best to avoid being categorized as a high-risk borrower.

- Keep the number of credit accounts to a minimum. Most credit counselors recommend carrying no more than two or three credit cards. The more cards you have, the greater the temptation to buy without thinking.

- Pay off your balances as quickly as you can. If you have the financial means to do so, pay off your balances in full to avoid interest charges. Carrying balances from month to month can hurt your credit score.

- Pay cash for small purchases. For many people, purchases under $25 represent daily commitments. You should not charge these unless you can pay them off at the end of the month. By paying as you go, you will avoid financing your current expenses. Paying cash will also help you realize how much you are spending. Thus, you may buy less and purchase only those items you really need.

- Understand the cost of credit and shop around. Think about the finance charge, the monthly payments, and the length of time you will be committed to paying off loans and credit card debt. Consider how this will affect your lifestyle and your budget for months or even years to come. Before getting a loan, shop around for the best credit terms. If the interest rate on your credit card rises, consider switching to one with a lower interest rate.

Source: Eva-Katalin/istock.com

How is unused credit both a good thing and potentially a bad thing?

Connections to Your World
Maxing out Credit Cards

A credit card is "maxed out" when you have reached your credit limit and your account has no room for additional charges. You cannot buy anything else on credit until you reduce the balance. Maxing out is not a good idea. Here's why:

- When you have a balance near your credit limit, exceeding it without realizing it is easy. If you have given your creditor permission to authorize purchases that put you over your credit limit, you will be charged an over-the-limit fee. Going over the limit also gives credit card issuers a reason to raise your interest rate. At the creditor's discretion, it may charge a penalty rate; the amount of a penalty rate depends on your creditor and account balance but can be a substantial increase in your interest rate.

(continues)

(continued)

- When your cards are maxed out, you cannot use the card. A credit card offers no advantages when you cannot use it for current purchases. You must be careful not to use it until you have created enough room for additional charges.
- A significant portion (30 percent) of your credit score is based on how much of your available credit you are using. If you max out credit cards, you will see a negative impact to your credit score. Potential creditors are likely to view this as an indicator that you are overextended and unable to pay down existing debts.
- People with maxed-out credit can fall victim to predatory lending or "easy access" credit, such as payday loans, no-credit-check loans, bad credit loans, and pawnshops. These forms of credit have very high interest rates and put you in a cycle of borrowing beyond your means.
- When you pay down your charges regularly, credit card companies will be more willing to raise your credit limit. But when the card is maxed out, the company will not likely extend additional credit, even if you need it for a major purchase.
- If you repeatedly max out your credit card, some companies will close or freeze your account, requiring you to pay the entire amount in full before you can use the card again.

It is best to avoid maxing out credit cards whenever possible. Keep a healthy amount of unused credit on hand in case you need it.

Think Critically

1. Using credit responsibly is essential to prevent maxing out credit cards. What questions could you ask yourself when making purchases to help assess whether you are financially responsible?
2. How might making purchases on credit that exceed your financial means impact your lifestyle?
3. If you were a creditor and someone with maxed out cards asked you for a loan, would you grant it? Explain.

- Take advantage of credit incentive programs. There are two major types of credit incentive programs: rewards and rebates. With an account that has a **rewards program**, you will earn points, cash back, airline miles, or other special awards that you can redeem later. With a **rebate program**, you get back a portion of what you spent in credit purchases over the year. For example, you may get a 1 percent rebate in the form of a credit to your account balance or a check from the credit card company to spend as you wish. While credit incentive programs offer many perks, they often have annual fees and/or high interest rates on unpaid balances.

✓ Checkpoint

How can you minimize credit costs?

7.1 Lesson Review

Check Your Understanding

1. List three responsibilities you have to your creditors. (LO 7.1.1)
2. What is phishing? How does it work? (LO 7.1.2)
3. Why should you only shop on secure websites? (LO 7.1.2)
4. Why is it important to pay off your credit balances as soon as you can? (LO 7.1.3)

Apply Your Understanding

1. Find a credit card application, either online or one that has arrived at your home via the postal service, and read the privacy policy. How does the company use your private information? (LO 7.1.2)
2. Ashwin just received his first credit card. He was excited to use it, so he used it to buy everything last month. When he received his statement, he was shocked at how much he owed. Explain to Ashwin why it is usually not a good idea to use credit to pay for day-to-day expenses, such as meals and groceries. (LO 7.1.3)

The Essential Question

What is involved in using credit wisely?

A: Using credit wisely involves meeting responsibilities, both to yourself and to your creditor. It also means taking measures to protect your account(s) from fraud and avoiding unnecessary credit costs.

7.2 Computing the Costs of Credit

The Essential Question   Why do credit costs vary, and how can you compute simple interest and finance charges on your credit?

Learning Objectives

By the end of this lesson, you should be able to:

LO 7.2.1 Explain why credit costs vary.
LO 7.2.2 Compute simple interest and annual percentage rate (APR).
LO 7.2.3 Compare methods of computing the finance charge on revolving credit.

Key Terms

- prime rate
- Federal Reserve
- fixed-rate loan
- variable-rate loan
- installment credit
- simple interest
- principal
- rate
- time
- down payment
- adjusted balance method
- previous balance method
- average daily balance method

LO 7.2.1 Why Credit Costs Vary

Several factors determine how much you will pay for the use of credit. One important factor is the method used to compute interest, which is explained later in the chapter. Other important factors include the following:

- Source of credit. Some lenders offer better credit plans than others.
- Amount financed and length of time. The more money you borrow and the longer you take to pay it back, the more interest you will pay.
- Ability to repay debt. The greater your ability to repay (creditworthiness), the better your chances of getting credit at reasonable rates.
- Collateral. Loans backed with collateral, such as a car, are known as secured loans. Because collateral offers some security to the lender in case the borrower fails to

pay back the loan, secured loans typically have lower interest rates than unsecured loans.
- Interest rates. The interest rates charged for the use of credit are usually affected by the prime rate. The **prime rate** is the interest rate that banks offer to their best business customers, such as large corporations, and is based on the Federal Reserve's federal funds overnight rate. The **Federal Reserve**, called the Fed, is the economic institution in the Unites States that sets interest rates, manages the money supply, and regulates financial markets. Changes to the overnight rate are often in the news. Individuals pay higher rates because the risk is greater for the lender. Generally, consumers will pay as much as 3 percent or more above the prime rate. Businesses are borrowing money to buy assets that will generate revenue to pay off the loan. These production loans are considered less risky than consumption (consumer) loans.

- Economic conditions. Interest rates are said to be an economic indicator. When you see interest rates rising, it is often because the economy is growing or inflation is rising. Falling interest rates are an indicator that the economy is slowing. Borrowers pay more for the use of credit during periods of economic growth. When prices are rising (inflation), money is more in demand to buy higher-priced goods and services. So, lenders can charge higher interest rates.
- Type of credit or loan. A **fixed-rate loan** is a loan for which the interest rate does not change (go up or down) over the life of the loan. For example, if you agree to a 3-year car loan with a fixed rate of 6 percent, the interest rate will remain at 6 percent for the life of the loan. With a **variable-rate loan**, the interest rate goes up and down with inflation and other economic conditions. Creditors can raise the rates on variable-rate loans and credit cards. Most borrowers find that rates go up faster during periods of rising prices than they go down during periods of falling prices. Sometimes variable-rate card agreements will state that the interest rate will rise and fall with the prime rate.

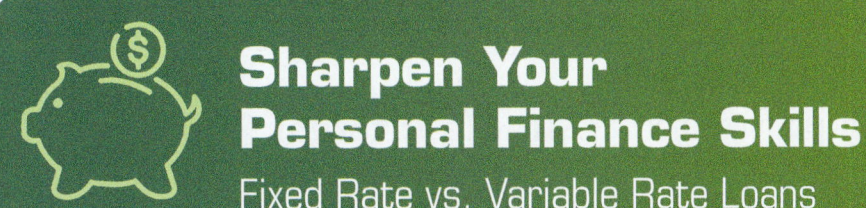

Sharpen Your Personal Finance Skills
Fixed Rate vs. Variable Rate Loans

Sasha begins working full-time and is excited to make her first vehicle purchase on her own. The vehicle costs $22,000, and she is looking to finance for 60 months. She is offered two financing options. The first has a fixed interest rate of 5%. The second has an interest rate of 4%, but the rate is a variable rate. Which loan would you recommend to Sasha?

Scenario 1: If Sasha takes the fixed interest loan, how much would she pay in interest? What would be the total price she pays for the vehicle?

Scenario 2: If Sasha takes the variable interest rate loan, how much would she pay in interest? Remember, a variable interest rate can change. Assume the rate increased to 7% after 1 year. What is the total price she would pay for the vehicle?

Think Critically

1. Based on the above scenarios, what are the risks associated with a variable rate loan?
2. In Scenario 2, the interest rate increased only one time during the life of the loan. What would happen if it had increased multiple times?

■ The business's costs of providing credit. Businesses pass along their costs for providing credit to consumers in the form of higher finance charges and higher product prices. These costs are related to delinquent accounts (overdue, but still collectible), bad debts (probably uncollectible), and bankruptcy. Other costs of issuing credit include printing and mailing monthly statements, electronic authorization of credit charges, and salaries and facilities for a credit department. When businesses accept Visa, MasterCard, or other all-purpose credit cards, they are charged a fee each time a customer uses the card. In turn, businesses may raise prices to pass along their cost of offering credit to customers. One example is at gas stations where they advertise one price for credit purchases and another price for cash. Restaurants may also offer a cash discount for customers who do not use a credit card.

What are the various costs for businesses that provide credit?

✓ Checkpoint

Why do credit costs vary?

LO 7.2.2 **Computing Cost of Credit**

In a previous chapter, you learned that interest is the money paid by a financial institution for the use of your deposit in a savings (or other) account. In the case of a loan, interest is the cost to you of borrowing money. Businesses such as banks make money by making loans to consumers; for them, debt is an investment.

Determining the cost of credit is easy using the formula for simple interest. The formula for calculating the total cost of installment credit is somewhat more complicated. **Installment credit** is a loan with fixed payments or installments, usually paid on a monthly basis.

Simple Interest Formula

Simple interest is interest computed only on the amount borrowed. The simple interest method of calculating interest assumes one payment at the end of the loan period. The cost is based on three elements: principal, rate, and time (based on one year). The formula for simple interest is:

$$\text{Interest (I)} = \text{Principal (P)} \times \text{Rate (R)} \times \text{Time (T)}$$

Principal

A loan's **principal** is the amount borrowed, or the unpaid portion of the amount borrowed, on which the borrower pays interest. For example, if you borrow $10,000 to buy a car, $10,000 is the principal, or the amount of the loan. Part of each payment you make goes toward paying down the principal. The rest of the payment is interest. As you make payments, the principal on your loan will decrease.

Rate

The **rate** is the percentage of interest you will pay on a loan. For example, you may agree to borrow $10,000 at 6 percent. The higher the rate, the higher the cost of the loan.

Time

Time is the period during which the borrower will repay a loan; it is expressed as a fraction of a year: 12 months, 52 weeks, or 360 days. (In most transactions, the standard practice is to use 360 rather than 365 as the number of days in a year for computing simple interest.) For example, for a 6-month loan, the time is expressed as ½, because 6 months is half a year. If money is borrowed for 3 months, the time is expressed as ¼ (one-quarter of a year). When a loan is for a certain number of days, such as 90, the time is expressed as 90/360, or ¼.

Figure 7.1 contains a simple interest problem showing the dollar cost of borrowing. In this problem, a person has borrowed $500 and will pay interest at the rate of 12 percent a year. The loan will be paid back in 4 months.

The simple interest formula can also be used to find principal, rate, or time when any one of these factors is unknown. As shown in **Figure 7.2** and **Figure 7.3**, you

Figure 7.1	Simple Interest

$$I = P \times R \times T$$

To multiply by a percent, first change it to a decimal: drop the percent sign, and then move the decimal point two places to the left.

$$I = ?$$
$$P = \$500$$
$$R = 12\%$$
$$T = 4 \text{ months}$$

$$
\begin{aligned}
I &= \$500 \times .12 \times {}^{4}\!/_{12} \\
&= \$500 \times .12 \times \tfrac{1}{3} \quad \text{(Four months is } {}^{4}\!/_{12} \text{ or } \tfrac{1}{3} \text{ of a year)} \\
&= \$60 \times .3333 \\
&= \$20
\end{aligned}
$$

Figure 7.2	Simple Interest (Principal)

$$I = P \times R \times T$$

Or change the formula to read:

$$P = \frac{I}{R \times T}$$

$$I = \$26$$
$$P = ?$$
$$R = 18\%$$
$$T = 18 \text{ months}$$

$$
\begin{aligned}
\$26 &= P \times .18 \times {}^{18}\!/_{12} \\
&= P \times .18 \times \tfrac{3}{2}\,(1.50) \\
&= P \times .27
\end{aligned}
$$

$$= \frac{\$26}{.18 \times 1.50}$$

$$
\begin{aligned}
P &= \$26 \div .27 \\
&= \$96.30
\end{aligned}
$$

$$= \frac{\$26}{.27}$$

$$= \$96.30$$

Figure 7.3 Simple Interest (Rate)

I = P × R × T

I = $18
P = $300
R = ?
T = 240 days

$18 = $300 × R × 240/360
    = $300 × ⅔ × R
    = $200 × R

R = $18 ÷ $200
   = .09 or 9%

Or change the formula to read:

$$R = \frac{I}{P \times T}$$

$$= \frac{\$18}{\$300 \times ⅔}$$

$$= \frac{\$18}{\$200}$$

= .09 or 9%

Sharpen Your Personal Finance Skills
Financing Options

For each scenario below, use the information provided in this chapter to complete the necessary calculations.

Scenario 1: Sasha is considering financing a new $1,200 TV for her apartment. She is considering financing the TV for 6 months at a 6% annual interest rate.

How much would Sasha pay in interest? Based on the finance charge, would you recommend that Sasha make the purchase? Why or why not?

Scenario 2: Sasha is considering financing a laptop for school. She is considering a 24-month finance option with an annual interest rate of 12%. The total interest she would pay during the loan would be $192. She is unsure what the principal amount of the loan is; this is also the cash purchase price of the computer.

What is the principal amount (cash purchase price) in this example? Would you recommend that Sasha make the purchase? Why or why not?

either plug the numbers into the formula or rearrange the formula.

Annual Percentage Rate Formula

Instead of making one payment at the end of the loan period, consumers often use an installment plan in which they repay the loan by making regular payments over time. An installment plan is typically used to pay for a major purchase, such as a car, appliances, or furniture. An installment plan requires a **down payment**, which is part of the purchase price paid in cash at the time of purchase. For example, when you buy a car, you will be encouraged to pay at least 10 percent of the purchase price in cash. The value of a car you trade in can also act as part of your down payment. The down payment reduces the amount of the loan.

The annual percentage rate (APR) is the true rate of interest you are paying when you make installment loan payments and spread interest over the life of that loan. To determine the APR for installment plans, use the formula in **Figure 7.4**. Work through the examples outlined in the Sharpen Your Personal Finance Skills to see how to apply the formula. (You can also determine the APR for installment plans using APR tables, which are more precise than using the formula. These tables can be found online by searching for "annual percentage rate tables" or "APR tables.")

In the above examples, notice that the total price paid is more than the cash price. The total price includes all installment payments plus the down payment. Each installment payment includes principal and interest. The difference between the total price paid and the cash price is the finance charge.

Figure 7.4	Annual Percentage Rate

To calculate the finance charge, use the following formula:

$$\text{Finance Charge} = \text{Total Price Paid} - \text{Cash Price}$$

Where:
Total Price Paid = (number of payments × amount of each payment) + down payment
Cash Price = the total price you would have paid is you had paid in cash rather than with a loan

Then use the finance charge in the following formula to calculate the approximate annual percentage rate:

$$\text{APR} = \frac{2 \times n \times f}{P(N + 1)}$$

Where:
n = number of payment periods in one year
f = finance charge
P = principal or amount borrowed
N = total number of payments to pay off amount borrowed

Sharpen Your Personal Finance Skills

Computing Finance Charges and Annual Percentage Rates (APR)

Scenario 1: Sasha is planning to buy a new sofa for her first apartment. After spending beyond her means at the clothing sale she mentioned at the start of the chapter, she learned her lesson. As Sasha looks to buy a new sofa, she wants to be sure that she understands the true cost of her purchase before buying. She is now aware that she must consider the purchase price plus any finance fees or interest charges while making payments.

Sasha found a sofa that she really likes. The cash price is $800. She is considering paying for it with an installment loan rather than cash. She plans to put $100 down and borrow $700. Sasha will pay off the loan in one year and make 12 monthly payments of $66 each. To find the full amount that Sasha is spending on the sofa, she needs to consider her down payment plus her monthly payments:

$$\$100 + (12 \times 66) = \$892 = \text{Total Price}$$

To determine the finance charge, Sasha takes the total she will pay ($892) and subtracts the cash price of the couch ($800). The cost of financing the couch for 12 months is $92. Sasha is okay with paying the finance charges so that she can keep her savings account.

As Sasha learns more about responsibly using credit, she wants to calculate her APR for the loan. To determine her APR, Sasha begins with the finance charge of $92 that she calculated:

$$\text{Finance Charge} = \$892 \text{ Total Price} - \$800 \text{ Cash Price} = \$92$$

Then she uses the finance charge in the APR formula from Figure 7.4:

$$\text{APR} = \frac{2 \times 12 \text{ payments} \times \$92 \text{ finance charge}}{\$700 \text{ principal} \,(12 \text{ payments} + 1)} = \frac{\$2{,}208}{\$9{,}100}$$

$$= .2425 = 24.36\%$$

Based on the above scenario, the APR on Sasha's loan would be 24.26% Following the process outlined above, solve for the finance charge and APR for Marcus and Devyn in this scenario.

Scenario 2: Marcus and Devyn bought a new refrigerator. The cash price was $1,200. They put $49 down and borrowed $1,151, which they will repay in payments of $49 per month for the next 27 months.

How is simple interest different from APR?

How does the billing method affect what you ultimately pay for charged purchases?

Source: kitzcorner/istock.com

LO 7.2.3 Calculating Finance Charges

The cost of using an open-end (revolving) credit account such as a credit card varies with the method the creditor uses to compute the finance charge (interest) on the unpaid balance. Most creditors that offer revolving credit give you a grace period to pay your balance in full before imposing a finance charge. The grace period is for new purchases if you do not have a previous balance on the account. Most credit card companies do not offer a grace period if you have not paid your account in full the previous month. Creditors must tell you the method they use to calculate the finance charge because it can make a big difference in the size of your credit card bills. They must also tell you the amount of finance charges you will pay if you make only the minimum payment. Creditors may calculate the finance charge on open-end credit accounts using the adjusted balance method, the previous balance method, or the average daily balance method. Some installment loans will also offer a grace period after the due date before placing the loan into default. If you make your payment within the grace period, you may be able to avoid a late payment penalty although your payment may be considered as late.

Adjusted Balance Method

When creditors use the **adjusted balance method**, they apply the finance charge only to the amount owed after you have paid your bill each month. For example, suppose your previous month's balance was $400 and you paid $300. If the creditor uses the adjusted balance method, you will pay additional finance charges only on the unpaid balance ($400 − $300 = $100). As you can see in **Figure 7.5**, the adjusted balance method results in the lowest finance charge.

To calculate the finance charge for this month, first determine the monthly rate by dividing the annual rate (18 percent) by 12 months. In this case, the monthly rate is 1.5 percent (or .015). Then multiply the balance due of $100 by .015 to determine the finance charge of $1.50. Then add the finance charge to the balance to determine the new account balance for the next billing cycle ($101.50).

Previous Balance Method

When creditors use the **previous balance method**, they impose the finance charge on the entire amount owed from the previous month. Payments are not considered. As shown in Figure 7.5, this method applies the monthly rate to the entire $400 (the previous month's balance). The finance charge is

Figure 7.5   Three Billing Methods for Computing the Finance Charge

The adjusted balance method, the previous balance method, and the average daily balance method produce different results. This example is based on an APR of 18% and a billing period of 30 days.

	Adjusted Balance Method	Previous Balance Method	Average Daily Balance Method
Monthly Interest Rate	1.5% (.015)	1.5% (.015)	1.5% (.015)
Previous Balance	$400	$400	$400
Payments	$300	$300	$300 (on the 15th day)
Finance Charge	$1.50	$6.00	$3.75
	($100 × .015)	($400 × .015)	(average balance of $250 × .015)*

*To figure average daily balance:

$$\frac{(\$400 \times 15 \text{ days}) + (\$100 \times 15 \text{ days})}{30 \text{ days}} = \$250$$

added to the previous month's balance, and then the payment is deducted to arrive at the new balance ($400 + $6 − $300 = $106), which will be the amount used to calculate the finance charge for the next month. This is the most expensive way to calculate the finance charge for the credit user.

Average Daily Balance Method

Most creditors use the **average daily balance method** for computing finance charges. Using this method, creditors calculate your balance on each day of the billing cycle. Payments made during the billing cycle are applied to determine the daily balance. As shown in Figure 7.5, the credit user starts the 30-day billing cycle with a balance of $400. Then on the 15th day of the billing cycle, the credit user makes a payment of $300, leaving a balance of $100 for the remaining 15 days of the billing cycle. To compute the average daily balance, each day's balance for

the billing cycle is totaled [($400 × 15 days = $6,000) + ($100 × 15 days = $1,500)] and then divided by the total number of days in the billing cycle ($7,500 ÷ 30 = $250). The average daily balance is then multiplied by the monthly interest rate to determine the finance charge ($250 × .015 = $3.75). To determine the new account balance for the next billing cycle, add the finance charge to the balance ($100 + $3.75 = $103.75). Because payments made during the period reduce the average daily balance, this method often results in a lower finance charge than does the previous balance method.

✓ Checkpoint

Explain the three methods of computing finance charges?

Check Your Understanding

1. Explain how economic conditions affect the cost of credit. (LO 7.2.1)

2. What are three reasons for the costs of credit to vary? (LO 7.2.1)

3. What three elements make up the formula for simple interest? (LO 7.2.2)

4. Explain the average daily balance method for calculating finance charges. (LO 7.2.3)

Apply Your Understanding

1. Sasha's friend Thanh asked her why the interest rate on her credit card went up. Sasha was not sure, so she asked you to help Thanh. After talking to Thanh and Sasha, the only thing you can see to cause the interest rate to go up is that the prime rate recently increased. Explain to them about the prime rate and why it impacts the interest rate on a credit card. (LO 7.2.1)

2. Use the following information to compute interest using the simple interest formula: (a) principal is $500, rate is 18 percent, and time is 6 months; (b) principal is $1,000, rate is 13.5 percent, and time is 8 months; and (c) principal is $108, rate is 15 percent, and time is 3 months. (Round to the nearest penny.) (LO 7.2.2)

3. Use the average daily balance method to calculate the finance charges on a credit card statement. The billing cycle is 30 days. The APR is 24 percent. At the beginning of the month, the balance on the statement was $1,000. On the 10th day, the person made a payment of $750. On the 20th day, the person made a purchase for $250. Find the finance charge. (LO 7.2.3)

The Essential Question

Why do credit costs vary, and how can you compute simple interest and finance charges on your credit?

A: Credit costs vary based on the source of credit, the amount and length of time financed, the interest rate, your creditworthiness, the type of loan, and economic conditions. Interest can be computed by using either the simple interest formula or the APR formula.

Summary

7.1 Using Credit Wisely

- Accessing credit brings the responsibility of managing it carefully.

- Credit responsibilities to yourself include not going into debt beyond what you can comfortably repay, researching businesses before you buy, comparison shopping, avoiding impulse buying, and using credit with the attitude that you will meet your obligations.

- Your responsibilities to creditors involve understanding the terms of your credit agreement, limiting your spending to amounts you can repay, and contacting the creditor immediately if you find an error on your billing statement or if your card is lost or stolen.

- Creditors are responsible for assisting consumers in making purchases, informing customers about all rules and regulations, cooperating with credit bureaus by providing accurate and current information, making credit card statements available to customers, applying fair credit policies, using reasonable methods to contact customers who fail to meet their obligations, and keeping credit users informed when policy changes occur.

- Credit card fraud takes place in a variety of ways. The most common types are the illegal use of lost or stolen credit cards and credit card information intercepted online.

- It is your responsibility to protect your cards and credit accounts from unauthorized use.

- Ways to safeguard your cards include signing and activating your cards as soon as you receive them, carrying only the cards you need, monitoring your credit cards using an app or website, notifying creditors immediately of a lost or stolen card, and not lending your cards to others.

- To protect your accounts online, deal only with companies you trust, enter personal information only on secure websites, read the site's privacy policy, do not store your personal information on the merchant's website, and do not respond to phishing scams.

- To reduce your credit costs, make more than the minimum payment each month, do not increase spending when your income increases, accept only the amount of credit you need (avoid high amounts of unused credit), keep the number of credit cards to a minimum, pay off your balances as quickly as possible, pay cash for small purchases, understand the costs of credit and shop around, and take advantage of credit incentive programs.

7.2 Computing the Costs of Credit

- Factors that determine the cost of credit include the source of credit, the amount and length of time financed, the borrower's creditworthiness, interest rates, economic conditions, the type of credit or loan, and the business's costs of providing credit.

- A fixed-rate loan is a loan for which the interest rate does not change over the life of the loan. With a variable-rate loan, interest goes up and down with inflation and other economic conditions.

- In the case of loans, interest is the cost of borrowing money.

- The simple interest formula is : Interest (I) = Principal (P) × Rate (R) × Time (T).

- Principal is the amount borrowed, rate is the percentage of interest a borrower will pay on a loan, and time is the period during which the borrower will repay a loan.

- The annual percentage rate (APR) formula calculates the costs of installment credit.

It includes the down payment and all monthly payments in the total price. The difference between the total price and the cash price is the finance charge.

- Most creditors calculate the finance charge by using the adjusted balance method, previous balance method, or average daily balance method. The finance charge varies depending on the method used.

Check Your Knowledge

1. Explain why it is important for consumers to be responsible with credit. How will they personally benefit? (LO 7.1.1)

2. Why is it important to protect your information from fraud? (LO 7.1.2)

3. Why is making the minimum payment each month not a good plan for financial security? (LO 7.1.3)

4. What factors are used to determine credit costs to consumers? (LO 7.2.1)

5. What is the formula to calculate simple interest? (LO 7.2.2)

6. What is the formula to calculate annual percentage rate (APR)? (LO 7.2.2)

7. Explain why the three most common ways of computing finance charges on revolving credit result in different amounts of finance charges. (LO 7.2.3)

Apply Your Knowledge

1. Your friend Angelina is proud of her ability to have and use credit. She buys lunch every day on credit, and at the end of the month she pays only the minimum balance due. When she reaches the limit on one credit card, she switches to another credit card. Do you see any problems with Angelina's actions? Explain your answer. (LO 7.1.3)

2. You want to get a secured credit card from your local bank. Your parent(s) or guardian(s) are willing to cosign on the card for you because they want you to learn how to be a responsible credit consumer. But before they will cosign, they want you to be able to explain to them that you understand your rights and responsibilities of using credit, how you will use the credit card, and how you will plan to make the required payments. Create a document to share with them that answers all the questions and concerns that you think they will have about your use of a credit card. Include as much detail as possible. (LO 7.1.1, LO 7.1.2, LO 7.1.3)

3. Some retailers do not offer their own store credit card to consumers. Instead, they accept major credit cards such as Visa and MasterCard. These retailers pay fees for the charged sales—typically about 3 percent. How does accepting major credit cards benefit the retailer? (LO 7.2.1)

4. Using the simple interest formula, solve for the missing elements, rounding to the nearest penny: (a) interest is $8, rate is 12 percent, and time is 60 days; (b) interest is $54, rate is 18 percent, and time is 18 months; (c) principal is $2,100, interest is $510, and time is 2 years; and (d) principal is $108, interest is $36, and time is 18 months. (LO 7.2.2)

5. Calculate the APR in the following cases:

   a. A $700 purchase requires a down payment of $60 with the balance to be paid in 12 monthly payments of $60 each.

   b. A $2,000 purchase requires a down payment of $100 and 24 monthly payments of $90 each. (LO 7.2.2)

6. Create a comparison chart for the three main methods of calculating finance charges on revolving credit. Include a sample calculation for each method. (LO 7.2.3)

Share Your Knowledge

Work in teams of two to four students to complete the following activities.

1. Develop a presentation or infographic that details the responsibilities of consumers and creditors related to credit. Include legal protections for both groups as part of your presentation. (LO 7.1.1)

2. Search online to find three different credit card offers. Websites like The Motley Fool (www.fool.com) or Nerd Wallet (www.nerdwallet.com) are good sources to review credit card offers. Working with your team, create a chart to compare the three offers. At a minimum identify the following features for each card. (LO 7.2.1)

   - What is the annual fee?

   - What is the rewards offer (cash or points)?

   - Are there different rewards for different spending categories (restaurants, travel, fuel purchases, etc.)?

   - Is there an introductory offer? Describe the offer.

   - Does the card have a recommended credit score for approval?

   - What is the balance transfer rate?

   - What other rewards are available?

3. As a team, use the following details to explain how to calculate finance charges with the average daily balance method. Explain the formula and provide an example of the calculations. The billing cycle is the number of days in the month. The interest rate is 24% APR. (LO 7.2.3)

Date of Transaction	Item	Debit (purchase or charge to the account)	Credit (payment or return of merchandise to the account)	Balance
November 1	Previous balance			$250.00
November 10	Payment on account		$125.00	
November 15	Purchase	$75.00		
November 19	Purchase	$180.00		
November 29	Payment on account		$250.00	
November 30	Purchase return credit		$100.00	

Connect and Reflect

Base your answers to the following questions on your own personal thoughts, preferences, and experiences.

1. Comparison shopping is one way you can be a responsible consumer. Do you think it is important to shop around for the best price? Is there a threshold where you would comparison shop? If so, how much would the item have to cost before you would shop around for the best price? (LO 7.1.1)

2. Think about your future self. What will be your strategy for managing your credit cards? Will you pay the account balance in full each month? Would there ever be a situation where you would only pay the minimum payment? What process would you use for budgeting your credit usage? (LO 7.1.3)

3. The terms of agreement for credit cards are a legal contract. Find a credit card agreement and read the terms. Why do you think it is important to understand the terms of the agreement before opening a credit account? What terms would cause you to not want to do business with that company? (LO 7.2.1)

Your class has been asked to conduct a workshop for the graduating seniors at your school. Each person in the class is to create one to three slides and a handout on two topics related to using credit. Use what you have learned in the chapter and conduct online research. Select two of the topics below to prepare your slides and handouts.

- How to protect your credit cards

- How to protect yourself when making online purchases

- How to reduce the costs of credit

- Five popular credit card rewards or rebate programs that consumers might find beneficial

- Three different ways credit companies can calculate finance charges

8 Chapter

Problems with Credit

The Essential Question — What are the dangers of credit, and what can you do to avoid them?

Learning Objectives

By the end of this lesson, you should be able to:

LO 8.1.1 Discuss good credit management rules and warning signs that you are overextended.

LO 8.1.2 Describe different debt relief options for consumers.

LO 8.1.3 Explain how to identify and avoid credit scams.

LO 8.1.4 Discuss how to protect yourself from identity theft.

Key Terms

- credit management
- 20/10 rule
- credit payment plan
- credit counseling
- debt management plan
- debt settlement program
- debt consolidation
- credit repair
- identity theft

Consider This ...

Last year, Diego graduated college and started a new job in marketing; he was excited to start his career in Georgia with a starting salary of $45,000 per year. Diego created a budget for his estimated monthly take-home pay of $2,625. When he created his budget, he only had a few monthly expenses, so he decided to rent an apartment that was $1,350 per month. Diego could cover his expenses but realized that his budget was tighter than he expected after all his monthly bills (rent, utilities, groceries, gas, and other common expenses). He was cautious to ensure he did not overspend and that all his bills were paid on time.

However, in the last 6 months, Diego has had some difficulties; he had to have an expensive medical procedure, and his dog had to have surgery. In addition, his car broke down and could not be repaired, so he had to purchase a new vehicle. Luckily, Diego and his dog are both healthy, but he is behind on his monthly expenses and is in debt by roughly $11,000.

"I do not think I can get back on track without change." Diego told his friend. "I think I need to explore debt relief options."

(continues)

Read and Reflect

1. What options does Diego have for debt relief?

2. What advice would you have given Diego that would have potentially allowed him to avoid his current situation?

LO 8.1.1 Credit Management

Many people from all levels of income and social standing get into trouble with credit every year. Credit problems often happen slowly. Although emergencies that cause people to get buried in debt can occur, credit problems typically arise after months and years of poor planning, impulse buying, and careless budgeting. If you recognize early enough that you are falling into excessive debt, you can take steps to fix the problem.

Exercising good **credit management** means following an individual plan for using credit wisely. It involves recognizing your limits and planning your use of credit. There are ways to practice good credit management, including following the 20/10 rule, being aware of the warning signs that you are overextending your credit, and devising a credit payment plan.

The 20/10 Rule

Credit counselors often suggest using the **20/10 rule**—a plan to limit the use of credit to no more than 20 percent of your yearly take-home pay, with payments of no more than 10 percent of monthly take-home pay (see the Math Minute feature on the next page). These limits do not include mortgage loans and monthly payment commitments for housing. However, all other types of borrowing are included in the limits of the 20/10 rule.

Danger Signs

Another part of good credit management is recognizing when you are headed for trouble. Watch for these warning signs that you are overextending your credit:

- You pay for everything with credit.
- You can make only minimum payments on your balances.
- You often pay late or at the end of the grace period.
- You often pay one credit card by shifting the balance to another.
- You use cash advances to pay your balances.
- You worry about how you will be able to pay your bills.
- You recognize that if an emergency arises, you will have inadequate unused credit to take care of it.
- Your credit cards are all at or near the limit.
- The credit card companies are raising the interest rates on your accounts because of late payments and charges that have exceeded your credit limit.
- You must time your payments carefully because otherwise, you will not have enough income to pay your bills.
- You skip some payments to make other payments.
- Your credit score is falling because you have too much credit.

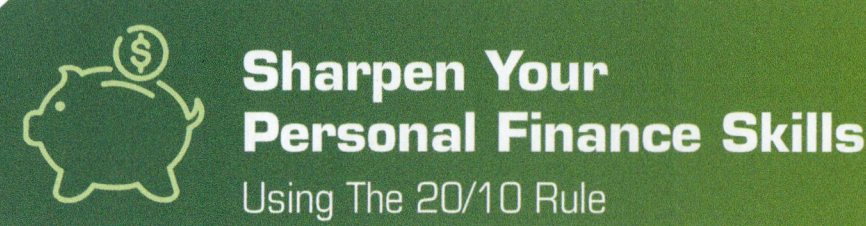

Sharpen Your Personal Finance Skills
Using The 20/10 Rule

Take-home pay is approximately 70 percent of gross pay. If your annual salary is $30,000, then your take-home pay (after taxes) is $21,000 ($30,000 × 0.70). If your annual salary is paid in 12 equal monthly payments of $2,500, your monthly take-home pay is $1,750 ($2,500 × 0.70).

Using the 20/10 rule, your total borrowing should not exceed 20 percent of annual take-home pay:

$$\$21{,}000 \times 0.20 = \$4{,}200 \text{ maximum borrowing}$$

Your monthly credit payments should not exceed 10 percent of your monthly take-home pay:

$$\$1{,}750 \times 0.10 = \$175 \text{ maximum monthly credit payments}$$

Following the 20/10 rule can help you keep your debt within your means to repay.

Try It Out!

1. Apply the 20/10 rule to Diego's situation: his annual salary at his new job is $45,000. Determine maximum borrowing and monthly credit payments.

2. Search the internet for the average starting salary for a career you are interested in. Salaries for similar positions will vary based on the location of the job. It is important to find salaries for the area you live in or plan to live in when you begin your career. Once you have found the average starting salary for your position, apply the 20/10 rule to determine your maximum borrowing and monthly credit payments if that was your starting salary.

A Credit Payment Plan

You can also practice good credit management by designing a credit payment plan. A **credit payment plan** records your debts and a strategy for paying them off.

To design a credit payment plan, gather your most recent credit card statements and list all the debts you owe, with enough information to analyze which ones should be paid first. Generally, accounts with the highest interest rates should be the priority. Using this method will reduce the total interest you pay on all credit. Focus on paying off one account at a time while making minimum payments on others. As one card gets paid off, begin paying the next highest priority card. Once you have listed and analyzed your debt, you can prepare a plan to pay off the balances.

Figure 8.1 Current Debt Schedule

Credit Card/ Account	Current Balance	Credit Limit	Interest Rate	Minimum Monthly Payment	Priority
1. Visa #1	$ 850	$900	18%	$ 55	2
2. Visa #2	450	500	22.9%	15	1
3. Store #1	300	200	14.9%	10	3
4. Store #2	600	400	11.9%	25	4
5. MasterCard	500	300	9.99%	20	5
Totals	$2,700			$125	

Figure 8.2 Credit Payment Plan

Credit Card/ Account	Current Balance	Monthly Payment	No. of Months Required	New Total Minimum Monthly Payment
1. Visa #2	$450	$ 90*	6**	$110***
2. Visa #1	850	145****	7	55
3. Store #1	300	155	3	45
4. Store #2	600	180	4	20
5. MasterCard	500	200	4	0
Total			24	

*$15 (Visa #2 minimum monthly payment) + $75 ($200 − $125) = $90.
**$450 ÷ $90 = 5 months + 1 (additional month to allow for added interest) = 6.
***$125 (total minimum monthly payments) − $15 (Visa #2 minimum monthly payment) = $110.
****$90 (monthly payment that was being paid to Visa #2) + $55 (Visa #1 minimum monthly payment) = $145.

Assume you have the debt listed in **Figure 8.1**, and you have a disposable income of $200 a month with which to pay credit card bills. When you add up the minimum monthly payments, it totals $125. This leaves $75 ($200 – $125) to add to the minimum payment of the card having the highest priority. **Figure 8.2** illustrates the credit payment plan.

Once Visa #2 is paid off, you can take the $90 you were paying on it and add it to the minimum monthly payment of Visa #1 (the next highest-priority card). You can continue this pattern until all cards are paid off. With this credit payment plan, you will have all your accounts paid off in 24 months.

In creating the credit payment plan, you should use the original balances for estimation purposes because by making minimum payments, balances will go down very slowly as interest accumulates. Also, the number of months required to pay off the debt will be different because you are adding an extra month to allow for accumulating interest charges. Finally, the credit payment plan works best when you are responsible and do not incur new debt.

LO 8.1.2 Debt Relief Options

If you cannot pay off your debt by practicing good credit management and still need help getting back on your feet, options are available to help you relieve your debt. Some of these options include contacting your creditors or seeking help from a debt relief service.

Contacting Your Creditors

Before contacting a debt relief service, talk with your creditors to try to work out a modified payment plan that reduces your payments to a more manageable level. By explaining your situation, you may be able to negotiate lower interest rates, reduced late fees, a discount on the principal, or even a temporary reduction of your payments.

Using Debt Relief Services

If you are still working out a modified payment plan with your creditors, consider seeking help from a company that offers debt relief services. There are various types of debt relief services. If you choose this route, your first option may be to get credit counseling.

Credit Counseling

Credit counseling is a service to help consumers manage their debt load and credit more wisely. It is available from nonprofit, government-sponsored, or commercial credit counseling services. Credit counselors are certified and trained in consumer credit, money and debt management, and budgeting.

Counseling sessions can be conducted in person, by phone, or online. During a typical credit counseling session, the counselor discusses your financial situation with you, including income, expenses, debt, the reasons for your current financial situation, and your goals. The counselor should also help you develop a personalized budget plan for your money problems.

When your financial situation is serious and needs immediate action, your credit counselor may suggest you enroll in a debt management plan. With a **debt management plan**, you will make a single monthly payment to a credit counseling organization that distributes the funds to creditors based on a payment schedule. The organization uses your money to pay your unsecured debts (such as credit cards) according to the payment plan the counselor develops with you and your creditors. Typically, the creditors have agreed to lower your interest rates and waive fees. These concessions may be available only through a credit counseling organization. Usually, debt management plans take 48 months or longer to complete. You also must agree to refrain from using credit while the plan is underway.

Credit counseling services are typically free, but clients may have to pay a fee for participating in the debt management plan. Most of the funding for credit counseling organizations comes from creditors who receive money owed to them through the debt management plan.

You can find consumer credit counseling services through an online search. Consumer Credit Counseling Services (CCCS)

What are the benefits of credit counseling?

is a nonprofit organization affiliated with the National Foundation for Credit Counseling (NFCC) and the Association of Independent Consumer Credit Counseling Agencies (AICCCA). Their websites will help you find a CCCS office near you. Some churches, private foundations, universities, military bases, credit unions, and state and federal housing authorities provide similar services.

Debt Settlement

A debt settlement or debt negotiation program is different from credit counseling or a debt management plan. In a **debt settlement program**, a company negotiates with your creditors on your behalf to reduce the amount of debt you owe. This type of program is typically offered by a for-profit company, meaning the services are not free. The company usually requires you to make monthly payments into an account administered by a third party. When enough money has accumulated, the company pays off the negotiated debt to the creditors in one lump sum.

While the thought of reducing your debt is appealing, numerous risks are associated with these programs. First, many debt settlement companies charge high fees for their services. Also, many make promises or guarantees they cannot keep (such as reducing your debts by 50 percent or more). In addition, your creditors have no obligation to agree to negotiate a settlement of the amount you owe. Therefore, there is a possibility that the company will not be able to settle some of your debts, even if you set aside the monthly amounts required by the program. Another risk is that these programs often encourage or instruct clients to stop making any monthly payments to their creditors. As a result, you may continue to accumulate late fees and penalties. This will negatively impact your credit report and will harm your ability to get credit in the future. Be sure to check with the attorney general's office of your state to verify that the debt settlement company is legally in business.

Debt Consolidation

With **debt consolidation**, a finance company loans you money to pay off your debt. They do this by offering you a debt consolidation loan, which consolidates some or all your debt into one loan. Rather than making monthly payments to your creditors, the debt consolidation loan requires a lower monthly payment to the finance company until the debt is repaid.

At first glance, it may seem that there is no downside to debt consolidation loans—you have a lower monthly payment and more cash on hand at the end of the month, while your debts still get paid off. However, debt consolidation loans do have some disadvantages. For example, although the monthly amount on a consolidated loan is less than the monthly amount that you would pay your creditors, the total amount of your debt does not change—you are just taking longer to pay it off. Therefore, depending on the terms of your loan, you may end up paying more in interest over time than if you keep paying your creditors. Also, to qualify for a debt consolidation loan, you must have some collateral that secures the payment of the debt. Debt consolidation loans can be in the form of a second mortgage, with your house acting as the collateral. If you fail to make your monthly payments as agreed, you lose your collateral. In the case of a second mortgage, you would lose your house in foreclosure—a legal process in which property used as collateral is sold to pay off debt.

> **✓ Checkpoint**
>
> Describe three forms of debt relief services.

LO 8.1.3 Credit Scams

Credit scams are common today. They can drain your finances and hurt your credit but can be avoided if you keep your guard up. It helps to be aware of some of the most common credit scams. You can find additional information on credit scams (as well as credit advice) at the Federal Trade Commission (FTC) website (www.ftc.gov) and at the MyMoney website (www.mymoney.gov).

Credit Repair Scams

Credit repair is the process of reestablishing a good credit rating. There are numerous companies who run ads in newspapers and on radio, TV, and the internet that aid consumers—for a price—to repair their credit. However, you can perform the same services they offer—for free. You can obtain copies of your credit reports, challenge incorrect information, and respond to disputes. Many of the claims these companies make are false. Regardless of what they say, these companies cannot remove negative information from your credit report. Beware of credit repair offers that do the following:

- Do not tell you your legal rights. The Credit Repair Organization Act requires that credit repair companies explain your legal rights in a written contract that details the services they will perform and the total cost.
- Require you to pay a fee before the company performs any service. The Credit Repair Organization Act also makes it illegal for credit repair companies to charge you before they have performed their services.
- Suggest that you create a "new credit identity." Companies that promise you a "new credit identity" often will provide you with a nine-digit number called a Credit Profile Number (CPN) that looks like a Social Security number, or they may direct you to apply for an Employer Identification Number (EIN) from the IRS. However, using these numbers to apply for new credit or default on previous debts is illegal.
- Recommend that you do not contact the credit bureau or creditors yourself. In many cases, it is recommended that you contact creditors when you are having problems paying a debt to try to work out a payment plan.

Advance-Fee Loans

With an advance-fee loan, scammers falsely promise that even consumers with bad credit histories can get a loan for an advance payment. The payment may range from $100 to several hundred dollars.

There are some red flags to watch for that can tip you off to an advance-fee loan scam. First, legitimate lenders never guarantee or say that you are likely to get a loan or a credit card before you apply, especially if you have bad credit. It is illegal for companies doing business by phone in the United States to promise you a loan or credit card and ask you to pay for it before they deliver.

Online Payday Loans

A payday loan is a cash advance from your next payroll check. Cash is received on the spot, but steep fees are charged for this service. Although these loans are legal, they should be considered a last resort due to their high interest rates.

Today, many people are tempted by ads for online payday loans. However, many online payday loan companies are scams. The payday lender asks the consumer to supply personal information along with bank account numbers so it can deposit the borrowed funds electronically. When the borrower's payment is due, the lender will withdraw the amount and a one-time finance fee. But consumers may find that the lender makes multiple withdrawals and charges a fee each time. By the time the last withdrawal is made, the consumer may have paid two to three times the original loan amount.

Why should consumers be cautious of online payday loans?

In addition, the lender may use the borrower's information to commit identity theft.

Credit Card Interest Rate Reduction Schemes

Many companies use prerecorded phone calls, or robocalls, to reach consumers. Some of these companies claim to have special relationships with credit card issuers, enabling them to negotiate significantly lower interest rates with creditors if you pay them an advance fee. They guarantee that their reduced rates will save you thousands of dollars in interest and finance charges, allowing you to pay off your credit card debt up to five times faster. They claim that lower interest rates are available for a limited time and that you must act now.

According to the FTC, most of these robocalls are scams. FTC investigators found that people who pay for these services do not receive interest rate reductions, save the promised amounts, or pay off their credit card debt any faster. Many people struggle to get their money back from the scammers and become victims of identity theft.

Prescreened Offers

A prescreened or preapproved offer of credit is simply the practice of identifying potential customers. These offers are based on information in your credit report that indicates you meet certain criteria, such as a minimum credit score. This is not an offer of credit. It is merely an offer for you to apply for credit. If other criteria are not met when you apply for credit, you will be turned down, which will adversely affect your credit score. You can opt out of receiving preapproved offers at www.optoutprescreen.com, and this will stop the credit bureaus from selling your information.

Why is it important to protect your credit cards, debit cards, and other sources of credit?

Source: RgStudio/istock.com

LO 8.1.4 Protecting Yourself from Identity Theft

Identity theft is one of the largest and fastest-growing crimes in the United States and around the world. If someone gets enough information about you to assume your identity, they can drain your bank account, run up charges on your credit card, and open new accounts. They may even take out mortgages or other loans.

Protecting Your Identity

In today's age of technology, most identity theft occurs when you give your personal information to others who do not protect it from thieves. You must be careful when you give out your personal information, such as your name, address, date of birth, and Social Security number. The business in possession of this information stores it in its database. Unless the business takes extreme measures to protect your information, hackers, dishonest employees, and others who gain access to your information can steal it. Be wary of a business that wants to make a photocopy of your driver's license or demands your Social Security number. Unless a business is giving you money that must be reported for tax purposes or granting you credit, it does not need your Social Security number.

You also must be careful about handing your debit and credit cards to others. Others can use information stored on those cards to obtain funds from your bank account or charge purchases to your account. Sometimes it is better to use cash or prepaid gift cards. These methods of payment do not contain information related to your identity. In certain situations, you are required to provide your personal information, such as when applying for a loan or receiving medical treatment. Checking your credit report frequently can help you identify early when someone has stolen your identity. In addition, several companies now offer identity theft protection services for a monthly fee. These services include monitoring your credit reports and scanning known criminal websites for the illegal sale of your personal information.

Guarding Your Privacy

Privacy is an important value in America. Some types of information should not be shared with others and should remain private. Information of this nature can hurt your reputation, your employment opportunities, and your credit—and it can even impair your ability to get insurance.

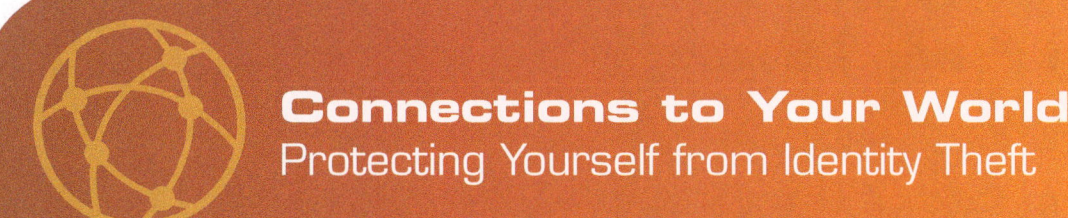

Connections to Your World
Protecting Yourself from Identity Theft

Based on a recent study from the Bureau of Justice Statistics, roughly 9 percent of individuals age 16 years and older were victims of identity theft within the previous 12 months. Although 9 percent of the population may not seem like a lot, it represents more than 20 million people in the United States. Of those impacted by identity theft, nearly all experience misuse or attempted misuse of existing bank accounts or credit cards. Establishing bank accounts and credit cards is a normal part of building credit and making responsible personal finance decisions. It is something that you will likely be doing in the near future if you have not already done so.

Think Critically

1. What can you do to ensure that you are protecting yourself from identity theft and financial fraud?
2. What advice would you give someone who believes they may be a victim of identity theft?

The internet is not private. Everything that is posted is stored electronically and can be accessed by virtually anyone. Therefore, be cautious of what you post online about yourself, your lifestyle, and others. Make sure the information posted does not harm you or others.

There are privacy laws designed to protect you. The Health Information Portability and Accountability Act (HIPAA) and the Family Educational Rights and Privacy Act (FERPA) are two laws that help protect your medical records and your school records. We will discuss these further in a later chapter.

You are the best person to protect your privacy. Be cautious with postings on social media sites. Keep them positive and avoid giving out personal information. Use the internet wisely. Privacy can seldom be restored once it is lost.

✓ Checkpoint

How can you protect yourself from identity theft?

Check Your Understanding

1. Does the 20/10 rule apply to all types of credit? Explain your answer. (LO 8.1.1)
2. Describe two different debt relief options. What are the advantages and disadvantages of each? (LO 8.1.2)
3. What are some warning signs of credit repair scams? (LO 8.1.3)
4. Why should you check your credit report frequently? (LO 8.1.4)

Apply Your Understanding

1. Your friend Adohi is concerned that he may be overextended with credit. He pays only the minimum on his credit card each month and has recently taken out a personal loan. What advice would you give to Adohi to help him determine if he is following good credit management rules? (LO 8.1.1)
2. If you are unable to pay off your debt by exercising good credit management, what other options do you have (list them in the order you would pursue them)? (LO 8.1.2)
3. You received an email telling you that a creditor can help you build excellent credit. How would you identify if the email is legitimate or a credit scam? What things do you look for when evaluating messages? (LO 8.1.3)
4. When you are posting on social media, why would you not want to share information such as your birthday and address? When would it be okay to share your private information? (LO 8.1.4)

The Essential Question

What are the dangers of credit, and what can you do to avoid them?

A: Danger signs include using credit for everything, paying late or shifting balances, and having cards at or near the limit. Avoid the dangers of credit by devising your own credit payment plan. You can also contact your creditors to work out a modified payment plan or seek help from debt relief services. Other dangers of credit are credit scams and identity theft.

The Essential Question   What are the types, common causes, and advantages and disadvantages of bankruptcy?

Learning Objectives

By the end of this lesson, you should be able to:

LO 8.2.1 Describe types of bankruptcy.

LO 8.2.2 Discuss common causes of bankruptcy.

LO 8.2.3 Explain the advantages and disadvantages of declaring bankruptcy.

Key Terms

- bankruptcy
- voluntary bankruptcy
- discharged debt
- involuntary bankruptcy
- Chapter 7 bankruptcy
- Chapter 13 bankruptcy
- Chapter 11 bankruptcy
- reaffirmation
- exempted property

Consider This ...

As Diego explored debt relief options, he continued to experience unfortunate events that continued to build his debt. His health concerns returned, and he required extensive testing, treatment, and medication. Diego accumulated roughly $30,000 more in medical bills. Also, Diego's medical condition forced him to miss a significant amount of work as he was receiving treatment. While he was off work, he charged his monthly expenses to his credit cards. His total debt is now nearly $60,000. Diego is considering declaring bankruptcy.

Read and Reflect

1. What are potential advantages to Diego declaring bankruptcy? What are potential disadvantages?

2. Would you recommend that Diego declare bankruptcy? Explain.

What Is Bankruptcy?

When a person gets into serious and irreversible debt and cannot pay the bills, the final and most serious step is bankruptcy. **Bankruptcy** is a legal process that relieves debtors of the responsibility of paying their debts or protects them while they try to repay. When you declare bankruptcy, you are said to be insolvent. This means you need more income and assets to pay your debts. Bankruptcy is a second chance, but it remains on an individual's credit record for 10 years.

Bankruptcy Laws

Bankruptcy laws in the United States have two goals. The first is to protect debtors by giving them a fresh start, free from creditors' claims. The second goal is to fairly treat creditors that are competing for debtors' assets.

Bankruptcy laws treat two general classes of debt: secured and unsecured. Secured debt is a loan backed by specific assets the debtor pledged as collateral to assure repayment. If the debtor does not pay, the creditor can take possession of the pledged assets. Unsecured debt is a loan not backed by any collateral. If you default, the creditor

What are the two main purposes of bankruptcy laws?

can obtain a court judgment against you to collect what you owe. Most of the debtor's assets can be used to repay unsecured debt.

Types of Bankruptcy

Bankruptcy petitions can be voluntary or involuntary. **Voluntary bankruptcy**, the most common kind, occurs when a debtor files a petition with a federal court asking to be declared bankrupt. The court notifies your creditors of the pending bankruptcy. Once notice is given, creditors may file claims. The court decides how much debt you will pay, what assets you can keep, and what debts will be canceled or discharged. **Discharged debt** refers to previous debts erased by the court during bankruptcy proceedings. Creditors can no longer seek payment for these debts. Some debts are not discharged and must still be paid. These include child support, alimony, income taxes and penalties, student loans, and court-ordered damages due to malicious or illegal acts.

Involuntary bankruptcy occurs when creditors petition the court, asking the court to declare the debtor bankrupt. Involuntary bankruptcy petitions do not occur very often because most creditors would prefer to be repaid in full over a set period rather than settle for only a portion of the debtor's remaining assets.

The bankruptcy process deals with debtors in one of two ways: liquidation or reorganization. Under liquidation, the court sells the debtor's assets and uses the proceeds to pay as much debt as possible. Usually, the value of the debtor's assets is not enough to pay off all the debts. The court appoints a trustee to sell the assets and give each creditor a share. Under reorganization, debtors may keep their property but must submit a payment plan to the court for repaying a substantial portion of their debts. The types of bankruptcy available to individuals can be distinguished by which of these two methods is used.

Chapter 7 Bankruptcy

Commonly called straight bankruptcy, **Chapter 7 bankruptcy** is a liquidation form of bankruptcy for individuals. It wipes out most debts in exchange for giving up most assets. Some assets that are considered necessary for survival may be retained.

The advantage of Chapter 7 bankruptcy is immediate debt relief—large debts and any payments on the debt are wiped out. As soon as bankruptcy is filed, all collections must stop. Debtors have a clean slate to start over. However, bankruptcy laws passed in 2005 have made it more difficult for a person to qualify for Chapter 7 bankruptcy.

Chapter 13 Bankruptcy

Chapter 13 bankruptcy is a reorganization form of bankruptcy for individuals. It allows debtors to keep most of their property and use their income to pay a portion of their debts over 3 to 5 years. Debtors work out a court-enforced repayment plan whereby they make a single monthly payment directly to the court. The court then disburses the funds to the creditors. Under Chapter 13, some debts are discharged, while others are paid off as agreed within the payment plan. Chapter 13 may seem like a better option for the debtor to reestablish credit. However, the blemish on the debtor's credit record caused by bankruptcy is hard to overcome for many years.

Chapter 11 Bankruptcy

Chapter 11 bankruptcy is a reorganization form of bankruptcy for businesses that allows them to continue operating under court supervision as they repay their restructured debts. Chapter 11 bankruptcy is most often associated with corporations but can be used by small businesses. In rare cases, individuals can file Chapter 11 bankruptcy. Wealthy individuals who have several investment properties may have debts that are too high to qualify for Chapter 13 but that do qualify for Chapter 11.

Reaffirmation of Debt

Creditors may ask debtors to agree to pay their debts, even after bankruptcy has discharged them. **Reaffirmation** is an agreement to pay debts that have been legally discharged. You may choose to reaffirm a particular debt if a friend or family member cosigned the loan, and you do not want to burden this person with the debt. Also, you may reaffirm rather than allow the collateral, such as a car, to be repossessed. Reaffirmation requires a court hearing, and debtors have 60 days to change their minds about promising to repay. A creditor is prohibited from harassing debtors to reaffirm after the court proceedings are over.

Bankruptcy Counseling

If you plan to file for bankruptcy, you must receive credit counseling from a government-approved organization within 180 days before you file. The counseling session should include evaluating your financial situation, discussing alternatives to bankruptcy, and a personal budget plan. You must also complete a debtor education course before your debts can be discharged. The debtor education course should include information on developing a budget, using credit wisely, and managing money.

A person who is considering filing for bankruptcy should also seek good legal advice. Since the passage of new bankruptcy laws in

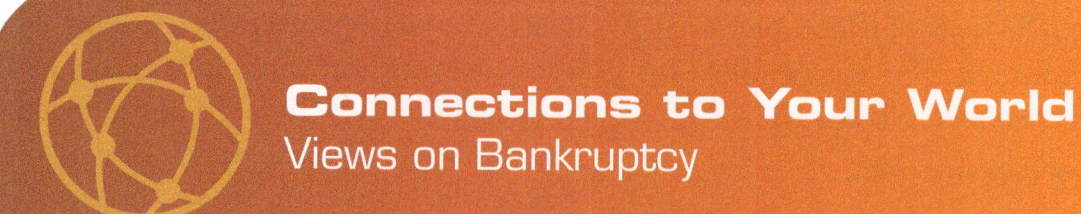

Connections to Your World
Views on Bankruptcy

Some businesses, such as credit card companies, believe consumers abuse credit laws and exploit creditors. They believe bankruptcy laws are too lenient and make it possible for people to run up debts and walk away from them. These businesses believe that credit is a privilege, not a right, and people should be held accountable for their decisions.

Others believe that credit laws are designed to protect consumers from unscrupulous businesses that would take advantage of them. Bankruptcy is the ultimate protection to give consumers a new start when they get buried in debt they can never repay. Those holding this viewpoint believe that creditors use deceptive practices to lure people into buying things they cannot afford and then raise interest rates when consumers fall behind on their payments, trapping consumers into a cycle of debt.

Think Critically

1. Which side do you agree with? How would you defend your stance to someone who does not agree with you? Create talking points or notes that could help you defend your belief.

2. Why might credit laws such as consumer bankruptcy protection sometimes be necessary? How can companies be protected to ensure that credit laws are not abused?

Source: Adam Gregor/Shutterstock.com

Why is it best to seek legal advice if you are filing for bankruptcy?

2005, the filing process has become very complex. A good bankruptcy attorney can assist you in deciding which bankruptcy plan will work best to help you solve your credit problems and help you navigate through the details and required forms you must complete.

✓ Checkpoint

List the types of bankruptcy options for individuals.

LO 8.2.2 Common Causes of Bankruptcy

There are many reasons why people are forced or choose to declare bankruptcy. Common causes include job loss, medical expenses, divorce, unexpected disasters, and poor financial planning.

Job Loss

According to Consumers Union, two-thirds of people who have filed for bankruptcy have been unemployed for a period of time before the filing. The loss of income from being laid off or terminated from a job can be catastrophic. Those who have debts and are unable to find full-time employment for an extended period may not be able to recover from this and are forced to file for bankruptcy. While you cannot control unexpected events, such as a layoff, you can plan and save for them. To help you get through rough financial times, save a portion each month rather than spending all your income.

Medical Expenses

Recent studies show that medical expenses and job losses are the biggest causes of bankruptcy. Many people are uninsured or underinsured. Serious illnesses or injuries can easily cost hundreds of thousands in medical bills. For example, a person hospitalized for a long period of time with a critical illness could easily owe $500,000 for medical care, drugs, room charges, and other fees. These bills can wipe out savings and retirement accounts in months. Once these have been exhausted, bankruptcy may be the only option left.

Divorce

Dissolution of marriage creates tremendous financial strain on both partners in the form of legal fees, child support, and/or alimony, as well as the burden of providing for a household on one income. The legal costs alone are enough to force some to file for bankruptcy, while wage garnishments to cover back child support or alimony can hinder others from paying the rest of their bills.

Unexpected Disasters

Loss of property due to theft or casualty, such as a house fire or natural disaster, can be nearly impossible to prepare for. As with medical insurance, many homeowners and renters are uninsured or underinsured. Those without homeowners or renters insurance may find it impossible to recover from debt related to these catastrophes and be forced into bankruptcy.

Poor Financial Planning

Many people who go bankrupt need a sound financial plan. They spend their money unwisely and need to follow a budget. Credit card bills, large mortgages, and other loan payments eventually spiral out of control. No matter what your financial position is, you must keep your spending and borrowing in proportion to your income. Most causes of bankruptcy can be avoided by careful planning and sound decision making based on good financial judgment, advice, and goals.

> **✓ Checkpoint**
>
> What things can lead to bankruptcy?

LO 8.2.3 Bankruptcy Advantages and Disadvantages

Bankruptcy has its advantages, but it also comes with disadvantages. A person considering bankruptcy should carefully weigh the advantages and disadvantages of declaring bankruptcy before deciding.

Advantages of Bankruptcy

For individuals whose debt situation seems hopeless, bankruptcy offers a solution. While this solution is not without a price, bankruptcy does offer the following advantages:

- Debts are erased. The biggest advantage that bankruptcy offers is a fresh start from most debts. It reduces or eliminates overwhelming bills, and the debtors can start over. With good financial planning and counseling, they can avoid future credit problems.
- An automatic stay is enacted. Once a bankruptcy petition is filed, an automatic stay is enforced, which stops lawsuits filed against the debtor and temporarily prevents creditor actions such as repossessions; garnishments; foreclosures; utility shutoffs; and in many cases, evictions. Although the automatic stay is temporary, in the case of foreclosure, it allows the debtor more time to find other housing, to work out a payment plan with the lender, or to sell the house before foreclosure.
- Exempted assets are retained. While Chapter 7 bankruptcy requires debtors to give up most of their assets to erase their debts, they can keep certain amounts and types of **exempted property**, or those assets considered necessary for survival. Exempted property includes a limited amount of equity in a residence; interest in a vehicle; personal property and furnishings;

clothing; some jewelry; and tools of a trade, including books and equipment. Exempted items allow the debtor to start over and have a base from which to begin.
- Certain incomes are unaffected. Bankruptcy will not affect certain types of income a debtor may have, such as Social Security; veterans' benefits; unemployment compensation; alimony; child support; disability payments; and payments from pension, profit-sharing, and annuity plans.

Disadvantages of Bankruptcy

While bankruptcy offers debt relief, it carries serious consequences. Bankruptcy should be considered a last resort. Some of the disadvantages of bankruptcy include the following:

- Credit is damaged. Filing for bankruptcy can destroy your credit rating. A bankruptcy judgment stays on your credit record for 7 years (Chapter 13 bankruptcy) or 10 years (Chapter 7 bankruptcy). During that time, you could find it difficult or impossible to obtain credit. If you can obtain credit, it will be at a very high interest rate because you will be considered high risk. Bankruptcy is a red flag to creditors and others that you were unable or unwilling to meet your financial responsibilities.
- Property is lost. Most of your property will be taken and sold to pay your debts. Even if you have an automatic stay, a creditor can file a motion to lift it. You may not even be able to keep exempt assets, such as your house. Assume that you own a house worth $120,000 with a mortgage of $90,000 against it. Your equity is $30,000. While the current bankruptcy code allows you to keep some of the equity in your home, you may be required to sell the home to pay off creditors.

- Some debts continue. Regardless of the type of bankruptcy selected; all debt is not erased. Certain obligations, such as child support and alimony, will remain after bankruptcy. Income taxes and related penalties that are less than 3 years old, student loans, and other debts at the bankruptcy court's discretion will also remain. Also, if a lender can prove that there was any false representation on the debtor's part in connection with a debt, the debt will not be discharged.

- Cosigners must pay. After you have been declared bankrupt under Chapter 7, any cosigners you had must repay the loans they cosigned. If you have missed loan payments, both your credit and the cosigner's credit may be harmed. Cosigners are likely to be your close friends or family members. Leaving them saddled with debt can damage your personal relationships.

What kind of debts are not erased by bankruptcy?

✓ Checkpoint

What are some major advantages and disadvantages of bankruptcy?

Lesson Review

Check Your Understanding

1. How is involuntary bankruptcy different from voluntary bankruptcy? (LO 8.2.1)

2. Why might someone choose to reaffirm a particular debt? (LO 8.2.1)

3. How can financial planning help you avoid bankruptcy? (LO 8.2.2)

4. Identify the advantages and disadvantages of filing for Chapter 7 bankruptcy. (LO 8.2.3)

Apply Your Understanding

1. If you were forced into a situation where bankruptcy is the only option, and you wanted to retain some assets through the reaffirmation process, what type of bankruptcy would be the best for your situation? Explain. (LO 8.2.1)

2. List the common causes cf bankruptcy for individuals. Next to each one, explain what you could do to avoid bankruptcy caused by these events. (LO 8.2.2)

3. If at some point in your future you were facing a large debt that would be extremely difficult to pay, what steps would you take related to debt relief? Explain what services you would use, such as credit counseling, and whether you would consider bankruptcy. Use a decision matrix to help you make the decision. (LO 8.2.3)

The Essential Question

What are the types, common causes, and advantages and disadvantages of bankruptcy?

A: Bankruptcy can be Chapter 7, 11, or 13. Bankruptcy may result from job loss, medical expenses, divorce, unexpected disasters, and/or poor financial planning. Although the advantage of bankruptcy is the erasure of most debts, the disadvantages to debtors include property loss and damage to their credit record.

Summary

8.1 Solving Credit Problems

- Consumers should have a responsible credit management plan. It involves recognizing your limits and planning your use of credit.

- The 20/10 rule suggests that your total debt not exceed 20 percent of yearly take-home pay and that your monthly payments not exceed 10 percent of your monthly take-home pay.

- Some danger signs that you are overextended include buying everything with credit, making only minimum payments on your balances, paying late, shifting balances between credit cards, paying off your balance with cash advances, and having inadequate unused credit to meet emergencies.

- Consumers with debt should manage their credit with a credit payment plan, which is a strategy to pay off accounts with the highest interest rate first.

- If exercising good credit management does not pay off your debt, contacting your creditors to try to work out a new payment plan, using debt relief services, and seeking help from a credit counseling service are options.

- Debt settlement programs are usually for-profit agencies that charge fees and may not be able to settle your debts without additional costs to you.

- Debt consolidation involves consolidating some or all your debt into one loan, but you may end up paying more interest over time or lose your collateral.

- Common credit scams include credit repair scams, advance-fee loans, online payday loans, credit card interest rate reduction schemes, and prescreened offers.

- Identity theft is one of the fastest-growing crimes in the United States. It can be devastating to a consumer's financial well-being.

- To protect yourself, you should secure your personal information, be careful when handling your debit and credit cards, possibly invest in identity theft protection services, be careful when posting information online, and be aware of privacy laws designed to protect you.

8.2 Bankruptcy

- Bankruptcy is a legal process that relieves debtors of the responsibility of paying their debts and protects them while they try to repay. It is used when a person gets into serious and irreversible debt.

- Bankruptcy is a second chance, but it remains on an individual's credit record for 7 to 10 years.

- Bankruptcy laws are designed to help people get a "fresh start" and to provide fair treatment to creditors competing for the debtor's assets.

- Bankruptcy may be voluntary (filed by the debtor) or involuntary (filed by creditors against the debtor).

- Chapter 7 bankruptcy is a liquidation form of bankruptcy for individuals in which debtors must give up most of their assets in exchange for having debts discharged.

- Chapter 13 bankruptcy is a reorganization form of bankruptcy for individuals in which debtors may keep most of their property and repay a portion of their debts following a court-enforced repayment plan.

- Chapter 11 bankruptcy is a reorganization form of bankruptcy primarily for businesses.

- If you file for bankruptcy, you must receive credit counseling from a government-approved organization within 180 days before you file.

- Common causes of bankruptcy are job loss, medical expenses, divorce, unexpected disasters, and poor financial planning.

- Advantages of bankruptcy are that debts are erased, an automatic stay is enacted, exempted assets are retained, and certain incomes are unaffected.

- Disadvantages of bankruptcy are that credit is damaged, property is lost, some debts continue, and cosigners must still pay.

Check Your Knowledge

1. Explain the 20/10 rule. (LO 8.1.1)

2. Where can you find credit counseling services, and what kind of help do they provide? (LO 8.1.2)

3. Describe two different credit scams. (LO 8.1.3)

4. To avoid identity theft, what personal information should you be careful not to give to others? (LO 8.1.4)

5. Define Chapter 7, Chapter 11, and Chapter 13 bankruptcy. (LO 8.2.1)

6. What are the most common causes of bankruptcy? (LO 8.2.2)

7. What is one advantage and one disadvantage of bankruptcy? (LO 8.2.3)

Apply Your Knowledge

1. Marcos and Elena have the following debts:

   - Credit Card #1: $2,000 balance, 18 percent interest, minimum payments of $30 per month

   - Credit Card #2: $1,000 balance, 15 percent interest, minimum payments of $20 per month

   - Credit Card #3: $3,000 balance, 24.99 percent interest, minimum payments of $50 per month

   - Store Account: $800 balance, 21 percent interest, minimum payments of $40 per month.

   Prepare a credit payment plan. How many months will it take to pay off their credit cards if they have $200 a month to apply toward credit payments? (LO 8.1.1)

2. Create a process chart or flowchart to develop a credit payment plan for a young adult who is overextended with credit. Write a description of what should be done at each step. (LO 8.1.2)

3. Refer to the two credit scams you described above. What would you do to avoid them? (LO 8.1.3)

4. Create a slide deck, poster, or blog post that explains how to protect yourself from identity theft. (LO 8.1.4)

5. Use a comparison chart to compare Chapter 7, Chapter 11, and Chapter 13 bankruptcy. (LO 8.2.1)

6. Jorj and Mandy both have full-time jobs, and Jorj is also taking on a part-time job so he can buy a boat. Neither set aside any of their income in savings. Explain the realities of this type of lifestyle, such as what would happen if the economy went bad or if one of them lost their job. (LO 8.2.2)

7. Do you believe the advantages of bankruptcy outweigh the disadvantages? Explain your answer. (LO 8.2.3)

Share Your Knowledge

Work in teams of two to four students to complete the following activities.

1. Choose one type of credit scam and as a team create a presentation, poster, or other way to explain how the scam works and what a consumer should do if they are the victim of a credit scam. (LO 8.1.3)

2. Visit the website www.identitytheft.gov. On the website, find the steps to recover from identity theft. Create a step-by-step process to follow to begin recovering from identity theft that can be shared with others. (LO 8.1.4)

3. Xiaodan is a small business owner. Her business has been losing money for some time, and she has been using her personal credit cards to pay for business expenses. She can no longer afford her payments. Use a decision matrix to determine which type of bankruptcy would be the most appropriate for Xiaodan. Explain your team's answer. (LO 8.2.1)

Base your answers to the following questions on your own personal thoughts, preferences, and experiences.

1. Write a set of credit management rules for yourself. Explain why you selected the rules you did and how you will apply them in the future. (LO 8.1.1)

2. Think about your personal online habits. Review the Texas Department of Insurance's website www.tdi.texas.gov/tips/how-to-protect-yourself-from-social-media-identity-theft.html. Have you ever done some of the things posted on this site? If so, what steps can you take now to protect your identity? (LO 8.1.4)

3. Divorce is one of the main reasons for financial trouble that can lead to bankruptcy. Why do you think divorce can have a negative impact on a person's financial well-being? (LO 8.2.2)

Chapter Project

Conduct research on federal bankruptcy laws, starting with the original Bankruptcy Act of 1898. As part of your research, learn about other major federal bankruptcy laws throughout history, including the Bankruptcy Abuse Prevention and Consumer Protection Act of 2005. Write a report that summarizes the most important provisions of the laws and explain why they were enacted. To enhance your report, use visuals, timelines, graphics, or charts depicting the progression of the laws and the number of bankruptcies over time.

Unit 2: Career Exploration

Researching Careers

It is important for students to ensure that their career goals align with future financial goals. By considering the earning potential of various careers, students can better assess how a career of interest aligns with their desired standard of living. To do this, students should research careers they are interested in. Education and skill requirements to enter the industry, job projections, and earning potential for careers of interest are all important for students to research. Once students have this information, they can compare their desired standard of living to the realistic prospects of a career they are interested in.

Based on the career cluster survey completed in the career exploration project in Unit 1, select one career cluster that you are interested in. For that career cluster, research various careers within the career cluster and gather information on education and skills required, salary projections (average starting salary and midpoint salary), and employment projections for each career. As a starting point, visit the U.S. Bureau of Labor Statistics Employment Projections Page (https://www.bls.gov/emp/). On the EP Data tab, you will find valuable resources to help you with your career cluster research. Use the graphic organizer below to compile information for at least five careers within your chosen career cluster.

Career Cluster Name:

Description:

Example Careers:

Career	Education/ Training	Skills Required	Salary Details	Employment Projections
			Avg. Starting: Midpoint:	
			Avg. Starting: Midpoint:	
			Avg. Starting: Midpoint:	
			Avg. Starting: Midpoint:	
			Avg. Starting: Midpoint:	

Share Your Knowledge

In groups of three to four students, share the information you gathered for your career cluster of interest. As a group, compare the different careers discussed and note any major differences in education and skills required, earning potential, and employment projections.

Reflect and Revisit

1. What does the employment projection data you found tell you about future job outlooks for the careers you researched?

2. Based on your research findings, how do the careers align with your desired standard of living? Will the jobs provide sufficient income to provide your desired standard of living? Why or why not?

3. Reflecting on the small group share-out, were there any details about career clusters that surprised you? How do the career clusters that others shared align with your interests and desired standard of living?

4. Based on your findings, would you reconsider the career cluster you originally chose? Explain.

How to Build a Credit History and Improve Your Credit Score

Sasha learned her lesson about overusing credit. She wants to set goals to plan for and use credit wisely. Her friend Diego suggested she learn more about building a good credit score by visiting the website of one of the three main credit bureaus for reliable credit information. Sasha decided to visit the Experian website. She found an article titled "How to Build Credit" and used it to help her set goals.

She considered three options to establish credit:

1. She could ask her parents to add her as an authorized user on one of their credit card accounts.
2. She could apply for a secured credit card.
3. She could have her apartment rent payments added to her credit report.

Using the website of one of the credit bureaus, identify at least two pros and two cons of each option. Sasha is considering using a T-chart, such as those included on the Companion Site, for each option.

Think Critically

1. Which option would you recommend to Sasha? Explain your answer.
2. What other methods of building credit are available to young adults?
3. What are five ways an individual can improve their credit score?

The Importance of Building a Credit History as a Young Adult

Sasha is curious about why you should be concerned about your credit score as a young person. So that you can share the information with Sasha, use online resources to research why building a credit history while young is important. Prepare a presentation to demonstrate what you learned about how your credit history is used for the various life events listed below.

1. Leasing an apartment
2. Setting up utilities for a home
3. Applying for a job
4. Buying a vehicle
5. Buying a home
6. Getting a cell phone
7. Insuring a car or home

Then create for yourself at least one short-term, intermediate-term, and long-term SMART goal related to credit. Explain why the goal is important to securing your financial future.

Example intermediate-term goal:
In the next 12 months, I will open a checking account. A checking account will allow me to create a personal budget, track income and expenses, and save for future goals.

Think Critically

1. Name five reasons why it is important to set financial goals and explain why each is important.

Warning Signs Related to the Misuse of Credit

Sasha has been approved for her first credit card. She has heard so many stories about people "getting into trouble" with their credit cards and wants to avoid any problems. She knows that credit cards are part of an overall financial wellness plan, and she wants to understand how credit can impact her financial future. Sasha is also interested in helping others learn about good credit practices. To help her learn more and help others, Sasha has asked you to help her research the warning signs associated with the misuse of credit. Help Sasha with her research and create a video or blog post to share. Include the sources you found. Submit your final product to your teacher.

Protecting Yourself from Identity Theft

Using the Identity Theft website (https://www.identitytheft.gov/#/) and the Federal Trade Commission website (https://consumer.ftc.gov/features/identity-theft), create a professional way to share the warning signs of identity theft, including the steps you can take to help protect yourself and what to do if your information is lost or stolen.

Think Critically

1. What preventative measures can be implemented to reduce the risk of identity theft?

2. Why is it important to protect your personal information?

3. What are some unintended ways teenagers place themselves at risk of identity theft?

4. Review the list below and identify the things you do regularly. Indicate if each is a safe or unsafe practice. If it is an unsafe practice, explain why.

   - Shop online
   - Share personal details on social media
     - Name
     - Birthday
     - Location (are your pictures geotagged, or do you check into places?)
     - Phone number
     - Where you go to school
     - Names of your parents or grandparents

- Use the same password on multiple websites
- Use simple passwords because they are easy to remember
- Use two-factor authentication
- Click links in emails or social media posts
- Use public wi-fi
- Update security settings on your phone and computer

Personal Financial Literacy

The Personal Financial Literacy Event measures your personal finance knowledge. Students must be able to apply reliable information and systematic decision making to personal financial decisions. The Personal Financial Literacy Event consists of a financial literacy exam and a role-play scenario with a business executive. Finalists will compete in a second role-play event. Participants will have 10 minutes to review the scenario and develop a professional approach to solving the problem. Participants will have 10 minutes to present their action plan to the judge. After each participant's explanation, the judge can ask questions about the scenario.

Go to DECA.org/compete for more detailed information.

Performance Indicators

- Compare and contrast a positive credit history with an adverse credit history.

- Discuss the information on a credit report, including how long the information will appear on the report.

- Explain the rights a consumer has to review and correct their personal credit report.

Try It Out!

You are a customer service representative at the local credit union. Your client, Diego (the judge), is a young adult seeking his first automobile loan. Diego has completed the loan application correctly, and you are reviewing it with him. Diego was unaware that the credit union would need to submit the loan application to the underwriting department, where his credit score and credit report would be considered for loan approval. He asked you to explain the purpose of the credit report and credit score.

Diego does have a credit card, but the application was a simple online form that only required him to enter his Social Security number, income, and birthdate. Diego does not understand why the credit union's process is so complicated. You must explain to Diego why a credit report and score are needed. You must also explain what is included in the credit report and why it is important to determine if the credit union will grant the loan to Diego. You must also explain consumer rights to Diego, including his right to examine the credit report.

The meeting takes place in your office. Diego will begin the meeting with a greeting and introduction before asking you for information about credit reports and credit scores. After you have presented the information to Diego, he may ask you questions. The meeting will end with Diego thanking you for your time and helpful information.

www.deca.org/compete

Managing Resources

Source: blackCAT/istock.com

Unit 3 focuses on the importance of personal decision making in all aspects of your life, including decisions related to where you will live, what you drive, your educational path, and your family when you are an adult. You will learn to make good decisions based on your values, needs and wants, and personal goals. You can apply the decision-making process to most aspects of your life, including whether to buy or rent your home and moving decisions, selecting and maintaining a vehicle, and determining if you will complete postsecondary education or training and how to pay for it. You can even apply the decision-making process to life decisions related to family and family goals and dealing with both foreseen and unforeseen life events. Although your goals will change over time, the decision-making or problem-solving process will remain constant and can be used for guidance throughout your life.

Unit 3: Profile

Source: lev radin/Shutterstock.com

Robert F. Smith

Robert F. Smith is the founder, chairperson, and chief executive officer (CEO) of Vista Equity Partners in Austin, Texas. He was born to working-class parents in Denver, Colorado, on December 1, 1962. His father was an elementary school principal, and his mother was a high school principal. His parents instilled in him the importance of supporting the community, a lesson he has followed.

While in high school, Smith was selected to be an intern at Bell Laboratories. He says that the internship changed his life. Smith earned his bachelor's degree in chemical engineering from Cornell University. Cornell University honored Smith in 2016 by naming the engineering school after him. Smith continues to support the school with his time as a member of the Cornell Engineering College Council as well as financially.

Although a successful businessperson, Smith is known for his philanthropy, which is the desire to promote the welfare of others, often through generous donations of money. Smith has donated millions of dollars to organizations, and he has signed the Giving Pledge, which is an agreement to donate the majority of his wealth to philanthropic causes. Smith was the first African American to sign the pledge. He supports human rights and has received numerous awards. Smith is one of 15 Black billionaires in the world.

Smith began his career in engineering, and he obtained two U.S. and two European patents for coffee filtration systems. He joined the team at Goldman Sachs in the investment banking division after earning his Master of Business Administration (MBA) from Columbia Business School in 1994. In 2000, Smith founded Vista Equity Partners. Smith's belief in the value of internships is part of his investment strategy. When Vista Equity Partners provides investment dollars to new companies, part of the agreement is for the company to build an internship program as part of their business activities.

Connect and Reflect

Smith is committed to investing half his net worth "to causes that support equality of opportunity for African Americans, as well as causes that cultivate ecological protection to ensure a livable planet for future generations." Explore how such values can impact decision making:

1. Why do you think Smith has chosen to invest in such causes? What in his background may have impacted his values?

2. From your perspective, are there benefits to charitable giving? Explain.

3. Identify financial priorities you may have for the future and the decisions or sacrifices you may need to make to accomplish them.

9 Chapter

Personal Decision Making

How can the decision-making process help you prioritize your needs and wants?

Learning Objectives

By the end of this lesson, you should be able to:

LO 9.1.1 Apply the decision-making process to solve consumer problems.

LO 9.1.2 Explain how economic needs and wants and collective values influence consumer decision making.

Key Terms

- sunk cost
- trade-off
- opportunity cost
- loss aversion
- needs
- wants
- values
- personal preferences
- collective values
- innovations
- public goods

Consider This ...

Hector is preparing to go to college in the fall and is trying to decide how to spend the summer before moving away. He can work full time and save money, or he can spend time with his friends and enjoy the break between high school and college.

"Making this decision is really tough," Hector said. "I'd like to have a fun summer with my friends. On the other hand, if I work, I can set aside more money for college. For me, it's a toss-up. Most of my friends are taking the summer off, and I'd enjoy spending time with them and making more memories before we start the next chapter in our lives. Part of me says that's the right thing to do, but another part says it would be more responsible to set aside money to help pay for college."

"That's a good point," replies Hector's older brother. "When you're in college, you'll have to devote a lot of your time to classes and studying, so you may not have as much time to work; I learned this the hard way. I think it's a good idea to work over the summer and set aside some of your earnings for college expenses. Even though you are working, you can still spend time with friends before you leave for college."

Read and Reflect

1. What advice would you give to Hector? What factors would you suggest Hector consider when making his decision?

2. In what ways does Hector's decision now impact him in the future?

LO 9.1.1 The Decision-Making Process

To make better purchase decisions, you should use a rational, step-by-step process to define your needs and evaluate alternatives before making a final choice. This process helps you make many different types of decisions, including how to use your money in ways that will benefit you most.

Step 1: Identify the Goal or Problem

The first step in the decision-making or problem-solving process is to identify a goal you wish to achieve or a problem you want to solve. This is more challenging than it sounds. For example, say you want to buy a laptop or tablet. First, consider the device's purpose for school, home, work, and so on. How will it benefit you? Are there special features or programs the device must have for you to be proficient in doing your job, doing your homework, and planning your schedule? If you cannot define the problem or goal (what the device would be solving), purchasing it would not be a good decision.

Why should you approach purchase decisions with a step-by-step process?

Source: Olena_T/istock.com

Step 2: Gather Information

Once you have defined the problem or goal, gather information on all possible solutions. For example, how else could you be more proficient without buying a device? List all alternative solutions and the cost of each. In this example, you might list these possible solutions related to a laptop:

- Use a computer at school (on campus) or at a public library
- Buy a used laptop
- Buy a new laptop

Each solution has different costs to consider. To use the computer at school or a library, you should factor in the time involved and mileage (gas). Most libraries have computers for public use with free internet access. To purchase a new device, you may have to borrow money. Keep a written record of the information you collect about your various choices, as shown in **Figure 9.1**.

Do not consider sunk costs. A **sunk cost** is an expense that occurred in the past for which money was spent and cannot be recovered. For example, maybe you already have an old computer. It may be slow, not capable of running new programs, or obsolete. Assume you paid $400 for it 3 years ago. If you added more memory to your old computer, would it solve the problem? The concept of marginal benefit says that if the added benefit exceeds the added cost, you should fix the old computer. Either way, the original price ($400) is a sunk cost and irrelevant to the decision.

Step 3: List and Consider Options

The next step in the decision-making process is to compare each alternative solution based on your gathered information. When you

Figure 9.1   Comparison Shopping Data

	Per Month	Per Year
Option 1: Use library/school lab		
Time: 5 hours/weekend	20 hours	240 hours
Gas: 6-mile round trip/weekend	$ 8.00	$ 96.00
	$ 8.00	$ 96.00
Option 2: Purchase a used laptop		
From private person (one-time cost)		$ 500.00
High-speed/wireless Internet access	$ 80.00	960.00
	$ 80.00	$ 1,460.00
Option 3: Purchase a new laptop		
Cost: $900.00 or $1,125 at 25% simple interest for 1 year		
Payments on one-year loan at 25%	$ 93.75	$ 1,125
High-speed/wireless Internet access	80.00	960.00
	$ 173.75	$ 2,085

make choices, they often involve making a **trade-off** or getting something in return for giving up something else. The trade-off results in an **opportunity cost**, the value of your next best choice—what you are giving up. For example, in the chapter-opening scenario, Hector's resources (time and money) are limited, so he must make a trade-off between spending time with his friends and working. Both options have opportunity costs. Suppose Hector could earn $2,000 by working over the summer. If he decides to spend the summer with his friends, the opportunity cost of his choice is the $2,000 income he gives up. If he decides to work, the opportunity cost of that choice is the value to him of the time he could have spent with his friends. Part of comparing choices is considering the value of the options given up.

The concept of loss aversion is related to opportunity costs as part of decision-making behavior. **Loss aversion** implies that losses due to a decision are weighted more in the consumer's mind than gains that may occur from the decision. Loss aversion can impact the final decision someone makes.

When comparing choices, convenience should be considered as well. In some cases, convenience may be more important than cost if the cost is reasonable. Using the laptop example, you may decide that the convenience of having a computer and being able to use it anytime you need it is worth the extra dollar cost. You may also decide that even though the cost of buying a new laptop will be greater, you prefer to avoid the uncertainty of possible repairs if you buy a used one. Another consideration is the security of your information. When you use a public computer, your information may be at risk if you are using an unsecured wireless network. Someone could also view your computer screen or watch you enter your passwords. Finally, public computers are more likely to be infected with malware or spyware. When you own a computer, you can minimize these risks.

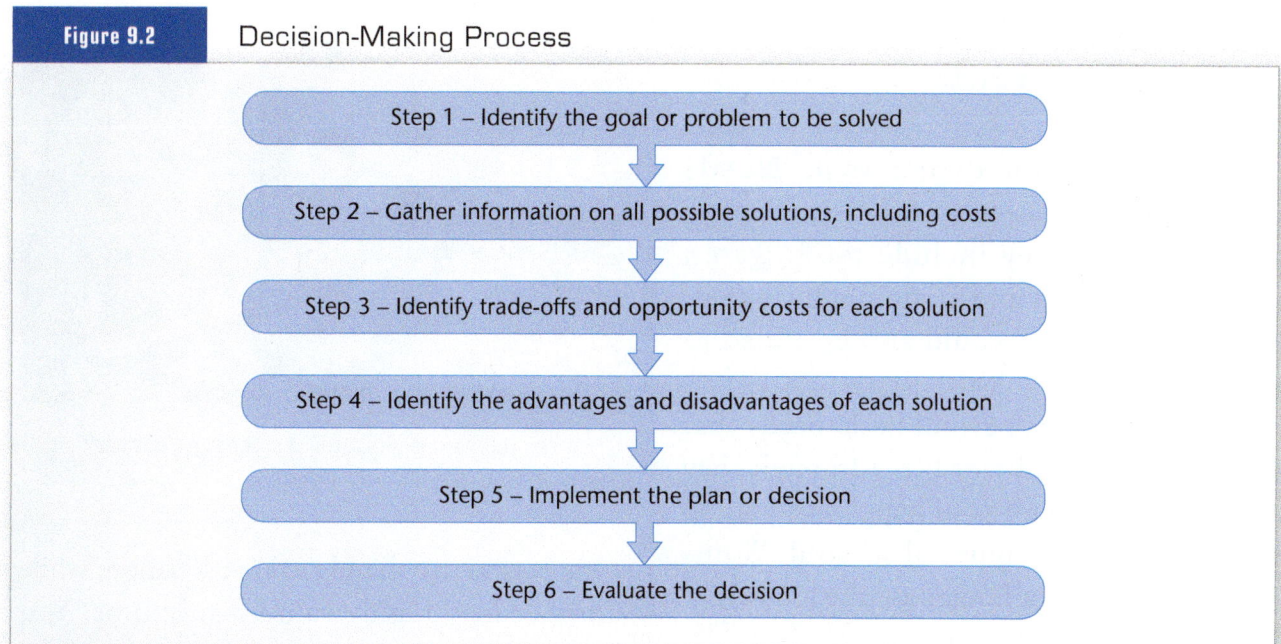

Figure 9.2   Decision-Making Process

Step 1 – Identify the goal or problem to be solved

Step 2 – Gather information on all possible solutions, including costs

Step 3 – Identify trade-offs and opportunity costs for each solution

Step 4 – Identify the advantages and disadvantages of each solution

Step 5 – Implement the plan or decision

Step 6 – Evaluate the decision

Step 4: Consider the Advantages and Disadvantages of Each Choice

Carefully consider the advantages and disadvantages of each option before making a decision. If you follow the steps outlined in the preceding paragraphs, your decision will be based on careful consideration of the problem, a thorough collection of data, and an analysis of that data. The wise decision in any situation is the one that best meets your needs, is within your budget, and gives you the most value for your dollar investment. Take the time you need to carefully evaluate the information you gathered about each choice before you decide, especially for expensive or complex products.

Step 5: Choose and Implement Your Decision

After you decide, take action to implement your chosen solution. Because you have made a thorough analysis of choices for solving your problem, you can be sure that you have made the best decision possible with the available information.

Step 6: Evaluate the Effectiveness of the Decision

After several months, revisit your decision and evaluate whether you "solved" the problem or met the goal you identified in step 1. Are you happy with the choice you made? If not, what could you do differently next time to make a better decision? Should you do something different now? If your needs have changed or your initial decision is not working out, go through the decision-making process again to decide whether to change.

Figure 9.2 is an example of a decision-making or problem-solving chart that can be used as a model or guide when going through the process.

✓ Checkpoint

What steps are involved in the decision-making process?

Economic Needs and Wants

Every person has needs and wants. **Needs** are the items necessary for maintaining physical life. They include food, water, shelter, clothing, and basic medical care. Safety and security could also be added to this list.

Wants are items beyond basic needs that improve your quality of life. Although they may be necessary for your happiness, you do not need them for physical survival. Wants include, but are not limited to, the following:

- Food, clothing, and shelter beyond what is necessary for biological survival; for example, eating out, name-brand clothing, or living in a house with a swimming pool are not necessary for survival
- Procedures such as cosmetic surgery, changing hair color, or teeth whitening to change your appearance may improve your self-esteem but are not medically necessary to survive
- Travel, vacations, and recreation to improve personal enjoyment of life
- Luxury items, such as a jet ski, the latest gaming system, or central air conditioning, to make life more fun or comfortable

Individual Wants

Beyond the basics, you decide what you want based on your values, personal preferences, income, and leisure time. Your wants, in turn, drive your buying decisions, and the best choice is different for everyone. These factors vary among individuals and societies. They also change throughout your life.

Values

Each person has their own set of values. **Values** are the principles by which a person lives. Different people value things differently.

How can your values affect your purchasing decisions?

Source: RyanJLane/istock.com

One person may highly value education, while another may highly value family time. You make economic choices based on your values. For example, if you highly value education, you may decide to save a large portion of your income for college. Someone who highly values time with family may choose to save for a family vacation. As you move through life, your values may change.

Personal Preferences

Personal preferences or tastes are your likes and dislikes. For example, one person may enjoy a weekend of hiking in the mountains, and another person may choose a visit to Disneyland. Based on personal preferences, we all make economic choices. We spend money on things consistent with our personal tastes.

Income

The amount you earn will influence the choices you make. As you learned previously, discretionary income is the money left over after you have paid your necessary expenses. This is the money you can spend or save as you wish. The more discretionary income you have, the higher the quality and quantity of products you can consider. The ability to afford goods and services to fulfill

Connections to Your World
Evaluating Your Wants

Prepare a list of the top five "wants" in your life today and briefly describe each one. Rank them in order of 1 to 5, assigning 1 to the most important and 5 to the least important item. Then answer these questions:

- How long have you wanted each of the five items?
- What is the cost of each choice (including opportunity costs)?
- Will you need to save or borrow money to purchase them?
- What benefits will you get from each item?
- Will the benefits be long-lasting, or will they be short-lived?
- How does each item relate to your values?
- How might your list be different 10 years from now?

your wants and meet your goals will impact the choices you make. For example, if owning many expensive things is important to you, you may want to pursue career goals leading to a high-paying job.

Leisure Time

The amount of free time you have and the activities you enjoy also affect how you spend your discretionary income. Leisure time is when you get to do things you like and enjoy. It allows opportunities for rest, relaxation, and enjoyment of life. You may use it to develop hobbies or a side job that you enjoy. Leisure time gives you the chance to participate in a variety of activities.

Collective Values

Collective values are ideals and values that are important to society. All citizens share in the costs and benefits related to collective values. Society influences our values, goals, and choices because it expects social

responsibility from its citizens. For example, owning a fuel-efficient vehicle or using an alternate energy source benefits everyone by reducing air pollution and our dependence on non-renewable energy sources.

Legal Protection

In a market economy, it is important to preserve legal and personal rights. Private property ownership and the freedom to make individual choices are important American values and part of our legal rights as U.S. citizens. Laws and their enforcement are the result of our desire to have and protect these freedoms. We pay for legal protection through taxes. The U.S. Constitution's Bill of Rights gives us individual freedoms and rights of citizenship.

Employment

Most people who are able will work because it is expected. It is a way to satisfy needs and wants in this society. Most of us are aware of the subtle, yet very real, pressure to perform in the work arena. Therefore, we strive to do the best we can and get a job that pays well for our effort. In this way, we can be personally satisfied with our productivity and, at the same time, satisfy society's demand for contributing citizens.

Progress

The relative state of progress of the country where you live, including its technological advances and perceptions about the importance of those advances, will affect your purchase decisions. The United States is technologically advanced and places a high value on innovations. **Innovations** are new ideas, products, or services that bring about changes in the way we live. Innovations can be fun and entertaining, but they also can add to the quality of life in various ways, such as by saving us time, effort, or money.

Environmental Impacts

Natural resources are of great value and concern because they are limited—some cannot be replaced. Because of our collective values, preserving a quality environment for future generations is a priority for some

How does society benefit from the gainful employment of individuals?

Source: Hoptocopter/istock.com

people and companies. Many people in our society support activities such as recycling and establishing air pollution standards. We have laws that require manufacturers to minimize the environmental damage caused by the production of their products and services. Environmental quality is an important part of our society. If this is an important value to individuals, they may support initiatives and make purchases related to the environmental impacts of their decisions.

Public Goods

Our country is organized to be "of the people, by the people, and for the people." We have a highly advanced and intricate system of government made up of the people, performing services for the people, with money contributed through taxes by the people. One of the roles of government is to provide its citizens with goods and services, such as police protection, highways, and national defense. These goods and services provided by the government to its citizens are known as **public goods**. The government provides them because the private business sector cannot do so efficiently. For example, national defense is necessary to protect our country from those who would do us harm. Each state, family, or business cannot reasonably provide for its own defense.

✓ Checkpoint

How do needs, wants, and collective values influence personal decision making?

Check Your Understanding

1. Besides the dollar cost, what other costs should you consider when comparing alternative solutions to a problem or goal? (LO 9.1.1)

2. How does discretionary income affect your choices for wants and needs? (LO 9.1.2)

Apply Your Understanding

1. Describe the last time you made a major purchase. Did you go through the six-step decision-making process? Was the decision a good one or would you choose something different today? (LO 9.1.1)

2. Explain how your wants can influence your decision-making process in purchasing goods or services. (LO 9.1.2)

The Essential Question

How can the decision-making process help you prioritize your needs and wants?

A: The decision-making process should be based on your needs and wants; as you analyze your purchases, they should also meet your personal values and the collective values of society.

The Essential Question How do personal and external factors, including marketing strategies, affect how you plan your major purchases?

Learning Objectives

By the end of this lesson, you should be able to:

LO 9.2.1 Describe factors that influence spending.
LO 9.2.2 Explain how to plan for major purchases.
LO 9.2.3 Analyze marketing strategies that influence spending.

Key Terms

- custom
- economy
- product advertising
- target market
- company advertising
- industry advertising
- odd-number pricing
- unit pricing
- loss leader

Consider This ...

Hector decided that it was best to work for the summer and save money for college. He has been working a lot of hours and has managed to save quite a bit of money. While watching TV with his brother, they see an advertisement for a new smartphone that just came out last week. "I think I'm going to upgrade my phone! Have you seen the features on that thing? It's amazing," said Hector. "I thought you were saving your money for college," replied Hector's brother. "I am, but everywhere I look, I see an advertisement for the new phone, and it makes me want it even more. We just saw it on TV. I see it almost every time I scroll through social media, and I just received a coupon for a free accessory if I buy it this week."

Read and Reflect

1. What advertising strategies are being used to influence Hector?
2. How could this advertising influence Hector's buying decision?
3. What questions should Hector ask himself before deciding to buy the phone?

LO 9.2.1 Factors That Influence Spending

Why do you buy the things you do? Consumer purchasing decisions are influenced by personal factors and external factors that encourage or discourage spending. When planning a major purchase, you should examine your motives. You should buy for the right reasons (to meet your needs and wants), instead of being swayed by outside influences that are not in your best interests.

Personal Factors

Personal factors influence your consumer spending choices. They include personal resources; position in life; customs, background, and religion; and values and goals.

Personal Resources

Personal resources include time, money, energy, skills and abilities, and available credit. The more you possess of any one of these factors, the greater your purchasing power. For example, the amount of time you have available to compare prices and options before purchasing a product will affect your ability to make better buying decisions. Your job skills will affect the amount of money you can earn and, consequently, your purchasing power.

Position in Life

Your position in life includes age, marital status, gender, employment status, living arrangements, and lifestyle. These factors have a big influence on an individual's purchasing decisions. For example, single people's spending patterns differ from those of married couples and families. Younger people tend to have different spending priorities than older people. Someone who has a high-wage job is more likely to make high-dollar purchases than someone who is working a minimum-wage job.

Customs, Background, and Religion

A custom is a long-established practice that takes on the force of an unwritten law. Families may be faithful to customs that they have followed for generations. Cultural, religious, and other groups share common customs. For example, people of a cultural or religious group may observe special holidays that are not observed nationally. The customs of the groups you belong to are likely to influence your buying patterns.

Values and Goals

Values are the principles by which a person lives. Values are intrinsic and slow to change, while goals change often; when you accomplish one goal, you move on to others. Your value system may change as your goals in life are met or not met. Individual and family values and goals are expressed through your choices of entertainment, literature, sports, luxuries, and so on. These choices are reflected in many ways, including the purchases you make, the use of your time, and your attitude toward accumulating possessions.

External Factors

Factors outside yourself and your family can affect your spending patterns. These factors include the economy, technological advances, the environment, and social pressures.

The Economy

Economy refers to all activities related to producing and distributing goods and services in a geographic area. The economy goes through stages in the business cycle, growing or slowing. Economists measure economic activity to describe the financial well-being of the region or the nation. The general condition of the economy affects everyone. We cut back and save more when we are concerned about the economy. For example, when interest rates on car loans are high, fewer people buy new cars. When the price of fuel skyrockets, people drive less and buy fewer luxury items. When the economy is strong and growing, people are more optimistic, so they travel, dine out, and buy more goods and services.

Technological Advances

Americans place a high value on new technological advances. Many people want the newest, most convenient, and most interesting gadgets, such as virtual reality headsets, or electric-powered cars. As new goods and services are created to raise our standard of living, many consumers willingly purchase them.

The Environment

Concern for the environment can affect buying decisions. Many citizens are interested in home projects, community activities, and statewide programs that beautify, preserve,

Why is the state of the economy an important factor in our buying decisions?

recycle, and protect existing resources and the environment. This interest in the environment affects consumers' actions and product preferences. Many people are buying more ecologically safe, biodegradable, recyclable, and organic products.

Social Pressures

Social pressures often persuade consumers to buy goods and services beyond their ability to pay for them. Your friends, family, and coworkers all influence your buying decisions. Through advertising, the media like radio, television, and the internet, also act as sources of social pressure for consumers.

> ### ✓ Checkpoint
>
> What are the personal and external factors that influence consumer purchasing decisions?

LO 9.2.2 Planning Major Purchases

Major purchases generally tie up future income or take a big bite of accumulated savings. Before making a major purchase, ask yourself the following questions and take time to reflect on your answers. Then make a final decision based on a rational—not emotional—perspective. Follow the decision-making process introduced earlier in this chapter to aid you in making the best decision possible.

- Why do I want this product?
- How long will this product last?
- What substitutes are available, and at what cost?

- By postponing this purchase, is it likely that I will choose not to buy it later?
- What additional costs are involved, such as supplies, maintenance, insurance, and financial risks?
- What are the trade-offs and opportunity costs of this purchase?
- What is the total cost of this product (cash price, interest, shipping charges, etc.), and will the cost be higher or lower if the purchase is made at a later date?

Cash or Credit?

Major purchase decisions involve whether to pay cash or use credit. Even though you may have cash available, you should only pay cash for some purchases to maintain a cash reserve for emergencies.

On the other hand, just because you have unused credit available does not mean you should charge a purchase. Examining your credit choices will lead you to your best options for each type of purchase. For example, you may choose a store financing plan that offers 0 percent interest for 2 years rather than using a credit card that charges 24 percent interest.

Figure 9.3 compares various options available for buying a refrigerator, with positive and negative consequences.

Research Before Buying

Comparison shopping will help you determine whether you are getting the best quality for the best price. The same brand often sells at considerably different prices at different retailers, depending on the sellers' markups. By shopping at multiple retailers, you may be able to save money. In addition, many stores offer sale prices at various times of the year or regular intervals.

The internet makes comparison shopping easy. Individuals can see different

Figure 9.3	Cash or Credit	
Item	**Cash**	**Credit**
New refrigerator		
Price	$800 + $15 delivery charge	$50/month for 18 months + $15 delivery charge
Total cost	$815	$915
Used refrigerator		
Price	$400 + $15 delivery charge	$30/month for 15 months + $15 delivery charge
Total cost	$415	$465
Considerations	Ties up cash; cannot make other purchases. No monthly payments. Reduced savings balance. No interest charges.	Allows for budgeting; ties up future income. Can make other purchases. Establishes credit. Interest charged.

prices for specific products through online stores and websites. These websites offer the convenience of comparing product prices without leaving your home.

When purchasing expensive items, take advantage of store policies that will refund part of your purchase price if the item you buy goes on sale within the next few weeks or months. This policy, together with a liberal return policy, should affect your choice of merchants. For example, a store that allows you to return a purchase within a reasonable period (a month or more) is much better than a store that will not accept returns or give refunds.

Quality and Price

The fact that you are paying a high price does not necessarily mean you are getting the best quality merchandise. It pays to know what good quality is and what you should expect from the merchandise.

For major purchases, it is important to check reviews in several sources before making your choice. *Consumer Reports* is an expert, independent, nonprofit organization that tests the quality of many products and compares different brands. It publishes the results in its *Consumer Reports* magazine and on its website; however, you may need to have a subscription or use the resources at a public library to see all the information. You can also find product reviews online through websites, apps, and social media.

✓ Checkpoint

How can planning and research help you make better buying decisions?

Marketing Strategies That Influence Spending

Numerous marketing strategies lure us to buy goods and services. Many of these strategies are subtle, and we often are unaware of their impact on our buying patterns.

Advertising

The primary goal of all advertising is to motivate consumers to purchase a product or service. Some advertising is informational and valuable; other advertising is false and misleading.

Advertising appears in a variety of media, including billboards, television, social media, and websites. All advertising is carefully coordinated to reach specific consumer groups. Marketers help businesses sell products and services by creating colorful and attractive campaigns, often appealing to emotion rather than reason. They hire celebrities or influencers, compose catchy jingles, create entertaining videos, design colorful logos, develop funny memes, and choose mascots to identify the business's products. There are three basic types of advertising: product, company, and industry.

Source: ChayTee/istock.com

What is the primary goal of advertising?

Product Advertising

Product advertising is advertising intended to convince consumers to buy a specific good or service. Advertisers repeat the product name several times during commercials and ads to help consumers remember it. Many ads feature famous athletes, actors, or other celebrities and influencers using the product. Advertisers hope your positive feelings for the celebrity will carry over to the product. Giveaways, testimonials from people who have used the product, and other promotional gimmicks are also used to persuade consumers to buy.

Ads are carefully planned to appeal to certain types of consumers. A **target market** is a specific consumer group to which the products are designed to appeal. In planning the advertising campaign, content creators consider many factors when placing their product ads, such as the day of the week, time of day, and type of platform for the ad. For example, products advertised during sporting events differ from those advertised on social media. The target markets differ depending on the delivery platform. Television ads are much different than ads found on social media. Even the type of social media will result in changes to the way a product is advertised.

Company Advertising

Advertising intended to promote the image of a store, company, or retail chain is known as **company advertising**. This type of advertising usually does not mention specific products or prices. Instead, it emphasizes the overall quality and reliability of the company and its products. For example, a company ad might feature company-sponsored community projects. A store ad might talk about the store's friendly employees or wide selection. These ads are designed to promote a favorable attitude toward the company so that you develop loyalty to the store and shop there frequently.

Industry Advertising

Advertising intended to promote a general product group without regard to where these products are purchased is called **industry advertising**. For example, the dairy industry emphasizes the nutritional value of milk and other dairy products. Consequently, the whole dairy industry benefits when people drink more milk and eat more dairy products. Often, industry ads stress concern about energy conservation or environmental protection. General health and safety ads often are presented as part of industry campaigns, such as ads by the tobacco industry that discourage teen smoking.

Pricing

The price of merchandise depends on several factors. Supply and demand determine what will be produced and the general price range. The cost of raw materials and labor, competitive pressures, and the seller's need to make a profit are some factors that determine a product's price. But there is more to pricing than adding up the production costs and including a profit.

Retailers understand the psychological aspects of selling goods and services and use pricing devices to persuade consumers to buy. For example, if buyers believe they are getting a bargain or are paying a lower price than they are, they are more inclined to buy the product or service. **Odd-number pricing** is setting prices at uneven amounts rather than whole dollars to make them

When does advertising "cross the line" and become offensive or inappropriate? Many consumers believe that the First Amendment's protection of free speech is important to our values as a country. They believe that when something is censored or controlled by the government, freedom of speech is in jeopardy. The U.S. Supreme Court has allowed wide latitude in interpreting what individuals and businesses can publish or make known to others. In 2010, the U.S. Supreme Court ruled that corporations have the same First Amendment freedom of speech rights as individuals.

However, many consumers feel that advertising should be appropriate, both in placement and in content. For example, certain advertisements would not be suitable during programs targeting young children. Thus, consumers believe that while businesses have a right to advertise their products, they should be sensitive about how, where, and when those ads appear as well as the possible effects of the ads.

Think Critically

1. Do you believe some television, internet, or social media ads are offensive or inappropriate? Why?
2. Do you think there should be more control over both content and placement in advertising? Explain.

seem lower. Consumers tend to perceive odd prices as significantly lower than they are. If a price tag reads $5.99 instead of $6.00, consumers tend to round the price down to $5.00, making it more likely that they will purchase the product.

Discounts are often available for buying in large quantities. However, you cannot assume that because you are buying the large economy size, you are paying less per unit than if you bought a smaller size. Compare unit prices on all sizes. **Unit pricing** tells you how much it costs per ounce or other unit of measure. By using unit pricing, you can compare various sizes of containers. Some

member-only stores, such as Sam's Club and Costco, sell only larger quantities of products. While the cost per unit may be lower, you are not saving money if you cannot use all the product before it spoils. You should also consider the cost of the annual fee to shop at stores such as Sam's Club and Costco. It may not be cost effective to be part of a members' only store if you do not shop there frequently.

Sales

Retailers advertise end-of-month sales, anniversary sales, clearance sales, inventory sales, holiday sales, pre-season sales, and post-season sales. They may mark down merchandise substantially, slightly, or not at all. To be sure that you are saving money by buying sale items, you must practice comparison shopping and know the regular prices. When an ad states that everything in the store or on the website is marked down, check carefully—items may only appear to be marked down. Some online merchants offer special pricing days; for example, Amazon offers Prime Day sales or lightning deals to drive consumers to the website on a regular basis.

A **loss leader** is an item of merchandise marked down to an unusually low price, sometimes below the retailer's cost. The store may lose money on the sale of this item because the cost of producing it is higher than the sale price. However, the loss leader is used to get customers into the store or visiting the website in the hope that they will also buy other products. Profits from the sale of other items are expected to make up for the loss incurred on the loss leader. There is nothing illegal or unethical about a loss leader if the product advertised is available to the customer on demand.

How can you be sure you are saving money by purchasing "sale" items?

Promotional Techniques

Retailers may use promotional techniques to lure customers, such as store displays, contests, coupons, rebates, frequent-buyer cards and customer-loyalty programs, packaging, sampling, target marketing, and cash back apps.

Store Displays

Retailers often use in-store displays to entice customers to buy. Variations of in-store displays include window displays, located prominently in the business's storefront area, and feature displays, located at the end of aisles to draw attention to a product. Many stores use point-of-sale displays located near cash registers to encourage impulse buying. Some stores use special racks, where shelf space is modified to make more space available for new or promoted products or seasonal items. Many displays have holiday themes, such as Halloween, Thanksgiving, or Christmas. Color schemes, decorations, music, and special effects often are used to make in-store displays more visually appealing to consumers.

Contests

Retail stores and restaurants that depend on repeat customers often use contests to bring customers into the business. The possibility of winning something or getting something free is appealing. Large and small prizes are offered to get customers to come back and buy more. Careful reading of the rules of the contest reveals the customer's chances of winning. Usually, the chances of winning a major prize are very small.

Coupons

Manufacturer coupons offer instantly redeemable savings on specific products and may be redeemed wherever the product is sold. Store coupons offer discounts on specific products, usually for a short period of time, and only at a specific store. Manufacturer and store coupons can be found inside or on a package, on the store's reward app, on a store shelf or in-store display, and online.

Rebates

Rebates offer money back to the consumer. They are offered by either the featured product's retailer or manufacturer. The most common types of rebates are online rebates and instant rebates with a few stores still offering a mail-in rebate. With a mail-in or online rebate, the consumer typically must mail or upload a filled-out rebate form, a receipt, and the product's barcode within a specified period to the retailer or manufacturer. In return, the store or manufacturer will send a check, gift card, or prepaid card for a specific amount to the consumer within 6 to 8 weeks. An instant rebate occurs when a product is advertised at a specific price and the discount is applied at the time of purchase. For example, an electronics store may advertise last year's television model for $699.99 with a $100.00 instant rebate. The $100.00 is taken off the total price by the cashier at checkout, and the consumer pays only $599.99 for the television.

Frequent-Buyer Cards and Customer-Loyalty Programs

Merchants continually look for ways to build customer loyalty and repeat business for future purchases. Kohl's Cash is one example of a reward that can be used in the future and helps bring customers back to the store. Some stores and restaurants use frequent-buyer rewards that can be tracked via your phone number or through a rewards app. Those customers who accumulate enough in rewards may receive free or discounted merchandise.

Customer-loyalty programs offer enrolled members lower prices, rebates, point-of-sale coupons, or other valued services. Each time the customer purchases at the store, their account is accessed. This practice allows the store to track purchasing patterns and target advertising accordingly. Customer-loyalty programs are often used by grocery stores, restaurants, and pharmacies.

Packaging

Packages do more than just protect the product. They are also promotional tools. A product's packaging often compels consumers to look at a new product. Manufacturers design packaging to appeal to the eye and provide the necessary product information. The visual aspects of the package—color, graphics, size, and shape—play an important part in attracting consumers' attention. Packaging should also emphasize special features about the product, such as "fat-free," "new and improved," and "organic." Manufacturers may also include coupons inside or on the package.

Sampling

Many companies promote their products through sampling. This can reduce consumers' apprehension about buying a new product or introduce them to a product with which they are unfamiliar. Samples are often given out in a store or shopping mall. Sometimes samples of nonperishable items are included in direct marketing mailings to households. Many companies now offer free samples through their websites or mobile apps. This encourages consumers to use the product and allows the company to gather data for marketing purposes.

Target Marketing

Many companies buy marketing data about consumers. Demographics include information about a person's age, gender, race, marital status, income, education level, and occupation. Psychographics describe consumers' lifestyle, interests, and attitudes. This information is gathered from purchases, customer-loyalty programs, public information, online shopping, and other sources provided by the government, postal service, banks, and credit bureaus.

Target marketing is a marketing strategy designed to target specific people likely to buy certain products. For example, when a couple has a child, they are likely to receive ads, samples, and coupons for baby products because the child's birth record is public information. These targeted promotions are efficient. Rather than pay the cost of mailing samples of baby products to everyone, baby product manufacturers can send samples only to consumers with babies.

Connections to Your World
Online Target Marketing

When you purchase a product from an online retailer, you will likely register with the site or app and provide information about yourself. The next time you visit, the site may present you with product recommendations. The products may be related to a previous purchase or products similar to items you are currently viewing on the site. Even if you do not officially register with the site, you can expect that it has captured information about you with the intent of selling products to you. How does the website know who you are and what you like?

When you visit an online retailer, the site places a cookie, or small data file, on your computer that stores basic information about you. The next time you visit the site, the cookie sends the stored information about you back to the site. This way, the site can recognize a returning customer. It also recognizes your specific computer. As you travel around the site, the cookie keeps track of the product pages you visit. The online retailer is building a database of your preferences. This is a form of target marketing. The advertising targets you—a target market of one customer. This custom-tailoring service benefits you because the ads you see might interest you. It benefits the retailer by increasing the chances of making another sale to you.

This type of marketing also occurs on other online platforms. For example, social media sites and apps use this approach to include ads that are relevant to your interests. As you scroll through a social media page, you may notice that the ads on the page are related to recent internet searches. In addition, the ads that you see are likely different than the ads a friend sees; this is because many social media sites use target marketing to personalize the ads on your page.

(continues)

(continued)

In addition, when you provide your e-mail address to an online retailer, you may receive e-mail advertisements in the future. By knowing your product preferences, the retailer can inform you of special offers and discounts on related products.

Although it has benefits, online target marketing also brings about privacy concerns. Many companies that collect customer information online sell their customer databases to other companies. In addition, the same technology that allows legitimate retailers to personalize their site for you can be used by criminals to steal information from you. In some cases, the cookies placed on your computer may contain spyware. This is a program installed on your computer without your knowledge that constantly collects data about you and uses your internet connection to send that data to advertisers. Although spyware is not illegal, the potential for abuse is cause for concern. Consumers have no control over the data collected or its use. There are many anti-spyware programs on the market that enable you to detect and remove these programs from your device.

Think Critically

1. Suppose you purchase some clothes through an online store. The next time you visit the website, a list of clothing of similar styles, shoes, and other related products pop up for your consideration, including some at a special low price. Is this kind of service worth the possible loss of privacy to you? Explain.

2. Do you like to receive e-mail or online advertising? What are potential benefits and downsides to online advertising?

3. How do you think target marketing influences consumer buying decisions? Do you think certain groups of individuals are more likely to be influenced by target marketing? Explain.

Cash Back Apps

Many companies will pay to have their products featured on cash back apps. Customers can shop at their favorite stores, such as Walmart, Target, and others. Customers who purchase one of the featured items receive credit in the rebate app. Once the credit reaches a specific threshold, usually $10, they can request a check or gift card from the app. Examples of online rebate apps are Ibotta, Rakuten, and Dosh.

✓ Checkpoint

How do marketing strategies and promotional techniques increase sales?

9.2 Lesson Review

Check Your Understanding

1. How do social pressures affect buying habits? (LO 9.2.1)

2. Explain what is meant by comparison shopping. (LO 9.2.2)

3. Why do companies use target marketing? (LO 9.2.3)

Apply Your Understanding

1. Which personal factors influence your spending the most and why? (LO 9.2.1)

2. You want to make a major purchase that will involve a large amount of cash and/or credit. What questions should you ask yourself before making such a commitment? Why is it important to make rational, rather than emotional, decisions regarding large purchases? (LO 9.2.2)

3. Compare two marketing strategies that influence spending and prepare a way to showcase the strategies to your classmates. (LO 9.2.3)

The Essential Question

How do personal and external factors, including marketing strategies, affect how you plan your major purchases?

A: Personal factors like resources, position in life, cultural or religious customs, and values, along with external factors, including marketing strategies, the economy, technological advances, the environment, and social pressures may influence your purchasing decisions. These factors encourage or discourage spending.

Summary

9.1 Making Better Decisions

- The decision-making or problem-solving process typically involves six steps: (1) identify a goal or problem to be solved, (2) gather information, (3) list and consider options, (4) consider advantages and disadvantages of each choice, (5) choose and implement a decision or solution, and (6) evaluate the effectiveness of the decision or solution.

- Giving up one option in exchange for another is called a trade-off. The opportunity cost is the value of what you give up. Loss aversion may impact final decisions.

- Needs include items necessary for maintaining physical life like food, water, shelter, clothing, and basic medical care. Wants are items beyond basic needs and improve quality of life but are not needed for physical survival.

- Individual wants are shaped by such factors as personal values and preferences, income, and leisure time.

- Values are the principles by which a person lives. For example, one person may highly value education while another values family time. People make economic choices based on their values.

- Collective values include the desire for legal protection, employment, progress (innovations), environmental quality, and public goods.

9.2 Spending Habits

- Personal factors that influence individual spending habits include personal resources; position in life; customs, background, and religion; and values and goals.

- External factors that affect spending habits include the economy, technological advances, the environment, and social pressures.

- When planning major purchases, make sure you want the product for rational, rather than emotional, reasons. Research and compare before you buy.

- The primary goal of all advertising is to motivate the consumer to purchase goods and services.

- There are three basic types of advertising: product, company, and industry. Product advertising promotes a specific good or service often to a target market, or specific consumer group. Company advertising promotes the image of a store, company, or retailer. Industry advertising promotes a general product group without regard to where these products are purchased.

- Pricing plays a large role in purchasing decisions. Consumers perceive odd-number pricing like $5.99 as being lower than it is.

- Retailers use loss leaders, or items marked down to an unusually low price, to lure customers to a store or online site, hoping they will buy other more profitable products while they are there.

- Promotional techniques to increase spending include store displays, contests, coupons, rebates, reward programs, customer-loyalty programs, packaging, sampling, target marketing, and cash back apps.

Check Your Knowledge

1. What are the steps in the decision-making or problem-solving process outlined in the chapter? (LO 9.1.1)

2. Define needs, wants, values, and collective values. (LO 9.1.2)

3. List the external factors that influence spending. (LO 9.2.1)

4. What are the steps involved in planning for a major purchase? (LO 9.2.2)

5. How do advertisers use product advertising to influence consumers? (LO 9.2.3)

Apply Your Knowledge

1. Using the steps in the decision-making process, make a decision that will satisfy your desire for a smart phone, gaming system, or other new technology product you have been wanting. Explain how you completed each step. (LO 9.1.1)

2. What community and national environmental concerns do you have? Explain how your concerns impact your spending decisions. (LO 9.1.2)

3. How do your spending patterns differ from those of your parent(s) or guardian(s)? What things do you buy that your parents also purchase? Can you trace any of these purchases to a strong family custom, background, or religion? (LO 9.2.1)

4. Use a search engine to find and select a price comparison website. Request a price comparison for a product in which you are interested. What is the range of prices for the product? What other features does the site offer to help you research and select products? (LO 9.2.2)

5. Spend time looking at the ads that appear when you are online. Identify which social media platform or web browser you were using for each ad. Identify the celebrities or social media influencers who may appear in the ads. Why do you think each celebrity was chosen for that product? Explain the emotional appeal behind at least five ads you saw. (LO 9.2.3)

Share Your Knowledge

Work in teams of two to four students to complete the following activities.

1. As a team, identify a project in your community you would like to see completed. Use the problem-solving process to generate ideas to present to the local community leaders. Develop an appropriate way to share the information with them. (LO 9.1.1)

2. As a group, identify the collective values you have. Why are these values important to you? Does everyone in the group agree? Explain. Prepare a poster or slide deck to share your group's collective values with the rest of the class. (LO 9.1.2)

3. With your team, compare the ads you found in a previous question. Were the ads the same? Were they different? If the ads were the same or similar, did you have the same reaction to the ad as your teammates? Explain. If they were not similar, why do you think you received different ads from the same social media platforms or web browsers? (LO 9.2.3)

Connect and Reflect

Base your answers to the following questions on your own personal thoughts, preferences, and experiences.

1. Think about a problem you had to tackle recently. Did you follow a problem-solving process? Evaluate the effectiveness of the solution you found to the problem. Write a paragraph or complete a problem-solving chart about the process you followed and the effectiveness of the solution you implemented. (LO 9.1.1)

2. Consider a purchase you made in the last year. Explain any trade-offs you made and describe what personal and external factors affected your decision. Are you satisfied with your purchase? Explain your answer. (LO 9.2.1)

3. Are you planning a major purchase soon, such as a new phone, gaming system, used car, or clothing for a formal event such as homecoming or prom? Explain your plans for this major purchase. Use the decision-making process introduced in the chapter to help you make the decision to purchase the item. (LO 9.1.1 and LO 9.2.2)

4. Have you ever bought something because you saw it in the store or online. Before you saw the item, did you want it? Is it something that you needed? How did marketing strategies influence your decision to purchase the item? (LO 9.2.3)

Chapter Project

Watch a sporting event or other program that interests you, either on television or online. Determine the program's target audience. Watch the commercials shown during the program and then do the following:

- List all the commercials and categorize each as product, company, or industry advertising. (Count public-service and political advertisements as industry advertisements.)

- Identify the target markets and rate each commercial as good, fair, or poor, depending on how well it is directed to the program's target audience.

- Explain which ads you think were most effective and why.

10 Chapter

Housing Decisions

What are your housing options, and what is involved in moving to your new home?

Learning Objectives

By the end of this lesson, you should be able to:

LO 10.1.1   Describe several housing options.
LO 10.1.2   Discuss potential living arrangements.
LO 10.1.3   Explain how to plan a successful move into your new home.

Key Terms

- residence hall
- studio apartment
- townhouse
- duplex
- condominium
- security deposit
- furnished rental
- unfurnished rental
- rent-to-own option

Consider This ...

Anisa is finishing her sophomore year in college. During her first two years, she lived in university housing, as required by the university. At age 20, she is ready to explore new housing options.

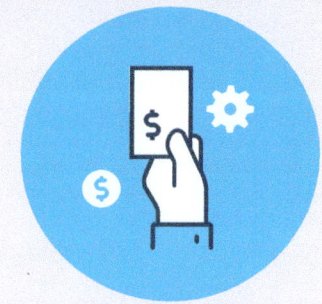

"We have lots of important decisions to make," she told her roommate, Nadia. "We could stay here in the dorm, but that may not be our best bet. Living off-campus has advantages, but there are also things to consider. For example, we'll have to pay rent and utility bills every month. We'll also need transportation to get to class and finding parking on campus can be a challenge. To afford rent for a house we'd want, we'd have to take in another roommate. On the other hand, if we rent an apartment or house, we'd have much more space. Plus, we would have a lot more privacy, freedom, and independence."

"Yes, there are a lot of advantages to being out on our own, but there are many challenges too," replied Nadia. "We would need to make some rules about our living arrangements and responsibilities that everyone agrees on. We don't want our living arrangements to distract us from our main goal—finishing our education. This is all pretty exciting to think about, and I'm looking forward to the change. How do we get started?"

(continues)

(continued)

Read and Reflect

1. What are the various housing options available for Anisa and Nadia? What are the advantages and disadvantages of each?

2. If you were Anisa, what housing choice would you make? Why?

3. What advice would you give Anisa and Nadia as they explore various housing options?

LO 10.1.1 Housing Options

You will soon have many important choices to make. One is where to live. You may decide to live at home with your parents and commute to college or postsecondary career education, which is usually less expensive than living alone or with a roommate. There are numerous housing options if you move out of your childhood home while attending school or beginning your first job. It is crucial that you weigh your options before you make a final decision.

Student Housing Options

Student housing options include on-campus housing like residence halls and off-campus housing like apartments or rental houses.

On-Campus Housing

Many students prefer to live on campus. Some colleges and universities will not allow first-year students or students under the legal age to live off campus. Living on campus has many benefits, including accessibility to classes and campus resources, such as the library, computer labs, and health center, and more social interaction as part of campus life. A college or university may also provide assistance with roommate issues.

For example, if your roommate does not pay their housing payments, your ability to stay in the residence hall is not impacted. The school may also help relocate students if there are major compatibility issues. The disadvantages to living on campus are little privacy and limited space.

If you live on campus, you will have several housing options: residence halls, university-owned apartments, or sorority or fraternity housing.

Residence Halls

Most students who choose to live on campus will live in a residence hall. A **residence hall** (or dormitory) is an on-campus building with many small rooms rented to students.

Source: SolStock/istock.com

When you first leave home, what are some student housing alternatives open to you?

The rooms usually come furnished with beds, dressers, and study desks. Some units have private bathrooms; however, most residence halls have communal bathroom facilities. Many rooms are intended for double occupancy, and some may be designed for three or four roommates, each with a private bedroom and shared common spaces such as small kitchens and a living room. It may be possible for students to request a private room for an additional charge if private rooms are available.

Most residence halls have centrally located lounges for watching television and group activities. Most have shared kitchen and laundry areas as well. Meals at the college cafeteria may also be included with the cost of the room (room and board). Although rooms are small, with limited space for living and studying, the cost per school term may be less than that of other housing options.

University-Owned Apartments

In addition to residence halls, many larger colleges and universities have student apartments. An apartment is a separate living space with one to three bedrooms. Although some schools permit only graduate students, married students, or students with families to live in the apartments, other colleges and universities allow undergraduate students to live in them as well. The apartments typically come furnished with beds, dressers, study desks, and chairs, and they include closets, bathrooms, a kitchen, and dining and living room areas.

Sororities and Fraternities

Many colleges have sororities and fraternities that provide housing on or near campus. A sorority is a social organization of female students who share a residence, and a fraternity is a similar organization for male students. Sorority and fraternity houses are often large homes that comfortably house 20 or more people.

To live in one of these houses, you must become a member of the sorority or fraternity in a process called pledging. Typically, sororities and fraternities seek new members with goals, abilities, and ideals like the organization's. For example, some require a certain grade point average. Others look for an interest in community service. The cost is usually higher for these facilities; however, you live with people with similar values and goals.

Off-Campus Housing

Some colleges and universities do not provide on-campus housing options. Even if the school you attend offers housing, you may choose to live off campus. Living off campus has advantages, such as more independence and privacy. Living off campus also helps you be more responsible because you will oversee paying your rent and bills every month, buying groceries, and planning your schedule. However, living off-campus comes with challenges. It may be more expensive than living on campus. You might also have to drive or use some form of public transportation to get to class.

When you live off campus, you have several choices, including apartments, duplexes, condominiums, and rental houses. You can also have one or more roommates if you live off-campus to share expenses. Roommates also present challenges. If one roommate decides to leave before the end of the lease, you will be responsible for their share of the expenses until the lease ends.

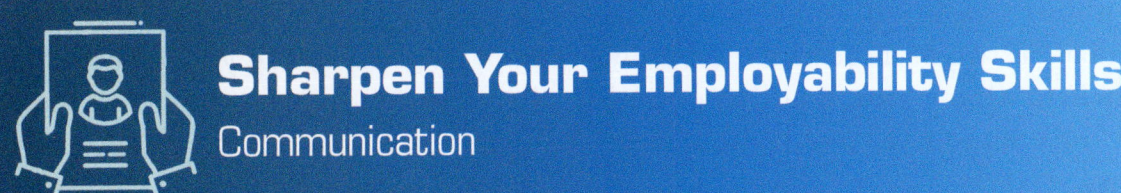
In just a couple years, you will likely be making housing decisions. Many young adults' first housing experiences include renting an apartment. Explore what apartment options might look like for you after you finish high school by answering the following questions:

- What kind of apartment building or complex would you find most desirable?
- What features would you want the apartment to have?
- What amenities would you want the apartment complex to offer?
- Where would you like the apartment to be located?
- Would you live by yourself or with a roommate?
- Would your ideal apartment be feasible based on your budget after high school?

Create a slide deck, video, or some other kind of presentation to communicate to a friend or family member the features you would desire in an apartment after high school. Keeping your budget in mind, explore apartment listings online and include links and pictures to two or three different apartments that meet your requirements. Outline advantages and disadvantages of living in an apartment. Based on your research, explain whether you think an apartment may be a good option for you after high school.

Additional Housing Options

Not everyone will attend college or university. But many young adults are eager to begin life outside of their family home, which could include a job that takes them to a different city or state.

Apartments

Many young adults choose to live in an apartment for their first home. An apartment complex is a large building or group of buildings that contain many units, often as many as a hundred or more. You can find an apartment in your chosen area in online ads and apartment guides.

Apartments come in a variety of floor plans. Typically, the smaller the apartment's square footage, the less expensive it is. A **studio apartment**, also known as an efficiency apartment, has one large room that serves as the living room, dining area, and bedroom. Kitchen facilities may be located in the central area or a separate room. Larger apartments with separate living, dining, and sleeping areas are also available. Many apartment units offer two- and three-bedroom apartments with considerably more living space. This is often a good option when two or more roommates are involved. Typically, a larger apartment is more expensive than a studio apartment but less expensive than a townhouse. A **townhouse** is a living space that has two or more levels. Typically, the kitchen, dining area, and living room are on the ground level, and bedrooms are upstairs.

Apartment amenities may include on-site laundry facilities, a storage area, parking, building security, a swimming pool, tennis courts, a clubhouse, and a fitness center. In addition, utilities like heat, water, gas, electric, and garbage service may be included in the rent. It is important to read the lease carefully before making a final decision. In some cases, you may have a washer and dryer or a hook-up for a washer and dryer in your apartment.

Apartment living provides independence and flexibility but also requires responsibility and good judgment. Most apartment buildings have rules that make close living more enjoyable for all.

Duplexes and Multiplexes

A **duplex** is a building with two separate living units that share a common central wall. Usually both living areas are the same with separate entrances. Duplexes usually offer more space than apartments and more privacy, with only one close neighbor. They may include a garage or carport, private laundry facilities, and other privileges and responsibilities like a house. A multiplex may be three or four living units connected by common walls.

Condominiums

A **condominium** (or condo) is an individually owned unit in a complex with shared ownership of common areas. The complex can be a building, similar to an apartment building, a group of duplexes,

or multiplexes. Although many owners choose to live in their condos, especially after retirement, many offer them for rent. Because condos are privately owned, the owner often has a larger financial investment. This usually means that the upkeep of the property is better. Also, a condo may offer more stylish and higher-end design elements than in apartments, such as granite countertops and stainless-steel appliances. The Condo Owners' Association (COA) maintains shared spaces in a condo complex. The COA is the governing board whose membership is made up of residents who own a condo in the building, complex, or neighborhood. The COA charges a fee that includes the costs of maintenance for the shared areas, insurance for the physical building, and any shared amenities such as swimming pools, gyms, and even roads if the complex is in a gated community. When renting a condo, you will have the same responsibilities for upkeep as the owner.

Rental Houses

Rental houses, also called single-family homes, offer many attractive features, such as a larger, more private living area, a driveway and garage or carport, a yard, and a patio or deck. Because you are getting many of the comforts of home ownership, the rent may be more expensive. When renting a house, you are likely to have many of the same restrictions as with other rentals, such as no pets allowed. Also, you may be responsible for upkeep, such as yard maintenance, and utility bills typically will be higher. In addition, because rented houses are investment properties that people buy and sell, the property may be shown to prospective new owners while you are living there.

If the property is sold, and the new owner is purchasing it for private use rather than as a rental, you may be asked to move.

✓ Checkpoint

What are common forms of housing?

LO 10.1.2   Living Arrangements

Your living arrangements will depend largely on the choices you make after high school. For college students who choose on-campus housing, many of the decisions regarding their living arrangements will be predetermined. Renting in the community involves more planning. You must determine whether you want a roommate, where you want to live, and what items you will need to furnish your new home.

Who to Live With

To share expenses, you may wish to have one or more roommates. Choosing a roommate can be difficult. Just because you are friends with someone does not mean that you can successfully live together. Your living habits may be very different. Be sure you are compatible with your potential roommate before you move in together. Discuss possible areas of disagreement that may cause trouble if not settled in advance. Some questions that each of you should answer include the following:

- Do you smoke or drink? How do you feel about others who do?
- Do you like a clean living area, or are you easygoing and casual about your environment?

- Do you have steady employment or another source of income to ensure that you can pay your share of expenses?
- What are some of your goals? Do you want to continue your education, work full time, or travel?
- What are your leisure activities? What activities will you share with (or impose on) your roommate?
- What type of transportation do you have? Will you share transportation? If so, what are the costs and how will you divide them?
- If you cannot make the living arrangements work, how will you separate the financial responsibilities that come with one person moving out?

You might also consider having more than one roommate. However, it is more difficult to have problem-free relationships when more personalities are involved. Matching similar personality types will increase the chances of a successful living arrangement.

Where to Live

Your finances will have a major impact on where you decide to live. You must determine how much rent you can comfortably pay. Then you can shop for the housing option that best meets your needs. There are additional considerations to consider as you decide where to live.

- Deposits and fees. A **security deposit** is a refundable amount paid in advance to protect the owner against damage or non-payment. If you take care of the property and pay your rent on time, you should get the security deposit back when you move. Utility companies may require you to make a security deposit when you first open an account. You may also have to pay fees, which are nonrefundable charges, usually for services provided.

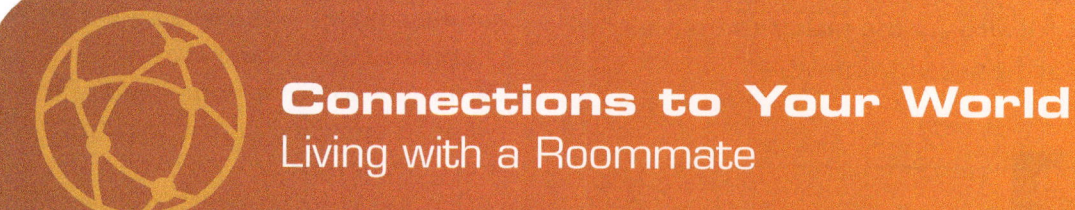

Connections to Your World
Living with a Roommate

Living with a roommate is challenging for many people. Even if you are close friends with someone before becoming roommates, living together presents new challenges that you must navigate. The division of responsibilities and financial obligations can cause tension and conflict.

Although Anisa and Nadia have previously been roommates, they are also very different. Anisa prefers things to be neat, clean, and tidy. Nadia, on the other hand, is not as concerned about clutter around the living space; she often leaves dishes out after meals and has clothes laying around.

Nadia prefers to pay bills early and in full, while Anisa often waits until the last minute and is sometimes short on money. These differences are a concern for them, as they will be sharing additional responsibilities and bills soon. They also have another friend, Margot, who will be moving into the new rental house with them. Margot told Anisa and Nadia, "I can't wait to have my own place so I can do whatever I want!"

As noted at the start of the chapter, Anisa, Nadia, and Margot should make rules about living arrangements and responsibilities.

Think Critically

1. What recommendations would you make to Anisa, Nadia, and Margot as they look at making rules?

2. What agreements should Anisa, Nadia, and Margot come to before deciding to become roommates?

3. What possible areas of misunderstandings can Anisa, Nadia, and Margot anticipate and what kind of plan can they develop to address them?

For example, the internet provider may charge a one-time installation fee. Or if you have a pet, you may have to pay a nonrefundable pet deposit, plus a surcharge on your monthly rent for the pet.

- Safety. You will want to try to live in a safe area. By researching the crime rates and statistics for various areas, you can learn more about the safety of a neighborhood.

- Length of time you plan to live in the residence. If you sign a lease for 6 months, you have committed to remain for that length of time. A lease is a legal contract. You may face penalties if you wish to move sooner. Usually, the shorter your commitment, the higher the monthly rent. Read the terms of the lease carefully before signing the document.

What factors might influence your decision of where to live?

- Distance from school and work. Your proximity to school or your job and access to public transportation are important considerations, especially if you do not own a vehicle or must share one.
- Distance from services. You will need access to shopping areas, gas stations, and other frequently used services. Your means of transportation can make a difference in how close you need to live to these services.
- Repairs and maintenance. As a renter, you may be responsible for maintaining the property in minor ways, such as replacing light bulbs, mowing lawns, and repairing damages—such as broken window screens—you have caused.

What to Take

Rental housing can come furnished or unfurnished. A **furnished rental** provides the basics—bed, dresser, sofa, chairs, lamps, dining table and chairs, and essential appliances. An **unfurnished rental** usually includes basic kitchen appliances, such as a stove and refrigerator, but little else. Usually, the fewer the items furnished, the lower the rent. If you have enough of these

furnishings or can acquire the essentials for an unfurnished residence, you can save a considerable amount on rent.

You can buy or rent furnishings. Compare purchase and rental payments carefully before you decide. For example, with a **rent-to-own option**, you rent furniture with an option to buy. At the end of the rental period (usually 6 months or longer), you can buy the furniture at a reduced price. However, rent-to-own options can be more expensive than paying for furniture you purchase outright with an installment plan. Renting furniture and appliances may be a good idea for those who will be moving long distances and do not want to take their old furniture with them.

Basic household and personal items necessary for setting up housekeeping include the following:

- Towels, wash cloths, sheets, and cleaning cloths
- Cleaning supplies (mops, brooms, buckets, vacuum cleaner, detergent, and cleansers)
- Personal items (shampoo, cosmetics, soap, and other personal hygiene items)
- Clothing (and clothes hangers), shoes, and other apparel
- Stereo, television, and computer
- Kitchen utensils (dishes, silverware, pots, and pans) and a trash can
- Tools (hammer, nails, duct tape), light bulbs, flashlight, extension cords, and batteries
- Lamps, artwork, pictures, and other decorations

You may also need to provide rugs, drapes, shower curtains, and mirrors. You or your roommate(s) may have some of these items, or you may decide to buy them. If you buy some things jointly, it is a good idea to make a list before purchasing them and agree on who will get the joint items if one of you decides to move.

✓ **Checkpoint**

What decisions must a person make regarding living arrangements?

LO 10.1.3 Planning Your Move

If possible, begin planning your move several months in advance. Others who have experienced a similar move can help you with advice. Here are some ways to prepare:

- Have savings. Set aside savings to cover the security deposit, first and last months' rent, fees, and initial expenses. If you have a pet, you may have to pay an additional security deposit and an additional monthly fee.
- Have income. Have a reliable source of income to pay monthly rent, utility bills, and expenses. Landlords typically require applicants to earn a specific

What are some ways you can prepare in advance before moving out on your own?

Source: Krakenimages.com/Shutterstock.com

income monthly. The standard income requirement is three times the monthly rent for the apartment or 30 percent of your net income. Because this is your first rental, the apartment complex may require a large deposit or cosigner on the lease or rental agreement to assume financial responsibility if you cannot pay your rent or other lease obligations.

- Have supplies. Gather what you need to live independently, such as clothing, towels, sheets, pillows, small appliances, and dishes, to minimize the items you need to buy when you move.
- Consider your goals. Plan the move with your goals in mind. If your goal is to finish college, your living plan should help you achieve this goal. For example, if you plan to go to college in September and live on campus, it would probably not be wise to move out on your own for the 3 summer months before the start of school. The expenses would be significant, and you probably would be better off saving your money to help meet college expenses.
- Make reservations. Plan for transporting furnishings. Professional movers can be expensive, and their services must be reserved. If you enlist friends to help you move, you may need to rent a moving truck that you reserve in advance. Also, plan to provide refreshments or a meal for your friends if the move takes several hours.

A good way to organize your preparations is to make a household needs inventory, such as the one shown in **Figure 10.1**. Decide what you will need and check each item as you fulfill the need. As you can see, getting ready for the move may take several months.

Moving Costs

Moving costs include the time and money spent in packing, loading, transporting, unloading, and unpacking. Professional

Figure 10.1   Household Needs Inventory

What Is Needed	Date Needed	Cost	Date Completed
1. Dishes/towels	October 1	$200	_____
2. First and last months' rent	October 1	$2,000	_____
3. Security deposit	October 1	$1,000	_____
4. Moving-in fees	October 1	$500	_____
5. Car (share of expenses)	September 1	$250	_____
6. Job (part-time)	August 1		_____
7. Household budget	September 1		_____
8. Plan with roommates	June 1		_____
9. Plan with parents	May 1		_____

movers typically charge based on the amount you must move, the distance traveled, and whether they do the packing. You can save money by doing your own packing.

You can save even more by renting a truck or trailer and using your own labor for loading, driving, and unloading. If it is just a local move, such as across town, the rental will likely be cheaper if you can return the vehicle to the place where you rented it. However, for a long-distance move, you can rent a truck or trailer one way and return it to the rental agency's branch in the new city.

When you reserve a moving truck or trailer, you may be asked if you would like to purchase additional insurance coverage for your move. This coverage may run up to $100 a day, but it may be well worth it, since many truck and trailer rentals are not covered on your auto insurance policy. If you choose not to purchase insurance, you will be held liable for any damage that occurs.

Utility and Other Fees

When you move into a new residence, you may be required to pay fees for internet or streaming services. You must also arrange to turn on the electricity and other utilities. Many utility companies charge new customers a refundable security deposit; others may charge a one-time nonrefundable fee.

Group Financial Decisions

As mentioned earlier in the chapter, you may decide to live with a roommate (or roommates) to share expenses. All roommates are responsible for meeting the obligations to which they agree. For example, each person must pay their share of the rent so that the total rent is paid on time. You should share utilities equally, as well as other expenses. But expenses such as cleaning supplies or groceries might be divided according to the use percentage. Laundry services usually are an individual expense.

Figure 10.2   Group Budget

Expense	Monthly Cost	Robert's Share	Carlos's Share	Ken's Share
Rent	$1,200	$400	$400	$400
Utilities (average)	300	100	100	100
Internet access	105	35	35	35
Gasoline	120	40	40	40
Groceries	600	200	200	200
Household supplies	90	30	30	30
Totals	$2,415	$805	$805	$805

Group budgeting allows for the careful allocation of expenses so that each person pays their share. The budget should be prepared and put into writing following a detailed discussion. **Figure 10.2** is an example of a group budget.

Part of the discussion will be to determine who is responsible for paying specific bills. It may be a good idea for one person to be responsible for paying the bills each month, and the roommates can use a cash transfer app to send the appropriate amount of money to that person. Most apartment leasing companies and utility companies require online payment for rent and services.

✓ Checkpoint

What are the key considerations in planning a move?

Check Your Understanding

1. Describe several housing options available to you after high school. (LO 10.1.1)
2. What questions should you and your potential roommate ask each other before deciding to live together? (LO 10.1.2)
3. What is a household needs inventory and why is it important? (LO 10.1.3)

Apply Your Understanding

1. If you were a first-year college student and had the choice of living on campus or off campus, which would you choose? Why? (LO 10.1.1)
2. If you plan to live in an apartment with multiple roommates, how would you handle the financial arrangements with the group? Why? (LO 10.1.2)
3. Use the problem-solving method you learned earlier. Create a plan to have a successful move within the next year. (LO 10.1.3)

The Essential Question

What are your housing choices, and what is involved in moving to your new home?

A: Housing choices include on-campus and off-campus options for students, apartments, townhouses, duplexes or multi-family units, condominiums, and houses. Moving involves deciding on living arrangements, paying deposits, meeting housing needs, and planning the move itself.

10.2 The Renting Process

The Essential Question When renting a place to live, what factors must be considered?

Learning Objectives

By the end of this lesson, you should be able to:

LO 10.2.1 List the advantages and disadvantages of renting.

LO 10.2.2 Describe the elements of the rental application, rental inventory, and lease forms.

LO 10.2.3 Discuss landlord and tenant responsibilities.

Key Terms

- renting
- landlord
- tenant
- lease
- lessor
- lessee
- rental agreement
- rental inventory
- eviction
- grace period

LO 10.2.1 Renting a Place to Live

Most people begin their independent lives as renters. **Renting** is the process of using another person's property for a fee. A **landlord** is the rental property's owner, or owner's representative. A person who rents property is called a **tenant** or renter.

Renting is a popular choice among young people who are just starting to live independently. There are numerous benefits to renting, but there are also some downsides. As with anything, it is important to weigh the pros and cons of renting an apartment, duplex, condo, or house before doing so. The more you know about the process, the better prepared you will be.

Advantages of Renting

Renting has several advantages over other forms of living choices.

1. Flexibility. If you have a short-term or month-to-month lease, you can move if you need to once your lease is up. If you are unsure whether you will stay in the same location for a long time, renting a residence is a wise choice.
2. Lower cost. Renting is usually cheaper than the cost of buying a house. Sharing expenses with roommates lowers individual costs even more.
3. Fewer responsibilities. Renting usually relieves you of many of the responsibilities of home ownership, such as costly repairs and maintenance.
4. Amenities. Many landlords provide several amenities for their tenants. For example, rental properties may have laundry, fitness, and recreational facilities.
5. Convenience. Rental units are often located near major shopping areas, public transportation, and area businesses.
6. Social life. Apartments offer the opportunity to meet others and socialize informally, especially where recreational facilities are provided.

How can neighbors make apartment living unpleasant?

Disadvantages of Renting

While there are many advantages to renting, there are also disadvantages.

1. Noise. Residents usually share common walls with neighbors above, below, and/or beside them. Consequently, neighbors' music, conversations, and other activities can be overheard. This can be irritating, especially if your neighbors keep unusual hours.
2. Lack of privacy. Because conversations and other activities can be overheard through common walls, tenants often feel a lack of privacy. Problems associated with shared facilities—laundry and recreation, for example—can also be annoying.
3. Small living and storage space. You will have a smaller living space unless you rent a house. The small size also means little cabinet and closet space. A few rental complexes offer additional storage space but may charge an extra fee for its use.
4. Scarcity of parking. Many rental properties need to provide garages or off-street parking. In complexes that do provide parking lots, parking is often limited. Parking spaces may also cost extra, especially when covered or reserved.
5. No tax benefits. While homeowners may receive a tax deduction, your monthly rent payment is not tax deductible; therefore, there are no tax benefits to you as a renter.

✓ **Checkpoint**

What are some advantages and disadvantages of renting?

LO 10.2.2 Rental Contracts

When you rent, you must fill out a rental application, typically online. The purpose of the application is to allow the landlord to verify your income, previous rental experience, and credit rating. The landlord does this to assure that you are a good risk—that you will likely pay your rent and be a good tenant. The landlord can refuse to rent you property or require you to have a cosigner because of your past rental history or lack of rental history, employment record, or credit rating. Rental may not be denied solely based on race, religion, national origin, sex, marital status, or having children. **Figure 10.3** shows a general rental agreement.

Figure 10.3   Rental Agreement

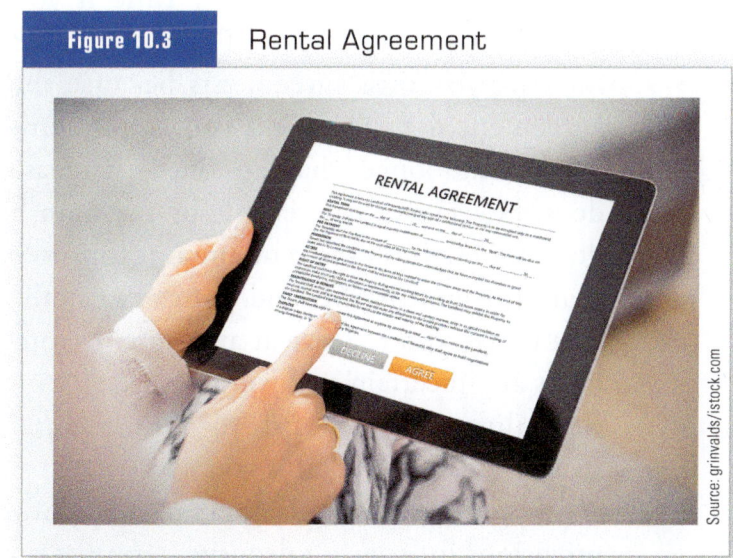

Leases and Month-to-Month Agreements

There are two types of rental contracts: leases and rental agreements. A **lease** is a written agreement that allows a tenant to use the property for a set period at a set rent payment. The landlord is called the **lessor**, or person responsible for the property. The tenant is called the **lessee**, or person who takes possession of the property. **Figure 10.4** is an example of a lease agreement.

You may sign a lease for 6 months, a year, or longer. During this time, rent remains constant. Before the lease expires, the landlord must inform you of any rent increases. If you do not wish to stay beyond the lease period, you can notify the landlord as specified. Often, leases require 30 days' written notice of rent increases and tenant departures. Most leases are completed online, using digital signatures. Make sure to carefully read the terms of the lease before signing. Once signed, you will want to print or save the lease and keep it in a safe place with your other important documents.

A **rental agreement**, also called a month-to-month agreement, is a written contract that allows you to leave any time if you give the required notice. These are called month-to-month agreements because the agreement does not bind you to pay rent for a period longer than a month, as a lease does. However, since renting by the month does not establish the rent amount for more than one month, the landlord can raise the rent or ask you to leave at any time. If your plans are uncertain and you need maximum flexibility, then a month-to-month rental may be a good option for you.

A lease and a rental agreement include provisions for security deposits, termination of rental, rent payments, tenant and landlord responsibilities, and various other matters. Both a lease and a month-to-month rental agreement are legally binding when signed. Therefore, ask the landlord to explain if you do not understand any part of the lease or rental agreement. If the answer is unsatisfactory and you still do not understand, do not sign the agreement until you have had a chance to meet with an attorney or trusted person to help you understand the terms of the lease.

Rental Inventory

When you move out of a rental property, it is expected to be in the same condition as when you moved in. Although normal wear and tear is expected and accepted, anything broken or damaged is unacceptable. To ensure that you are not accused of such acts as breaking, damaging, or taking furnishings, prepare an inventory of the premises when you move into the property.

The **rental inventory** is a detailed list of current property conditions. Noted are missing window screens, holes in walls, torn or stained carpeting, and broken items. **Figure 10.5** shows an inventory and condition report that can be used in various rental situations.

You and your landlord should tour the property together to take the inventory before you move into the apartment. Take pictures or videos of anything that could be considered damaged and note on the inventory that a picture was taken. Keep the images in a safe location. Once the inventory is complete, you and your landlord should sign it to indicate that you agree. Then you or the landlord should make a copy for each of you. When you move out, you and your landlord should take an

Figure 10.4 Lease Agreement

RESIDENTIAL LEASE AGREEMENT
AND SECURITY DEPOSIT RECEIPT

THIS INDENTURE, made this __29th__ day of _____ October _____ , 20 __-- __ , between

_____ Keisha Johnson _____ , hereinafter designated the Lessor

or Landlord, and _____ Alo Hernandez _____ , hereinafter designated the Lessee,

WITNESSETH: That the said Lessor/Landlord does by these presents lease and demise the residence

situated at __614 Dundas Street__ in _____ Cincinnati _____ City,

_____ Hamilton _____ County, _____ Ohio _____ State,

of which the real estate is described as follows:

614 Dundas Street, Cincinnati, Ohio,

upon the following terms and conditions:

1. **Term:** The premises are leased for a term of __one (1)__ year(s), commencing the __1st__ day of __November__ , 20 __--__ , and terminating the __31st__ day of __October__ , 20 __--__ .

2. **Rent:** The Lessee shall pay rent in the amount of $ _____ 1,200.00 _____ per month for the above premises on the __1st__ day of each month in advance to Landlord.

3. **Utilities:** Lessee shall pay for service and utilities supplied to the premises, except __None__ which will be furnished by Landlord.

4. **Sublet:** The Lessee agrees not to sublet said premises nor assign this agreement nor any part thereof without the prior written consent of Landlord.

5. **Inspection of Premises:** Lessee agrees that he has made inspection of the premises and accepts the condition of the premises in its present state, and that there are no repairs, changes, or modifications to said premises to be made by the Landlord other than as listed herein.

6. **Lessee Agrees:**
(1) To keep said premises in a clean and sanitary condition;
(2) To properly dispose of rubbish, garbage, and waste in a clean and sanitary manner at reasonable and regular intervals and to assume all costs of extermination and fumigation for infestation caused by Lessee;
(3) To properly use and operate all electrical, gas, heating, plumbing facilities, fixtures, and appliances;
(4) To not intentionally or negligently destroy, deface, damage, impair, or remove any part of the premises, their appurtenances, facilities, equipment, furniture, furnishings, and appliances, nor to permit any member of his family, invitee, licensee, or other person acting under his control to do so;
(5) Not to permit a nuisance or common waste.

7. **Maintenance of Premises:** Lessee agrees to mow and water the grass and lawn, and keep the grass, lawn, flowers, and shrubbery thereon in good order and condition, and to keep the sidewalk surrounding said premises free and clear of all obstructions; to replace in a neat and workmanlike manner all glass and doors broken during occupancy thereof; to use due precaution against freezing of water or waste pipes and stoppage of same in and about said premises and that in case water or waste pipes are frozen or become clogged by reason of neglect of Lessee, the Lessee shall repair the same at his own expense as well as all damage caused thereby.

8. **Alterations:** Lessee agrees not to make alterations or do or cause to be done any painting or wallpapering to said premises without the prior written consent of Landlord.

9. **Use of Premises:** Lessee shall not use said premises for any purpose other than that of a residence and shall not use said premises or any part thereof for any illegal purpose. Lessee agrees to conform to municipal, county and state codes, statutes, ordinances, and regulations concerning the use and occupation of said premises.

10. **Pets and Animals:** Lessee shall not maintain any pets or animals upon the premises without the prior written consent of Landlord.

11. **Access:** Landlord shall have the right to place and maintain "for rent" signs in a conspicuous place on said premises for thirty days prior to the vacation of said premises. Landlord reserves the right of access to the premises for the purpose of:
(a) Inspection;
(b) Repairs, alterations, or improvements;
(c) To supply services; or
(d) To exhibit or display the premises to prospective or actual purchasers, mortgagees, tenants, workmen, or contractors. Access shall be at reasonable times except in case of emergency or abandonment.

12. **Surrender of Premises:** In the event of default in payment of any installation of rent or at the expiration of said term of this lease, Lessee will quit and surrender the said premises to Landlord.

13. **Security Deposit:** The Lessee has deposited the sum of $ _____ 1,200.00 _____ , receipt of which is hereby acknowledged, which sum shall be deposited by Landlord in a trust account with __Citizens__ bank; savings and loan association, or licensed escrow, __Cincinnati__ branch, whose address is __201 Main Street, Cincinnati, Ohio__

All or a portion of such deposit may be retained by Landlord and a refund of any portion of such deposit is conditioned as follows:
(1) Lessee shall fully perform obligations hereunder and those pursuant to Chapter 207, Laws of 1973, 1st Ex Session or as may be subsequently amended.
(2) Lessee shall occupy said premises for __one (1)__ month(s) or longer from date hereof.
(3) Lessee shall clean and restore said residence and return the same to Landlord in its initial condition, except for reasonable wear and tear, upon the termination of this tenancy and vacation of apartment.
(4) Lessee shall have remedied or repaired any damage to apartment premises;
(5) Lessee shall surrender to Landlord the keys to premises;

Any refund from security deposit, as by itemized statement shown to be due to Lessee, shall be returned to Lessee within fourteen (14) days after termination of this tenancy and vacation of the premises.

IN WITNESS WHEREOF, the Lessee has hereunto set his hand and seal the day and year first above written.

__/s/ *Keisha Johnson*__   __/s/ *Alo Hernandez*__
LANDLORD   LESSEE
__614 Dundas Street__

__Cincinnati, Ohio__
ADDRESS

(Acknowledgment)

Figure 10.5 Rental Inventory

INVENTORY AND CONDITION REPORT

Use this report to record the contents and condition of your unit when you move in and before moving out. If you mark anything as being either dirty or damaged, describe it fully on an additional sheet. Use the blank before each item to indicate how many there are. Ask the landlord to sign your copy.

	Dirty Yes*	Dirty No	Damaged Yes*	Damaged No
Living Room				
___ Couch 1	☐	☐	☐	☐
___ Chair................. 2	☐	☐	☐	☐
___ End table 3	☐	☐	☐	☐
___ Easy chair 4	☐	☐	☐	☐
___ Floor lamp 5	☐	☐	☐	☐
___ Table lamp 6	☐	☐	☐	☐
___ Coffee table 7	☐	☐	☐	☐
___ Light fixture 8	☐	☐	☐	☐
___ Rug or carpet 9	☐	☐	☐	☐
___ Floor................ 10	☐	☐	☐	☐
___ Walls 11	☐	☐	☐	☐
___ Ceiling.............. 12	☐	☐	☐	☐
Bedroom (1)				
___ Bed frame(s) 13	☐	☐	☐	☐
___ Headboard(s) 14	☐	☐	☐	☐
___ Mattress 15	☐	☐	☐	☐
___ Mattress cover 16	☐	☐	☐	☐
___ Bedsprings 17	☐	☐	☐	☐
___ Dresser 18	☐	☐	☐	☐
___ Nightstand 19	☐	☐	☐	☐
___ Drapes or curtains .. 20	☐	☐	☐	☐
___ Mirror 21	☐	☐	☐	☐
___ Light fixture 22	☐	☐	☐	☐
___ Rug or carpet 23	☐	☐	☐	☐
___ Floor 24	☐	☐	☐	☐
___ Walls 25	☐	☐	☐	☐
___ Ceiling............. 26	☐	☐	☐	☐
Bedroom (2)				
___ Bed frame(s) 27	☐	☐	☐	☐
___ Headboard(s) 28	☐	☐	☐	☐
___ Mattress 29	☐	☐	☐	☐
___ Mattress cover 30	☐	☐	☐	☐
___ Bedsprings 31	☐	☐	☐	☐
___ Dresser 32	☐	☐	☐	☐
___ Nightstand 33	☐	☐	☐	☐
___ Drapes or curtains .. 34	☐	☐	☐	☐
___ Mirror 35	☐	☐	☐	☐
___ Light fixture 36	☐	☐	☐	☐
___ Rug or carpet 37	☐	☐	☐	☐
___ Floor 38	☐	☐	☐	☐
___ Walls 39	☐	☐	☐	☐
___ Ceiling............. 40	☐	☐	☐	☐
Kitchen				
___ Working stove 41	☐	☐	☐	☐
___ Working oven 42	☐	☐	☐	☐

	Dirty Yes*	Dirty No	Damaged Yes*	Damaged No
___ Oven racks 43	☐	☐	☐	☐
___ Broiler pan 44	☐	☐	☐	☐
___ Working refrigerator 45	☐	☐	☐	☐
___ Ice trays............... 46	☐	☐	☐	☐
___ Working sink 47	☐	☐	☐	☐
___ Working garbage disposal .. 48	☐	☐	☐	☐
___ Countertops 49	☐	☐	☐	☐
___ Range hood w/working fan .. 50	☐	☐	☐	☐
___ Working dishwasher 51	☐	☐	☐	☐
___ Hot and cold running water .. 52	☐	☐	☐	☐
___ Drawers 53	☐	☐	☐	☐
___ Dinette table 54	☐	☐	☐	☐
___ Dinette chairs 55	☐	☐	☐	☐
___ Light fixture 56	☐	☐	☐	☐
___ Floor 57	☐	☐	☐	☐
___ Walls 58	☐	☐	☐	☐
___ Ceiling 59	☐	☐	☐	☐
Bathroom				
___ Towel racks 60	☐	☐	☐	☐
___ Tissue holder 61	☐	☐	☐	☐
___ Mirror 62	☐	☐	☐	☐
___ Medicine cabinet 63	☐	☐	☐	☐
___ Countertop 64	☐	☐	☐	☐
___ Working sink 65	☐	☐	☐	☐
___ Working tub 66	☐	☐	☐	☐
___ Working shower 67	☐	☐	☐	☐
___ Working toilet 68	☐	☐	☐	☐
___ Toilet seat 69	☐	☐	☐	☐
___ Shower curtain 70	☐	☐	☐	☐
___ Cabinet 71	☐	☐	☐	☐
___ Light fixture 72	☐	☐	☐	☐
___ Hot and cold running water .. 73	☐	☐	☐	☐
___ Floor................... 74	☐	☐	☐	☐
___ Walls 75	☐	☐	☐	☐
___ Ceiling 76	☐	☐	☐	☐
Miscellaneous				
___ Door key 77	☐	☐	☐	☐
___ Windows 78	☐	☐	☐	☐
___ Window screens 79	☐	☐	☐	☐
___ Mailbox 80	☐	☐	☐	☐
___ Mailbox key 81	☐	☐	☐	☐
___ Thermostat 82	☐	☐	☐	☐
___ Other 83	☐	☐	☐	☐
___ 84	☐	☐	☐	☐

Do all the windows work?_____

Does the heat work properly? _____

_____
Tenant

_____
Witness

_____
Date

_____
Landlord

_____
Date

*Describe fully on an additional sheet.

inventory again. Comparing this inventory and the initial one will often determine if you get your security deposit back.

If your landlord does not do or require a rental inventory, it is advisable to do one anyway. Videotape or take photos of the property's conditions when you move in as supporting evidence. Make sure the videos and/or photos are date-stamped. Provide a copy of the inventory and any supporting evidence to the landlord, even if the landlord does not ask for it. Keep your copy of the rental inventory and supporting documents in a safe place to prevent damage.

✓ Checkpoint

Describe the elements of a rental application, inventory, and lease agreement.

LO 10.2.3 Landlord and Tenant Responsibilities

Most states have passed landlord–tenant laws detailing the legal rights and obligations of landlords and tenants. A successful landlord–tenant relationship depends heavily on landlords and tenants knowing and complying with these laws.

Landlord Obligations

Housing laws in most states require that landlords provide a dwelling that is always habitable and in living condition. A dwelling is considered habitable if:

- The exterior is weatherproof and waterproof. The exterior includes the roof, walls, doors, and windows.

- Floors, walls, ceilings, stairs, and railings are in good repair.
- Elevators, halls, stairwells, and exits meet fire and safety regulations. Smoke detectors are required in each unit in most states. Tenants may be responsible for testing the alarms, replacing batteries, and reporting any defects.
- Adequate locks are provided for all outside doors, and working latches are provided for all windows.
- Plumbing facilities comply with local and state sanitation laws and are in good working condition.
- The water supply provided is safe and adequate.
- Lighting, wiring, heating, air-conditioning, and appliances are in good condition and comply with local and state building and safety codes.
- Buildings and grounds are clean and sanitary; garbage receptacles are adequate.

Tenant Obligations

Tenants have numerous responsibilities not only to landlords but to other tenants. These obligations are usually stated specifically in the lease or rental agreement. Even when not stated, tenants should:

- Read, understand, and abide by the rental contract terms.
- Pay the rent on or before the due date. Failure to make a rent payment as stated in the rental contract may result in late fees, termination of the contract, or eviction. **Eviction** is the legal process of removing a tenant from rental property. If the eviction goes to court and the judge rules in favor of the landlord, it will be reported to credit bureaus. This reflects poorly on the tenant's credit score and makes it difficult for the tenant to rent property in the future. Some landlords offer a grace period. The **grace period** is specified in the lease and allows 3 to 7 days before late fees are applied.

Many owners of rental property would rather lease space to you for a year or more rather than renting it to you on a short-term lease (typically three or six months) or on a month-to-month basis. A lease gives both the lessor (the landlord) and the lessee (the tenant) the security of knowing the property is committed for a fixed period. But a lease can be a trap if you do not understand everything included in the lease before you sign.

For example, many lessors offer "specials" to those who sign leases for a year or more. These specials may include reduced monthly rent, reduced deposits and fees, and other concessions. But in most cases, if you need to terminate the lease before the agreed-upon time, there can be large financial penalties.

A typical lease is for one year. By signing a one-year lease, you typically save money in comparison to a short-term lease or month-to-month rental. For example, a month-to-month rental may cost $1,300. If the lessee signs a one-year lease, the rent is reduced to $1,200. Other "special" lease offers for signing a one-year lease of longer may include reduced fees and deposits. The savings can be significant. But the lease also states that if the lessee terminates the agreement prior to one year, they must repay the entire rent reduction and a fee of $350.

Suppose you are the lessee, and you must move out early, say at the beginning of the 8th month. If your lease agreement prohibits subleasing, which allows you to find another tenant to take over the rest of your lease, you would have to pay back 7 months' worth of reduced rent ($100 × 7) plus the additional $350 fee, for a total of $1,050. In addition, you are still obligated to pay the remaining 5 months' rent (at the regular rate of $1,200) until the lessor can find another tenant to take your place. While the lessor must make every "reasonable" effort to re-rent your place, they have no incentive to try to lease yours first if there are other units available. Therefore, these "special" deals can be very expensive.

Before you sign the lease, be sure to read it carefully and understand your commitments. You may be able to negotiate better terms before you sign.

Think Critically

1. What are the potential advantages and disadvantages of signing a longer-term lease?

2. Are certain age groups or people at specific stages in life more likely to be interested in a longer-term lease? Explain.

3. What recommendations would you have for a young adult looking to sign their first lease?

- Give at least 30 days written notice of intent to move. This notice will prevent the loss of the security deposit and allow the landlord time to find another renter before you leave.
- Keep the premises clean to prevent unnecessary wear and tear or damage to the unit.
- Use a rental unit only for the purpose for which it is intended. For example, if the tenant plans to rent a place to use for a business, the tenant must discuss that with the landlord.
- Allow the landlord access to the living unit to make repairs or improvements.
- Obey the rules specified in the rental contract for the residents of the rental community, covering such things as quiet hours, use of recreational facilities, use of laundry facilities, and parking regulations.
- Maintain renters insurance for personal contents and liability if it is required in the lease.

> **✓ Checkpoint**
>
> What are a tenant's obligations when renting property? What are the landlord's obligations to the tenant?

10.2 **Lesson** Review

Check Your Understanding

1. Why do some people prefer to rent instead of buying a home? Describe the advantages of being a renter. (LO 10.2.1)

2. What is the purpose of a rental inventory? (LO 10.2.2)

3. What obligations does a landlord have to their tenants? (LO 10.2.3)

Apply Your Understanding

1. Review the disadvantages of renting. Using the problem-solving method learned in a previous chapter, how would you attempt to solve three of these disadvantages? (LO 10.2.1)

2. Review the rental lease example in Figure 10.4. List five things that are in the lease agreement that are important to you as the lessor. What is the impact of violating these things? (LO 10.2.2)

3. What should you do if the landlord is not providing a secure place to live? (LO 10.2.3)

The Essential Question

When renting a place to live, what factors must be considered?

A: Factors to consider include the advantages and disadvantages of renting, the rental application process, the type of rental contract desired, and the obligations of both the landlord and tenant.

The Essential Question

What are the advantages, costs, responsibilities, and processes involved with buying and owning a home?

Learning Objectives

By the end of this lesson, you should be able to:

LO 10.3.1   Discuss the advantages of home ownership.

LO 10.3.2   Describe the costs and responsibilities of buying and owning a home.

LO 10.3.3   Outline the steps in the home-buying process.

Key Terms

- market value
- appraised value
- assessed value
- equity
- mortgage
- escrow account
- loan origination fee
- conventional loan
- FHA loan
- closing costs
- covenants, conditions, and restrictions (CC&Rs)
- prequalify
- preapproval
- offer
- earnest money
- contingencies
- inspection report
- seller's acceptance
- seller's counteroffer
- escrow closer
- title
- title insurance
- deed

Consider This ...

During college, Anisa began dating Omar. Anisa and Omar graduated college and have been married for 5 years. They have been saving money with the goal of buying their own home.

"I think we have enough money saved to put a down payment on a four-bedroom home, though we really only need two bedrooms right now," stated Omar.

"I'm not sure we have as large of a down payment as you think," Anisa replied. "We'll have to pay other costs as well, such as closing costs and moving expenses."

"Okay," Omar agreed. "Let's start out with a smaller house that meets our needs now and has potential for improvement. We can sell and move to another house when we start our family. By then, we'll have built up some equity. Now how do we go about finding the right home?"

(continues)

(continued)

Read and Reflect

1. What factors will impact the amount of equity Anisa and Omar build up in a home?
2. Besides mortgage payments, what costs should Anisa and Omar consider?
3. What is the process of buying a home?

LO 10.3.1 Advantages of Home Ownership

There are many advantages to owning your own home. Homeownership builds equity, increases your quality of life, and may help you save on your income taxes. However, purchasing a home requires a large up-front investment, a commitment to stay on one place for a longer time, maintenance and up-keep on the home, and a potential decrease in home value.

Value and Equity

There are four valuation methods commonly used in real estate:

1. Market value. The **market value** of a home is the highest price the property will bring on the market. It means what a ready and willing buyer and seller would agree upon as the price.
2. Appraised value. Real estate appraisers can prepare an **appraised value** by comparing the house to similar homes in the same geographic area. The recent selling price of a similar home in your area is a good estimate of the current value of your home.
3. Assessed value. To compute property taxes owed against your home, the city or county in which you live annually sets an **assessed value**. The assessed value is based on the cost and quality of the construction, the cost of improvements, and

the cost of comparable properties. It is usually a percentage of the market value. Rather than visual inspection, computer programs are often used to determine assessed value.

4. Estimated value. Real estate agents also estimate the value of homes to help sellers establish a list price. To do this, they evaluate your house to comparable properties, called comps, recently sold in a close geographic area. Using these comps gives a general idea of a property's value and establishes a point to begin negotiations.

The value of most homes appreciates or increases in market value over time. For example, if you buy a home for $150,000 and 2 years later you can sell it for $160,000, then your property has appreciated by $10,000. Appreciation is one way that the equity in your home increases. **Equity** is the difference between the market value of the property and the amount owed.

Equity also increases because each loan payment you make decreases your debt. Equity turns to cash when you sell your home. For example, if you purchase a home valued at $150,000 and have a loan of $120,000, your initial equity is $30,000. Suppose that when you decide to sell, the market value has increased to $170,000, and your loan debt is down to $100,000. Your equity would be $70,000 (the $170,000 market value minus the $100,000 owed).

What kinds of quality-of-life advantages do homeowners enjoy?

Quality of Life

Owning a home offers many benefits that enhance a person's quality of life. Homeowners usually have more privacy and larger living and storage space than renters. Homeowners also have more personal freedom. In your own home, you can redecorate or remodel to accommodate your needs and personal style. Knowing that the home is yours to do with as you wish can be very satisfying. Owning a home may also provide security, stability, and independence. You may also get a sense of belonging by becoming part of a neighborhood.

Although neighborhood living involves responsibilities to surrounding neighbors, the homeowner can have a voice in helping to set the tone of the neighborhood. Neighborhood associations are homeowners in geographic areas that voluntarily meet and work to set quality-of-life standards for the area. Some neighborhoods have homeowner associations that are legal entities; they make rules for living in the area to protect home values. Similar to condominium owner associations described earlier in the chapter, homeowner associations, known as HOAs, may charge a fee to pay for common areas in the neighborhood such as a park, walking path, lake, or playground.

Tax Savings

Tax savings may result when deducting money paid for certain expenses from your tax liability. Renters cannot deduct any part of their rent payments from their income taxes. However, the interest you pay on your home loan and the property taxes you pay may be tax deductible, if the taxpayer itemizes deductions. If the homeowner qualifies for these tax deductions, the cost of home-ownership may be lowered.

Even though the equity in your home may increase each year, you pay tax on the equity only once you sell your home if the profit you make when selling exceeds $250,000 for a single person or $500,000 for a married couple who files a joint annual income tax return.

✓ Checkpoint

What are the advantages of home ownership?

LO 10.3.2 Costs and Responsibilities of Home Ownership

Home ownership carries significant costs and responsibilities. Before deciding to buy a home, you should ensure that you are financially able to handle the costs and are personally ready to accept the responsibilities.

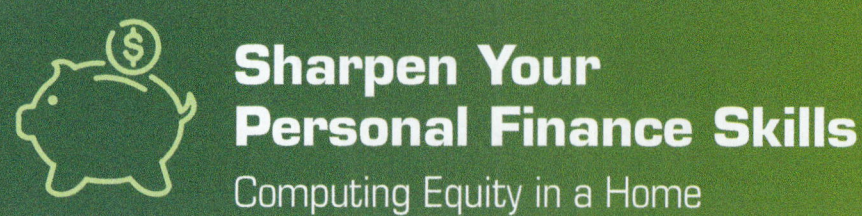

Sharpen Your Personal Finance Skills

Computing Equity in a Home

Suppose you bought a home for $200,000. Your lender required a 20 percent down payment. Therefore, your down payment was:

$$\$200,000 \times 0.20 = \$40,000$$

Your initial loan amount (not including other costs) was:

$$\$200,000 - \$40,000 = \$160,000$$

Now let's say that you have been making payments on your house for 2 years, reducing your debt (principal) by $8,000. Therefore, you now owe:

$$\$160,000 - \$8,000 = \$152,000$$

Your house has been appreciating at 5 percent per year for 2 years. As a result, the current market value is:

$$\$200,000 \times 1.05 = \$210,000 \text{ after year 1}$$
$$\$210,000 \times 1.05 = \$220,500 \text{ after year 2}$$

Your equity is now:

$$\$220,500 \text{ market value} - \$152,000 \text{ remaining debt} = \$68,500$$

Try It Out!

Anisa and Omar bought a house 2 years ago for $175,000. They put 15 percent down. Their payments have reduced their debt by $6,000. Houses in their area have been appreciating at 4 percent per year.

Based on the information above, compute the amount for Anisa and Omar's:

- Down payment
- Initial loan amount
- Current debt
- Current market value
- Current equity

Mortgage Payments

A **mortgage** is a loan to purchase real estate. Mortgages are long-term loans of 10–30 years.

Monthly loan payments include principal and interest. Most mortgages require an escrow account. An **escrow account** is used to collect property taxes and insurance on the home. The financial institution will collect 1/12 of the insurance premium and property taxes each month as part of the mortgage payment to pay the taxes and insurance that are due during the year. For example, if your property taxes are estimated to be $2,400 a year, an additional $200 a month will be added to your loan payment.

When buying a house, borrowers may have the option to purchase points to lower the mortgage interest rate. Typically, one point equals 1 percent of the loan amount. For example, three points on a $100,000 loan would be $3,000.

Although points increase closing costs, they reduce the amount of interest paid of the term of the loan. Each point typically reduces the interest rate by 0.25%. So, if three points were purchased, it would likely reduce the interest rate on the loan by 0.75%. When you compare loan rates, be sure to consider the points. Points paid may be tax deductible.

A **loan origination fee** also called a mortgage loan fee, is the amount a bank or other lender charges to process the loan papers. This fee compensates the loan officer or broker for the time spent qualifying buyers, preparing paperwork, and working with loan underwriters.

Down Payment

Mortgage lenders usually require that borrowers pay a certain amount of money as a down payment toward the purchase price of a house which will lower the total amount of the mortgage loan. A **conventional loan** is a mortgage agreement that does not have government backing and is offered through a commercial bank or mortgage broker. This type of loan often requires a 10 to 30 percent down payment. For example, if you purchase a home for $150,000, you will need $15,000 to $45,000 for the down payment. The typical down payment is 20 percent. To qualify for a conventional loan, a borrower must have a good credit score, and their monthly mortgage payment and debt load must fall within certain percentages related to gross monthly income, typically less the 30 percent of net income.

Those who do not qualify for a conventional loan may be able to obtain a loan through the Federal Housing

Sharpen Your Personal Finance Skills
Mortgage Points

When Anisa and Omar purchased their home for $175,000, their interest rate for their loan was 6%. They had the option to purchase points to lower the interest rate. If they purchased three points, what would the additional closing cost be for the purchase of the points?

Authority (FHA). An **FHA loan** is a government-sponsored loan that carries mortgage insurance. In other words, borrowers may pay a monthly insurance premium, and their loan payments are guaranteed through the FHA insurance program, making it less risky for banks to lend the money. FHA loans may require down payments of as little as 3.5 percent. FHA loans are often available for first-time homebuyers and low-income buyers.

A few types of loans may not require a down payment. Military veterans may qualify for a loan backed by the Veteran's Administration (VA). A Rural Development loan is another government-backed loan available through the United States Department of Agriculture (USDA). To qualify, houses must be in an eligible rural area as defined by the USDA.

Closing Costs

Closing costs are the expenses incurred in transferring ownership from buyer to seller in a real estate transaction. The buyer usually pays several fees:

- Credit report fee. Credit bureaus charge a fee to provide a credit report on the potential borrower. The mortgage company or bank adds this fee to the closing costs.
- Title search fee. A title search verifies the seller is the legal owner and that no one else has a claim on the property.
- Loan origination fee. This fee is to cover the cost of preparing and processing the loan paperwork.
- Loan assumption fee. A fee that the buyer pays if the seller still has a mortgage on the property.
- Closing fee. The closing fee is charged for preparing the paperwork to transfer ownership from the seller to the buyer.

- Recording fee. The city, county, and state may charge a fee to transfer the deed from the seller to the buyer. This fee is added into the closing costs.
- Prorate taxes. The annual taxes for the property are split between the current owner and the new owner, with each paying for the amount of time in the year they will own the property.
- Current interest. The buyer will need to pay the interest that accrues on the property between the sale date and the date of the first mortgage payment.
- Points, if applicable, are also part of the closing costs.

Typically, homebuyers pay between two and five percent of the purchase price of their home in closing costs. For example, paying $150,000 for a house will require closing costs between $3,000 and $7,500. Truth-in-Lending laws require lenders to provide a good faith estimate of what the closing costs on your home will be within three days of when you apply for a loan.

Property Taxes

Homeowners pay real estate property taxes based on the assessed value of land and buildings. A local taxing authority determines the assessed value of property, usually a percentage of the market value. For example, a home worth $200,000 might have an assessed value of $180,000 (or 90 percent of its market value). If the property tax rate is $15 per thousand of assessed value, you will pay $2,700 (180 × $15) in property taxes per year. Property taxes may be tax deductible.

Property Insurance

A homeowner must have property insurance covering the structure. This is usually a requirement of the loan agreement to protect the interests of the mortgage lender and the homeowner. Standard homeowners insurance includes both fire and liability protection. A more detailed explanation of homeowners insurance is in a future chapter.

Utilities

Because most homes are larger than apartments or other rental units, the utility bills are typically higher. The homeowner pays for all utilities and garbage services. In contrast, a renter may pay for some but not all these services. Utilities may include water and sewer charges, storm drain assessments, gas, electricity, and public safety fees.

CC&Rs and Zoning Laws

Many housing subdivisions are governed by homeowners' associations (HOAs) that set **covenants, conditions, and restrictions (CC&Rs)**, which are rules designed to maintain property values and protect the interests of all property owners. Most HOAs charge an annual fee to pay expenses of the common areas of the housing subdivision. CC&Rs include things such as maintaining your lawn, limiting the color(s) you can paint your house, specifying where vehicles can be parked, controlling the kinds of fences or storage buildings that can be built, specifying the type of roof that can be installed, along with other items that the homeowners agree upon. When purchasing a home located within an HOA, it is important to understand the CC&R rules and costs before purchasing the home and what fees may be required. The CC&Rs are a legal contract.

Homeowners must obey all zoning laws and local ordinances. These are laws passed by local governments to preserve the quality of life for all people in the community. They require

As a potential homebuyer, what kinds of CC&Rs and zoning laws might you encounter?

Source: valentinrussanov/istock.com

you to obtain a building permit when you add to or modify your home and adhere to rules regarding the kinds and types of buildings that can be constructed in the area. In addition, you must follow setback requirements that force buildings and improvements to be set back a minimum number of feet from streets and other properties.

Maintenance and Repairs

As a homeowner, you will be responsible for maintenance and repairs inside and outside of your home. Ongoing maintenance includes painting, mowing, weeding, landscaping, and fixing things that break or wear out from normal use. You are responsible for these tasks or arranging to have them done.

In addition to ongoing maintenance, you will occasionally have to make expensive repairs or improvements to your home. These can range from replacing your roof to removing a dead tree from your yard or replacing a major appliance, such as the furnace or water heater. Before you choose to buy, make sure you are willing to spend the time and money needed to keep your home in good condition. This will prolong the life of your home.

LO 10.3.3 ## The Home-Buying Process

When buying a home, factors to consider include location, accessibility, nearness to employment, type and quality of construction, cost and effort of maintenance, and personal likes and dislikes. Before starting your search, determine the price range you can afford. It is also a good idea to list the features you want your home and neighborhood to have and then prioritize the list according to what features are most important to you.

You can look for a new home by yourself or use the services of a real estate agent. If you choose to do your own search, there are many places you can look. You can find homes for sale listed on multiple websites, like Realtor.com or Zillow.com. All these sites contain photos and list the features of each home, and you can often take a virtual video tour of the house.

Working with a Real Estate Agent

It may be in your best interest to work with a real estate agent. Real estate agents function as an intermediary between sellers and buyers of real estate. They earn commission income. The commission is a percentage of the home sale price, usually between five and eight percent. The seller pays the commission, and the agents working for the buyer and seller split it. As the purchaser, you do not pay the agents' commission. If you buy directly from an owner without the assistance of an agent, you might be able to negotiate a lower price because the seller will not have to pay this fee. You should still seek advice from a professional, such as a lawyer or title company, to protect your interests before signing any contracts.

There are many advantages to working with a real estate agent. Agents know the market and can use their knowledge and expertise to help find the right home for you. They will also assist you with the purchasing, financing, inspection, and closing processes. Agents help protect your interests in a complex, sometimes confusing, marketplace. Having an agent also gives you access to multiple listings. The Multiple Listing Service (MLS) is a real estate marketing service in which agents from multiple real estate agencies pool their home listings and agree to share commissions on the sales. Sellers gain wide exposure for their properties. Buyers can sift through the large pool of property descriptions to select those they want to visit.

Source: monkeybusinessimages/istock.com

Why is it a good idea to work with a real estate agent when buying your first home?

One of the first things an agent will have you do is go to a mortgage lender and prequalify for a real estate loan. To **prequalify** you will fill out an application asking about your job, income, and monthly debts to help determine how much money you are qualified to borrow. This will guide you and your real estate agent to look for houses in your price range. Prequalification is the first step toward buying a home and is based on consumer submitted data. Prequalification is intended to give you an idea of the mortgage amount you will likely qualify for. Most prequalification applications are free and do not include a credit history report.

After you have been prequalified for your loan and have narrowed your choices of homes in your price range that match your criteria, you should visit the homes with your agent. Take notes, both pro and con, on the features of each house and neighborhood. Do not decide on the spot. After you have made a careful comparison and are certain you have made your best choice, take the next step: obtain preapproval for a mortgage and make an offer.

Preapproval and Making an Offer

Preapproval speeds up the buying process and can begin as soon as you find a home you like and can afford. The buyer completes the mortgage application and provides the documentation required to perform an extensive credit and financial background check. The preapproval process will help the borrower know specific loan details like the interest rate to be charged, the amount of down payment required, and the maximum loan amount.

While going through the preapproval process, you can let the homeowner know of your interest in buying the home and the price you are willing to pay, by signing an agreement called an offer. An **offer** is a serious intent to be bound to an agreement. In real estate, when you make an offer to buy property the offer is accompanied by a deposit called **earnest money**. For example, in an offer to buy a house selling for $200,000, the earnest money deposit could be $2,000 or more. The amount of the earnest money deposit is usually 1 percent of the offer. The money is held in an escrow account until the transaction is completed.

Earnest money protects the seller if you fail to meet the terms of the agreement. If you and the seller have agreed on the transaction, the seller will take the house off the market. During that time, the house cannot be sold to anyone else. If you later back out of the deal, you will forfeit your earnest money to the seller.

One way to avoid losing your earnest money is to include contingencies in your offer. **Contingencies** are conditions that limit a buyer's liability in case one or more of the conditions are not met. For example, you can make your offer contingent on obtaining financing. That way, if you do not qualify for a mortgage on the property, you will not have violated the contract and will get your earnest money back. Another contingency may be dependent on the property passing an inspection. During a home inspection, an independent, certified, licensed inspector checks every surface in the house from the roof to the basement, including appliances, windows, doors, flooring, and subflooring, electrical, plumbing, and wall safety. The inspector should look for leaks, substandard materials, dry rot, mold, insect damage, and any other issues that may impact the house's value. The inspector then prepares a written **inspection report**, which details the existing conditions of the house and property. If the inspection report brings any problems to light, you can negotiate with the seller on how any necessary repairs will be completed and who will pay for them. If the seller refuses to negotiate, you can withdraw the deal and keep your earnest money.

The seller may or may not accept your initial offer. When the seller agrees to your offer exactly as stated, you have acceptance. A **seller's acceptance** is a formal agreement to the terms of the buyer's offer, forming a contract between the parties. You may withdraw your offer before the seller accepts it; however, the offer becomes a binding contract once accepted.

If the seller wants to change any part of the offer, they make a counteroffer. A **seller's counteroffer** rejects the original offer with a listing of what terms would be acceptable. In effect, it is a new offer the seller makes to the buyer. For example, if you offered to buy a house at a lower price than the seller was willing to accept, the seller may make a counteroffer with a higher price. The buyer and seller negotiate until they either agree on mutually acceptable terms or decide not to complete the transaction.

Financing Your Home Purchase

After you have agreed with the seller, you will have to arrange for your loan. To finance your purchase, you must have funds for a down payment, meet certain lending

Connections to Your World
Planning for a Home

When looking to purchase a home, there are a lot of things to consider. It is never too early to begin thinking about your ideal home and setting goals to work toward obtaining it. One key consideration when planning and budgeting for your ideal home is location. The cost of homes with similar features and square footage can be very different depending on where they are located. For example, a $300,000 home in the Midwest may cost over $1 million in California or New York.

Create a list outlining the features you would desire in your ideal house. Be sure to include number of bedrooms, bathrooms, square footage, type or style, and other features you would like. Then, go online to find house listings that meet these requirements in different parts of the country. Copy links to house listings from at least three different locations. Based on your research, have a discussion with a classmate about your ideal house and your findings when exploring houses. Explain how housing prices of your ideal home varies in different parts of the country.

institution requirements, and select the type of mortgage you want. This process is faster if you have been preapproved for a mortgage.

Down Payment Sources

There are various sources available for your down payment. Personal savings is often the first source. Because the down payment can be expensive and many first-time homebuyers need more money in savings to cover it, some buyers receive help from their parents or other family members in the form of a monetary gift. If any of your down payment is part of a gift, your lender will require the donor to submit a gift letter. This letter will state the loan applicant's relationship to the donor and the gift amount. Most importantly, since many lending institutions will not allow mortgage applicants to borrow their down payment formally, the donor will have to state that the gift fund is indeed a gift and not a loan.

If you do not have the necessary funds for a down payment from your savings account or family, your retirement account is another option. First-time homebuyers can withdraw up to $10,000 to purchase a home from an individual retirement account (IRA) without paying the 10 percent early withdrawal penalty.

Qualifying for a Mortgage

To qualify for a mortgage, you must complete an extensive loan application. The lender will check your credit history, employment history, and references. The lender will also look at the type and amount of your current debts, the amount and source of your income, and your creditworthiness. Based on this information, the lender will judge if you can afford the monthly mortgage

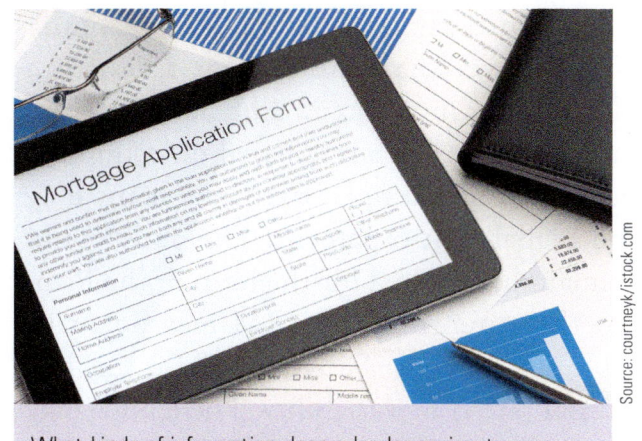

What kinds of information does a lender review to determine whether you qualify for a mortgage?

payments which should not exceed 25 to 35 percent of your take-home (net) pay. The lender will also require a real estate appraisal by a certified real estate appraiser. This is to assure the lender that the property is worth more than the loan amount. If the appraisal comes back less than the offer on the house, the lender will only loan an amount equal to the appraised value.

The lender collaborates with an underwriter, which secures the funding for the loan. The underwriter typically evaluates the same factors as the lender but may have additional qualifications that must be met.

Types of Mortgage Loans

There are two basic types of mortgages: fixed-rate mortgages and adjustable-rate mortgages. A fixed-rate mortgage is a mortgage on which the interest rate does not change during the loan term. Your monthly payments and the total amount of interest paid on the loan remain constant throughout the loan. An adjustable-rate mortgage (ARM) is a mortgage whose interest rate changes in response to the movement of interest rates in the economy.

The interest rate for an ARM usually starts lower than the current rates for a fixed-rate mortgage. The lender then adjusts the ARM's rate based on economic activity. For example, fixed-rate loans may be available at 6 percent. This rate would remain unchanged for the term of the loan. At the same time, an ARM may be available at 4 percent. The trade-off for this low initial rate is its variability. The lender may raise the rate over time to 7 or 8 percent as interest rates increase. Most ARMs specify maximum rate increases per year and a maximum ceiling interest rate. Read the mortgage contact carefully to ensure you understand the terms and conditions of any mortgage.

Taking Title to Property

After you and the seller have reached an agreement and you have arranged your financing, the next step is to prepare for the closing. During the closing process, you will work with an escrow closer. An **escrow closer** is an independent person who gathers and verifies information, prepares the closing statement of what the buyer owes and the credits that have been applied. The escrow closer will also make sure that title of the property passes to the buyer. The **title** is proof of your ownership.

Before you take ownership, you will want to ensure that the title is clear—that is, free of any liens. A lien is a financial claim against the property. For example, if the previous owner used the home as collateral for a loan other than the mortgage, then that lender has a financial claim or lien on the property. This claim must be paid before ownership of the property can be transferred.

What does an escrow closer do during the closing process?

To ensure that a property has a clear title, the escrow closer orders a title search. A title search is searching public records to check for ownership and claims to a piece of property. When the title insurance company confirms that the title is clear, it will issue title insurance. **Title insurance** protects the buyer from any claims arising from a defective title. Most lenders also require title insurance to protect the lender's interests. Buyers and sellers often negotiate who will pay the title insurance fees.

Before the closing, the lending institution prepares the loan papers and sends them to the escrow closer. The escrow closer will then prepare the closing statement and schedule a closing date. Before the closing date, you should make a final walk-through of the property to ensure that the seller has completed all of the requested repairs and that the property has yet to have any changes since you signed the sales agreement. Also, ensure that any items included in the sales agreement are present and in satisfactory condition and that all items

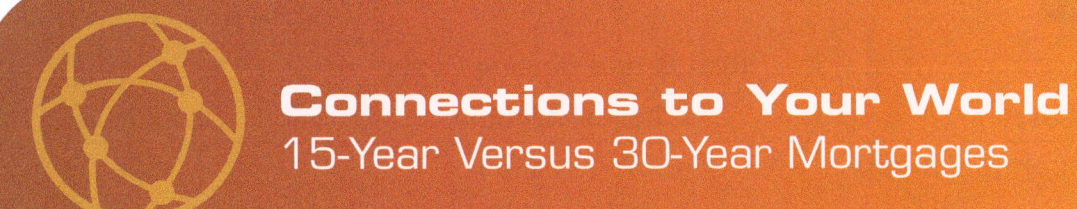

Connections to Your World
15-Year Versus 30-Year Mortgages

Lenders typically offer mortgages that run for a term of 15 years or 30 years. Before choosing a loan term, consider the differences. A 15-year mortgage has significant advantages:

- Because the loan term is shorter, lenders consider a 15-year mortgage less risky. Thus, 15-year loans have lower interest rates than 30-year loans. For example, if a 30-year fixed-rate mortgage has a rate of 6.375 percent, you could likely get a 15-year fixed-rate mortgage for 5 percent or less. Thus, you will pay much less total interest over the life of the loan.
- You will pay off a 15-year mortgage in half the time of a 30-year mortgage, enabling you to build equity at a much faster rate and enjoy the payment-free status sooner.

A 15-year mortgage also has disadvantages that make a 30-year loan more attractive to many homebuyers:

- Because the loan will be paid off in 15 years rather than 30, the monthly payments will be significantly higher. Many homebuyers do not earn enough income to qualify for a 15-year loan because of the payment size.
- The 15-year loan payment may put a strain on your budget, even though you are paying off the house at a faster rate. The payment may take such a large percentage of your paycheck that you would not have enough left over to live comfortably. Some people prefer to get a 30-year loan with a lower monthly payment and then pay off the loan earlier by making extra payments toward the principal. Because the extra payments are optional, there is less strain on the budget.

Whether to get a 15-year or 30-year mortgage is an important decision for homebuyers because your choice will affect your budget in a major way. Things to take into consideration include your age, current financial situation, and long-term financial goals.

Think Critically

1. Which mortgage term (15 or 30 years) sounds better to you? Does your age impact your decision?
2. Would your choice of mortgage be different in 10 years? 15 years? 20 years? Explain.

Figure 10.6   Typical Closing Costs

Real Estate Closing Costs

Type of Cost	Typical Amount	Who Pays
Credit report (on buyer)	$50 to $100	Buyer
Property appraisal fee	$350 to $500	Buyer
Pest/damage inspection	$250 to $500	Buyer
Electrical/plumbing/ water inspection report	$250 to $500	Buyer
Loan origination fee	Varies; often 1% of loan amount	Buyer
Points	Varies; often 1% of loan amount	Buyer
Loan assumption fee	Varies; often $500 to $1,500	Buyer
Escrow closing fee	Depends on selling price of property; usually $750 to $1,500	Buyer and Seller
Notary and filing fees	$50 to $150	Buyer and Seller
Title search and title insurance	Depends on selling price of property; usually $750 to $2,000	Buyer and Seller
Survey	$500 to $1,500	Seller
Home warranty (optional)	Depends on selling price of property; usually $300 to $1,000	Seller
Real estate commission	Percentage of sales price of home; usually between 6% and 8%	Seller
Attorney's fees	Varies; depends on services provided, such as preparing contract	Buyer and Seller
Prorated interest and taxes	Depends on date of possession and when title passes	Buyer and Seller
Transfer taxes and fees	Varies by state	Seller

excluded in the sales agreement have been removed from the property.

If the final walk-through does not present any issues, then you and the seller will meet at the closing location to sign the papers and pay all related closing costs, such as those shown in **Figure 10.6**. If you have a real estate agent, the agent will attend the meeting and help you through the process. Once the closing costs are paid, the seller receives their money, and the **deed** to transfer ownership is recorded.

✓ **Checkpoint**

Summarize the steps in the home-buying process.

Check Your Knowledge

1. Why do some people choose to buy a house rather than rent a residence? (LO 10.3.1)

2. What costs come with home ownership? (LO 10.3.2)

3. What is the difference between a fixed-rate mortgage and an adjustable-rate mortgage (ARM)? (LO 10.3.3)

4. What responsibilities do sellers have before the closing? (LO 10.3.3)

Apply Your Knowledge

1. If you were trying to decide how much a home was worth for the purpose of making an offer to purchase it, what types of value would you consider? Which valuation method is the best? Why? (LO 10.3.1)

2. Anisa is excited to buy her first home. She knows that her budget will be tight but will make it work. When she shares her list of houses to view and her budget with Nadia, Nadia notices that Anisa has not budgeted for property insurance or property taxes. What should Nadia tell Anisa about the importance of understanding the cost of homeowners property insurance and property taxes when considering purchasing a home? (LO 10.3.2)

3. If you were in the market for a new home, would you look by yourself or use a real estate agent to help you through the process? Explain. (LO 10.3.3)

The Essential Question

What are the advantages, costs, responsibilities, and processes involved with buying and owning a home?

A: Buying a home offers many advantages, such as tax savings, privacy, freedom, and quality of life. Costs and responsibilities include making payments; paying closing costs, property taxes, insurance, and utilities; adhering to CC&Rs and zoning laws; and maintaining your property. Purchasing a home is a lengthy process that includes qualifying for and obtaining a mortgage, making an offer on a home, completing the closing process, and transferring the title from the previous owner to you.

Summary

10.1 Housing Choices

- There are many housing options available for students and working adults. These include on-campus and off-campus housing for students, apartments, duplexes and multiplexes, condominiums, and single-family homes.

- To live together successfully, roommates must have compatible living habits and work out responsibilities in advance.

- When deciding where to live, consider required security deposits and fees, safety of the area, length of time you plan to live there, distance from school or work, distance from services, and repairs and maintenance.

- Prepare to move by saving money and having a steady income, accumulating needed items, and planning to transport belongings. A good way to organize your preparations is to create a household needs inventory.

- When you move in, you will have to arrange to turn on electricity and other utilities and may have to pay fees for internet or streaming services.

- All roommates are responsible for meeting obligations to which they agree. Developing a group budget is one way to discuss responsibilities and allocate expenses.

10.2 The Renting Process

- Renting is the process of using another person's property for a fee. A landlord is the rental property's owner; the person who rents the property is a tenant.

- Advantages of renting include flexibility, lower cost, fewer responsibilities, amenities, convenience, and social life.

- Disadvantages of renting include noise, lack of privacy, small living and storage space, scarcity of parking, and no tax benefits.

- Landlords use the rental application to determine if you are a good risk as a tenant.

- If you lease, you (the lessee) agree to rent the space for a set period at a set rent payment. During this time, the landlord (the lessor) cannot raise the rent, but there are penalties if you leave early.

- If you enter a rental agreement, or a month-to-month agreement, you can leave at any time with proper notice, but the landlord can also raise the rent or ask you to leave at any time.

- To protect yourself from being held responsible for preexisting problems, complete a rental inventory when you move in.

- Landlords are responsible for providing a safe and habitable place for tenants to live.

- Tenant responsibilities include paying rent on time, obeying the rules, and taking reasonable care of the property. Failure to meet obligations could result in eviction.

10.3 Purchasing a Home

- There are four valuation methods commonly used in real estate: market value, appraised value, assessed value, and estimated value.

- Financial advantages of home ownership include an increase in equity as property values increase and the loan balance is paid down.

- Quality-of-life advantages for homeowners, as compared to renters, generally include more privacy, space, and personal freedom; a feeling of security, stability, and independence; a sense of belonging to a community; and a sense of pride and accomplishment.

- Real estate may be considered a tax shelter because mortgage interest and property taxes on primary residences may be tax deductible.

- Home ownership carries significant costs and responsibilities, such as a down payment, mortgage payments, closing costs, property taxes, property insurance, utilities, CC&Rs and zoning laws, and maintenance and repairs.

- A conventional loan requires a larger down payment; an FHA or other government-backed loan often requires a smaller down payment but also requires the borrower to carry mortgage insurance.

- Before starting your house search, determine the price range you can afford and prioritize a list of the features you want. Search the multiple listings for homes that meet your criteria. Once you have narrowed your choices, visit these homes and note their good and bad points.

- Real estate agents' commission is a percentage of the home sales price, paid by the seller. The commission is usually between five and eight percent.

- It is important to prequalify for a real estate loan. This guides you and your real estate agent when looking for homes.

- Preapproval, which involves an extensive credit and financial background check, can speed up the home-buying process.

- Once you have selected a home, you will make an earnest money offer to buy it. The seller may accept your offer or make a counteroffer.

- Once you have agreed on a price and terms of the sale, the offer becomes a contract.

- To finance your purchase, you must have funds for a down payment, fill out a loan application and meet the lender's requirements, and select whether you want a fixed-rate mortgage or an adjustable-rate mortgage.

- Prior to closing, you will want to have the title verified as free of any liens. You will also want to conduct a final walk-through of the property.

- At the closing, you will sign papers and money will change hands. Then the deed will transfer title to you.

Check Your Knowledge

1. List the housing options available for a young adult moving into their first home and discuss the advantages of each option. (LO 10.1.1)

2. What are the advantages and disadvantages of living with a roommate? (LO 10.1.2)

3. Why is a group budget important if you are going to live with roommates? (LO 10.1.3)

4. What are three advantages and three disadvantages of renting? (LO 10.2.1)

5. What is the purpose of a rental application? (LO 10.2.2)

6. What is the primary responsibility of a landlord to their tenants? (LO 10.2.3)

7. Compare the advantages and disadvantages of renting vs. buying. (LO 10.3.1)

8. What is the biggest cost to consider when purchasing a home? (LO 10.3.2)

9. Use a sequence chain graphic organizer or some other organizer or matrix to outline the steps in purchasing a home. (LO 10.3.3)

Apply Your Knowledge

1. Use a comparison chart to compare two different housing options. How are they different? How are they similar? Based on your comparison, explain which option you would choose for your first home. (LO 10.1.1)

2. Conduct research of the rental housing market in your area. Compare today's prices to those of ten years earlier. Explain how rentals have changed: How many new rental properties are in the area? Are there more or fewer houses for rent? What types of rental properties are available around local universities? (LO 10.1.1)

3. Make a list of the things you consider to be essential for a successful living arrangement with a roommate. Consider personal preferences, habits, and financial responsibilities. Then, create a list of questions you would ask a potential roommate. Brainstorm how you would handle a situation where your roommate eats the food your purchased for the week and refuses to replace it or a situation where your roommate does not pay their share of the rent on time, forcing you to cover the full rent until they repay you. (LO 10.1.2)

4. Use Zillow.com or Realtor.com to find a house for sale that interests you. Pick a house that has a video tour. Watch the video and view the pictures. Write a description of the property, including the asking price, tax history, and estimated homeowners insurance. Create a list of things that you like and dislike about the property. If you were to tour the house in person, what things would you want to inspect more closely? (LO 10.3.3)

Share Your Knowledge

Work in teams of two to four students to complete the following activities.

1. Anisa and Nadia just graduated from high school and are planning to attend the same college. They want to get an apartment and be roommates. Help them prepare a list of topics to discuss and prepare a tentative budget, assuming that they will share expenses equally. (LO 10.1.2)

2. Search online for a sample lease agreement. With your team, read the agreement and find the following information:

   a. Length of the lease

   b. What is included in the rent (utilities, parking, amenities, etc.)

   c. The due date for rent

   d. The grace period

   e. Information about security deposits and if they are refundable

   f. Requirement for renters insurance

   g. Notice before moving out

   h. Penalties that may be assessed

   i. Contact information for emergency maintenance

   j. Landlord inspection schedule

   k. Pet policy

   l. Guest policy

   Create a poster, infographic, or other visual media to help others understand what the terms of the lease mean. (LO 10.2.2)

3. Assume you have been appointed president of your homeowners' association. Create a brochure to be distributed to new homeowners that explains their responsibilities as a homeowner in your neighborhood, including the CC&Rs of the subdivision. Include suggestions on how to be a good neighbor and how to maintain the quality of life and property values in the area. (LO 10.3.2)

Connect and Reflect

Base your answers to the following questions on your own personal thoughts, preferences, and experiences.

1. Have you ever shared a room with a sibling? If so, what were some of the challenges and rewards of sharing space with them? How can that experience help you if you have a roommate in the future? If you have never shared a room with a sibling, consider how you would handle the potential challenges and rewards of having a roommate. How will you plan to be successful with the roommate living arrangement? (LO 10.1.2)

2. Find a "Moving out for the first time checklist" and review it. What things on the list surprised you? How can you prepare now for your first move? (LO 10.1.3)

3. Would you prefer to be a homeowner or a renter? Consider the advantages and disadvantages of each and explain your answer. (LO 10.1.1 and 10.3.1)

Select a large city in another state where you might want to live in the future. Search online for rental properties in that city. Create a table outlining three of your rental options. Include columns for the cost of rent and security deposit, amenities available, and the pros and cons of each property. Based on the city you selected, estimate your moving costs by determining the mileage and the cost of renting a truck or paying a moving company. Make a list of the furnishings and other household and personal items you will take. If you need to purchase any furniture, research and list the costs. Finally, assume you will have one roommate and prepare a group budget. Compile and save your findings to help prepare for your future move.

11 Chapter

Personal Transportation Decisions

What steps are involved in selecting a car to buy or lease?

Learning Objectives

By the end of this lesson, you should be able to:

LO 11.1.1 Explain the steps in choosing a vehicle.
LO 11.1.2 Discuss forms of consumer protection for car buyers.

Key Terms

- leasing
- car warranty
- upside-down
- vehicle identification number (VIN)
- compression test
- vehicle emission test
- extended warranty
- lemon
- lemon laws
- Used Car Rule

Consider This ...

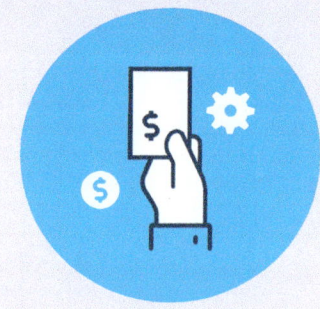

Rya works part time and attends school full time. She lives at home with her parents, and her take-home pay is just over $600 a month.

"I'm ready to buy a car," Rya tells her parents. "This ad says that with just $100 down, I can finance the purchase of a new car. I'd have to make 72 payments of $350 each. I make nearly twice that much each month, so I can afford the car. But I'm not sure I want that particular car. My friend Ishaq just bought a car from an auto dealer that gave him a good deal on last year's model. So that's something to consider too."

"Something else to think about is whether I might be able to get a better deal if I finance a car through my credit union. I've been a member there for several years now, and I have maintained my accounts well. I've never bounced a check or had an overdraft. They also have a car-buying service at the credit union. Would that be the way to get the best deal?"

Read and Reflect

1. What different options does Rya have for financing the purchase of a car?
2. What costs are associated with the purchase of a car?
3. What maintenance costs should Rya plan for after the purchase of a vehicle?

The Car-Selection Process

Because it is a large purchase, buying or leasing an automobile should involve taking the time to make a good decision—one that you will not regret later. Following a decision-making model, such as the one presented in a previous chapter, may help you make better choices as you get ready to select a car.

Identify Your Needs and Wants

Selecting a car starts with identifying both your needs and wants. To begin, ask yourself some basic questions:

- How far do I need to drive each day or week?
- Do I need to have a vehicle that is fuel-efficient?
- Do I need to haul several people or a lot of gear?
- Do I need to use a vehicle for towing or hauling?
- How much money do I have to spend on a vehicle? How much will it cost to maintain the vehicle?
- Do I want a new car or a used car? Which is more affordable?
- Should I buy or lease?
- Do I want a vehicle I can take off-road?
- What features do I want to have on the vehicle?

After you have made your list of needs and wants, decide which ones are most important. Prioritizing helps you identify what you must have and what you can give up if necessary to keep the price affordable.

Decide What You Can Afford

Before shopping for a car, determine how much you can afford to spend. One general guideline is that you can afford monthly car payments and maintenance costs of approximately 10 to 15 percent of your net income. When setting your transportation budget, consider your regular monthly expenses, such as rent or mortgage payment, utilities, credit card payments, and other expenses. Remember to figure in your budget the costs of maintaining your car as well as the costs of fuel and auto insurance. Cars can be expensive when you decide to add special features, such as special wheels and stereo equipment. Sometimes these features can be added later at a lesser cost than the cost of later at a lesser cost than buying a fully loaded car.

Identify and Research Your Choices

Select several types of cars that would meet your wants and needs and your budget. Then, research the features for each of your selections. Several magazines or websites, such as *Car and Driver* and *Consumer Reports*, offer abundant information on car models. Look for articles about performance, repair records, safety records, fuel economy, and prices. Websites such as Car and Driver Reviews (https://www.caranddriver.com/reviews) can provide important information about possible vehicles.

Compare the features of the models you are considering against your list of wants and needs. Note the pros and cons of each model. Use your list and price range to narrow your choices to a few that best meet your criteria. When comparing prices, be sure to compare models that have the same options.

Decide Whether to Buy or Lease

The primary decision is whether to buy or lease a vehicle. **Leasing** is a type of car financing where you rent a car from the dealership. If you decide to purchase a vehicle, you must decide if you should buy a new or used car. Cost is a major factor in this decision. A new car will be more expensive than buying a used car. Also, a new car loses much of its market value when you drive it off the lot. A new car can lose approximately 20 percent of its resale value in its first year. However, a new car likely will not need new tires, brakes, or any major repairs during its first few years of ownership. Most new cars have a car warranty. The **car warranty** protects the owner from costly mechanical repairs. A car warranty will not cover routine maintenance such as tires or oil changes.

On the other hand, a used car is likely to need more maintenance and repairs. Even if you have a mechanic check the car's overall condition before buying it, a used car is still somewhat unknown. A car dealer may offer a used-car warranty you would not get from an individual seller, but a dealer typically charges more for the used car.

Leasing can help lower the monthly costs of a new vehicle. Still, most lease agreements will restrict the number of miles you can drive in a year, and you may be responsible for items considered excessive wear and tear on the vehicle.

Decide How You Will Pay for It

If you plan to borrow money to purchase a car or to enter into a lease agreement, you should first work with a lender to determine a preapproved amount that you can afford to pay for the vehicle. Preapproval is getting a new or used-car loan prearranged through your bank or credit union. Preapproval separates financing from the process of negotiating the price of the car. It also allows you to compare the total costs of buying, including credit rates. You may or may not take

Why is getting preapproved before buying or leasing a car so important?

the preapproved loan, but you will know how much you can spend and the interest rate you can get before you shop for a car. If you consider leasing a new car, you will also want to obtain pre-approval through the manufacturer. It is always smart to compare the monthly lease and purchase payments.

To get preapproved for a car loan, visit your credit union or bank and fill out a loan application. Based on the information you supply; the loan officer will determine how much the institution would be willing to lend you. The loan officer will then give you a form stating this preapproved amount and rate. Typically, the preapproval expires in 30 or 60 days, after which time you must reapply if you want the loan. Another important consideration is to consider the actual cost of purchasing a vehicle. Many people consider only if they can afford the monthly payment instead of determining how much the car will cost. Many consumers find themselves upside-down on their car loans when they consider only the monthly payment. Knowing how much you can afford to pay for a vehicle allows you to have control during negotiations. Many dealerships will ask you how much you can afford per month and manipulate the loan details to meet the monthly payment. This does not always give you the best price on the vehicle.

If you plan to trade in your current vehicle, you may find yourself upside-down. You are **upside-down** when you owe more on the loan than the vehicle is worth. If you are upside-down, you will be required to pay the difference before you can sell or trade your car. This is important because many consumers agree to car loans that last 6, 7, or even 8 years. The longer your car loan, the greater the chance that you will be upside-down on your loan.

If you are considering a car lease, you will usually negotiate with the car manufacturer through the dealership where you are leasing the vehicle. Some financial institutions will also allow you to lease a vehicle. Check with your local bank or credit union about leasing options and preapproval.

Check Insurance Rates

Check out the insurance rates on your vehicle choices. Car insurance rates can differ widely from one car to another. For example, SUVs and pickup trucks cost less to insure than sports cars. A call to your insurance agent to get this information helps rule out choices that may result in high insurance premiums that you may not be able to afford.

Your driving record may also influence your choice of car. If you have numerous moving violations, including accidents and/ or speeding tickets, you may be deemed a risky driver by the state and qualify only for assigned risk insurance. Assigned risk pools are state-run (or regionally run) programs that allow people who cannot otherwise obtain needed insurance to purchase affordable coverage. Typical coverage is for liability only (to cover damages to the other driver). With a car loan, you will need full coverage (to protect the lender). Thus, your car choices are more limited if you are in a high-risk pool. You will learn more about insurance in future chapters. Also, check with your insurance company if you are considering a lease. Most lease agreements require higher insurance coverage than is needed if you purchase a vehicle.

Search for Available Vehicles and Purchase or Lease Options

Search online for cars available from car dealers and individual sellers in your area. Many websites, such as AutoTrader, Cars.com, and Kelley Blue Book, allow you to search for specific models, both new and used. Many websites will even give you price quotes. Most car dealerships also list their inventory on the dealership's website. It is also possible to purchase a vehicle through online buying sites such as Carvana, CarMax, and CarGurus. Buying a vehicle online can save you time, and often the price is fixed. One disadvantage of buying online is it may be difficult to test drive the vehicle. Research is key. Check to see if the online site has a return policy and understand how the car will be delivered to you. The downside of buying online is that you do not have the opportunity to inspect the car or test drive the vehicle. Financing choices for online purchases are more limited than buying through a local dealership. One of the biggest disadvantages of buying online is the inability to trade-in your old car, if you have one. Another way to purchase a vehicle is through large box store auto programs. Companies like Costco have a program with prearranged pricing for consumers wanting to buy a new car. When buying a vehicle in

Connections to Your World
Online Car Shopping

In recent years, many people have begun exploring options to purchase cars online. Buying a car online has especially been embraced by individuals between the ages of 18 and 24 years. There are many different online options for purchasing vehicles; CarGurus, CarMax, and Carvana are all examples of online car shopping websites. As Rya begins her search for a car, she is considering using an online automobile retailer. She has worked with her credit union and knows that she can get an interest rate of 5 percent, maybe better, for her loan. She has also learned that there will be additional cost for her purchase (such as sales tax, registration, and title fee). Rya is anticipating a purchase price in the range of $17,000 to $22,000. Explore an online car retailer and find potential vehicles that Rya could purchase.

Think Critically

1. What recommendations would you give Rya as she explores online car retailers?
2. What are potential advantages of shopping for a vehicle online? What are potential disadvantages?
3. Would you consider purchasing a vehicle online? Why or why not?

person, you may be able to negotiate a lower price through the dealership.

Make a list of the available cars that match your criteria, including their features and prices. These are your finalists—the cars that you think are worth investigating further.

Test Drive Vehicles

Sometimes, descriptions are quite different from the actual car. That is why it is important to test drive cars of interest before choosing one. A test drive is a simple road test where you drive the car for several miles in typical traffic and road conditions.

Begin the test drive by simply sitting in the car and asking yourself a few questions to help you decide whether the car is a good fit:

- Is it easy to get in and out of the car?
- Is there enough legroom and headroom?
- Is there enough storage for devices and other items?
- Are seats comfortable and adjustable?
- Are mirrors easy to adjust and is visibility satisfactory?
- Are the gauges and controls easy to locate, read, and use?
- Does the vehicle have the features that you consider important?

The top features to consider in your vehicle should include:

- Climate control. Do you need or want air conditioning? If you live in a cold climate, do you need an engine block heater? Are heated seats important to you?

- Electronic features. Is the car smartphone compatible and equipped with features like touch-screen display, remote start, or a digital key?
- Automatic or manual transmission. Although most cars have automatic transmissions, some people prefer the control that comes with a manual transmission. Manual transmissions are also more fuel-efficient and require less maintenance.
- Engine size. Smaller engines are more fuel-efficient, while larger engines provide more power.
- Safety features and ratings. What safety features do you want? Is a back-up camera important to you? Do you want crash detection or drive assist features?
- Hauling capacity. Will you need to tow a trailer, boat, or RV? If so, what towing capacity do you need?

Once you begin the test drive, evaluate the ride, steering and handling, acceleration, power, visibility, and braking. Try out the car's features, such as climate control and sound system, to see how well they work. Once you test the sound system, turn it off so that you can hear the car as you drive. Especially when evaluating used cars, listen for noises that might indicate a problem. When you accelerate, look for dark smoke from the exhaust. This is a sign that the car is burning oil, which would require an expensive repair. If you test drive a used car, look for rust and mismatched paint on the body. This may mean the car has been in an accident.

After the test drive, some salespeople will pressure you into buying immediately. However, resist that temptation and take your time. You will enhance your bargaining position with patience and knowledge of the car you plan to buy. When buying a car, check the dealer's reputation first. Checking with the Better Business Bureau will give you valuable information about consumer complaints about this dealer.

Check the History of a Used Vehicle

If you are considering a used car, you should learn about its history. You can do so by looking up the car's **vehicle identification number (VIN)**, an alphanumeric number that identifies each vehicle manufactured or sold in the United States. This number is available on vehicle documents and the dashboard on the driver's side. It is visible through the front windshield.

Get the VIN from the used vehicle(s) you are considering and enter it into the online search tool at the CARFAX website. A detailed history for one vehicle costs approximately $40, or you can get reports on an unlimited number of vehicles for around $55. You can also request the seller to provide you with a CARFAX report. The full report provides information, such as whether the vehicle has been in an accident serious enough to report to the insurance company, how many times the vehicle has been sold, and the mileage readings each time it was sold so that you can check for odometer rollbacks. Cars totaled (wrecked) or used as rental cars will show a branded title to alert you to possible condition issues or high mileage. The maintenance records of the car may also be included if the car was serviced by a dealership.

Get the Vehicle Checked Mechanically

After the used vehicle has passed the VIN check and you have decided to buy it, have the car checked out by an independent mechanic. For around $100 to $150, the mechanic can provide a general indication of the vehicle's mechanical condition. The vehicle inspection will determine whether the engine is in good shape. A **compression test** can tell you whether to expect serious engine trouble ahead, such as head gaskets about to fail. You will also want to be sure that the transmission is working properly. If the vehicle passes these two critical tests, then ask for a complete check to see what repairs might need to be made soon and how much they might cost. For example, you will want to know how much longer the brakes will last, whether new tires are needed, and other common issues with used vehicles. Once the vehicle has been inspected, ask the mechanic for a written report with a cost estimate for all necessary repairs. If you decide to make an offer after considering the inspection results, you can use the estimated repair costs to negotiate the price of the vehicle.

Many states require vehicles to pass a **vehicle emission test**, which verifies that a vehicle meets the minimum clean-air standards. If buying a used car, ask the seller

What is the difference between the sticker price and invoice price of a vehicle?

for the record showing that it passed the most recent vehicle emission test. If the seller cannot produce the record, ask the seller to have the vehicle tested before you buy it.

> **✓ Checkpoint**
>
> Explain the steps involved in choosing a vehicle.

Why is it important to get a vehicle checked mechanically before purchasing it?

LO 11.1.2 Consumer Protection for Vehicle Owners

Once you have completed your transaction and have your new vehicle, you need to know what to do if you have any problems. As you learned previously, a warranty is a written statement about a product or service's qualities or performance that the seller assures are true. A warranty clearly states what the manufacturer will do if the product or service does not perform as it should. A new-car warranty provides a buyer with some assurance of quality. Car warranties vary in the time and mileage of the protection they offer and in the parts they cover. The important aspects of a warranty are the coverage of basic automobile parts against manufacturer defects and the power train coverage for the engine, transmission, and drive train. In addition to the basic warranty, there are several other ways that new- and used-car owners are protected.

Extended Warranties

Many car dealers offer their customers extended warranties. For a flat fee car buyers can purchase an **extended warranty** to cover the costs of expensive repairs and defects not covered by the standard warranty or that occur after the standard warranty expires. However, most extended warranties are nothing more than extended service plans. You are simply paying upfront for things that need repairing or replacing later.

Extended warranties can be purchased through the dealer or a third-party provider. Dealer warranties often require you to have the repair made at the dealership. Therefore, if you are on a trip or if you move to another city, you will need to take the car back to the dealer where the extended warranty was purchased to get any repairs done.

Lemon Laws

A **lemon** is a car with substantial defects that the manufacturer has been unable to fix after repeated attempts. You have a lemon if, in the first year of ownership or 12,000 miles, you have taken the car into the dealer for four or more unsuccessful attempts to repair the same substantial defect or your car has been out of service for a total of at least 30 days.

Lemon laws exist in many states and protect consumers from the consequences of owning or leasing a defective car. Lemon laws

allow you to get a new car or your money back. Unfortunately, this protection is not automatic. You need to have good documentation and be prepared for a long process. An arbitration proceeding and a possible lawsuit may be necessary to enforce your state's law.

Although very few cars are lemons, there are things you can do to protect yourself if you end up with a car with major defects:

- When you take a car in for repairs, provide a written list of problems.
- Review the repair receipt to ensure all the list's issues have been addressed.
- Keep copies of the list and receipt with your other important papers.
- If you need to have the same repair completed again, document it with the dealership. Have the dealership note that the problem is ongoing and was not resolved with the previous repair.
- If your vehicle qualifies as a lemon, notify the dealership. Provide copies of your lists and repair records.
- If the dealership does not help, contact the manufacturer. Follow-up, in writing, after each interaction with the dealership and manufacturer. Keep a copy of all communications for your records.
- Be persistent. Follow up quickly after each communication.
- If the defect is serious and makes the vehicle dangerous to drive, request arbitration if the issue is not resolved immediately.
- Demand a quick hearing. Under Section 703 of the Magnuson-Moss Warranty Act, you are entitled to a hearing within 40 days of filing the complaint.
- The Center for Auto Safety in Washington, D.C., may be able to assist you in the process.

The FTC Used Car Rule

People who buy a used car must be concerned about whether it has some hidden defects or potentially expensive repairs ahead. The

Do you think lemon laws are necessary? Why or why not?

Federal Trade Commission's (FTC's) **Used Car Rule** requires that dealers fully disclose to buyers what is and is not covered under warranty for the used vehicle. This rule also requires used-car dealers to inform consumers before purchase about who will be responsible for paying for certain repairs if they occur after the sale.

The rule requires dealers to place a sticker, called the "Buyer's Guide," on all used cars they offer. **Figure 11.1** illustrates this sticker. The buyer must pay all repair costs

Figure 11.1	Buyer's Guide (FTC Used Car Rule)

BUYER'S GUIDE

IMPORTANT: Spoken promises are difficult to enforce. Ask the dealer to put all promises in writing. Keep this form.

Ford	Focus	2023	A0A085C147961
VEHICLE MAKE	MODEL	YEAR	VIN NUMBER

T6204B

DEALER STOCK NUMBER (Optional)

WARRANTIES FOR THIS VEHICLE:

☒ # AS IS – NO WARRANTY

YOU WILL PAY ALL COSTS FOR ANY REPAIRS. The dealer assumes no responsibility for any repairs regardless of any oral statements about the vehicle.

☐ # WARRANTY

☐ FULL ☐ LIMITED WARRANTY. The dealer will pay ___% of the labor and ___% of the parts for the covered systems that fail during the warranty period. Ask the dealer for a copy of the warranty document for a full explanation of warranty coverage, exclusions, and the dealer's repair obligations. Under state law, "implied warranties" may give you even more rights.

SYSTEMS COVERED: **DURATION:**

_____   _____

_____   _____

_____   _____

_____   _____

☒ **SERVICE CONTRACT.** A service contract is available at an extra charge on this vehicle. Ask for details as to coverage, deductible, price, and exclusions. If you buy a service contract within 90 days of the time of sale, state law "implied warranties" may give you additional rights.

PRE-PURCHASE INSPECTION: ASK THE DEALER IF YOU MAY HAVE THIS VEHICLE INSPECTED BY YOUR MECHANIC EITHER ON OR OFF THE LOT.

SEE THE BACK OF THIS FORM for important additional information, including a list of some major defects that may occur in used motor vehicles.

if the "As Is – No Warranty" box is checked. If the "Warranty" box is checked, the dealer pays for the items listed for the specified period. If the "As Is" box is checked, it is recommended that you have an independent mechanic conduct a prepurchase vehicle inspection.

✓ Checkpoint

What are the consumer protections available when purchasing or leasing a vehicle?

Check Your Understanding

1. Why should you turn the sound system off when you are test driving a car? (LO 11.1.1)

2. Why should you obtain a preauthorization from a financial institution when shopping for a vehicle? (LO 11.1.1)

3. Explain the FTC Used Car Rule. (LO 1.1.2)

Apply Your Understanding

1. Describe the vehicle that would be your first choice, based on your needs and wants. Describe the process you would use to research your choices. (LO 11.1.1)

2. Outline the steps you should follow if you think you have purchased a lemon. (LO 11.1.2)

The Essential Question

What steps are involved in selecting a car to buy or lease?

A: Steps in the process include identifying your needs and wants, deciding what you can afford, researching your choices, searching for cars, test driving vehicles, checking their histories, and arranging the financing. It is also important to understand consumer protection laws related to auto purchases.

What is the process for buying or leasing a vehicle, including financing options?

Learning Objectives

By the end of this lesson, you should be able to:

LO 11.2.1   Outline the car buying and leasing process.

LO 11.2.2   Discuss the differences between buying and leasing a vehicle, including the advantages and disadvantages of each.

LO 11.2.3   Explain vehicle financing choices, including leasing.

Key Terms

- sticker price
- invoice price
- gap insurance
- car-buying service
- dealer add-ons
- residual value
- rent charge

LO 11.2.1   The Buying Process

When buying a car, there are several steps that you should follow. As with any big purchase, you should use a decision-making process to help you make the best decision possible.

Determine a Fair Price

Decide what price you feel is fair before you make any offer for a car. Several websites provide accurate estimates of the market price for vehicles. TrueCar and Kelley Blue Book are two popular pricing guides for cars. The guides include current trade-in values and suggested retail values on almost all new and used vehicle models. You can also get a feel for a fair price by checking ads for cars of the same model and year to see what other sellers are charging.

For a new car, the **sticker price**, or manufacturer's suggested retail price (MSRP), is shown on the tag in the car's window. A fair price for a new car usually lies somewhere between the sticker price and the price the dealer paid for it, called the **invoice price**. Typically, the more expensive a vehicle, the greater the difference between the MSRP and the invoice price. Depending on the vehicle's popularity and the number of vehicles currently on the market, a fair price will likely be 3 to 6 percent above the invoice. You can use a site such as Edmunds.com to help determine the invoice prices through their True Market Value pricing system. The pricing system researches the amounts that consumers have actually paid for vehicles.

Negotiate the Price

When it comes time to negotiate the price of a vehicle, you can do it yourself or use someone else to negotiate on your behalf. If you do your own negotiating, there are a few things to remember. First, be relaxed and do not be intimidated by the salesperson. Stick to facts and do not reveal emotions to sellers.

For example, do not say, "This car is just what I want." Saying how much you love or want the car can weaken your bargaining position. Also, make your initial offer lower than your top price. In addition, do not be pressured into paying more than you think is fair. Walk away from the deal if you feel you are being pressured or the dealer will not meet a price you feel is fair.

When negotiating, you should also be aware of common dealer negotiating tactics. For example, the salesperson might initially act positively toward your offer, allowing you to get your heart set on the car. Then, the salesperson may tell you they need approval from the sales manager, leave you for several minutes, and then return to say your offer is unacceptable. If this occurs, and the new price the dealer offers is still below the maximum you set for yourself as the fair price, then make a counteroffer that is a little higher but still lower than your top price. If the dealer will not come down any, then walk away. Always negotiate on the vehicle's total price, not the monthly payment amount. Because you have pre-approval, you will know how much you can afford for the car and the approximate monthly payment. If the dealership knows your monthly budget, they may extend the loan length to 7 or even 8 years to meet your monthly payment budget. As discussed earlier in the chapter, long-term car loans almost always lead to being upside-down on the vehicle. Consider gap insurance if you purchase a car with a long-term loan contract or make a minimal down payment. **Gap insurance** is an optional type of car insurance that will help pay off your loan if the car is totaled or stolen and you are upside-down. Gap insurance is also called loan/lease gap coverage.

Sometimes, you will have a car you want to trade in when buying a new one. To ensure clarity in determining the true price of the new car, negotiate the price for it separately from the price for your trade-in. After settling on a fair price for the new car, ask how much the dealer will give you for your old car. If the dealer does not offer an amount close to the trade-in value found during your research, plan to sell your old car yourself rather than trading it in. Selling the car yourself can be a hassle, but you will likely get more money for it that way.

If you are uncomfortable negotiating the price of a vehicle, consider using the services of a professional. Through your automobile club, a wholesale club (such as Costco), your credit union, or an online car-buying service, you can get a price based on the cost to the dealer. A **car-buying service** allows you to choose the vehicle features you want and have a professional car buyer handle the price negotiation. Once you know exactly what car you want, the service will locate the car, negotiate the price, and arrange delivery. This service is not free, but it can save you money.

Avoid Dealer Add-Ons

After you have agreed on the price of a car, the dealer may try to increase the purchase price with **dealer add-ons**—high-priced, high-profit dealer services that add little or no value. For example, dealer preparation is nothing more than cleaning the car and checking the air in the tires and the oil in the engine. These services should be provided without extra charge. Other common dealer add-ons include protective wax or polish, pinstriping, rustproofing, and other services. Rarely are these special services worth the cost. If you consider adding special features to your car, such as chrome-plated wheels, headlight covers, or window tinting, check with outside companies first. Usually, these features can be added at a lesser cost by a specialty shop rather than the car dealership.

Buying Private-Party Cars

Many people prefer to sell their own vehicles using online listings and local advertising. You may see cars for sale parked along the street, in driveways, or posted on social media.

Private sellers are not covered under the FTC Used Car Rule and do not have to display the Buyer's Guide sticker. A car purchased from a private seller typically will be sold "as is." Be sure to test drive the car.

Taking someone with you who is knowledgeable about cars and can give you good advice is always a good idea. The best protection you can get is having an independent mechanic inspect the vehicle. Used cars will not be perfect, but they should be in good running condition so that you will not experience major repairs within the next 30 to 90 days.

If you buy from a private party, pay for the vehicle and exchange ownership information (title and registration) at your state department of motor vehicles (DMV). This will ensure that the seller is the true owner and has the right to transfer title to you as the buyer.

Connections to Your World
Selling a Used Car

If you decide to sell your old car yourself, here are some steps that will help you make a quicker sale and get what it is worth:

1. Give your car "curb appeal." Wash and polish the outside, vacuum and clean the inside, and shampoo the upholstery. Remove all personal property. Make sure the car is mechanically sound. A car that appears well cared for will bring a higher price.

2. Set a reasonable price. Check Kelley Blue Book (www.kbb.com), Edmunds.com, or another online appraisal tool to determine the fair market value of your car. Check online classified ads to be sure this price is within the range advertised by other people selling the same model and year as your car.

3. Advertise your car. Advertise your vehicle on websites such as Auto-Trader, Cars.com, or in social media marketplaces. Putting a "For Sale" sign in the car window is an inexpensive advertising technique that can be an effective way to sell it.

(continues)

(continued)

4. Screen potential buyers. Use your intuition to evaluate potential buyers. If they seem suspicious, difficult, or pushy, wait for another buyer. If you do not feel comfortable having buyers come to your house to see the car, arrange to show the car at a neutral place, such as the parking lot in a shopping center. If you are uncomfortable, consider having a family member or friend with you when meeting potential buyers. Also, if selling online, be cautious of potential scams. Do not provide banking or personal information to anyone requesting to purchase the vehicle and transfer money to you.

5. Be truthful. Present the truth to prospective buyers—what is good about the car as well as its weaknesses. Disclose the last time you had a tune-up and allow prospective buyers to check maintenance records.

6. Accompany the potential buyer on the test drive. Prospective buyers will want to test drive the car. Consider riding along with them so you can answer any questions about the car's performance. If you do ride along with the potential buyer, it is wise to bring along a trusted adult or guardian.

7. Be prepared to negotiate. The buyer's offer may be lower than the price you have advertised, so be prepared to negotiate. Once a price has been agreed upon, always ask for payment in the form of cash or a cashier's check.

8. Finalize the sale. Once you have money for the sale, prepare and sign a bill of sale and any other documents your state may require. Make copies of all paperwork. Remove the license plates if they cannot be transferred. Sign the title and provide it to the buyer or meet the buyer at the department of motor vehicles to transfer title if is required in your state. Never let a new owner drive away with a car that is still in your name.

9. After you sell the car, remove all registration and other documents that contain your name and address. Also, notify your insurance company immediately to cancel your policy.

Think Critically

1. Why should you tell the truth about your car when you are trying to sell it? What consequences might you face if you do not?

2. Why is it best to go along on a potential buyer's test drive?

3. If you were selling your car, what kind of payment would you accept? Explain.

The Leasing Process

Rather than purchasing a new car, you may consider leasing. A car lease is like an apartment lease. It is a written agreement that allows you to use the property (in this case, a car) for a specified time and monthly payment. You do not own the car; you are simply renting its use. However, at the end of the lease period, you usually have the option to buy the car for a price specified in the lease agreement. The selling price is based on the car's expected value at the end of the lease term.

For some people, leasing is an attractive alternative to buying a car. Lease payments are usually lower than monthly loan payments. Like purchasing a vehicle, you should understand the process and the steps.

1. Negotiate the sale price of the vehicle. This process is the same if you lease or buy.
2. Determine the length of the lease. Typically, 36 months is a standard lease. Most new cars have a 36-month warranty so most repair costs will be covered by the warranty.
3. Determine the maximum miles you can drive in one year. A standard lease will be either 12,000 or 15,000 miles per year. The higher your annual mileage allotment, the higher your monthly payment will be. Remember, if you exceed the maximum number of miles, you must pay for every mile over the maximum. This charge can be very expensive, often exceeding $1.00 per mile.
4. Determine the car's residual value. The **residual value** is the car's value at the end of the lease period. If you decide to buy the car at the end of the lease, this is the amount you will need to pay to keep the car.
5. Determine the rent charge. The **rent charge** is similar to the interest rate you would pay on a vehicle loan. This amount will be written into the lease agreement as a dollar amount you will pay each month.
6. Determine taxes and fees. You may be responsible for sales taxes and other fees as part of the lease agreement. You may also be required to make a down payment.

✓ Checkpoint

What are the steps involved in buying or leasing a vehicle?

Buying vs. Leasing

Understanding the pros and cons of buying rather than leasing a vehicle is important. Identifying the advantages and disadvantages of each will be helpful as you follow a decision-making process to make the best choice.

Advantages and Disadvantages of Leasing

When leasing a vehicle, you may have a smaller down payment and monthly costs than purchasing a vehicle. For some consumers, this may allow them to drive a car they may not have been able to afford if purchasing the vehicle. Another advantage of leasing is that you can return the car at the end of the lease and get a new car, allowing you to always have the newest features. At the end of your lease, you can return the car and need to pay only the negotiated end-of-lease costs for the vehicle. One of the most attractive advantages of leasing a car comes if you own a business. You may be able to use business tax deductions if you use the car for business purposes.

A major disadvantage of leasing a car is that you will not own the car. You are also limited to the maximum miles you can drive during the lease. It is expensive to exceed the allowable mileage. Because you do not own the car, you cannot modify the car. If you do make modifications, you may be required to pay the costs of returning the car to its original features. Another disadvantage of not owning the car is that at the end of the lease, you will need to return it and either lease or buy another car. You will always have a car payment when you lease. Often, at the end of the lease, you will be surprised with end-of-lease costs you were not expecting, such as excessive wear and tear, cleaning costs to prepare the vehicle for the next owner, and damages such as door dings or hail damage you may not have noticed.

Advantages and Disadvantages of Buying

When you buy a car, you own it. Once you have made all of your loan payments, the only expenses are insurance and maintenance on the vehicle. You will not have any restrictions on how many miles you can drive and will not owe any fees for excessive wear and tear on the vehicle. You can also modify the car's appearance or add extra features that allow you to enjoy driving the car. Overall, it is less expensive to buy a car than it is to lease one.

The biggest disadvantage of owning a car is depreciation. Most cars will lose up to 25 percent of their value during the first few years of ownership. Cars should not be considered investments. Another disadvantage is that once the warranty period has ended, you will be responsible for any car repairs that are needed.

✓ Checkpoint

What are the advantages and disadvantages of buying rather than leasing a vehicle?

LO 11.2.3 Financing Your Car

After you have narrowed your choices based on your wants, needs, and budget, the next step is to decide how you will pay for the car. While some people opt to pay cash and avoid interest charges, most people cannot afford to make one lump-sum payment. Therefore, many car buyers finance their cars with an auto loan or lease. When financing a car, you have two main options. You can finance the car through direct lending options at a financial institution or use dealership financing.

Financial Institutions

Banks and credit unions typically offer car loans for 36, 48, 60, or 72 months. It is now possible to finance a vehicle for 84 or even 96 months. Longer-term loans mean lower monthly payments but increase the interest paid because you use the money for longer. You may also be upside-down with the vehicle's value versus the amount of your auto loan. The age of a used vehicle will also impact the length of the auto loan. Financial institutions will not finance an older vehicle for as long as a newer vehicle. Your local credit union will often offer the best deal on a car loan. A credit union may finance more of your purchase, require a lower down payment, have lower interest rates, and require smaller monthly payments. Some financial institutions also provide financing for a lease. When you lease a vehicle, you will pay the rental fee instead of paying interest. Financial institutions call this fee the money factor, similar to the interest rate on a loan.

Dealership Financing

Most car dealerships also offer financing. On some models and at certain times of the year, they may offer you better terms than those available from other sources. These special deals are sponsored by the auto manufacturers, or the manufacturers' financing agencies, to stimulate sales or to promote a particular model. Although you finance through the dealer, you will pay the finance company. GM Financial is an example of a finance company that makes loans on cars through dealerships.

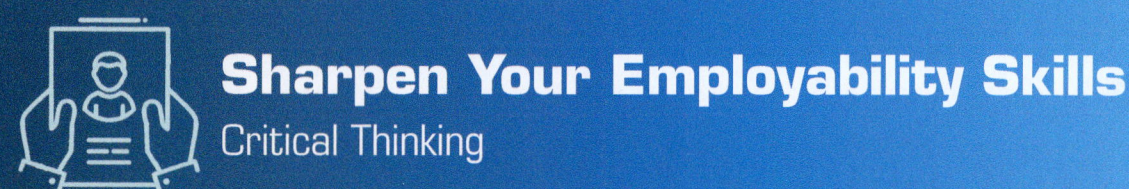

Sharpen Your Employability Skills
Critical Thinking

It is common for car dealerships to offer dealer financing to potential buyers. Dealer financing may be advertised as special rates for those with good credit. In addition, dealerships may often encourage using dealer financing for longer loan terms to lower monthly payments and increase the potential purchase price of a vehicle. It is important for you to consider your financing options and the cost associated with different options.

Option 1: Rya has been preapproved through her credit union for an automobile loan. She was approved for a loan of $19,000 with an interest rate of 4.5% for 60 months. If she puts no money down, her monthly payment would be just over $350 per month.

Option 2: The dealership has offered Rya a longer loan term and informed her that she can consider a more expensive car. Through dealer financing, Rya can obtain a $25,000 loan at 5.5% interest for 84 months. The dealership informs her that with this financing offer, she can now get more features on a vehicle, and her payment will only increase $5 per month.

Think Critically

1. What are the advantages and disadvantages of each financing option?
2. What advice would you provide Rya in this situation?
3. How does extending the term of a loan impact the overall amount paid for a vehicle?
4. What are potential risks associated with taking out a longer loan term?

Use caution with this type of financing. Do not allow a special promotional loan rate to influence you to buy a more expensive car that does not fit your budget. In most cases, the financing is handled by the dealership's finance department. The finance manager works directly with the financial institution to process the loan on your behalf. Always compare dealer financing with a loan from a financial institution. Calculate the total price paid using both options to determine which is the most affordable.

It is important to know your rights when financing a vehicle. The Equal Credit Opportunity Act prohibits lenders from discriminating against borrowers based on race, color, religion, sex, or marital status. As with any loan, the Truth-in-Lending Act requires you to be provided with information about the loan. These disclosures include the annual percentage rate, finance charges, amount financed, total number of payments, and the total sales price.

✓ Checkpoint

What are your financing options when buying or leasing a car?

Check Your Understanding

1. Why is it important to follow the steps in the car buying process? (LO 11.2.1)

2. Why is it important to follow the steps in the car leasing process? (LO 11.2.1)

3. Explain two main differences between buying and leasing a car. (LO 11.2.2)

4. Describe the two main financing options available to consumers. (LO 11.2.3)

Apply Your Understanding

1. Why would you want to keep the negotiations related to purchasing your new car and the value of your trade-in separate? (LO 11.2.1)

2. Use a problem-solving process to determine if you would prefer to purchase or lease a vehicle. Explain how and why you made your decision. (LO 11.2.2)

3. Rya cannot decide if she should buy or lease a vehicle. She thinks that buying may be best, but she does not understand the financing of leasing a vehicle. Explain the main differences between financing to purchase a vehicle and financing to lease a vehicle to help Rya make a decision. (LO 11.2.3)

The Essential Question

What is the process of buying or leasing a vehicle, including financing options?

A: Whether buying or leasing, the process is similar. You will want to determine a fair price before vehicle shopping, negotiate the price of the vehicle, determine if buying or leasing is your best option, and then secure financing.

11.3 Maintaining a Vehicle

The Essential Question   What are the costs of maintaining a vehicle, and how can you preserve its resale value?

Learning Objectives

By the end of this lesson, you should be able to:

LO 11.3.1 Identify the costs of operating and maintaining a vehicle.

LO 11.3.2 Describe methods for extending the life of your vehicle and preserving its resale value.

Key Terms

- hybrid
- electric cars
- depreciation
- classic cars
- appreciation
- car title
- car registration
- oxidize
- polishing compound
- car detail
- paintless dent removal

LO 11.3.1 Costs of Maintaining a Vehicle

Most people spend more of their income on transportation than any other item, except housing. Costs of operating a car include the monthly loan or lease payment and car insurance, discussed in a future chapter. Other costs associated with having a car include fuel, depreciation, registration and title fees, vehicle emission fees, maintenance and repairs, and accessories.

Fuel

Most engines today are gas powered. Gasoline is a nonrenewable source of fuel that is refined from crude oil taken from the earth. The cost of gas depends on world supplies of crude oil, political conditions, and world energy markets. The amount of gas you consume depends on your car's fuel efficiency, the number of miles you drive, and your driving habits.

Because of environmental concerns and the volatility of gas prices, you may want to buy a hybrid, electric, or other alternative fuel vehicle. A **hybrid** vehicle combines an internal combustion (gas-powered) engine with an electric motor. Hybrids get better gas mileage than cars that use conventional fuel. **Electric cars** run on batteries that you charge through a special plug at your home or at charging stations. Car manufacturers are also developing vehicles that use other types of energy including biodiesel

Why is fuel efficiency an important factor when shopping for a car?

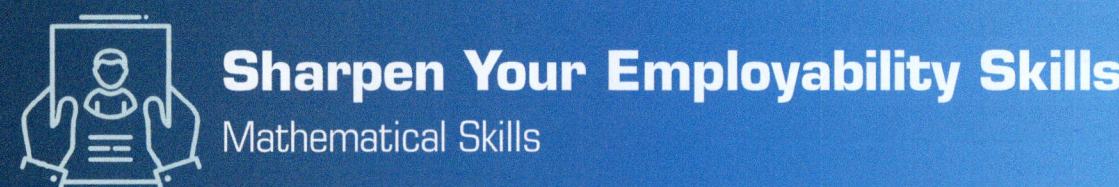

Sharpen Your Employability Skills
Mathematical Skills

Because of rising fuel prices, fuel efficiency is more important than ever. Determining how many miles per gallon your car gets is very useful. You can calculate MPG as follows:

1. Go to the gas station and fill up your tank. It does not matter if it is empty or partially full before filling up.

2. Record the mileage on your odometer before leaving the gas station.

3. Drive your normal route until your tank is almost empty.

4. Return to the gas station, record the mileage on your odometer, and fill up your tank again. Look at the pump to see how many gallons of gas were needed to fill up your tank.

5. Subtract the first odometer reading from the last odometer reading. Then divide this number by the number of gallons needed to refill your tank to calculate the MPG.

Try It Out!

Suppose Rya filled up her tank and had an odometer reading of 11,300 miles. After driving her normal route all week, she refilled her car, which now has an odometer reading of 11,631 miles. It takes 12 gallons of gas to refill the car. What is Rya's MPG?

and hydrogen. Alternative fuel vehicles not only reduce consumers' fuel costs but also reduce fossil fuel emissions from cars, thus helping to preserve and enhance air quality. To promote the use of alternative fuels, the federal government and many state governments offer tax incentives to consumers who purchase qualifying vehicles.

Depreciation

As a car ages, the number of miles it has been driven increases, the physical condition begins to deteriorate, and mechanical difficulties may arise. Also, styles and consumer tastes change over time. All these factors lead to **depreciation**, which is a decline in property value due to normal wear and tear. However, not all cars depreciate. Rare cars and older vehicles that are kept in excellent condition, called **classic cars**, may experience **appreciation** or an increase in value if valued as collectors' items.

Depreciation is the single greatest cost of owning a car. The cost of gasoline is the second largest expense. In most cases, the age of a car is the most important factor in determining its resale or trade-in value. Other factors include mileage, mechanical condition, model popularity, size, and color. Cars that maintain a high demand and low supply typically have better resale values.

Registration and Other Fees

All states charge fees for title and registration. Some states, counties, and cities charge sales tax or excise tax on vehicle purchases.

A **car title** is a legal document that establishes ownership of the vehicle. A car title lists the legal owner (usually the lending institution) and the registered owner (you). You must pay title fees only at the time you buy the car. In addition, you must also pay an annual **car registration** or license tag fee. Your vehicle's license plate carries a sticker showing you have paid the current year's renewal registration fee.

Vehicle Emission Fee

As mentioned earlier in the chapter, many states require vehicles to be tested to ensure they meet environmental emissions standards. Whether a car needs this testing usually depends on the type and model year of the vehicle and the county in which you reside. Cars that require vehicle emission tests usually must be tested every two years once the car is four or more years old. The fee for the test is usually about $15 to $30.

Maintenance and Repairs

To keep a well-maintained car, you must perform regular maintenance. The owner's manual for the vehicle provides a maintenance schedule that tells you what services are needed and how often. For gasoline-powered and hybrid vehicles, you can expect to change the oil every 3,000 to 7,000 miles or every 3 months—whichever comes first; have a major engine tune-up every 20,000 to 30,000 miles; and perform other maintenance, such as rotation of your tires, at scheduled intervals. Car systems that you should monitor and maintain include emissions control, air conditioning, brakes, and transmission. Hybrid and electric vehicles will also have many of the same maintenance requirements with additional maintenance for the battery, battery filter, and the high voltage cooling system.

You should also plan for unscheduled repairs. Broken belts and leaky hoses happen from time to time, and these repairs can be expensive. Setting aside money for car repairs should be part of your monthly budget. The American Automobile Association (AAA) suggests that you budget approximately $700 per year. Other experts suggest saving as much as $100 per month. As your car gets older, repair costs will increase. You should expect to replace relatively inexpensive parts, such as fan belts, hoses, the battery, and the muffler, but also plan for occasional expensive repairs, such as replacing the alternator and buying new tires.

Accessories

Many people choose to add certain features to their car to make it safer or more functional, attractive, or efficient. These items may include snow tires, wheel covers, window tinting, pinstriping, alarm systems, and sound systems. In some cases, these accessories will add to the vehicle's value; in other cases, they will subtract from it. As mentioned earlier in the chapter, many dealers offer these features as add-ons when you purchase a car; however, you can usually get accessories added to your car at a much lower cost by going to a specialty shop.

What are some examples of the regular maintenance you will be expected to perform when you own a car?

Connections to Your World
Distracted Driving

Many states have passed laws making it illegal to use a handheld cell phone while driving. They usually allow a hands-free system, which may include earphones, a Bluetooth, a mounted cell phone, or a cell phone speaker through the sound system. The laws are based on safety. Many of these laws specifically target teenagers. When people are talking or texting on the phone, especially inexperienced drivers, they become distracted, which can be dangerous and cause accidents. Their driving skills are also impaired when they have only one hand available to drive. For example, distracted drivers often fail to signal when changing lanes.

Many motorists believe, however, that a cell phone is no more dangerous than speaking to a passenger, using a GPS, eating, or any other distraction. They advocate that cell phones are a great convenience and help people get where they need to go. When on long trips or in traffic jams, they can save time and allow for multitasking.

Think Critically

1. With which side do you agree? Why?
2. How do such laws impact teenagers specifically? How do such laws impact others?
3. Do you think laws targeting teenagers are discriminatory? Explain your answer.

> **✓ Checkpoint**
>
> What are the costs of operating and maintaining a car?

LO 11.3.2 Extending the Life of Your Car

Because a car is expensive, you will get your best value if you take care of your investment. You can keep your car running well and looking good by performing routine maintenance, keeping your car in a garage, taking care of the interior and exterior, and practicing good driving habits.

Perform Routine Maintenance

Performing regular maintenance is vital to keeping your car on the road. For example, you should regularly check and maintain the proper fluid levels for your transmission, power steering, windshield washer, radiator, and brakes. These car functions must have fluid to work properly. Regular maintenance also includes rotating and balancing your tires. Rotating the tires extends their life by ensuring all tires get equal wear. Treadwear puts you in danger of a blowout or accident. You should also regularly inspect belts, hoses, and spark plugs.

Another important part of routine maintenance is having your oil changed. Oil lubricates the engine's moving parts and keeps it running smoothly and efficiently. Oil must be changed to eliminate accumulated dirt and sludge. Your individual driving habits will dictate how often you should change the oil. For example, the frequent starting and stopping of city driving uses more oil than long highway driving trips. However, as a rule, most experts advise having your oil changed every 3,000 to 7,000 miles or every 3 months—whichever comes first. You should also replace the oil filter when you change the oil. The filter helps clean the oil circulating through the engine. The average cost of an oil change service is $50 to $100, depending on the size and type of engine and the type of oil your vehicle uses.

Consult the vehicle maintenance schedule in the owner's manual to determine when these and other preventive maintenance checks and services should be performed. Regular vehicle maintenance can seem like a lot of work, but the time and effort you put into keeping up with scheduled maintenance can save you big money in the long run.

Keep Your Car in a Garage

If possible, keep your vehicle in a garage or in a covered area such as a carport. Using a garage protects the vehicle from theft and vandalism. Covered parking also protects it from weather, which can damage or destroy the vehicle's finish and even affect its mechanical condition. Low temperatures, for example, affect almost every component of the vehicle. The engine is harder to start, and the battery is weaker. Thus, the starter must work harder, and the charging system is stressed.

Preserve the Interior

The condition of the inside of your vehicle is very important for a higher resale value.

The upholstery is seat-covering material. Generally, cloth upholstery is more durable than vinyl. Although spills and dirt are more difficult to clean on cloth upholstery, vinyl can crack and tear when it gets too hot or cold. Leather upholstery holds up best, but it is more expensive and requires regular cleaning and lubricating to keep it soft and to prevent cracking.

Floor mats will protect the carpet and are a good investment. You can cover the interior of your trunk with an insert or an old blanket to protect it. Avoid eating in the car, especially messy foods, and vacuum frequently to keep your car's interior in good condition. Products are available to rub on vinyl dashboards and plastic interior surfaces to protect them from fading and cracking from exposure to the sun's rays. If you must park your car in the sun for long periods of time, you might consider covering the inside of your windshield and windows with a sunshade.

Preserve the Exterior

Proper care of your car's exterior finish is one of the most important ways to extend the life of your car. Your car's body picks up dust and grime while you are driving. All that grime slowly chips away at your vehicle's paint. Regular car washes to clean off the road dust and grime will protect the car's undersurface areas and protect the finish.

In addition to regularly washing your car, it is recommended that you wax the paint twice a year—before the cold and rainy/snowy winter and before the hot and dry summer. Protective wax can guard your paint from the snow-melting chemicals spread on streets in cold climates and the sun's damaging rays. If you live near the coast, wax is essential for protecting the car's finish from the salty spray of ocean breezes. Once the paint has begun to **oxidize** (permanently lose its color and shine because of a chemical reaction with the air), it is not easy to restore the original gloss. In most cases, a vehicle with oxidized paint must be repainted to restore its shine. A **polishing compound** is a substance that can smooth out surface scratches, scuffs, and stains. Often called cleaners or pre-waxes, polishing compounds can be tricky to use. They may contain abrasives, coarse materials that scour or rub away a surface. An abrasive can gently remove the paint's top layer and expose the shiny paint underneath. But an abrasive will strip away the paint when rubbed too vigorously or too much. Make sure to read your owner's manual for the car to determine the best way to protect it from the elements.

Many people choose to have their vehicles detailed. A **car detail** is a service provided by specialists who clean and polish the exterior and cleaning and treating the interior. These specialists can provide high-shine polishes that help restore the shine to your vehicle paint job. They can also remove stains and even dye the carpet to cover damage. Car detailing prices vary depending on what type of package you select and the size of your vehicle. Experts recommend the service twice yearly (as seasons change from hot to cold and vice versa). To save money, you can detail your car using products available at large box stores or auto parts stores.

It is also important to repair paint chips and dents before rust can form. You can buy vehicle paint that matches your car's color from a dealer that sells your make of car and, in many cases, auto parts stores. When something nicks your paint, such as a rock that hits your car while you are driving, it is a good idea to touch up the ding. Clean the area with mild soap, dry it, and then apply the touch-up paint in very small amounts. **Paintless dent removal** is a service in which a suction device is attached to your car to remove small dents. The suction pops out the indention but usually does not require painting or other repair. This service is relatively inexpensive, and it keeps your car looking good. If larger dents are involved, such as scratches or scrapes where the paint is damaged, you should take your car to a body shop and repair it professionally.

Follow Wise Driving Habits

Your driving habits have a direct effect on the life span of your car. For example, many new vehicles have a recommended break-in period, during which you may need to drive differently. Breaking in your car can impact the way it performs. Your owner's manual will likely include information if your car has a recommended break-in period. During the first 1,000 miles of driving a new car, you will want to avoid driving at a constant speed for long distances, avoid sudden starts or stops, and try to avoid long trips.

You should follow several driving tips during and after your car's break-in period. You can keep your vehicle running efficiently for years by practicing good driving habits.

Source: RichLegg/istock.com

What can you do to preserve the exterior of your vehicle?

Check Your Understanding

1. Why do vehicles usually depreciate? What might cause a particular vehicle to appreciate? (LO 11.3.1)
2. Considering all vehicle costs, which ones will be the most expensive over time? (LO 11.3.1)
3. Why should you perform regular maintenance on a vehicle? (LO 11.3.2)

Apply Your Understanding

1. Research the differences between the purchase price and maintenance costs of gasoline-powered, diesel-powered, hybrid, and electric cars. Using the information you find, which car would you be most interested in getting? Why? (LO 11.3.1)
2. Detailing a vehicle is an important step in prolonging the life of the car. Using a shopping site, calculate how much it would cost to purchase the items necessary to detail a car. You will need basic cleaning supplies, interior and exterior detailing spray, glass cleaner, small and large scrubbing brushes, car wax, microfiber rags, and a way to vacuum the car. (LO 11.3.2)

The Essential Question

What are the costs of maintaining a vehicle, and how can you preserve its resale value?

A: Costs of maintaining a car include the monthly car or lease payment, car insurance, fuel, depreciation, registration and title fees, vehicle emission fee, maintenance and repairs, and accessories. You can maintain your car's resale value by performing routine maintenance, keeping the car in a covered area, caring for the interior and exterior, and practicing good driving habits.

Summary

11.1 Selecting a Vehicle

- The car-selection process begins with identifying and prioritizing your needs and wants. Then determine what you can afford. Research and compare features and narrow your choices to a few. Decide whether to buy new or used or to lease a vehicle.

- Rather than purchasing a new car, you can also lease. Leasing is renting the use of a vehicle, often with an option to buy at the end of the lease term.

- If you determine you need to finance part of the cost, obtaining pre-approval at your bank or credit union will let you know how much you can borrow and at what rate before you commit to a purchase or lease contract.

- Check insurance rates on your vehicle choices since rates can differ widely.

- Search for cars available at car dealers, other sellers, or online. There are many resources that allow you to search for specific models and give you price quotes. It is also possible to purchase a vehicle through online buying sites.

- Test drive your top choices. Before buying a used vehicle, check its history by looking up its vehicle identification number (VIN) at the CARFAX website and have a mechanic perform a vehicle inspection.

- All new cars come with warranties to provide the buyer with some assurance of quality. Lemon laws help consumers get a new car or their money back if the car they purchased has substantial, unfixable defects. The FTC's Used Car Rule is designed to protect consumers who buy used cars from dealers.

11.2 Buying or Leasing a Vehicle

- The buying or leasing process begins with determining a fair price for the vehicle. Next, negotiate with the dealer to reach an agreement on price.

- The fair price for a vehicle is somewhere between the sticker price and invoice price. Make your initial offer below your top price. Then negotiate but be prepared to walk away if the seller pressures you or will not come down to a fair price. If you are uncomfortable with negotiations, you can hire a car-buying service to negotiate the purchase for you.

- Keep negotiations about the price of the new vehicle separate from any negotiations related to a potential trade-in vehicle.

- Dealer add-ons—or high-priced, high-profit dealer services—will increase the purchase price and add little value to the car.

- The advantages of leasing may include a smaller down payment and lower monthly charges, the ability to have a new car every three to four years, and possible tax advantages if you lease the vehicle for business purposes.

- The disadvantages of leasing are you will not own the vehicle, your mileage is limited, and the car must be returned at the end of the lease.

- You have two options for financing a car. You can finance through a financial institution such as a bank or credit union, or you can finance with dealership financing services.

- The Equal Credit Opportunity Act prohibits lenders from discriminating against borrowers.

11.3 Maintaining a Vehicle

- Costs of operating a vehicle include the monthly car or lease payment, car insurance, fuel, depreciation, registration and title fees, vehicle emission fees, maintenance and repairs, and the cost of accessories.

- Most vehicles depreciate, or decline in value, over time. However, older vehicles in excellent condition (classic cars) may appreciate.

- You can extend the life of your car by performing routine maintenance as prescribed in your owner's manual, keeping your car in a garage or other covered area, preserving the interior and exterior, and following wise driving habits.

- A car's interior can be preserved by regularly cleaning upholstery and other interior surfaces. Car paint can oxidize, so it is important to protect the exterior with wax. A polishing compound with abrasives gently applied can restore shine. A car detail service does these tasks for you.

Check Your Knowledge

1. Using a sequence chart, list the steps necessary to select a vehicle. (LO 11.1.1)

2. Explain the importance of lemon laws for consumer protection of car buyers. (LO 11.1.2)

3. Use a comparison chart to document the differences between buying or leasing a vehicle. (LO 11.2.1 and LO 11.2.2)

4. Why is it important to shop around and then negotiate for the best price when you are planning to buy or lease a vehicle? (LO 11.2.3)

5. Why should you consider the costs of replacing the batteries on an electric vehicle as part of the buying or leasing process? (LO 11.3.1)

6. Describe two different ways to extend the life of your car and preserve its resale value. (LO 11.3.2)

Apply Your Knowledge

1. Visit the Kelley Blue Book or other car value website and look up the trade-in value of your car or your family's car. This is the estimated amount a dealer will give you for your car. Now look up the used-car retail price for the same car. This is an estimate of a fair price that a buyer can expect to pay for the car. Subtract the two figures. What is the difference? What does this number represent? (LO 11.1.1)

2. Conduct online research about the lemon laws in your state. Create a one-page summary explaining what qualifies as a lemon, how long you have to file a claim, and what the burden of proof is. Include any additional information that you think is pertinent. (LO 11.1.2)

3. Research the costs of registration, title, and driver's license fees in your county. Also research whether your county requires vehicle emission testing and what the fees are if required. You can get this information by calling or visiting the website or local office of your state's department of motor vehicles (DMV) or other agency that may oversee car registration. What should someone in your county expect to pay for all these fees? (LO 11.2.1)

4. Obtain the owner's manual for your car or a family member's car. Find the section related to maintenance of the vehicle. Make a list of the required maintenance and the intervals between maintenance services. Search online to find prices for the various services. If you drive your vehicle 15,000 miles per year, what would your annual costs be for basic maintenance of the vehicle? (LO 11.3.1)

Share Your Knowledge

Work in teams of two to four students to complete the following activities.

1. As a team, identify three or four new technological advances in vehicles in the past 3 to 5 years. Explain how they have improved safety, efficiency, and/or comfort for the owners. Then research technological advances that are currently under development. Select two and explain the purposes (benefits) of each one. Be prepared to present your findings to the class. (LO 11.1.1)

2. Rya needs help determining whether she should buy a new or used car. She has saved $2,000 toward her purchase. She can afford to finance up to $25,000. Find four options for Rya. Prepare a comparison chart for her. Include price, options, safety features, gas mileage, maintenance costs, and any other detail your team thinks is important to help Rya make her decision. (LO 11.2.1 and LO 11.3.1)

3. Make a list of car dealers in your area. Visit their websites. Find information about interest rates when purchasing or leasing a vehicle. As a group, report on your findings. What kinds of loans do they offer (interest rate, length of loan)? Is it a better deal to lease or buy? Explain. (LO 11.2.3)

4. Rya decided to purchase a vehicle. She plans to drive the car at least 100,000 miles and then sell it to get as much money as she can for it. What advice can you give Rya about extending the life of the car and improving its resale value? Prepare an infographic or report with charts and graphs to present to Rya with the team's advice. (LO 11.3.2)

Base your answers to the following questions on your own personal thoughts, preferences, and experiences.

1. Purchasing or leasing your first vehicle is an important step for most young adults.

   a. If you already have a car, describe the process you used to select the vehicle. How did you feel the first time you drove your car? What would you do differently if you could do it again?

   b. If you do not have a car, think about what you want in your first vehicle. Make a list of the things you will need in your car and the things you want in your car. (LO 11.1.1)

2. Would you consider getting a hybrid, electric, or alternative-fuel vehicle? Explain. (LO 11.1.1)

3. Research what it takes to receive a driver's license in your state. What kinds of questions are on the driver's exam? What must you do to prove you will be a safe driver? What documents will you need to take with you to your state's agency to complete the process? In your own words, explain why the state requires you to do these things before licensing you to drive a vehicle. (LO 11.3.1)

Chapter Project

Understanding the cost differences between buying or leasing a vehicle is important. Search online for a lease versus buy car calculator. Forbes.com, Bankrate.com, CreditKarma.com, and Edmunds.com are reliable sources you can use. Compare the two options using the following details.

Purchase Details

- Select a new vehicle to use for the example.

- Find the manufacturer's suggested retail price (MSRP) for the vehicle using one of the tools introduced in the chapter.

- Find your local sales tax rate for new cars.

- Assume you have negotiated a sales price for the vehicle equal to 95 percent of the MSRP. Calculate the sales price.

- Assume you have negotiated a trade-in value for your current car of $6,500.

- If your trade-in value is more than 10 percent of the sales price, you will not add any additional cash for a down payment. If your trade-in value is less than 10 percent of the sales price, you will add enough cash to have a 10 percent down payment.

- Assume depreciation rate is 17 percent per year.

- Find the current auto loan interest rate from a local bank or credit union. You can find the interest rate on the financial institution's website.

- Select a loan term you prefer.

Leasing Details

- For the lease interest rate, use six percent or 0.0025 for the lease money factor. (*Note:* Different calculators may ask for either the interest rate or the lease money factor, not both.)

- Use the same down payment you calculated above.

- Select the lease term you prefer.

- Use the table below to determine the residual value of the vehicle at the end of your lease term.

Lease Term	Residual Value Factor
12 months	75% of the sales price
24 months	65% of the sales price
36 months	55% of the sales price
48 months	45% of the sales price
60 months	35% of the sales price

- Assume additional fees equal to 2 percent of the sales price.

Think Critically

1. Which option is the most cost effective?
2. Would you purchase or lease the vehicle? Explain your answer.

12 Chapter

Postsecondary Education Decisions

The Essential Question

What options for education and training exist for students after high school, and what are the factors to consider when making postsecondary education decisions?

Learning Objectives

By the end of this lesson, you should be able to:

LO 12.1.1 Explain educational opportunities after high school.

LO 12.1.2 Explain the factors to consider when making postsecondary education decisions.

LO 12.1.3 Discuss alternatives to formal education after high school.

Key Terms

- technical school
- trade school
- internship programs
- early college
- community colleges
- open access
- dual enrollment
- university
- apprenticeship program

Consider This ...

Adohi and Sequoia are finishing their junior year of high school. Both have taken part in career exploration activities and a variety of career and technical education classes while in high school to help them determine a career of interest.

"I really liked my classes this year. They helped me decide that I want to become an electrician or pursue a career in business," Adohi told his friend Sequoia. "That's great," Sequoia replied. "How does that impact your plans after high school?"

"Well, I'm not quite sure. If I want to become an electrician, I need to go to a technical school and complete an apprenticeship. If I decide to pursue business, I need to start taking college classes. I heard that financing trade school is different than college, but I'm not exactly sure how. I think I need to find ways to explore the careers more this year and find someone who can help me better understand what the path and costs for each looks like," stated Adohi. "That sounds like a great plan. They both seem like great careers. Finding more information sooner rather than later would give you a better idea of the advantages and disadvantages of each and help you decide," replied Sequoia.

(continues)

(continued)

Read and Reflect

1. What kinds of education and training options are available to Adohi after high school?

2. What are the major differences between the two options Adohi is considering?

3. What other ways can Adohi explore these two career options this year?

LO 12.1.1 Postsecondary Education Opportunities

You will have choices to make about what to do after high school. Cost is often a primary factor in determining what a student decides to do. If you are a high school senior, you may have already been asked where you are going to college. The term *college* needs to be clarified for students and parents because it refers to several educational institutions. College is often used interchangeably with university to indicate attending a 4-year school where students often live on or near the school's campus. However, college refers to many educational opportunities students can pursue after high school.

Technical Schools

Technical school programs provide students with authentic learning experiences and opportunities to develop academic and technical skills that can help prepare them for the next step on their career path through hands-on learning. Students may earn industry certifications and college credit by attending a technical school. Examples of technical school programs include business management and administration, marketing, information technology, engineering, manufacturing, hospitality services, agriculture, health science, education, transportation, skilled trades, and public safety.

Many students are encouraged to attend college after high school; however, the United States faces shortages of skilled labor in the trades, such as agriculture, electrical, plumbing, HVAC, health care, and other technical fields. A **trade school** allows students to learn specific skills related to a technical career. The Bureau of Labor Statistics estimates that about 1/3 of all new jobs in 2022 were in construction, health care, and personal care. Plumbers and electricians will also be in high demand, along with jobs to rebuild and add to the nation's infrastructure. Completing a technical education program in as little as 3 to 18 months is possible.

Several types of schools offer technical training. Students may find technical

Source: gorodenkoff/istock.com

What are the advantages of attending a technical program as a high school student?

programs in their local high schools, community colleges, or trade schools. Technical education is hands-on, meaning you learn workplace skills to prepare you for a specific job.

Trade schools can be for-profit, nonprofit, or public institutions. It is important to research the school. You will want to know the programs' costs, job placement rates, and accreditation. Accredited trade schools may offer scholarships and participate in the federal financial aid programs, covered later in this chapter. When you complete a program at a trade school, you do not graduate with a bachelor's degree. Instead, you will earn a diploma or industry certification. Some trade schools offer an associate degree, the same degree you would earn by graduating from a two-year community college. Trade schools that offer associate degrees may be called technical colleges. Once you graduate, you should have the skills and credentials to enter the workforce in your field of study.

High school programs allow students to take specialized courses and participate in work-based or **internship programs** where they can earn industry credentials and even college credit while completing their core academic requirements for high school graduation. These programs allow students to earn the credentials to enter the workforce immediately after high school graduation. One example is Oklahoma's Career and Technical Education (CTE) system. Students in Oklahoma high schools can apply to attend an area CTE Center. If accepted, these students spend half the school day learning the skills related to their program, participating in work-based learning or internships, and preparing for certifications while earning credit toward high school graduation. They are in classes

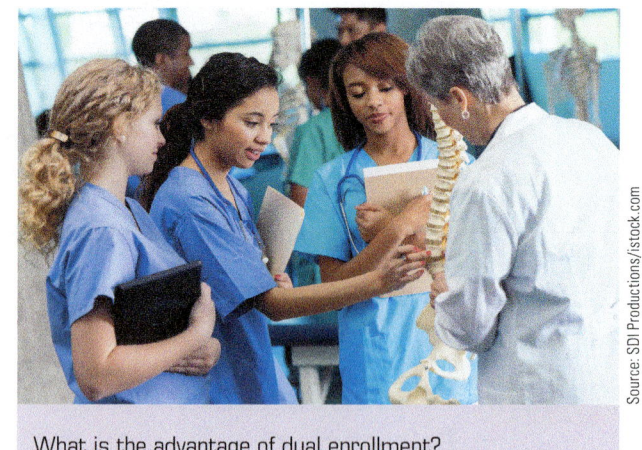

What is the advantage of dual enrollment?

at their home high schools for half the school day, completing their core academic courses in history, science, math, English, and elective courses. Many states have similar options, either within the home high school or through an area technical school or college.

Another option for high school students in many states is early college. **Early college** is an initiative that began in 2002 with funding from multiple philanthropic organizations. Early colleges can be found on college campuses, within traditional high schools, or through community colleges. Students who participate in early college programs receive both a high school diploma and an associate degree (up to 2 years of college credit) by taking a combination of high school and college courses.

Community College

The community college system in the United States was developed to provide educational training that emphasizes the needs of local students and labor markets. **Community colleges** offer various degree and certificate options and operate under an open-access admissions policy. **Open access** means anyone with a high school diploma or GED may attend classes at the community college. Also, most community colleges and some universities offer concurrent or dual enrollment to high school students who want to begin earning college credit while still in high school. **Dual enrollment** allows high school students to earn both college credit and complete requirements for high school graduation simultaneously. Many students in dual enrollment programs can earn up to 2 years' worth of college credit by the time they graduate from high school.

Many community colleges work directly with local businesses and CTE schools to provide education to meet the needs of the local workforce. Students can earn an associate degree in several fields, including business, medical, information technology, law enforcement, and many others. In many cases, the associate degree can be transferred to a university where you can complete a bachelor's degree. Community colleges also offer applied associate of science degrees, which are college degrees related to a career and technical field. Most towns and cities are within easy driving distance of a community college campus, allowing students to live at home while learning a skill or beginning a college education or both. Because community colleges offer programs for working adults, the course offerings are at convenient times, such as evenings, weekends, and online, providing more flexibility than traditional university course offerings.

University

Many students are encouraged to attend a **university** after high school. Universities are typically larger institutions that offer undergraduate (bachelor's degrees) and advanced degrees (master's and doctoral degrees). At universities, the professors teach and conduct research in specialized fields. Universities also offer student housing and activities to create the "college experience." To attend university, students must complete an application, pay an enrollment deposit, and possibly meet academic requirements for entry. Many universities have a competitive entrance policy, and some applicants may not be accepted. Universities can either be public or private. Private universities charge higher tuition and fees than public universities, which receive a portion (typically 12 to 50 percent) of their funding from taxes.

✓ **Checkpoint**

List educational opportunities available after high school.

LO 12.1.2 Postsecondary Education Decisions

According to the National Postsecondary Education Cooperative, there are three stages to planning postsecondary education. Stage 1 is the predisposition stage, followed by the search stage, and then making a choice. Predisposition is the stage where students reflect on their options. A student's background and environment will be important at this stage. Factors such as parental education levels, trusted adult encouragement, and personal achievement are important. In the search stage, students gather information about their postsecondary education options. The student's personal network of mentors, friends, and extended family may have the

Why should you consider multiple options for postsecondary education?

Source: Edwin Tan/istock.com

most influence. The final stage is choice. By this point, the student and their family have gathered information and compared options, leading to a final decision about postsecondary educational choices.

To determine your path after high school, create a pros and cons list for your options. Start by researching a career that interests you. Then, learn as much as you can about success in that career. What type of education, if any, is required to begin working in the field? You have many options, such as attending a university or college, community college, or technical school, or you can enter the military or workforce. You may be able to work for a company, serve as an apprentice, or participate in on-the-job training to learn a skill.

To help you decide, consider the following things:

- Cost. The overall cost to attend the institution. Most programs will provide the "cost of attendance" on their website. As a student, you can visit the website of any reputable educational institution to learn the cost to attend.
- Program length. College and university degrees require credit hours to complete the program. A typical associate degree is 60 credit hours, which takes 2 years to complete if you attend full-time. A typical bachelor's degree is 120 hours, which takes 4 years to complete. Certificate programs and industry certifications can be completed in less time than a college degree.
- Scheduling flexibility. Most universities have limited flexibility in scheduling classes. Classes tend to be offered Monday through Friday during the day. There may also be limited options to begin your education outside the typical academic year. Sections often fill quickly, and students may be unable to enroll in the classes they need to progress quickly toward a degree. Community colleges and technical schools often have more scheduling opportunities, including online, weekend, and evening options. Classes may also begin at different times of the year.
- Admission requirements. University admission requirements typically include standardized testing. Although some institutions eliminated these requirements during the COVID-19 pandemic, the requirements are beginning to return at many institutions. Other postsecondary options may have fewer admission requirements or even open entry.
- Class sizes. Class sizes can vary at different educational institutions: the more hands-on activities, the smaller the class sizes. Community colleges and technical schools tend to have smaller class sizes than most universities.
- Career growth. Some careers require a degree for advancement, but many do not. College degrees often provide a broad base of knowledge that does not prepare a student for specialized careers. In contrast, technical degrees or associate degrees may allow you to specialize in a high-demand career option.
- Financial aid. Most educational institutions offer multiple types of financial aid. It is essential to research your financial aid options for any educational choice.

- Transferability of credits. Community college credits can be transferred to universities for students who want to earn a bachelor's degree. If you are planning to transfer to a university, make sure you work with an academic advisor to maximize the number of credits you can transfer to the university—because universities will not accept some community college courses. Credit earned from noncollege options may not transfer to a college or university.
- Diversity of students. Most universities have faculty and students from countries around the globe. You can attend classes and social activities with diverse students and be taught by faculty from many countries and cultures. Community college students tend to live and work within the community, potentially limiting exposure to students from other backgrounds.
- Campus life. Community colleges are focused on offering affordable education. Many campuses will not have the campus activities and social interactions commonly associated with attending college. The facilities at community colleges may not include amenities that students often expect of a college campus, such as athletics, recreational facilities, food options, and other things that make up the traditional college experience. Universities are usually residential programs, meaning the students live on or very close to campus. The social activities and nonacademic opportunities allow students to engage with other students and have options to join student organizations, participate in athletic events, and enjoy the traditional college experience.

✓ Checkpoint

What are the most important factors to consider when determining what to do after high school?

Alternatives to Formal Education After High School

Students may have many reasons for not wanting to attend college or pursue technical education after high school. Some students may want to invest less time to earn a degree, and others may want to begin their careers immediately. For some students, they may not know what interests them. For others, educational costs may be a major factor.

Some careers do not require formal education. There are many free or inexpensive resources available to learn skills today. Some students may have developed skills in graphic design, video production, coding, or other technical skills while in high school. Others may have turned a part-time job, such as lawn care or babysitting, into a small business. Developing a business plan and working hard can lead to a career as an entrepreneur.

Apprenticeship Programs

Several careers can be learned on the job or through an apprenticeship program. An **apprenticeship program** is an opportunity

Source: Jovanmandic/istock.com

Why are apprenticeship programs a good way to learn a skill or trade?

to learn an art, trade, or skill from an expert. The website Apprenticeship.gov offers information about apprenticeship programs across the country. Most apprenticeship programs are in skilled labor industries such as electrical, plumbing, masonry, carpentry, and so on. You can learn from a skilled professional to gain the necessary skills to open a business or work for a general contractor.

Military

The military is also an option for high school graduates. Military careers offer training for various skills, travel to other locations, and the opportunity to serve the country. Military training programs include engineering, aviation, law enforcement, human resources, and supply chain management. It is possible to earn college credit for military training. After you have completed your military service, you may be eligible for educational benefits to earn a college degree.

If you want to join the military, consider the following before deciding. First, make sure you can explain why you want to join the military. When you join the military, you are making a life-defining decision. Next, are you ready for the physical demands of a career in the military? Service careers require physical strength and stamina. Third, take the Armed Services Vocational Aptitude Battery (ASVAB). It is usually offered during your time in high school. Your score on the ASVAB can help determine the best place for you in the military. The ASVAB measures aptitude and acquired skills, which can be used to help predict future academic and occupational success. It is an excellent career guidance tool.

Source: gorodenkoff/istock.com

How can joining the military help you with a career?

✓ Checkpoint

What are some alternatives to a formal education after high school?

Check Your Understanding

1. What are the advantages of CTE programs when compared to university programs? (LO 12.1.1)
2. What are the three stages in planning for postsecondary education? (LO 12.1.2)
3. What are the advantages of completing an apprenticeship program? (LO 12.1.3)

Apply Your Understanding

1. Visit the website of your local community college. Select two different programs that may interest you. Compare the requirements to complete a certificate and an associate degree. (LO 12.1.1)
2. You are trying to decide what to do after high school. Create a list of things to consider and explain the importance of each item on the list and how it impacts your decision making. (LO 12.1.2)
3. You are very artistic and want to learn how to create custom jewelry. What do you think is the best educational or training path for you? What should you explore before deciding? (LO 12.1.3)

The Essential Question

What options for education and training exist for students after high school, and what are the factors to consider when making postsecondary education decisions?

A: Students can attend technical and trade schools, community college, or university. They can also complete an apprenticeship program or join the military. Factors to consider when deciding on postsecondary education include cost, program length, scheduling flexibility, admission requirements, class sizes, career growth, financial aid, transferability of credits, diversity, and campus life.

What are the costs associated with educational opportunities after high school, and how can you pay for those costs?

Learning Objectives

By the end of this lesson, you should be able to:

LO 12.2.1 Explain the costs associated with postsecondary educational opportunities.

LO 12.2.2 Discuss financial aid and cost-saving options for college or career training.

LO 12.2.3 Complete a Free Application for Federal Student Aid (FAFSA).

Key Terms

- differentiated tuition
- grants
- work-study
- student loan
- undergraduate student
- repayment plans
- scholarships
- 529 College Savings Plan
- opportunity cost
- FAFSA (Free Application for Federal Student Aid)
- dependent student

LO 12.2.1 Postsecondary Education Costs

The typical costs of education include tuition and fees, books and supplies, room and board if you are not living at home, transportation to and from school, and personal expenses. According to the College Board,

What are the typical costs of attending college?

tuition and fees at a public 4-year school averaged $11,000 annually in 2022–2023. Two-year schools average almost $4,000 annually, while private 4-year schools average almost $40,000 annually. Room and board average between $10,000 and $14,000 annually. The total cost of a four-year degree from a public university can cost between $80,000 and $100,000. The fees associated with attending college contribute to the costs of your education. Standard fees may include registration, activity, technology, student health, and other fees that are used to support campus services. Depending on your major, you may also be required to pay differentiated tuition. **Differentiated tuition** may be required for highly technical fields such as engineering, business, and the lab sciences. Upper-division courses, or courses above the 100 or 200 levels, may also cost more per credit hour.

Source: Hispanilistic/istock.com

There are many options for postsecondary education. The costs of these options vary greatly based on several factors, including the type of education, the organization or institution offering the education, the length of education, and location. Regardless of your education plans after high school, it is important to research and understand the cost of each option.

Identify three institutions or organizations that provide postsecondary education related to a career you are interested in. Examples of institutions include trade schools, apprenticeship programs, community colleges, and universities. If you are unsure of specific programs offered by these institutions, begin by searching online to find options.

Then, research each institution to gather information about the cost of attendance. Use the table below to help organize the information you find. At a minimum, find the costs outlined in the table, but do not limit your research to these costs; include all applicable costs for each option. When looking at the cost of tuition or attendance, be sure to factor in the cost difference between in-state and out-of-state tuition.

	Option 1	Option 2	Option 3
Name of program or school			
Location			
Cost of tuition or cost of attendance			
Room and board			
Fees			
Books			
Other costs			
Estimated total			

Think Critically

1. Based on your findings, what costs are similar for each education option you listed? What costs are different?
2. How does the cost of different options vary from program to program? Explain.
3. Does the cost of the different options impact your education plans? Why or why not?

Textbooks are another big expense for college students. The average textbook cost over $100 in 2022. Some students may find textbook options to reduce costs, such as renting the textbook, using an electronic version of the textbook, or utilizing a service that allows the student to electronically "check out" a chapter of the book as needed. In addition, students will need various supplies like book bags, notebooks, pens and pencils, paper, and other accessories. Most schools also require students to have a laptop or personal computer.

Other fees associated with attending college include parking, furnishings for your dorm room or apartment, clothing, transportation, and personal expenses.

Most universities, community colleges, and technical schools will provide a cost calculator to estimate the costs of attending the school. You can find the information on the school's website using the search term *costs for attendance*.

The Rising Cost of College

Over time, college education costs have been growing faster than costs for other goods and services. There are several factors that impact the rising costs of a college education, some of which are discussed below.

Colleges are providing more student support services than ever before. Since the COVID pandemic, colleges have increased mental health support for students. Colleges also help students who may need housing, food, transportation, and childcare support. These services have not been provided previously. Through assistance programs like these, students who may have dropped out of college without a degree can continue

their education and graduate. The need for academic advising has also grown. By adding support services, the colleges have added staff support positions to help students finish school.

State and local funding has also changed for many public colleges and universities. When state and local funding decreases, the costs of providing educational and support services are passed onto students through increases in tuition and fees.

Colleges are part of the service industry. There is little that can be done to increase efficiency in college classrooms. Costs can be reduced by increasing classroom sizes, but that leads to less personalized attention for students. Large class sizes also mean that there is less interaction between the students and the professor, fewer opportunities

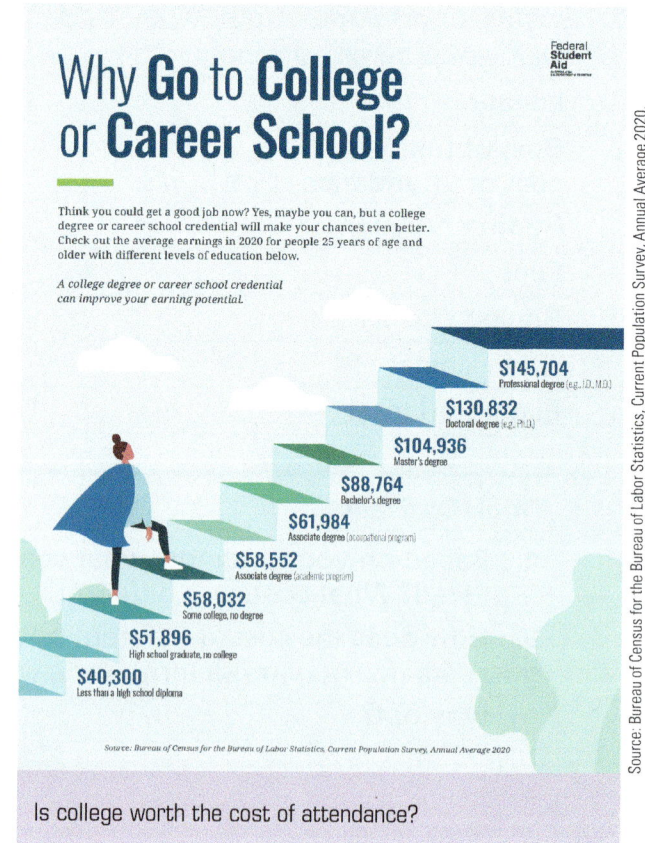

Why Go to College or Career School?

Federal Student Aid

Think you could get a good job now? Yes, maybe you can, but a college degree or career school credential will make your chances even better. Check out the average earnings in 2020 for people 25 years of age and older with different levels of education below.

A college degree or career school credential can improve your earning potential.

$145,704
Professional degree (e.g., J.D., M.D.)

$130,832
Doctoral degree (e.g., Ph.D.)

$104,936
Master's degree

$88,764
Bachelor's degree

$61,984
Associate degree (occupational program)

$58,552
Associate degree (academic program)

$58,032
Some college, no degree

$51,896
High school graduate, no college

$40,300
Less than a high school diploma

Source: Bureau of Census for the Bureau of Labor Statistics, Current Population Survey, Annual Average 2020.

Is college worth the cost of attendance?

Source: Bureau of Census for the Bureau of Labor Statistics, Current Population Survey, Annual Average 2020.

Connections to Your World
Average Salaries

The salaries one can earn vary greatly from occupation to occupation. Work in a group with two to three of your classmates to research and discuss salaries of various occupations. First, create a list of 5 to 10 occupations that members of your group are potentially interested in. Then, search online to find the national average salary for each position. In addition, find the average salary for each occupation in your state or local area.

After compiling the above information, discuss the questions below with your group:

1. Were you surprised by the average salaries for any of the occupations you researched? Were they higher or lower than expected?
2. How do the local average salaries differ from the national averages? Why might this be?
3. What factors do you think impact the starting salaries for the occupations you researched? Explain.

for lessons and activities that require class participation, and fewer projects that lead to deeper learning.

Another reason for increasing costs is that colleges, like other businesses, must pay higher salaries to hire qualified professors, administrators, and staff. The costs of purchasing the latest technologies to provide a quality education are also rising.

Is College Worth the Cost?

The question of whether college is worth the cost is an important one to consider before you decide to attend college. According to the Social Security Administration, men with a bachelor's degree earn about $655,000 more in their lifetime than those with a high school diploma. Women with a bachelor's degree will earn $450,000 more in their lifetime than those with a high school diploma. Earning a graduate degree can increase those differences. How much you earn depends in part on your choice of majors. Engineering is one of the highest-paying fields for college graduates. The average starting salary for a chemical engineer in the United States is $75,000. Computer science and business analytics are also high-paying careers. Studying science, math, engineering, or technology fields (STEM) allows graduates to earn the most money after college. The lowest-paying college degrees include theology, social services, teaching, and liberal arts. Occupations in the technical trades will often earn higher salaries than some college degrees.

It is important to do your own research to learn about the careers that interest you and their potential return on investment (ROI). Calculating ROI is a good way to answer the question of whether college is worth the cost. To calculate a simple ROI, you must know the following things:

- The salary or wages you can earn if you do not complete a college program

- The salary or wages you can earn in the first year after you have completed a college program
- The full costs of the college program, including tuition, books, fees, supplies, and other costs

To find these numbers, use the Occupational Outlook Handbook or similar source to determine salary or wages.

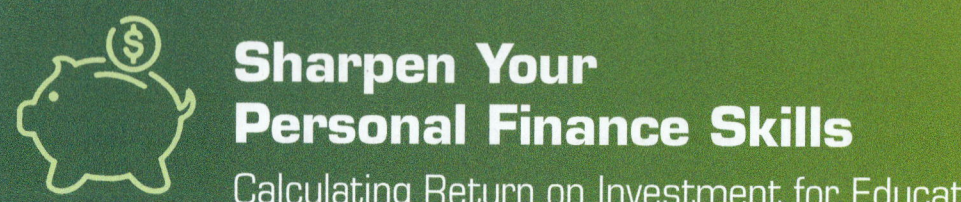

Sharpen Your Personal Finance Skills
Calculating Return on Investment for Education

"Hey Adohi, I was talking with our career counselor, and they recommended that I calculate the return on investment, or ROI, for the various education options I am considering to make sure I am getting my money's worth. This may be a good idea for you as you continue to explore your options," stated Sequoia.

"That's a great idea! I know different options have different value, but I am not sure exactly how much. Thanks for the idea," replied Adohi.

Try It Out!

Using the information below, calculate the ROI for the education requirements if Adohi decides to pursue postsecondary training to become an electrician. If Adohi does not complete any postsecondary education, he can work 30 hours per week at his current job that pays $11 per hour.

It takes 700 hours over 7 months to complete the electrician training program Adohi is considering; during this time, he can continue working 30 hours per week at his current job.

The costs to attend electrician trade school include:
- $16,900 for tuition
- $2,500 in fees
- $100 for accident insurance
- $1,950 for course materials, tools, and textbooks

After completing the program, Adohi would be able to obtain an entry-level position in the electrical industry with a starting hourly rate of $26.00 per hour. He would be able to work full-time (40 hours per week).

What would the ROI be for Adohi after his first year working full time as an electrician?

The cost of the college program can be found on the educational institution's website.

Here is an example to help you see the math calculations.

- Salary or wages without attending a college program. Michaela can earn $15 per hour at her current job and has been promised 32 hours per week.
  - $15 × 32 = $480 per week
  - $480 × 52 weeks = $24,960 per year
- Salary or wages if Michaela attends a nursing program to become a licensed practical nurse. Michaela can earn $24 per hour as a full-time nurse working 40 hours per week.
  - $24 × 40 = $960 per week
  - $960 × 52 weeks = $49,920 per year
- The nursing program Michaela selected at a local school will take her 7 months to complete. She can continue to work her current job for 32 hours per week. Costs of the program include:
  - $2,194.50 for tuition
  - $1,826 in fees
  - $3,010 for books and supplies
  - $2,194.50 + $1,826 + $3,010 = $7,030.50
- Net Return on Investment = First Year Salary – Cost of the Program
  - $49,920 – $7,030.50 = $42,889.50
- ROI = Net Return/Cost of the Program
  - $42,889.50/$7,030.50 = 6.1
  - Michaela would have a 610 percent return on her investment after the first year.

✓ Checkpoint

What cost factors should you consider before you make postsecondary education decisions?

Financial Aid and Cost-Savings Options for College or Career Training

Federal financial aid for postsecondary education is available for many students. The three main types of aid are grants, work-study jobs, and loans.

Grants

Grants are a form of financial aid that needs to be repaid only if you withdraw from school or do not complete the required service obligation. You may qualify for a grant to attend college or a CTE program. Funding for grants comes from either the federal government or your state government. Through the federal government, the main grants are the Federal Pell Grant, Federal Supplemental Educational Opportunity Grants (FSEOG), Iraq and Afghanistan Service Grants, and the Teacher Education Assistance for College and Higher Education (TEACH) Grants. Most grants are awarded based on financial need, and you must remain eligible to receive the grant each year you are in school.

Work-Study

Work-Study is a federal program that pays you to work part time while in school. The program is based on financial need and is used to help pay for your educational expenses. When possible, your school will try to place you in a job that is related to your studies or in a civic education program. Most jobs will be located on your college campus but can also be in the local community, usually in a private nonprofit organization or a public agency. The number of hours you can work each week is determined by the amount of aid you are to receive.

Student Loans

Student loans are the third type of federal financial aid. A **student loan** must be repaid with interest, and if you ever file for bankruptcy, student loans cannot be discharged through bankruptcy proceedings. The U.S. Department of Education loan program is the William D. Ford Federal Direct Loan Program, simply called Direct Loan. There are four types of Direct Loans available to students.

- Direct Subsidized Loans are for undergraduate students. An **undergraduate student** is a student who has not yet earned a bachelor's degree. The loan is based on financial need. While you are a student, the U.S. Department of Education pays the interest on your loan if you are enrolled as a half-time or more student. They will also pay the interest for the first 6 months after you leave school and if your loan is deferred due to hardship.
- Direct Unsubsidized Loans are available to both undergraduate and graduate students. Eligibility for unsubsidized loans is not based on financial need. You are responsible for paying the interest on an unsubsidized loan. Although you do not need to make loan payments while enrolled as a half-time or more student, the interest will continue to be added to the loan.
- Direct PLUS Loans are available to graduate students and the parents of dependent undergraduate students. Eligibility is not based on financial need. Anyone applying for a PLUS loan must have a credit check. The interest rate in 2023 was 8.05% on a PLUS loan. Generally, PLUS loan payments must be made as soon as the loan has been received.
- Direct Consolidation Loans allow the student to combine all federal loans received into one loan with a single payment.

It is important to understand your loan type and how interest is charged. Keep track of how much you are borrowing. Only borrow the amount that you need to pay your educational expenses. Understand the terms of your loan and keep copies of all loan documents in a safe place. You are responsible for repaying your loans even if you do not graduate, cannot find a job, or end up not working in the field you studied.

As with any loan, make all payments on time. Failure to repay your student loans will impact your credit score and ability to obtain loans for a house or car. Federal student loans are an obligation that cannot be discharged via bankruptcy.

Repayment Plans

Student loans must be repaid. There are several **repayment plans** to consider.

The Standard Repayment Plan is available for all student loan borrowers. The monthly payment is a fixed amount. You are expected to repay your loan within 10 years of graduation or leaving school. If you have consolidated your loans, the timeframe can be extended up to 30 years. The Standard Plan will usually result in less interest being paid over the life of the loan.

A Graduated Repayment Plan is also available to all student loan borrowers. Under this plan, payments are lower at first and then increase every other year. Again, the payments are designed to pay off the loan within 10 years unless you have a consolidated loan.

The Extended Repayment Plan is available only if you have more than $30,000 in student loans. Payments can be either fixed or graduated and are structured to allow you to pay the entire loan within 25 years.

Two other types of repayment plans are based on income after graduation. The Saving on Valuable Education (SAVE) Plan sets your monthly payment at 10 percent of your net income. Payments are recalculated each year. If you are married, your spouse's income will be considered if you file a joint tax return. Any outstanding balance on the loan may be forgiven if you have not repaid the loan in full after 20 years for an undergraduate degree or after 25 years for a graduate degree. You may have to pay income taxes on any amount forgiven on this repayment plan. The second option is the Pay as You Earn Repayment Plan (PAYE). Under this plan, you will also pay 10 percent of your net income, but your payment will never be more than the amount you would have paid under the 10-year Standard Repayment Plan.

There are other types of plans that are income-based. Your financial aid office at the school you attend can explain all options available when you need to repay your loans.

Student loans can be a significant expense after graduation. The average monthly student loan payment is just over $500 per month, and most students take 20 years to repay their debt. The Federal Student Aid website (https://studentaid.gov/) provides a loan simulator to explore more about student loan payments.

Source: carlofranco/istock.com

What resources are available to students with a family member in the military or through personal military service?

Military Benefits for Students

If you are the spouse or child of a veteran or plan to enter the military, various forms of aid are available. Examples include Army, Air Force, Navy, and Navy-Marine ROTC scholarships available at over 1,000 colleges. You may be eligible for additional benefits if your parent or guardian lost their life or was injured due to military service. The Federal Student Aid website has details about military benefits for students.

The Reserve Officers' Training Corps (ROTC) offers scholarships based on merit, not financial need. Students who join the ROTC may be eligible for scholarships through the Army, Air Force, Navy, or Navy ROTC Marine Option. Students who enter a ROTC program will graduate as an officer within the branch of service selected. ROTC programs offer up to 100 percent tuition coverage and other monetary support. For example, the Army currently offers scholarships based on grades or other merit for tuition and fees, $420 per month for personal expenses, and up to $1,200 per year for textbooks.

The Department of Veterans Affairs (VA) offers education benefits for veterans, their widows, and dependents. If you are a dependent of a veteran who lost their life in military service, explore options on the veterans affairs website (https://www.va.gov/).

The Iraq and Afghanistan Service Grant is available to dependents of veterans who lost their life because of military service in Iraq or Afghanistan. You must be under 24 years old or enrolled part-time in a college or CTE program. If you meet these requirements, you should apply for these grants.

Other service organizations may also offer benefits for military service or family members of military personnel. These national organizations include the American Legion, AMVETS, Paralyzed Veterans of America, and Veterans of Foreign Wars. You should also check with the local military organizations for scholarships available in your city or state.

International Study

If you want to study outside the United States and earn a degree at an international school, you may be eligible for financial aid related to study abroad programs. Some international schools also participate in Federal Student Loan Programs.

Other Federal Benefits

Other federal benefits include tax benefits; education awards for community service like AmeriCorps; financial support for students who are in or were in foster care; and programs for individuals who may qualify through the Department of Health and Human Services Indian Health Service, National Institutes of Health, or the National Health Service Corp.

State and School Aid

Most states use the FAFSA as the first step in applying for state aid and scholarships. The FAFSA will be covered in the next section. Most states offer grants for qualifying students. You may also qualify for financial aid through the school you attend. Visit the school's financial aid website to learn about scholarships and other financial aid programs.

Scholarships

Scholarships may be merit-based or based on financial need, sometimes both. **Scholarships** are gifts of money that you do not need to repay and can be offered through multiple sources, such as the educational institution, nonprofit agencies, professional associations, businesses, and local organizations. You can learn about scholarships through the financial aid office of your school. You should never pay for a scholarship search or any other financial aid search. The information is available for free.

Applying for a scholarship is time-consuming, but it is worth it when you receive the scholarship. Deadlines can be as early as a year before you start school. It is important to begin your scholarship search between your junior and senior years of high school. Each scholarship will have its own requirements for you to meet. Read the scholarship application carefully. You can search for scholarships through the financial aid office of your school(s) of choice, through your high school counselor's office, on the free scholarship finder tool found on the CareerOneStop.org website, and through state or local foundations.

Other Cost-Savings Options

A 529 College Savings Plan is one way to help save money for college. A **529 College Savings Plan** is a tax-advantaged savings plan to allow families to save for future education costs. Parents or guardians (and grandparents) can open a 529 Plan. 529 Plans can be used for any child in the family. The plans offer federal and sometimes state tax benefits. They are flexible and easy to maintain.

Opportunity Costs

If you are planning any type of postsecondary education, you should consider the opportunity costs of your education. An **opportunity cost** is the loss of a benefit that could have been derived from the option not chosen. In simple terms, the opportunity cost of going to college is the cost of what you gave up by going to college. When you decide to invest in postsecondary education, you will be required to pay the school expenses. In addition, you must also think about the lost income you could have earned if you had started working when you graduated from high school. You must also consider things that you could not do because you were in college.

> **✓ Checkpoint**
>
> What are the different sources available to help save and pay for college?

LO 12.2.3 Federal Financial Aid

The first step for anyone considering postsecondary education is to complete the FAFSA. The **FAFSA** is the Free Application for Federal Student Aid. To learn more about the FAFSA, visit their website (https://studentaid.gov/). On the website, you can learn how to apply for federal aid, including many grants, loans, and scholarships. Starting the process early, even if you are unsure of your postsecondary plans, is important. The website offers checklists for students and their families to begin planning as early as elementary school. The high school checklists are broken down by year in high school. They can be used to support families and help you focus on how to succeed academically and provide guidance throughout the application process. There is even a checklist for those who have been accepted into a college or technical school and have yet to apply for financial aid. High school seniors should complete the FAFSA by October of their senior year. Some states require all high school seniors to complete the FAFSA. Some private colleges will ask you to complete the College Scholarship Service Profile, or the CSS Profile.

FAFSA is part of the Federal Student Aid Office and the Department of Education. The Federal Student Aid Office manages student financial assistance programs authorized under Title IV of the Higher Education Act of 1965.

When you complete the FAFSA, you apply for federal grants, loans, and work-study assistance. Many students may qualify for federal or state grants. Completing the FAFSA is also the first step in applying for a student loan. A student loan must be repaid unless you study a field with student loan forgiveness. Students who become teachers, government employees, or non-profit employees, or those who enter the medical profession may qualify for student loan forgiveness. To qualify for student loan forgiveness, you must meet the eligibility standards found on the student aid website.

To complete the FAFSA, you must begin on the StudentAid.gov website. From there, you will follow the steps provided.

Free Application for Federal Student Aid

Source: Good_Stock/istock.com

Why is it important to complete a FAFSA as part of your postsecondary education plans?

Most high school students are considered dependent students. This means that you will need to report information and income of your parents on your FAFSA.

A **dependent student** is one who is younger than age 24, working on an undergraduate degree, unmarried, not a parent, along with a few other situations that you can learn more about on the StudentAid.gov website.

Steps to Complete the FAFSA

1. Obtain an FSA ID. You will need your Social Security Number and your own mobile phone number and/or email address.

Connections to Your World
Understanding the FAFSA

Understanding financial aid options and the requirements for completing the FAFSA is essential as you begin planning for your future. This process may seem overwhelming; familiarizing yourself with the different financial aid options that may be available to you and the information that is required for the FAFSA can reduce stress and ensure that you are better prepared to make informed financial decisions regarding your postsecondary education.

With a parent or guardian, complete the steps below.

1. Use the Federal Student Aid Estimator found at https://studentaid.gov/aid-estimator/ to help you understand your options for paying for college or career school. This estimator will provide you an early estimate of how much federal student aid you may be eligible for.

2. Gather all necessary information and complete the "FAFSA on the Web Worksheet" found at https://studentaid.gov/sites/default/files/2023-24-fafsa-worksheet.pdf. This is a practice worksheet that allows you to preview the questions and information needed to complete the FAFSA.

Think Critically

1. Why is it important for high school students to complete the FAFSA?

2. What recommendations would you make to a friend who is planning to complete the FAFSA for the first time?

3. What challenges did you face as you completed the practice FAFSA worksheet? How did you overcome these challenges?

2. Gather the documents you will need to apply. These documents include:

    - Your FSA ID
    - Your parents' or guardians' Social Security numbers
    - Your driver's license number if you have one
    - Your Alien Registration number if you are not a U.S. citizen
    - Federal tax information, tax documents, or tax returns, including IRS W-2 information, for you and your parents
    - Records of your untaxed income, such as child support, interest income, and veteran's noneducation benefits

    - Information on cash and bank accounts, investments, and real estate

3. Fill out the online form with the required information.

You can view help videos on the student aid website and find additional help information.

✓ Checkpoint

What are the steps to complete the FAFSA?

Lesson Review

Check Your Understanding

1. What are the typical costs of college? (LO 12.2.1)

2. Define the three main types of financial aid. (LO 12.2.2)

3. List the information that you need to have available to complete the FAFSA. (LO 12.2.3)

Apply Your Understanding

1. Calculate the return on investment (ROI) of a short-term CTE program using the following information. The formula for calculating a simple ROI is Net Return on Investment/Cost of Investment.

   a. Without completing the program, you can earn $15 per hour for 32 hours per week. You can continue to work 32 hours per week while attending the program.

   b. If you complete the program, you will have a starting wage of $26 per hour for 40 hours per week.

   c. Tuition: $1,995

   d. Fees: $250

   e. Books and other supplies: $650 (LO 12.2.1)

2. Visit the Financial Aid Office website for any school you are interested in attending after high school. Read the information available about the financial aid process. What are the eligibility requirements for financial aid at the school? What is the cost of attendance at the school? What are the options for financing and payments? Write a summary of what you learned. (LO 12.2.2)

3. Visit the resources section of the FAFSA website (https://studentaid.gov/resources#fafsa). Find the most recent "FAFSA on the Web Worksheet" and work with your parent(s) or guardian(s) to complete it. (LO 12.2.3)

The Essential Question

What are the costs associated with educational opportunities after high school, and how can you pay for those costs?

A: The costs to attend a postsecondary education program include tuition and fees, books and supplies, room and board, transportation, and personal expenses. Students can apply for financial aid, including grants, loans, work-study programs, and scholarships. Personal savings can also help with school expenses.

Summary

12.1 Postsecondary Education Opportunities

- Cost is often the primary factor in determining what a student will do after high school.

- College refers to the many educational opportunities available after high school, including 4-year schools where students often live on or near the school's campus.

- Career and technical education (CTE) programs provide both academic and technical skills that can help students prepare for the next step on their career path. This can include entering the workforce, completing an apprenticeship, attending a technical or trade school, or pursuing another form of postsecondary education such as community college or university.

- Trade schools allow you to learn specific job skills related to a technical career.

- Technical schools offer certification programs.

- Community colleges offer both degrees and certificates, including associate degrees. They operate under an open-access admissions policy, meaning anyone with a high school diploma or GED may attend classes.

- Universities offer undergraduate (bachelor's degrees) and graduate degrees (master's and doctoral degrees). Universities can be either public or private, and admission is usually competitive.

- There are three stages to planning for postsecondary education: the predisposition stage, the search stage, and the choice stage.

- Students should list the pros and cons of each educational option.

- It is important to consider several factors when deciding on postsecondary education, including cost, program length, scheduling flexibility, admission requirements, class sizes, career growth, financial aid, transferability of credits, diversity, and campus life.

- Alternatives to formal postsecondary education include apprenticeship programs and the military.

12.2 Costs of Postsecondary Education

- The typical costs of postsecondary education include tuition and fees, books and supplies, room and board, transportation, and personal expenses.

- The cost of college is rising faster than other goods and services.

- It is important to determine if college is worth the cost before deciding to attend college or other postsecondary education. One way to determine this is by calculating the return on investment (ROI).

- Federal financial aid is available for many students.

- Financial aid may include grants, work-study, and student loans. Grants generally do not need to be repaid, work-study programs pay you to work part while in school, and student loans must be repaid with interest.

- There are multiple student loan repayment plans, most of which are based on your income and/or future profession.

- Some students may be able to access military benefits for college, including scholarships.

- States and schools may also offer financial aid for students.

- Scholarships are gifts of money that do not need to be repaid. Many different types of organizations offer scholarships, including educational institutions, nonprofits, businesses, and local organizations. They can be merit-based or based on financial need. The scholarship application process can be time-consuming, so begin during the summer before your senior year of high school.

- 529 College Saving Plans are a way for families to save money for college expenses. The plans offer federal and sometimes state tax benefits.

- Understanding the opportunity costs of postsecondary education is an important part of the decision-making process.

- Applying for federal financial aid begins with the Free Application for Federal Student Aid (FAFSA), which is available on the StudentAid.gov website. Anyone considering postsecondary education should complete the FAFSA.

Check Your Knowledge

1. What are the main factors to consider when selecting options for postsecondary education? (LO 12.1.2)

2. What is an apprenticeship program? (LO 12.1.3)

3. Why is the cost of college rising faster than other goods and services? (LO 12.2.1)

4. Define the different types of student loan repayment options. (LO 12.2.2)

5. What is the 529 College Savings Plan? (LO 12.2.2)

6. What is the purpose of the FAFSA? (LO 12.2.3)

Apply Your Knowledge

1. Visit the website TodaysMilitary.com and find the Education and Training page. How can the military help pay for postsecondary education? (LO 12.1.3)

2. Use the Occupational Outlook Handbook (www.bls.gov/ooh) to select an occupation group. Select three occupations from the group list and then select occupations by education level. Choose one from high school diploma or equivalent, one from postsecondary nondegree award or associate degree, and one from bachelor's degree. Complete the table below to compare the occupations. Then answer the following questions. (LO 12.2.1)

   a. Did the median pay surprise you?

   b. Which occupation would provide you with the highest potential income?

   c. How would knowing this information help you select a future career and education choices?

	Occupation 1	Occupation 2	Occupation 3
Most recent median pay			
Typical entry-level education			
Number of jobs			
Job outlook			
Employment change			

3. Visit the FAFSA website at https://studentaid.gov. Read the information about Public Service Loan Forgiveness. Create a brochure for others to explain how to qualify for forgiveness. Include information about degree programs that are included and the requirements to receive loan forgiveness. (LO 12.2.3)

Share Your Knowledge

Work in teams of two to four students to complete the following activities.

1. Recently, different groups, including students, parents, businesses, and the media, have questioned if college is worth the cost. Your team has been asked to create talking points for both the pros and the cons of earning a degree from a university. Prepare a slide deck with speaker's notes to highlight at least four reasons why college is worth the cost and four reasons why college may not be worth the cost. Include statistics, graphics, and specific examples. All data must be cited using appropriate citation standards, and you will need to submit a bibliography of your sources. (LO 12.2.1)

2. Develop an infographic to explain the types of student loan repayment plans. (LO 12.2.2)

3. Create a comparison chart of the various student grant and loan options introduced in this chapter, including private and federal loans. (LO 12.2.3)

4. Research 529 College Savings Plans. As a team, develop a way to explain the purpose of a 529 Plan, how to start a 529 Plan, and what will happen to the plan if the person who is supposed to use the plan decides not to attend college. (LO 12.2.3)

Connect and Reflect

Base your answers to the following questions on your own personal thoughts, preferences, and experiences.

1. Think about your own career goals. If you have not documented your goals, write a long-term SMART goal for your future plans. Next, use a sequencing tool to help you identify the steps you will need to take to meet your long-term goal. When you have completed the task, review it with a trusted adult. What feedback did you receive? How would you change the steps you created to meet your goal based on the feedback? Why is it important to begin thinking about your future career plans while you are still in high school? (LO 12.1.1)

2. You have not yet decided what to do after high school. Search online to learn about careers that may interest you but do not require a college degree. Select two of the occupations to research. Use a variety of sources such as the Occupational Outlook Handbook and the Bureau of Labor Statistics. Would you consider pursuing these careers after high school? Why or why not? (LO 12.1.1)

3. Look back at the FAFSA worksheet you completed earlier in the chapter. Why do you think students are considered dependent upon their parent(s) or guardian(s) until they turn 24? Do you think this is fair? Explain your reasoning. (LO 12.2.3)

Chapter Project

Working with a team or alone, refer to the Department of Education's website (https://studentaid.gov/apply-for-aid/fafsa/review-and-correct/sar-student-aid-report) for information about Student Aid Reports (SARs). Review the information and answer the following questions.

1. What is the purpose of a SAR?

2. What kinds of information does a SAR contain?

3. Why is a SAR important?

4. How can a person access their SAR?

5. What should a person do if there is a mistake on their SAR?

Chapter 13

Family Decisions

What are the financial implications of family unit decisions, and why is it important to plan for major life celebrations?

Learning Objectives

By the end of this lesson, you should be able to:

LO 13.1.1 Discuss the financial implications of family decisions.

LO 13.1.2 Discuss the importance of planning major life celebrations.

Key Terms

- nuclear family
- single-parent family
- extended family
- blended family
- skipped-generation family
- family budget

Consider This ...

Thanh and Tu'ong recently took a weekend trip during which they became engaged. After the engagement, they were excited to share the news with their families. They shared the news through a video call with their immediate family members and crafted a simple text message text message to other family and friends that exclaimed, "We're getting married!"

Upon arriving home, they began discussing possibilities for their wedding. They quickly identified a few things that will shape the planning process. They noted that they both have large families and want them to be involved, they want a formal wedding, and would like it to be inclusive of family and cultural traditions.

"Wow, we have a lot of planning to do! I think we should set a date at least a year in advance. By waiting a year, we'll be able to plan this wedding thoroughly," Thanh said to Tu'ong. "It also gives us time to save additional money since we can't expect our parents to pay for all the costs of such a large wedding."

"You're right," replied Tu'ong. "There are a million details, and I'd like to enjoy the planning process. I think a year gives us enough time to thoroughly plan without being stressed."

(continues)

(continued)

Read and Reflect

1. Why is it important for Thanh and Tu'ong to develop a budget for their wedding?

2. What factors should they consider when planning and making decisions about their wedding?

LO 13.1.1 Family Financial Decisions

When people live together in a committed relationship, they form a new family unit. The family should make major decisions based on each person's needs, wants, and values. Religious and cultural customs often impact family decisions. Couples must discuss their values when considering whether to form a family unit.

Family Units

Families can take many forms. The family unit is a group of family members who live together. The traditional family structure is the nuclear family. A **nuclear family** consists of two parents and at least one child. A nuclear family may include parents who are married or cohabitating parents. A recent study indicates that one-in-four parents in the United States are unmarried. A **single-parent family** is one parent raising at least one child. Mothers comprise most single-parent families. **Extended family** units, also called multi-generational families, consist of three or more generations living as a family unit. In many multi-generational families, a grandparent often serves as a caregiver to their grandchildren. Blended families are almost as common as the nuclear family unit. A **blended family** brings two separate families together to form a new family unit. Another type of family is the **skipped-generation family**. In this family unit, children are raised by one or more grandparents. The type of family unit often impacts the financial situation of families. Nuclear and blended families often have higher incomes because both parents may be working, or one parent works while the other provides the majority of childcare. In single-parent families, only one adult may be providing for the family's financial needs.

Family Goals

All family units should work together to examine their needs and set goals for their future. Short-term goals involve decisions about the near term, such as major purchases to make this year and next and leisure activities. Intermediate-term goals are those the family wants to pursue in the next 5 or so years: whether they want children, where to live, and training or education needs. Long-term goals are for the distant future. They include decisions about savings and investments, job changes, and retirement.

When setting goals, especially financial goals, you should use SMART goals covered in an earlier chapter. For example, a goal of accumulating $9,000 in a savings account within 5 years by depositing $150 in it each month is SMART because it is specific, measurable, attainable, realistic, and time bound. The goal of saving money for the future is not a SMART goal.

The Family Budget

In an earlier chapter, you learned how to create a personal budget. You can follow these same steps in creating a budget for your family. A **family budget** is a plan that allocates spending, saving, borrowing, and investing of the family's pooled resources to meet future goals.

Unlike an individual budget, a family budget must consider the needs, goals, and values of each family member in allocating resources. Joint decisions can be difficult because more people are involved in the decision-making. Nevertheless, family budgeting and communication are essential parts of successful family relationships.

Dividing Responsibilities

Maintaining a household means sharing responsibilities, both financial and domestic. Successful division of household responsibilities involves communication and compromise.

Many families choose to have individual banking accounts, with each partner responsible for part of the income and part of the bills. For example, a couple may decide that one will pay the utilities, groceries, and car payment, while the other will pay the mortgage or rent, insurance premiums, and other miscellaneous expenses. Then each partner is responsible for balancing their own financial accounts and meeting their part of the budget. Other families may choose to have a joint checking account, where all income is deposited and bills are paid out of one account. If a family chooses to have a joint checking account, managing the account will be easier if only one person pays the bills. Otherwise, accidental overdrawing can easily occur. Many families

choose a hybrid model where each person maintains their accounts and contributes to a joint account to cover joint expenses such as rent/mortgage, utilities, insurance, and other expenses. Each person will use their accounts to pay for their expenses. Families can use the decision matrix introduced earlier in this unit to start the conversation about dividing financial responsibilities.

> ### ✓ Checkpoint
>
> Why is it important to discuss financial planning within a family unit?

LO 13.1.2 Planning for Major Life Celebrations

Family celebrations are common in many cultures. Some families celebrate cultural or religious holidays; most families celebrate weddings, births, and birthdays; and others celebrate life milestones. Planning for major life celebrations is an important part of financial planning.

What are the financial considerations related to a wedding?

Source: PeopleImages/istock.com

Marriage and Commitment

Marriage has changed dramatically in the last half-century. Statistics show that more and more people today choose to remain single or wait until later in life to get married and start families. The planning process can be vastly rewarding and surprisingly complex for those who decide to get married. In some cultures, the couple becomes engaged before the wedding or commitment ceremony. There are many customs around the world surrounding an engagement. Some couples may skip the engagement, and others may exchange promise/engagement rings or another symbol of their commitment. No matter what the cultural customs include, the couple will want to consider the financial implications of the celebration ceremony.

Many couples attend premarital counseling sessions to help prepare for marriage. Some religions require premarital counseling. Some states also have laws related to premarital counseling. For example, several states will reduce or waive the marriage license fee if the couple completes counseling before marriage. Other states enforce a waiting period for the license to be effective if counseling still needs to be completed. Premarital counseling helps partners improve their ability to communicate, set SMART goals for the future, and develop conflict-resolution skills. The couple meets with a designated counselor or clergy member, together and separately, to discuss issues vital to family's success. Topics most often discussed include money and budgeting, the meaning of commitment, beliefs and values, children and parenting, family relationships, and religious aspects of commitment that are unique to each partner's culture.

Ceremony Customs and Costs

Wedding costs vary widely and depend on cultural, religious, and social values. In some cultures, one person's family is responsible for all celebration costs. In other cultures, both families may contribute to the ceremony. For some families, the couple is responsible for the entire cost of the celebration. Weddings can vary in style from informal to formal, small affairs to destination weddings, and justice of the peace to days-long affairs. Couples and their families should discuss priorities and the financial implications of any ceremony. For some, a simple ceremony with minimal costs may allow the couple to meet their goals sooner, such as buying a house or having children. Others may want a large celebration because of cultural expectations.

Planning for Children

Many couples want children. An important part of any financial plan should include setting financial goals related to children. According to a recent study, it can cost as much as $160,000 to raise a child until they are 17 years old. This amount does not include the costs of sending a child to college or helping them financially as they transition from child to adult. The decision to become a parent has trade-offs for the family's financial plan, including housing, education, and retirement. If the family decides to adopt a child, the adoption costs can range between $20,000 and $45,000 or more. Families who may want to have children and face medical issues related to fertility may face much higher costs to have a child. If children are part of your family plan, careful

Sharpen Your Employability Skills
Critical Thinking

As Thanh and Tư'ong begin planning their wedding, they find themselves having several conversations around finances. They quickly realize these conversations will continue to evolve as they look beyond the wedding and begin planning their lives together.

"I appreciate that we both chip in to ensure all bills are paid, but would it help us to be more strategic with our financial responsibilities?" asked Tư'ong. "I think that's a great idea, but I know that financial conversations can also cause tension between couples," replied Thanh. "I heard that using a decision-making tool helps guide people these tough conversations."

Refer to the decision-making matrix on the Companion Site and then answer the following questions.

Think Critically

1. What should Thanh and Tư'ong consider as they complete the decision matrix to help them evaluate dividing financial responsibilities?
2. What are the potential pros of dividing financial responsibilities? What are the potential cons?

Why should a family plan for the costs of religious or cultural celebrations?

Source: Alex Potemkin/istock.com

consideration about budgeting for children is an important part of your financial plan.

Other Life Celebrations

Holidays, birthdays, and graduations are times of celebration for many families. For example, the average cost of the traditional Thanksgiving dinner in 2022 for a family of ten was approximately $70. If you have a large family, this cost could double or triple. If your family custom includes a bar/bat mitzvah celebration, a religious event to celebrate a child reaching the legal age of adulthood under Jewish law, the average costs in

If you have not already done so, you will likely plan travel in the coming years. Whether it is a spring break trip with friends, a weekend trip to visit family, or a family vacation, travel requires planning. Today, many people do all their travel planning online. The internet offers several travel-planning websites. Many websites, such as Expedia, Hotwire, Priceline, Orbitz, and Travelocity, allow you to search for and plan various components of a trip or an entire trip. You can do airfare searches; check seat availability; and book flights, hotel rooms, rental cars, or complete vacation packages. While there are some risks of using these sites, the savings and convenience can be substantial.

Some travel websites also allow users to receive special prices, promotional benefits, and other perks. For example, Priceline offers travelers "Express Deals" in which customers can book a hotel in a designated area for a reduced price. Although the traveler can designate a specific star rating for the hotel, they do not know the specific hotel until after booking and paying. Priceline has similar offers for airfare and other travel packages. The benefit of using this program is that you can get substantial discounts—sometimes 40 percent or more off the regular price. The downside is that you must be flexible with your travel plans. While you can select a general location and price, Priceline takes care of everything else, and you do not receive the details until the booking is confirmed. After the purchase has gone through, you cannot cancel it.

Many travel sites also offer special pricing and promotion that is clearly identified prior to booking. For example, Priceline offers "Priceline VIP" customers reduced rates on many travel options. Expedia offers a tiered rewards program in which travelers earn funds that can be applied to a future trip; many of Expedia's partner hotels also offer members special perks during their stay. These types of rewards programs are common with online travel sites and typically increase rewards and offers as usage is increased. These programs are intended to encourage customer loyalty.

Conducting online research when planning trips can save you both time and money. Even if you book your tickets by phone, you can still benefit from the information and online search-and-compare features prior to booking your trip.

Think Critically

1. What distant vacation destination appeals to you most? Use a travel planning website to find the best airfare and hotel rate for this destination. Do travel dates affect the cost? What other factors impact the cost?

2. As you explore your ideal vacation, what factors influence your plans the most? As you build the trip based on your needs, wants, and/or values, what adjustments may be needed to ensure cost is manageable?

New York can exceed $10,000. Similarly, a quinceanera is a traditional ceremony for Latinas representing a young woman entering adulthood. It is a formal celebration with a cost that can also exceed $10,000. Many cultures commemorate their children's "coming of age" through celebrations.

Family Vacations

For some families, planning a vacation is a family goal. Some families may plan an annual camping trip to a local state or national park; others may want to visit a large amusement park or take their family to the ocean if they live in the middle of the country. Family vacations need to be part of your financial plan if this is an important goal for your family. Well-planned vacations maximize the time available for fun, while managing costs and timelines. Apply the decision-making process you learned earlier to help you choose a vacation that meets your goals and fits into your budget. First, define the problem or goal: What does your family want most from a vacation—relaxation, excitement, travel, adventure, time with relatives, or a combination of these items? Based on the goals of your vacation and the time and money available, identify your options. Then gather information about each option, weigh the pros and cons of each, and make a final decision. A successful vacation depends on selecting the trip that will best satisfy family members, saving for it, and planning it carefully.

> **✓ Checkpoint**
>
> What are major life events that may be celebrated, and why is it important to plan for these events?

Check Your Understanding

1. Describe one conversation that is necessary to have before creating a family unit. (LO 13.1.1)

2. Why is it important to plan for major life celebrations? (LO 13.1.2)

Apply Your Understanding

1. Compare the advantages and disadvantages of using a hybrid model for paying expenses as a family with using a joint model of paying expenses. (LO 13.1.1)

2. Explain why the family budget can be both complicated and controversial. (LO 13.1.2)

The Essential Question

What are the financial implications of family unit decisions, and why is it important to plan for major life celebrations?

A: The type of family unit can impact the financial decisions of the family and the family's goals. Life celebrations can be costly but very rewarding experiences. Planning ahead maximizes your money and time.

13.2 Life Events

The Essential Question How can life events affect your personal finances?

Learning Objectives

By the end of this lesson, you should be able to:

LO 13.2.1 Describe the financial implications related to family or job changes.

LO 13.2.2 Explain the financial implications of a major illness or injury.

LO 13.2.3 Discuss financial planning steps for end-of-life considerations.

Key Terms

- dissolution of marriage
- divorce decree
- custodial parent
- child support
- spousal support
- unemployment insurance
- Family and Medical Leave Act (FMLA)
- short-term disability
- long-term disability
- adult foster care
- employee assistance plan (EAP)
- hospice
- cremation

Consider This ...

Thanh and Tu'ong have been happily married for 5 years. Since getting married, they have purchased a home together and started a family. Their daughter, Linh, is almost 2 years old. Unfortunately, Thanh received news at work that she is losing her job due to the company closing. "I lose my job at the end of the month. What will we do? How will we afford to live? I am so stressed out over this," said Thanh. "You're right. This is a stressful time, but if we make smart decisions, we'll get through until you are able to find a new job. We have an emergency fund built up, and we can take Linh out of day care to help reduce costs," replied Tu'ong. "I am so glad that we have been saving. I have started applying to jobs and hope to get some interviews soon," stated Thanh.

(continues)

(continued)

Read and Reflect

1. What are the potential financial implications of this unplanned life event?

2. How will Thanh and Tu'ong's savings help them in this situation?

3. How could unemployment insurance potentially help Thanh and Tu'ong?

LO 13.2.1 Family and Job Changes

No matter how well you plan, planning for all of life's surprises is impossible. Many life events can happen unexpectedly, making it hard to set intermediate-term or long-term goals to help meet the financial needs that arise from these events. Examples of the unexpected include changes in the family situation due to accidents, injuries, major illnesses, or divorce.

Family Changes

Family changes can include adding a family member if a niece, nephew, or grandchild needs care; a grown child returning home for an extended time due to their own life changes; or divorce.

Many marriages end in divorce each year. A divorce, or **dissolution of marriage**, is a legal process in which a judge dissolves the marriage. Divorce in the United States is governed by state law rather than federal law. Although divorce laws vary by state, all 50 states allow for a no-fault divorce, which means that one partner does not have to prove fault by the other to be granted a divorce. It can be done if one partner wants the marriage to be dissolved.

Steps in Divorce

Dissolving a marriage is often a lengthy and unpleasant process. The divorce process begins when one party contacts an attorney to file a Petition for Dissolution of Marriage. The petition states the grounds for divorce and specifies how the petitioner proposes to divide property and award custody, amounts desired for any child support, visitation rights, and spousal support.

Because it often takes many months, even a year or more, for the case to be heard in court, a temporary hearing may be held to establish temporary custody, child support, visitation rights of the noncustodial parent, and other matters. Many of these temporary provisions tend to become permanent. Often, both parties agree in writing to property settlement, child custody and visitation, and other matters before the court date. When the judge approves the written agreement, it is entered as part of the **divorce decree**, a final statement of the dissolution decisions. A decree is final and binding on both parties until modified by the court.

If the parties cannot reach an agreement, the case goes to court for a judge's decision. There is no jury in divorce cases. Both parties present their cases. Witnesses may be called in child-custody cases to determine which parent would be the better custodial parent. The judge bases the final decision on the evidence presented. Once the decree is entered, the court usually imposes a waiting period before either party may remarry.

What costs are involved in getting a divorce?

Costs of Divorce

Expenses involved in divorce are high. They may include attorneys' fees, court costs and filing fees, child support and spousal support, division of assets, and other settlement costs. The more issues the divorcing couple can settle out of court, the less the divorce proceedings will cost.

Child Support and Spousal Support

When dissolving a marriage, the court can order two kinds of support: child support and spousal support. The **custodial parent**, or the parent with whom the children will live, fulfills most support obligations by caring for the children daily. In most cases, the parent not granted custody will be required to pay **child support**—monthly payments to the custodial parent to help provide food, clothing, and shelter for the children. The amount of the payments will depend on the income of both parents and their ability to pay. Sometimes, both parents have joint custody, and the children live part of the year with each parent.

Spousal support, also called alimony or maintenance, is money one former spouse pays to support the other. The money may be paid as one lump sum or monthly payments, usually for a set number of years until the former spouse can become self-supporting. Spousal support is sometimes awarded when one spouse has been dependent on the other for many years and has little means of self-support.

Child and spousal support are at the court's discretion and become binding on the parties under the divorce decree. The amount of support can be modified only by another court order.

Division of Assets

When a couple goes through a divorce, they will have to decide how to divide assets. For example, they will have to decide who will keep the family home, who will keep the furniture and other tangible property, and how they will divide retirement benefits and savings. If they cannot agree on these issues, a judge will divide their property for them.

Consequences of Divorce

Divorce can be a devastating life event leading to emotional distress and financial hardship for one or both partners. In addition to the costs of the divorce proceedings, the family will have to establish new living arrangements. If children are involved, each parent will need a home to accommodate children who travel between the parents. Another cost of divorce is that your tax filing status will change. You can no longer file a tax return as a couple, often putting both partners into a higher tax bracket. You will no longer be able to share expenses such as streaming services and insurance. Creating a new financial plan as you transition from a couple to a single person is important.

One of the most devasting aspects of divorce is the possibility of bankruptcy for one or both partners. If there is considerable debt in the family, that debt is split between the two people when they divorce. Bankruptcy is a real possibility. After divorce, income typically falls for both parties, yet the household expenses may remain the same or even increase. Making financial decisions around divorce should be part of the divorce negotiations.

Job Changes

Another major life disruption happens when one person has a job change. Job changes can be promotions, layoffs, or transfers. Financial costs are involved if a job promotion or transfer results in the family needing to move from one city to another. The family may need to buy a home or rent an apartment in the new city, sell their current home or end a lease, hire a moving company, or rent a moving van to transport their things from one home to another. When you move into your new home, you may have to pay utility deposits, purchase items for your new home, restock supplies and groceries, and other unexpected expenses. Some companies will help pay moving costs, but that assistance often does not cover all costs.

The family budget may be drastically reduced if the job change is a job loss. The family must evaluate their expenses and update the budget until the person can find a new job. If you are unable to find a new job quickly, unemployment insurance may be available to help offset some of the lost income. **Unemployment insurance** is state-provided insurance that pays a worker who has lost their job and meets the state eligibility requirements for the funds. As

described in an earlier chapter, an emergency fund can help with these unexpected expenses.

Accidental or Unexpected Death of a Family Member

One of the hardest conversations a couple can have is what to do if one partner passes away unexpectedly due to an accident or illness. As a couple, you should discuss your wishes and prepare a will. Life insurance, covered in a later chapter, can help offset the lost income when a partner passes away. Regardless of which partner handles most financial decisions, both need to understand the household finances. It is important to know where the financial accounts are located and the account numbers. A record of all important information should also be kept in a safe place.

As part of your financial plan, you should determine how much your spouse will need to pay off debt and live comfortably until they can provide for themselves. If you have children, a plan for their education should be in place. You will also want to discuss investment and retirement plans.

These situations are challenging to discuss but ignoring them in your financial

How can unexpected injuries impact your personal budget?

Source: iStock.com/FatCamera

planning can lead to financial consequences such as not being able to pay the bills or provide for your family's future.

✓ **Checkpoint**

What are the financial implications of a family or job change?

LO 13.2.2 Major Illness or Injury

Accidents and illnesses happen. Such occurrences will interrupt finances and plans. But there are certain things to know and do that will ease the financial burden on the family.

Absence from Work

If you or a close family member suffers from a major illness or accident, it is often necessary to miss work. Part-time workers, gig workers, and people who work for small companies may not have sick leave or other paid time off benefits. Missing work can devastate your family budget if you need to miss work due to illness or injury. If possible, you should be building an emergency fund to help you manage short-term absences. Some companies offer sick leave or paid time off. If so, you may be able to use your accumulated sick or personal leave to miss work without losing pay. Companies with at least 50 employees must follow the Family and Medical Leave Act (FMLA). The **Family and Medical Leave Act (FMLA)** provides up to 13 weeks of unpaid time from work in any 13-month period. To qualify, you must meet certain eligibility requirements. If you take FMLA leave, your employer must continue your health insurance as if you were not on leave. However, when a wage earner's salary is lost, expenses must still be paid. There are several types of insurance that can provide financial help in this situation.

Short-Term Disability

Many employers offer short-term disability insurance that replaces a wage earner's salary up to a certain percentage (typically 70 percent or more). The **short-term disability** benefit generally lasts between 3 and 6 months. If your employer does not have such a group plan, private insurance can provide individual coverage.

Long-Term Disability

If you cannot return to work after your short-term disability runs out, you need long-term disability coverage. Most **long-term disability** coverage begins when short-term benefits end, and the plans usually cover 50 to 70 percent of monthly salary. The benefits last until you can return to work or for the number of years stated in the policy. Should the disability become permanent, long-term disability can bridge the gap between injury or illness and retirement. As with short-term disability, if your employer does not offer long-term disability insurance, individual coverage can be provided through private insurance.

Long-term disability coverage is also available through the Social Security Administration (SSA). Social Security Disability Insurance (SSDI) pays monthly benefits to you if you become disabled before you reach retirement age and are not able to work. To qualify for SSDI, you must have worked a certain number of years in a job where you paid Social Security taxes, and you also must have a medical condition that meets the SSA's definition of disability. When applying for SSDI, forms, paperwork, and detailed documentation must be provided. It often takes a year or longer to get approved and for monthly payments to begin.

Extended Care Expenses

Some types of insurance policies provide coverage so people can remain at home and receive nursing care, physical rehabilitation, and other services when needed. When family members cannot provide adequate care for the injured or ill person, **adult foster care**, which is personal care and services provided for adults in a facility outside of the home, may be required. Sometimes, the care is temporary; other times, it is permanent. For example, a person who suffers a stroke may need physical therapy and recovery treatment for 6 months to a year. After that time, they may recover well enough to return home. Other people will not recover and must have ongoing care.

Private or group health insurance will cover some of these expenses, but there are limits in dollars and time. Special insurance needed to cover these expenses will be discussed later. Many people use savings and home equity extensively to pay for the costs of treatment and recovery. If they use all their funds, public assistance may be available to help them.

There are also private and nonprofit groups that help families with certain extended care expenses. For example, the Shriners help uninsured children get adequate eyeglasses and other essential services. St. Jude's Hospital was founded to help poor children receive life-saving care when they have diseases such as cancer. Ronald McDonald House is a program sponsored by McDonald's to help families of critically ill children. The Make-a-Wish Foundation also provides support services for very ill children.

Under what circumstances would adult foster care be needed?

Keith Brofsky/Getty Images

Mental Health Services

Sometimes the impact of a major illness or injury within a family creates the need for mental health services. Counseling may also be needed when dealing with marital problems or depression, addiction, or dependency issues. Larger companies may offer an **employee assistance plan (EAP)**, a group benefit that allows employees and their families to seek counseling and other services. This program is usually not offered to part-time or gig workers, and it is not a required benefit that employers must offer. If available, these plans are limited regarding the types of services and number of appointments allowed. Thus, many families must bear the cost of continuing these services if needed for an extended period.

✓ Checkpoint

What are the financial implications of an accident or illness on a family's budget?

Financial Planning for End-of-Life Considerations

Many people often prefer to avoid discussing or even thinking about death. However, death is a part of life. Planning for end-of-life expenses makes the process easier for loved ones left behind.

End-of-Life Care

End-of-life planning includes choosing where you want to spend your final days and what type of care you would like to receive. When asked, most people say they would prefer to die at home. That may not be possible, and they may need to receive round-the-clock care at a nursing home or hospital, which can be expensive.

For terminally ill patients with less than six months to live, an end-of-life-care option is hospice. **Hospice** is a nonprofit program consisting of medical and support services provided by a team of professionals and volunteers for those who are dying and their families. Hospice care can be provided in the patient's home or an outside facility. The goal of hospice is not to prolong life but rather relieve pain and provide the patient the highest quality of remaining life. In addition, hospice also provides counseling and grief recovery programs for those who have lost their loved ones. The hospice team will also help make final arrangements for transporting the deceased's body when a person dies at home. This relieves the family from dealing with police and other governmental agencies.

Final Instructions

All adults should prepare for death to help ensure their final wishes are fulfilled. Many people prepare a final instruction letter that offers family members guidance. It may include financial details, names and contact information of financial planners and insurance agents, a list of bank and retirement accounts, information on other financial accounts, and memorial or funeral instructions. In today's world, the final instructions should include information about how to handle your digital assets, including online banking, utility accounts, and social media.

Many people also fill out a Do Not Resuscitate (DNR) directive. A DNR tells physicians, EMT workers, and other medical providers that once a person's heart has stopped beating and they are no longer breathing, no extraordinary measures should be taken. Medical professionals will not perform CPR or other medical processes. This allows people to die with dignity instead of being put on life-support for long periods of time when there is no hope for survival.

As part of your financial planning for end-of-life situations, you may want to appoint a medical representative and durable power of attorney to handle medical and financial decisions if you cannot make decisions for yourself. Working with an attorney to create your will and final instructions will ensure that your wishes meet state legal requirements.

Preparing these final instructions in advance will spare survivors the anguish of making these difficult decisions. It is critical that these last wishes be spoken, written, and made available to persons who will be expected to follow them. Placing the instructions in a safe deposit box with other important documents may mean that these wishes are not known until it is too late to fulfill them. Some states require the DNR to be placed in a visible place, especially if the person is at home on hospice. If the person is a patient at a hospital or other medical facility, they may have a wristband that indicates they have a DNR.

Last Expenses

The costs involved when a person dies can range from a few hundred dollars to thousands of dollars. These expenses include final medical and hospital bills and the funeral or cremation service cost.

Medical and Hospital Bills

Typically, the deceased's estate is liable for unpaid medical and hospital bills, which can be sizable. Any assets the deceased had at the time of death become a part of their estate. The estate sells these assets and uses the proceeds to pay the bills. Collection agencies may try to convince grieving family members that they are responsible for any unpaid medical bills, but the family is not personally responsible. If they feel pressured, an attorney may need to be contacted to deal with the collectors.

Funerals

Funeral costs can range from $5,000 to $10,000 or more, depending on the type of services provided, the casket, and the burial. Typical funeral charges include moving the body from the place of death to the funeral home or crematory, then to the funeral location, and the final resting place. The charges will also include embalming and preparation of the body for public viewing, casket, use of facilities, and funeral staff fees. They may also include the hearse, escort to the cemetery, obituary, clergy fees, printed memorial folders, memorial book, death certificates, and all necessary permits. The costs of a burial

plot and marker (gravestone) are significant additional expenses that the deceased or family will pay.

Many funeral homes have prearranged funeral plans available at guaranteed costs. Payments are made in advance for the funeral and other arrangements. You should be able to get a full refund if you cancel the plan. It is wise to carefully review any prepayment plan you consider. It may lock you into using the services of a particular funeral home at uncertain future prices. If you move away or the funeral home goes out of business, you may have trouble getting your money back.

Cremation

Cremation is becoming more popular for families. **Cremation** is the process of reducing a body to ashes in a high-temperature oven. The ashes are then placed in an urn or other memorial keepsake. Cremation is a less expensive alternative to embalming and preparing the body for public viewing.

Survivors' Benefits

The surviving spouse and children may receive death benefits. For example, if the deceased had a life insurance policy, beneficiaries may receive a nontaxable, lump-sum payment. Benefits from a life insurance policy can be obtained by mailing a copy of the death certificate, the original life insurance policy, and a claim form to the insurance company.

The Veterans Administration pays a benefit to survivors of armed service veterans. The benefit may include a grave marker, funeral service, and small cash. Children of veterans may also be entitled to scholarships and educational grant benefits.

What types of death benefits are available to survivors?

The Social Security Administration also pays a monthly death benefit to surviving eligible family members. The more the deceased person earned over their lifetime, the larger the payment. An estimated death benefit will appear on your annual Social Security statement. The SSA also pays a one-time death benefit of $255 to the surviving spouse or minor children who qualify.

Many employer-provided life insurance, pension, and retirement plans may also pay lump-sum or monthly benefits to the surviving families. In most cases, the family must apply to receive these benefits.

✓ **Checkpoint**

Why should you plan for the end of life?

13.2 Lesson Review

Check Your Understanding

1. What are the major life events that can impact a family budget? (LO 13.2.1)

2. What is the purpose of FMLA, short-term, and long-term disability benefits? (LO 13.2.2)

3 List the costs involved with planning and paying for a funeral or cremation. (LO 13.2.3)

Apply Your Understanding

1. Thanh's sister just learned that her company is downsizing, and she will need to relocate to stay employed. She has asked Thanh to explain how an unexpected job change can impact a family's financial situation. What information should Thanh's explanation include? (LO 13.2.1)

2. Jessica's 18-year-old son Kaidon has trouble saving. In his final football game as a high school senior, he was injured. The injury is minor, but he cannot work for the next 2 weeks, and his truck insurance is due. Jessica needs to describe how an emergency savings plan can help offset the financial strain of an unexpected short-term injury or illness to Kaidon. What should she say? (LO 13.2.2)

3. Rhiann's family comes from a culture where they do not like to discuss issues related to illness or death. Rhiann, as the eldest daughter, has the duty to take care of her parents. She needs to know her parents' wishes, but she must first explain to them the purpose of planning for end-of-life decisions. Rhiann has asked you to help her plan what she needs to say. (LO 13.2.3)

The Essential Question

How can life events affect your personal finances?

A: Divorce, illness, and death are not things people like to think about, but each comes with costs. If you are not prepared for these events, you could be facing huge bills that may become a financial burden on you and/or your family.

Summary

13.1 Family Financial Decisions

- There are many types of family units, including nuclear, single-parent, extended, blended, and skipped-generation families.

- Family financial decisions should be based on common goals, and a family budget should be agreed upon by all family members.

- Maintaining a household entails sharing responsibilities, both financial and domestic.

- Planning for life celebrations is an important part of family decision-making and financial planning. Celebrations can include cultural or religious holidays, weddings, births, birthdays, and coming-of-age ceremonies.

- A family's culture, values, needs, and wants factor into the priority placed on these celebrations and impact decision-making and costs.

13.2 Life Events

- Many life events happen unexpectedly and are hard to plan for. Examples include accidents, injuries, major illnesses, and divorce.

- Divorce, or dissolution of marriage, is a legal process in which a judge dissolves the bonds of matrimony between two people. All states now allow no-fault divorces.

- Divorce is often a lengthy and unpleasant process. It can also be expensive. Costs can include attorney's fees, court costs and filing fees, child and spousal support, division of assets, and other settlement costs.

- Steps In getting a divorce include filing a petition, agreeing to a property settlement, attending a court hearing, and obtaining a divorce decree.

- One consequence of divorce is the possibility of bankruptcy for one or both partners. Divorce negotiations should include financial decision-making.

- Job changes such as promotions, layoffs, or transfers can impact a family's budget and decision-making.

- If a family member loses their job, the family must evaluate their expenses and update their budget. Unemployment insurance may be available to offset lost income.

- The death of a family member will impact a family's financial situation.

- An emergency fund can help offset unexpected events for a family.

- Short- and long-term disability insurance can help cover lost wages resulting from injury or illness. If family members are unable to provide adequate care, adult foster care may be required.

- Mental health services are sometimes covered by health insurance policies or employee assistance plans (EAPs) but are often limited in scope.

- All adults should prepare for their death to ensure their final wishes are carried out and to help make the process easier for their loved ones left behind.

- Last expenses include final medical and hospital bills and the cost of the funeral or cremation service.

Check Your Knowledge

1. Why can the type of family unit impact a family's financial situation? (LO 13.1.1)

2. When planning for important family celebrations, why is it important to create and follow a budget? (LO 13.1.2)

3. How would a job promotion that involves relocation impact the family budget? (LO 13.2.1)

4. What is the difference between short-term and long-term disability insurance? (LO 13.2.2)

5. What types of decisions are important for end-of-life planning? (LO 13.2.3)

Apply Your Knowledge

1. As couples set their future goals, they often include short-term, intermediate-term, and long-term goals. Thanh and Tu'ong want to write their own goals. Help them determine what types of goals might appear in each of these categories. Explain why families as a unit should set goals in addition to individual goals. Then, help Thanh and Tu'ong write one goal in each category. (LO 13.1.1)

2. Consider a major family celebration in your own family such as a major holiday, graduation, or birthday. List what is involved in the celebration, such as food, who is invited, if gifts are involved, or other things that are involved in having a successful event. Use online resources to develop a preliminary budget for this type of family event. (LO 13.1.2)

3. Explain the purpose of child support and spousal support and then research the way such support is calculated in your state. How long is support required to be paid? Prepare a way to share what you learned. (LO 13.2.1)

4. Develop a list of pros and cons related to short-term and long-term disability insurance and its importance in family financial planning. (LO 13.2.2)

5. Write a letter of last instructions for yourself. Include the things that would be most important for your family to know. (LO 13.2.3)

Share Your Knowledge

Work in teams of two to four students to complete the following activities.

1. Find a legitimate research source that provides a current profile of parents in the United States. One example of a reliable source is the Pew Research Center. As a team, prepare a report or presentation that includes information about marriage rates, unmarried parenting, demographic profiles of single or cohabiting parents, and the public views related to the information. (LO 13.1.1)

2. Thanh and Tu'ong are planning to get married. They have asked for your opinion on how to divide household responsibilities. Thanh earns approximately 40 percent of the couple's net income. Tu'ong earns approximately 60 percent of the couple's net income. Devise a plan for dividing financial responsibilities. Explain your team's reasoning. (LO 13.1.2)

3. As a team, investigate the steps involved in planning for a funeral in your local area. What are the factors to consider and the costs involved? (LO 13.2.3)

Connect and Reflect

Base your answers to the following questions on your own personal thoughts, preferences, and experiences.

1. If you are part of a blended family, or if you know someone in a blended family, what are some of the issues that are part of living in such a family? How does the family make decisions? What would you do differently? (LO 13.1.1)

2. Have you ever been on a family vacation? If so, how much were you involved in the planning process? If not, what type of family vacation would you plan? Would others in your family enjoy the same type of vacation you would plan? Explain your answer. (LO 13.1.2)

3. How will you plan for the end of your life? What decisions should you make in advance? (LO 13.2.3)

Chapter Project

Describe a special celebration you would choose for yourself, including the setting, type of celebration, size, and other important considerations. Use online resources to help you plan the event and create a budget for the celebration.

Unit 3: Career Exploration

Skills Assessment

Part 1

Once you have identified a career cluster of interest and have completed initial research, it is necessary to dive deeper into the skills needed to be successful in different career paths within that cluster. It is important to gain an understanding of the skills needed, assess your skillset, and identify areas of strength and potential growth. By assessing skills now, you can work to develop skills that may be lacking. Strengthening and enhancing your skillset will increase the likelihood of you being successful in a career of interest.

There are many skills assessments available online. One to try is the Skills Matcher assessment from the U.S. Department of Labor, which can be found at https://www.careeronestop.org/ExploreCareers/Assessments/skills.aspx. Take the assessment, review the suggested career matches, and click the link to view your full list of skills.

Reflect and Revise

1. Do you agree or disagree with the list of skills generated? Explain.

2. Do the suggested careers align with the career cluster that you selected in Unit 2? If not, what skills do you think you may be missing?

Part 2

Advance CTE provides Knowledge & Skills Statements for each career cluster within their National Career Cluster Framework. These statements outline essential and foundational knowledge and skills that apply to each of the 16 career clusters. They also provide Knowledge & Skills Statements for specific career pathways within each cluster. These statements focus on skills workers need to demonstrate competence within that specific pathway.

Visit https://careertech.org/what-we-do/career-clusters/ and select the icon for the career cluster you chose to research in the Unit 2 project. Open the Knowledge & Skills Statement for your chosen cluster. As you review the statement, take notes on skills that you believe are your strengths, skills that you believe you may need to further develop, and skills that stand out to you. Use a three-column graphic organizer like the one below or another strategy to help collect and organize your notes.

Skills That Are Strengths for Me	Skills That I Should Further Develop	Skills That Stood Out to Me and Why

Reflect and Revise

1. How well does your current skillset align with the skills needed to be successful within your chosen career path? Explain.

2. How can you develop skills that will help prepare you for a career in your chosen career path?

Scenario 1: Postsecondary Education Decisions

Sequoia is trying to decide what she wants to do after high school. She remembered her conversation with her friend Adohi and decided to follow her own advice and start planning for what she might do when she graduates. Sequoia decided to complete a decision-making or problem-solving matrix to help her decide between several options. She wanted to use a matrix that would allow her to compare and weigh options against a standard set of criteria, or factors to consider, to make the most informed decision. Using the problem-solving matrix on the Companion Site, help Sequoia make her decision.

Think Critically

1. Which option was best for Sequoia? Explain your answer.

2. How can weighing factors to consider impact the overall score of each option in the problem-solving matrix?

3. Compare the problem-solving matrix you completed for Sequoia with that of a partner. How did your matrix differ from theirs? Why do you think the scores were different?

4. How do personal values influence the weight and impact of factors to consider when solving problems and making decisions?

Scenario 2: Housing Decisions

Sequoia has decided that she wants to continue her education. The school she selected is in a different town from where her parents live. She plans to share an apartment or house with two friends, Jazmin and Sasha.

Sequoia knows she wants to be near the school and where she will be working, but she is willing to drive or take public transportation if it helps lower her rent costs. She also knows that the most she can pay for her share of the rent is $500 per month plus another $150 for utilities and other services, and she would prefer to have a private bedroom. Her parents want her to be in a safe neighborhood. Sequoia does not have a pet, so she does not care if pets are allowed. She wants access to a washer and dryer at any time and considers this very important because she has only two work uniforms.

Use the problem-solving matrix and housing options on the Companion Site to help Sequoia determine which type of housing would work best for her.

Think Critically

1. Using the criteria outlined above and on the Companion Site, which housing option would best meet Sequoia's needs? Explain your answer.

2. Sequoia, Jazmin, and Sasha met to discuss their options. Each of them brought their completed problem-solving matrix. Compare the three matrices and determine the best option for them. All three go to the same school and work near each other. Jazmin has a dog and would like the dog to live with her. All three would prefer their own room but would consider sharing if there is a master bedroom with its own bathroom.

   • Which option did each of them rank number one?

   • Which option would you recommend to them? Explain your answer.

3. What compromises do they need to make to select a housing option?

Making Your Own Decisions

Create a problem-solving matrix for a personal decision you need to make. After you complete the matrix, answer the following questions.

1. Why did you select the criteria, or factors to consider, used in the matrix?
2. How did you select the criteria weight for each factor to consider listed in your matrix?
3. Did completing the matrix help you make your decision or solve your problem? Why or why not?
4. What is the benefit of using a problem-solving matrix when you have a complex decision to make?
5. What did you find most and least useful about the matrix? What would you change to help you make better decisions in the future?

Personal Financial Literacy

The Personal Financial Literacy Event measures your personal finance knowledge. Students must be able to apply reliable information and systematic decision making to personal financial decisions. The Personal Financial Literacy Event consists of a financial literacy exam and a role-play scenario with a business executive. Finalists will compete in a second role-play event. Participants will have 10 minutes to review the scenario and develop a professional approach to solving the problem. Participants will have 10 minutes to present their action plan to the judge. After the participant's explanation, the judge can ask questions about the scenario.

Go to DECA.org/compete for more detailed information.

Performance Indicators

- Give an example of how education and training can affect lifetime income
- Compare the costs of postsecondary education with the potential increase in income from a career of choice
- Discuss how nonincome factors such as childcare options, cost of living, and work conditions can influence job choice

Try It Out!

You are to assume the role of a guidance and career counselor at the local high school. One of your responsibilities is to meet with the high school juniors and seniors to discuss postsecondary options, including the decision to attend postsecondary education.

Your next appointment is with a high school senior (the judge), Adohi, who has yet to decide whether to attend college. Adohi is interested in working in health care but does not think earning a degree to be a doctor or nurse is necessary. Adohi thinks getting a job as a nurse's aide right out of high school will be less expensive and less time consuming.

Your goal is to showcase to Adohi the benefits of attending some postsecondary training and how it can affect future choices. You may use the information below, if needed.

City Hospital Starting Salaries

- Nurse's aide—The starting salary is $12.50 per hour, with an annual 2 percent cost of living increase and an additional $2.00 per hour raise after 3 years of employment. A nurse's aide would work 12 hours per day, 3 days per week, and be paid 40 hours per week (even though they work only 36 hours). This job requires completion of a certified nursing assistant program that costs approximately $2,000 and would take 120 hours of education.

- Registered nurse—The starting salary for a nurse is $70,000 per year, with an annual 2 percent cost of living increase and additional salary increases of $600 per year. An RN would work 12 hours per day, 3 days per week, and be paid 40 hours per week (even though they work only 36 hours). Job requirements include being licensed by the state, which requires completing a 2-year nursing program. The cost is approximately $24,000 for tuition, fees, books, and supplies.

- Bachelor of Science in Nursing (BSN)—A BSN is a registered nurse who has earned a bachelor's degree. The starting salary is $85,000 per year, with an annual 3 percent cost of living increase and additional salary increases of $1,800 per year. A BSN would work 12 hours per day, 3 days per week, and be paid 40 hours per week (even though they only work 36 hours). Job requirements include being licensed by the state, which requires completing a bachelor's degree program. The cost is approximately $48,000 for tuition, fees, books, and supplies. City Hospital offers tuition reimbursement for RNs who want to complete the BSN program.

You will discuss with Adohi how education affects career choices and income. You must also discuss nonincome factors that may affect career choices. You will meet with Adohi in your office. The meeting will begin with Adohi greeting you and asking about education choices. At the end of the presentation, Adohi may ask you questions and conclude the meeting by thanking you for your time.

www.deca.org/compete

Source: Monkey Business Images/Shutterstock

4 Unit

Managing Risk

14 Introduction to Risk Management

15 Property and Liability Insurance

16 Health and Life Insurance

Unit 4 provides you with practical skills that can promote financial literacy, responsible decision making, and a deeper understanding of risk and its management. Risk management is an essential life skill that allows you to protect yourself from unforeseen events such as accidents, natural disasters, or health issues. It is important to understand how to budget for protection against unexpected expenses by learning about the appropriate types and amounts of insurance needed to protect your property, health, life, and financial resources. As part of your risk management plan, you will be able to assess risk and make better choices in evaluating potential risk and taking the necessary precautions.

Source: Lyndsie Schlink/Illinois State University

Tricia Griffith

Tricia Griffith was born in October 1964 in Illinois. She is a business executive currently serving as the president and chief executive officer (CEO) of the Progressive Corporation, an insurance company founded in 1937. The company offers vehicle, home, life, and pet insurance and is headquartered in Mayfield Village, Ohio. Progressive also offers automobile insurance in Australia. Progressive Corporation is in the Fortune 100, which means it is one of the largest corporations in the United States.

Griffith attended Illinois State University (ISU) for her undergraduate degree in marketing. She credits her education and experiences at ISU for starting her leadership journey. In an interview with ISU, she talked about her summer job as a preview guide, stating, "It was a life-changing summer. I realized then that if you lead with your values, you can really influence people." Griffith also studied advanced management at the University of Pennsylvania's Wharton School of Business.

Griffith was named the president and CEO of Progressive Corporation in July 2016. She is the first woman to hold the position in the history of Progressive. Griffith joined the Progressive Corporation as an entry-level employee, a claims representative, when she was 22 years old. Before being named CEO, she served the company in many roles, including chief human resources officer, group president of the claims division, personal lines chief operating officer, and president of customer operations. She launched the first-ever diversity and inclusion program at Progressive. While Griffith was CEO, the company launched a mobile app called Snapshot. The app uses telematics to charge drivers premiums based on their driving style. The data from over 1.5 billion miles of driving was used to create an algorithm to measure distracted driving, placing Progressive as an innovator in the insurance industry.

In 2016, Fortune ranked Griffith as 18th in their list of Most Powerful Women in Business, and she was ranked 13th in 2018. She was also the first woman named Fortune's Businessperson of the Year. She has worked hard to bring a diverse and inclusive environment to Progressive. In 2018, the company was in the 96th percentile of all companies that use Gallup's Culture Survey. Progressive's employees credit Griffith's leadership style as a key to the company's success. Griffith believes that "it's very important to have a fair and inclusive work environment, reflect the customers we serve, and for our leaders to reflect the people they lead."

Connect and Reflect

Griffith is known for her authentic and inclusive leadership style. Reflect on how effective leadership impacts the direction of a team or organization and the effect it can have on productivity, morale, and organizational culture.

1. What do you think Griffith means when she says, "[I]f you lead with your values, you can really influence people"? Do you agree? Explain.

2. What qualities do you think make an effective and authentic leader?

3. What do you think it means to have a fair and inclusive work environment?

14 Chapter

Introduction to Risk Management

Learning Objectives

By the end of this lesson, you should be able to:

LO 14.1.1 Explain the different types of risk.
LO 14.1.2 Explain the basics of insurance and how risk is managed by insurers.
LO 14.1.3 Identify ways to reduce the costs of insurance.

Key Terms

- risk
- pure risk
- insurance
- insurable risk
- insurable interest
- personal risk
- property risk
- liability risk
- economic risk
- speculative risk
- risk management
- premium
- indemnification
- deductible
- policy limits
- copayment
- multipolicy discount
- multiline discount

Consider This ...

Sosi has had a full-time job for almost a year and is working hard to establish financial stability. She met with a financial planner to discuss strategies for purchases and investments in the future. The financial planner asked Sosi to share details about her risk management plan.

"I have basic insurance on my car," Sosi answered, "but I don't really know if it's adequate. I hear a lot about life insurance, but I haven't bought a policy. I have health insurance but don't know what it really covers. I'm renting an apartment, so I have considered getting renters insurance. However, I don't have much room in my budget, and I can't afford to make big insurance payments. On the other hand, I don't want to take chances that could drain my savings if an unfortunate event occurs and I'm not properly insured. You've mentioned having a risk management plan. What is that? Is that the same thing as buying insurance?"

Read and Reflect

1. What is insurance and how does it help minimize risk?

2. What types of insurance might Sosi need as a teenager? What types of insurance are needed by adults?

3. What is a risk management plan, and why would it be beneficial for Sosi to have one?

Types of Risk

Risk is a state of uncertainty where certain situations may result in loss or another undesirable outcome. Uncertainty is the likelihood that something will or will not happen. In other words, there is more than one possible outcome. For example, the weather forecast may call for a 50 percent chance of rain.

A future chapter will describe one type of risk (investing risk) as the chance of financial loss from a decline in an investment's value. There are many other types of risks you will face in your lifetime.

Pure Risk

Pure risk is a chance of loss with no chance for gain. Pure risks are random, meaning they can happen to anyone. Examples of pure risk include:

- Accidents resulting in physical injury and damage to property
- Illnesses that people get throughout life as a part of aging
- Acts of nature resulting in damage to persons and property

It is possible to do things to help protect yourself from the consequences of these types of risk. Everyone should have a plan in place in the event of a pure risk because the consequences are often serious and can even be catastrophic, affecting your life and your lifestyle.

Insurable Risk

You can reduce negative consequences of pure risk by purchasing insurance. **Insurance** is a method for spreading individual risk among a large group of people to make losses more affordable for all. An **insurable risk** is a pure risk faced by many people for

What are some types of risk that we experience during our lives?

Source: iStock.com/Brian Sevald

which the amount of the loss can be predicted. Insurance companies can make these predictions by examining the loss incurred from past events, such as flooding.

To purchase insurance, you must have an insurable interest to protect. An **insurable interest** is any financial interest in life or property such that the insured would suffer financially if the life or property were lost or harmed. For example, you cannot buy insurance on someone else's house. Unless you own the house, you would not suffer a financial loss if it burned down. But, if you depend on your spouse's income to live, you have an insurable interest in your spouse and can buy life insurance on them.

There are three major insurable risks: personal, property, and liability. You should consider these risks as you plan to protect your financial interests. **Figure 14.1** gives examples of common insurable risks and ways to protect yourself or reduce their financial impact.

Personal Risk

A **personal risk** is the chance of loss involving your income and standard of living. You can protect yourself and others who depend on your income from personal risks by buying life, health, and disability insurance.

Figure 14.1   Common Insurable Risks

Risks	Causes (Perils)	Ways to Protect Yourself
1. Losing job (income)	Poor economy Company's financial condition Job-skills obsolescence	Unemployment insurance Learn new skills; make yourself more valuable
2. Illness or injury	On-the-job accident Chronic health condition or handicap	Health insurance Disability insurance Retraining programs
3. Death of wage earner	Dangerous activities including sports or job illness	Life insurance Get training/lessons Take safety precautions
4. Liability for others' injuries	Careless driving Hazard at home/place of work	Liability insurance Signs, warnings, supervised uses
5. Loss of property to theft	Vehicle stolen Robbery	Property insurance Park in well-lit and secure places Locks/security devices

Property Risk

The chance of loss or harm to personal or real property is called **property risk**. For example, your home, car, or other possessions could be damaged or destroyed by fire, theft, wind, rain, accident, and other hazards. To protect against such risks, you can buy property insurance.

Liability Risk

A **liability risk** is the chance of loss that may occur when your errors or actions result in injuries to others or damage to their property. For example, you could accidentally cause injury or damage to others or their property while driving a car. Or a person could fall and break an arm because of your home's crumbling front steps. Liability insurance protects you if others sue you for causing injuring or damaging their property.

Economic Risk

Everyone faces risks due to the current state of the economy. **Economic risk** may result in gain or loss because of changing economic conditions. For example, when the business cycle is in a period of recovery or growth, most people and businesses are realizing gains in their financial position. However, the economy can slow down and go into a recession if the slowdown lasts for several months or years. During this time, many people lose their jobs and are unable to buy goods and services. As a result, many businesses find themselves unable to meet their debts. **Figure 14.2** is an illustration of the business cycle.

Speculative Risk

A **speculative risk** may result in either gain or loss. For example, if you buy gold, futures, options, crypto, or commodities as

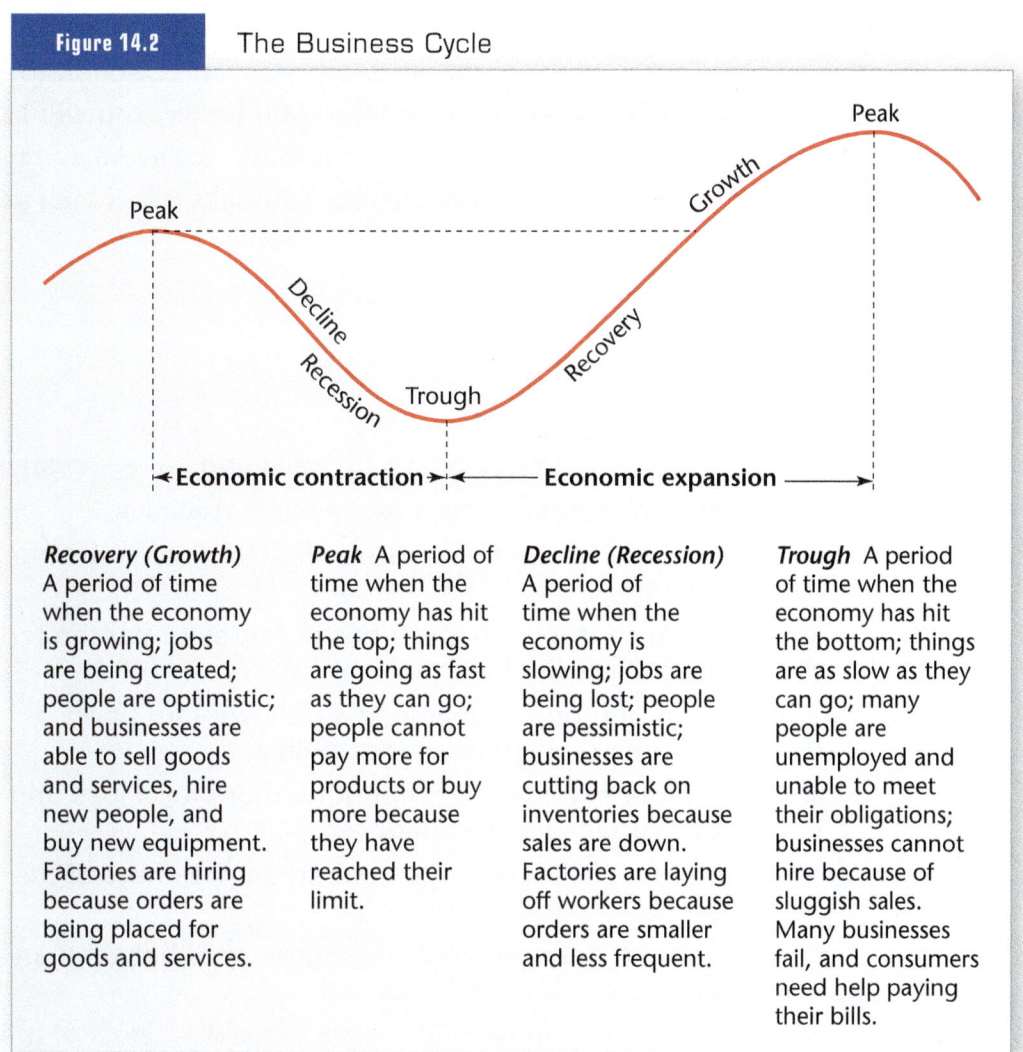

Figure 14.2 The Business Cycle

Peak

Peak

Growth

Decline

Recovery

Recession

Trough

←— Economic contraction —→ ←— Economic expansion —→

Recovery (Growth) A period of time when the economy is growing; jobs are being created; people are optimistic; and businesses are able to sell goods and services, hire new people, and buy new equipment. Factories are hiring because orders are being placed for goods and services.

Peak A period of time when the economy has hit the top; things are going as fast as they can go; people cannot pay more for products or buy more because they have reached their limit.

Decline (Recession) A period of time when the economy is slowing; jobs are being lost; people are pessimistic; businesses are cutting back on inventories because sales are down. Factories are laying off workers because orders are smaller and less frequent.

Trough A period of time when the economy has hit the bottom; things are as slow as they can go; many people are unemployed and unable to meet their obligations; businesses cannot hire because of sluggish sales. Many businesses fail, and consumers need help paying their bills.

investments, you could either make a lot of money or lose a lot of money. Because speculative risks are not accidental or random and may result in either gain or loss, you cannot protect yourself from losses in a traditional manner. While hedging (making an investment to help offset against loss) is a technique used to help reduce losses from such risky acts, it does not reduce the risk itself.

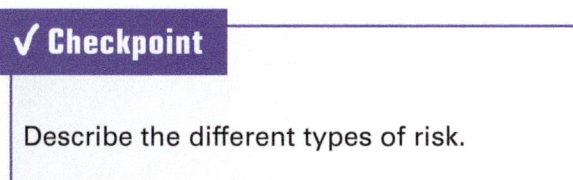

✓ Checkpoint

Describe the different types of risk.

LO 14.1.2 Insurance Basics

You face risks every day. From the moment you get out of bed, you take chances. You could slip and fall. You could have an accident in the kitchen. You could have your mobile phone stolen or injure another person or damage their property while driving your car. Insurance serves as an excellent risk management tool. It provides relief from fear of severe financial loss due to events beyond your control. Although most adults purchase some form of insurance during their lifetime, such as life, health, liability, disability, homeowners, and auto, many do not understand how insurance works. It is helpful to familiarize yourself with some basic insurance terminology. **Figure 14.3** illustrates the many insurance terms that all consumers need to understand.

Here is an example of how insurance works. Suppose your textbook for this class costs $60. If you lose it, you will have to pay that amount to replace it. An average of 1 out of every 10 textbooks is lost each school year.

Figure 14.3   Insurance Terminology

Term	Definition
Actuarial table	A table of premium rates based on ages and life expectancies
Actuary	A specialist in insurance calculations and statistics
Beneficiary	A person named on an insurance policy to receive the benefits from the policy
Benefits	Money to be paid for specific types of losses under the terms of an insurance policy
Cash value	The amount of money payable to a policyholder upon discontinuation of a life insurance policy
Claim	A policyholder's request for reimbursement for a loss under the terms of an insurance policy
Coinsurance	A type of insurance where the insured pays a share of the payment made against a claim
Contract	The document that represents the agreement between an insurance company and the insured
Copayment	The amount an insured person pays toward the cost of medical treatment or other services
Coverage	The protection provided by the terms of an insurance policy
Deductible	The specified amount of a loss that the policyholder pays before the insurer is obligated to pay anything; the insurance company pays only the amount above the deductible
Exclusions	Specified losses that the insurance policy does not cover
Face amount	The amount stated in a life insurance policy to be paid upon death
Grace period	The additional time after the premium due date that the insurer allows the policyholder to make the payment without penalty
Hazard	A condition that creates or increases the likelihood of some loss; for example, defective house wiring can increase the likelihood of a fire
Insurance agent	A professional insurance representative who acts for the insurer in negotiating, servicing, or writing an insurance policy
Insured	The person or company who is protected against loss; the Insured does not have to be the owner

(continues)

Figure 14.3 Insurance Terminology *(continued)*

Term	Definition
Lifetime limit	A maximum amount of total lifetime benefits you may get from your insurance company
Loss	An unexpected reduction in the value of the insured's property caused by a covered peril; the basis of a valid claim for reimbursement under the terms of an insurance policy
Peril	An event whose occurrence can cause a loss; people buy policies for protection against such perils as a fire, storm, explosion, accident, or robbery
Policy limits	A maximum benefit an insurance company will pay when an insured event happens
Premium	The amount you pay for an insurance policy
Probability	The mathematics of chance, or the statistical likelihood that something will happen
Proof of loss	The written verification of the amount of a loss that must be provided by the insured to the insurer before a claim can be settled
Standard policy	The contract form that has been adopted by many insurers, approved by state insurance departments, or prescribed by law; modifications are made to meet individual needs
Unearned premium	The portion of a paid premium that the insurer has yet to earn because the policy term has not ended; the unearned premium is returned to the policyholder when a policy is canceled. Also called pre-paid insurance

Based on this statistic, the expected losses in a class of 30 students would be 3 books, at a total cost of $180 (3 × $60). To lower the cost of these expected losses to each student, the class could establish an insurance company. An insurance company, or insurer, is a business that agrees to pay the cost of potential future losses in exchange for regular fee payments. If every student contributed $6 to the company, the total of $180 collected would be used to replace lost books. The cost to each student for a lost book would be only $6, rather than the full $60. When a business or individual does this, they are practicing **risk management**.

Risk management is forecasting and evaluating financial risk then developing a plan to avoid or minimize the impact of the risk.

When people buy insurance, they join a risk-sharing group by purchasing a written insurance contract called a policy. Under the policy, the insurer agrees to assume an identified risk for a fee, called the **premium**. The premium is paid at regular intervals by the owner of the policy, known as the policyholder. The insurer collects insurance premiums from policyholders under the assumption that only a few policyholders will have financial losses at any given time.

How does insurance help protect you from financial loss?

Insurers set premiums based on statistical probability, which estimates the likelihood of potential losses. They gather and analyze historical data to determine how many of a particular type of loss occurred, on average, in a population over a given period. From this analysis, they can predict approximately how many such losses to expect among their policyholders over a similar future period, such as a year. For example, in a sample of 100,000 drivers under 18, an insurer can predict approximately how many will have accidents each year.

The higher the probability of a loss occurring, the higher the premium for insuring against it. Remember that insurers deal in averages. They cannot predict which specific individuals will suffer losses. To make a profit, the insurer must

Connections to Your World
Reducing Driving Accidents

Experts believe that to reduce teen driving accidents, the most effective tactic is to limit teens' driving risk exposure. For example, some states impose night driving and passenger restrictions for beginning drivers and require higher ages for initial licensure. At the same time, very few states have laws that regulate elderly drivers. This group often continues to drive after their vision, reflexes, hearing, and other skills necessary for safe driving have diminished.

Think Critically

1. Do you think that stricter teen driving rules are effective? Why or why not?

2. Do rules aimed at reducing risk for teen drivers infringe on teens' rights? Explain.

3. Do you think that restrictions should be placed on older drivers? What would you recommend? Explain.

collect more in premiums than it pays out for losses and operating expenses. In years when a catastrophic disaster or multiple major disasters occur, such as hurricanes, floods, and earthquakes, an insurer may pay out more in benefits than it receives in premiums. This is why in some states, such as Florida, the cost of homeowners insurance is higher than in other states. The probability of a hurricane or other large storm happening is very likely, so the insurance companies are taking considerable risk with these policies.

Insurance is not meant to enrich—only to compensate for actual losses incurred. This principle is called indemnification. **Indemnification** is the process of putting the policyholder back in the same financial condition he or she was in before the loss occurred. If the insured tries to make money by filing false insurance claims, they are committing insurance fraud, which is deception for the purpose of unlawful gain. Insurance fraud is a crime punishable by law, and it results in higher insurance rates for everyone.

✓ Checkpoint

How is risk managed by insurers?

LO 14.1.3 Reducing Insurance Costs

Insurance can be expensive. As you consider an insurance plan, think about the following ways to save on insurance costs.

- Increase deductibles. A **deductible** is the specified amount of a loss that the insured must pay. The insurer's obligation to pay begins only after you have paid your full deductible. Generally, the higher the deductible, the lower the insurance premium. For example, premiums for a policy with a $500 deductible will be higher than for a policy with a $1,000 deductible. To reduce your premiums, accept a higher deductible.
- Consider policy limits. Some types of insurance, such as health or dental insurance, have lifetime maximum benefits called policy limits. **Policy limits** are a cap on the total lifetime benefits you may receive from your insurance company.
- Purchase group insurance. Premiums for group plans are usually much lower than for individual plans, especially for health insurance. If group plans are available through your job, credit union, a social or professional organization, or other similar group, you will likely save money by enrolling in them.
- Consider copayment amounts. A **copayment** is the specified amount that the insured must pay for each doctor or hospital visit. By selecting a health insurance policy with a higher copayment amount, the insurance premium will be lower.
- Consider payment options. How you pay premiums can save you considerable money over a short period of time. Monthly payments usually contain an extra charge, but annual or semiannual payments do not. Agreeing to have your premiums automatically deducted from your checking account or paying electronically may also reduce your costs.
- Look for discount opportunities. Many insurance companies offer discounts for special conditions. For example, nonsmokers can get lower premiums on health insurance. Taking driver's education courses and getting good

grades can reduce auto insurance costs for teenagers. Good driving records can lower costs. Insuring more than one vehicle with the same company can result in a **multipolicy discount**. Having more than one type of policy (such as auto insurance and homeowners insurance) with a company can result in a **multiline discount**.

- Comparison shop. Like many other things you buy, it pays to shop around for insurance. Get quotes from several insurers. Be sure to give each insurer the same information so that you can compare exact coverage and costs. It is also important to know exactly what coverage you need—and do not need—before talking to insurers.

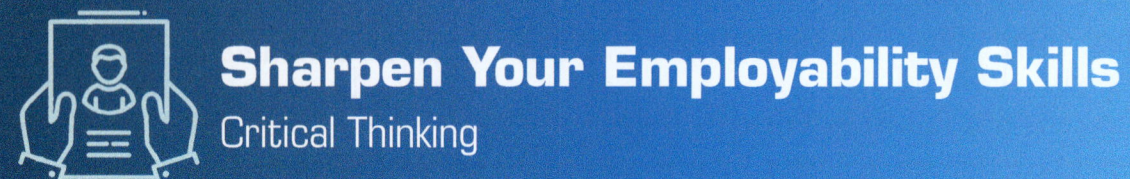

Sharpen Your Employability Skills
Critical Thinking

Since the Great Depression, the United States has had many programs designed to protect people from the harsh realities of risk in their lives. Transfer payments are government grants to some citizens that are paid with taxes collected from other citizens. Essentially, the government uses taxes to transfer some wealth from those who have it to those who do not. Some transfer payments are made in cash; others are made "in kind." That is, the government provides the needed item rather than cash. The following programs are available to U.S. citizens:

In-Cash Payments

- Unemployment compensation. When workers are laid off, they are eligible to receive a percentage of their pay for a specified number of weeks, or until they get a new job (whichever comes first).
- Disability payments. For injured workers, the disability portion of Social Security pays a monthly benefit until the workers recover, or for the rest of their lives if they remain disabled.
- Temporary Assistance for Needy Families (TANF). Low-income families with children can receive a monthly payment for up to five years. To receive the benefit, adults in the family must work a minimum of 30 hours per week (20 hours for parents with children under 6 years old) to gain the experience needed to become economically self-sufficient.

In-Kind Payments

- Supplemental Nutritional Assistance Program (SNAP). People with insufficient income or resources to buy food may qualify to receive government vouchers or debit cards that can be exchanged for food items.
- Housing subsidies. Special housing programs allow low-income individuals and families to rent apartments and other residences at a lower rate than the market rate. The difference is subsidized or paid by the government.

(continues)

(continued)

- National School Lunch Program. Children from low-income families may receive free or low-cost lunches at school. The schools receive cash subsidies and donated food from the government for each meal they serve.
- Medicaid. Medicaid is government-sponsored health insurance for people living in poverty who cannot afford private health insurance.

These programs are temporary, rather than permanent, solutions. They are designed to help sustain people while they are retraining, recovering, or working to get back on their feet financially.

Think Critically

1. What would you do if you lost your job and had no immediate source of cash for food and other necessities? How would you cope?
2. Visit your state government website and list resources that are available to people in need.
3. Do you think that these government programs are necessary and beneficial? How might these programs benefit society and the economy? Explain.

There are many sources that can help you when shopping for insurance. For example, ask people you know for recommendations about insurers they have used. Also, check with your state insurance commissioner to see which companies are legally doing business in the state and whether any complaints have been filed against them. The financial strength of the insurer may be a major factor in keeping down insurance costs. You can find ratings for different insurers in print and online publications of AM Best Company and Standard & Poor's. You can also find insurance comparison sites online.

You should consider looking for a new insurance company when premiums rise. Many companies offer low rates to new customers, but then steadily raise them after a few years. It pays to shop around periodically.

✓ Checkpoint

What can you do to save money on insurance premiums?

14.1 **Lesson** Review

Check Your Understanding

1. Explain the concept of an insurable risk. (LO 14.1.1)

2. What is the purpose of insurance? (LO 14.1.2)

3. How can changing the deductible reduce an insurance premium? (LO 14.1.3)

Apply Your Understanding

1. What is the difference between pure risk and speculative risk? Provide an example of each type. (LO 14.1.1)

2. How do insurance companies use the law of averages to manage risk? (LO 14.1.2)

3. Why should you comparison shop when looking for insurance? (LO 14.1.3)

The Essential Question

What is risk, and how is insurance used to manage risk?

A: Types of risk include pure risk, insurable risks (personal, property, and liability risks), economic risk, and speculative risk. You can purchase insurance to spread the costs of insurable risk and lower your financial exposure.

The Essential Question What is the risk management process, and how can you develop a risk management plan?

Learning Objectives

By the end of this lesson, you should be able to:

LO 14.2.1 Explain the risk management process.
LO 14.2.2 Create a risk management plan.

Key Terms

- risk assessment
- risk transfer
- risk avoidance
- risk reduction
- risk retention
- risk management plan

LO 14.2.1 The Risk Management Process

While you cannot eliminate risk, you can manage it so that a loss does not become financially devastating. As defined in the previous section, risk management is forecasting and evaluating financial risk then developing a plan to avoid or minimize the impact of the risk. It is an organized strategy for controlling financial loss from pure risks. It begins as soon as you have something to lose. In other words, as soon as you have assets, wealth, income, and anything that others could take from you, you must begin to think about how you can protect yourself from loss. Risk management should remain in effect throughout your life. Even after death your estate can be vulnerable, so steps should be taken to protect it.

Risk management involves more than buying insurance for every possible hazard that could occur. Some risks are not serious enough to insure. Others are better handled by taking steps to avoid the risk or reduce the chances that the risk will occur. Risk management is a three-step process, as illustrated in **Figure 14.4**.

Step 1: Identify Risks of Loss

The first step in risk management is to identify potential risks. Begin by asking yourself what financial risks you take on a regular basis, such as the risks you incur by driving a car or renting an apartment. As you will see in later chapters, many potential losses could occur. Even though they may not happen because you make an error or are at fault, you can still be held responsible for damage to others and to property.

Step 2: Assess Seriousness of Risks

Once risks have been identified, they should be assessed to determine the probability of occurrence and the potential severity and impact on you if they do occur. **Risk assessment** is a systematic study of the risks that you face. It involves understanding the types of risk you will face and their potential consequences.

Figure 14.4   Risk Management Process

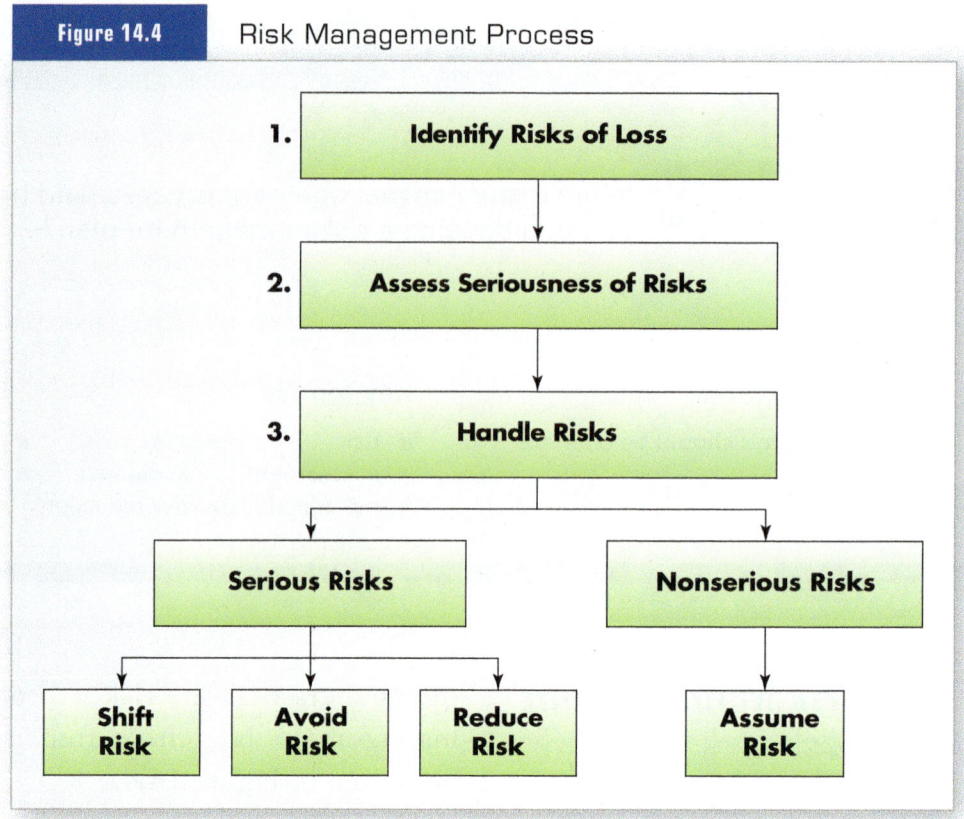

Human activities and the ownership of property reflect a certain amount of risk. Some risks are high priority because they could have serious financial consequences. For example, when driving your car, you could destroy the property of others, injure others, or even kill someone. Because potential losses are very great, driving is a high-priority risk. Other types of risk may have a relatively low financial consequence or may have a very small chance of occurring. Therefore, these types of risk are a lower priority. By understanding the risks you face and their consequences, you can better plan to protect yourself and others.

Step 3: Handle Risks

Based on the nature and seriousness of the risks you identify, you should select a risk management technique that best addresses each risk. There are four techniques you can consider for handling risk: shifting, avoiding, reducing, or assuming risk. A good risk management plan uses a combination of these strategies to balance risk, the cost of insurance, and your potential losses.

1. **Risk transfer**, also called risk sharing, passes risk to another party. An example is when you buy insurance to cover financial losses caused by damaging events, such as auto accidents, fire, theft, injury, or death. By making insurance premium payments, you transfer the risk of major financial loss to the insurance company. This is the most common method of dealing with pure risks that can carry high costs.

2. **Risk avoidance** lowers the chance for loss by not engaging in the activity that could result in the loss. For example, instead of having a party at your house and risking damage, you could reserve

a section of a restaurant. Instead of participating in a dangerous sport, such as bungee jumping, you could go camping. You can avoid certain health issues by practicing a healthy lifestyle, avoiding substances that cause health issues, and receiving medical care when needed.

3. **Risk reduction** lowers the chance of loss by taking measures to lessen the frequency or severity of losses that may occur. For example, you may put studded snow tires on your car if you live in an area that receives snow in the winter, install fire alarms or sprinklers in your home, or use seat belts. All these steps would lessen the financial risk of potential losses as well as the severity of damages from the loss.

4. **Risk retention,** also called risk assumption, is the process of accepting the consequences of risk. To help reduce your financial burden, you could establish a monetary fund to help cover the cost of a loss. People who self-insure are planning to absorb the costs of some risks themselves. This strategy can reduce the cost of insurance. In some cases, the cost of insuring against a particular risk may be too great, or the probability that the risk will occur may be too low, to justify paying an insurance premium. For example, an older car may not be worth much money. So instead of fully insuring it, you may retain the risk of paying for repairs yourself if it is damaged.

✓ Checkpoint

What are the four techniques used to handle risk?

The Risk Management Plan

Everyone faces risks and the potential losses they bring. Some people do nothing—but this is, in fact, a choice. When you allow events to control your life, they can drain your finances unpredictably. To avoid possible financial disaster, you should create a **risk management plan**, which lists the risks you have identified, your assessment of their financial impacts, and the techniques that you plan to use to manage each risk.

Figure 14.5 outlines a risk management plan that a young person might develop. A good risk management plan uses various techniques to lower overall risk. As you progress through life, your priorities will change, and you will need to adjust your plan. For example, life insurance may become a higher priority when you have children who depend on your income.

Insurance is an important part of any risk management plan. In general, financial advisers say that a basic insurance plan should help reduce risk and protect against the following:

- Potential loss of income due to the premature death, illness, accident, or unemployment of a wage earner
- Potential loss of income and extra expense resulting from the illness, disability, or death of a spouse or other family member
- Potential loss of real or personal property due to fire, theft, or other hazards
- Potential loss of income, savings, and property resulting from personal liability (injuring a person or damaging the property of others)

Figure 14.5   Risk Management Plan

Risk	Seriousness of Financial Impact	Method for Handling
1. Auto accidents	High	Collision and liability insurance Reduce risk—driver's education class
2. Theft or damage to personal property in my apartment	Medium	Renters insurance Reduce risk—add deadbolt lock to door
3. Theft or damage to personal property at work or in my car	Medium	Renters/homeowners standard policy Floater policy (for higher-priced items) Reduce risk—install an alarm in my car; keep items locked and out of sight
4. Injury to my apartment visitors	Medium	Renters insurance Low probability of occurring—assume risk above renters insurance coverage
5. Personal illness and sports injuries	High	Health insurance Avoid some risk—stop bungee jumping Reduce some risk—wear a helmet for mountain biking Reduce risk—get special training
6. Vision and dental needs	Low	Assume risk—contribute $10 a month to a fund to pay for new glasses and dental work when needed (self-insure)
7. Income protection	Medium/low (depending on life situation)	Life insurance (to protect dependents) Disability insurance (to provide income if I can't work) Insurance to make minimum payments when I am unemployed

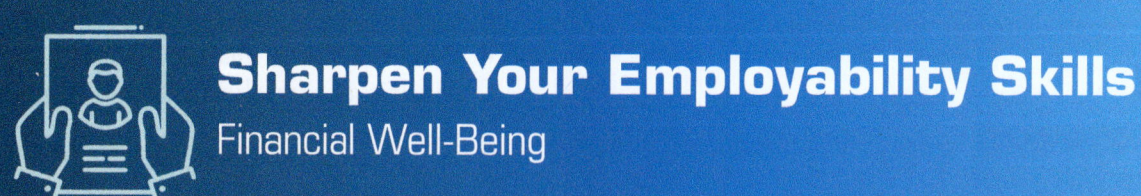

Sharpen Your Employability Skills
Financial Well-Being

Developing a risk management plan is important to ensure financial well-being and stability. Risk management plans are not just for adults; it is wise for teenagers to develop a risk management plan as they start planning their path after high school. It is important to understand that the risks you face will change as you

(continues)

(continued)

progress through life. For this reason, it is necessary to revisit and update your risk management plan at different stages of your life.

Following the format in Figure 14.5, create a risk management plan that outlines your remaining high school years and your transition from high school to your post-secondary education or occupation. List as many potential risks as you can identify. Be sure to outline the seriousness of financial impact and method for handling the risk.

Think Critically

1. What are the greatest risks for teenagers and young adults? Explain.

2. How might your risks be different than someone who is 30 years old, is married, recently bought a home, and has a newborn child?

3. What type(s) of insurance would you recommend to a friend to help manage risk?

When a risk is significant and can have drastic consequences, shifting the risk by purchasing insurance is a good idea. In the next chapters, you will learn more about types of insurance.

✓ Checkpoint

What is a risk management plan?

14.2 Lesson Review

Check Your Understanding

1. Provide an example of risk transfer, risk avoidance, risk reduction, and risk retention. (LO 14.2.1)

2. What role does insurance play in a risk management plan? (LO 14.2.2)

Apply Your Understanding

1. Why is it important to perform a risk assessment before developing a plan to manage risk? (LO 14.2.1)

2. Consider the types of risk you may face when you move into your first apartment or home. Create a risk management plan. (LO 14.2.2)

The Essential Question

What is the risk management process, and how can you develop a risk management plan?

A: Risk management is an organized strategy for controlling financial loss from pure risks. The purpose of a risk management plan is to lower overall financial risk and protect from loss of income, property, and other forms of wealth.

14 Chapter Review

Summary

14.1 Understanding Risk

- Risk is a state of uncertainty where certain situations may result in loss or another undesirable outcome.

- Pure risk is a chance of loss with no chance for gain. Pure risks are random and related to events that are beyond the risk-taker's control.

- Insurance is a method of spreading risk across a large group, so that no one member must endure the full cost of a devastating loss.

- To be insurable, a risk must be a pure risk faced by many people and for which the amount of the loss can be predicted. Insurable risks include personal risks, property risks, and liability risks.

- Everyone is affected by what happens in the economy; economic risk is not avoidable, but there are ways to lessen its impact (such as saving during good economic times to help prepare for slow economic times).

- Speculative risk may result in either loss or gain.

- It is important for consumers to understand basic insurance terminology, such as premiums, deductibles, and policy limits.

- Risk management is forecasting and evaluating financial risk than then developing a plan to avoid or minimize the impact of the risk.

- Insurers analyze historical data to help predict how many losses to expect among their policyholders over a given period.

They base premiums on these statistical averages.

- Insurers make a profit by collecting more in premiums than they pay out in losses and operating expenses.

- Insurance is not meant to enrich, but to provide indemnification, or return the policyholder to the same financial condition as before the loss occurred.

- To reduce insurance costs, increase your deductibles, buy group plans, choose cost-effective payment options, take advantage of discounts, and comparison shop.

14.2 Managing Risk

- Risk management is an organized strategy for controlling financial loss from pure risks. It should begin as soon as you have assets, wealth, and income and remain in effect throughout your life.

- Risk management is a three-step process that involves identifying risks, assessing the seriousness of the risks, and considering the techniques for handling the risks.

- You can choose to handle risks through risk transfer, risk avoidance, risk reduction, or risk retention.

- A good risk management plan uses a combination of techniques to lower overall risk.

Check Your Knowledge

1. Compare the three types of risk. (LO 14.1.1)

2. Explain the basic concept of insurance. Why would insurance be part of a risk management plan? (LO 14.1.2)

3. Describe at least three ways to reduce the costs of insurance. Rank the cost reduction measures from the easiest to complete to the hardest. (LO 14.1.3)

4. Explain the risk management process. (LO 14.2.1)

5. Why is it important to have a risk management plan? (LO 14.2.2)

Apply Your Knowledge

1. Using Figure 14.1 as a guide, list any current or anticipated risks that you and your family face or will face soon. Analyze your current personal, property, and liability risks. Then assume that you are now 10 years older. Based on where you would like to be and what your current goals dictate, analyze your personal, property, and liability risks for this stage in your life. (LO 14.1.1)

2. Insurance premiums are based on statistical probability. Explain what this means and what you can do to reduce your personal risk. (LO 14.1.2)

3. Why would an insurance company offer a multiline policy discount to a family? If you are unsure, email or call an insurance agent. (LO 14.1.3)

4. Using the three-step risk management process (see Figure 14.4), interview a family member or another person to help identify, assess, and handle their risks. Then using Figure 14.5 as a guide, prepare a risk management plan for them. (LO 14.2.1)

5. Explain three techniques you would use to minimize risk in your personal risk management plan. (LO 14.2.2)

Share Your Knowledge

Work in teams of two to four students to complete the following activities.

1. Search online to learn more about the economic risks facing the United States today. How do you think this type of risk will impact you in the future? What can you do now to protect yourself from the economic risks? As a team, prepare a presentation to share what you find with your classmates. (LO 14.1.2 and 14.2.2)

2. Research the various types of insurance that are available, such as pet insurance. Create an infographic or other product that explains the many different types of insurance a consumer can buy and includes an assessment of the importance of each type of insurance. (LO 14.1.2)

3. Teenagers pay the most for car insurance. Research why teenagers pay more and develop a way to share information about ways teens can lower their premiums. (LO 14.1.3)

Connect and Reflect

Base your answers to the following questions on your own personal thoughts, preferences, and experiences.

1. There are many terms related to insurance. Refer to the table of insurance terms. Identify five terms that you had never heard before. Why are these terms important? How can you use your new understanding of insurance basics to set long-term goals for yourself related to risk management? (LO 14.1.2)

2. Sosi made the following statement: "I don't take any chances. Everything I own is insured, including my life and ability to provide money for my family. In fact, I pay so much in insurance premiums that there is little money left for entertainment. Am I doing something wrong?" What advice would you give to Sosi? Explain. (LO 14.1.3)

3. Look at the risk management plan that you created in an earlier activity. Explain each part of the risk management process that you followed to develop the plan. Discuss the plan with a trusted adult. Ask for their guidance related to insurance. Then summarize what you learned to demonstrate your understanding of risk management. (LO 14.2.2)

Chapter Project

Assume you will be attending college next year. Using Figure 14.4 as a guide, identify your most significant risks as a college student and the perils that cause them. Then list ways that you can protect yourself by shifting, avoiding, or reducing the risks and financial impact. Then based on the risks you identified, use Figure 14.5 as a guide to prepare a risk management plan for yourself. Present your plan to the class using the presentation method assigned by your teacher.

Chapter 15

Property and Liability Insurance

The Essential Question What is the purpose of renters and homeowners insurance, and what kind of coverage do they provide?

Learning Objectives

By the end of this lesson, you should be able to:

LO 15.1.1 Explain the purpose of and coverage provided by renters insurance.

LO 15.1.2 Explain the purpose of and coverage provided by homeowners insurance.

Key Terms

- renters insurance
- homeowners insurance
- personal property floater
- liability coverage
- guest
- uninvited guest
- trespasser
- attractive nuisance
- endorsement
- coinsurance clause
- 80 percent rule
- overinsuring
- replacement value
- indemnification
- claims adjustors

Consider This ...

Louis attends college full-time and shares an apartment with two housemates. "As renters, we need to insure our personal possessions, and we're responsible for what happens on the property, even though we're only renting," he tells his housemates. "I've talked to my insurance agent about renters insurance. It would protect us in case of theft, fire, or freezing pipes. It would even cover people's injuries if they were visiting and had some kind of accident at our apartment. The good news is that it doesn't cost very much—probably between $150 and $300 a year. That's only about $50 to $100 per person for the year. It's good coverage for the price, and it takes care of risks that we face as renters. I think we should include it in our monthly budget. What do you think?"

Read and Reflect

1. How might renters insurance protect Louis and his housemates?

2. Would you recommend that Louis and his housemates get renters insurance? Explain.

3. Do you think that renters insurance is worth it? Explain.

Renters Insurance

If you rent your residence, the landlord will insure the building; however, your personal belongings are your responsibility to protect— not the landlord's responsibility because the landlord has no insurable interest in your assets. You are also responsible for personal injuries that occur inside your home. **Renters insurance** protects renters from property and liability risks. For example, it protects you from damage to personal property, loss of personal possessions you carry outside the home, and liability for injuries to your guests. Many landlords require renters insurance.

Personal Property

Personal possessions inside the rental property can be damaged or destroyed by fire, smoke, water, moisture, freezing temperatures, or heat. For example, if you rent an apartment and there is a fire in the building, your personal property (couch, chairs, bed, clothing, computer, and other things) may suffer damage from the fire, smoke, or water to put out the fire. Your rental insurance policy will cover repairing or replacing damaged or destroyed property.

Source: iStock.com/KLH49

What protection is available with renters insurance?

Personal Liability

The landlord is not responsible for what happens inside your residence; that is your responsibility because you have control over those events. Renters insurance can help protect you if someone is injured in your rented home. For example, if someone trips and falls harming themselves seriously enough to warrant medical attention, your renters insurance policy will pay for their medical costs. It is important to note that you can be held legally liable even if the injury was not your fault.

Extended Coverage

A renters insurance policy may also cover the contents of your vehicle and luggage while traveling. For example, if an item is stolen from your car, it likely will be covered by renters insurance. Also, if your suitcase is lost, most airlines will reimburse you only up to a certain amount. Renters insurance may cover the remaining cost of the lost items.

You might need to buy special coverage if you have treasured possessions at your home, in storage, or with you as you travel. For example, expensive jewelry, computers or other technology, or valuable antiques beyond the primary policy's limits may need extended coverage. To insure such items, you will likely need an appraisal or expert opinion on the asset's market value. An appraisal will give you proof of value if the item is damaged, stolen, or destroyed. Appraisals cost anywhere from $50 to $300 or more, depending on the property's value.

Cost of Renters Insurance

Renters insurance rates vary from state to state, and the cost of renters insurance also depends on the insurance company, the amount of coverage, and the deductible you select. However, renters insurance is relatively inexpensive. The average policy costs between $15 and $30 a month. Most people's personal property (furniture, clothing, television, computer, and other such items) would cost $25,000 or more out of pocket to replace. Purchasing renters insurance is an excellent idea to protect your personal property from loss.

> ✓ **Checkpoint**
>
> Why do you need insurance as a renter?

LO 15.1.2 Homeowners Insurance

When you buy a home, you will spend a large amount of money on the house and its contents. It would be best to protect your investment by limiting your risks. If you have a mortgage, homeowners insurance will be required by the financial institution. **Homeowners insurance** protects property owners from property and liability risks. It is similar to renters insurance, except that it includes coverage for the building in addition to the owner's possessions inside the building. Homeowners insurance policies offer varying levels of protection depending on the homeowner's needs. **Figure 15.1** lists common types of homeowners insurance policies. Package policies that include several types of coverage in

a single contract usually carry a lower premium than you would pay for each type of coverage purchased separately. One benefit of homeowners insurance if you have a child attending postsecondary school full-time and they live in an apartment near campus is that their property may be covered under your homeowners insurance policy, saving you the expense of purchasing a separate renters insurance policy to protect their possessions.

Homeowners insurance typically covers property owners' losses from these three types of risks:

1. Hazards—fire, water, wind, and smoke that may cause physical damage
2. Crimes—criminal activity, such as robbery, burglary, arson, and vandalism
3. Liability—the cost of another person's losses for injuries at your property

Physical Damage Coverage

The main component of homeowners insurance is protection against financial loss due to damage or destruction. Hazards such as fire, water, wind, and smoke may damage or destroy your home or temporarily cause you to lose use of it. Coverage extends to household belongings, including appliances, clothing, and furniture. Some policies will even provide limited coverage for refrigerated items that spoil due to a power outage. Detached structures on your property, such as a garage or shed, as well as trees, plants, and fences, are also covered by homeowners insurance. Suppose damage from a concealed hazard prevents you from using your property while it is being repaired or replaced. In that case, your homeowners insurance policy will pay for temporary housing for a limited time.

Figure 15.1   Homeowners Insurance Policy Coverage

Type of Policy	Type of Coverage	Description of Coverage
HO-1	Basic Coverage	Fire, lightning, windstorm, hail, explosion, riot, civil commotion, aircraft, nonowned vehicles, smoke, vandalism, malicious mischief, theft, and glass breakage. Limits apply, such as $500 or 5 percent of policy value.
HO-2	Broad Form	Broader list of perils; broader definition; still has restrictions and limits, such as fire from fireplaces being excluded; limit of $1,000 or 10 percent of policy value.
HO-3	Special Form	All-risk coverage on dwelling itself; a loss not specifically excluded (such as flood) is covered.
HO-4	Renters	Insuring personal property on a broad-form basis with advantages of homeowners policy (such as special coverage in event of flood or water damage).
HO-5	Comprehensive	Most complete coverage available; dwelling and contents are covered on an all-risk basis.
HO-6	Condominium Owner's	HO-4 coverage for condominium owners (wording is adjusted to fit legal status of condominium owner).
HO-7	Mobile Homes	Protects owners of manufactured homes.
HO-8	Older Homes	Meets special needs of owners of older buildings with high replacement costs (actual cash value basis rather than replacement cost basis).

Theft and Vandalism Coverage

Theft and vandalism coverage protects your personal belongings against loss from criminal activity, such as robbery and physical damage from vandals. Not only does homeowners insurance cover your possessions when they are in your home, but most policies contain off-premises coverage to protect your possessions if they are with you when you are away.

A **personal property floater** is additional insurance coverage for valuable items not covered by the primary policy.

People sometimes buy floaters to protect items of high value, such as jewelry, tools, coin and stamp collections, fine art, musical instruments, and other valuable property not generally covered by an insurance policy. A standard homeowners insurance policy has limits on coverage of personal property. For example, your policy may pay up to only $2,000 for jewelry and $1,000 for collections and collectibles. If you have personal property worth more than these minimum amounts, you can protect it with a floater. You may need to get an appraisal to insure these items.

Liability Coverage

Liability coverage is insurance to protect against claims resulting from injuries and damage to people and/or property. For instance, if a guest in your home falls and breaks a leg, you may be liable for medical expenses. If you own a dog, you are responsible if the dog bites someone or another dog. If your child hits a baseball through your neighbor's window, you are responsible for the damage. Read your policy carefully, especially if you own animals. Some breeds of dogs or other animals may be excluded.

Homeowners are responsible for acts occurring on their property, both for guests and uninvited guests. A **guest** is someone you specifically ask to come to your house. An **uninvited guest** is presumed to have permission to be on your property, such as door-to-door solicitors or delivery people. In most cases, homeowners will not be held liable for damage caused by or injuries to a **trespasser** or an unlawful intruder.

An **attractive nuisance** is a dangerous place, condition, or object particularly attractive to children, such as a swimming pool. For example, suppose a child sneaks into a private pool without permission and is hurt. In that case, the homeowner will be held liable for the child's injuries, even if the homeowner has taken steps to prevent entry into the pool.

What's Not Covered

While homeowners insurance covers most losses, not every loss will be covered. Exclusions are items that homeowners insurance policies will not cover, as shown in **Figure 15.2**.

A basic homeowners policy generally does not cover damage resulting from floods and earthquakes. For these perils, policyholders often use endorsements to add coverage to their policy for an additional premium. An **endorsement** is a written amendment to an insurance policy that reflects its changes. For example, you can add flood or earthquake insurance as an endorsement to your homeowners insurance policy. If you live in an identified flood zone, your mortgage company may require you to purchase flood insurance.

| Figure 15.2 | Exclusions from Homeowners Insurance |

Items Not Covered by Most Homeowners Insurance Policies

- Articles insured separately (floater) such as jewelry, collections, and fine art
- Animals, birds, fish, and other pets
- Motorized land vehicles (licensed for use), except for lawn mowers and things used on the property exclusively
- Entertainment or infotainment systems in vehicles
- Aircraft and parts of aircraft
- Property of renters, boarders, and other tenants (unless they are related to the owner and not paying rent)
- Business property in storage, such as samples
- Business property pertaining to a business that is conducted at the residence (separate insurance is required)
- Business property away from the residence

How Much Coverage Is Needed?

Insurance companies typically require you to insure your home using the 80 percent rule known as a **coinsurance clause.** The **80 percent rule** requires homeowners to have insurance equal to 80 percent of the replacement costs for the house to receive full coverage from the insurance company. If it would take $200,000 to rebuild your home after a disaster, you would need to be insured for at least $160,000. Insurers do not require 100 percent coverage because even if your property is destroyed, the land and the building foundation will still be usable. You must meet the coinsurance minimum coverage to receive the full amount for the damages.

Generally, people insure the contents of their home for at least half the value of the building. For example, a building insured for $200,000 will likely cover contents for at least $100,000. This includes all personal possessions, from furniture and appliances to clothing and other personal property and assets kept at the property.

To ensure you are reimbursed for all damaged or destroyed property, complete a household inventory, as shown in **Figure 15.3**. This inventory is like the

Figure 15.3   Household Inventory for Insurance

Household Inventory

Room	Item	Quantity	Year Bought	Make/ Model	Serial Number	Proof of Purchase (receipt and/or picture)	Cost
Living Room	Television	1	2021	LG	LG21-89456		$899.00
	Sofa, recliner, loveseat set		2023	Lazy Boy	LB 23SFA56		$2,285.00
	End table	2	2023	N/A	530483u		$175.00 ea.
	Wall art	3	2019	N/A	N/A		$50.00 ea.
	Floor and table lamps	3	2020	Acme	29045092		$119.00
	Rug	1	2024	Americana Rugs			$295.00
Dining Room	Dining room set with 6 chairs		2024	Franklin	24eifn042		$1,875.00
	Wall décor		2020	HB Designs			$250.00
Kitchen	Refrigerator		2025	Maytag	M25em469		$1,376.00
	Dishwasher		2024	Maytag	M24e3593		$899.99
	Range/stove		2024	Maytag	M24ein523		$749.98
	Microwave		2018	GE	18mwv938		$79.00
	Handheld appliances		Various	Various			$395.00

(continues)

Figure 15.3   Household Inventory for Insurance *(continued)*

Household Inventory

Room	Item	Quantity	Year Bought	Make/ Model	Serial Number	Proof of Purchase (receipt and/or picture)	Cost
	12 place dishes		2022	Pioneer Woman			$350.00
	Glassware/cups/ mugs		Various	Various			$85.00
	Flatware		2022	Oneida			$79.00
	Pots and pans		2025	Rock			$299.00
Bathrooms	Electronic devices (toothbrushes, shavers, hair dryer, flat iron, etc.)		Various	Various			$350.00
	Towels		Various	Various			$120.00
Bedrooms	Beds	3	Various	Various			$3,500.00
	Linens and comforters	5 sets linens 3 comforters	Various	Various			$895.00
	Clothing	Jeans, sweaters, shirts, suits, socks, under garments, shoes, etc.	Various	Various			$1,500.00
	Lamps	6	Various	Various			$200.00
	Dressers/chests	6	2022	American West			$900.00
	Game stations	2	2025	Nintendo			$600.00
	Television	1	2025	Vizio			$397.00
Basement/ Garage	Hand tools		Various	Craftsman			$750.00
	Power tools		Various	Black and Decker			$2,300.00
	Lawn mower		2019	John Deere			$1,846.00
	Bicycles	4	Various	Schwinn			$1,200.00
Miscellaneous	Antiques						$5,200.00
	Photography equipment		2025	Canon			$2,300.00
	Musical instruments		Various	Various			$1,250.00
	Window treatments	14 windows	Various	Various			$1,395.00

personal property inventory you prepared in an earlier chapter, except that a homeowner's inventory checklist usually needs to be more detailed. Your inventory should include documentation that shows proof of ownership and value. Some people keep receipts and take pictures or record a video. Keep this documentation in a safe place, such as a safe deposit box or a fireproof vault. If you have an appraisal that was prepared, that document should also be stored with the inventory.

Connections to Your World
Creating a Household Inventory

When you go to college or start working full-time, you will likely begin exploring options for living on your own. Whether your first living space is an apartment or a house, it is important to be sure that you have the needed insurance.

Assume that you will be looking to rent an apartment in the next few years; you will want to be sure to have renters insurance. As noted, it is important to have a home inventory to provide documentation of personal property within your home.

Step 1: Use a spreadsheet software program to create a template for a household inventory for insurance similar to the one in Figure 15.3.

Step 2: Create a list of items that you currently have, would plan to take with you to your first apartment, and would want to be sure are insured. Input these items in your household inventory.

Step 3: Search online for five items that you do not currently have but would need to purchase for your first apartment. Look for larger items that you will likely need and would want to document for insurance. Input these items in your household inventory.

When you begin building your household inventory, it is a good idea to take advantage of technology to help you document your possessions. You can take pictures of items to show proof of ownership; in addition, you can take pictures of or scan receipts to show proof of purchase. These photos can then be stored in cloud storage and linked to your household inventory for receipt or proof of purchase. Technology can provide a convenient way to assist with documentation and storage of related files.

After completing the steps above, discuss the questions below with a small group of classmates.

1. Why is it important to create a household inventory?
2. What items are most common for young adults just beginning to live on their own?
3. How do you expect the inventory of items and your insurance needs to change throughout your life?

Avoid **overinsuring**—that is, buying more insurance than is necessary. An insurer will pay no more than the actual replacement value of the house. The **replacement value** is the cost of replacing an item regardless of its actual cash (market) value. The home inventory will provide the documentation needed for the replacement of your items within the home. For larger or expensive items, keep a copy of the receipt with your inventory. Your insurance company will calculate the replacement value for the structure based on the standards of your city or state. For example, if your home has a market value of $150,000 and it is lost in a fire, it may cost $200,000 to rebuild the home using material of similar quality due to rising costs. If a house with a replacement value of $200,000 and contents worth $100,000 is destroyed, the insurer would pay no more than $300,000 ($200,000 + $100,000). If you owned a $400,000 homeowners insurance policy, you would still receive no more than $300,000 reimbursement to rebuild the house and replace its contents. Insurance follows the legal principle of indemnification. **Indemnification** means that the insurance company agrees to protect the policyholder against any damages that may occur. The insurance company will reimburse the actual cash value of a loss, which includes depreciation, unless your policy includes a replacement value clause, in which case it will reimburse the amount needed to restore you to your preloss financial position, up to the amount of insurance you purchased.

Claims adjusters, also known as insurance adjusters, determine the value of the property destroyed or damaged by a covered hazard. Also, insurers employ insurance investigators who look for evidence of destroyed or damaged property. They also investigate cases where people fraudulently claim damages that did not occur.

Cost of Homeowners Insurance

As with renters insurance, rates for homeowners insurance vary from state to state. The most expensive states for home

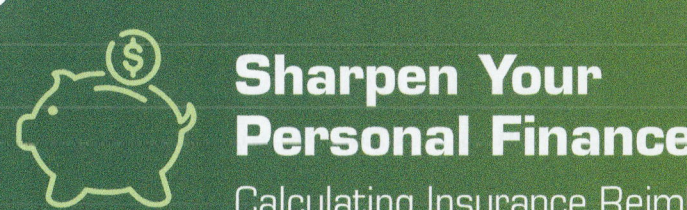

Sharpen Your Personal Finance Skills
Calculating Insurance Reimbursements (Coinsurance)

The coinsurance clause in a homeowners policy requires that you buy coverage equal to a stated percentage of the property's replacement value to receive full reimbursement for a loss. For example, if Roseline and Louis purchase a $150,000 house and have an 80 percent coinsurance clause, their policy would require the following coverage:

$$\$150,000 \times 0.80 = \$120,000 \text{ coverage required}$$

(continues)

(continued)

Many homeowners believe they can save money by underinsuring. Say Roseline and Louis decide to only buy $100,000 of insurance instead of the required $120,000, thinking that $100,000 will cover most losses. Then, they have a fire that results in a loss valued at $50,000. They think their $100,000 policy will cover the loss, but that is not the case. Because they did not meet the $120,000 requirement, the insurer will reimburse based on the percentage of coverage they do have:

$$\$100,000 \div \$120,000 = 0.833 \text{ or } 83.3\%$$

To determine the amount of reimbursement, the insurer will multiply the value of the loss by this percentage:

$$\$50,000 \times 0.833 = \$41,650$$

For the $50,000 loss in this example, Roseline and Louis will receive only $41,650, or 83.3 percent of the loss.

Try It Out!

Based on the example above, compute the insurance reimbursement in the following situation: Roseline and Louis bought a house for $200,000. Their coinsurance requirement is 85 percent. Roseline and Louis bought insurance for $120,000 to save money on insurance premiums. Last month, a storm caused $60,000 damage to their house. How much will the insurer reimburse?

insurance are those most susceptible to large-scale natural disasters, such as fires, floods, tornadoes, and hurricanes. Due to rising costs and the increasing frequency of natural disasters, some insurance companies no longer insure any homes in areas that are high-risk. The cost of homeowners insurance also depends on the insurance company you select, how much coverage you choose to have, and the amount of your deductible. Other variables that can affect the cost of homeowners insurance include your zip code, the size of the house, and its condition.

When shopping for homeowners insurance, the internet is a valuable resource. Many insurers have websites where you can find information about their policies and premiums. Websites such as Insure.com and NetQuote allow you to comparison shop for quotes.

✓ Checkpoint

Why should a person insure their home against potential risk?

15.1 Lesson Review

Check Your Understanding

1. What is covered by renters insurance? (LO 15.1.1)
2. Explain why a renter would need liability insurance coverage. (LO 15.1.1)
3. What is covered by homeowners insurance? (LO 15.1.2)

Apply Your Understanding

1. Explain why renters and homeowners have liability for injuries to invited and uninvited guests. What can they do to lower the risks? (LO 15.1.1 and LO 15.1.2)
2. Explain the concept of a coinsurance clause. Why do most homeowners insurance policies contain this clause? (LO 15.1.2)

The Essential Question

What is the purpose of renters and homeowners insurance, and what kind of coverage do they provide?

A: Renters and homeowners insurance protects you from damage to your personal property, loss of personal possessions that you may have with you outside the home, and liability for injuries to guests in your home.

The Essential Question | What is the purpose of auto insurance and umbrella liability insurance, and what kind of coverage do they provide?

Learning Objectives

By the end of this lesson, you should be able to:

LO 15.2.1 Explain the purpose of auto insurance and the coverage it provides.

LO 15.2.2 Explain the purpose of an umbrella liability insurance policy and the coverage it provides.

Key Terms

- driving record
- infraction
- moving violation
- nonmoving violation
- full coverage
- collision coverage
- deductible
- comprehensive coverage
- medical coverage
- uninsured/underinsured motorist coverage
- no-fault insurance
- assigned risk pool
- umbrella liability insurance

LO 15.2.1 Auto Insurance

Auto insurance covers the costs of damage to the vehicle, its owner, and any passengers. It also covers the costs of repairs to other vehicles, medical expenses of occupants in other cars, and property damage, such as to shrubs, trees, and fences, caused by an accident. Standard policies also cover theft of the vehicle and its contents.

Cost of Auto Insurance

People pay premiums to an insurance company to insure their vehicles. In return, the company pays most of the costs of an accident or other vehicle damage. Premiums are based on several factors, such as:

- Type of car (model, style, age)
- Driver classification (age, sex, marital status)
- Driving record

- Location (city, county) of the driver and car
- Distances driven
- Purpose of driving (such as work)
- Age, sex, and marital status of other regular drivers of the car

How are premiums set for car insurance?

© Rick Becker-Leckrone/Shutterstock.com

Premium discounts are available for certain conditions, such as insuring more than one vehicle with the same company, taking driver's education courses, having safety features such as airbags and rear-view cameras in your car, and getting good grades in high school and college (usually a "B" average or better).

Type of Car

Besides vintage (antique) cars, older cars should require less insurance than newer ones because older cars are worth less. New and expensive cars cost more to insure because they are worth more and would be more costly to repair or replace. Statistics show that sports cars have an increased risk of being in an accident and that the accident will be more serious. Thus, sports cars often have higher premiums.

Different makes and models of cars are rated by insurance companies on the risk of damage, both to the vehicle and its occupants and to other cars and their occupants. These ratings can cause premium increases. The results of crash tests, where cars are intentionally wrecked to see how they will perform, can also affect premiums. In addition, vehicles that are common targets among thieves usually carry higher auto insurance premiums.

Driver Classification

As you learned in the previous chapter, insurers base their premiums on statistical probabilities. From their analysis, insurers determine that some drivers are more likely to get into accidents than others. For example, young, single drivers are statistically more likely to be involved in an accident than married drivers over age 25. Thus, young drivers pay higher premiums.

Also, women generally have fewer and less costly accidents than men and pay less for auto insurance.

Driving Record

Your **driving record** includes the number and type of traffic tickets you have received for driving infractions and misdemeanors, along with the number of accidents in which you have been involved. An **infraction** is a minor violation and is punishable by a fine. Infractions can be moving violations or nonmoving violations.

A **moving violation** is any violation of the law committed by the driver of a vehicle while it is in motion. Moving violations include failing to come to a complete stop at a stop sign, making an improper left-hand turn, or following the vehicle in front of you too closely. A **nonmoving violation** is any violation of the law involving a car that is not in motion. Nonmoving violations may include expired license tags, malfunctioning equipment, such as a headlight or turn signal light not working, excessive noise, and parking tickets.

More serious offenses, called misdemeanors, may incur fines and jail time. Examples include excessive speeding, driving without a license, and reckless driving. Severe traffic violations, such as driving under the influence (DUI) of alcohol or drugs, hit-and-run, or leaving the scene of an accident, can cause insurance premiums to rise dramatically and may result in large fines or jail time. Many insurance companies use point systems to calculate premiums. Points are assigned for different types of accidents and traffic violations. One serious accident or offense such as a DUI may result in a significant increase in the premium you pay or could even result in having your insurance canceled.

Other Factors

Other factors determine auto insurance premiums. For example, specific geographic locations (such as large cities) have higher accident rates. As a result, insurers charge higher premiums to drivers in these areas. In addition, how much you drive influences how much your auto insurance costs. For example, someone commuting 50 miles a day may pay a higher premium than someone whose commute is only 10 miles because more miles behind the wheel means more risk exposure. Who will be driving the car is also a factor in setting premiums. Adding a teenage driver to an existing policy will increase premiums.

Another important consideration is the number of claims filed. When you file too many claims, your premiums rise. Also, when you are in an accident that is your fault, and your insurance company must pay claims, you will likely see a surcharge, which effectively increases your premium for 3 years or longer.

Types of Auto Insurance Coverage

There are five basic types of auto insurance (**Figure 15.4**):

- Liability
- Collision
- Comprehensive
- Personal injury protection (PIP)
- Uninsured/underinsured motorist

When all these types are purchased together in a single policy, it is known as

Figure 15.4 Protection by Automobile Insurance Type

	Who Is Protected	
	Policyholder	**Other Persons**
Liability coverage:		
Personal injuries	No	Yes
Property damage	No	Yes
Collision coverage:		
Damage to insured vehicle	Yes	No
No-fault provision	Yes	No
Comprehensive coverage:		
Damage to insured vehicle	Yes	No
Personal injury protection:		
Medical payments	Yes	Yes
Pedestrian coverage	Yes	No
Uninsured/underinsured motorist coverage:		
Bodily injury	Yes	Yes

What is the difference between collision coverage and comprehensive coverage?

full coverage. When you have a loan on a car, the lender will require full coverage to protect its interests.

Liability Coverage

Most states require all drivers to at least purchase liability coverage. Each state sets its minimum limits for liability coverage. The purpose of liability coverage protects against claims resulting from injuries and damage to people and/or property. It pays nothing toward the insured's losses, either personal injury or damage to the vehicle. However, if an accident is legally not your fault, the other driver's liability coverage will pay for damage to your car. If the accident is your fault and all you have is liability coverage, your insurance will not pay for the damage to your vehicle.

Liability insurance coverage is usually described using numbers, such as 100/300/50. These numbers mean that the insurer will pay up to $100,000 for injury to one person, $300,000 total for all people, and $50,000 for property damage per accident. Premiums charged for liability insurance vary according to the amount of coverage. If your liability coverage is insufficient to cover the costs of an accident where you are at fault, you will be personally responsible for the remaining charges. Most insurance companies now recommend a policy with at least 100/300/100 liability limits, and many insurance companies are recommending liability limits of 250/500/250 for policy-holders who may own a home.

Collision Coverage

Collision coverage is auto insurance that protects your car against damage from accidents. This coverage will pay for the damage to your car if you are at fault for the accident.

Most collision coverage has a deductible. A deductible is the amount of money you pay toward a covered claim. For example, you may have to pay the first $500 for repairs, and the insurer will pay the rest. Many minor traffic accidents involve damage that costs less than the deductible. A higher deductible will lower your premiums and may be wise to save money. In other words, paying the first $1,000 for each accident may be less expensive in the long run than having a $500 deductible and paying higher premiums.

Comprehensive Coverage

Comprehensive coverage is auto insurance that protects you from damage to your car from causes other than a collision. The causes might be fire, theft, severe weather, natural disasters, falling objects, acts of vandalism, and impacts from hitting an animal, such as a deer. For example, if your car receives hail damage from a storm, your comprehensive insurance pays for the repair.

As with collision coverage, comprehensive coverage has a deductible. The higher you set your deductible, the lower your premium.

Sharpen Your Personal Finance Skills
Calculating Liability Coverage

It is important to understand how the amount of insurance coverage impacts your liability in the event of an accident. For the scenarios below, work with your teacher and class to calculate the amount that would be paid by insurance and the amount Louis would be liable for based on his insurance coverage in each example.

Scenario:

Louis is at fault in an automobile accident. In this accident, the other car was totaled. The car's value was $23,000. The car's driver was injured, and his medical care cost $15,000. A second passenger in the car had $12,000 in medical expenses. A third passenger in the car received $24,000 in medical care. The driver and both passengers sue Louis, arguing that he was negligent as he ran a stop sign while texting. The court awarded the three people $50,000 each for their pain and suffering and lost wages as a result of the accident. Louis also incurred medical expenses of $10,000 related to his injuries, and his car was totaled. The value of his car was $7,500. Fortunately, Louis did not have any passengers with him. How much will the accident cost Louis's insurance company? How much will Louis be required to pay?

Example 1: Louis had the state mandated minimum coverage of 20/40/15. He did not have any other coverage. This means he has $20,000 per person for bodily injuries up to a maximum of $40,000. He also has a maximum of $15,000 in property damage.

20/40/15 Insurance Coverage	Insurance Pays	Louis Pays
$23,000 in damage to the other vehicle		
$15,000 liability to the other car's driver for medical expenses		
$12,000 liability to other car's passenger (person #2) for medical expenses		
$24,000 liability to other car's passenger (person #3) for medical expenses		
$150,000 court award ($50,000 per person)		
$7,500 damage to Louis's car		
$10,000 for Louis's medical expenses		
Totals		

(continues)

(continued)

Example 2: Louis had 100/300/100 coverage; collision coverage with a $1,000 deductible; $10,000 medical coverage; and comprehensive coverage with a $1,000 deductible.

This means that he had $100,000 in bodily insurance coverage per person up to a maximum of $300,000 in bodily injuries for others. Collision coverage with a $1,000 deductible means that the insurance company will pay all damages to Louis's car after he pays the first $1,000. Louis also has up to a maximum of $10,000 available for his personal injuries.

100/300/100 Insurance Coverage	Insurance Pays	Louis Pays
$23,000 in damage to the other vehicle		
$15,000 liability to the other car's driver for medical expenses		
$12,000 liability to other car's passenger (person #2) for medical expenses		
$24,000 liability to other car's passenger (person #3) for medical expenses		
$150,000 court award ($50,000 per person)		
$7,500 damage to Louis's car		
$10,000 for Louis's medical expenses		
Totals		

Think Critically

1. Why did the insurance company not pay any of Louis's damages in the first example?
2. Given the examples above, what recommendations would you make to a friend who is unsure how much liability insurance they should have as part of their automobile insurance?

Medical Coverage

Also known as personal injury protection (PIP), **medical coverage** is auto insurance that pays for medical, hospital, and funeral costs of the insured and their family and passengers, regardless of fault. If the insured is injured as a pedestrian or bicyclist, this insurance will pay the medical costs. In some cases, the medical coverage will also cover lost wages if the insured cannot work due to accident-related injuries.

Medical coverage is mandatory in some states. If you have health insurance with excellent postaccident benefits, the lowest legally required medical limits may be sufficient. On the other hand, if you do

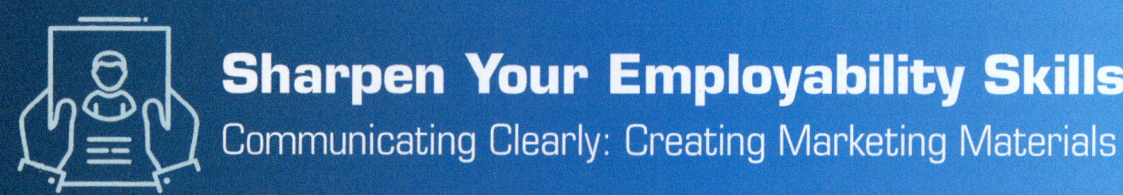

not have good health insurance or have a plan that does not offer all the benefits of a medical coverage insurance clause, it might be in your best interest to get as much medical coverage as you can comfortably afford. To reduce costs for this kind of insurance, consider buying a car with extra airbags, antilock brakes, and other safety devices that lower the risk of injury.

Uninsured/Underinsured Motorist Coverage

Uninsured/underinsured motorist coverage is auto insurance that pays for injuries to you and your passengers when the other driver is legally liable but unable to pay. In other words, if the other driver is legally at fault for the accident but has insufficient insurance or no insurance to cover the costs, your insurer will pay your medical expenses. This coverage also protects you as a pedestrian or a bicyclist if you are hit by an uninsured vehicle. Because of the high number of uninsured drivers on the road, many states require drivers to carry uninsured motorist coverage.

No-Fault Insurance

Many states have passed no-fault insurance laws. These laws set up a compensation system for auto accidents that do not require a legal determination of who was at fault before claims are paid. **No-fault insurance** is auto insurance in which drivers receive reimbursement for expenses from their insurer, no matter who caused the accident.

The basic idea behind no-fault insurance is to avoid the years of legal battling required to settle a case and determine fault. Even then, drivers with no assets and no insurance would be unable to fix the other driver's car or pay for damages resulting from their negligence. Also, by reducing the number of lawsuits, more money can go to injured people in a shorter timeframe and lower insurance costs.

Assigned Risk Policies

If you have an accident that costs your insurer large sums of money, the insurer may cancel your policy. The number of traffic citations and fines on your driving record may also cause your insurer to drop you. If so, you may be deemed a high-risk driver by the state and may be unable to find another insurer willing to insure you.

Every state has an **assigned risk pool** that consists of people who cannot obtain auto insurance due to the high risk they present. The state assigns these people to different insurers in the state. The insurers must then provide coverage. However, the insurance premiums may cost the insured considerably more than the average rate until the risky driver can reestablish a good driving record. In addition, basic liability coverage may be all that is available for the high-risk pool.

✓ Checkpoint

What are the five basic types of auto insurance?

LO 15.2.2 Umbrella Liability Insurance

People who maintain required liability coverage on their vehicle and residence can also purchase an umbrella policy that picks up where the other coverage ends. **Umbrella liability insurance**, also called personal umbrella policy (PUP), supplements your basic auto and home liability coverage by expanding limits and including additional risks. Personal liability insurance protects you if you are responsible for damages or injuries to others. It also protects against defamation, vandalism, and invasion of privacy. For example, a PUP will protect you when a guest falls and is injured on your property and requires expensive surgery, or if you post a negative review about a company online and the owner sues you for defamation (injuring the business' reputation). With personal injury lawsuits yielding verdicts in the millions of dollars, it is a good idea when you have built up your assets and your income to protect yourself from this type of catastrophic loss.

Umbrella liability insurance protects you from extraordinary losses, which result in incredibly high claims because of unusual circumstances. It can be very beneficial if you are sued, and the dollar limit of your original policy has been exhausted. For example, you may be involved in a car accident in which a person receives a permanent injury. If you are sued and found liable for $1 million, but your auto liability policy covers only $250,000, you would be responsible for the remaining $750,000. However, if you have $1 million in umbrella liability insurance coverage, your umbrella policy will cover it.

Insurance companies that offer auto and property (renters and homeowners) insurance policies also offer umbrella policies. Premiums for umbrella insurance are reasonable. For example, a policy for $1 million would typically cost between

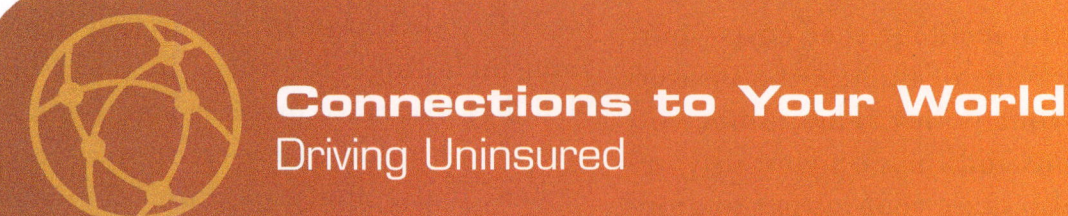

In most states, drivers are legally required to have liability insurance. This insurance protects others from loss when the accident is not their fault. Still, many people drive uninsured, even though it is against the law. In fact, it is estimated that one in eight drivers go uninsured. Some likely consequences for uninsured drivers include the following:

- They may be cited for failure to have insurance. The fine for this offense can be severe. Continued lack of insurance, following a citation, can result in jail time, loss of driving privileges, and large fines.
- Their citation may subject them to state financial responsibility laws. These laws would require them to file a special form (an SR-22) with the state for a period of one to three years, proving they have insurance or the ability to pay for damages they may cause. Filing these forms result in even higher insurance rates.
- Because they do not have insurance, an accident may be deemed their fault automatically This would require them to pay for damages.

Uninsured motorists also cause consequences to others on the road:

- Because people drive without insurance, or without enough insurance, other drivers must carry uninsured/underinsured motorist coverage. This raises the cost of insurance for everyone.
- When insured drivers file claims that their insurance company must pay because the other driver is uninsured, this loss may be counted against the policyholders. This means that another person's failure to have insurance can result in an increase in your premiums.
- It may take longer to process claims and get your car repaired when an uninsured driver is at fault.

It is a bad idea to drive uninsured. You should obey the law and carry the required insurance. You, as well as everyone else, will benefit.

Think Critically

1. If you are in an accident with a driver who does not have insurance, what are the potential consequences and impacts for that driver? What are the potential impacts to you?
2. What are the requirements for car insurance in your state? Does your state have a no-fault law? What is the penalty for those who disobey your state law?

$150 and $300 a year, depending on where you live and the probabilities calculated by the insurance company for your geographic area. This premium is in addition to the premiums for your auto and renters or homeowners insurance.

✓ **Checkpoint**

Why does a person or family need umbrella liability insurance?

Check Your Understanding

1. What are the basic types of auto insurance? (LO 15.2.1)

2. What types of protection does umbrella liability insurance provide? (LO 15.2.2)

Apply Your Understanding

1. Liability coverage is required in most states. What is the reasoning behind this requirement? What would an accident's total policy limit be if the insured had 100/300/100 liability insurance? (LO 15.2.1)

2. If you had 100/300/100 liability insurance and a $2 million umbrella policy, what is the maximum amount that could be paid if you were at fault in an accident? (LO 15.2.2)

The Essential Question

What is the purpose of auto insurance and umbrella liability insurance, and what kind of coverage do they provide?

A: Full-coverage auto insurance includes liability, comprehensive, collision, uninsured/underinsured, and medical coverage. Full-coverage auto insurance with an umbrella policy will protect you from exposure to risk and lawsuits resulting in personal liability.

Summary

15.1 Property Insurance

- Renters insurance protects you from damage to personal property, loss of personal possessions you carry with you outside the home, and liability for injuries to guests in your rented home.

- Renters insurance rates vary from state to state. The cost also depends on the insurance company, the amount of coverage, and the deductible you select.

- Homeowners insurance includes personal property and liability protections plus coverage for the building itself. It protects against three types of risks: hazards, crimes, and liability.

- A personal property floater provides additional insurance coverage for items generally not covered by basic policies.

- Liability coverage protects you if a guest, invited or uninvited, is injured on your property and for damage caused to others' property.

- An endorsement is a written amendment to an insurance policy often used to add coverage, such as for damage caused by a flood or earthquake.

- Insurers will reimburse no more than the replacement value; therefore, overinsuring will result in higher premiums with no additional benefits.

- The coinsurance clause requires you to insure your building for a stated percentage, usually 80 percent, of its replacement value to receive full reimbursement for a loss.

- A claims adjuster will determine the value of any destroyed property.

- Rates for homeowners insurance vary from state to state. States most susceptible to large-scale natural disasters have higher insurance rates. Costs also depend on the insurance company selected, how much coverage you choose to have, and the amount of the deductible.

15.2 Auto and Umbrella Insurance

- Auto insurance covers the costs of damage to the vehicle, its owner, and any passengers. It also covers the costs of repairs to other vehicles, medical expenses of occupants in other cars, and property damage. Standard policies also cover theft of the vehicle and its contents.

- Factors such as type of car, driver classification, driving record, coverage desired, distances driven, purpose of driving, and deductibles affect auto insurance premiums.

- Liability coverage protects others who may be injured or have property damage because of your actions or negligence.

- Collision coverage pays for damage to your vehicle when you are at fault in an accident.

- Comprehensive coverage protects your vehicle from non-collision losses, such as from theft, storms, and falling objects.

- Medical coverage, also known as personal injury protection (PIP), pays for medical, hospital, and funeral costs of the insured and their family and passengers, regardless of fault.

- Uninsured/underinsured motorist coverage protects you in the event the other driver is uninsured or does not have enough insurance.

- No-fault insurance laws require insurers to pay the losses of their own policyholders rather than require the at-fault driver's insurer to pay.

- Umbrella liability insurance, also called personal umbrella policy (PUP), may be purchased to expand coverage and reimbursement limits. It protects you if you are responsible for damages or injuries to others.

Check Your Knowledge

1. Why would your landlord's insurance policy not cover your personal possessions? (LO 15.1.1)

2. Why are homeowners insurance premiums more expensive than renters insurance premiums? (LO 15.1.2)

3. What is the purpose of liability insurance for your automobile? (LO 15.2.1)

4. Explain the difference between collision and comprehensive auto insurance coverage. (LO 15.2.1)

5. Describe the purpose of a personal umbrella policy. (15.2.2)

6. Explain the difference between a guest, an uninvited guest, and a trespasser. Who is responsible for damages to the property of the insured with regards to each of these individuals? (LO 15.1.2)

Apply Your Knowledge

1. Develop a plan that will protect valuables from being stolen from your home and share with your parent(s) or guardian(s). (LO 15.1.2)

2. A home is valued at $180,000. The homeowners have an insurance policy with an 80 percent coinsurance clause. The property is insured for $140,000. Calculate the insurance payout if there was $25,000 in damages to the home. How much more insurance coverage would have been required for the owner to receive the full amount of damages? (LO 15.1.2)

3. Calculate how much the insurance company will pay to repair your car if you have a $1,000 deductible for your comprehensive coverage and you hit a deer that causes $2,400 in damage to your car. (LO 15.2.1)

4. If you are responsible for an automobile accident that causes severe injury to multiple people resulting in $500,000 in damages, would your automobile insurance pay all the medical expenses if you had a maximum of 100/300/100 liability limits on your auto insurance? Explain your answer. (LO 15.2.1)

5. Tia has the following auto insurance coverage: comprehensive ($250 deductible); bodily injury and property liability (100/200/25); and collision ($250 deductible). As a result of an accident that was her fault, the other driver was awarded $9,800 for injuries and $2,100 in damages to his car. Tia's car was damaged at a cost of $820. Her medical bills were $135. How much did the insurer have to pay in accident claims? What is the most that Tia's policy would pay for injuries to the other driver? (LO 15.2.1)

6. Assume that you also have a personal umbrella insurance policy worth $2,000,000. How much would you be personally responsible to pay in the accident described above? (LO 15.2.2)

7. If you write an online review about a local restaurant, and the owner sues you for defamation and wins, what type of insurance policy would pay for the damages to the restaurant? (LO 15.2.2)

Share Your Knowledge

Work in teams of two to four students to complete the following activities.

1. Develop an insurance plan for Aman, a first-time homebuyer. He also owns a car. Describe the types of insurance that he might consider. (LO 15.1.2, LO 15.2.1, and LO 15.2.2)

2. Create a poster, blog, or other creative way to explain coinsurance to other teens. Include a definition, an explanation of why it is an important consideration for homeowners, and provide two examples of how it works. One example should focus on a homeowner who had less than the required coinsurance coverage and the second example should focus on someone who had the correct amount of coinsurance coverage. (LO 15.1.2)

3. Research the reasons young drivers often have higher auto insurance premiums. As a team, develop a way to teach young drivers how to minimize their premiums. (LO 15.2.1)

Connect and Reflect

Base your answers to the following questions on your own personal thoughts, preferences, and experiences.

1. Ask your parent(s) or guardian(s) if you can read their homeowners insurance policy. Look for the terms you learned in this chapter. What discounts are they receiving? If you were the one purchasing the insurance policy, what would you do differently? (LO 15.1.1)

2. If you have been involved in an automobile accident, what questions were you required to answer by the insurance company? Why do you think they asked those questions? If you were at fault, what happened to your automobile insurance the next time it renewed? (LO 15.2.1)

3. Think about your future. What types of coverage would you want for your own automobile and home insurance? Would you want an umbrella policy? Explain your answers. (LO 15.1.1, 15.1.2, 15.2.1, and 15.2.2)

Chapter Project

Assume you are helping your family with its insurance needs. For insurance claim purposes, prepare a household inventory, listing the contents of each room in your home. Use Figure 15.3 as an example. Next to each item, record its approximate value and indicate whether you have a receipt to prove its cost. Take a photo of particularly valuable or collectible items to include with the inventory. Then help your family find insurance for a new car of your choice that you will be permitted to drive. Get a price quote for full-coverage auto insurance. Determine ways to reduce premium costs through discounts or other methods. Organize and save all the information you have collected.

16 Chapter

Health and Life Insurance

What is the difference between group and individual health insurance, and what types of coverage and plans are available?

Learning Objectives

By the end of this lesson, you should be able to:

LO 16.1.1 Distinguish between group and individual health insurance.

LO 16.1.2 Explain common types of health insurance coverage and plans.

Key Terms

- health insurance
- group health insurance
- Flex 125 Plan
- health savings account (HSA)
- Affordable Care Act (ACA)
- pre-existing condition
- health insurance exchange
- COBRA
- coordination of benefits
- basic health insurance
- major medical coverage
- out-of-pocket maximum
- unmanaged care plans
- managed care plans
- preferred provider organization (PPO)
- health maintenance organization (HMO)
- high deductible health plan (HDHP)
- point of service (POS)
- Medicare
- Medicaid

Consider This ...

Aja wasn't feeling well and was sure it was strep throat. Because she'd had it before, she knew the symptoms.

"I need a doctor's appointment," she told her partner Sahil. "I'm insured under my mother's policy at work. I have an insurance card that allows me to see the doctor, but I have to pay a $30 copayment at the time I go to the clinic. The doctor will give me a test to be sure that I have strep. I'll also have to pay 20 percent of the cost of that test. Then, I'll need a prescription, and I have a $15 copayment for that. Even with insurance, this illness will cost me $70 or more plus another $80 for time lost from work. Health care is expensive! Soon, I won't be able to stay on my mom's policy any longer and will need to get my own insurance if I'm not employed. This really worries me."

(continues)

Read and Reflect

1. Why is it important to have health insurance?

2. Why has Aja been able to stay on her mother's health insurance policy? Why won't she be able to stay on it much longer?

3. What factors impact the copayments Aja has to pay?

4. What types of health insurance plans may be available for Aja if she gets a job that provides health insurance?

LO 16.1.1 — Group and Individual Health Insurance

Health insurance is a plan for sharing the risk of high medical costs from injury or illness. Like other forms of insurance, health insurance reduces individual risk by spreading it among many people. In exchange for regular premiums, the insurer promises to pay medical expenses for the treatments covered by the policy.

If you are employed, health insurance may be provided through your employer. Still, if you are self-employed, unemployed, or work for an employer that does not offer health insurance, you will want to explore other ways to buy health insurance. In that case, you may find that purchasing an individual health insurance policy is your only option. Monthly premiums for individual plans are often high, and some people cannot afford coverage. Many reforms instituted by the Affordable Care Act of 2010 were designed to extend healthcare coverage to those without it.

Group Policies

The most common type of health insurance is group insurance, which may be called employer-based coverage. **Group health insurance** is a type of health insurance plan offered by an employer or member organization for their employees (the group). Employers with 50 or more full-time employees must offer affordable health insurance to their full-time employees and their dependents. Dependents can stay on their parents' or guardians' health insurance until the end of the month when they turn 26. Employers with fewer than 50 full-time employees are not required to offer health insurance benefits.

The employees or members usually receive coverage at a lower cost because the risk to the insurer is distributed across all employees or members of the organization. The group members have the same coverage and pay a set premium. It is most often obtained through employers. Because a group represents a large portion of potential business for an insurer, a group can usually negotiate better coverage and lower premiums than individuals can get on their own.

Some employers pay the premiums as a benefit to their employees. More commonly, however, the employer and employee share the premium costs. Due to rising insurance costs, employees now pay more for their health care and insurance. The rationale is that if employees share more expenses, they will better manage their use of health care services.

Flexible Benefit Plans

Many employers provide flexible benefit plans. A Section 125 Flex Plan, or **Flex 125 Plan**, is an employee benefit program that allows employees to set aside money, pre-tax, to help pay deductibles, copayments, and other health expenses during the year that are not covered by insurance. A Flex 125 Plan is often offered as part of an employee benefits program that allows employees to choose the benefits that best meet their needs. However, the Flex 125 Plan has one significant disadvantage: the money the employee sets aside may be forfeited at the end of the year unless used.

A **health savings account (HSA)** is associated with a medical plan with a higher annual deductible than typical health plans. The insured takes the money that would have gone toward the premiums for basic health coverage and deposits it into an HSA. The account is then used to pay qualified medical expenses not covered by insurance, including deductibles and copayments. Contributions to the account are made pretax and are tax-deductible. If the HSA is sponsored through the employer, the employer may also contribute to the account. Money withdrawn from an HSA to pay qualified medical expenses is tax-free. Unlike the Flex 125 Plan, unused money in an HSA is not forfeited at the end of the year; it continues to grow on a tax-deferred basis, like an IRA.

Individual Policies

People can also buy individual health insurance policies. The premiums are often higher than group coverage and depend on the type of coverage an individual purchases. If you are not eligible to purchase group health insurance, you can get coverage under the Affordable Care Act of 2010. The **Affordable Care Act (ACA)** became law in March 2010, making health insurance available to more people. Anyone living in the United States legally, not incarcerated, and not covered by Medicare can enroll in an ACA plan. This sweeping law aimed to increase the availability and affordability of health insurance while controlling rising medical costs for individuals and the government. The law prevents health insurance companies from refusing to cover an individual or to charge more if the person has a pre-existing condition. A **pre-existing condition** is a health problem, such as diabetes or cancer, that the person had before the new health insurance coverage began. The law also prevents insurance companies from charging women more than men for health insurance.

The law mandates that everyone has health insurance. The rationale is that if everyone is insured, the overall insurance cost should drop because younger people (usually with lower health risks) who chose to be uninsured previously would now be added to the pool. Many young people think health insurance is optional. However, the average doctor visit for illness can exceed $100 per visit. A trip to urgent care can cost $150 or more, and one day in the hospital can cost $1,500 to $5,000. A sound financial plan should include decisions about health care.

Since the ACA mandates health insurance, the risk is spread, and everyone pays a minimum insurance rate based on age rather than physical condition or other arbitrary factors. Congress removed the penalty for not being insured in 2017, but some states have health insurance mandates with penalties for noncompliance.

What is the purpose of the Affordable Care Act?

The law set up health insurance exchanges to facilitate the purchase of health insurance in each state. A **health insurance exchange** provides a set of government-regulated and standardized health care plans from which uninsured and underinsured individuals may purchase health insurance policies. The states control the coverage cost to help ensure reasonable premium rates. Individuals who meet low-income requirements can receive federal subsidies to help pay the premium costs of insurance purchased through a health insurance exchange.

The Affordable Care Act mandates that qualified health insurance plans must provide minimum essential coverage. The coverages include:

- Lab services. Your insurance plan must cover testing costs if you need a lab test.
- Emergency services. Your insurance must cover the cost if you need to go to the emergency department.
- Prescription drugs. Your insurance should cover prescription drug costs for both acute and chronic conditions.
- Mental health and substance use services. Your insurance plan should cover treatment for mental health issues such as anxiety and depression and pay if you must go to an inpatient treatment facility for substance abuse or mental health care.

- Maternity and newborn care. Qualified plans must provide coverage for prenatal expenses, labor and delivery, and the costs of a newborn.
- Pediatric services. Children should receive routine medical care along with dental and vision care.
- Rehabilitative services and devices. If you require rehabilitation as a treatment after an accident or illness, the insurance plan should pay to restore you to full functionality and mobility.
- Ambulatory patient services. This type of service refers to outpatient care and urgent care visits.
- Hospitalization. If you become sick and need to be in the hospital, your plan should cover some of the costs.

As with all health insurance plans, you may be required to pay the deductible and copayments as described in your policy.

Other Insurance Considerations

Individuals may have other insurance needs or options due to job changes, life changes, or personal preferences. For example, a family may be concerned about a genetic risk for cancer. If so, they may want to purchase supplemental cancer insurance.

Supplemental Insurance

Sometimes, medical costs can exceed the limits of a standard health policy, either a group or an individual policy. To protect against this risk, people can buy supplemental health insurance. This secondary policy is designed to pay high deductibles, copayments, and higher medical fees than the insured's standard policy allows. For example, a traditional plan may pay up to $450 daily for a hospital room, but the actual charges may come to $500 daily. A supplemental policy would pay the difference of $50 a day.

COBRA

The Consolidated Omnibus Budget Reconciliation Act, or **COBRA**, is a federal law enacted in 1986 that allows people who leave their job to continue their health insurance under the company plan for a limited period (usually 18 months). During this period, former employees pay premiums individually for the same group coverage they had while employed. This law aims to give former employees financial security while trying to obtain other insurance, either on their own or through a new employer.

Double Coverage

If a family has more than one insurance plan, the insurers will share the costs of a claim. **Coordination of benefits** is a health insurance provision that specifies how the insurers will share the fee when more than one policy covers a claim. This provision ensures that reimbursement will not exceed 100 percent of allowable expenses. For example, if a couple has two policies—one through the husband's employer and one through the wife's employer—then one policy may pay 80 percent of the medical expenses and the other the remaining 20 percent.

> **✓ Checkpoint**
>
> What are the main differences between group and individual health insurance plans?

LO 16.1.2 Types of Coverage and Plans

Both group and individual health insurance have similar types of coverage and plans. In most cases, there is an annual enrollment period during which the insured can change their plans, including adding or deleting certain types of coverage.

Types of Coverage

Health insurance policies typically cover medical, hospital, and surgical expenses and significant medical costs. This coverage helps protect consumers by paying most doctor and hospital bills. Some policies cover dental and vision costs for an additional premium.

Basic Health Insurance

Basic health insurance usually includes medical, hospital, and surgical costs. Medical coverage helps pay for routine physician services, including doctor office visits, annual physical exams, recommended immunizations, screenings, X-rays, and laboratory tests. Policies that cover prescriptions will usually pay the cost of generic medications. If the consumer prefers name-brand drugs, a surcharge above the amount of the generic prices must be paid. Hospital coverage pays hospital bills for room, board, and medication. Surgical coverage pays the majority of surgical costs. Usually, basic health insurance covers only necessary (not cosmetic or elective) surgery and excludes certain types of procedures. Under the ACA, preventive health care, such as vaccines and healthcare screenings are covered under healthcare plans. For example, screenings for blood pressure, diabetes, cholesterol, and many types of cancer are covered. Counseling for quitting smoking, losing weight, and depression as well as well-baby care and routine vaccines are also covered. You may be required to pay an office visit charge, but the cost of the screening or vaccine is paid through your insurance.

While playing tennis with friends, Aja took a nasty spill. She was scraped up, was bleeding, and her ankle immediately began swelling. Her friend drove her to an urgent care, where her wounds were treated and her ankle was examined. She received an X-ray of her ankle and was informed it was not broken. Aja was provided with a brace and instructed to follow up with her primary care doctor in 3 days if it was not improving. After 3 days, she had seen no improvement, so she called her doctor to follow up. Her doctor asked her to come in for an examination, where he recommended that Aja have an MRI. Estimated costs of Aja's medical treatment are outlined in the table below:

Urgent care visit	$175
X-ray of ankle	$160
Ankle brace	$40
Prescription anti-inflammatory	$40
Follow-up visit with primary care doctor	$120
MRI	$2,200

Scenario 1: Aja has a PPO plan with a $500 deductible; 90% coinsurance; and a $1,500 out-of-pocket maximum.

Scenario 2: Aja has a high deductible plan with a deductible of $5,000; 80% coinsurance; and out-of-pocket maximum of $7,500.

Calculate the amount that Aja would pay in each scenario.

Think Critically

1. Increased insurance coverage typically results in a higher monthly premium. What are the advantages and disadvantages of paying higher monthly premium to have increased health coverage?

2. What factors may influence the type of insurance an individual needs? Would the necessary insurance be different for someone who is 55 years old? Explain.

3. A friend is trying to select an insurance plan through their new employer, and they are not sure what coverage they should take. What would you recommend they consider as they decide?

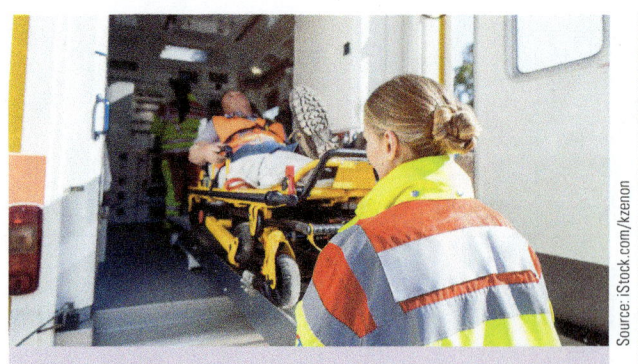

Why is major medical coverage so important?

Source: iStock.com/kzenon

Major Medical Insurance

Major medical coverage protects against the catastrophic expenses of a severe injury or illness. For example, when a patient is admitted to the hospital for an organ transplant or other major surgery, the cost can be $500,000 or more. Major medical coverage is beyond basic health insurance; by law, there can no longer be a limit on the dollar amount of lifetime benefits paid. Major medical insurance requires the insured to pay a deductible before the insurance pays anything. These plans are also called high deductible plans. Someone selecting this type of plan may qualify for a health savings account (HSA).

Major medical coverage often has a coinsurance provision requiring the insured to pay some medical bills even after the deductible is met. The typical coinsurance amount is 20 percent. For a higher premium, an out-of-pocket maximum, sometimes called a stop-loss requirement, is often included. An **out-of-pocket maximum** is an insurance clause that caps or sets a maximum that the insured must pay out of pocket during any calendar year. For example, a $5,000 stop-loss means the insured will pay no more than $5,000 for copayments and deductibles in a year.

Dental and Vision Insurance

Dental insurance covers essential dental services, such as exams, cleanings, X-rays, and fillings. Dental plans usually have low deductibles and coinsurance requirements of 20 percent. The insurance will typically set a maximum amount paid per person. The standard upper limit range is $1,000 to $2,000 per year. Insurers usually pay less for some services, such as crowns and bridges.

Vision insurance often pays for exams, prescription adjustments, and lenses. Policies usually cover a periodic eye examination and the purchase of single-vision corrective lenses and basic frames. Some policies offer limited coverage for prescription sunglasses and contact lenses.

Managed and Unmanaged Health Care Plans

Employee or private health care plans are grouped into unmanaged and managed categories.

Unmanaged Care

Unmanaged care plans are also called fee-for-service plans. Unmanaged care plans allow participants to choose any doctor and be reimbursed for a percentage of the expenses incurred after a deductible is met. Deductibles often range from $100 to $1,000 per patient or $500 or more per family. This type of plan is often the most expensive because control over costs and services is relaxed.

Managed Care

Managed care plans rely on a network of healthcare providers. To receive maximum reimbursement, participants in a managed care plan must select doctors from the

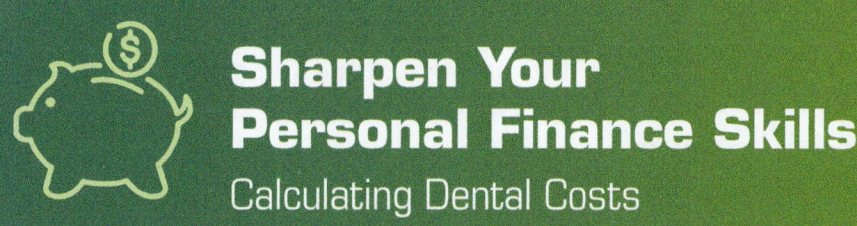

Sharpen Your Personal Finance Skills

Calculating Dental Costs

Aja needs to have a root canal. Her dental insurance will pay 50 percent of the cost. The policy sets an allowable limit for a root canal at $800. The dentist bills Aja's insurer for $1,200. How much will insurance pay? How much will Aja have to pay?

First, compute how much insurance will pay on the root canal:

$$\$800 \times 0.50 = \$400 \text{ will be paid by insurance}$$

Then, subtract the amount paid by insurance from the total for the root canal:

$$\$1,200 - \$400 = \$800 \text{ due from Aja}$$

Based on the example above, compute the out-of-pocket expenses in the following situation:

Sahil's dental insurance will pay 70 percent of the cost of a porcelain crown. The policy sets an allowable limit for a crown at $2,000. The dentist bills Sahil's insurer for $2,250. How much will Sahil have to pay?

---

network. The policy requires participants to obtain preapproval for any surgery or hospital admission. Some insurance plans will require a second opinion before they approve treatment. The insurer exercises significant control over the types of services provided and the maximum benefits allowed for those services. Health maintenance organizations (HMOs), preferred provider organizations (PPOs), and point of service (POS) plans are the most common types of managed care plans. As of 2022, PPOs were the most common plan type. Forty-nine percent of covered workers were enrolled in PPOs, followed by HDHP/SOs (29%), HMOs (12%), POS plans (9%), and conventional plans (1%). HDHP is a high deductible health plan that combines HSAs or Health Reimbursement Arrangements (HRAs).

Preferred Provider Organization

A **preferred provider organization (PPO)** is a network of healthcare providers that includes doctors and hospitals who band together to provide health services for set fees. Patients can choose doctors from an approved provider list, but they can also go outside of the plan for health care. However, if they choose to obtain treatment from a provider outside the network, they will have to pay a higher percentage of the costs. Patients are not required to select a primary care physician and do not need a referral to see a specialist, but the price will be higher. There are limits on the types of services that can be provided and fees that can be charged. Patients who stay within the network of providers usually must make a small copayment, such as $30 to $35 per office visit or prescription.

Health Maintenance Organization

A **health maintenance organization (HMO)** is a group plan offering prepaid medical care to its members. An HMO often has facilities and provides full medical services. Patients must choose doctors on the HMO staff, including one doctor to be their primary care physician (PCP). To see a specialist, patients usually need a referral from their PCP first. Otherwise, the insurance will not cover the visit. In this way, the PCP acts as a gatekeeper. HMO patients usually make a copayment of $25 to $50 for an office visit. Capitated HMOs receive a fixed monthly premium for each patient, regardless of whether the patient seeks medical care.

High Deductible Health Plan

A **high deductible health plan (HDHP)** is a plan that combines a Health Savings Account (HAS) or a Health Reimbursement Arrangement (HRA) with a high deductible conventional medical plan. The monthly premium is typically lower than other types of plans, but the insured will pay more of the costs before insurance pays anything. You can use the HAS or HRA to cover your share of the costs.

Point of Service

Hybrid medical insurance plans are rare but are available in some locations. **Point of service (POS)** plans provide people with more choices and control over medical benefits. These plans combine the features of HMOs and PPOs. Like an HMO, patients may be required to choose a primary care physician, but like a PPO, patients can choose to go outside of the plan for health care. However, unless referred by the primary care physician, patients will pay more for going outside the program than they would with a PPO. Although a POS gives you more flexibility than an HMO, its cost structure is designed to encourage participants to stay within the plan. HSA plans may offer this type of option for maximum flexibility.

Types of Government Health Care Plans

Medicare and Medicaid are government-sponsored programs designed to help cover healthcare costs. While both programs were established by the federal government in 1965 and are taxpayer-funded, they are very different programs with differing eligibility requirements and coverage. People with Medicare and Medicaid do not qualify for the health insurance exchanges under the Affordable Care Act.

Medicare

Medicare is government-sponsored health insurance for people aged 65 or older. Medicare is run by the Social Security Administration (SSA) and funded by employee payroll deductions and matching employer contributions. Like other plans, maximum benefits, exclusions, and other requirements exist. Retired people pay a monthly premium for Medicare insurance, which is deducted from their Social Security payments.

Medicare has four parts: Part A (hospital insurance), Part B (medical insurance), Part C (Medicare Advantage health plans), and Part D (prescription drug costs). Part A provides payments for inpatient hospital or nursing care facility services, home health care services, and hospice care. Part B offers payments to physicians and surgeons for medically necessary outpatient hospital services, such as going to the emergency department, laboratory tests, and X-rays. Part C is not a benefit but rather an option. It allows private health insurance companies to provide Medicare benefits. Medicare Advantage plans must offer at least the same benefits as Parts A and B but can do so with different costs and coverage restrictions. Part D of Medicare covers prescription drugs. It is provided only through private insurance companies that have government contracts. Anyone with Part A or B is eligible for Part D. Medicare Advantage plans may also offer prescription drug coverage.

Medicare will not cover all healthcare costs for Medicare enrollees, also called beneficiaries. Many beneficiaries purchase supplemental Medigap insurance to help pay the copayments and deductibles not covered by Medicare. Private insurance companies sell Medigap insurance.

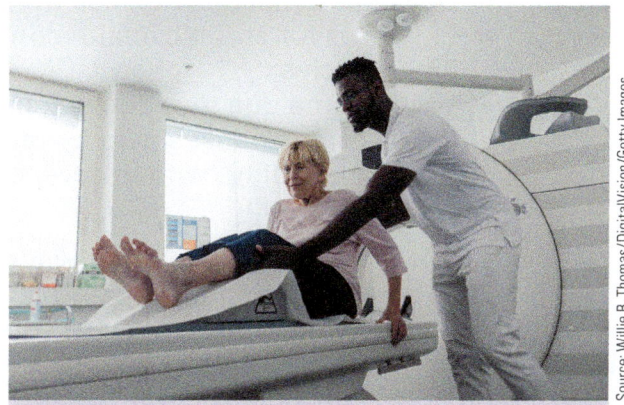

Source: Willie B. Thomas/DigitalVision/Getty Images

Why do many Medicare enrollees purchase Medigap insurance?

Connections to Your World
The Affordable Care Act

The Affordable Care Act is a federal statute signed into law by President Barack Obama on March 23, 2010. Together with the Health Care and Education Reconciliation Act, it became the most significant overhaul of the healthcare system since the passage of Medicare and Medicaid in 1965. The goals of the new law are to decrease the number of uninsured, to expand public and private health insurance coverage, and to reduce overall costs of health care.

(continues)

(continued)

Some are critical of the law. Opponents are against mandatory coverage that requires all citizens to buy insurance. On June 28, 2012, the U.S. Supreme Court upheld the constitutionality of the law's mandate to obtain insurance. However, many conservative political advocacy groups, small business organizations, and some state governments continue to challenge the law.

On the other hand, proponents say that the Affordable Care Act puts consumers back in charge of their health care. Under this law, a new "Patient's Bill of Rights" gives the American people the stability and flexibility they need to make informed choices about their health. Supporters argue that lack of health insurance results in poor health and shorter lives for many Americans. They also argue that there are costs to society as well, such as the following:

- Developmental deficiencies from insufficient health care during infancy
- Expenses for chronic health conditions not treated until they become emergencies
- Lost income due to reduced job productivity and employment
- Healthcare expenses paid by taxpayers for uninsured patients
- Social inequality (with lower-income Americans being at a definite health disadvantage)

Many people propose other ways to provide access to affordable health care. Some say a single-payer, government-sponsored health plan is the answer. In a single-payer system, individuals and businesses pay taxes to raise revenue that covers insurance expenses for the entire population. This type of system exists in many other nations, such as Canada and most western European countries. Others say we can reform the system we have so that health insurance becomes portable—meaning you can take it with you from job to job. Whatever the answer, the United States must find a way to reduce the costs of health care and provide access to affordable health insurance for all Americans.

Think Critically

1. Suppose you have no health insurance. How would this fact affect the decisions you make about your health care?
2. What are the potential advantages and disadvantages of the Affordable Care Act?
3. Do you believe it is a violation of your freedom of choice (life, liberty, and pursuit of happiness) to be required to buy health insurance? Explain.

Medicaid

Medicaid is government-sponsored health insurance for people with low incomes and limited resources. This program helps families who live in poverty and cannot afford private health insurance to pay the costs of long-term medical and custodial care.

Unlike Medicare, which is solely a federal program, Medicaid is a joint federal and state program. Each state operates its own Medicaid system. The federal government funds up to 50 percent of the cost of each state's Medicaid program. All states must cover certain mandatory benefits, such as comprehensive inpatient and outpatient health care coverage.

Not everyone is eligible for Medicaid. There are income, age, disability, and citizenship requirements that must be met. The Affordable Care Act expanded Medicaid eligibility starting in 2014. Under the law, states that choose to participate in the Expanded Medicaid program must allow people with income up to 133 percent of the poverty line to qualify for coverage. Those enrolled in Medicaid receive coverage like the coverage provided by the Affordable Care Act but at little or no cost.

✓ Checkpoint

Define the common types of health insurance coverage and plans.

16.1 Lesson Review

Check Your Understanding

1. Explain the differences between group health insurance choices and individual health insurance choices. (LO 16.1.1)
2. Define the various types of managed care plans. (LO 16.1.2)

Apply Your Understanding

1. Under the ACA, young adults can be covered on their parent(s) or guardian(s) insurance until they turn 26. Assume you are turning 26 this year. What should you know about purchasing your own health insurance, including how the health insurance exchange works? (LO 16.1.1)
2. Sahil needs to find new insurance. He is curious about the minimum essential benefits that were established under the ACA. Explain to Sahil what the minimum essential benefits are and why they were established as part of the ACA. (LO 16.1.1)
3. Explain the advantages and disadvantages of choosing a managed care plan over an unmanaged one. (LO 16.1.2)

The Essential Question

What is the difference between group and individual health insurance, and what types of coverage and plans are available?

A: With group insurance, often called employer-provided coverage, all those insured have the same coverage and pay a set premium, which is usually lower than individuals can get on their own or through health insurance exchanges offered through the Affordable Care Act. Basic health coverage, major medical coverage, and dental and vision insurance are available through unmanaged and managed care plans, such as HMOs and PPOs. Medicare and Medicaid are government-sponsored health insurance plans.

The Essential Question — Why do individuals need disability insurance, life insurance, and long-term care insurance?

Learning Objectives

By the end of this lesson, you should be able to:

LO 16.2.1 Explain types of disability insurance plans.

LO 16.2.2 Explain types of life insurance plans.

LO 16.2.3 Explain types of long-term care insurance plans.

Key Terms

- disability insurance
- waiting period
- worker's compensation
- life insurance
- beneficiaries
- portability
- incontestable clause
- double indemnity
- acceleration of benefits
- term life insurance
- permanent life insurance
- cash value
- long-term care insurance

LO 16.2.1 Disability Insurance

Of all the types of insurance, disability insurance is the most often overlooked. **Disability insurance** is a plan that makes regular payments to replace income lost when illness or injury prevents the insured from working. This type of insurance is often called income protection because coverage compensates workers for loss of income resulting from severe illness or injury. People often think nothing can happen to them that will interrupt their earning power or believe the insurance premiums are too expensive. Unfortunately, recovery from an accident or an illness can go on for weeks or months. Yet while you are disabled and unable to perform your job, your regular living expenses continue.

Generally, there are two types of disability insurance: short-term and long-term. Short-term disability insurance usually lasts between three and six months. Long-term disability insurance usually picks up where short-term disability leaves off and can provide coverage until retirement.

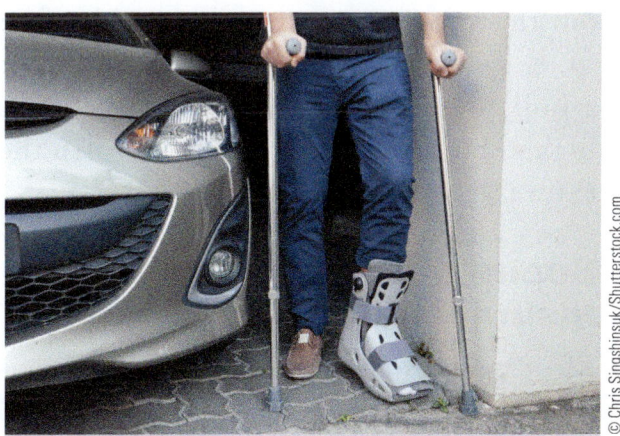

What is the primary purpose of disability insurance?

© Chris Singshinsuk/Shutterstock.com

Short-term and long-term disability plans typically cover 50 to 70 percent of the monthly salary.

Most employers offer both short-term and long-term disability group plans. In many cases, the employer pays a portion of the premium. However, the insurance is good only if you work for the employer. If you leave the company, you lose all policy benefits. If your employer does not have a group plan, individual coverage can be provided at a higher premium through private insurance.

Disability benefits do not begin the day you become disabled. Instead, coverage requires a **waiting period**, also known as an elimination period. The waiting period can range from 30 days to 6 months before disability insurance begins. You may be on sick leave from work collecting regular pay during this time. Private disability insurance policies that require longer waiting periods have lower premiums.

The maximum duration of benefits under most disability policies is until age 65 or early retirement if you qualify. A few policies pay benefits for life if you become permanently disabled. Guaranteed renewability of coverage will protect you against cancellation if your health declines. Without this provision, an insurer could refuse to renew your insurance. The premium for a policy with guaranteed renewability is higher, but the coverage may be worth the extra cost.

Social Security Disability Insurance

Most workers in the United States participate in the Social Security program. Social Security is more than retirement income. It is old age, survivors, and disability insurance

(OSDI) and health insurance (HI) through the Medicare program. If you have Social Security taxes deducted from your paycheck, you are entitled to disability payments from Social Security in the event you become disabled and cannot work.

To qualify, you must prove the extent of your disability, fill out forms, and have medical exams as required by the Social Security Administration. Workers are considered disabled if they have a physical or mental condition that prevents them from doing any gainful work, and the situation is expected to last for at least 12 months or result in death. Benefits are determined in part by your pay and the years you have been covered under Social Security. The work requirement may be waived for specific individuals, including the blind, widows or widowers with disabilities, children with disabilities, and wounded military service members.

Workers' Compensation Insurance

Workers' compensation is a form of insurance that covers an employee who has suffered an injury or illness from job-related duties. Coverage includes payment of medical bills and compensation for lost wages. This insurance also carries a death benefit. It provides a burial payment and an allowance for living expenses for survivors of people killed on the job. Like Social Security benefits, these benefits are determined by your earnings and your work history.

Workers' compensation insurance is administered at the state level. Each state has its laws and programs for workers' compensation. In most states, workers' compensation coverage is not optional;

almost all employers must carry this insurance. Employees do not pay for workers' compensation insurance. The employers pay for it.

Workers' compensation should not be confused with short-term and long-term disability; it pays workers only when injured on the job, whereas disability insurance pays regardless of when or where the insured is impaired or disabled.

> **✓ Checkpoint**
>
> What are the most common types of disability insurance?

LO 16.2.2 Life Insurance

Life insurance provides funds to the beneficiaries when the insured dies. **Beneficiaries** are those who will receive the proceeds of an insurance policy when the insured person dies. Consider the financial needs that a family will face after the death of a wage earner—and how much income will be needed to pay the ongoing expenses of daily living.

Like all types of insurance, life insurance is based on risk sharing and probability. To predict the likelihood of death at different ages, insurers use mortality tables. These tables are based on statistics gathered about life expectancy and death rates among various groups of people. Insurers set premiums based on these tables. For example, older people are more likely to die while the policy is in effect than younger people. As a result, insurers generally charge older adults higher premiums. Other factors enter the

calculation as well. For example, smokers tend to die sooner than nonsmokers, and premiums reflect this.

To buy an individual life insurance policy, you must supply a detailed medical history. You may also be required to have a medical exam, especially for policies with high values. Someone with a severe health problem, such as heart disease, may be unable to buy an individual life insurance policy.

You may be able to buy group life insurance through your employer. A group life insurance plan insures many people under the terms of a single policy without requiring a medical exam. Employers often provide group life insurance as an employee benefit. Group coverage costs much less than an individual policy. Today, recent laws require that group policies be portable. **Portability** means that when you leave your employer, you can continue paying the premiums and convert your group policy into an individual policy.

Provisions of Life Insurance Policies

Although life insurance policies differ from company to company, many standard provisions are usually found in all policies. It is important to understand these provisions before purchasing a life insurance policy to know what is expected of you and the insurer.

Beneficiary Clause

A necessary provision in a life insurance policy is the right to name your beneficiaries. The beneficiaries of a life insurance policy will receive the amount specified in the policy upon the insured's death. Beneficiaries can be anyone; if children

Figure 16.1   Other Purposes of Life Insurance

- Provides cash to pay for a funeral.
- Can be used to pay off a home mortgage and other debts at the time of death.
- Provides a lump-sum payment to children when they reach a specified age.
- Provides an education or income for children.
- Allows you to make charitable bequests after death.
- Provides for retirement income.
- Allows you to accumulate savings.
- Can be used to make estate and inheritance tax payments.
- Takes care of children's needs as they are growing up (including child care services in the event of the death of a parent).
- Provides cash value that can be borrowed.

are minors, parents may name a trustee or guardian to handle the money on behalf of the children. Both primary and secondary beneficiaries can be designated. The benefits will go to the secondary beneficiary if the primary beneficiary is deceased. You also can change the beneficiaries anytime during the term of the policy.

There are also other purposes that life insurance can fulfill, as shown in **Figure 16.1.** As you can see, life insurance can also provide savings benefits in addition to death benefits.

Incontestable Clause

An **incontestable clause** is a provision of a life insurance policy stating that once the policy has been in effect for a specified time, usually 2 years, the insurer may no longer question items on the application to deny coverage. For example, an applicant may lie about their age or conceal a severe medical condition to get a lower premium. If the insurer discovers this, it will not pay the claim on the insured's death if it occurs during the policy's first 2 years, or other specified time. After the specified period,

the insurer cannot dispute the policy's validity during the lifetime and after the insured's death for any reason. One reason for this provision is to protect the beneficiaries from financial loss. They should not be made to suffer because of the acts of the insured.

Suicide Clause

A suicide clause is a provision of a life insurance policy that specifies that the insurance company will not pay the claim if the insured commits suicide within the first two years, or other specified time of the policy's

Source: iStock.com/StefaNikolic

What are the various provisions commonly found in life insurance policies?

purchase. If the insured's death results from suicide, the insurer will likely only return previously paid premiums to the family. Some policies will pay death benefits after a waiting period, such as two years, from the date of death.

Riders

Insurers offer a variety of riders to life insurance policies. A life insurance rider is a small insurance addendum that modifies the coverage of the main policy. A rider usually adds or excludes some types of coverage or alters policy benefits. Riders result in higher premiums.

A waiver of premium rider allows you to stop paying premiums and keep your coverage in force if you become disabled and cannot work. This rider usually does not kick in until you have been disabled for at least 6 months.

Guaranteed insurability riders give you the right to renew a policy or buy additional coverage regardless of changes in health. If your health declines with age, you can apply for extra coverage without a medical exam.

Many insurers also offer accidental death riders. In the case of accidental death, some riders provide for double indemnity. **Double indemnity** means that the beneficiary is paid double the face amount of the insurance policy.

The acceleration of benefits rider is also offered by many insurers. **Acceleration of benefits** allows people diagnosed with a severe medical condition that will likely lead to their death in 12 or 24 months, or other specified period, to collect a portion of their life insurance benefits before death. Typical benefits are between 50 to 90 percent of the face value of the policy, depending on the insurer. The purpose of this provision is to allow the person to pay off debts and prepare for expenses that will occur. If the person does not die within the specified time, they do not have to repay the accelerated benefits received.

Types of Life Insurance

There are two main types of life insurance: term life and permanent life. Both types come in different forms and have advantages and disadvantages.

Term Life Insurance

Term life insurance remains in effect for a specified period, such as 20 years. Coverage ceases if the insured survives beyond that time with no remaining value. Term life insurance has no savings component, as permanent life policies do. However, the premiums for these policies are significantly lower than the costs for permanent life insurance. Parents often buy term policies to cover the financial needs of their children in case they should die while the children are still young. By the time the term policy ends, the children will be grown and independent, so the parents no longer need to provide for their children.

Decreasing Term Insurance

There are several variations of term life insurance. With decreasing term insurance, coverage decreases yearly while the premium remains the same. For example, assume a person buys a 20-year decreasing term policy worth $100,000. The policy decreases in coverage yearly until the value reaches zero at the end of 20 years. If the insured dies during the first year of the policy, it pays the full benefit of $100,000. If the insured dies during the second year, death benefits decrease to $95,000. If the insured dies during the third year, benefits reduce to $90,000 until the policy has no value after 20 years. Therefore, the policy coverage reduces by a specified amount each year. In contrast, the death benefit on level-term insurance remains constant from beginning to end, while the premium may increase at designated intervals. Although it can be used for any purpose, decreasing term insurance is often sold to pay off a mortgage in the event of death. The value of decreasing term insurance decreases over time, as does the principal in a mortgage.

Renewable Term Insurance

Renewable term insurance gives the insured the right to renew the policy yearly without passing a physical exam.

Premiums increase with each renewal because the policyholder is older and the risk of death is greater, but the death benefits remain the same.

Convertible Term Insurance

Convertible term insurance permits the insured to convert the policy to permanent coverage within a specific period without providing additional evidence of insurability, such as a medical exam. This type of policy offers the benefit of purchasing less expensive term life insurance now with the option to convert to a permanent policy later as insurance needs and financial resources change. Converting the policy to permanent insurance will raise the premium.

Sharpen Your Personal Finance Skills
Calculating Life Insurance Needs

Aja and Sahil recently married and had their first child. They begin discussing life insurance to ensure that the family will be financially stable in the event of an unexpected passing. They know there are a lot of factors that impact the amount of life insurance they need. They begin by exploring life insurance policies for Aja.

Aja currently has an annual salary of $72,000. Aja and Sahil have a mortgage on their house for $185,000, and Aja has $18,000 in student loans. They pay $800 a month for daycare and will have this expense for 3 more years. If something happens, Aja wants her family to receive the equivalent of 2 years' worth of her income as a supplement. They estimate the cost of a funeral at $8,500. Aja and Sahil want to allocate $80,000 for college or postsecondary expenses for their child.

Aja currently has life insurance through her employer equal to her annual salary. In addition, she has $35,000 in a retirement account. Aja and Sahil have $8,500 in savings.

Using the information above and the two-step method below, calculate the amount of life insurance that Aja would need.

(continues)

(continued)

Step 1: Determine Aja's financial obligations

- Annual salary × 2 years = $72,000 × 2 = $144,000
- Mortgage balance = $185,000
- Other debt (student loans) = $18,000
- Future college needs = $80,000
- Funeral cost = $8,500
- Daycare expenses = $800 × 12 months × 3 years = $28,800

Total financial obligations = $464,300

Step 2: Subtract liquid assets from financial obligations calculated in Step 1. This is the amount of life insurance Aja will need.

To find liquid assets add:

- Employer-provided life insurance = $72,000
- Retirement account = $35,000
- Savings = $8,500

Total assets = $115,500

How much life insurance would you recommend for Aja?

Permanent Life Insurance

Permanent life insurance remains in effect for the insured's lifetime and builds a cash value. **Cash value** is the savings accumulated in a permanent life insurance policy you would receive if you cancelled your policy. A portion of your premiums is deposited into an investment account, where it earns interest to build cash value. The interest rate varies with short-term rates in the economy. You can borrow money using your policy's cash value as collateral. If you do not repay the loan, the policy will repay it out of the death benefit when you die. For example, if you have a $100,000 policy and borrow $20,000 but do not repay it, your beneficiaries will receive only $80,000 upon death.

Permanent life insurance comes in many forms. Four common types of permanent life policies are whole life, limited-pay life, universal life, and variable life.

Whole Life

A whole life policy, also known as straight or ordinary life, is insurance for which you pay fixed premiums throughout your life. Upon your death, a stated sum is paid to your beneficiary. The amount of your premium depends primarily on the age at which you purchase the policy. The premiums are high enough to pay for the death benefit plus contribute to the policy's cash value.

Limited-Pay Life

With a limited-pay life policy, premiums are limited to a specific number of years or until age 65. At the end of the payment

Is it wise to borrow against the cash value of your life insurance policy? Why or why not?

benefit and cash value rise (or fall) with the investment results. While a minimum death benefit is guaranteed, cash value is not guaranteed. With some variable life policies, policyholders pay fixed premiums. With others, the premiums can fluctuate because the interest earned on investments may be applied to the premiums, thus reducing the amount the policyholder pays.

✓ **Checkpoint**

What are the differences between the various types of life insurance?

period, the policy is considered "paid up." However, you remain insured for life, and the company will pay the face value of the policy at your death.

Universal Life

Unlike the other types of permanent life policies, the premiums and death benefits on a universal life policy are not fixed. The policyholder can choose to change the death benefit and the amount or timing of premiums during the policy's life. Thus, the face value of the policy can be lowered or raised without rewriting the policy. When interest rates are high, you can move large sums of money into your policy, by paying higher premiums, and let the earnings grow tax deferred.

Variable Life

Variable life combines a death benefit with investment options. At the designation of the policyholder, the insurer invests part of the premium in securities, such as stocks, bonds, and money market funds, within the insurance company's portfolio. The death

LO 16.2.3 **Long-Term Care Insurance**

Long-term care insurance will pay for some of your long-term care if you become unable to care for yourself in the future. **Long-term care insurance** is designed to cover the expenses of long-term services and support such as help with daily living activities or provide payment for staying in a long-term care facility.

Types of Long-Term Care Insurance

There are three main types of long-term care insurance policies: traditional long-term care insurance, hybrid long-term care insurance, and life insurance with a long-term care rider.

Traditional Long-Term Care Insurance

A traditional long-term care insurance policy is a standalone policy that will cover your expenses for in-home care or for care in a nursing home or other long-term care facility.

Hybrid Long-Term Care Insurance

A hybrid policy allows the insured to link benefits of long-term care with a life insurance policy or an annuity. If you need long-term care, your life insurance or annuity will pay the costs necessary for your care. But, if you never need long-term care, your family will receive the proceeds of the life insurance policy or the remaining value of the annuity.

Life Insurance with a Long-Term Care Rider

Some life insurance policies will add a long-term care rider as additional coverage to your life insurance policy. You may be able to use some of the life insurance for your care.

Costs of Long-Term Care and Insurance

Long-term care prices vary widely depending upon your geographic location. Medicare generally will not pay for extended care in a nursing home or assisted living facility. Neither does Medicare pay for most in-home care for routine tasks such as bathing and getting dressed. Medicaid may pay for some of these services, but only for people with limited assets. Long-term care insurance can cost between $200 and $300 per month if you purchase the insurance while in your 50s and maintain the insurance throughout the rest of your life. The long-term care insurance premiums are based upon your age, health condition, and the extra features built into the insurance policy.

The costs for long-term care can be expensive. The average price for a semiprivate room in a nursing home is almost $8,000 per month. Without long-term care insurance, you or your family will be responsible for paying for your care. Everyone may not need long-term care. The American Association for Long-Term Care Insurance estimates that only 35 percent of people will need to be in a nursing facility, and the average time is less than a year. If you have sufficient assets, you may be able to pay for your care without insurance. Those who have limited assets may have their care paid for by Medicaid.

Before purchasing long-term care insurance, investigate the advantages and disadvantages for your personal situation and speak to a financial advisor. If you have a health savings account, you can increase the amount you save each month to put toward your long-term care.

✔ Checkpoint

What is the purpose of long-term care insurance?

Check Your Understanding

1. What is the difference between short-term disability insurance and long-term disability insurance? (LO 16.2.1)

2. Explain why disability insurance is an important part of a financial plan. (LO 16.2.1)

3. What are standard provisions found in most life insurance policies? (LO 16.2.2)

4. What are the three main types of long-term care insurance policies? (LO 16.2.3)

Apply Your Understanding

1. Sahil was injured playing soccer, and he will need to miss work for at least 2 weeks because he cannot drive. He has short-term and long-term disability insurance, but he does not understand the difference. Explain to Sahil which insurance will be used to help cover the time he is away from work. (LO 16.2.1)

2. How do life insurance needs change over a lifetime? Describe a life insurance plan for a single adult, a person who is in a long-term relationship, a person who has children, and parent(s) who have adult children who no longer rely on them for support. (LO 16.2.2)

3. Think about your future family situation. Why should you consider long-term care needs when determining your insurance needs? (LO 16.2.3)

The Essential Question

Why do individuals need disability insurance, life insurance, and long-term care insurance?

A: Disability insurance protects the family from loss of income when the wage earner cannot work. Life insurance protects those left behind when a wage earner dies. Long-term care insurance helps pay the costs for daily activities or a stay in a long-term care facility if you are unable to care for yourself.

Summary

16.1 Health Insurance

- Health insurance is a plan for sharing risk of high medical costs among many individuals.

- Group health insurance policies, offered by an employer or member organization, provide broad coverage at lower premiums than do individual policies.

- A Flex 125 Plan allows employees to set aside money, pretax, to help pay deductibles, copayments, and other health expenses that are not covered by insurance.

- Health savings accounts are available for people who have high annual deductibles and can be used to pay health care costs not paid by insurance.

- People without a group plan can buy individual health insurance, but they may have to meet certain requirements.

- The Affordable Care Act (ACA) of 2010 made health insurance available to more people and placed safeguards for those who may have been denied health insurance before the law was in place.

- Health insurance exchanges, established by the ACA, provide a set of government-regulated and standardized health care plans from which uninsured and under-insured individuals may purchase health insurance policies.

- The ACA also mandates that qualified health insurance plans must provide minimum essential coverage, including lab, emergency, and mental health services, among others.

- Individuals may have other insurance needs or options due to job changes, life changes, or personal preferences. This can include supplemental insurance, or a secondary health insurance policy.

- COBRA allows people who leave their jobs to keep their employer-provided health insurance for a limited time.

- Some families may have more than one health insurance plan. When this happens, the two insurance companies coordinate benefits.

- Typical health insurance includes basic medical and major medical coverage. Some cover dental and vision needs for a higher premium.

- Unmanaged care plans allow employees to select their own providers and be reimbursed a percentage of expenses after a deductible is met. Managed care plans contract with a network of healthcare providers.

- The most common managed care programs include preferred provider organizations (PPOs), health maintenance organizations (HMOs), high deductible health plans (HDHPs), and point of service (POS) plans.

- Medicare is government-sponsored health insurance for people aged 65 or older.

- Medicaid is government-sponsored health insurance for people with low incomes and limited resources.

16.2 Disability Insurance, Life Insurance, and Long-Term Care Insurance

- Disability insurance replaces income if you are injured or ill and cannot work. Social Security and workers' compensation insurance also provide disability coverage.

- Life insurance provides funds to beneficiaries when the insured dies.

- Insurers set life insurance premiums based on life expectancy and death rates compiled in mortality tables.

- Most life insurance policies offer standard provisions like a beneficiary clause, an incontestable clause, and a suicide clause. Riders can be added to modify the coverage of the main policy.

- Term life insurance remains in effect for a specified time. If the insured survives beyond that time, coverage ceases with no remaining value. Types of term life insurance include decreasing term insurance, renewable term insurance, and convertible term insurance.

- Permanent life insurance remains in effect for the insured's lifetime and has a savings component (cash value) as well as a death benefit. Common types of permanent life policies are whole life, limited-pay life, universal life, and variable life.

- Long-term care insurance covers the costs associated with daily living if you are unable to take care of yourself.

- Types include traditional long-term care insurance, hybrid long-term care insurance, and life insurance with a long-term care rider.

Check Your Knowledge

1. What is the most common type of health insurance policy? (LO 16.1.1)

2. What is the purpose of an HSA? (LO 16.1.1)

3. What is the ACA? (LO 16.1.1)

4. Define PPO, HMO, HDHP, and POS. (LO 16.1.2)

5. Write a short summary of each type of disability insurance. (LO 16.2.1)

6. Explain the main difference between term-life insurance and permanent life insurance. (LO 16.2.2)

7. What are the advantages and disadvantages of long-term care insurance? (LO 16.2.3)

Apply Your Knowledge

1. Create a comparison chart to show the similarities and the differences between the various types of health insurance policies. (LO 16.1.1)

2. Compute the out-of-pocket expenses in the following situation: Lia's medical insurance will pay 80 percent of the cost of a procedure. The policy sets an allowable limit for the procedure at $1,000. Lia's doctor bills the insurer for $1,300. How much will Lia have to pay? (LO 16.1.2)

3. You have just been offered your first full-time job with benefits. You need to select your health insurance coverage from a list of managed care programs. Which one would you select as part of your benefits package for health insurance? Explain your choice. (LO 16.1.2)

4. Use online resources to review the rights a person injured at work has in your state. What are the most important things to know if you are injured on the job? (LO 16.2.1)

5. Pick one of the calculations for life insurance introduced in the chapter. Calculate your life insurance needs based on the following criteria: Income $60,000 per year; debt $25,000; funeral expenses $10,000; mortgage $275,000; two children. (LO 16.2.2)

6. Using the following information, decide if you should purchase long-term care insurance or save the monthly premium for your future care. Which is the better financial choice?

   Purchase a long-term care policy for $250 per month beginning at age 50. Assume that you will earn 5 percent per year on your savings if you do not purchase the insurance.

   You enter a long-term care facility when you are 80 and live there for 18 months. The monthly cost is $8,500. (LO 16.2.3)

Share Your Knowledge

Work in teams of two to four students to complete the following activities.

1. Working as a team, research the Affordable Care Act and the number of uninsured people in the United States. What can be done to increase the number of insured? How can we control medical costs to make medical care more affordable for everyone? (LO 16.1.1)

2. Create a way to explain the various types of managed health care. Include information about the average costs for doctor visits, prescriptions, urgent care visits, and hospital stays. (LO 16.1.2)

3. Aja is considering purchasing life insurance. Create a comparison chart for the various types of life insurance, including the advantages and disadvantages of each to give to her. (LO 16.2.2)

Connect and Reflect

Base your answers to the following questions on your own personal thoughts, preferences, and experiences.

1. It is becoming common practice today for employers to require employees to participate in wellness programs to manage their health. These programs include mandatory exercise and diet programs and weight management. If employees refuse to participate, they pay higher premiums for their health insurance. Do you feel this practice invades a person's rights? Or do you believe that forcing people to get well and stay well is a benefit worth having? Explain your answer. (LO 16.1.1)

2. Think about your need for health insurance as an adult. Use a decision-making matrix to determine which type of health insurance would be most beneficial for you. (LO 16.1.2)

3. Explore the various types of life insurance. At what point would you consider it important to purchase life insurance? List the reasons for having a life insurance policy, identify the people who would be your beneficiaries, and explain the type of life insurance you would purchase. (LO 16.2.2)

Chapter Project

Visit https://www.healthcare.gov/quick-guide. Find the section on HSA-eligible plans. Read the information available. Prepare a summary of what you learned in the form of a paper, slide deck, blog post, or video. Would you consider an HSA-eligible plan for yourself if you had to purchase health insurance? Explain in your summary.

Setting Career Goals

Once you have explored and researched a career of interest as part of career exploration projects in earlier units, it is important to set goals to help you work toward that career. Setting SMART goals—or goals that are specific, measurable, achievable, relevant, and time-bound—will help ensure that all important factors are considered and included in your goals. Your SMART goals should factor in, at a minimum, education and/or training required, skill development needs, and salary or other factors related to your desired standard of living. Set one short-term, one intermediate-term, and one long-term career goal. Be sure that they are SMART and include all the components listed above.

Think Critically

1. Why is it important for you to set career goals now? How does waiting to do this until after high school impact your ability to pursue a career of interest?

2. How do your SMART goals help your work toward obtaining the future career you desire? How do your short-term goals support your long-term goals?

Unit 4: Project

After discussing health insurance needs with Aja, Sahil decided to plan his risk management strategy. He had never considered risk management or mitigation before; as a young adult, he thinks it is time.

Risk Management Terminology

Sahil has come to you to help him get started. He has several questions. His first question is about risk management terminology he has seen while researching online. Help Sahil understand the following terms by providing a simple explanation for each.

- Risk
- Risk management
- Risk avoidance
- Risk transfer
- Risk reduction
- Risk mitigation

Automobile Insurance Risk Management Plan

Now that he understands the terms, help Sahil work through the following scenarios to develop his automobile insurance risk management plan.

Scenario 1

Sahil owns a vehicle. He currently has full coverage insurance on the vehicle, and he would like to reduce his premiums while staying protected.

The vehicle is not financed. It is a Subaru Outback valued at approximately $15,000. Sahil has a safe driving record and has had no accidents or traffic violations in the past 5 years. He is 25 years old and lives in an apartment in Austin, Texas. If something happens to his vehicle, he does not have enough savings to buy a new car without making payments.

Think Critically

1. What are the automobile liability limits required in Texas? Why is it important to know this information?

2. Should Sahil carry the minimum liability insurance or increase the limits? Explain your answer.

3. Provide Sahil with three advantages and disadvantages regarding purchasing comprehensive and collision coverage.

Scenario 2

Sahil wonders if it would be more cost-effective to purchase liability insurance only and place the amount he saves on automobile insurance into his long-term savings account. Calculate the amount of savings Sahil would accumulate if he did this.

Sahil's current insurance premium for full-coverage automobile insurance is $360 per month. The liability portion of the insurance is only $120 per month. If Sahil were to place the $240 monthly savings into a long-term savings account that earns 3 percent interest per year, calculate his savings over the next 5 years by completing the table below.

Apply Your Knowledge

1. How much would Sahil pay for full-coverage insurance over the next 60 months?
2. How much would Sahil pay for liability-only insurance coverage over the next 60 months?
3. How much would Sahil save if he had only liability insurance over the next 60 months?
4. Create a spreadsheet to show the accumulated savings for the next 60 months, assuming that Sahil allows the savings to grow and does not withdraw any money from the account. The formulas to use are shown below.

Month	Beginning Balance	Deposit Amount	Interest	Ending Balance
Month 1	0.00	240.00	= Beginning Balance × (0.03/12)	= Beginning Balance + Deposit Amount + Interest
Month 2	= Previous Month Ending Balance			

Example:

Month	Beginning Balance	Deposit Amount	Interest	Ending Balance
Month 1	0.00	$240.00	0.00	$240.00
Month 2	$240.00	$240.00	$0.60	$480.60
Month 3	$480.60	$240.00	$1.20	$721.80
Month 4	$721.80	$240.00	$1.80	$963.61
Continue for a total of 60 months				

Think Critically

1. What risks will Sahil be taking if he does not have full coverage insurance?
2. What would you recommend to Sahil about liability versus full coverage insurance on his vehicle? Explain your answer.

Rights and Responsibilities Presentation

Research what to do if you are ever in a car accident. Create a blog, video, or flyer that can be used to help other new drivers understand their rights and responsibilities if they are in an accident.

Preparing a Personal Insurance Plan

Refer to the questions and information below to prepare a personal insurance plan.

1. Based on your current situation, what types of insurance do you have? You may need to speak to your parent(s) or guardian(s) to answer this question.
2. Think about your future self. What types of insurance do you anticipate needing when you are 20, 25, 30, 50, and 65? Explain the type of coverage, the amounts, and why you think you will need the coverage for each category below.
   - Homeowners insurance
   - Automobile insurance
   - Health insurance
   - Disability insurance
   - Life insurance

Risk Mitigation Emergency Plan

Part of risk management is the ability to mitigate risk. This means you attempt to find ways to reduce risk by preparing for an event that may happen.

Prepare an emergency plan for severe weather based upon the types of weather events that may occur where you live. Include the following in your plan:
   - Type of weather event (e.g., tornado, hurricane, earthquake, fire, flood, blizzard).
   - What do you need to do to prepare? For example, if you lose electricity due to an ice storm, what can you do to prepare to survive? How will you prepare food? How will you keep warm?
   - What must you have available in your home for this emergency? For example, what do you need to have on hand if you are in the path of a hurricane?

Once your emergency plan is developed, work with a partner or team to develop an informational product (e.g., video, presentation, poster, flyer) to share with the local community.

Personal Financial Literacy

The Personal Financial Literacy Event measures your personal finance knowledge. Students must be able to apply reliable information and systematic decision making to personal financial decisions. The Personal Financial Literacy Event consists of a financial literacy exam and a role-play scenario with a business executive. Finalists will compete in a second role-play event. Participants will have 10 minutes to review the scenario and develop a professional approach to solving the problem. Participants will have 10 minutes to present their action plan to the judge. After the participant's explanation, the judge can ask questions about the scenario.

Go to DECA.org/compete for more detailed information.

Performance Indicators

- Recommend insurance for the types of risk that young adults might face.
- Discuss factors that affect insurance premiums.
- Predict the consequences of accepting risk with insufficient or no insurance.

Try It Out!

You are to assume the role of an insurance agent. You will meet with a new client (judge), Sahil, who wants to know about the different types of insurance that would benefit a young professional. Sahil is a 24-year-old who is working full-time. Sahil's employer provides health insurance for all full-time employees, so he does not need information about health insurance. Sahil does not have any other insurance coverage or a risk management plan in place. Your task is to explain the factors that impact the cost of insurance premiums and the possible consequences of not having each type of insurance. Below are Sahil's current life circumstances:

- Plans to purchase a vehicle soon
- Rents an apartment
- Has a young child
- Has inherited several pieces of expensive jewelry from his grandmother worth more than $50,000

You will meet with Sahil in your office. The meeting will begin with Sahil greeting you and asking about insurance choices. After you have explained the options available for risk management, Sahil may ask you questions and will conclude the meeting by thanking you for your time.

www.deca.org/compete

5 Unit

Providing Financial Security

source: SaiArLawKa2/Shutterstock.com

17 Investing for the Future

18 Investing in Securities

19 Real Estate Investing, Other Investments, and Retirement Planning

Unit 5 emphasizes the importance of developing responsible financial habits by fostering a proactive approach toward money management. The concepts covered will help you make informed financial decisions that can lead to financial independence. You will learn the importance of starting to save and invest early as part of your financial plan, including how to use compound interest to allow your money to grow over time. The importance of setting financial goals and prioritizing spending is also emphasized. This allows you to allocate money toward savings and investments to help you meet your long-term goals. By understanding your personal investments, you will also learn how the financial markets operate and the impact of economic events on investments as part of your larger role as a consumer in a market economy. A solid financial plan can help you make informed decisions and use financial tools to accumulate wealth gradually over time, potentially leading to a more secure financial future.

Unit 5: Profile

Janet Yellen

Janet Yellen was born on August 13, 1946, in Bay Ridge, Brooklyn, New York. She is the 78th U.S. secretary of the Treasury. President Joe Biden nominated Yellen to this position, and the U.S. Senate confirmed her on January 26, 2021. She had previously served as the 15th chair of the Federal Reserve (2014–2018). She is the first woman to hold these positions.

Yellen graduated from Brown University in 1967 and completed a PhD in economics from Yale University in 1971. She was an assistant professor at Harvard, teaching economics between 1971 and 1976. She became a staff economist for the Federal Reserve, commonly referred to as the Fed, after failing to receive tenure at Harvard. Since 1980, Yellen has been a faculty member at the Haas School of Business, where she is currently a professor emeritus.

Yellen has had a distinguished career in economics. Among other positions, she has served as chair of the Council of Economic Advisors under President Bill Clinton and president and chief executive officer (CEO) of the Federal Reserve Bank of San Francisco.

President Biden nominated Yellen to be his treasury secretary during his presidency. During her tenure, Yellen outlined the benefits of an international global minimum corporate tax rate. In June 2021, the finance ministers from the Group of Seven (G7) agreed to reinstate a worldwide corporate tax rate of at least 15 percent to modernize the international tax system. In July 2021, the G20 countries agreed to enforce a requirement that multinational corporations pay an appropriate tax.

Yellen is considered a "dove" on monetary policy. She is more concerned with unemployment than inflation and favors lower Federal Reserve interest rates. A "hawk" on monetary policy, in contrast, is in favor of raising Federal Reserve interest rates to combat inflation. Yellen believes that investing in economically distressed regions provides greater benefits for American workers and the nation's economy than investing in more wealthy communities.

Connect and Reflect

Yellen has stated that "much of my life has been dedicated to creating an economy that lifts workers and families up, rather than weighing them down. If I've learned one lesson from my time in economics, it's this: American workers are central to our nation's economic progress." Consider how Yellen's economic policies can be considered an investment in the nation's future.

1. In what ways is Yellen's statement that "American workers are central to our nation's economic progress" supported by the idea that prioritizing the well-being of workers and families is crucial for economic development?

2. How can investment in economically distressed areas help American workers and the nation's economy?

3. How does Yellen's approach to fiscal policy align with the idea that personal financial security allows people to contribute more fully to their own career success and to society?

17 | Chapter

Investing for the Future

What are the basic concepts and stages of investing, and what risks and strategies are involved?

Learning Objectives

By the end of this lesson, you should be able to:

LO 17.1.1 Explain the underlying value of investing.

LO 17.1.2 Discuss the stages of investing.

LO 17.1.3 Explain the concept of risk.

LO 17.1.4 Describe investment strategies.

Key Terms

- investing
- securities
- exchange platforms
- inflation
- rule of 72
- portfolio
- strategic investing
- speculative investing

- investing risk
- risk capacity
- risk tolerance
- risk adverse
- diversification
- political risk

- market risk
- company risk
- industry risk
- temporary investments
- permanent investments

Consider This ...

Rory has saved some money that he will use for college expenses in a few years. Right now, it is in a regular savings account, earning 1.5 percent per year.

"My parents say I can earn more with the money I've saved," Rory tells his friend Genevieve. "If I invest the money, I could earn 6 to 8 percent, or maybe even more. I've been checking my options. So far, I've found that investing is filled with risk, and there are many types of risk. If I'm willing to take more risk, then I may be able to earn more money. But I also stand a chance of losing some or all of my money. I've never invested before and don't want to lose the money that I have worked hard to save. I have to decide what my goals are, weigh the trade-offs, and make the best choice to meet my goals. Looking into investment options is interesting, but getting started isn't as easy as it sounds."

Read and Reflect

1. What investment options does Rory have if he wants to earn more with the money he has saved?

2. What are the pros and cons of different investment options?

3. Knowing that Rory wants to minimize risk of losing his initial investment (principal), what investment options would you recommend to Rory?

Why Should You Invest?

Investing is using long-term savings to grow money over time. It is common to invest in securities. **Securities** are a type of financial instrument with monetary value. Securities are traded on **exchange platforms**. Investing is a proven and powerful way to strengthen your financial position in the future. It is an essential part of supporting future needs. It provides a source of income, allowing you to make money on money.

Investing Is a Way to Beat Inflation

Inflation is a rise in the general level of prices. Inflation reduces your purchasing power over time. As prices rise, buying the same goods and services takes more money. Thus, investors seek investments that will grow faster than the inflation rate. For example, if the annual inflation rate is 4 percent, you will want your investments to yield a rate of return higher than 4 percent.

Thus, investing will help protect your purchasing power. As prices rise, your investments will keep your net worth rising. Investments allow your net worth to grow faster than general price levels.

How can you protect yourself from the effects of inflation?

Source: Ljupco Smokovski/Shutterstock.com

A quick way to evaluate an investment's rate of return is to use the rule of 72. The **rule of 72** is a technique for estimating the years required to double your money at a given rate of return. Divide the percentage rate of return into 72. For example, if an investment yields an average of 6 percent, it will take 12 years to double your investment (72 ÷ 6). As shown in the Sharpen Your Personal Finance Skills feature, you can also use the rule of 72 to estimate the rate of return needed to double your earnings in a given number of years.

Investing Increases Wealth

Financial success grows from the assets that you build up over time. Investing helps you accumulate wealth faster than saving excess cash in a savings account does. Because you are taking part in helping businesses make and sell new products and services when you invest in stocks and bonds, you will be rewarded with dividends and interest.

Investing Can Be Rewarding and Challenging

Investors make choices and hope to invest in things that increase in value over time. Once you gain experience, you can have fun choosing investments, buying and selling when the time is right, and using your knowledge to plan for your financial security. The challenging aspects of investing involve risk. As an investor, it is possible to predict only some situations that can cause an investment to gain or lose value. Researching potential investments is a critical part of any good investment portfolio. You can also work with a financial planner to learn more about investing. Remember that the greater the potential reward, the greater the risk involved with the investment.

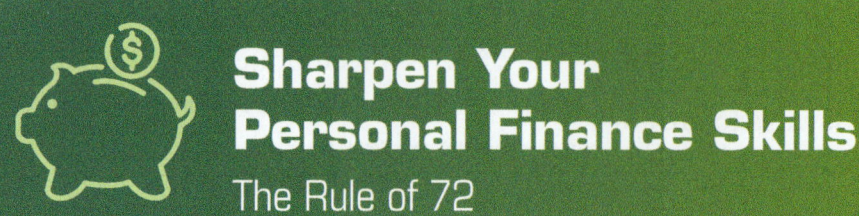

Sharpen Your Personal Finance Skills
The Rule of 72

The rule of 72 can be used to estimate either the number of years or rate of return needed to double your money.

If you want to find the number of years, divide 72 by the rate of return.

Example: You are earning 10 percent on your money. How long will it take to double your money?

Answer: 72 ÷ 10 = 7.2 years

If you want to find the rate of return, divide 72 by the number of years in which you want your money to double.

Example: You have $5,000 and want to double it in 6 years. What rate must your investment earn to achieve $10,000 in six years?

Answer: 72 ÷ 6 = 12%

At 12 percent, your money will double in 6 years.

Try It Out!

- Rory has $6,400 saved that he is looking to invest. He has found an investment option that will pay him 4.25 percent. How long will it take Rory to double his money if he chooses this investment option?
- Rory has decided that he would like to double his money in 8 years. What rate must an investment earn for Rory to achieve this?

✓ Checkpoint

What are three reasons you should consider investing, and what is the risk of each?

LO 17.1.2 Stages of Investing

Before investing, you must consider your budget, income, expenses, and savings. As your income grows and exceeds your expenses, you can progress through stages from temporary savings to various kinds of investing that include greater risk (**Figure 17.1**).

Stage 1: Emergency Fund

When you begin to earn a paycheck, you will put it into an account and take money out as needed to pay your bills. This money is your emergency fund. The purpose of this money is to pay for your short-term emergency needs, with enough left over to cover unexpected expenses. Thus, you

Figure 17.1   Stages of Investing

Stages of Investing*	Type of Investment	Strategy	Considerations
Stage 1: Emergency Fund	Short-term savings (equal to 3-6 months of net pay)	Safety	• Security • Liquidity of assets • Short-term needs
Stage 2: Initial Investing for Future Needs	Conservative, low-risk securities	Higher rates of return than traditional savings	• Liquidity of assets • Intermediate-term needs • Low initial investment
Stage 3: Systematic Investing	Retirement funding	Long-range planning focusing on growth	• Growth investments • Future financial security
Stage 4: Strategic Investing	Portfolio expansion	Maximization of return on investment in the medium term of 5-10 years	• Diversifying portfolio holdings • Planning for long-term future • Mitigating future risk
Stage 5: Speculative Investing	High-risk options	High rate of return on investments	• Increased risk of loss of initial investment due to speculative nature of investments • Short-term profit potential • Only used when funding for long-term needs is available and in secure investments

*Once a stage is fully funded, begin investing for the next stage.

should put your money in an account that offers security. Experts recommend setting aside 3 to 6 months of your net pay in an emergency fund.

Stage 2: Initial Investing

Investing begins when you have excess savings beyond what you need for daily expenses and emergencies. Your initial investing, which is your first amount set aside for investment purposes only, should be conservative with low risk. You have only a little money to invest, so you want to avoid losing it. Once you have established a safe investment cushion, you can afford to make riskier and potentially more profitable investments.

Stage 3: Systematic Investing

You can enter a systematic investing stage once you are comfortable with your initial investments. Systematic investing involves making investments on a regular and planned basis. Money is set aside regularly for investing each month. As income grows, the amount invested also grows. At this stage, your investing goals are long-term. You are investing in a financially secure future. Some jobs offer systemic investing via a 401(k), a 403(b), or some other type of investing account. It is wise to take advantage of this opportunity through your employer if offered. Some companies will match a percentage of what you place in the account. You will learn more about this in a future chapter.

Stage 4: Strategic Investing

Once you can make investments regularly, you can begin to build a **portfolio** or collection of investments. **Strategic investing** is the careful management of investment alternatives to maximize the growth of your portfolio over the next 5 to 10 years. Many people like to keep their portfolios growing and diversified. In other words, they want to make various investment choices with various risk factors. This minimizes the overall risk of the portfolio itself. When the growth prospects for one investment seem to be declining, you can move your money into another investment where the prospects for growth seem greater. To maximize your returns, you should invest in diverse securities such as stocks, bonds, index funds, and mutual funds.

Stage 5: Speculative Investing

When you are investing regularly in a broad collection of investments, but you still have money available to take bigger risks, then you can choose to move into the final stage, called speculation. **Speculative investing** happens when you make bold and high-risk investment choices. In this stage, you can make—or lose—a great deal of money in a brief period. Typically, odds are small that you will make a profit in a speculative investment; however, when it does pay off, the profit is higher. High-risk investing is not for everyone, though. Beginning investors should especially avoid speculative investments because they cannot afford the likely loss.

✓ **Checkpoint**

What are the five stages of investing?

LO 17.1.3 The Role of Risk

Investing risk is the chance that an investment's value will decrease. All types of investing involve a degree of risk. Short-term investments are generally less risky than long-term investments. It is important to determine your risk capacity. **Risk capacity** depends on your personal and financial goals and your timeline to achieve those goals.

The greater the risk you are willing to take, the greater the potential returns. Some people are willing to take more risks than

Why is it wise to invest in diverse types of securities?

© Ryan R Fox/Shutterstock.com

others. Your risk tolerance is the amount of uncertainty that is acceptable to you. Risk-takers are investors willing to take on a great deal of risk, and they may make considerably more in the long run than investors who are risk averse. A risk-adverse investor approaches investing with more caution. The best plan for most investors is to plot a moderate course, somewhere between no risk and extreme risk.

Diversification Lowers Risk

One way to minimize risk is through diversification, which spreads risk among diverse types of investments. Rather than buying only one security, you should choose different types, such as stocks, bonds, and real estate. Also, you should diversify among types of stocks. For example, you might select low-risk stocks to balance others with greater risk. Diversification reduces overall risk because only some choices will perform poorly simultaneously. If one choice does not perform well, the others will likely make up some or all the loss.

Types of Risk

Numerous types of risk can affect the performance of an investment. These include interest rates, political, market, nonmarket, company, and industry risks.

Interest-Rate Risk

Interest-rate risk is the chance that inflation will rise faster than the return on your investments. Inflation makes your fixed-rate investments worth less because they are locked in at lower rates. The value of a fixed-rate investment decreases when overall interest rates increase. Their value increases when overall interest rates decrease. For example, if you own a security paying a fixed interest rate of 5 percent and interest rates are increasing to a level greater than 5 percent, your investment will be worth less over time.

Political Risk

Political risk refers to political changes or instability in the government that may reduce the value of your investment. Political risk can include changes in economic policy, environmental policy, and laws that govern business. Increased taxes and certain regulations can make some investments less attractive.

Market Risk

Market risk is caused by the business cycle—periods of economic growth or decline. When the economy is doing well, the financial markets usually follow (and vice versa).

Nonmarket Risk

Nonmarket risk is unrelated to market trends. Nonmarket risk is entirely unpredictable and uncontrollable. For example, terrorism, global pandemics, and civil unrest are examples of threats that may affect investments in the short term. Because of the unpredictable nature of such events, people change their behavior and seek ways to protect themselves. This causes markets to suffer as people sell their investments to hold more cash for personal security.

Company and Industry Risk

Company risk is associated with owning one company's stock. Bad management decisions, other internal missteps, or even external situations can have a negative impact on a company's performance and, therefore, on the value of your investment in that company.

Industry risk affects groups of businesses. For example, if you invest in the candy industry, a nationwide trend toward dieting or the avoidance of sugar may adversely affect your investment.

> ✓ **Checkpoint**
>
> What are five types of risk you can face while investing?

LO 17.1.4 Investment Strategies

Many individuals do not start an investment program because they think they do not have enough money. Even a small amount of money, such as $50 or $100 per month, will grow over time. Others may have the benefit of receiving gifts of money, such as an inheritance from a family member. Rather than choosing to spend this extra money on something that may have only limited value, a better choice might be to invest it. Regardless of the amount of money you have, start investing as soon as you can and continue to invest over your lifetime to achieve financial security.

Criteria for Choosing an Investment

When deciding whether an investment is appropriate for you, evaluate your choice based on these factors:

- Degree of safety/risk of loss
- Degree of liquidity which is the ability to get your money quickly
- Expected dividends or interest
- Expected growth in value, preferably exceeding the inflation rate
- Reasonable purchase price and fees
- Tax benefits that result in tax savings or postponing tax liability

No investment offers all things. Each investment choice has an opportunity cost. For example, in exchange for tax benefits, you would likely have to give up a high return and liquidity. You should choose investments that offer the highest degree of safety you can get for the expected return. A diversified portfolio of investments achieves a balance among these factors. It would include some safe but low-yield investments, some riskier, higher-growth choices, and some tax-deferred investments that allow investors to pay taxes on income earned from investments later.

Wise Investment Practices

People commonly make investment mistakes. Some mistakes are minor and can be corrected easily; others cause serious financial damage. The suggestions that follow will help you avoid making investment mistakes while at the same time maximize your investing returns.

Define Your Financial Goals

Clearly defined financial goals will help you to find which investments to purchase. To be useful, investment goals must be SMART goals. That is, the goals need to be specific, measurable, achievable, relevant, and timely or time bound. Identify how you plan to use the money and how soon you need to accomplish each goal.

Go Slowly

Before making investments, gather the information you need to make a wise decision. Make temporary investments until you are certain they will meet your needs. **Temporary investments** are choices that should be reevaluated within a year or less.

Follow Through

A common mistake is keeping temporary investments too long and not reevaluating them regularly to determine how well they are performing. If they are not performing as expected, they should be sold, and other choices selected. Temporary investments that perform well often end up becoming permanent investments. **Permanent investments** are investment choices that are held for the long run—5 or 10 years, or longer. These securities will become the critical mass of your investment portfolio. They will sustain good solid returns over long periods of time and will grow substantially in principal (the initial amount invested) as well.

Keep Good Records

Good record-keeping is an essential part of investing. Keeping good financial records will help you keep a clear view of your progress toward future needs and goals and help with tax return preparation. Pay attention to how your investments are doing.

What are some suggestions that can help you make wise investment decisions?

Every year, compare your investments' current balances with their previous years' balances. Keep statements to verify your account balances and make transfers when needed. Recordkeeping can be completed using spreadsheets. Unless you know where you have been and where you are now, it is difficult to plan where you are going. It is important to keep records of how much you paid for your investments because you are responsible for any profit you earn when you sell the investment.

Seek Good Investment Advice

Do not be afraid to ask questions. Seek advice from a trained professional as you make investment decisions. One of the first places to seek advice is at your current financial institution. Most banks and credit unions have an investment department. If your employer offers a 401(k) plan, the company that manages the plan usually provides free advice to you. Once you know more about investing, online brokerage companies offer educational resources. Be wary of those offering investments that deliver higher than usual returns. Avoid get-rich-quick schemes—if they sound too good to be true, they probably are.

Keep Investment Knowledge Current

Be aware of what is new in the financial market, what kinds of investments are currently good prospects, when to sell, and when to buy. It is your responsibility to know when to ask questions and to make the final decisions about your investments. Understanding the economy and how it works will help you make better investment

Sharpen Your Personal Finance Skills

Using Spreadsheets to Track Financial Records and Investments

Spreadsheets can be utilized to improve efficiency in both your professional and personal life. No matter the spreadsheet program or app you use, spreadsheets provide an easy method for tracking financial records and investments.

Try It Out!

Rory began investing and keeping records, but he wants to transition his record-keeping to a spreadsheet. He knows that this will allow him to have quick access to previous years' information and he can safely keep all his records in one location. Rory has gathered the following information from his records:

Initial Investment	$4,600
Balance after 1 year	$4,876
Balance after 2 years	$5,168.56
Balance after 3 years	$5,478.67

Create a spreadsheet template that Rory could use to track his investments. Be sure the spreadsheet includes the starting and ending balance for each year, a way to track earnings/losses of investments, and any other information that you feel is important for Rory to keep record of.

Remember, using formulas in spreadsheets improves efficiency and reduces the chance of human error in calculations. Use formulas, when possible, to have the spreadsheet software complete calculations for you.

choices. For example, you should expect that stock prices are rising, and people are investing during periods of economic growth. But when economic decline begins, stock prices often fall as people take their money out of the markets. A common piece of investment advice is to "Buy low and sell high." This means that with research, you can invest in securities when the prices are lower and sell the securities for a profit, when the prices are high.

Know Your Limits

Understand your risk tolerance and the amount of money you can afford to risk, so

Connections to Your World
Understanding Your Risk Tolerance

Identifying your risk tolerance may sound simple, but it is more complicated than many people think. It is important for all investors to identify their risk tolerance so that they can make appropriate investment decisions.

Review information on the risk tolerance spectrum and how to determine your risk tolerance at https://www.forbes.com/advisor/investing/what-is-your-risk-tolerance/ or a similar website.

Think Critically

1. Based on the information you find, where on the risk tolerance spectrum would you fall? Conservative, moderately conservative, moderate, moderately aggressive, or aggressive?

2. Based on where you fall on the spectrum, what types of investments would be appropriate for you?

3. Why might young adults have a higher risk tolerance than those who are nearing retirement?

you can maximize returns within your risk comfort zone. If you are uncomfortable taking large risks, then avoid them. The chance of making huge profits is not worth being stressed by the risk.

✓ Checkpoint

Identify basic investment strategies.

Check Your Understanding

1. How does investing help you beat inflation? (LO 17.1.1)

2. Why do you need to establish an emergency fund before investing? (LO 17.1.2)

3. What is diversification and what is its purpose? (LO 17.1.3)

4. What are the criteria for choosing investing opportunities? (LO 17.1.4)

Apply Your Understanding

1. You have $500 saved from your job and are considering investing in stocks, but a friend told you stocks are a risky investment, and you should put your money into your savings account instead. Before deciding, research the benefits and risks associated with investing in securities as a long-term financial strategy compared to only placing money in a traditional savings account. Based on your findings, what should you do with your $500? Explain. (LO 17.1.1)

2. Describe the five stages of investing. Which stage do you think is most important and why? (LO 17.1.2)

3. What is your personal risk tolerance? Why is it important to understand your risk tolerance level? (LO 17.1.3)

4. You have six months of savings in your emergency fund and have opened a Roth IRA to which you have contributed the maximum this year. You would like to begin to do more to save for retirement. What investment strategies should you be considering and why? (LO 17.1.4)

The Essential Question

What are the basic concepts and stages of investing, and what risks and strategies are involved?

A: Stages of investing include an emergency fund, initial investing, systematic investing, strategic investing, and speculative investing. You should evaluate investment options for safety, liquidity, dividends or interest, growth, cost, and tax benefits. Your goal when investing is to find ways to reduce risk while maximizing your return.

The Essential Question | Where can investors find financial information, and how do investment choices vary by risk?

Learning Objectives

By the end of this lesson, you should be able to:

LO 17.2.1 Describe sources of investing information.

LO 17.2.2 Describe investing choices and rate them by risk.

Key Terms

- brokerage firm
- discount brokers
- full-service brokers
- robo-advisor
- fiduciary financial advisor
- annual report
- bond
- stock
- mutual fund
- annuity
- real estate
- futures
- commodity
- option
- penny stocks
- collectible

LO 17.2.1 Sources of Financial Information

To make sound investment choices, you must have good information. Investment information can be found both online and in print as well as through other sources to help you evaluate investment options.

Online Sources

The most common way for potential investors to be informed is via the internet. Financial websites provide data and analysis for investors and often provide up-to-date information via RSS feeds, X (formerly known as Twitter), Facebook, and other communication channels. The wise investor will read multiple sites before making an informed decision about investments. According to Investopedia, Google Finance, Yahoo! Finance, and Bloomsburg.com are the three most common sources for investment information.

The *Wall Street Journal* is a daily newspaper, available in both print and online formats, which provides detailed coverage of the business and financial world. *Barron's* is a publication that also provides charts of trends, financial news, and technical analysis

What information is found in the financial pages of a newspaper?

Source: iStock.com/Sarinyapinngam

of financial data. Other news sources include *The Financial Times, MoneyWeek,* and *The Economist.* All three are based in London and provide global financial information. The *MIT Sloan Management Review* and *MorningStar.com* are U.S.-based publications from research institutions.

Brokerage Firms

A **brokerage firm** acts as the intermediary to connect buyers and sellers of securities. They make money through commissions and fees for completing transactions between buyers and sellers. There are two broad categories of brokers: discount and full-service. **Discount brokers** buy and sell securities for clients for a reduced commission or zero commission fees. They make money through fee payments from the security exchanges and trading fees on mutual funds and bonds, which are covered in a later chapter. Discount brokers provide little or no direct investment advice to their clients. Their websites offer online investment education and financial information for investors to use when making decisions. Examples of discount brokers include Charles Schwab and E*TRADE. Robinhood and Acorn are newer companies that also offer online investment services through mobile apps. Many young investors use mobile apps for investing and investment education resources.

Full-service brokers provide analysis and opinions based on their judgments and experts' opinions at the company they represent. In addition to buying and selling securities for their clients, full-service brokers research various investments and keep clients up to date on market trends and stock performance while providing investment ideas and recommendations. Well-known full-service brokerage companies include Edward Jones, JP Morgan Wealth Management, Morgan Stanley, Charles Schwab, Fidelity, and others.

Because of the increasing popularity of inexpensive trading, many full-service brokers also offer discount trading on their websites. Some banks, credit unions, and other financial institutions also assist their customers with buying and selling securities. Money can be transferred from your checking or savings account to pay for securities purchased and sold. You will receive statements showing the current value of your securities.

With most types of brokerage accounts, you can manage them online. You can give buy and sell orders; transfer money among investment accounts; and track the progress of your investments, either with your software or with a platform supplied by the broker or bank.

Another type of brokerage company is a robo-advisor. A **robo-advisor** is a digital platform that follows an automated long-term passive index strategy based upon algorithms. There is limited human interaction. The investor answers questions about their financial situation and future goals. The robo-advisor will then automatically invest their money for them. Betterment and Wealthfront are two robo-advisors.

Financial Advisers and Independent Brokers

Professional financial advisers are trained to give investment advice and manage your investments. Certified financial planners (CFPs) have completed education requirements and have passed CFP Board certification exams. CFPs must have at least 3 years of experience in the financial planning process.

Advice given is based on your goals, age, lifestyle, and other factors. The adviser will ask you to supply confidential information about your assets, liabilities, net worth, income, budget, and financial goals. The adviser usually receives a fee for consulting services, although some also receive a commission when they sell you investment products (such as stocks, bonds, or life insurance policies). Generally, you will get better overall advice when the adviser does not stand to make a profit on the investments you choose to buy.

Financial planners may also be independent brokers. The most common is a registered investment advisor (RIA). An RIA is not affiliated with a company and may be able to offer more options and products to their clients.

When selecting a financial advisor, it is important to do your research and select someone who is certified and trustworthy. A **fiduciary financial advisor** is legally required to only make recommendations to the client if it is in the client's best interest. Not all financial advisors are fiduciaries. A fiduciary financial advisor typically works for an RIA, and most chartered financial analysts (CFAs) act as a fiduciary. Nonfiduciary financial advisors are required to offer recommendations that are suitable for you, but they may offer you products that have higher fees.

Annual Reports

An **annual report** is a summary of a corporation's financial results for the year and its prospects for the future. The Securities and

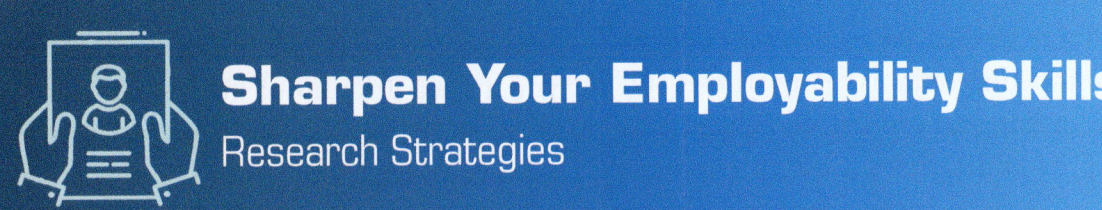

Sharpen Your Employability Skills
Research Strategies

When selecting a financial advisor, it is important to do your research and select someone who is certified and trustworthy. This helps ensure that you are not taken advantage of. As Rory looks to begin investing, he wants to find a financial advisor. He has no idea how to select a trustworthy advisor who can help him. Use the internet to research factors that should be considered when selecting a financial advisor. Based on your research, compile a list of factors for Rory to consider and tips that can help him in the process of selecting a financial advisor. In small groups, discuss the list of factors and tips you created.

Think Critically

1. Why is it important to be sure that you do your research prior to selecting a financial advisor?
2. What factors do you think are the most important to consider when selecting a financial advisor? Explain.

Exchange Commission (SEC) requires all public corporations to prepare this report each year and send it to their stockholders. Investors can use the information to evaluate the corporation as an investment prospect.

Annual reports are found online at the SEC's website (www.sec.gov). Corporations often publish their financial performance data in their websites' "Investors" section. Also, libraries have access to annual reports of major corporations.

Online Investor Education

In addition to the financial websites for publications and brokers, the internet offers several free educational sites for new investors. For example, Teenvestor is a website dedicated to helping teens learn how to invest and manage their money. The Motley Fool website offers investing advice, commentary, analysis, and articles. BetterInvesting is a nonprofit site dedicated to investor education. Investopedia contains many articles and tutorials covering all aspects of finance and investing, in addition to a comprehensive financial dictionary. Investopedia also offers free weekly newsletters and interactive tools, such as its stock market simulator, which allows individuals to set up a brokerage account with play money and trade publicly traded stocks on stock exchanges. These are just a few educational sites available to investors online. An online search using a search engine will produce more.

✓ Checkpoint

Where can you find information related to investing?

Investment Choices

Once you are ready to make investments, it is time to consider your investment choices. Investments can be categorized by their degree of risk and expected return. The remaining chapters in this unit will allow you to explore each investment type more thoroughly.

Low Risk/Low Return

For your first investments, you will likely want to consider safe investments, even though their returns will be relatively low. You should continue to include low-risk investments as part of your diversified portfolio even as you become a more sophisticated investor.

Corporate and Municipal Bonds

A bond is a debt obligation of a corporation or a state or local government. When a corporation or government body sells a bond, it borrows from an investor. When you invest in a corporate bond, the corporation pays you a fixed amount of interest, usually every six months. The corporation also must repay the principal at maturity. The maturity date of a bond is the date on which the borrowed money must be repaid.

When you loan money to a state or local government unit, such as a city, county, community college district, or utility district, you are also paid interest on your investment. Your principal is repaid when the bond matures. Typically, interest earned on municipal bonds is tax-free, giving the investor a tax advantage. Bonds are explained in detail in a future chapter.

U.S. Government Savings Bonds

When you buy a savings bond, you are lending money to the U.S. government. Savings bonds help pay for the U.S. government's borrowing needs. They are considered one of the safest investments because the full faith and credit of the U.S. government backs them. You can buy savings bonds online at the U.S. Department of Treasury's Treasury-Direct website (www.treasurydirect.gov); paper certificates are no longer issued.

U.S. savings bonds are available in Series EE and Series I. Both Series EE and Series I savings bonds are sold at face value. For example, you would pay $50 for a $50 bond. They must be held for a minimum of one year and can be held for a maximum of 30 years. Bonds redeemed within 5 years must pay a 3-month interest penalty. The two forms of bonds differ in how they earn their interest. Series EE savings bonds earn a fixed rate of interest. Series I savings bonds earn a fixed interest rate in combination with a semiannual adjustment for inflation. The interest that both Series EE and Series I savings bonds earn is subject to federal income tax but not state or local income tax. However, if the bond is used to finance a college education, you may not have to pay federal income tax on your interest.

U.S. Government Treasury Securities

Like savings bonds, U.S. Treasury securities are considered safe investments because the U.S. government backs them. They are subject to federal taxes but are exempt from state and local taxes. You can buy U.S. Treasury securities at the TreasuryDirect website or through a bank or broker. There are three types.

- Treasury bills. These bills, called T-bills, are available for a minimum purchase of $100. They are issued for terms of 4, 13, 26, and 52 weeks. T-bills are typically sold at a discount rather than face value. For example, you might pay $990 for a $1,000 bill. When the bill matures, you will be paid $1,000. The difference between the purchase price and face value constitutes the earnings on the bill.
- Treasury notes. These notes, called T-notes, are available for a minimum purchase of $100. They are issued for terms of 2, 3, 5, 7, and 10 years. They earn a fixed rate of interest every 6 months until maturity.
- Treasury bonds. These bonds, called T-bonds, are issued for a minimum of $100 with a 30-year maturity. They pay interest every 6 months until they mature. Interest rates are generally higher than rates for either T-bills or T-notes because of the longer maturity.

Medium Risk/Medium Return

When you feel secure enough to take more risk, and you have additional money to invest, you are ready to step up to the medium-risk range to increase your return. Some medium-risk options involve investing with companies that manage the investment.

Stocks

Stock is a unit of ownership in a corporation. The owner of stock is called a stockholder. When you are a stockholder, you may share in a corporation's profits, which are paid to you as dividends. Some companies do not pay dividends because they are investing their earnings back in the company to help it grow. This should result in greater value for your investment in the future. If the company does well, you also earn returns in the increased value of your stock, called capital gains.

Stocks generally carry more risk than investment choices with a fixed interest rate because a stockholder's earnings can go up or down, depending on the company's profits. Stocks in well-established companies are reasonably safe, whereas stocks in less stable companies can be risky. However, a diversified portfolio of stocks of various risk levels can achieve a medium overall risk. You will learn more about investing in stocks in a future chapter.

Mutual Funds

Suppose you have $500, which is insufficient to buy a diversified portfolio of stocks. Instead, you can purchase shares in a large, professionally managed group of investments called a mutual fund. A **mutual fund** pools money from many investors to buy a large selection of securities. Security funds are grouped to meet the fund's stated investment goals. Two significant advantages of a mutual fund for investors are professional management and diversification. Because the fund invests in various securities, it provides diversification that small investors could not otherwise achieve with their limited resources.

Although some mutual funds fall in the speculative category and others fall in the low-risk category, such as those specializing in money market securities, most mutual funds fall somewhere in the broad medium range regarding risk and return. You can diversify your portfolio by investing in mutual funds with different objectives. For example, some funds buy securities in riskier small companies, hoping to earn a higher return. Others stick to well-established, safe companies for a lower but stable return. By investing money in both funds, you are diversifying your investments. If your riskier fund does not do well, your stable fund will limit your losses. Mutual funds are the fastest-growing segment of the American financial services industry. You will learn more about mutual funds in a future chapter.

Annuities

An **annuity** is a contract in which you make a lump-sum payment or series of payments that earn interest in return for regular disbursements, often after retirement. You usually buy an annuity directly from a life insurance company. Generally, you will receive income monthly, with disbursements continuing as long as you live or for a specified number of years. The interest on the principal and the interest compounded on that interest builds up free of current income tax. Taxes are deferred until you receive disbursements from your annuity. This type of annuity is called a tax-deferred annuity.

The payments from an annuity are commonly used to supplement retirement income. An annuity is often described as the opposite of life insurance. It pays while you are alive; life insurance pays when you die.

Real Estate

Many people like to invest in **real estate**— buildings and land. If you own a house, it will be one of your most significant investments. While this type of investment usually represents a significant and often nonliquid investment of cash, it generally has proven to be protected against inflation in most parts of the United States. In some areas, the market value of homes have increased faster than the inflation rate. However, during recessionary periods in the economy, real estate may lose value. But in the long run, real estate generally is a good investment.

Real estate investments also have tax benefits. Certain costs associated with homeownership may be deductible from gross income, thus lowering taxable income. While investing in a home carries little risk, investing in other types of real estate can be very risky. Investing in real estate is covered in greater depth in a future chapter.

High Risk/High Return

High-risk/high-return choices involve considerable uncertainty. Returns can be high, but they can also be low or even negative, resulting in a loss of principal (the amount of the original investment). If you are willing to take the risks of these choices, you stand to make high returns over time. But you also risk high losses if your investments could be better performers.

Futures

A **futures** contract obligates the buyer to purchase, or the seller to sell, stock or a commodity for a specified price at a date in the future. A **commodity** is a raw material or agricultural product. Examples include minerals such as gold, silver, or copper along with crops such as coffee, corn, or livestock. The investor is betting that the cost of the stock or commodity will be higher on that date than at the time of the contract. Thus, trading in futures is a very risky speculation. If prices rise, the investor can make a lot of money; if prices fall, the investor loses. This type of investment is not for beginners or individuals who cannot afford to lose their investment.

Options

An **option** is the right, but not the obligation, to buy or sell stock or a commodity for a specified price within a specified period. As with futures, the investor is betting that the cost of the stock or commodity will rise during the option period. If it does, the investor can buy it at the lower option price, resulting in an instant profit. Typically,

options are short-term investment devices speculators use to make a quick profit. They are risky for inexperienced investors.

Penny Stocks

Penny stocks are low-priced stocks of small companies that have a limited history of success. Stock usually sells below $5 per share. Small companies often need higher revenues and more assets to assure future growth. Dot-com and internet companies typically begin this way. Many of them fail, making the stock worthless. Occasionally, a penny stock booms, and the investor earns a significant amount of profit. Generally, penny stocks are considered high risk.

Collectibles

A **collectible** is any physical asset that appreciates over time because it is rare or desired by many. Collectibles can be things such as coins, art, stamps, ceramics, or other items that are popular from time to time, such as comic books, dolls and toys, and trading cards such as Pokemon or baseball cards. If you collect an item that goes up in value rapidly, you can reap significant

What are the pros and cons of investing in collectibles?

Sharpen Your Employability Skills
Communicating Investment Options

This past month, Rory worked several hours of overtime and managed to save additional money. He is excited about his extra savings and wants to begin investing some of his savings. Rory is new to investing and does not know what investment options he has. Create a slide deck or other multimedia presentation to outline investment options for Rory. Be sure to include a brief description, potential pros and cons, and the risk level for each. Finally, conclude with your recommendations for how Rory should invest his money. Be sure to include reasoning for your recommendations.

rewards. However, if you do not sell when your item is at the peak of popularity, it will likely lose its value just as quickly, making it a risky investment. Collectors must be aware of the market and realize that their collections are subject to changing public tastes and can be difficult to resell.

✓ Checkpoint

Give three examples each for low-risk, medium-risk, and high-risk investment choices.

17.2 Lesson Review

Check Your Understanding

1. List four sources for investment information. (LO 17.2.1)
2. Why is investing in stocks riskier than investing in bonds? (LO 17.2.2)

Apply Your Understanding

1. Research three sources of financial information mentioned in the chapter. What source did you find the most helpful, and how would you use information from this source as you consider investments of your own? (LO 17.2.1)
2. Create a chart that compares different investment choices. Include a column for risks and a column for benefits. Given this information, what investment choices would you consider either currently or in the future and why? (LO 17.2.2)

The Essential Question

Where can investors find financial information, and how do investment choices vary by risk?

A: Sources of information include online sources, investor services and news-letters, financial magazines, brokers, financial advisers, annual reports, and websites. Investment choices can either be low risk, such as bonds; medium risk, such as stocks and mutual funds; or high risk, such as futures and options.

Summary

17.1 Basic Concepts of Investing

- Investing is using long-term savings to grow money over time and is a way to strengthen your financial position and support future needs.

- Securities are a common type of investment. They are traded on exchange platforms.

- Investing helps you beat inflation when your investments give you a return that is higher than the inflation rate.

- The rule of 72 is a technique for estimating the years required to double your money at a given rate of return.

- As your income grows beyond current needs, you can progress through five investment stages involving greater amounts of risk.

- Before investing, consider your budget, income, expenses, and savings.

- The five stages of investing are creating your emergency fund, initial investing, systematic investing, strategic investing, and speculative investing.

- It is important to know your personal risk capacity and risk tolerance.

- All investments involve risk that your investment will lose value and potential reward when your investment increases in value.

- Diversification, or selecting different types of investments, helps minimize overall risk.

- Types of investment risk include interest-rate risk, political risk, market risk, nonmarket risk, and company and industry risk.

- Evaluate investment options for their degree of safety, degree of liquidity, expected dividends or interest, expected growth in value, cost, and tax benefits. All investment choices involve trade-offs among these criteria.

- To make wise investments, define your financial goals, go slowly, follow through, keep good records, seek good investment advice, keep your investment knowledge current, and know your limits.

17.2 Making Investment Choices

- You can get investment information from online sources, brokerage firms, financial advisors and independent brokers, and annual reports.

- Full-service brokers give you advice in buying and selling securities; discount brokers do not give advice, but their cost is lower.

- Robo-advisors are automated investment programs with lower costs than discount and full-service brokers, but they have little human interaction.

- Fiduciary financial advisors are legally required to make recommendations in their clients' best interests.

- Generally, the more risk you are willing to take, the more you stand to gain or lose from an investment.

- Investment choices can be low risk, medium risk, or high risk—depending on the investor's ability and willingness to take risks.

- Low-risk/low-return investment options include corporate and municipal bonds, U.S. government savings bonds, and U.S. government Treasury securities.

- Medium-risk/medium-return investments include stocks, mutual funds, annuities, and real estate.

- High-risk/high return investments include futures, options, penny stocks, and collectibles.

Check Your Knowledge

1. How do inflation and investment affect purchasing power? (LO 17.1.1)

2. Why is an investment strategy an important part of a financial plan? (LO 17.1.1)

3. Describe the five stages of investing. Include the type of investment, the investment strategy, and things to consider at each stage. (LO 17.1.2)

4. What is the difference between political, market, nonmarket, company, and industry risk? Provide an example of how each affects investment. (LO 17.1.3)

5. Identify criteria you can use when choosing an investment. (LO 17.1.4)

6. Select four sources of investing information. Describe each and explain why using multiple sources of information is an important part of being a wise investor. (LO 17.2.1)

7. Describe the investing choices presented in the chapter. Identify the level of risk associated with each and where they would fit into the stages of investing. (LO 17.1.2 and 17.2.2)

Apply Your Knowledge

1. You would like to buy a house in about 10 years. You have already saved $5,000 for a down payment and would like to move your savings into an investment account. Calculate how long it will take to double your initial investment at the following annual rates.

   1. 4 percent

   2. 6 percent

   3. 8 percent

   4. 12 percent (LO 17.1.1)

2. You have been working at your current job for a year. You have an emergency fund to cover you for 3 months and are ready to move on to the next stage of investing. What factors should you consider before you make your first investment? (LO 17.1.2)

3. You have determined that you have an aggressive risk tolerance, but you do not have an emergency fund and have not set any financial goals. Create a three-step plan that will help you begin your investment journey. (LO 17.1.3)

4. Write a short-term, intermediate-term, and long-term goal related to investing for your future. Make sure goals are SMART goals—specific, measurable, achievable, relevant, and timely or time bound. (LO 17.1.4)

5. You would like to invest in XYZ Corporation but do not know much about it. What kinds of information should you collect before you invest in this company? Where can you find this information? (LO 17.2.1)

6. List three different investment choices and rate them by their risk level. Provide an explanation for each rating. (LO 17.2.2)

Share Your Knowledge

Work in teams of two to four students to complete the following activities.

1. Find an historical chart for one of the major stock market indexes (Dow Jones, S&P 500, or NASDAQ). As a group, research the interest-rate, political, and/or market risk for the three most recent declines in the index. Create a timeline with graphics and explanations about what was happening in the world when the declines occurred. (LO 17.1.3)

2. Using the media of your choice, develop a resource that helps explain investment strategies to others. Be sure to include a text explanation and supporting visuals. Product examples include slide decks, blog posts, and infographics. (LO 17.1.4)

3. Your team has been asked to provide information about investing apps that teens like to use. Create a video to explain the rules for teens under 18 to open an account, what parental controls are available, and the pros and cons of three investment apps. (LO 17.2.1)

Connect and Reflect

Base your answers to the following questions on your own personal thoughts, preferences, and experiences.

1. Find a risk tolerance quiz online. Take the quiz. What did you learn about yourself and your risk tolerance? Based on what you learned, how would you approach each stage of investing? Explain. (LO 17.1.2 and 17.1.3)

2. Refer to the goals you wrote for Question 4 under Apply Your Knowledge. Why did you select these goals? How do they fit into the stages of investing, and what do you need to consider to meet these goals? (LO 17.1.4)

3. Refer to the investing apps for teens that the groups investigated. Select one app to learn more about. Read the information at the apps' website. What type of investment education do they provide? How do they secure your information? Do they offer human customer service? If so, how? Would you want to use this app for your early investment strategies? Explain your answer. (LO 17.2.1)

Chapter Project

Create a personal investment plan using the five stages of investing. Consider your personal risk tolerance and the goals you wrote earlier. Identify where you would find the information to help you be successful at each stage of investing and the risks associated with the choices you added to your plan.

Chapter 18

Investing in Securities

How are securities bought and sold, and what strategies are available for buying and selling them?

Learning Objectives

By the end of this lesson, you should be able to:

LO 18.1.1 Describe the channels involved in buying and selling securities.

LO 18.1.2 Describe short-term and long-term strategies for buying and selling securities.

Key Terms

- securities
- securities exchange
- auction market
- leverage
- short selling
- dividends
- stock split
- dollar-cost averaging
- dividend reinvestment

Consider This ...

Zander worked during the summer and managed to save $500 to invest. He decided he wanted to make an investment and try to double his money in the next year or two.

"I've been doing research on different types of investments," Zander told his friend Mia. "There's so many options. We can invest in stocks, bonds, mutual funds, and more! I came across a medical research company, and it may be on the verge of something big. I've done a lot of reading about this company, and I think the stock price is low now because the company isn't paying dividends. Instead, it's using company profits to develop new products. All of the information I've gathered suggests that the company is solid, steadily growing, and will be a leader in its industry. I think this company's stock is worth the risk, so I think I am going to buy as many shares as my money will purchase."

"That seems risky," Mila replied, "but it sounds like you've done your research. It may be a good option for you, but I am much more conservative with my money. I want to be certain my money is safe and will be available when I need it to start my business."

(continues)

(continued)

Read and Reflect

1. How does the investment goals of Zander and Mila shape their investment decisions?

2. Zander has a higher risk tolerance than Mila. What investment options should Zander consider as he looks to double his money in the next year or two?

3. What low-risk investment options does Mila have that will ensure her money is available when she needs it? Of these options, which has the potential to yield the greatest return on her money?

4. What are the pros and cons of different investment options?

LO 18.1.1 The Securities Market

The securities market consists of the channels where securities can be bought and sold. **Securities** is the term for stocks, bonds, and other financial investments. Trading agents buy and sell securities in a securities marketplace, an exchange, or an over-the-counter market. Most people use trading agents to buy and sell securities. To purchase common or preferred stock, you need a trading agent. Some people use a financial planning expert for a brokerage firm such as Edwards Jones, Charles Swab, or another service agency. Individuals can also open an online account through many sources and manage their purchases through a mobile app. Individuals cannot directly access the stock market. They are required to use a securities exchange.

Securities Exchange

A **securities exchange** is a marketplace where brokers representing investors meet to buy and sell securities. The largest organized exchange in the United States is the New York Stock Exchange (NYSE). To have a stock listed on the NYSE, a company must meet a minimum number of public shares and dollar market-value requirements. Securities listed with the NYSE are traded only during official trading hours—9:30 a.m. to 4 p.m. (EST), Monday through Friday (except holidays).

In the NYSE building, the trading floor where stocks are bought and sold is about two-thirds the size of a football field. Around the edge of the trading floor are booths with computer terminals and room inside for a dozen or more floor brokers. Floor brokers buy and sell stocks on the exchange. Brokers must be members of the exchange to do business there.

Horseshoe-shaped counters, called trading posts, are spaced regularly around the trading floor, each occupying about 100 square feet. Behind each counter are specialists—from the brokers to the floor brokers. All buying and selling are done around trading posts. About 90 different stocks are assigned to each post. Post display units above each counter show which stocks are sold in each section, the last price of that stock, and whether that price represents an increase or a decrease from the previous price.

Orders received at a brokerage firm or discount brokerage are phoned or sent by computer to that firm's booth at the exchange. When the transaction is completed, the brokers who bought and sold the stock report back to their respective brokerage firms. Then, the buyer and seller are advised that the transaction has been concluded.

The NYSE is a form of **auction market** where buyers enter competitive bids, and sellers enter competitive offers simultaneously. Stock is sold to the highest bidder and bought from the lowest offeror.

NASDAQ is another popular U.S. securities exchange. It is a dealer market, not an auction market, because dealers work directly with other dealers to buy and sell NASDAQ securities without using brokers. NASDAQ is a completely computerized network and does not have a physical location.

Over-the-Counter Market

When securities are bought and sold through brokers but not through a stock exchange, the transaction is over the counter (OTC). The OTC market is a network of brokers who buy and sell securities of corporations that are not listed on a securities exchange. A stock might be traded in the OTC market because the company is small and unable to meet exchange listing requirements. However, some large, well-known companies also are traded over the counter. Brokers in the OTC market do not deal face-to-face with other brokers. Instead, trades with other brokers are completed by telephone or computer networks. Brokers operating in the OTC market use the OTC Bulletin Board (OTCBB) or the OTC Link LLC. Both electronic quotation systems display quotes, last-sale prices, and volume information for stock that is not listed on a securities exchange. The difference between companies listed on the OTCBB and the OTC Link is that the Securities and Exchange Commission regulates companies listed on the OTCBB but not on the OTC Link.

✓ Checkpoint

What channels can investors use to purchase securities?

LO 18.1.2 Investing Strategies

You can approach investing with either a short-term or a long-term strategy. Only experienced investors with a high risk tolerance should use short-term investment strategies. Generally, you are a speculator or day trader if you buy and sell stock quickly. If you hold your investment for a long time (a year or more), you are an investor.

Short-Term Techniques

You play the stock market when you buy and sell stocks for quick profits. The goal is to buy a stock that will soon increase in value. Then, when the price rises, you sell the stock. Many investors make short-term gains through buying on margin and selling short.

Buy on Margin

Buying on margin involves borrowing money from your broker to buy stock. This strategy is called **leverage**—using borrowed money to buy securities. You use less of your own money; therefore, can buy more stocks with less cash. With a margin purchase, you are betting that the stock will increase in value. If it does, you sell the stock, repay the loan with interest and commission, and take your short-term profit. Unfortunately, if the value of the stock does not increase, you will have to pay the difference. A great deal of money can be made using leverage. At the same time, large sums of money can be lost quickly, creating the need for immediate cash.

Sell Short

Short selling involves selling stock borrowed from a broker that must be replaced later. To sell short, you borrow a certain number of shares from the broker. You then sell the borrowed stock, knowing you must repurchase it later and return it to the broker. You are betting that the price will drop so that you can repurchase it at a lower price than you sold it, thus making a profit. However, if the stock price increases, you will lose money because you must replace the borrowed stock with stock purchased at a higher price.

Long-Term Techniques

Investing in the stock market for short-term gains can be extremely risky. Most financial consultants advise investing in the long term. Research has shown that over a long time, stock investments have consistently beaten rates for savings accounts, CDs, and other conservative options. Long-term investment strategies include buy and hold, dollar-cost averaging, and reinvesting **dividends** (money paid to stockholders from the corporation's earnings or profits).

Buy and Hold

Most investors consider stock purchases as long-term investments. All stocks go up and down, but the overall trend of nonspeculative stocks is for them to rise. Remember, a profit or loss occurs only when you sell the stock. When you sell years later, your stock will have likely gained value. In addition, many stocks pay dividends, so you earn income while holding the stock.

A stock split can also add to the value of the stock over time. A **stock split** is an increase in the number of outstanding shares of a company's stock. When a company increases its number of outstanding shares,

it lowers the selling price in direct proportion. For example, if there were 1,000 shares outstanding with a market value of $60, then a 2:1 (two-for-one) stock split would result in 2,000 shares outstanding selling for $30. Notice that the stock is still worth a total of $60,000. A stock split lowers the stock's selling price, making the shares more affordable and encouraging investors to buy more. The share price often rises as investors buy more stock at a lower price. If you held the stock before the split, this price increase makes your stock worth more.

Dollar-Cost Averaging

The **dollar-cost averaging** technique involves systematically purchasing an equal dollar amount of the same security at regular intervals, regardless of the share price. The result is usually a lower average cost per share.

Investors use this technique so they do not have to worry about timing their investment purchases. A regular purchase over a year usually averages a reasonable price per share. The investor profits when the selling price per share is higher than the average cost per share.

Reinvesting Dividends

You can also save money by reinvesting the dividends you earn. **Dividend reinvestment** is using dividends previously made on the stock to buy more shares. Buying stock this way avoids a broker fee and other costs that apply, such as taxes, when you receive cash dividends on the stock.

> ✓ **Checkpoint**
>
> What are some short-term and long-term investment strategies?

18.1 Lesson Review

Check Your Understanding

1. What kinds of stocks are traded over the counter? (LO 18.1.1)

2. How is an investor different from a speculator? (LO 18.1.2)

Apply Your Understanding

1. You have heard that you can make a lot of money quickly through day trading. After researching the rewards and risks of short-term investment strategies, do you think you should pursue day trading? Explain. (LO 18.1.2)

2. Why would dollar-cost averaging be a good investment strategy for a new investor? (LO 18.1.2)

The Essential Question

How are securities bought and sold, and what strategies are available for buying and selling them?

A: Securities are bought and sold through securities exchanges or in over-the-counter markets. When to buy or sell depends on your interpretation of how the stock is doing compared to other investment choices you have and if you are following a short-term or long-term investment strategy. Your risk tolerance will help determine your investment strategy.

The Essential Question

What are the reasons for owning stocks, what types of stocks are available, and how do you determine a stock's value and read stock listings and indexes?

Learning Objectives

By the end of this lesson, you should be able to:

LO 18.2.1 Explain the reasons for owning stocks and the types and categories of stocks.

LO 18.2.2 Explain how to determine a stock's value.

LO 18.2.3 Explain how to read stock listings and indexes.

Key Terms

- public corporation
- capital gains
- capital loss
- common stock
- proxy
- preferred stock
- income stocks
- growth stocks
- blue chip stocks
- emerging stocks
- cyclical stocks
- defensive stocks
- par value
- market value
- P/E ratio
- earnings per share (EPS)
- bull market
- bear market
- return on investment (ROI)
- stock symbol

LO 18.2.1 Owning Stocks

Investing in stocks is often viewed as one of the best ways to build up wealth and reach long-term financial goals. Today, around 60 percent of Americans own stocks. When you buy a share of stock, you are purchasing an ownership interest in a company. A **public corporation** is a company whose stock is traded openly on stock markets.

People who own shares of stock are called stockholders, or shareholders, of the corporation. If the corporation does well, stockholders will profit in two ways. One way stockholders make money is through dividends. Dividends are money paid to stockholders from the corporation's earnings or profits. For example, if you owned 100 shares and a company declared a $1 dividend per share, you would receive $100.

The other way that stockholders profit is through capital gains. **Capital gains** are an increase in the value of a stock over time. For example, if you bought stock for $5 per share and the corporation thrived, its stock price might increase to $10. If it did, you could sell it for a substantial profit. However, part of the risk in owning stock is that the price could also go below the price initially paid, resulting in a **capital loss**. Also, a capital gain becomes profit, and a capital loss is a loss only when you sell the stock. Until then, it is called an unrealized gain or loss.

Why is owning stock risky?

Stockholders can also lose all their investment if the company fails or goes out of business. However, one advantage to owning stock is that stockholders can lose no more than their investment. On the other hand, the owner of a small business can also lose personal assets if the business fails.

Common Stock

Common stock represents a type of stock that pays a variable dividend and gives the holder voting rights. The common stockholders elect the board of directors, which guides the corporation and decides the amount of dividends, if any, to pay each year. Common stockholders vote on major policy decisions, such as issuing additional stock, selling the company, or changing the board of directors. Each share of common stock has the same voting power; therefore, the more shares a stockholder owns, the greater their power to influence corporate policy.

Common stockholders may vote in person at the stockholders' meeting or by proxy. A **proxy** is a stockholder's written authorization to transfer their voting rights to someone else, usually a company manager. Most common stockholders vote by proxy.

Preferred Stock

Preferred stock represents a type of stock that pays a fixed dividend, but stockholders have no voting rights. Preferred stockholders earn the stated dividend, regardless of company performance. Thus, preferred stock is less risky than common stock. If the company fails, preferred stockholders are paid before common stockholders. However, as with most investments, the trade-off for lower risk is lower return. Dividends on preferred stock may be lower than the dividends common stockholders would earn if the company were thriving.

Categories of Stocks

Investors often classify stocks, both common and preferred, into different categories. Categories of stocks include income, growth, blue chip, emerging, cyclical, and defensive. Some stocks may fall into more than one category. Which category is best for you will depend on how much risk you are willing to assume for a chance to earn large returns. Most investors buy stocks in several of these categories to diversify their risk.

Income Stocks

Corporations can use their profits in two ways. They can reinvest the profits in the business to help it grow, or they can distribute the profits to stockholders as dividends. **Income stocks** are stocks in corporations with a consistent history of paying high dividends to stockholders. Investors choose income stocks to receive current income in the form of dividends. Investors can either collect the dividends as income or reinvest the dividend by purchasing additional stock. Income stocks are ideally suited for investors seeking a relatively safe and regular source of current income from their investment capital. Thus, income stocks are a popular choice for retirees.

Growth Stocks

Growth stocks are stocks in corporations that reinvest their profits into the business so that it can grow. These corporations may pay little or no dividends. Instead of current income, investors buy growth stocks for future capital gains. If the reinvested profits grow the business, the stock will be worth more, and the investor can sell their shares of stock to make a profit. Thus, growth stocks are long-term investments. They are often selected by younger people who have more time to let investments grow.

Blue Chip Stocks

Blue chip stocks are stocks of large, well-established corporations with a solid record of profitability. These companies generally sell high-quality, widely known products and services. They include Apple, Johnson & Johnson, and the Coca-Cola Company. Blue chip stocks are a conservative investment. Investors choose them for relatively safe and stable but moderate returns.

Emerging Stocks

Stocks in young, often small, corporations with higher overall risk than those of companies that have been successful for many years are called **emerging stocks**. These young companies may be on their way to becoming highly profitable. Or they may be among the many small companies that fail every year. Because the future of these companies is so uncertain, their stocks are often inexpensive but risky. Tesla was an example of an emerging stock in 2023.

Cyclical Stocks

Cyclical stocks are affected by ups and downs in the economy. Examples include travel-related companies, such as airlines and resorts, car manufacturers, and housing/construction companies. When the economy is doing well, people can afford to travel, buy new cars, and buy or build new houses. However, during a recession, many people lose their jobs or earn less than they would during good economic times. As a result, these discretionary expenses are some of the first things consumers will cut. This, in turn, causes reduced profits for these companies. In response to poor profit performance, the value of the stocks in these companies will likely decline.

Defensive Stocks

Defensive stocks, or noncyclical stocks, are stocks that remain stable and pay dividends during an economic decline. They are not affected as much by the ups and downs of business cycles. Examples include utility, pharmaceutical, healthcare, and food companies. These companies generally have a history of stable earnings because the demand for these products remains consistent regardless of economic conditions. Therefore, stocks in these industries protect the investor from sharp losses during bad economic times.

✓ Checkpoint

What are the different categories of stock available for investment?

LO 18.2.2 Valuing Stock

When you purchase stock, you can track your investments through a mobile app. All major brokerage firms have mobile apps where you can easily see the number of shares you own, the name of the company, the type of stock, and the par value. The **par value** is an assigned dollar value given to each share of stock. For preferred stock, par value is used to calculate dividend payments. However, par value is generally meaningless for common stocks since they can be issued without a par value.

Par value has nothing to do with a stock's **market value**, or the price for which the stock is bought and sold in the marketplace. A stock's market value reflects the price investors are willing to pay for the stock. How a company performs, its track record, and how well it is expected to perform determine market value.

Some stocks perform very well, yet their market value seems too low. These undervalued stocks are worth more than the price for which they are selling. Stocks that are undervalued make good bargains for investors, while creating a dangerous situation for businesses by leaving them vulnerable to a takeover by a large investor or company. Takeovers may be unfavorable for employees but can be very favorable for stockholders

Sharpen Your Personal Finance Skills
Calculating and Analyzing P/E Ratios

As Zander and Mila explore investment options, they are considering investing in different stocks. They have spent time researching various stocks and calculating the P/E ratio for each to assess if it is a good investment. For example, they are looking at investing in Amazon stock (stock symbol AMZN). When they look at purchasing Amazon stock, they see the current price per share is $146.74 and the earnings per share is $1.95. Zander and Mila compute the P/E ratio for AMZN by dividing the market value price per share ($146.74) by the earning per share ($1.95):

$$\$146.74/\$1.95 = \$75.25$$

Mila and Zander also find that the average P/E ratio over the past 3 years was $90.61 and over the past 5 years was $87.30. Based on this information, would you recommend that they invest in AMZN stock? Explain.

Try It Out!

Choose five companies that you would be interested in investing in. Research each company to find the information needed to calculate the P/E ratio for each company. Based on your findings, would you invest in these companies? Why or why not?

because the stock's market value is likely to rise. On the other hand, stocks can be overvalued, which means they sell at a price that is perceived as too high. The price of the stock is not justified by its earnings but is based on its superior growth potential in the future. This situation is very risky for the investor because it is likely that the price of the stock will drop. The wider the price swings, the riskier the stock. To help determine if a stock is undervalued or overvalued, investors can use the price to earnings ratio, known as the **P/E ratio**, to determine if the current stock price is low relative to the company's earnings. To calculate the P/E ratio, divide the market value price per share by the company's earnings per share. If the P/E ratio is high, the stock's price may be overvalued when compared to the company earnings or that investors are expecting high growth rates in the future.

Stock Price

Several factors affect the price you will pay for a share of stock. These factors include the company's financial situation, current interest rates, the market for the company's products or services, the company's earnings per share, and the current condition of the stock market.

The Company

When a company is performing well, the company's stock is attractive. Investors consider the company's earning power and its debt. If the company seems to be in a good financial position, the stock price will continue to rise.

Stock analysts review information about companies, both public news and information from the company's financial statements as found in its annual reports and SEC filings. These analysts prepare ratios and compare a company to its past performance, the performance of other companies, and industry standards. Analysts rate stocks using the terms buy, hold, or sell. Public corporations desire to be on the buy list, or at worst, to drop to the hold list. Stock prices can drop dramatically when analysts tell their customers to sell the stock.

Interest Rates

When interest rates are low, people who would normally put money in savings accounts and CDs look for more profitable places to invest their money. As interest rates rise, however, people tend to move their money to safer investments. Generally, when

© photo.ua/Shutterstock.com

What is the difference between a bull market and a bear market?

interest rates fall below the current rate of inflation, people buy more stocks, and stock prices rise.

The Market

The marketplace determines a company's ability to sell its products or services. If the company is in a popular industry and its products or services are selling well, its stock price should rise. For example, when people are buying computers, software, and related items, companies in the technology industry are considered wise investments. The stock price will decline if the demand for a particular product or service declines.

Earnings per Share

Earnings per share (EPS) are a corporation's after-tax earnings, called net profit, divided by the number of common stock shares outstanding. Outstanding shares are the shares of stock owned by investors. For example, assume that in a given year, XYZ Corporation had a net profit of $1,000,000 and 100,000 shares of common stock outstanding. Therefore, its EPS is $10, which is calculated by dividing the net profit by the number of outstanding shares: $1,000,000 ÷ 100,000. EPS indicates a company's profitability and is the most quoted measure for determining a stock's value.

Sharpen Your Personal Finance Skills
Stock Market Conditions

Many people struggle to remember the difference between a bull market and a bear market. To differentiate, remember that bulls are known for being aggressive and charging ahead, like stock prices in a rising market. On the other hand, bears are known for hibernating, similar to how investors might scale back investments during market downturns. Another way to differentiate is to remember that a bull will thrust its horns into the air, while a bear will swipe downward. These actions can be correlated to the movement of the market. If a market is trending up, it is considered a bull market. If the market is trending down, it is considered a bear market.

Think Critically

1. How would you explain the difference between a bull market and a bear market to a friend who is struggling to remember the difference?
2. What are potential pros and cons of bull and bear markets?
3. Do you think we are currently in a bear or bull market? Explain.

Stock Market Conditions

The stock market goes through cycles of rising and falling prices. A **bull market** is a prolonged period of rising stock prices and a general feeling of investor optimism. Confidence in the country's economy also serves to drive up stock prices. A **bear market** is a prolonged period of falling stock prices and a general feeling of investor pessimism. It develops when investors become negative about the overall economy and start to sell stocks. In bear markets, stock prices may fall 20 percent or more. Bear markets are usually short and savage. The average bull market often lasts three to four times as long as a bear market. Whether the stock market is bullish or bearish affects people's decisions about when to buy stocks, which ones to buy, and how much to pay for them.

Return on Investment

Return on investment (ROI) is used to evaluate the efficiency of an investment. Because you can make money on stocks from dividends and from an increase in the price of the stock, you should consider both when computing the return on your investment.

Figure 18.1 shows the formula for computing a stock's ROI. Your profit is the difference between what you paid for the stock and what you sold it for, plus any dividends you earned. To compute the total costs, add any commission you paid to the stockbroker to the purchase price of the stock.

Stock Indexes

A stock index is a benchmark that investors use to judge the performance of their investments. The Dow Jones Industrial Average is the oldest and most widely known stock index. Often called the Dow, it is an average of the price movements of 30 major, blue chip stocks listed on the New York Stock Exchange (NYSE). This average provides a general overview of how stock prices are doing in the stock market. Investors compare the price fluctuations of their stocks against

---

Figure 18.1   Computing Return on Investment

Computing a Stock's One-Year ROI

$$\frac{\text{Current Profit on Stock}}{\text{Purchase Price} + \text{Commission}} = \text{Return on Investment (ROI)}$$

Example: Selling price (or current stock price): $40/share
Dividends received during the year: $1/share
Purchase price: $38/share
Discount brokerage fee: $19
Number of shares owned: 100

Computations:
Current profit: $40/share − $38/share = $2/share × 100 = $200 + $100
dividends = total profits of $300

$$\frac{\$300}{(100 \times \$38) + \$19} = \frac{\$300}{\$3,819} = 7.86\%$$

this average to judge how well their stocks are performing compared to the overall stock market. Indexes for judging the performance of all kinds of stocks are available online and in print publications. Other commonly used indexes are the Standard & Poor's 500, called the S&P 500, and the NASDAQ Composite Index.

✓ **Checkpoint**

How do you determine a stock's value?

LO 18.2.3 Reading the Stock Listings

To make wise investments in the stock market, it is a good idea to track the progress of your assets to see how they are performing. You can track your stock through financial news publications, such as the *Wall Street Journal* or *Investor's Business Daily*, or online at various financial websites. Many sites allow you to sign up for daily portfolio email updates, and some have smartphone apps that let you track your investments on the go. Whether you follow your stock portfolio in the mobile app or online, you should see a listing like **Figure 18.2**. Follow along in the figure as you read the following explanations of each column.

- Name of stock. The top portion of the image shows the stock symbol, also known as the ticker symbol, and name of the company. The **stock symbol** is a unique series of letters that identify the security for trading purposes. On the NYSE, the symbol is one to four letters. This image represents Apple, Inc. Company.

- Annual scale. This shows the highest and lowest price of the stock over the past 52 weeks, along with the date of the value. The highest amount that Apple stock sold for was $198.23 on July 19, 2023. The lowest stock price was $124.17 on January 3, 2023. In the middle of the scale, the numbers indicate the daily range for the previous day of trading during the official trading day, which was October 27, 2023. *Note:* Many stocks are part of the after-hours trading, and the daily range of the stock's value can change when the U.S. stock markets are closed.

- Open. Indicates the value of the stock at the beginning of the official trading day.

- Previous Close. Indicates the value of the stock at the end of the official trading day.

- Average Volume. The number of shares that were bought and sold over the indicated period. In this case, 56.74 million shares of Apple stock were traded in the past 10 days.

- P/E. Apple stock had a price-to-earnings ratio of 28.03. This is calculated as the price per share divided by the corporation's earnings per share over the past 12 months. The P/E ratio is a critical factor that serious investors use to evaluate stock investments. A low P/E ratio may indicate a solid investment, while a high P/E ratio may indicate higher risk.

- EPS. Earnings per share for Apple stock were $5.95 per share.

- Next Earnings Date. The next earnings date is the next time the company will make a public announcement about their year-to-date earnings.

- Market Cap. The market cap is how large the company is. This is calculated by the value of a company's outstanding shares of stock plus any restricted shares held by company officers and insiders. Apple was worth almost $2630 billion dollars.

- Shares Outstanding. This is the number of shares of Apple stock available in the public marketplace. Apple had 15.63 billion shares of stock on this date.

Figure 18.2   Reading the Stock Listings

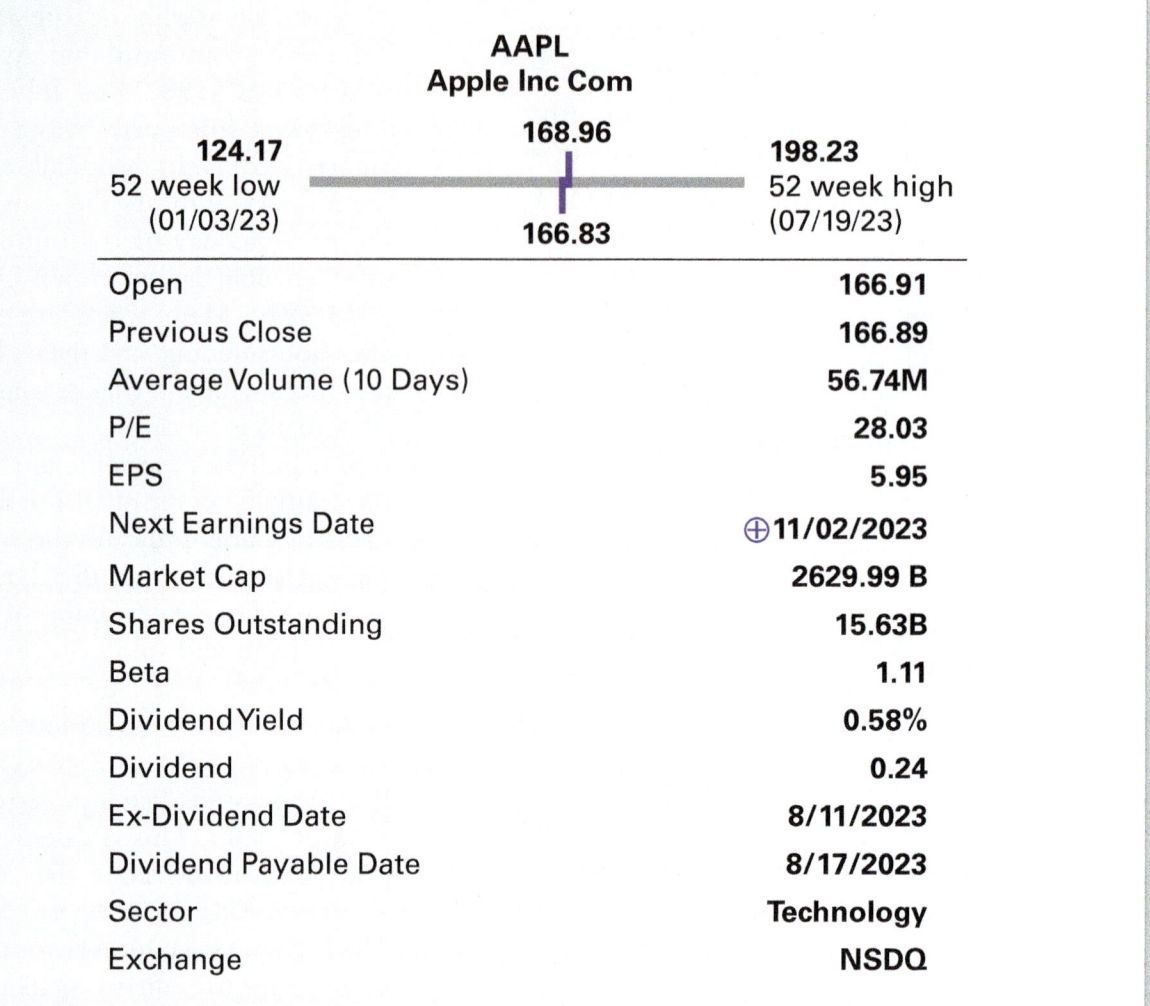

AAPL
Apple Inc Com

168.96

124.17		198.23
52 week low		52 week high
(01/03/23)	**166.83**	(07/19/23)

Open	166.91
Previous Close	166.89
Average Volume (10 Days)	56.74M
P/E	28.03
EPS	5.95
Next Earnings Date	⊕11/02/2023
Market Cap	2629.99 B
Shares Outstanding	15.63B
Beta	1.11
Dividend Yield	0.58%
Dividend	0.24
Ex-Dividend Date	8/11/2023
Dividend Payable Date	8/17/2023
Sector	Technology
Exchange	NSDQ

- Beta. This is the volatility measure of a stock. If the beta is greater than 1.0, the stock value changes more than the broader market. In this case, Apple's beta is 1.11, making it slightly more volatile than the overall NASDAQ market.
- Dividend Yield. The dividend yield (DY) is calculated by dividing the dividend per share by the market price and multiplying by 100. A DY of 0.58% indicates that Apple pays less than 1% of the stock price as a dividend and retains more than 99% of the value to invest back into the company.

- Dividend. The dividend paid on one share of Apple stock was 24 cents.
- Ex-Dividend Date. If you owned Apple stock on August 11, 2023, you would have received a 24-cent dividend for every share of stock you owned on the dividend payable date.
- Dividend Payable Date. The date dividends are paid to shareholders.
- Sector. This indicated the type of industry the company is in. Apple is a technology stock.
- Exchange. This indicates which stock exchange is used to trade stock. Apple is part of the NASDAQ stock exchange.

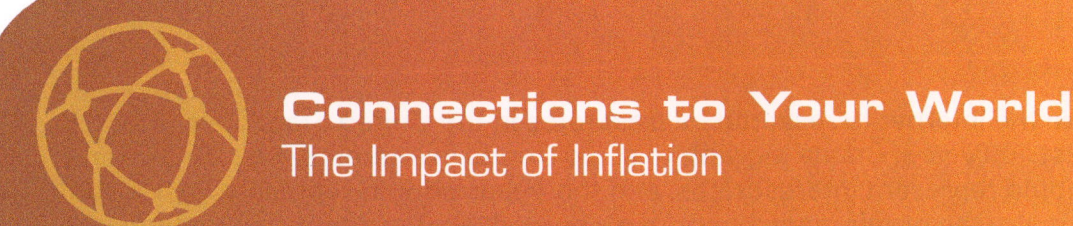

Inflation is an increase in the general level of prices. It is measured yearly to see how much prices are rising. The consumer price index (CPI) is the instrument most often used as a measure of rising prices. The CPI measures price changes for a "market basket" of goods and services typically purchased by consumers; items commonly included in a market basket are housing, transportation, recreation, apparel, and education. In addition, inflation is evident in rising interest rates. Interest rates reflect the cost of lending and borrowing money. As prices increase, interest rates go up as well.

Some people get hurt by rapidly rising prices and interest rates. People who are more likely to be affected by inflation include the following:

- **People on fixed incomes.** Many retired people live on a fixed monthly retirement benefit. When prices rise, their fixed income stays the same. Thus, they are unable to maintain the same standard of living in inflationary times.
- **People with a lot of debt.** During inflationary times, interest rates charged by credit card companies rise. As your interest rate goes up, so does your monthly payment. More of each month's payment goes toward interest rather than paying off the debt. This makes it difficult for people with a lot of debt to pay down their credit cards.
- **People who have to borrow.** If you need to borrow money, you will pay higher interest rates in times of inflation. As a result, your monthly payments will be higher, or you will have to make payments for a longer time to pay off the loan.
- **People working as employees.** As an employee, you work for a salary or wage. Although you may get a yearly raise, it may not be enough to keep up with price increases. When inflation hits, you must adapt by making changes in your lifestyle. This lowers your standard of living because rapidly rising prices erode your purchasing power.
- **People who have fixed-rate investments.** Many investors buy fixed-income securities because they want a stable return on their investment, which comes in the form of interest payments. However, because the interest rate on fixed-income securities remains the same over time, the purchasing power of the interest payments declines as inflation rises.

To prepare for periods of inflation, you should save so that you will have resources during hard times. You should also look for investments that consistently (over time) bring you a rate of return that is higher than the rate of inflation so that your wealth grows rather than falls behind as price levels continue to rise.

(continues)

(continued)

Think Critically

1. Use the internet to research interest rates in the United States over the past 100 years. Create a graph to show trends in interest rates; the *x*-axis should represent interest rates, and the *y*-axis should represent years. You can plot the graph manually or use a spreadsheet program to create the graph for you. What trends do you notice from the graph? What factors may have impacted fluctuations in interest rates over time?

2. Have you noticed goods or services you buy frequently increasing in price? How have prices of those goods or services affected your lifestyle?

Figure 18.3   Stock Progress Chart

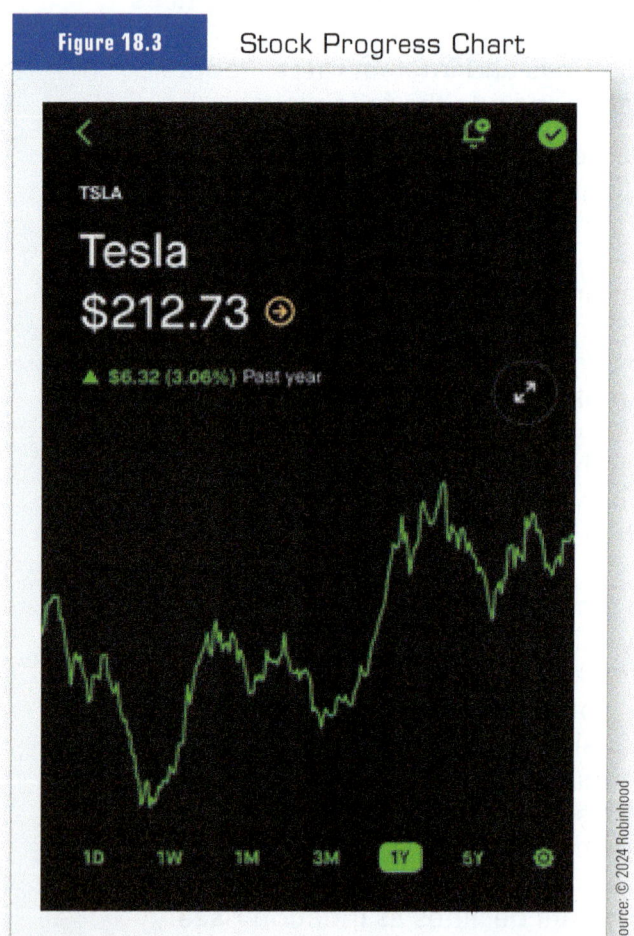

TSLA

Tesla
$212.73 ⊕

▲ $6.32 (3.06%) Past year

1D   1W   1M   3M   **1Y**   5Y   ⚙

Source: © 2024 Robinhood

Keeping track of your stock portfolio and holdings can be as simple as checking the closing prices periodically through the online broker account or website where your investment accounts are located. The image in **Figure 18.3** shows the stock price for Tesla for the past year. It does not consider dividends received or the appreciation in value since the stock was purchased. The stock progress chart is merely a device for monitoring changes in the closing prices of stocks.

✓ Checkpoint

What information can you obtain from stock listings?

Check Your Understanding

1. How do investors profit from owning stock? (LO 18.2.1)

2. Define the different categories of stocks. (LO 18.2.1)

3. How can an investor determine if a stock price is over- or undervalued? (LO 18.2.2)

4. How can you keep track of a stock's value over time? (LO 18.2.3)

Apply Your Understanding

1. Consider the various stages of investing from a previous chapter. At which stage should an investor include blue chip, emerging, cyclical, and defensive stocks? Explain your answer. (LO 18.2.1)

2. Use an online resource to find the P/E ratio for one of the blue chip stocks mentioned in this chapter. Do you consider the stock to be over or undervalued? Why? (LO 18.2.2)

3. Select five stocks from the Dow. Create a stock listing for the stocks like the one in this chapter. Use spreadsheet software to create the listing. Based on the P/E ratio, rank the stocks in order of the best value to the worst value. (LO 18.2.3)

The Essential Question

What are the reasons for owning stocks, what types of stocks are available, and how do you determine a stock's value and read stock listings and indexes?

A: Owning stock is a good way to earn income (dividends) and save for the future (capital gains). Income, growth, blue chip, emerging, cyclical, and defensive stocks are available. A stock's market value is based on a combination of the company's financial standing, interest rates, the market, earnings per share, and the current condition of the stock market. You can find information to determine a stock's value through the stock listing.

18.3 Investing in Bonds

The Essential Question

What are the different types of corporate and government bonds, what factors should be considered when buying and selling bonds, and how do you read bond listings?

Learning Objectives

By the end of this lesson, you should be able to:

LO 18.3.1 Describe the characteristics and different types of corporate bonds.

LO 18.3.2 Describe different types of government bonds.

LO 18.3.3 Explain how to buy and sell bonds, considering both risk and return.

LO 18.3.4 Explain how to read bond listings.

Key Terms

- bonds
- fixed-rate investment
- maturity date
- bond redemption
- face value
- debenture
- secured bond
- convertible bond
- callable bond
- zero-coupon bond
- municipal bond
- revenue bond
- general obligation (GO) bond
- U.S. savings bond
- U.S. Treasury securities
- agency bond
- hedge
- primary market
- secondary market
- bond rating
- investment-grade bond
- junk bond
- bond default
- bond fund
- bond listings

LO 18.3.1 Corporate Bonds

Companies need funds for new technology, long-term operating expenses, and expansion into new markets. While a corporation may use bonds and stocks to finance business activities, there are important distinctions between the two. First, **bonds** are loans that must be repaid at maturity. Stocks are shares of ownership in the corporation, not loans. Second, corporations must make semiannual interest payments on their bonds. Corporations are not required to pay dividends on stocks. The board of directors decides whether to pay stock dividends.

Characteristics of Corporate Bonds

Bonds are known as **fixed-rate investments** because they pay a specified amount of interest on a regular schedule. In other words, a bond's interest does not go up or down, unlike stock dividends. Usually, bond interest is paid to bondholders twice a year.

All bonds have a maturity date. The **maturity date** is when the bonds can be redeemed. Bond maturities typically range from 1 to 30 years. **Bond redemption** occurs when the bond is paid off at maturity. **Face value** is the amount the bondholder will be repaid at maturity. Face value is also

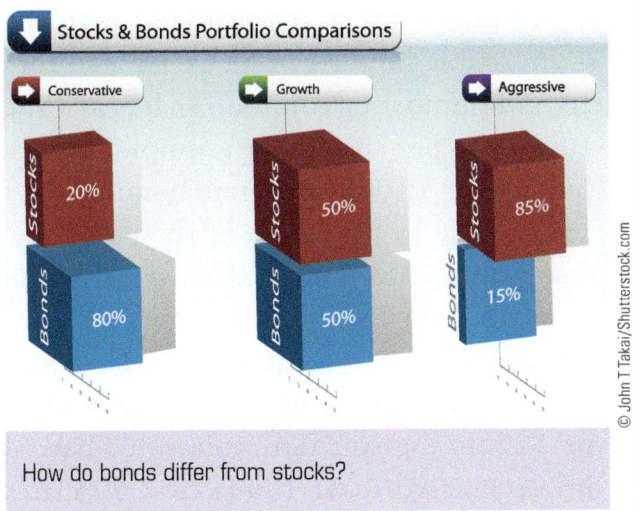

Stocks & Bonds Portfolio Comparisons

Conservative — Stocks 20%, Bonds 80%
Growth — Stocks 50%, Bonds 50%
Aggressive — Stocks 85%, Bonds 15%

How do bonds differ from stocks?

© John T Takai/Shutterstock.com

Figure 18.4 shows interest payments on a 10-year, 6 percent corporate bond with a face value of $10,000. Assume that the bond was issued on January 1, 2025, and interest payments are due on June 30 and December 31 each year. The bondholder would receive semiannual payments of $300 for 10 years. There is no compounding of interest. The bond has a maturity date of January 1, 2035, or 10 years from the issue date. On this date, the principal of $10,000 is repaid to the bondholder by the issuer.

The process for collecting the interest on a bond depends on whether it is a registered bond or a coupon bond. The issuing company records a registered bond in the owner's name. Interest checks for registered bonds are mailed semiannually directly to the bondholder. The issuing company does not register a coupon bond or bearer bond. To collect interest on a coupon bond, bondholders must clip a coupon and then

referred to as par value because the face value is the dollar amount printed on the certificate. All corporate bonds are issued with a stated face value and fixed contract rate. A bond's interest rate, called the contract rate, is the percentage of face value the bondholder will receive as interest each year. Interest received on corporate bonds is taxable and must be reported as ordinary income on your tax return.

Figure 18.4	Earnings on a 10-Year, 6% Corporate Bond	
Year	**June 30 Interest**	**December 31 Interest**
1	$300.00	$300.00
2	300.00	300.00
3	300.00	300.00
4	300.00	300.00
5	300.00	300.00
6	300.00	300.00
7	300.00	300.00
8	300.00	300.00
9	300.00	300.00
10	300.00	300.00

January 1, 2035: $10,000 principal is repaid

cash it in at a bank, following the procedures outlined by the issuer. Today, most bonds are registered.

A major disadvantage for individual investors is the cost of corporate bonds. Very few corporate bonds are sold in units of less than $1,000. Bonds are commonly sold in $5,000 units.

Types of Corporate Bonds

There are many types of corporate bonds. Some common types include debentures, secured mortgage, convertible, callable, and zero-coupon bonds.

Debentures

A **debenture** is a corporate bond based on the company's general creditworthiness and reputation. The issuer does not pledge any specific assets to assure loan repayment. Because of this, debentures are considered unsecured bonds. An investor relies on the full faith and credit of the bond issuer for repayment of the interest and principal. When issued by reliable companies, debentures are relatively safe investments.

Secured Bonds

A **secured bond**, also called a mortgage bond, is backed by specific assets that serve as security to assure debt repayment. If the corporation fails to repay the loan as agreed, the bondholder may claim the property used as security for the debt. The asset most often used for security is real estate, a building, or some other property type.

Convertible Bonds

A **convertible bond** is a corporate bond that can be converted to shares of common stock. The bondholder has the option of switching to a stock investment. If the bond-holder converts to common stock, the bond

is no longer due and payable at maturity. Convertible bonds can be exchanged for a certain number of common shares at a specific price per share. For example, say you purchase a $1,000 corporate bond which is convertible to 50 shares of the company's common stock. You should convert the bond to stock whenever the company's common stock price is $20 ($1,000 ÷ 50 shares) or higher. Assume the company's stock is selling for $22. In this situation, you would have an investment worth $1,100 ($22 × 50 shares) on conversion.

Callable Bonds

A bond may be issued with a call provision. A **callable bond** is one that the issuer has the right to pay off (call back) before its maturity date. The date when a bond can be called is identified when it is offered for sale. For example, a 10-year bond issued in 2025 with a maturity date of 2035 may be callable in the year 2030. Because they can reissue them at a lower interest rate, Corporations may call the bonds if interest rates fall. Generally, it is cost-effective for corporations to pay the costs of calling and reissuing when interest rates drop by 2 percent or more. Corporations usually agree not to call bonds for the first 5 years after issuance. When the corporation does exercise its right to call the bond, it generally pays the bondholders a small premium that is an amount above the face value of the bond. For example, a $1,000 bond may be called at a value of $1,020.

Zero-Coupon Bonds

Another type of corporate bond is a zero-coupon bond. A **zero-coupon bond** is sold at a deep discount, makes no interest payments, and is redeemable for its face value at maturity. The U.S. government or municipalities may also issue these bonds.

They are sold at as much as 50 to 75 percent below the face value of the bond. As the bond progresses toward maturity, it may increase in value. The bondholders make money by selling the bonds before maturity at a higher price than they paid, or they can hold the bonds to maturity and receive the face value and interest.

With a zero-coupon corporate bond, you must pay taxes on any interest you gain yearly, even though you receive it once the bond is paid at maturity. Interest on zero-coupon municipal bonds, however, is not subject to taxation. Prices on zero-coupon bonds tend to fluctuate widely. You may face a loss if you need to sell the bond before maturity.

> **✓ Checkpoint**
>
> What are the different types of corporate bonds?

LO 18.3.2 **Government Bonds**

In addition to loaning money to corporations, you can also loan money to the government. Bonds are issued by the federal government as well as by state and local governments. There are four major types of government bonds: municipal bonds, savings bonds, Treasury securities, and agency bonds.

Municipal Bonds

A bond issued by state or local governments is called a **municipal bond**. The minimum investment in a municipal bond is usually $5,000, although brokers often ask for a multiple of this amount as a minimum investment. Municipal bonds generally pay a lower interest rate than corporate bonds. However, the interest is exempt from federal taxes, and often state and local taxes, so the effective rate is higher than the stated rate. As **Figure 18.5** shows, the tax advantage of municipal bonds sometimes makes them a better deal than a corporate bond that pays a higher interest rate. Figure 18.5 calculates net interest on both kinds of bonds for an investor in the 28 percent tax bracket. Municipal bonds, called munis, come in revenue and general obligation bonds.

Revenue Bonds

A **revenue bond** is a municipal bond issued to raise money for a public-works project. The revenues generated by the project are used to pay the interest and repay the bonds at maturity. For example, if a revenue bond is issued to build a new toll road, the tolls that are collected from motorists who drive

Figure 18.5	Comparing Taxable and Tax-Exempt Bonds

	Corporate Bond	Municipal Bond
Face value (principal)	$10,000	$10,000
Rate of interest	× 6%	× 5%
Amount of annual interest	$ 600	$ 500
Tax on interest earned (28%)	−168	− 0
Net interest	$ 432	$ 500

Borrowing by the federal government creates the national debt. Each year, the national deficit (excess of spending over revenue collected) is added to that debt. In late 2023, the national debt was more than $33 trillion. In historical times, the national debt was used to finance wars. Currently, it is still used to fund the military, but it is also applied to funding recommendations outlined in annual federal budgets. The national debt is represented by Treasury notes, bills, and bonds.

Many people think the debt is overwhelming and represents obligations that must be paid by future generations. Others think the national debt is needed to fund major government functions, including income security programs such as unemployment compensation and food and nutrition assistance, Social Security, healthcare services and research, national defense, and Medicare.

Think Critically

1. Which side do you agree with? Explain.

2. Search online to find the current amount of the national debt. What do you think the country should do about the national debt?

3. Unexpected events such as wars and national crises like the COVID-19 pandemic cause drastic increases in spending that result in higher levels of national debt. Search online to research events from the past two decades that have significantly contributed to the national debt level. What caused the increased debt during these times? How was the increased spending intended to benefit the country or stabilize the economy?

on the road are used to pay off the bond. In addition to toll roads, other major projects financed by revenue bonds include airports, hospitals, and public housing facilities.

General Obligation Bonds

A **general obligation (GO) bond** is a municipal bond backed by the power of the issuing state or local government to levy taxes to pay back the debt. For example, school districts may issue bonds to finance the construction of new buildings. A city may issue bonds to pay for a new police or administrative center. States may issue bonds to pay for a new college campus or a new road system.

A GO bond is repaid with the government's general revenue and borrowings. In contrast, a revenue bond is repaid from the revenue generated by the facility built with the borrowed funds. Cities pay off GO bonds by using funds collected from city income and sales taxes, fees, fines, and other sources. Schools and colleges pay off the bonds with property taxes, tuition, fees, state funding, and other sources.

Savings Bonds

U.S. savings bonds are available as Series EE and Series I bonds. When you purchase a **U.S. savings bond**, you are loaning funds to the U.S. government that will be repaid to you with interest at a later date. Both types of savings bonds are sold at face value. The bonds are available in any amount from $25 to $10,000, and you can buy up to $10,000 worth of bonds in a year. The interest that both Series EE and Series I savings bonds earn is taxable at the federal level but exempt from state and local income taxes.

You can no longer purchase Series EE or Series I savings bonds at a local bank, financial institution, or credit union. These savings bonds are sold online only at the U.S. Department of Treasury's TreasuryDirect website (www.treasurydirect.gov). Paper certificates are also no longer issued. The only exceptions are for those who (1) are replacing lost bonds or changing a beneficiary or co-owner name and (2) wish to exchange their tax refund for a Series I bond.

Treasury Securities

Treasury securities (Treasury bills, notes, and bonds) can be purchased at the TreasuryDirect website or through a bank or broker. **U.S. Treasury securities**, called Treasuries, are debt obligations issued by the U.S. government and are secured by the full faith and credit of the United States. These investments exist as bookkeeping entries in the records of the U.S. Department of

Treasury or in the records of commercial banks. Like savings bonds, U.S. Treasury securities are taxed by the federal government but are exempt from state and local income taxes. They are virtually risk-free because they have the backing of the U.S. government.

Agency Bonds

A bond issued by government agencies or by government-sponsored enterprises (GSEs) is called an **agency bond**. GSEs are federally chartered corporations that are publicly owned by stockholders. They help investors create a more diversified portfolio without creating more credit or inflation risk. Examples of GSEs include the Federal Home Loan Mortgage Corporation (Freddie Mac), the Federal National Mortgage Association (Fannie Mae), and the Federal Farm Credit Banks. Because stockholders own GSEs, and they are not part of the federal government, bonds issued by these corporations are not backed by the full faith and credit of the federal government and, thus, have a certain amount of default risk.

In contrast, bonds issued by government agencies, such as the Small Business Administration (SBA), the Federal Housing Administration (FHA), and the Government National Mortgage Association (Ginnie Mae), are backed by the full faith and credit of the U.S. federal government. These agencies may not issue bonds directly. Instead, they may insure or guarantee securities issued by other companies.

When you purchase an agency bond, you are loaning money to one of these agencies. The agencies use this funding to finance activities related to specific purposes, such as increasing home ownership or providing agricultural assistance. There is usually a

Source: iStock.com/JHVEPhoto

What is the purpose of an agency bond?

minimum investment required to buy an agency bond. For example, investing in a Ginnie Mae bond requires a $25,000 minimum investment.

Agency bonds help investors create a more diversified portfolio. They are basically risk-free and offer a slightly higher yield than Treasury securities. They are usually taxable at the federal level but exempt from state and local income taxes. Agency bonds can be purchased through a bank or broker.

✓ Checkpoint

What are the four major types of government bonds?

LO 18.3.3 Buying and Selling Bonds

In addition to buying stocks, many investors also choose to invest in bonds. Bonds are generally a safe investment because they have a fixed interest rate and represent a loan the issuer must repay. Bonds play an essential role in a diversified portfolio. Bond prices tend to remain steadier than do stock prices. Also, bond prices often react in a manner opposite to the reaction of stock prices. When stock prices fall, bond prices tend to rise, and vice versa. As a result, bond investments help offset the risk of the stocks in your portfolio. A **hedge** is any investment or action that offsets against loss from another investment.

Full-service and discount brokers can assist you in buying and selling bonds. If you decide to use a broker, you will be charged a commission or flat fee for this service. Some bonds can also be purchased through banks.

Buying Bonds

You cannot purchase U.S. savings bonds at financial institutions. Instead, you can buy them at the TreasuryDirect website (www .treasurydirect.gov). To purchase a savings bond, you must have a TreasuryDirect account and a checking or savings account. When you buy a bond at TreasuryDirect, the purchase price is withdrawn from your designated bank account. When the bond matures, TreasuryDirect deposits the payment into your bank account.

TreasuryDirect also offers a payroll savings plan to buy savings bonds. Participating employers automatically withhold money from paychecks and directly deposit it into a TreasuryDirect account. The employee decides what type and dollar value of savings bond they want to buy, and TreasuryDirect automatically purchases it once there are enough funds in the employee's account.

You can also buy Treasury securities at the TreasuryDirect website. Interest earned is deposited directly into the designated bank account when you set up your

TreasuryDirect account. When the security matures, you can redeem it by having the principal deposited into your bank account or reinvest it by using the proceeds from the matured security to buy another one. Treasury securities can also be purchased through a bank or broker.

You can buy corporate, municipal, and agency bonds through banks or brokers. You can set up a bank account in most states to buy municipal bonds. Often, you are purchasing a bond from the inventory your bank has on hand. Banks buy large blocks of municipal bonds and make them available to their customers. There is a fee for this service.

Primary and Secondary Markets

Corporate, municipal, and agency bonds can be purchased on the **primary market**, also known as the new issue market, because investors can buy stocks and bonds when a company or group first issues them. However, most of these bonds are purchased on the **secondary market**, created when investors buy and sell previously issued stocks and bonds from one another with the help of brokers. One of the most significant differences between buying bonds on the primary and secondary markets is the price.

In the primary market, investors pay only the face value of the bond. The issuing corporation—not the investor—pays the broker commission for the sale. In the secondary market, the bond price is affected by interest rates in the market as well as supply and demand.

Return on Bonds

Investors earn a return on bonds through the interest that accumulates each day they own the bond and through the principal they receive when they redeem the bond for its face value at maturity. Investors can also earn a return if they sell the bond before maturity. While the interest rate on a bond is fixed, the market price can change. Bonds often appreciate, especially when interest rates are dropping, and bondholders may be able to sell the bond before maturity for a price higher than they paid for it. When bonds sell for more than their face value, they sell at a premium. For example, **Figure 18.6** shows that the yield (or return) is 6 percent on a $10,000 bond selling for face value, or 100. But if the bond is sold for 104, it would have a premium of 4 percent. At 104, the market price would be $10,400.

$$\$10,000 \times 0.04 = \$400 \,\text{premium}$$
$$\$10,000 + \$400 = \$10,400 \,\text{market price}$$

Figure 18.6   Yield on a $10,000, 6 Percent Bond

$$\frac{\text{Annual Interest Dollar Amount}}{\text{Market Price}} = \text{Yield}$$

	Annual Interest/Market Price	= Yield
If you buy the $10,000 bond at face value	$600/$10,000 =	6%
If you buy the bond at 104	$600/$10,400 =	5.8%
If you buy the bond at 96	$600/$9,600 =	6.3%

In this case, the buyer's yield would be lower than 6 percent because the buyer had to pay more than face value to buy the bond.

Bonds can also sell below face value. Investors are unwilling to pay face value for a bond yielding 6 percent when current interest rates are higher than 6 percent and rising. Therefore, the bond may have to be sold at a discount or for an amount lower than face value to attract buyers. If a bond sold for 96, it was sold at a 4 percent discount. The bond purchaser would pay only $9,600 for a $10,000 bond.

$$\$10,000 \times 0.04 = \$400 \text{ discount}$$
$$\$10,000 - \$400 = \$9,600 \text{ market price}$$

In this case, the buyer's yield would be higher than 6 percent because the buyer paid less than face value for the bond. As these examples show, yield is not the same thing as the contract rate of interest.

Risk on Bonds

Like all investments, bonds have risk. However, the risk is not the same for all bonds. To help investors evaluate the risk level of different bonds, independent rating services rate bonds according to their safety. A **bond rating** tells the investor the risk category assigned to a bond. Bond rating services, such as Moody's and Standard & Poor's, base their ratings on the creditworthiness of the issuing corporation or municipality. **Figure 18.7** shows the bond rating scales for both Moody's and Standard & Poor's.

An **investment-grade bond** is considered a high-quality, low-risk bond. It has a rating of Baa or higher by Moody's or BBB or Standard & Poor's. These bonds are considered safe because the issuers are stable and dependable. For example, U.S. Treasury bonds provide maximum safety because the federal government itself backs them. Unfortunately, the higher the bond's rating, the lower the interest rate you will earn.

If a company falls below a certain credit rating, its grade changes from investment quality to junk status. A **junk bond** has a low rating or no rating at all. Any bond with a Ba/BB or lower rating is called a junk bond and is categorized as speculative. Junk bonds have higher yields and, at times, appear to have reasonable levels of risk. However,

Figure 18.7	Bond Rating Scales		
Moody's	**Standard & Poor's**	**Grade**	**Risk**
Aaa	AAA	Investment	Highest quality
Aa	AA	Investment	High quality
A	A	Investment	Strong
Baa	BBB	Investment	Medium
Ba, B	BB, B	Junk	Speculative
Caa, Ca	CCC, CC, C	Junk	Highly speculative
C	D	Junk	In default

in most cases, interest rates on junk bonds are high because they are at increased risk since the companies issuing them are not financially sound.

A bond rating of C by Moody's or D by Standard & Poor's indicates that the bond is in default. **Bond default** occurs when the issuer cannot meet the interest or principal payments. Because bonds are not insured, investors can lose their money if the corporation or municipality defaults.

Lowering Risk

To lower risk in owning bonds, many investors buy into investment pools of various types of bonds rather than buying individual ones. A **bond fund** is a group of bonds that have been bundled together and sold to investors in shares, like stock. Typically, a bond fund will contain some investment-grade bonds along with bonds of some newer companies, foreign bonds, and a few junk bonds. Mutual funds, brokers, and investment services at financial institutions offer bond funds to their customers as a method of hedging against the risk of loss from other investments.

✓ Checkpoint

What are the different ways bonds can be bought or sold, and what are the risks associated with bonds?

LO 18.3.4

Reading Bond Listings

Bond listings are extensive tables that contain information about recent trades of bonds. You can find them in financial news publications such as the *Wall Street Journal*, *Investor's Business Daily*, *Barron's*, and many financial and investor websites. Bond listings contain bond quotes or the prices at which bonds are trading expressed as a percentage of face value. Interest rates affect bond prices. When interest rates rise, the value of bonds decreases. The bonds are paying less in comparison to other fixed-rate investments. Conversely, because they are locked in at higher rates, fixed-rate bonds will become attractive when interest rates drop.

The bond listings you will find will look like the one shown in **Figure 18.8**. To track bond prices, you need to understand the various columns in the bond listings.

- Column 1. This column lists the abbreviated name of the bond issuer.
- Column 2. This column indicates the type of bond and its rating. An "a" stands for senior bond, a "b" stands for split coupon, a "c" is a zero-coupon bond, a "d" is an unsecured bond, and an "e" is a secured bond.
- Column 3. This column shows the coupon rate of the bond (the guaranteed, fixed interest rate that will be paid annually on the bond).
- Column 4. This column shows the maturity date. Typically, the month and year are listed. For example, "12/27" means December 2027
- Column 5. This column tells you what the final closing bid for the day was for the bond. It is like the closing price for stocks. Prices (bond quotes) are given as a percentage of face value, which is usually $1,000. For example, the last sale price for AK Steel was 98½, which translates into $985 on a $1,000 bond, or 98.5 percent of the face value.
- Column 6. This column compares the last price paid for the bond today with that paid on the previous day. A minus

Figure 18.8   Reading Corporate Bond Listings

Excerpt from stock exchange (bond) listings:

Name	Type/ Rating	Coup.	Mat.	Last Sale	Net Chg.	Yld
1	2	3	4	5	6	7
AK Steel	a/BB	9.125	12/23	98½	+.38	9.46
Allied Waste	b/B	10.000	8/26	102	unch	9.57
Am Std	a/BB	7.375	2/25	98½	−1.25	7.56
Chanclr	b/BB	8.125	12/27	103	unch	7.36
Echostar	a/B	9.375	2/26	101¼	unch	9.52

Connections to Your World
Investment Tax Strategies

When choosing investment options, one important consideration to keep in mind is taxability. Some investments are fully taxable, while others are tax-free. There are numerous options in between. The choice of an investment might hinge on its tax status.

An investment is tax-exempt when there is no tax due on the interest income earned, either now or in the future. Tax-exempt investments include municipal bonds sold by state and local governments. However, to be free from both federal and state taxes, you must live in the state where the bond is issued. For example, if you live in California and own a municipal bond issued in the state of Oregon, the bond will be tax-free in Oregon but will be subject to state income taxes in California.

An investment is tax-deferred when income will be taxed later. Tax-deferred investments include annuities. While earnings are credited to your account now, you do not pay taxes on the earnings until you withdraw them. Withdrawals from these accounts commonly occur during retirement when you are in a lower tax bracket because your income is lower.

Taxes also are deferred on assets that appreciate in value. Capital gains, the profits from the sale of assets such as stocks, bonds, or real estate, are not taxed until the asset is sold. For example, if shares of stock you own are currently worth more than you paid for them, you will owe no taxes on the gain until you sell the stock.

(continues)

(continued)

Income and tax deductions can be shifted by postponing them to the following tax year, or by accelerating them forward into a current year, depending on when they will be more beneficial. If your income is higher than usual this year, you can shift some deductions to help offset this increased income.

Taxes can be avoided by selling securities on which you lost money to offset gains on the sale of other securities. You can deduct losses to reduce capital gains on securities you sold at a profit. For example, you may sell shares of stock that are worth more than you paid for them and make a profit. However, you may own a bond that has dropped in value. If you sell the bond before maturity, you can use the losses from the sale of the bond to reduce the gains from the sale of stock. This strategy is called tax avoidance. Tax avoidance is different from tax evasion, which is the use of illegal actions to reduce your taxes.

Think Critically

1. Why is it important to consider tax consequences when choosing investment alternatives?
2. What type of investor would likely choose a tax-exempt investment? What type of investor would choose a tax-deferred investment?
3. Why is it beneficial to seek professional advice when shifting income and avoiding taxes?

---

means the price has gone down; a plus means the price has risen. "Unch" means "unchanged"—the price has not changed from the previous day.

- Column 7. This column states the current yield for the bond. The current yield is computed by dividing the bond's coupon rate by its average market value (not its closing price). This yield figure varies as market interest conditions change; therefore, the current yield may be above or below the actual coupon rate. The current yield is an important indicator because it tells you what your bond is worth relative to other bonds you may have in your portfolio and other bond choices in the marketplace.

✓ Checkpoint

What kind of information can you find in bond listings?

Check Your Understanding

1. What is the difference between a debenture and a secured bond? (LO 18.3.1)
2. Describe the different types of government bonds. (LO 18.3.2)
3. How do investors buy and sell bonds? (LO 18.3.3)
4. What are risks and returns for different types of bonds? (LO 18.3.3)
5. What are the categories on a bond listing? Describe each category. (LO 18.3.4)

Apply Your Understanding

1. How would incorporating bonds into an investment portfolio benefit an investor seeking to balance risk and return? Explain the role of bonds in diversification, income generation, and risk management. (LO 18.3.1)
2. Mila does not understand the difference between the risk of corporate bonds and owning stock. Explain in two or three sentences which one is more secure and why. (LO 18.3.1)
3. You are interested in purchasing government bonds. After looking into options, which type would you purchase and why? (LO 18.3.2)
4. Research the price of U.S. Treasury Bonds, the rate of inflation, and interest rates over the past ten years. Create a chart or some other graphic organizer to show how the three items are related. (LO 18.3.3)

The Essential Question

What are the different types of corporate and government bonds, what factors should be considered when buying and selling bonds, and how do you read bond listings?

A: Corporate bonds are fixed-rate investments that pay a specified amount of interest at regular intervals. Government bonds are issued by the federal government as well as by state and local governments. A return on bonds is earned in one of three ways: (1) by collecting interest, (2) by redeeming the bond at maturity, and (3) by selling the bond for a premium before its maturity. The risk of owning bonds can be reduced by checking their ratings, buying a bond fund, and reading and understanding bond listings.

The Essential Question

Why are mutual funds a good investment for less experienced investors, what types of mutual funds are available, and how do you buy and sell mutual funds?

Learning Objectives

By the end of this lesson, you should be able to:

LO 18.4.1 Explain mutual funds as an investment strategy and the types of mutual funds available.

LO 18.4.2 Explain how to buy and sell mutual funds.

Key Terms

- mutual fund
- growth fund
- income fund
- growth and income fund
- balanced fund
- money market fund
- global fund
- index fund
- exchange-traded fund (ETF)
- prospectus
- load
- net asset value (NAV)

LO 18.4.1 | Mutual Funds

A **mutual fund** is a professionally managed group of investments bought using a pool of money from many investors. Individuals buy shares in the mutual fund. Mutual funds are operated by professional fund managers who use the pooled money to buy stocks, bonds, and other securities based on market research they have conducted. The kinds of securities they buy depend on the fund's stated investment objectives. For example, some mutual funds specialize in aggressive growth stocks. Others specialize in more conservative investments like bonds or money market securities.

Most mutual fund companies offer a family of funds, which is a variety of funds covering a whole range of investment objectives. You can choose the family member(s) that best match your goals. You are allowed to move back and forth among the company's funds. For example, you can buy one type of fund, such as a stock fund, and later switch to another, such as a bond fund, all within the same family of funds.

Fund investors share in any profits made by the mutual fund. They receive profits as dividends and capital gains, which may

Why do most mutual funds companies offer a family of funds?

be reinvested in the fund or distributed to investors as cash payments. Capital gains come from the profits made when the managers sell some of the fund's securities for more than they paid.

Advantages of Mutual Funds

Investors often choose mutual funds for several good reasons:

- Professional management. The primary advantage of investing in mutual funds is professional money management. A mutual fund is a relatively inexpensive way for investors who do not have the time or expertise to manage their own portfolio to get a full-time manager to do so.
- Diversification. When you invest in mutual funds, you are diversifying because mutual funds purchase various stocks and bonds. When you have enough money to invest in more than one fund, you can further diversify by buying shares in funds with different investment objectives. For example, you can buy some shares in

riskier aggressive mutual funds and limit the risk by purchasing shares in more conservative funds.

- Liquidity. Mutual funds allow you to convert your shares into cash at any time. However, there is some risk of loss if the fund's price is low when you choose to sell.
- Small initial and ongoing purchases. Many funds require only a small minimum investment. Once you buy into a fund, you can make additional purchases as often as you like. Also, by pooling your money with other investors in the fund, you can own, for example, part of a $10,000 government bond without having to pay $10,000 to buy the whole bond yourself.

Mutual Fund Risk

Individual funds within a family have different investment goals and risk levels. In their publications and websites, investment companies describe each fund's investment goals and level of risk. You can choose funds that match your goals and risk tolerance. As with any investment, the greater the potential return, the higher the risk. **Figure 18.9** shows the general risk/return profiles for general categories of mutual funds.

Growth Fund

A **growth fund** is a mutual fund whose investment goal is to buy stocks that will increase in value over time. To do this, the fund managers select stocks in companies that reinvest their profit in the company

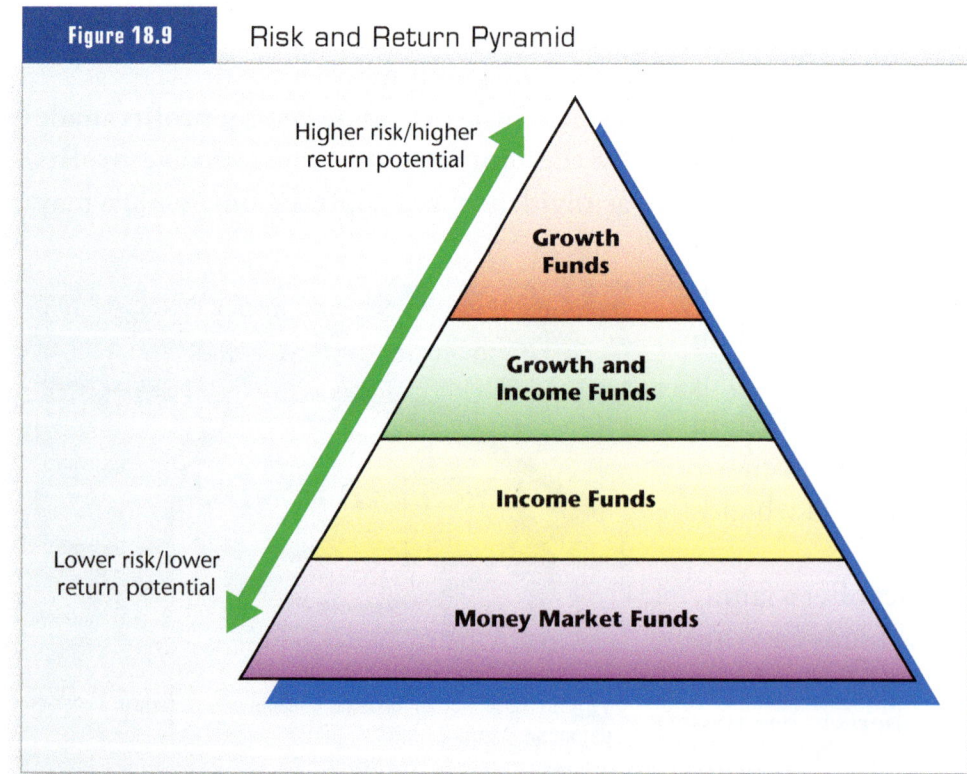

Figure 18.9 Risk and Return Pyramid

Higher risk/higher return potential

Growth Funds

Growth and Income Funds

Income Funds

Money Market Funds

Lower risk/lower return potential

rather than distribute it to investors as dividends. Investors in growth funds earn their return through capital gains rather than dividends.

There are different levels of growth funds. An aggressive growth fund invests in the stock of new or out-of-favor companies and industries that the fund managers think will achieve above-average increases in value. The philosophy behind aggressive growth funds is to accept high risk of loss in exchange for a chance to earn high returns. Other growth funds follow a less risky philosophy. They invest in more stable companies that the fund managers expect to increase in value but at a slower, steadier rate than the stocks of aggressive growth funds.

Income Funds

An **income fund** is a mutual fund whose investment goal is to produce current income on a steady basis in the form of interest or dividends. Investors in income funds seek income from their investments now rather than capital gains later. Income funds are of low-to-moderate risk and are less risky than growth funds.

Some income funds specialize in tax-exempt bonds. Their goal is to provide tax-free income for investors. Tax-exempt bond funds appeal to investors in high-income tax brackets.

Growth and Income Funds

A **growth and income fund** is a mutual fund whose investment aims to earn returns from dividends and capital gains. Managers of these funds try to select stocks that pay dividends and stocks that increase in market value over time. The risk level of this type of fund is moderate—between the riskier growth funds and less risky income funds.

A **balanced fund** is a mutual fund that seeks growth and income but attempts to minimize risk by investing in a mixture of stocks and bonds rather than stocks alone. Like growth and income funds, the goal of a balanced fund is to earn returns from current income and capital gains. Balanced funds have moderate risk. They are less risky than growth and income funds that invest only in stocks.

Money Market Funds

A **money market fund** is a mutual fund that invests in safe, liquid securities, such as Treasury bills and bonds that mature in less than a year. These short-term maturities provide modest current income with little risk. The goals of a money market fund are the preservation of principal and high liquidity.

Many investors put their money into money market funds during unfavorable market conditions. For example, if returns from income funds are dropping, an investor might transfer their balance to a money market fund until the income funds rise again.

Global Funds

A **global fund** is a mutual fund that purchases international stocks and bonds as well as U.S. securities. Global funds fall into various risk categories, depending on the investment objective of the individual fund. For example, a global fund can be risky if its goal is to invest in aggressive growth international stocks, whereas a global fund that invests in a conservative mix of international stocks and bonds would be less risky. However, most global funds have risks that U.S. stock funds do not have. Fluctuations

Sharpen Your Employability Skills
Investment Decisions

Zander and Mila dated for a few years and recently got married. They are having difficulty deciding what investments to make and how much money to keep in liquid savings. As outlined in the start of the chapter, Zander is a risk-taker and wants to do aggressive, high-risk investing; Mila is risk averse and wants to put all their savings into a money market account.

How can Zander and Mila resolve their investment perspective into one that is compatible for both? What kinds of stock or other investment would you suggest they invest in to meet their needs now and in the future?

Create a slide deck, write a one-page report, or create another form of media presentation that outlines your investing advice.

in currency exchange rates and political instability in other countries can affect the value of global stocks. These uncertainties make global funds generally riskier than U.S. stock funds.

Index Funds

An index is an average of the price movements of certain selected securities. Investors use indexes as benchmarks for comparison to judge how well their investments are doing. An **index fund** is a mutual fund that tries to match the performance of a particular index by investing in the companies included in that index. For example, an index fund might invest in companies included in the Standard & Poor's 500 or Dow Jones Industrial Average indexes. The risk level of an index fund depends on the index to which it is tied. Since the Dow includes only blue chip stocks, funds tied to this index would be relatively low risk. The NASDAQ Composite index, on the other hand, includes stocks of some volatile high-tech companies. Funds tied to this index could be risky.

One type of index fund is an **exchange-traded fund (ETF)**. An ETF is a pooled investment security like a mutual fund. Like a mutual fund, the ETF tracks an index fund or similar security. The primary difference between a mutual fund and an ETF is that investors can purchase an ETF on the stock exchange just like a regular stock. The first ETF was the SPDR S&P 500 fund with the ticker symbol SPY. It tracks the S&P 500 Index. One advantage of an ETF is low expense ratios and lower broker commissions than purchasing individual stock.

✓ Checkpoint

Describe the different types of mutual funds.

Buying and Selling Mutual Funds

Thousands of mutual funds cover the whole range of investment objectives and risk levels. You must know your investment goals and risk tolerance to choose the right mutual fund for you. Do you want income from your investments now, or can you wait for capital gains in the future? Do you need a tax-free or tax-deferred investment to reduce your current income taxes? Are you comfortable risking your investment for big returns, or do you prefer a safe but lower return? Once you know your own requirements, you can read about the objectives and risk profiles of different funds and find one that matches your requirements.

Selecting a Mutual Fund Company

The most important decision you will make with mutual fund investing is selecting the right company or companies. Because mutual fund investments are not insured, the investor is taking a risk when placing money with these companies. Conducting extensive research on potential mutual fund companies is an important factor in selecting a mutual fund company.

To reduce your risk, you should choose a mutual fund company with the following characteristics:

- It has been in business for 20 or more years.
- It has a good track record of providing solid returns to its investors.
- It is a large company that manages investments for millions of investors.
- It is a well-known company that is highly respected among investment advisers and experts.

- It exists both in brick-and-mortar and in cyberspace.
- It is customer-friendly and responsive to customer questions and needs.
- It provides customers with easy-to-read statements and reports and offers daily online access.

Sources of Mutual Fund Information

Financial publications such as *Forbes*, *Fortune*, and *Money* regularly review and rank mutual funds. They compare 1-year, 5-year, and 10-year performances of various funds with similar objectives.

A great deal of information about mutual funds is available online. The Morningstar website issues reports that compare mutual funds. At the Yahoo! Finance website, you can get up-to-date news and market data on mutual funds. Another good website is the Mutual Fund Investor's Center. In addition to educational information and news articles, the site features daily pricing and performance information on more than 7,000 mutual funds. You can also search for the sites of fund families by name, such as Dreyfus and Vanguard. You can find detailed descriptions at these sites, including risk/return profiles for all funds in their fund families.

The Prospectus

You can refer to its prospectus to find information on the mutual funds a company offers. A **prospectus** is a legal document issued by an investment company that details the securities it offers for sale. A fund prospectus contains a summary of the fund's portfolio of investments, its objectives and investment strategies, and financial statements showing past performance.

In the United States, companies are legally required to provide potential buyers with a prospectus. They are also required to file their prospectus with the Securities and Exchange Commission (SEC). You can find company prospectuses at EDGAR, a database maintained by the SEC. You may also find a company's prospectus on its corporate website.

Costs and Fees

You can buy and sell mutual funds through a broker or through the fund company directly. If you buy a mutual fund through a broker, you will likely have to pay a sales fee, called a **load**. The broker's commission comes from this fee. A front-end load is a sales charge paid when you buy an investment. Sometimes you pay this fee on reinvested dividends as well. A back-end load is a sales charge paid when you sell an asset. Either way, loads can range from 2 to 8 percent of the value of the shares purchased.

Sometimes, you can buy mutual funds directly from investment companies by phone or on their websites. This kind of fund, a no-load fund, does not charge a sales fee when you buy or sell because no salespeople are involved.

Mutual fund companies make money by charging fees to their customers for the professional services provided. Funds often charge an annual management fee, which averages about 1 to 1.5 percent of a fund's total assets. This charge is for the services of professional fund managers and for maintaining your account. The fund may also charge a 12b-1 fee to cover the costs of marketing and distributing a mutual fund. These fees are part of the fund's expense ratio, expressed as a percentage of assets deducted yearly for fund expenses. Mutual funds publish their expense ratios with their fund descriptions. When you consider investing in mutual funds, compare expense ratios as part of your evaluation.

Connections to Your World
Checking Investment Balances

Some investors believe that once you have selected a mutual fund, you should check on it only periodically—maybe once every year or two—and resist making changes. Others believe that it is important to check your account balances almost daily. These investors frequently move their balances from one fund to another as they constantly look for choices that pay higher returns.

Think Critically

1. Which view do you agree with? Explain.
2. How often do you think you should check your investment balances and make changes? Why?

Mutual Fund Prices

Unlike stocks, mutual fund prices are not determined by what people are willing to pay for them. The net asset value determines them. The **net asset value (NAV)** tells you the market price for a share of a mutual fund. The NAV is the total value of a fund's investment portfolio minus its liabilities, divided by the number of outstanding shares of the fund.

$$NAV = \frac{\text{Value of Portfolio} - \text{Liabilities}}{\text{Number of Shares}}$$

For example, suppose the value of all stocks in a fund's portfolio is currently $100,000. The fund has $90,000 in liabilities and has sold 500 shares of its fund to investors. The price for one of its shares, or its NAV, would be $20.

$$\frac{\$100,000 - \$90,000}{500} = \$20$$

Because the portfolio's value changes as stocks and other securities are traded throughout the day, the NAV is calculated at the end of each business day. Thus, the value of your investment depends on that fund's performance in the securities market.

✓ **Checkpoint**

What are some factors to consider when selecting a mutual fund company?

Check Your Understanding

1. Why are mutual funds an important part of an investment strategy? (LO 18.4.1)

2. How are mutual funds bought and sold? (LO 18.4.2)

Apply Your Understanding

1. Describe the type of investor (in terms of goals and risk tolerance) who would be interested in each of the following types of mutual funds: (a) growth funds, (b) income funds, (c) growth and income funds, and (d) money market funds. (LO 18.4.1)

2. You want to begin investing in mutual funds but do not know where to start. Create a flowchart that identifies the steps you should follow. At each step in the flowchart, add questions that you should think about and answer before moving to the next stage. (LO 18.4.2)

The Essential Question

Why are mutual funds a good investment for less experienced investors, what types of mutual funds are available, and how do you buy and sell mutual funds?

A: Mutual funds are good investments for less experienced investors because they are operated by professional fund managers, are comprised of a diversified group of investments, are highly liquid, require only a small minimum investment, and are focused on particular investment goals. Mutual fund types include growth funds, growth and income funds, income funds, and money market funds. You purchase mutual funds through a securities exchange, in the same manner used to purchase stocks and bonds.

Summary

18.1 Buying and Selling Securities

- The securities market consists of channels where securities can be bought and sold.

- Securities include stocks, bonds, and other financial investments.

- Securities can be bought and sold in a securities marketplace, a securities exchange, or over the counter (by phone, computer, or mobile app).

- A securities exchange is a form of auction market where stock is sold to the highest bidder (buyer) and bought from the lowest offeror (seller).

- The largest exchange in the United States is the New York Stock Exchange (NYSE).

- Investing can be approached through short- or long-term strategies.

- Short-term investors are speculators with higher risk tolerance who try to make a quick profit by buying on margin or selling short.

- Long-term investment strategies are generally lower risk and include buy and hold, dollar-cost averaging, and reinvestment of dividends.

18.2 Investing in Stocks

- Investing in stocks is a way to build wealth and reach long-term financial goals.

- When you buy a share of stock, you purchase ownership interest in a company. People who own shares of stocks are called stockholders.

- Public corporations are companies whose stock is traded openly on stock markets.

- Stockholders profit through dividends and capital gains.

- Common stocks pay a variable dividend and give stockholders voting rights.

- Preferred stocks pay a fixed dividend, which is less risky than common stocks, but stockholders do not have voting rights.

- Stocks generally fall into the following categories: income stocks, growth stocks, blue chip stocks, emerging stocks, cyclical stocks, and defensive stocks.

- Corporations that issue income stocks pay profits to stockholders in the form of dividends, whereas corporations that issue growth stocks reinvest profits in the business so that it can grow.

- Blue chip stocks provide a relatively safe but moderate return.

- Emerging stocks are issued by young, often small, companies and have a higher overall risk.

- Cyclical stocks are affected by ups and downs in the economy. They do well when the economy is growing but do poorly during recessions.

- Defensive (noncyclical) stocks are not affected by the ups and downs of business cycles. They remain relatively stable during both good and bad economic times.

- Par value is an assigned dollar value given to each share of stock. It has nothing to do with the market value, which is the price investors pay for a stock.

- Stock price depends on the company's financial situation, current interest rates, the market for the company's products or services, the company's earnings per share, and the current conditions of the stock market.

- Dividends and capital gains are used to determine a stock's return on investment (ROI).

- Investors use stock indexes to judge the performance of their investments. The Dow Jones Industrial Average is the oldest and most widely known stock index.

- You can track your stock's progress by reading the stock listings online and in print publications.

18.3 Investing in Bonds

- Bonds are loans that a corporation or government body must repay at face value, with interest. They are a fixed-rate investment because they pay a specified amount of interest at regular intervals.

- All bonds have a maturity date, or a date when the bonds can be redeemed.

- Types of corporate bonds include debentures, secured bonds, convertible, callable, and zero-coupon bonds.

- Debentures are unsecured bonds. Secured bonds (such as mortgage bonds) are secured by a specific asset.

- Owners of convertible bonds can exchange their bonds for common stock if they want to take advantage of higher stock prices.

- A callable bond may be "called" (paid off) by the issuer before maturity.

- Zero-coupon bonds sell at a deep discount and make no interest payments until maturity. Holders make money by selling them at a profit before maturity or redeeming them at face value at maturity.

- Government bonds are issued by the federal government as well as by state and local governments. The four major types of government bonds are municipal bonds, savings bonds, Treasury securities, and agency bonds.

- Municipal bonds generally are tax-free. Revenue bonds are issued to raise money for public projects. General obligation bonds are backed by the power of the issuing government unit to levy taxes to pay back the debt.

- U.S. savings bonds and Treasury securities are considered one of the safest investments because they are backed by the full faith and credit of the U.S. government.

- Agency bonds are issued by government agencies and by government-sponsored enterprises.

- You can buy corporate, municipal, and agency bonds through a bank or broker. U.S. savings bonds can be purchased only at the TreasuryDirect website, while Treasury securities can be purchased at the TreasuryDirect website or through a bank or broker.

- Investors can earn a return on bonds from interest, by redeeming the bonds for their face value at maturity, or by selling them before maturity for a price higher than they paid for them.

- Bonds whose interest rates are higher than the current market rate will sell at a premium. Bonds whose interest rates are lower than the current market rate will sell at a discount.

- Rating services rate bonds based on the financial condition of the issuing corporation or municipality. Investment-grade bonds are the highest-quality, lowest-risk bonds. Junk bonds have a low rating.

- Bond listings are extensive tables that contain information about bonds in recent trades.

18.4 Investing in Mutual Funds

- A mutual fund is a professionally managed group of investments.

- Mutual funds use money pooled from many investors to buy securities that fit the fund's stated objectives.

- Investors choose mutual funds for their professional management, diversification, liquidity, and relatively small minimum investment required.

- Individual funds within a mutual fund family have different investment goals and risk levels.

- Growth funds invest in stocks that are expected to earn future capital gains, whereas income funds invest to provide current income on a steady basis in the form of interest and dividends.

- Growth and income funds as well as balanced funds seek returns from both dividends and capital gains.

- Money market funds invest in safe, liquid securities.

- Global funds invest in international stocks and bonds as well as U.S. securities.

- Index funds try to match the performance of a particular index.

- To evaluate a mutual fund, examine its prospectus and other information about the fund and learn about the fees involved. A great deal of information is available online.

- Mutual fund prices are determined by net asset value (NAV). This is calculated as the total value of the fund's investments minus its liabilities, divided by the number of outstanding shares.

Check Your Knowledge

1. What is a securities exchange? (LO 18.1.1)

2. Describe the over-the-counter (OTC) market. (LO 18.1.1)

3. What is the main difference between short-term and long-term investment strategies? (LO 18.1.2)

4. List the different types of stocks and discuss the advantages and disadvantages of each. (LO 18.2.1)

5. Explain the difference between par value and market value. Explain which is most useful in determining a stock's actual value for the investor. (LO 18.2.2)

6. How would you know the amount of and the date you would receive a dividend? (LO 18.2.3)

7. Explain the difference between various types of corporate bonds. (LO 18.3.1)

8. Which government bonds are exempt from income taxes? Identify the type of bond and the exemption for each. (LO 18.3.2)

9. What are the risks and returns of owning bonds? (LO 18.3.3)

10. How do interest rates impact the selling price of bonds? (LO 18.3.4)

11. List and explain three advantages and three disadvantages of investing in mutual funds. (LO 18.4.1)

12. How can you invest in mutual funds? (LO 18.4.2)

1. List the pros and cons of using online brokerage platforms versus traditional brokerage services. How would the type of brokerage account influence an investor's strategy? Which type of service would you prefer to use? Explain your choice. (LO 18.1.1)

2. Consider the type of investor who is best suited to be a day trader. Do you have the characteristics to be a day trader? Why or why not? (LO 18.1.2)

3. Your neighbors, Mr. and Mrs. Nelson, are in their late 50s and plan to retire within the next 5 years. They want to take some of the money they have saved through the years and invest in the stock market. Which of these options would you recommend to them: Income or growth? Blue chip or emerging? Cyclical or defensive? Give a brief reason for each choice. (LO 18.2.1)

4. Suppose you purchased 100 shares of stock in January for $48 a share. You received dividends of $1.25 a share on April 1 and July 1 and $0.95 a share on September 1. You sold the stock in December for $50 a share. What would be the stock's return on investment for the year? Assume a broker commission of 3 percent on the purchase and 3 percent on the sale of the stock. (*Hint:* Use the formula in Figure 18.1.) (LO 18.2.2)

5. Your brother bought stock using an online stock app. When he was checking his stock, he noticed that a dividend had been reinvested. He did not know the stock had a dividend. Explain to your brother how he would know what date the dividend would be paid and how much the dividend would be. (LO 18.2.3)

6. You bought a $10,000, 6 percent corporate bond at face value that matures in 5 years. What would be your total earnings during that 5-year period? (LO 18.3.1)

7. A new bond you are considering buying has a face value of $1,000; an interest rate of 5 percent; and a maturity date 8 years away. The average market price of the bond is 104. What is the yield? What amount of interest would you earn in that period? (LO 18.3.3)

8. Xiaodon is trying to read the bond listings for an assignment. Explain to her the difference between a bond that is quoted at 99 versus a bond that is trading at 102. (LO 18.3.4)

9. Your friend, Levi, is 16 years old and wants to retire when he is 65. He plans to invest the maximum amount into a Roth IRA every year. Use an online Roth IRA calculator to calculate how much Levi would have in the account when he turns 65. Assume that he can earn a rate of return at 7% and he is in the 22 percent tax bracket. (LO 18.4.1)

10. Research how to open a Roth IRA. Create an infographic or video to explain the process. (LO 18.4.2)

Share Your Knowledge

Work in teams of two to four students to complete the following activities.

1. The Securities and Exchange Commission (SEC) was formed in 1933 to protect investors from corporations that would deceive them into buying stock. Visit the SEC's website (www.sec.gov) and discuss the role of the SEC in the past and today. What does it do to protect investors? What kinds of reports do corporations file with the SEC that are made available to the public on the SEC's website? Create a slide deck to share your group's findings. (LO 18.1.1)

2. Visit the TreasuryDirect website (www.treasurydirect.gov) and find the answers to the questions below.

   a. What are STRIPS?
   b. How can you buy Treasuries from this site?
   c. How can you replace a lost, stolen, or destroyed savings bond? (LO 18.3.2)

3. Your group has been given $100,000 to invest. Research the best securities to invest in, assuming you have a long-term investment strategy for the next 40 years. What securities would you include? Calculate what the value of your portfolio would be today if you had started your investment strategy 5, 10, and 20 years ago. (Multiple LOs)

Connect and Reflect

Base your answers to the following questions on your own personal thoughts, preferences, and experiences.

1. Given your current circumstances, what would your personal investment strategy be? Explain your answer. (LO 18.1.2)

2. Many people select mutual funds based upon personal goals, such as environmental sustainability. To do this, you must understand your investment goals; research investment funds that match your goals; review the fund's holdings; and then consider the fund's environmental, social, and governance impact. Select one fund that meets your goals and explain why you selected this fund. (LO 18.4.1)

Chapter Project

Research the historical background of the NYSE, S&P 500, and NASDAQ using online sources. Create a product that illustrates the historical performance of each exchange. Explain the factors behind significant fluctuations in their values. Include recommendations for a young investor planning to use dollar-cost averaging as an investment strategy for the next 25 years.

Chapter 19

Real Estate Investing, Other Investments, and Retirement Planning

The Essential Question

How is investing in real estate, collectibles, and commodities similar and different in terms of risk and reward?

Learning Objectives

By the end of this lesson, you should be able to:

LO 19.1.1   Explain real estate investing, both direct and indirect.

LO 19.1.2   Describe other investments, including metals, gems, collectibles, and commodities.

Key Terms

- commercial property
- depreciation
- real estate investment trust (REIT)
- real estate syndicate
- certificate of participation (COP)
- precious metals
- gems
- commodities

Consider This ...

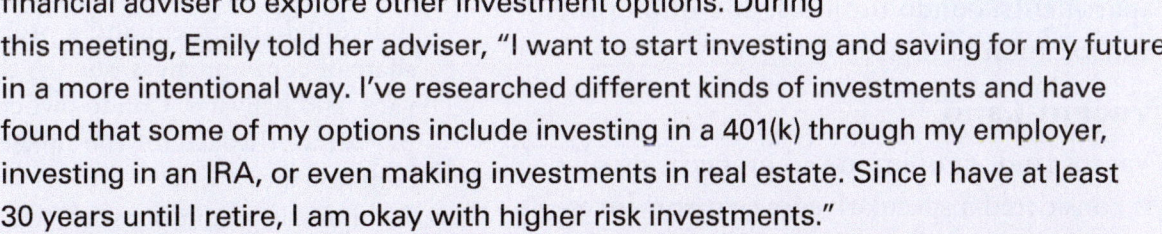

Emily has been working full-time for the past 10 years. She has established financial stability and wants to begin investing more for retirement. Upon reviewing her budget, Emily believes she can set aside 10 percent of income to invest toward her retirement.

Emily has been making small, consistent investments since she started working, but she recently met with a financial adviser to explore other investment options. During this meeting, Emily told her adviser, "I want to start investing and saving for my future in a more intentional way. I've researched different kinds of investments and have found that some of my options include investing in a 401(k) through my employer, investing in an IRA, or even making investments in real estate. Since I have at least 30 years until I retire, I am okay with higher risk investments."

Emily's financial adviser replied, "It's great that you're looking to invest now! You must know your goals and risk tolerance before we begin exploring investment options. Let's take a look at different options to see what is right for you!"

Read and Reflect

1. Why would Emily be willing to invest in higher risk investments right now? How might this be different for someone who plans to retire in 5 years?

2. What recommendations would you make to Emily as she explores investment options?

3. Why is investing at a young age important? How would waiting 10 years impact Emily's required investment to meet retirement goals?

Real Estate Investing

When investing in real estate, you buy land and any buildings on that land. **Commercial property** is land and buildings that produce income through leasing or renting. Such property includes office buildings, stores, hotels, duplexes, and multiunit apartments. Investing in real estate is an excellent way to combat inflation because it usually increases in value over the years at rates equal to or higher than inflation. However, real estate is one of the least liquid investments because a property can take months or even years to sell. Also, some real estate investments are speculative and can result in a substantial loss. You can invest in real estate directly or indirectly.

Direct Investing

With direct investing, the investor holds legal title to the property and controls management decisions. There are numerous types of real estate properties that you can buy directly. These include vacant land, single-family houses, rental properties (such as apartments, condominiums, and duplexes), and vacation homes.

Vacant Land

Vacant land, or unimproved property, usually is considered a speculative investment. Investors hold the property, expecting it to increase substantially in value over time. Other people purchase a vacant lot with plans for building a house or a small business. In either case, you may have to pay cash for vacant land. Because it is considered speculative, some banks are unwilling to make loans. When purchasing vacant land, it is essential to check zoning laws that regulate the type of structure built on the property.

Single-Family Houses

In addition to owning your own home, you can purchase a single-family house and rent it to others. Because the property is not owner-occupied, you may find that banks are reluctant to grant you a mortgage loan to buy a house as a rental property. As a condition for a loan, you may have to make a larger down payment or pay a higher interest rate.

When a renter takes possession of your house, you still have responsibilities as the owner. For example, you must maintain the premises in a livable condition. This involves running water, electricity, sewer or septic hookups, and routine maintenance.

Rental Properties

Several types of rental properties are designed for owners to rent to tenants continuously.

- An apartment complex is a large building or group of buildings that contain many housing units and have shared facilities such as a recreation area, clubhouse, laundry room, and parking lots.
- A condominium (or condo) is an individually owned unit in an apartment-style complex with shared ownership of common areas. The condo owner owns the individual apartment and a proportional share of common areas, such as the lobby, yard, and hallways. Condo owners usually pay a monthly fee for the upkeep of the common areas.
- A duplex is a building with two separate living units with a common wall. A triplex is a building with three individual housing units, while a quad has four individual housing units. Usually, the living areas are the same, with separate entrances.

By pooling your cash with other investors, you can afford to buy larger, more expensive property pieces. For example, if you and three others formed a partnership to buy an eight-unit apartment building, each of you

Do you think vacation homes are good investments? Why or why not?

would have to pay only one-fourth of the total costs of purchasing and maintaining the property.

Vacation Homes

Many people buy second homes for vacations, which may become their primary residence after they retire. Often, the owners rent these properties out to others to generate income when they are not using them.

Vacation property includes beaches, mountain cabins, and even vacant land near recreational sites such as rivers, lakes, or an ocean. The owner can use and enjoy the property on weekends and during vacations and rent out the property at other times using short-term rental agencies such as AirBnB and VRBO. However, absent owners may need to arrange for someone else to take care of the property and manage the rental process. Real estate companies in popular vacation areas can provide these services for a fee.

Buying and Owning Rental Property

When buying real estate directly, most people make a down payment and get a mortgage (or trust deed) to pay the balance.

A mortgage is a loan to purchase real estate. Borrowing money to buy an investment is called leverage, which means only a small amount of the purchase price is your own money. For example, if you buy a duplex for $300,000 and make a down payment of $60,000 (a 20 percent down payment is usually required for rental property), you borrow $240,000 from the bank. As the property gains in value, the mortgage payments remain fixed. When you eventually sell the property, you keep the difference between the sales price and the mortgage balance. This difference is the equity or ownership interest.

Monthly Payments

As your tenant makes rent payments, you pay the bank mortgage payments. You would use the difference between the amount of rent collected and the mortgage payment to pay property taxes and the cost of upkeep on the property. You have a positive cash flow if you have money left over after paying these expenses. If you cannot collect enough rent to pay the mortgage, property taxes, repairs, and maintenance, you have a negative cash flow and must make up the shortfall from your own pocket.

Managing Rental Property

To manage a multiunit rental property, you can be a resident landlord or hire a resident landlord or property manager. A resident landlord lives at the rental site, handles all repairs and maintenance, collects the rent, and assures suitable living conditions. A property manager collects rent, hires, and pays people to repair and maintain the property, charges a fee for their services, and remits the difference to the owner. Property managers do not live on-site and usually manage several rental properties simultaneously.

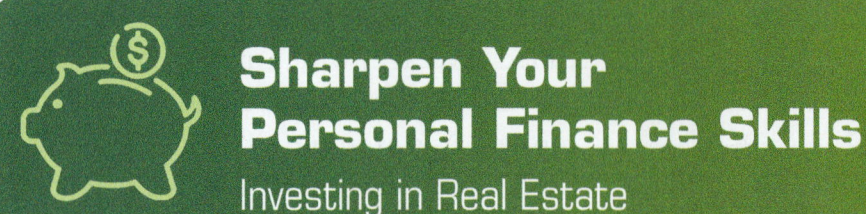

Emily has been working full-time and investing for 10 years. She has started investing in different types of investments to diversify her portfolio. Recently, Emily purchased a house that she plans to rent out. The purchase price of the house was $140,000. Emily took out a 20-year mortgage with a fixed interest rate of 4.85 percent; her monthly mortgage payment will be $912. In addition, Emily has gathered the following information as she evaluates her costs to set a rental price:

- Annual property taxes = $2,240
- Annual homeowners insurance = $1,130

Based on this information, Emily has determined that her monthly costs (not including potential repairs) are:

- Monthly mortgage payment = $912
- Monthly property taxes = ($2,240/12) = $186.67
- Monthly homeowners insurance = ($1,130/12) = $94.17
- Total monthly cost = ($912 + $186.67 + $94.17) = $1,192.84

Emily wants to be sure she saves for needed repairs that may come up and that she makes a profit on her investment. Initially she decides that she will add 10 percent of the total monthly cost to establish savings for future repairs and 10 percent for profit. This helped Emily find her rental price as outlined below:

- $1,192.84 × 0.1 = $119.28
- $1,192.84 + $119.28 + $119.28 = $1,431.40

Knowing that rental amounts are typically round numbers, Emily considered a rental price of $1,425 or $1,450. She decided on renting the property for $1,450 to provide a little more return on her investment.

Try It Out!

Emily has been successful renting her property and has decided to look at buying a second investment property. This house is smaller, so it does not cost as much. At the same time, she will not be able to charge as much in rent. Use the information below to calculate monthly costs and recommended rental price for this property:

- Purchase price = $90,000
- 15-year mortgage with a fixed interest rate of 4.25 percent
- Monthly mortgage payment = $715
- Annual property taxes = $1,425
- Annual homeowners insurance = $ 1,055

(continues)

(continued)

Emily wants to continue accounting for future repairs and profit on investment as outlined above.

What price would you recommend Emily set the monthly rent at for this property?

Think Critically

1. How is investing in real estate a long-term investment? Why would someone invest in real-estate if they were going to profit only $100 to $200 a month on a large financial investment?

2. The length of a mortgage can be 10 years, 15 years, 20 years, or 30 years. How does the length of a mortgage impact the return that the investor sees in the short term? How does the length impact the return the investor sees long term?

3. What recommendations would you make to someone who is considering investing in real estate?

Tax Advantages

Depreciation is the decline in property value due to normal wear and tear. Even though your property may be increasing in overall market value, you can deduct depreciation expense on your rental property when filing your tax return. In addition, property taxes and other costs of maintaining rental property can be deducted to help reduce the taxes you must pay on your rental income. However, when you sell your rental property, you must pay taxes on the capital gain.

Risks of Owning Rentals

It would be best to consider the risks of owning and renting property. Renters can damage or destroy your property far exceeding what a security deposit will cover. When your units have vacancies, your rental income will decline, yet you still must pay the mortgage and other expenses, thus cutting your profits.

Real estate is also subject to zoning laws and other local use restrictions. Cities have laws regulating what type of structure, for example, single-family residences, apartment complexes, and office buildings, can be built in each city area. Before buying property, you should check the zoning laws to ensure you can use the property as you intend.

Indirect Investing

With indirect investing, investors have a third person do the actual buying and selling of property. A trustee is an individual or institution that manages assets for someone else. The trustee holds the title to the property. Real estate investment trusts, real estate syndicates, and mortgage pools (in the form of certificates of participation) are examples of indirect investments using a third-party trustee.

Real Estate Investment Trusts

A **real estate investment trust (REIT)** is a corporation that pools the money of many individuals to invest in a diversified class of properties. Properties may include warehouses, shopping malls, apartment buildings, and hotels. A REIT is like a mutual fund in that it makes all buy-and-sell decisions for properties. REITs may invest in the properties themselves, generating income through rent collection, or they may invest in mortgages tied to the properties, generating revenue through the interest they earn on the mortgage loans.

REITs allow you to invest in portfolios of large-scale properties through the purchase of shares of stock. You can buy and sell REIT shares at will, making them highly liquid. REITs are traded on stock exchanges or over the counter. Like stocks, REIT shares fluctuate with market conditions, and dividends are paid when the real estate investments do well. REIT listings can be found online at various financial websites.

Real Estate Syndicates

A **real estate syndicate** (often called a limited partnership) is a group of investors who pool their money to purchase high-priced real estate as a short-term investment. This is a temporary association of individuals organized to raise a large amount of capital. A real estate syndicate often owns several properties for diversification, which are managed professionally. Unlike a REIT that pays dividends periodically, a real estate syndicate only distributes cash at the end of the investment.

The organizer of the syndicate is called the general partner or syndicator. The people who contribute capital are called limited partners. In a real estate syndicate, the general partner forms a partnership and assumes unlimited liability for all the obligations or debts of the partnership. Assuming unlimited liability, the general partner's responsibility extends beyond the initial investment to their assets if the investment incurs debt. The general partner then sells participation units to limited partners whose liability is limited to the amount of their investment. This means the limited partners can lose no more than they invested if the investment fails. Limited liability is significant in real estate partnerships because the mortgage acquired to purchase real estate often exceeds the net worth of the individual partners.

Certificates of Participation

A **certificate of participation (COP)** is an investment in a pool of mortgages purchased by a government agency or government-sponsored enterprise. COPs (also known as pass-through securities) are issued by the Government National Mortgage Association (Ginnie Mae), the Federal Home Loan Mortgage Corporation (Freddie Mac), and the Federal National Mortgage Association (Fannie Mae). As the name suggests, the cash flow from the mortgage payments is passed through to the investor through monthly payments of principal and interest.

COPs are also issued when individuals buy shares of lease revenues associated with government projects. Payments are made to the investor for the project's duration, based on the percentage of shares the investor has in the lease agreement.

✓ Checkpoint

What are some types of direct and indirect real estate investments?

LO 19.1.2 Other Investing Choices

You may invest your money in just about anything you think will bring you a return in value over time or provide some other form of income. Often these choices depend on personal values and tastes.

Metals, Gems, and Collectibles

Investments in this category are often speculative. They can return large profits or losses when sold. Sometimes, the investment's enjoyment will far exceed any resale value. Although expensive, precious metals, gems, and collectibles are easy to purchase. However, they can be tough to sell quickly and do not provide any current income in the form of interest or dividends. Therefore, be cautious when making this type of investment.

Precious Metals

Precious metals are tangible metals with known and universal value worldwide. Examples include gold, silver, and platinum. They are usually rare, natural substances that have high economic value. However, prices of precious metals can swing widely over

Sharpen Your Employability Skills
Thinking Critically about Bitcoin as an Investment

A bitcoin is a digital "currency" created in 2009 as open-source software by an unknown person using the alias of Satoshi Nakamoto. Bitcoins allow transactions without intermediaries—no banks or credit card companies. Without transaction fees, people can do business anonymously. Several online merchants have begun to accept bitcoins as a form of payment. There are differing views on the use of bitcoin. A bitcoin is not tied to any one country and is more difficult for countries to regulate. Some believe that this adds convenience by making international payments easy and cheap. Because they have been mostly unregulated, many governments are concerned about their lack of control over the currency and have made attempts to implement restrictions and regulations on the use of bitcoins. On the other hand, some countries and several private businesses have embraced the digital currency, accepting bitcoin as a form of legal tender and a viable investments option.

Think Critically

1. Some people buy bitcoins as an investment, expecting them to increase in value. Would you consider investing in bitcoins? Explain.
2. Do you think bitcoins have become an integral part of the global financial system since being introduced in 2009? Will this change in the future? Explain.
3. Do you see bitcoin as a possible competitor to paper currency? Why or why not?

time. These swings are what make investments in precious metals very risky.

You can buy gold, silver, and platinum as coins, medallions, jewelry, and bullion. Storing precious metals safely may be a problem because of bulk and weight. Instead of keeping your investment, you can buy gold and silver as a certificate stating how much you own of the metal being stored for you. You can also own gold indirectly by investing in gold-mining stocks or mutual funds specializing in these stocks. Other metals you can invest in include aluminum, tin, copper, lead, nickel, and zinc. Prices for precious metals can be found in the financial pages of newspapers and online at various financial sites.

Gems and Jewelry

Gems are natural, precious stones like diamonds, rubies, sapphires, and emeralds. Their prices are high and subject to drastic change. Gems have their most significant value as jewelry. However, when you purchase jewelry at retail prices, you are paying 50 to 500 percent or more in markups. Prices must increase substantially in the world market before you can recover the cost and make a profit from reselling your jewelry.

Why might you want to avoid investing in gems?

The most significant disadvantage of investing in gems is the risk that you will not be able to resell them. The gems market can be tiny and unpredictable, and no ready need may exist when you decide to sell. The process of buying and selling can also be hazardous, as most such transactions require the use of cash. Fraud is also a common risk that investors will face when purchasing gems. Judging whether a stone is natural can be tricky unless you work with a professional appraiser. However, despite these drawbacks, the returns from investing in gems can be high.

Collectibles

Collectibles are physical assets that appreciate value over time because they are rare or desired by many. Collectibles can be things such as antiques, art, baseball cards, stamps, and comic books. Collectibles are valuable because they are old, no longer produced, unusual, irreplaceable, or historic. Coins are the most collected items. Silver coins often are worth more than 20 times their face value.

People collect items in hopes that someday their collection will be valuable. If you collect an item that goes up in value rapidly, you can reap significant rewards. Unfortunately, collectibles can take a very long time to increase in value and may not increase in value at all, making them a risky investment. If you want to be a collector, buy what you can personally appreciate and enjoy through the years, knowing that your collection may or may not result in a profit when you decide to sell it.

Commodities

Commodities are products that are mined or grown. These include farm products (such as wheat, corn, and cattle) and metals (such as gold and silver). Commodity prices are volatile

Sharpen Your Employability Skills
Researching Collectibles as an Investment Option

Collectibles attract a specific type of investor. They can be found almost any-where—swap meets, flea markets, antique stores, auctions, and garage sales. They also can be found on several websites. All types of things are offered to buy, sell, and exchange.

Use the internet to research collectibles and find listings for collectibles that are for sale.

Based on your research, answer the following questions:

1. What types of items are most commonly considered collectibles?
2. What types of collectibles may be purchased as an investment?
3. Would you consider buying collectibles as a potential investment? Explain.

Prepare a summary of your findings to share in a class discussion.

because commodity supply and demand are disrupted by all kinds of largely unpredictable situations, from political upheaval to the weather.

Commodities may be sold for cash or traded in the futures market. A futures contract obliges the buyer to purchase or the seller to sell stock or a commodity for a specified price on a selected date in the future. People enter the futures market for protection against volatile prices. For example, a farmer could agree to deliver 5,000 bushels of wheat one year from today at a specific price. In this case, the farmer knows what they will earn for the grain in advance. If prices of wheat fall during the year, the farmer can make money because they are being paid a set price; if prices rise, however, the farmer will lose money. Thus, trading in futures can be hazardous.

An option is the right, but not the obligation, to buy (or sell) stock or a commodity for a specified price within a specified period. A call option is a right to purchase shares of stock at a set price by a specific expiration date. You can exercise the right at any time before the option expires. A put option is the right to sell stock at a fixed price until expiration. An investor who thinks a stock's price will increase during a short period of time may decide to purchase a call option. On the other hand, an investor who feels a stock's price will decrease during a short time may buy to safeguard the investment. Options are risky business and not for the inexperienced investor.

✓ Checkpoint

Why are investments in real estate, collectibles, and commodities risky?

19.1 Lesson Review

Check Your Understanding

1. What are some advantages of owning real estate as an investment? (LO 19.1.1)

2. How is direct investing in real estate different from indirect investing? (LO 19.1.1)

3. Why do collectibles often not increase in value over a long period of time? (LO 19.1.2)

4. What is the purpose of a futures contract? (LO 19.1.2)

Apply Your Understanding

1. Describe what it would be like to be a landlord (your responsibilities and duties) if you owned: (a) a single-family house rented to a family, (b) an eight-unit apartment building where you were the resident landlord, and (c) a second home on the beach that you rented to vacationers. (LO 19.1.1)

2. How would including nontraditional assets like cryptocurrency, gems, or real estate impact the risk and return for investment portfolios? Discuss the potential benefits and challenges of diversifying with nontraditional assets. (LO 19.1.2)

The Essential Question

How is investing in real estate, collectibles, and commodities similar and different in terms of risk and reward?

A: Real estate, collectibles, and commodities are similar in that they can be difficult to sell and can sometimes result in large losses when sold. However, real estate investments have ongoing value, whereas collectibles and commodities do not provide any current income until sold.

The Essential Question | What are the factors to consider when determining retirement needs, and how does estate planning minimize taxes?

Learning Objectives

By the end of this lesson, you should be able to:

LO 19.2.1 Explain the factors to consider when determining retirement needs for most individuals and families.

LO 19.2.2 Discuss estate planning documents and methods to minimize taxes on estates.

Key Terms

- appreciation
- reverse mortgage
- estate
- will
- codicil
- trust
- probate
- power of attorney
- estate tax
- inheritance tax
- gift tax

LO 19.2.1 Retirement Needs

When you retire, you will want to have enough financial resources to live comfortably. At that point, many people also want to be able to afford to do the things they did not have time for while working. There may need to be more than just Social Security and a retirement plan to cover living costs because inflation will decrease the purchasing power of your retirement savings.

How Much Income Will You Need?

Many financial advisers suggest you need between 75 and 85 percent of your preretirement income to live comfortably. This percentage may seem high, and you may wonder how you can have that kind of income when you are no longer working. To achieve a comfortable retirement, most people need to limit current spending and start saving at the beginning of their work life.

There will be times when you will not have much cash to set aside. You may be paying for a college education, cars, houses, furniture, and other things for your family. However, it is important to save when you can. As your expenses go down, you can save more. With regular saving and investing, your nest egg will grow.

Why is it important to save for retirement during your work life?

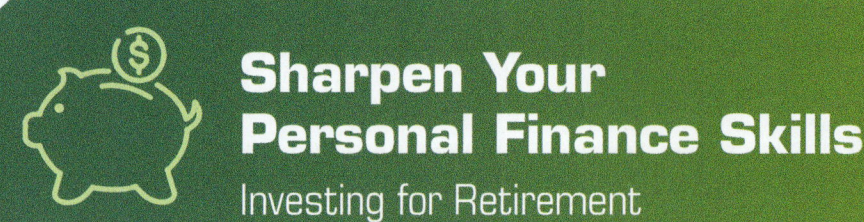

Sharpen Your Personal Finance Skills
Investing for Retirement

When Emily met with her financial advisor, the importance of investing for retirement at a young age was emphasized. Assuming that Emily can invest $435 a month (10 percent of her income), earns 7 percent return (compounded annually) on her investment, and will retire when she is 67, her financial advisor created the following table:

Age When Investments Begin	Monthly Investment Amount	Total Dollars Invested before Retirement	Investment Balance at Retirement
22	$435	$234,900	$1,538,883
25	$435	$219,240	$1,242,054
30	$435	$193,140	$ 863,486
35	$435	$167,040	$ 593,572
40	$435	$140,940	$ 401,127
45	$435	$114,840	$ 263,917
50	$435	$ 88,740	$ 166,088

Try It Out!

Emily wants to have $2,000,000 by the time she retires at age 67. Use the online investment calculator found at https://www.bankrate.com/investing/investment-goal-calculator/ or a similar site to find how much Emily would need to invest each month to reach her goal if she begins investing at 22 years old, 25 years old, 30 years old, and 40 years old. Assume she has no initial investment and that she expects to earn 8 percent annually on her investment.

Think Critically

1. Using the information above, explain the impact of compounding interest.
2. How would you explain the importance of investing at a young age to a friend who believes they can wait 10 or 20 years to start saving for retirement?

Keep the House or Move?

If you own a home, one decision in retirement may be whether to keep the home or move to a smaller living space or retirement home/community. Many people keep their house because they may no longer have a mortgage, and moving can be expensive. Others may choose to sell their home and find something smaller and easier to maintain. Current tax law allows married couples to sell the house they have lived in for at least 2 years without paying taxes on the profits of up to $500,000. For a single person, the tax-free profit limit is $250,000. Therefore, if you choose to sell your home, you can keep the proceeds.

The value of most homes appreciates, or increases in value, over time. **Appreciation** is one way that the equity in your home increases. Equity in a house is the difference between the property's market value, the amount for which you could sell your home now, and the mortgage balance. As you make mortgage payments over the years, the equity in your home increases while the mortgage decreases. However, equity is not income. It is money that is part of the property value. You can turn equity into income without selling your house by getting a reverse mortgage.

A **reverse mortgage** is a loan available to homeowners age 62 or older that allows them to convert their home equity into income. It works the opposite of a mortgage; hence the name reverse mortgage. Instead of the homeowner making payments to the lender, the lender makes tax-free monthly payments to the homeowner. This is a loan, however, and it must be repaid in the future. Also, there is a limit on the loan amount. Most reverse mortgages are a percentage of equity. The monthly payments to you will continue until they add up with interest to the agreed-upon loan limit. Once the full loan amount has been reached, you may have to sell the home or get a regular mortgage to pay off the loan. If you die during the loan term, your heirs must pay the loan. An heir is a person who will inherit property from someone who dies. Typically, heirs are the deceased's spouse and/or children. If the property must be sold to pay off the mortgage, the property will not pass to heirs.

What Type of Investment Strategy?

Retired people view investments from a different perspective than when they were younger. Rather than saving for the future, investors at this stage are trying to preserve their financial position. They want to maintain the principal while earning a reasonable return. Thus, fixed-income, low-risk investments become a more practical choice. Many retirees and people approaching retirement move more of their investments into low-risk options, trading high-potential earnings for lower, but more certain, returns. Also, because monthly income is often their main need, retirees may want to take dividends rather than reinvest them. They often move some of their money out of growth stocks, which earn capital gains in the future, and into income stocks and bonds that produce interest and dividends now.

How Much Insurance?

When you retire, your insurance needs also change. While your need for life insurance decreases, your need for other insurance increases.

For retired people, health insurance is crucial to ensure an illness or injury will not wipe out a lifetime of saving and investing. The rapidly rising cost of prescription medications may be a major obstacle, along with high payments for health insurance coverage. In the United States, Medicare is a national social insurance program administered by the U.S. government that guarantees access to health insurance for Americans age 65 and older who have worked and paid into the system. However, since you must be age 65 to be eligible for Medicare, there may be an interim period between your retirement and the start of your Medicare coverage. In this case, you

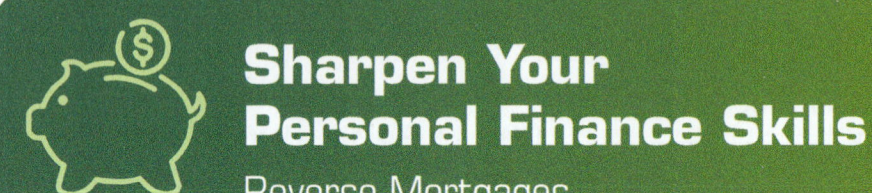

Sharpen Your Personal Finance Skills
Reverse Mortgages

A couple owns a home with a market value of $200,000. The unpaid mortgage balance is $40,000. With a reverse mortgage that allows them to borrow up to 80 percent of their equity, they could borrow $128,000 ($160,000 × 0.80). Amortized over their remaining life expectancy of 20 years and at 7 percent interest, how much could they receive in monthly payments? (*Hint:* Find a mortgage payment calculator online and plug in the years and the interest rate to determine payment.)

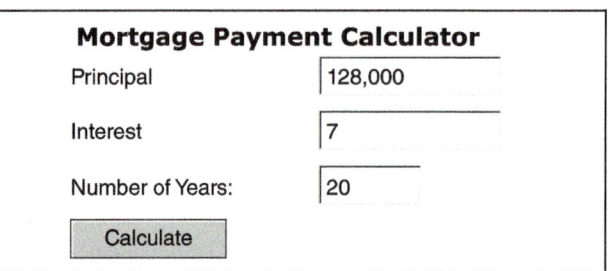

Mortgage Payment Calculator

Principal	128,000
Interest	7
Number of Years:	20

Calculate

Think Critically

1. What are pros and cons of reverse mortgages?
2. What happens if all equity is paid out in a reverse mortgage and the person is still living?
3. How does a reverse mortgage potentially impact more than the individual(s) taking out the reverse mortgage?
4. How could investing for retirement at an early age prevent the need for a reverse mortgage?

must pay for your health insurance. Also, Medicare may not cover all healthcare costs. So, you will likely need supplemental insurance to cover out-of-pocket expenses. In addition, retired people may need coverage for long-term care in a nursing facility.

How Do You Beat Inflation?

The probable loss of buying power due to inflation is one reason that planning for retirement is so important. As you will recall, inflation is a general increase in prices. Because of inflation, the cost of living goes up over time. Price increases reduce buying power. For instance, if prices are increasing at a faster rate than your retirement income, you will have to cut out something from your budget or dip into your principal to maintain your living standard. Therefore, budgeting must continue throughout retirement. Many seniors choose to work part-time to earn more income to offset inflation.

What are the various goals of estate planning?

Source: iStock.com/Charday Penn

preparing a plan for transferring property during one's lifetime and at one's death. Your goals in estate planning should be to minimize taxes on the estate, to make known how you want your possessions distributed, and to provide for a smooth transfer of your possessions to your loved ones upon your death.

> ### ✓ Checkpoint
>
> What needs should a person consider as they create an investment strategy for retirement?

Estate Planning Tools

To provide for proper disposal of assets and to avoid taxes whenever possible, there are several good estate planning tools. These include wills, trusts, joint ownership of assets, and powers of attorney.

Wills

A **will**, or testament, is a legal document that tells how an estate is to be distributed when a person dies. The person who makes the will is called the testator. In your will, you name an executor or personal representative to carry out your wishes when you die.

Any person who is age 18 or older and of sound mind can make a legally valid will. If your estate is relatively uncomplicated, you can prepare a simple will yourself. A simple will is a short document listing the people you want to be your heirs and what you

LO 19.2.2 **Estate Planning**

An **estate** is all that a person owns, less debts owed, at the time of the person's death. When people die, their possessions pass to other people, either as directed by the person who died, called the decedent, or by the laws of the state in which the person died. The estate may be taxed by the federal and/or state governments. Estate planning involves want each to receive. A simple will takes a short time to prepare and is a standard document. Whether you draft your will or use a lawyer, you will need two witnesses to watch you sign the will. Usually, the witnesses must be people not mentioned in the will who are age 18 or older, unrelated to you, and able to attest to your mental competency when you signed the will. An example of a simple will is shown in **Figure 19.1**.

A holographic will is written in a person's own handwriting. It does not require witnesses. In some states, a handwritten will is legally valid if it is entirely written in your own handwriting, is dated and signed, and clearly expresses your intent to make it your will.

Figure 19.1   Simple Will

LAST WILL AND TESTAMENT OF ANTHONY JOHN HINTON

I, Anthony John Hinton, of the city of Dayton and state of Ohio, do make, publish, and declare this to be my Last Will and Testament in manner following:

FIRST: I direct that all of my just debts, funeral expenses, and the cost of administering my estate be paid by my personal representative hereinafter named.

SECOND: I give, devise, and bequeath to my beloved daughter, Carol Hinton Campbell, now residing in Englewood, New Jersey, that certain piece of real estate, with all improvements thereon, situated in the same city and at the corner of Hudson Avenue and Tenafly Road.

THIRD: All the remainder and residue of my property, real, personal, and mixed, I give to my beloved wife, Kimberly Sue Hinton, personal representative of this, my Last Will and Testament, and I direct that she not be required to give bond or security for the performance of her duties as such.

LASTLY: I hereby revoke any and all former wills by me made.

IN WITNESS WHEREOF, I have hereunto set my hand this tenth day of October, in the year two thousand --.

Anthony John Hinton
_____
Anthony John Hinton

We, the undersigned, certify that the foregoing instrument was, on the date thereof, signed and declared by Anthony John Hinton as his Last Will and Testament, in the presence of us who, in his presence and in the presence of each other, have, at his request, hereunto signed our names as witnesses of the execution thereof, this tenth day of October 20--; and we hereby certify that we believe the said Anthony John Hinton to be of sound mind and memory.

Vilbin Schaenbar
_____ residing at   251 Wonderly Avenue
                                Dayton, Ohio 45419-2521

Samuel Vance
_____ residing at   3024 James Hill Road
                                Kettering, Ohio 45429-2454

Irene Vasilhous
_____ residing at   423 Goldengate Drive
                                Centerville, Ohio 45459-2459

When handwritten, people may be more likely to contest the will, which means that a lawsuit is filed challenging the validity of the will.

A person can make a will and make small changes later. A **codicil** is a legal document that modifies parts of a will and reaffirms the rest. A will cannot be legally amended by crossing out or adding words, by removing or adding pages, or by making erasures. A codicil is drawn by an attorney and is executed and witnessed the same as a will.

When people die without a will, they are said to be intestate. In that event, the person's property is distributed according to the laws of the state where the decedent died. By having a valid will, you can control what your heirs get, rather than allowing the state to make those decisions. Property reverts to the state when a person dies without heirs.

Trusts

A **trust** is a legal document in which an individual, called the trustor, gives someone else, called the trustee, control of property for ultimate distribution to another person who is the beneficiary. The trustee may be a financial institution or a person, while the beneficiary can be one or multiple parties.

There are two types of trusts. A trust that exists during the lifetime of the trustor is called *inter vivos*, or a living trust. With a living trust, you simply transfer some property to a trustee, giving them instructions regarding its management and disposition while you are alive and after your death.

The other type of trust is called a testamentary trust or trust will. It takes effect upon the death of a trustor. This type of trust is often used when a trustor wants to leave assets to a beneficiary but does not want the beneficiary to receive the assets until a specified time. Such a trust can be valuable if your beneficiaries are minor children. For money and property to be left to a minor child, the child must have a legal guardian who accounts for the child's property and money. Parents of small children typically create trust wills to provide for their children's education and living expenses. Then the balance of the estate is given to the children at some later age when they have reached adulthood.

The purpose of a trust is twofold. First, trusts provide for beneficiaries who might need help to effectively manage assets for themselves. The trustee is held accountable for how money is spent and how the trust is administered. The trustee must file papers yearly with the court, reporting on how the trust is progressing. Also, the trustee typically receives a fee for these services. Second, a trust can minimize inheritance or estate taxes and avoid probate. **Probate** is the legal process of proving that a deceased person's will is valid and then administering and distributing that person's estate upon death. Probate can be a lengthy process because the estate pays all creditors and probate fees

How does joint ownership between spouses affect an estate?

before the balance of the estate is distributed to heirs. Property held in a trust is not subject to probate. Therefore, the property can pass to beneficiaries quickly without a prolonged court proceeding and without the costs of probate.

Joint Ownership

Many people opt to hold title to property through joint ownership. By putting property in joint ownership, two or more people own an undivided interest in the property. Joint ownership of property can exist between spouses, parents and children, other relatives, or any two or more people.

Joint tenancy between spouses is perhaps the most widely used property ownership arrangement. If you and your spouse own property as joint tenants with right of survivorship (JTWROS), the ownership is split 50/50 for the purpose of the estate. If one spouse dies, the surviving spouse automatically becomes the sole owner of the property. No legal action is necessary to transfer title. This form of ownership is commonly used for land, automobiles, residences, bank accounts, and securities.

Two or more people can own property without survivorship. This form of property ownership is known as tenancy in common. With tenancy in common, the interest in the property does not automatically pass to the remaining owners as in JTWROS. Instead, each owner leaves his or her share of the property to a beneficiary of his or her choosing.

Joint ownership offers many advantages over holding ownership of property singly. Upon death, title to the property automatically passes to the joint owner or named beneficiary, making probate unnecessary.

Joint ownership is also an effective way to avoid inheritance taxes in some states.

Power of Attorney

At some time in your life, you may become incapacitated and unable to make your own decisions. A **power of attorney** is a legal document authorizing someone to act on your behalf. For example, if you become incapable of caring for yourself, the power of attorney gives your appointed person the power to use money from your savings and other accounts or assets to pay your bills and hire people to care for you.

The power of attorney may be limited or general in time or in scope. A limited power of attorney may be good for a specified amount of time, such as 30 days or a year, or it may pertain to a particular transaction. A general power of attorney gives another person the right to act for you completely.

When you give a power of attorney to another person, you give that person the power to do anything you could have done. Therefore, you should choose a trusted family member, a proven friend, or a reputable and honest professional.

Figure 19.2 shows a power of attorney form. You can hire a lawyer to write your power of attorney, or you can do your own using a kit or software designed for creating legal documents. Often software packages for writing wills contain templates for creating powers of attorney. Websites such as LegalZoom also provide power of attorney forms.

Taxation of Estates

Federal and state governments levy various types of taxes that must be taken into consideration when planning your estate, including estate, inheritance, and gift taxes.

Figure 19.2   Power of Attorney Form

GENERAL POWER OF ATTORNEY

I, [YOUR FULL LEGAL NAME], residing at [YOUR FULL ADDRESS], hereby appoint
_____ of _____, as my Attorney-in-Fact ("Agent").

    I hereby revoke any and all general powers of attorney that previously have been signed by me. However, the preceding sentence shall not have the effect of revoking any powers of attorney that are directly related to my health care that previously have been signed by me.

    My Agent shall have full power and authority to act on my behalf. This power and authority shall authorize my Agent to manage and conduct all of my affairs and to exercise all of my legal rights and powers, including all rights and powers that I may acquire in the future. My Agent's powers shall include, but not be limited to, the power to:

1. Open, maintain, or close bank accounts (including, but not limited to, checking accounts, savings accounts, and certificates of deposit), brokerage accounts, and other similar accounts with financial institutions.

2. Sell, exchange, buy, invest, or reinvest any assets or property owned by me. Such assets or property may include income-producing or non-income-producing assets and property.

3. Purchase and/or maintain insurance, including life insurance upon my life or the life of any other appropriate person.

4. Take any and all legal steps necessary to collect any amount or debt owed to me, or to settle any claim, whether made against me or asserted on my behalf against any other person or entity.

5. Enter into binding contracts on my behalf.

6. Exercise all stock rights on my behalf as my proxy, including all rights with respect to stocks, bonds, debentures, or other investments.

7. Maintain and/or operate any business that I may own.

    My Agent shall be entitled to reasonable compensation for any services provided as my Agent. My Agent shall be entitled to reimbursement of all reasonable expenses incurred in connection with this Power of Attorney.

    My Agent shall provide an accounting for all funds handled and all acts performed as my Agent, if I so request or if such a request is made by any authorized personal representative or fiduciary acting on my behalf.

    This Power of Attorney shall become effective immediately, and shall not be affected by my disability or lack of mental competence, except as may be provided otherwise by an applicable state statute. This is a Durable Power of Attorney. This Power of Attorney shall continue effective until my death. This Power of Attorney may be revoked by me at any time by providing written notice to my Agent.

Dated _____, 20-- at _____, _____.

[YOUR SIGNATURE]
_____
[YOUR FULL LEGAL NAME]

[WITNESS' SIGNATURE]   [WITNESS' SIGNATURE]
_____   _____
[WITNESS' FULL LEGAL NAME]   [WITNESS' FULL LEGAL NAME]

STATE OF _____, COUNTY OF _____, ss:

    The foregoing instrument was acknowledged before me this _____ day of _____, 20-- by [YOUR FULL LEGAL NAME], who is personally known to me or who has produced _____ as identification.

_____
Signature of person taking acknowledgment

_____
Name typed, printed, or stamped

_____
Title or rank

_____
Serial number (if applicable)

Federal Estate Tax

The federal government levies an **estate tax**, which is a tax on property transferred from an estate to its heirs. An estate must be worth more than a certain amount to be subject to this tax. In 2023, the estate tax applied only to estates worth more than $12.9 million. The estate tax is paid from the assets of the estate before anything can be distributed to heirs. An estate may have to sell property or investments to pay this tax.

State Inheritance Tax

People who inherit property may also have to pay a separate state inheritance tax. The state **inheritance tax** is imposed on an heir who inherits property from an estate. The difference between the federal estate tax and a state inheritance tax lies in who pays the tax. The estate tax is deducted from the value of the estate before distribution to heirs, but the heir pays inheritance taxes on property received. The amount of tax is based on the value of the property in the estate. In states where inheritance taxes are imposed, laws vary widely as to the rate of taxation and the treatment of property to be taxed.

Federal Gift Tax

Gifts are a popular way of distributing some property to loved ones before death to avoid estate and inheritance taxes. However, you may be subject to federal gift tax if you give someone money or property during your life. A **gift tax** is applied to a gift of money or property. The gift tax is paid by the giver, not the receiver, of the gift.

In 2023, you could have given up to $17,000 per person per year without paying a gift tax. Spouses may use gift splitting, allowing married couples to combine their annual exclusion amounts. Therefore, in 2023, spouses together could have given as much as $34,000 to any one person, tax-free. For gifts that exceed the limit, you can either pay the tax on the excess or take advantage of the unified gift tax credit, which allows a person to give away up to a specific amount during their lifetime. Gifts to your spouse or to a charity are exempt from the gift tax.

The timing of the gift also matters. A gift of personal property given within 3 years of a person's death may be considered a gift in contemplation of death. In this event, the gift is included in the value of the estate, rather than the gift being subject to a separate federal gift tax that would be charged to the gift giver. The gift receiver would have to pay the appropriate inheritance taxes on the value of the gift.

It is important not to distribute property that you need to live comfortably prior to your death. One way to retain possession is to create a life estate. A life estate allows you to pass title to real property to a loved one but retain your right to live on the premises for as long as you live. This means that you cannot be evicted even after the property is in another person's name.

Federal/State Income Taxes

When someone dies, income taxes must be paid on the income that the decedent earned that year and on any income earned by the estate while its assets remain undistributed, such as interest or dividends. The executor or attorney representing the estate must file this tax return and pay the taxes from the estate before the estate can be distributed to heirs.

> ### ✓ Checkpoint
>
> What is the purpose of estate planning?

Check Your Understanding

1. What are the most common needs in retirement? (LO 19.2.1)
2. Why is it important to have a will? (LO 19.2.2)

Apply Your Understanding

1. At what age would you like to retire? Briefly describe your plans for retirement, such as travel and recreation. What things should you consider soon to meet your retirement goals? (LO 19.2.1)
2. Conduct online research to determine if a holographic will, or a will handwritten and signed by the testator, is legal in your state. If it is legal, what must be included in the document. If it is not legal, what is a legal will in your state? (LO 19.2.2)

The Essential Question

What are the factors to consider when determining retirement needs, and how does estate planning minimize taxes?

A: Planning for retirement involves such things as determining how much income you will need to live comfortably, deciding whether to keep your home or move, creating an investment strategy, determining your insurance needs, minimizing estate taxes, and preparing a plan for transferring property.

The Essential Question   What are personal, employer-sponsored, and government sources of retirement income?

Learning Objectives

By the end of this lesson, you should be able to:

LO 19.3.1   Discuss features and types of personal retirement plans.

LO 19.3.2   Discuss features and types of employer-sponsored retirement plans.

LO 19.3.3   Explain benefits available through government-sponsored plans.

Key Terms

- individual retirement account (IRA)
- traditional IRA
- Roth IRA
- Keogh plan
- Simplified Employee Pension (SEP) plan
- annuity
- defined-benefit plan
- defined-contribution plan
- 401(k) plan
- 403(b) plan

LO 19.3.1   Personal Retirement Plans

Personal or individual retirement accounts are an excellent way to set aside money for the future. Private retirement plans are essential for the self-employed or those not covered by employer-sponsored plans. You can select from tax-sheltered plans, such as individual retirement accounts, Keoghs, simplified employee pensions if you qualify, and annuities. You should also include some savings and investments you have paid taxes on.

Individual Retirement Accounts

An **individual retirement account (IRA)** is a retirement savings plan that offers tax advantages and allows individuals to set aside a specified amount each year. The total amount that can be contributed to an IRA is limited. In 2023, the contribution limit was $6,500 per year or $7,500 if you were over age 50. People not covered by a retirement plan at work may contribute the full amount per year if they wish. Those who do participate in a retirement plan at work can also contribute to an IRA, but they may not be able to contribute the maximum, depending on their income.

There are different types of IRAs, each with its own tax implications. With a **traditional IRA**, you can deduct your contribution each year from your taxable income. This allows you to delay paying tax on that income and the earnings it accumulates until you begin withdrawing the money after age 59½. At that time, your income will likely be lower than it was while you were working. As a result, you would be in a lower tax bracket and pay less tax. Although you do not have to start making withdrawals when you turn 59½, you must begin making withdrawals, or required minimum distributions (RMDs), from your traditional IRA by age 72; otherwise, a penalty will be assessed.

Source: iStock.com/Designer491

What are the benefits of contributing to an IRA?

A **Roth IRA** is an IRA where contributions are taxed, but earnings are not. With a Roth IRA, you pay tax on your income before you put it into the account. After a 5-year holding period, and at 59½, you can begin making tax-free withdrawals. This is the opposite of a traditional IRA, for which you pay tax on the earnings and the contributions when you withdraw the money at retirement. RMDs do not apply to Roth IRAs.

For early withdrawals from a traditional or Roth IRA before age 59½ or before having the account for five years, a 10 percent tax penalty will be applied. In addition, the money withdrawn is subject to federal and state income taxes in the year of withdrawal.

To help lessen your expenses during retirement, you should set up a Coverdell Education Savings Account (CESA), formerly an educational IRA, if you have children under age 18. Contributions to a CESA are not tax-deductible. It is a trust created to pay higher education expenses. Withdrawals for qualified expenses, such as tuition, books, fees, and supplies, are not taxable when withdrawn. This is like how a Roth IRA works.

Keogh Plans

A **Keogh plan** is a tax-deferred retirement savings plan available to self-employed individuals. In addition, if you own a small business and have employees, they can participate in your Keogh plan. However, employees do not contribute to the plan. All contributions come from the business owner, and the contribution rate set by the business owner must be applied uniformly to all employees.

Keogh plans can be structured in various ways. A self-employed person may set an annual goal for funding the plan. In 2023, Keogh contributions were limited to $66,000 or up to 25 percent of self-employment income, whichever is less. Some Keogh plans may have higher contribution limits than other retirement accounts.

The amounts that a self-employed individual contributes are fully tax-deductible. Earnings on Keogh plans are also tax-deferred. Withdrawals cannot be made before age 59½ without penalty.

Simplified Employee Pension Plans

A **Simplified Employee Pension (SEP) plan**, or a SEP-IRA, is a tax-deferred retirement plan available to small businesses. SEPs were authorized by Congress to encourage smaller employers to establish employee pension plans with IRAs as a funding method. Many self-employed individuals also use SEPs because they are easier to set up than Keogh plans.

With a SEP plan, all contributions come from the employer; employees cannot contribute. In 2023, employers could make an annual tax-deductible contribution of up to 25 percent of the employee's salary or $66,000, whichever is less. These contributions go into a traditional IRA each employee sets up at a financial institution. Withdrawals cannot be made before age 59½ without penalty and must begin by age 70½. The SEP-IRA works much the same way for self-employed individuals.

Annuities

An **annuity** is a contract between you and an insurance company. You make a lump-sum payment or series of payments that earn interest in return for regular disbursements, often at retirement. You can receive your payments for a specific period, such as 20 years, or receive them until your death. In recent years, tax-sheltered annuities (TSAs) have become popular because of the tax-free buildup of interest or dividends during the time the annuity contract remains in effect. Younger people often use such annuities to save money for retirement. Before purchasing an annuity, check the financial standing of the insurance company offering it. Ask about charges, fees, and the expected rate of return.

Pretaxed Savings

Not all your retirement savings should be tax deferred. Some should be savings and investments made with income on which you have already paid tax. In fact, many financial advisers recommend that at least half of your retirement savings be pretaxed. By having pretaxed savings and investments as part of your personal retirement plan, you will be able to withdraw these funds at any time without tax consequences. However, because there is no early withdrawal penalty for these funds, you will have to restrain yourself from spending this part of your nest egg so that it will be there when you retire.

✓ **Checkpoint**

Why should you have a variety of retirement plans in your portfolio?

LO 19.3.2 Employer-Sponsored Retirement Plans

Another source of retirement income may be the retirement plan offered by your company. With employer-sponsored retirement plans, you and often your employer contributes to your retirement savings. Contributions and earnings on employer-sponsored plans accumulate tax-free until you receive them.

When participating in employer-sponsored retirement plans, employees are protected under the Employee Retirement Income Security Act (ERISA), enacted in 1974. In addition to safeguarding retirement funds from employer mismanagement, ERISA does the following:

- Requires employers to provide participants with information about the plan's features and funding
- Requires that all participants be treated equally under the plan
- Defines how long a person may be required to work before becoming eligible to participate in a plan, to accumulate benefits, and to have a nonforfeitable right to those benefits (vesting)
- Guarantees payment of certain benefits if a defined plan is terminated

Defined-Benefit Plans

A few larger employers may provide defined-benefit plans or pensions for their employees. A **defined-benefit plan** is a company-sponsored retirement plan in which employees receive a set monthly amount for life beginning at retirement based on wages earned and the number of years of service. To become vested or entitled to the total amount in the plan, you may have to work for the company for a specified number of years.

Employees who are vested but leave the company before retirement may withdraw the account balance in cash or transfer the money to an IRA. This is called a rollover contribution to the IRA. In this situation, most people roll the money into an IRA to delay paying taxes until retirement. If they take it as cash when they leave the company, they will have to pay tax on the total amount plus a 10 percent penalty if they are under age 59½.

Defined-Contribution Plans

A **defined-contribution plan** is a company-sponsored retirement plan in which employees receive a periodic or lump-sum payment based on their account balance and the performance of the investments in their account. Defined-contribution plans are more common than defined-benefit plans at most companies today.

Each company's plan specifies the percentage of salary an employee may contribute to their account each year. These contributions are often tax-deferred until withdrawn at retirement. The employer may or may not make contributions to the plan. The plan specifies the amount the employer will contribute, if anything. When a plan participant retires or otherwise becomes eligible, their benefit is the total amount of money accumulated in the account, including investment earnings on contributions to the account. Two types of defined-contribution plans are 401(k) and 403(b) plans.

401(k) Plans

A **401(k) plan** is a defined-contribution plan for employees of companies that operate for a profit. Under a 401(k) plan, employees choose the percentage of salary they want to contribute to their account. The employer deducts this amount from their paychecks and puts it into the employees' accounts. This amount is not part of the employee's taxable income for the year, so they do not have to pay taxes until they withdraw the money at retirement. An investment company manages the accounts and invests the money. Usually, employees may select the types of investments they want from among several options the plan offers.

Frequently, employers match employee contributions by some percentage. For example, for every $1 of salary that employees contribute to their account, the employer may add 50 cents (a 50 percent match). This contribution is pure profit to the employee. In the preceding example, the 50 percent match is the same as making an immediate 50 percent return on your investment!

Employees cannot withdraw funds from their 401(k) without penalty before age 59½, except for death, disability, or financial hardship. They must also begin making withdrawals by age 72 or otherwise pay a penalty.

Why are 401(k) plans a wise investment choice?

403(b) Plans

A **403(b) plan** is a defined-contribution plan for employees of schools, nonprofit organizations, and government units. Under a 403(b) plan, employees contribute a percentage of their salary toward this tax-deferred account. While the rules may vary slightly, the 403(b) plan operates like a 401(k).

These plans are also known as tax-sheltered annuities because, initially, annuities were the only type of investments in these plans as permitted by law. Today, 403(b) plans are no longer restricted to annuities and can choose other assets, such as mutual funds. However, investment options are still fewer than under a 401(k) plan. Earnings are tax-deferred, and early withdrawal penalties apply. Should an employee leave their employer, the 403(b) funds can be rolled into an IRA within a specific period.

> ### ✓ Checkpoint
>
> What are the main differences between the various employer-sponsored retirement plans?

LO 19.3.3 Government-Sponsored Plans

You may be entitled to benefits from the federal government—in the form of Social Security, military retirement, or veterans' benefits. Many state, county, and city governments also have employee retirement plans.

Social Security Benefits

You are eligible for Social Security benefits if you worked for at least 10 years and paid Social Security taxes. Your benefit amount is based on your earnings and contributions to Social Security over your lifetime.

Benefits are funded by taxes imposed on the wages of employees and self-employed individuals. The employer and employee are each responsible for one-half of the Social Security tax, with the employee's half withheld from their paycheck. Self-employed workers are responsible for the entire amount of Social Security tax.

Social Security replaces only about 40 percent or less of an average wage earner's income after retiring; therefore, it was never intended to fully support people in retirement. Instead, Social Security is designed as a safety net or supplement to an individual's retirement savings. You must have accumulated your nest egg apart from Social Security to retire comfortably. Social Security laws allow seniors at retirement age to continue working without losing Social Security benefits, which many seniors choose to do to supplement their Social Security income. Until you reach full retirement age, there may be a limit on how much you can earn during the year and continue to collect your Social Security benefits. In 2023, if you earned more than $21,240, your Social Security benefits would be reduced.

Once you have started paying into the system, you can view and print a Social Security benefits statement online by signing up for an account at the Social Security Administration's website (www.ssa.gov). This statement shows a record of the income on which you paid Social Security taxes, how much you can expect to earn in monthly Social Security benefits when you reach retirement age, plus your estimated disability and Medicare benefits. Medicare premiums are deducted from your monthly Social Security payments.

Full Social Security retirement benefits are available at the full retirement age of 67 for people born after 1960. If you delay collecting your Social Security benefits beyond your full retirement age, benefits are increased by a certain percentage up to 70 years old. The earliest age at which reduced benefits are payable is 62. In addition, if you have been married for 10 years or more, you may be entitled to receive Social Security benefits based on your spouse's income, even if you are divorced.

Most of Social Security retirement benefits are taxable if your total income from all sources exceeds maximum limits adjusted from time to time. Cost-of-living adjustments to Social Security benefits are made periodically, subject to the approval of Congress.

Military Benefits

Retired military personnel receive pensions after 20 years of active duty in the U.S. armed forces. Pensions are payable in full regardless of other sources of income and are subject to income taxes. In addition, military retirees may have special privileges, such as purchasing goods through military posts. These benefits can be attractive, especially for people who retire from the military in their early 40s and continue working in different jobs until retirement age.

The Veterans Administration provides regular pensions for survivors of men and women who died while in the armed forces and disability pensions for veterans who were permanently injured while in the armed forces. Veterans may also be entitled to additional benefits, such as low-interest mortgage loans; educational assistance; burial and memorial services; and low-rate car, home, and life insurance.

✓ Checkpoint

Explain the types of government plans available for retirement.

Check Your Understanding

1. List and describe the types of personal retirement plans. (LO 19.3.1)

2. What types of retirement plans are offered by some employers? (LO 19.3.2)

3. What makes a person eligible for Social Security benefits? (LO 19.3.3)

Apply Your Understanding

1. You are considering opening an IRA. Given your current circumstances, should you open a Roth IRA or a traditional IRA? Explain your reasoning. (LO 19.3.1)

2. You have been offered your first full-time job, and one of the benefits is a defined-contribution plan. The company will match 3 percent if you contribute 3 percent. What does this mean for you? (LO 19.3.2)

3. Create a personal retirement plan. Set your long-term financial goals while considering your investment risk tolerance. Include the following in your plan:
   a. Types of retirement accounts
   b. How you will make contributions to the accounts
   c. Plans for healthcare in retirement
   d. How you can be debt-free when you retire (LO 19.3.3)

The Essential Question

What are personal, employer-sponsored, and government sources of retirement income?

A: Personal retirement plans include IRAs, Keogh plans, SEP-IRAs, and annuities. Employer-sponsored retirement plans include 401(k) plans and 403(b) plans. Government sources include Social Security and military benefits.

Summary

19.1 Real Estate and Other Investments

- Real estate investing includes buying land and/or buildings.

- Commercial property is land or buildings that produce income through leasing or renting such as office buildings, stores, and apartments.

- Real estate investing can combat inflation, but it is one of the least liquid investments.

- If you invest in real estate directly, you own legal title to it. If you invest indirectly, a trustee holds legal title on behalf of the investor group.

- Types of real estate properties you can invest in directly include vacant land, single-family houses, rental properties (such as apartment units, condominiums, and duplexes), and vacation homes.

- As the owner of rental property, you benefit from tax advantages for depreciation and other expenses. However, there is a risk of having bad tenants or prolonged vacancies, and it may be difficult to resell.

- If your rental income from rental property exceeds your mortgage payment, property taxes, and upkeep expenses, then you have a positive cash flow.

- You can invest in real estate indirectly through real estate investment trusts (REITs), real estate syndicates, or mortgage pools (in the form of certificates of participation).

- Investments in precious metals, gems, collectibles, and commodities are risky and not for the novice investor.

19.2 Planning for Retirement

- To have a comfortable retirement, you need to start saving at the beginning of your work life.

- Most people need between 75 and 85 percent of their preretirement income to live comfortably.

- The equity built in a home can be a source of retirement income with a reverse mortgage.

- As you near retirement, you may want to switch to less risky investments that emphasize current income over future capital gains.

- For retired people, health insurance is a crucial need that can be costly. It must be part of a retirement plan.

- Some seniors may choose to work part time to offset inflation.

- Estate planning involves preparing a plan for transferring property during one's lifetime and at one's death.

- A will specifies how to distribute your assets. A trust is a legal document in which an individual gives someone else control of property, for ultimate distribution to another person.

- Probate is the legal process of proving a deceased person's will is valid and then distributing that person's estate upon death. It can be a lengthy process.

- Joint tenants with right of survivorship (JTWROS) transfers property at death without the costs and time involved in probate.

- A power of attorney empowers someone else to act on your behalf.

- Various federal and state taxes, such as estate taxes, inheritance taxes, and gift taxes, may be applied to an estate. Estate planning can minimize these taxes.

19.3 Saving for Retirement

- Personal retirement plans, such as an individual retirement account (IRA) or an annuity, are a good way to set aside money for the future.

- A traditional IRA allows you to delay paying income tax on the contributions until you withdraw the money at retirement age.

- With a Roth IRA, you pay taxes on the contributions but pay no taxes on the earnings when withdrawals are made at retirement.

- A Keogh plan is a tax-deferred plan for self-employed people. Simplified Employee Pension (SEP) plans are tax-deferred plans for employees of small businesses.

- An annuity is a contract between you and an insurance company in which you make a lump-sum payment or series of payments that earn interest in return for regular disbursements, often at retirement.

- Employer-sponsored retirement plans are another possible source of retirement income.

- Under a defined-benefit plan (such as a pension), retired employees receive a set monthly amount for life based on wages earned and number of years of service.

- Defined-contribution plans, such as 401(k) and 403(b) plans, allow employees to contribute part of their salary to tax-deferred investments. Employers may or may not contribute matching funds.

- Government-sponsored retirement plans include Social Security benefits and military benefits for veterans.

- You are eligible for Social Security benefits at retirement if you worked and paid Social Security taxes for at least 10 years. Social Security benefits generally replace only 40 percent of an average wage earner's income after retirement and are meant to supplement an individual's retirement savings.

Check Your Knowledge

1. Why is it important to check a city's zoning laws before purchasing vacant land? (LO 19.1.1)

2. What benefits does a vacation home offer to an investor? If you do not plan on living in the home full time until you retire, why might you buy it now? (LO 19.1.1)

3. Explain the factors individuals and families need to consider when determining retirement needs. (LO 19.2.1)

4. What are some advantages of owning property jointly with another person? Why would people own property as joint tenants with right of survivorship? (LO 19.2.2)

5. Explain the difference between a traditional IRA and a SEP-IRA. Explain who can have these types of accounts. (LO 19.3.1)

6. Explain the difference between a defined-benefit plan and a defined-contribution plan for retirement. (LO 19.3.2)

7. How can a veteran or their family be eligible for military benefits for retirement? (LO 19.3.3)

1. Alena has decided to invest in real estate. She cannot decide whether to buy a vacant lot for $25,000 or a one-fourth interest in a four-unit apartment building selling for $400,000. Explain to her the pros and cons of both options. (LO 19.1.1)

2. You are considering buying a ruby ring from a friend because you think you can sell it and make a profit. After researching the pros and cons of this type of investment, do you think you should purchase the ring? Why or why not? (LO 19.1.2)

3. Search for websites about a collectible that interests you. How is this item bought and sold online and does this impact your decision making around the purchase? Explain. (LO 19.1.2)

4. You were talking to your parent(s)/guardian(s) about what you are learning in this class. They have not yet started saving for retirement. They are in their early 40s, have a solid emergency fund, and owe five more years on their mortgage. They have invested in a postsecondary savings account to help pay for your education. What advice would you offer? (LO 19.2.1)

5. Prepare a simple will for yourself, using Figure 19.1 as a guide. What questions do you have as you prepare the document? (LO 19.2.2)

6. Bob works and earns under $35,000 a year. He has never had an individual retirement account (IRA) because he thinks he does not make enough money to save for retirement yet. Explain how investing even a small amount can help Bob be more financially secure. (LO 19.3.1)

7. One of your friends just graduated from their career training program and was offered a job with a 401(k) with a 4 percent match. Participation in the program is voluntary. They tell you that they cannot afford to start saving now because they have too many bills to pay. What advice would you give them about their option to start the 401(k)? (LO 19.3.2)

8. Jackson served in the military for 20 years and retired with an honorable discharge. Conduct online research about the types of military benefits Jackson might be able to receive when he retires. (LO 19.3.3)

Share Your Knowledge

Work in teams of two to four students to complete the following activities.

1. Investigate real estate investment trusts (REITs). What types of REITs exist? What types of assets do they own? How do they make money? As a group, identify a REIT you would be interested in purchasing and explain why you selected it. (LO 19.1.1)

2. Conduct online research about the requirements for wills and the probate laws in your state. Create a chart that outlines each. (LO 19.2.2)

3. Discuss the features, types, and advantages and disadvantages for one of the following categories of retirement plans: personal retirement plans, employer-sponsored retirement plans, or government-sponsored plans. Then, as a group, report out on your findings. (LO 19.3.1, 19.3.2, and 19.3.3)

Connect and Reflect

Base your answers to the following questions on your own personal thoughts, preferences, and experiences.

1. Why do you think planning for retirement should happen early in your life rather than waiting until you are in your 40s or 50s? What are the advantages of early planning? (LO 19.2.1)

2. Why do you think most people are reluctant to plan, write, and discuss issues around wills? (LO 19.2.2)

3. In 2023, it was estimated that the trust fund that pays Social Security benefits would be exhausted in 2037. What do you think this means for your future retirement plans? Explain. (LO 19.3.3)

Chapter Project

When people die, they often leave their estates (assets) to beneficiaries. What is the difference between estate taxes and inheritance taxes? If you inherited $25,000, what federal, state, or other taxes would you have to pay? Could these taxes have been avoided? Explain why or why not. How might you invest your large inheritance for retirement? Find a retirement calculator to estimate how much you can save by the age of 65 if you deposit the full $25,000 into an investment with an expected rate of return of 7 percent. Prepare a report explaining your findings on taxes and your investment choices. Include tables and graphs as visual aids.

Personal Plan of Study

It is important to prepare for a future career while in high school. Taking high school courses related to a future career not only confirms your interest but allows you to begin developing skills and be more prepared for additional career-focused training or education after high school. Students may also be able to take courses in high school to earn college credit, gain industry certification, or make them more qualified to enter a training program. Taking advantage of these opportunities in high school can potentially yield financial benefits and reduce the overall expense of preparing for your career of interest.

Using career exploration and research findings from previous unit activities, determine courses and/or activities that you can take in high school to help prepare you for your desired career and postsecondary education/training. Then, develop a personal plan of study, making sure to leverage available resources such as school counselors and career exploration/college and career readiness platforms.

Think Critically

1. How do the classes and activities included in your personal plan help prepare you for postsecondary education/training or your career of interest?

2. Looking at your personal plan, what focus areas are missing or what skills will you not be able to fully develop from the courses offered? What opportunities can you seek to address these gaps?

Unit 5: Project

Planning for the future is not just a good idea but a crucial step toward financial security for young adults. And the best part? You can start as soon as you have your first part-time job. If you are among those who have federal income taxes withheld from their paycheck, you may be eligible to contribute to a Roth IRA. A Roth IRA is an individual retirement account that allows you to contribute after-tax dollars. The beauty of it is that all your contributions and earnings from interest and dividends can grow tax-free and be withdrawn at 59½ years of age. The only requirement is that you must open the account 5 years before any withdrawals are made. On average, a Roth IRA can earn between 7 and 10 percent annually.

In 2024, individuals who earn less than $161,000 a year or married couples who earn less than $240,000 a year can contribute to a Roth IRA. The maximum contribution to the Roth IRA in 2024 is $7,000. The federal government increases the maximum contributions and earnings yearly based on inflation. The 2024 full retirement age is 67.

A Roth IRA can be opened with most brokerage firms or at a local bank. And here is another benefit to a Roth IRA: As a first-time home buyer, you can use up to $10,000 toward the purchase price of your home.

Apply Your Knowledge

1. Using online resources, find a Roth IRA calculator such as the one at Bankrate.com. Use the following information to plan your contributions:
    *   Enter $0 as your starting balance.
    *   Enter your current age as the starting age for the calculations.
    *   Enter the maximum amount the calculator allows as the amount you can contribute annually.
    *   Set your retirement age at the full retirement age for the current year. In 2024, the full retirement age is 67.
    *   Enter an expected rate of return of 7 percent.
    *   Assume that you will be in the 24 percent tax bracket.

    Answer the following questions using the criteria above:

    1. How many years would you be contributing to the Roth IRA?
    2. How much would you contribute to the account based on your answer to question 1?
    3. What is your estimated Roth IRA balance when you retire?
    4. Edit the expected rate of return to 10 percent. What is your new balance?
    5. Continue changing the variables on the calculator to show what you would earn if you waited until you were 25, 35, or 45 to begin saving, using both and 10 percent as the expected rate of return. How did the numbers change at the different starting ages? How did the numbers change at the different rates of return?

Think Critically

1. What are the potential consequences of delaying starting to save for retirement until you are older?

2. What factors contribute to the compounding effect of early retirement savings, and how does this impact long-term financial growth?

3. How does starting to save for retirement early provide flexibility and freedom in retirement choices compared to starting later?

Personal Financial Literacy

The Personal Financial Literacy Event measures your personal finance knowledge. Students must be able to apply reliable information and systematic decision making to personal financial decisions. The Personal Financial Literacy Event consists of a financial literacy exam and a role-play scenario with a business executive. Finalists will compete in a second role-play event. Participants will have 30 minutes to review the scenario and develop a professional approach to solving the problem. Participants will have 15 minutes to present their action plan to the judge. After the participant's explanation, the judge can ask questions about the scenario.

Go to DECA.org/compete for more detailed information.

Performance Indicators

- Explain the need to save and invest.
- Explain types of financial markets.
- Describe the role of financial institutions.
- Explain the time value of money.
- Interpret business policies for customers/clients.
- Write informational messages.
- Select and utilize appropriate formats for professional writing.

Try It Out!

You are a financial advisor at a local banking institution. The bank president (the judge), Aiyana, wants you to work with your team to create an informational flyer to promote the long-term investing option of a Roth IRA. Most bank customers keep their money in savings or checking accounts, sometimes both, that earn very little interest. Aiyana thinks that most of the bank's customers do not understand how investing works and wants to help educate the customers about the importance of planning for retirement.

The bank offers a Roth IRA option to customers, but less than 5 percent of the customers are taking advantage of the opportunity.

Aiyana wants the bank customers to better understand the value of investing in a Roth IRA and wants your team to create an informational flyer that will be mailed to all customers, placed at each bank teller's station, and featured on the bank's social media platforms. To encourage the bank customers to open a Roth IRA, Aiyana has planned a promotion for all new Roth IRA customers. When a customer opens a Roth IRA, the bank will match up to $100 of the opening deposit if the account stays active for 12 months. The informational flyer must include:

- Easy-to-understand explanation of Roth IRAs
- The current promotion
- The need to save and invest
- Why delaying investment is a lost opportunity

You will present and explain the planned promotional campaign to Aiyana in a meeting in their office. The meeting will begin with Aiyana greeting you and asking about your promotional ideas. At the end of the presentation, Aiyana may ask you questions and conclude the meeting by thanking you for your work.

www.deca.org/compete

6 Unit

Consumer Rights and Responsibilities

Sergii Figurnyi/Shutterstock.com

20 Role of Consumers in a Market Economy

21 Consumer Protection and Dispute Resolution

Unit 6 helps you understand the role of consumers in a market economy and how consumer protection and dispute resolution is crucial. Consumers influence demand, which then affects supply, prices, and product quality. Understanding your rights as a consumer regarding fair pricing, product quality, safety, and accurate information will allow you to make informed decisions and protect you from fraud. If you are a victim of fraud, it is important to know how to address conflicts appropriately, such as through mediation, arbitration, or small claims court. As a consumer, when you understand your rights, your responsibilities, and the impact of your decisions, you can become a more confident and informed decision maker.

Rohit Chopra

Source: United States Government

Rohit Chopra was born on January 30, 1982, in Plainfield, New Jersey. His parents are first-generation immigrants from India. He was appointed director of the Consumer Financial Protection Bureau (CFPB) in October 2021 and is the third director of the bureau, which was formed in 2011. The CFPB is part of the Federal Reserve and is responsible for consumer protection in the financial sector of our economy. The agency was created through the Dodd-Frank Act in response to the financial crisis that led to the Great Recession of 2008–2009. Chopra was the first CFPB student loan ombudsman. As an ombudsperson, he helped resolve issues between parties through informal meditation. Chopra has also served on the Federal Trade Commission (FTC), where he was only the second Asian American to serve. Chopra is one of the youngest directors of a government regulatory agency.

Chopra graduated from Harvard University in 2004 and then attended the Wharton School at the University of Pennsylvania, where he earned his Master of Business Administration (MBA). He was a Fulbright fellow in South Korea and began his career as a management consultant.

Chopra was part of the team that created the CFPB in 2011, and he helped document the student loan overcharging scheme that impacted many military members. He is passionate about student loan reform and wants to improve the status of people with large student loan debts. His efforts have led to more oversight of predatory educational institutions and student loan service providers.

As CFPB director, Chopra closely monitors how big tech companies, such as Amazon and Google, utilize financial institutions for payments. Chopra also closely monitors how college-sponsored financial products have higher fees and unfavorable terms than typical financial products. "Many students get their first credit card or deposit account when they enroll in college, and banks know that consumers are unlikely to move to a different provider once a product is integrated into their financial life," Chopra had said. "Schools should take a hard look at the fees and terms of the products they pitch to their students and alumni." The CFPB examines these practices and looks for possible violations of federal consumer financial protection law.

Connect and Reflect

Throughout his career, Chopra has been a strong consumer advocate, particularly in the areas of student debt reform and banking and credit fees and terms. Reflect on the impact of Chopra's work protecting consumers against fraud, lack of transparency, and deceptive practices.

1. Do you think consumer advocacy and regulation of financial institutions are important? Explain.

2. Why do you think Chopra has focused on student debt reform and the oversight of student loans? Does his work in this area affect you? Explain.

3. Chopra has stated that "a handful of very large banks and financial firms control much of the market," leaving consumers with fewer options. Do you agree with this statement? Why or why not?

20 Chapter

Role of Consumers in a Market Economy

The Essential Question

What are the characteristics of the various types of economic systems, and what is the role of money?

Learning Objectives

By the end of this lesson, you should be able to:

LO 20.1.1   Compare economic systems.
LO 20.1.2   Discuss the basic characteristics of a market economy.
LO 20.1.3   Explain the role of money in a market economy.

Key Terms

- communist economic system
- socialist economic system
- traditional economic system
- capitalism
- market economy
- producers
- consumers
- scarcity
- utility
- opportunity cost
- production possibility frontier (PPF)
- supply
- demand
- competition
- oligopoly
- monopoly
- money
- fiat money

Consider This ...

Justin is a full-time student. He works part time at a gym to earn money during the school year. He often wants to buy new things but does not always have money for them. He just heard about the newest cell phone that was recently released. His friends are talking about it, and he has seen several advertisements while scrolling through social media. Justin really wants the new phone, but the price is very high. He does not have enough money, but he could use credit to purchase it.

"If I wait to buy this device until I can save enough money for it, I won't be able to enjoy it now while it's new and loaded with features other phones don't have. On the other hand, if I wait, the price will come down, and then I can afford it. By then, other similar phones may be on the market. I'm not sure what to do, since my money is tight! What would you do?" he asks his friend.

(continues)

(continued)

LO 20.1.1 — Economic Systems

An economic system refers to the process used by a society to decide what to produce, how to produce it, and for whom to produce it. There are three major types of economic systems: hands-on, hands-off, and mixed.

Hands-On Systems

A hands-on system is where the government or central authority controls most decisions involving what will be produced, how, and for whom. This type of system grew from the feudalism of the Middle Ages, where people lived together for safety and to provide for group needs. Today, two basic hands-on economic systems exist: communism and socialism.

- Communism. Within a **communist economic system,** also known as a command system, the government owns and controls most, if not all, of the productive resources of a nation. Parts of China, North Korea, and Russia are examples of communist systems. Based on the Marxist theories of sharing resources for the greater benefit of all, this system excludes most private property and ownership of resources; it also limits individual choices.

- Socialism. A **socialist economic system,** also called a planned system, is characterized by a large degree of government control of many of the decisions within the nation. Examples include Sweden, Germany, and other nations that have high tax rates but provide universal access to services, such as education and health care. While private ownership of resources and property exists, many of the nation's choices are predetermined.

Hands-Off Systems

A hands-off system is one where there is a limited role for the government or a central authority. Decisions about what will be produced, how, and for whom are made by the people, acting rather than individually.

- Traditional. Within a **traditional economic system**, the people decide what decisions will be made and how they will be made. Often, these systems are based on long-established traditions, religion, or cultural values. Middle Eastern countries and some small nations in Africa and Asia are organized as traditional economies.

- Capitalism. When the United States began, it started as a pure free-enterprise, or capitalist, system. **Capitalism** is an economic system in which producers and consumers are free to operate and compete in business transactions with minimal, if any, government interference or regulation. A hands-off economy follows the *laissez-faire* economic theory that says the government should not interfere in the economy except to protect an individual's inalienable rights. The power to make decisions regarding resources belongs to individuals and businesses rather than society as a whole, without much, if any, governmental interference.

- Others. Other hands-off economic models include anarchism, mutualism, and libertarianism. These models reject the role of government and instead embrace self-rule for all choices.

Why are most economic systems around the world mixed economies?

Mixed Economic Systems

Most nations today have some form of a mixed economy, which contains elements of more than one type of economic system. For example, a capitalist system can become a survival of the fittest society over time unless it accepts a growing need to protect those who would not otherwise survive. Our U.S. economy is considered a **market economy** because market forces, based on individual freedoms and government decisions, determine which goods and services are

Connections to Your World
Debating Government Intervention

Many people in the United States believe that a market economy will work most efficiently if it is left alone; that is, without government intervention when the economy is faltering. When the government takes action—such as offering company bailouts during the Great Recession of 2008 and economic relief packages during the COVID-19 pandemic—it can lead to saved jobs, financial support to businesses to pay employees and remain open, and stimulus funds to keep money flowing within the economy. However, taxpayers ultimately pay the bill for these economic interventions. Some people feel that government actions do little for the economy; these individuals believe that the economy would recover on its own, although at a slower pace, and that the money spent could have been used to create new jobs or for other better purposes. Others argue that government action is sometimes needed to save jobs, protect small businesses, and stabilize the economy.

(continues)

(continued)

Think Critically

1. What side do you agree with in this argument? Explain.

2. Do you think that the government should bail out large companies to avoid the impact of numerous job losses on the economy? Why or why not?

3. Do you think that government should step in to help stabilize the economy during pandemics, natural disasters, or other events that impact a large part of the population? Explain.

produced and how they are distributed. The government produces some goods and services rather than leaving them to private enterprise.

In a market economy, the government also influences and controls some choices. For example, the government collects taxes, borrows money that it spends, and redistributes according to governmental priorities. The government is also able to impose price controls and other regulations. For example, a price floor is imposed on the market when the government sets a minimum wage. Employers must pay at least the floor. When the government sets a price ceiling, sellers cannot charge more. The government protects some buyers who cannot afford certain items. For example, the government might set a price ceiling on milk and insulin to protect young families and those with diabetes, respectively.

In our market economy, government influence also exists through fiscal policy. Fiscal policy refers to actions of the government to stimulate or slow the economy, such as tax increases or decreases and tax rebates or adjustments to the interest rate. A market economy recognizes the need for such actions to protect consumers from adverse economic conditions.

Today, there are few, if any, pure economic systems. For example, a country may be a command system mixed with individual choices and ownership of some resources. Or it may be a free-enterprise system mixed with some degree of governmental controls. The degree of those centralized or group decisions determines the classification for each country.

✓ Checkpoint

Describe the main differences between hands-on, hands-off, and mixed economic systems.

LO 20.1.2   **Elements of a Market Economy**

In a market economy, both producers and consumers must play active roles. **Producers** are the manufacturers or makers of goods and services for sale. **Consumers** are the buyers and users of goods and services. Producers and consumers engage in self-interest, forcing wise use of scarce resources.

Scarcity

In any economy, consumers' wants are unlimited, while the resources for producing the products to satisfy these wants are limited. This basic economic problem is called **scarcity**. A country's economic system determines what products will be produced with limited resources. Consumers play a key role in determining what is produced in our market economy.

As an individual consumer, you have limited resources. You must decide what to buy with your limited income to achieve the greatest satisfaction or utility. **Utility** is a measurement of something's usefulness. When you decide how to use your limited resources, you are considering the opportunity costs of your alternative. An **opportunity cost** is the value of the choice you did not select. Your spending decisions and those of other consumers determine which products will succeed and which will fail and leave the market. Producers take cues from the marketplace to know which products will be profitable.

One economic model to illustrate this concept is the **production possibility frontier (PPF)** (also called a production possibilities curve). A PPF (**Figure 20.1**) is a curve on a graph that shows the possible quantities of two products that can be produced using the same resources. The PPF shows the most efficient use of scarce resources and the trade-off between the two items. At point A, all resources would be spent on infrastructure, with no funding provided for public safety. At Point F, all resources would be spent on public safety, with nothing being provided for infrastructure. The PPF can help decision makers determine the most efficient use of

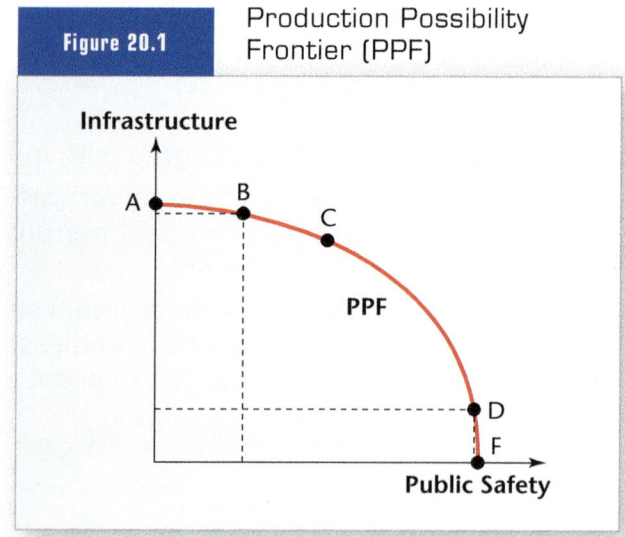

Figure 20.1 Production Possibility Frontier (PPF)

resources. At each point along the graph, the decision makers must consider their decisions' scarcity, choice, and opportunity costs.

Supply and Demand

Supply is the quantity of goods and services that producers can provide at various prices. **Demand** is the willingness and ability of consumers to purchase goods and services at various prices. Generally, if enough consumers demand a product and are willing and able to buy it, producers are willing to produce and sell it. The system works like this:

1. Increased demand creates a situation in which the product's supply is insufficient to satisfy all consumers who want to buy it. As a result, producers can raise their prices.
2. The high prices bring large profits to the producers.
3. Large profits prompt current producers to make more of the product and attract other producers to start providing the product, thus increasing supply.
4. Supply then exceeds demand, giving consumers more of a selection. To entice

consumers to buy their products instead of their competitors' products, producers must reduce their prices.

5. Reducing prices, in turn, lowers profits, and producers begin to produce less.

6. Eventually, the product reaches the equilibrium price. This is the price at which the quantity supplied equals the quantity demanded of the product. At this price, there is just enough of the product available for all consumers who want to buy it.

Figure 20.2 represents a supply and demand curve (D=demand and S=supply). Notice that the equilibrium price goes up when demand increases (D₁ to D₂).

Consumer Power

Consumers have the ultimate power in a market economy; this is known as consumer sovereignty. Consumers determine what is produced and at what price. Collectively, consumer buying decisions direct the production of goods and services. When consumers purchase a good or service, they are casting dollar "votes" for its continued production.

If consumers refuse to buy a good or service, the price will drop. If the good or

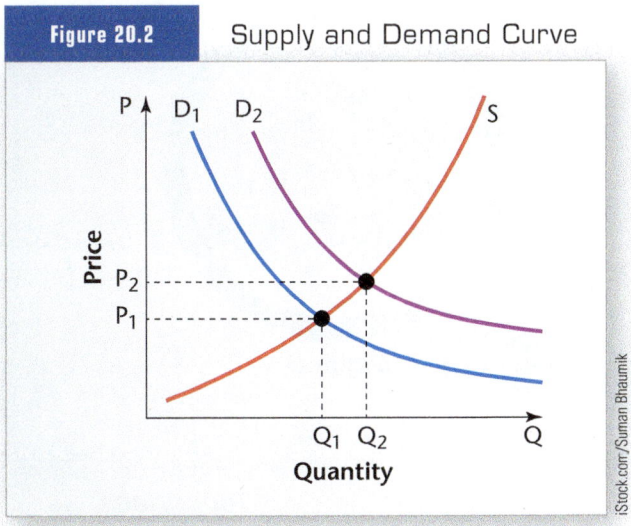

| Figure 20.2 | Supply and Demand Curve |

service still does not sell or sales do not generate a profit, producers will no longer provide it.

Producer Power

Producers also have power in a free-enterprise system because they can employ various techniques to influence consumer buying decisions. They use advertising and other marketing strategies to try to increase demand for their products. Advertising can be informative and provide important facts about the quality and features of products. Unfortunately, it can also be false and misleading—thus, the saying, "Let the buyer beware."

Parts of the Economic System

Three essential parts of a market economy are: (1) competition, (2) purchasing power, and (3) informed consumers. If one of these parts is missing or not functioning properly, the system begins to fail. The economy gains strength when each component functions properly.

Competition

Competition must exist for prices to rise and fall resulting in shifts in the quantity of goods available for sale. **Competition** is the rivalry among sellers in the same market to win customers. There are three forms of competition in a market economy:

1. Pure competition. With pure competition, many sellers in the market produce nearly identical products, resulting in improved quality and lower prices. Because of the freedom of both producers and consumers to enter and leave the market, supply and demand are free to interact to set equilibrium prices.

Sharpen Your Employability Skills
Thinking Critically about the Circular Flow Model

The circular flow model, shown below, illustrates how different sectors interact within the U.S. market economy. There are three main sectors in the U.S. economic system: households, businesses or firms, and the government. The circular flow model shows how money moves between these sectors. For example, money moves from businesses to households as wages and back again as workers spend money on products and services. Additionally, money flows from businesses and households to the government in the form of taxes. The money flows from the government to households and businesses in the form of benefit programs, public services, and other programs. Review the graphic below to better understand the flow of goods and services between these sectors.

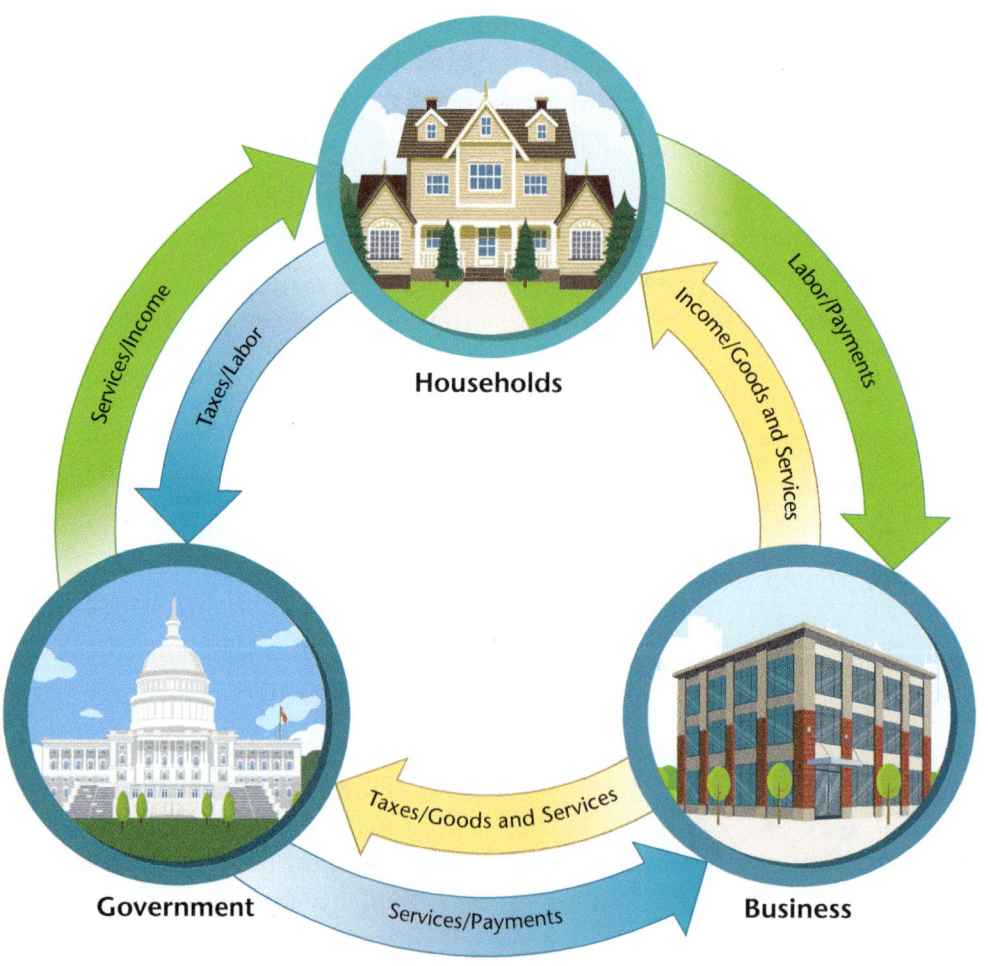

(continues)

(continued)

2. Oligopoly. An **oligopoly** exists when only a few sellers produce a similar product or service. Because of the dominance of a few businesses, it is difficult for competitors to enter the industry. For example, the automobile industry has only a few manufacturers. An oligopoly works properly when buyers shop carefully and negotiate prices effectively.

3. Monopoly. A **monopoly** is a market with many buyers but only one seller. Without competition, the one seller has no incentive to improve quality or lower prices. Sometimes a monopoly is necessary within a market economy. Examples of monopolies include power and utility companies. Because consumers cannot shop for the product or service elsewhere, monopolies must be controlled (by government) to ensure they provide fair prices to consumers.

Illegal business practices can reduce competition and result in higher prices. Price fixing is an illegal agreement among competitors to sell a good or service for a set price. There is no real competition because prices have been predetermined, or fixed. Because price fixing prevents the forces of supply and demand from determining prices freely in the marketplace, it impedes free enterprise. Therefore, laws were passed to make it illegal.

Purchasing Power

For a market economy to operate, citizens must be able to buy goods and services. In the United States, most adults have income from their jobs to spend on goods and services. However, the dollar's purchasing power increases or decreases with the economy. Purchasing power is the value of money, measured in the goods and services it can buy.

In a period of inflation, when prices are generally rising in the economy, purchasing power decreases. For example, if coffee prices rise from $3.50 to $5.00, then your income will buy fewer coffee drinks. Purchasing power also declines during periods of recession when production, employment, and income are declining. People who lose their jobs or have their wages reduced cannot buy as many goods. The result is an overall loss of purchasing power in the economy.

The government also shifts purchasing power among citizens by making transfer payments, which are government grants to some citizens paid with money collected from other citizens, generally through taxes. Transfer payments are unearned income for the recipients because they are not providing any services in exchange for the payments. However, transfer payments provide purchasing power for needy people. Medicare, Social Security, and veterans' benefits are all transfer payments. SNAP benefits, reduced-price school lunches, and housing assistance also fall into this category.

The Federal Reserve uses monetary policy to promote maximum employment, stable prices, and moderate long-term interest rates. The Federal Reserve's policies are meant to achieve the economic goals of Congress. Congressional goals include high employment rates, sustainable long-term growth, and stable prices. Monetary policy impacts short-term interest rates, which can then influence the government's and consumers' economic activity and long-term interest rates.

Informed Consumers

A market economy must have informed consumers who know their rights and responsibilities in the marketplace. Informed consumers compare products and prices. When consumers make wise decisions, the system works to weed out inferior products and keep prices at acceptable levels.

> **✓ Checkpoint**
>
> What are the basic characteristics of a market economy?

LO 20.1.3   The Role of Money

All economic systems use some form of money or medium of exchange. **Money** is anything that can be used to settle debt. It should be easily exchangeable and readily accepted in the marketplace. To meet these requirements and be functional, money must be readily divisible, durable, and recognizable as a store of value.

- Divisibility. In the United States, money, or currency, is divided into denominations to ease transactions. The dollar bill is easily recognizable, and coins are used for sums less than a dollar. The largest denomination produced for circulation is the $100 bill. In recent years, the Bureau of Engraving and Printing has added color and new security features to help prevent counterfeiting. When money is counted, it is divided into units. For example, 50 cents equals one-half of a dollar. Ten dollars is 10 times one dollar. Because money is readily divisible, you can buy and sell goods and give and receive the exact change for your money.

- Durability. Money must be transferred from one person to another. Currency lasts a long time before it must be reissued. Coins are produced by the U.S. Mint, and paper money is produced by the Bureau of Engraving and Printing. As money wears out, new coins and bills replace old ones, which are destroyed.

- Store of value. To serve as a medium of exchange, money must have a store of value, or be recognized to represent that value. For example, a $5 bill is readily exchangeable for merchandise of that value. When you accept a $5 bill for something you have sold, you expect to be able to reuse that $5 bill when you wish to do so. Because you have confidence that the paper money can be used again, you will accept it in exchange for goods and services.

The Gold Standard

When our nation was young, our money was based on a gold standard. With a gold standard, each dollar bill was backed by that same amount of gold in storage at a safe place. Much of the U.S. gold supply is stored at Ft. Knox, Kentucky. In the early days of our country, a citizen could go into a bank and demand $20 of gold in exchange for a $20 bill. Banks issued their own money, called gold or silver certificates, because they could produce the gold or silver on demand.

Today our money is referred to as **fiat money**, which is not backed by gold, but by faith in the general economy and government of the country. You readily accept dollar bills and other currencies because you are confident that you will be able to exchange them for other goods and services when you wish.

Supply and Demand of Money

Like most other commodities, money is also subject to the forces of supply and demand. The government's efforts to stabilize the economy by managing the money supply and setting interest rates are referred to as monetary policy. The Federal Reserve System (the Fed) controls our money supply, or the total amount of money in circulation. Using the reserve requirement, the Fed can increase or decrease the money supply. The reserve requirement indicates how much money a bank can loan out from its transaction deposits from customers and how much it must keep on reserve. For example, with a 20 percent reserve requirement, 20 percent of all demand account deposits, such as checking accounts, must be retained by the bank in its vaults. Raising that percentage means the banks have less money they can lend. When they have less to lend, the price of borrowing (the interest rate) will rise.

The Fed also controls the discount rate and the federal funds rate. The discount

What is the purpose of the reserve requirement?

rate is the interest rate charged to banks that borrow from the Fed. The federal funds rate is the interest rate at which banks can borrow from the excess reserves of other banks. As these rates increase, the money supply shrinks because it is more expensive to borrow money. As these rates drop, banks can borrow and loan more money. When more money is available, its price (interest rate) will be lower.

The creation of money helps the economy to grow. A growing economy can provide more jobs for workers and more products for consumers to purchase. Thus, the supply and demand for money affects our lives in a significant way.

The Money Multiplier

When banks can lend money they have on deposit from customers, they can create more money. The money multiplier indicates how much more money can be made when banks lend out a portion of each customer's deposit. The formula is as follows:

$$\text{Money Multiplier (MM)} = \frac{1}{\text{RR}} \text{(reserve requirement)}$$

With a reserve requirement of 20 percent, the formula would work like this:

$$MM = \frac{1}{0.20} = 5$$

Thus, if one customer deposits $100 in their checking account, the bank must keep 20 percent on reserve, or $20, and can lend the rest of the deposit, $80, to another customer, which creates a new deposit in another account. Of that new $80, 80 percent, or $64, can also be loaned to others, and so on. This will result in a multiplier of 5, or a maximum of $500 ($100 × 5) in additional money that can be created from the initial deposit.

If the Fed lowers the reserve requirement, the money multiplier gets larger. If the Fed raises the reserve requirement, the money multiplier gets smaller.

✓ **Checkpoint**

Describe the role of money in the economy.

Lesson Review

Check Your Understanding

1. List and define each of the economic systems presented in the chapter. (LO 20.1.1)

2. What group has the ultimate power to determine what will be produced and at what prices in a market economy? (LO 20.1.1)

3. Why is purchasing power important in a market economy? (LO 20.1.2)

4. How does the money multiplier create more money in the economy? (LO 20.1.3)

Apply Your Understanding

1. To help another student understand the concepts, your teacher has asked you to create a comparison chart to demonstrate the characteristics of hands-on and hands-off economic systems. How does each type of system impact economic efficiency, individual freedoms, and societal welfare? (LO 20.1.1)

2. How is the market price of a good or service affected by (a) an increase in demand; (b) a decrease in demand; (c) an increase in supply; and (d) a decrease in supply? (LO 20.1.2)

3. Explain the three requirements for money to be functional in an economic system. (LO 20.1.3)

The Essential Question

What are the characteristics of the various types of economic systems, and what is the role of money?

A: Hands-on and hands-off economic systems are characterized by the degree of government control. Hands-on systems, such as communism and socialism, have a high degree of governmental control. Hands-off systems, such as traditional and pure capitalism systems, have limited governmental control. Most economic systems are mixed systems that include characteristics of more than one type. Money provides a medium of exchange that is divisible, durable, and a store of value.

20.2 Consumer Responsibilities

The Essential Question What are some major forms of deception in the marketplace, and how can consumers protect themselves?

Learning Objectives

By the end of this lesson, you should be able to:

LO 20.2.1 Summarize deceptive practices used to defraud consumers.

LO 20.2.2 Discuss how to be a responsible consumer and protect yourself from fraudsters.

Key Terms

- deception
- imposter scam
- online shopping fraud
- bait and switch
- infomercial
- malware
- low-balling
- pyramid scheme
- Ponzi scheme
- clearance
- liquidation

LO 20.2.1 Recognizing Fraud and Deception

The marketplace is full of deceptive and misleading promotions that persuade consumers to buy goods and services of inferior quality or that they do not need or want. **Deception** occurs when false or misleading claims are made about a particular product's quality, price, or purpose. In many cases, little can be done once the consumer has been fooled into purchasing. Dishonest sellers quickly disappear or deny wrongdoing. In a market economy, consumers must learn to recognize potential fraud before becoming victims. Prevention is still the best safeguard against financial misfortune. Fraud can lead to identity theft. Identity theft, as covered in a previous chapter, is stealing someone's personal information to gain access to their finances.

Imposter Scams

The most common type of fraud is the imposter scam. In an **imposter scam**, the fraudsters will target people by pretending to be someone else. Examples include frantic calls or texts on behalf of a child or grandchild who is stranded or imprisoned in a foreign country and needs money wired immediately. Others include phone calls, texts, or emails from legitimate sounding sources such as the IRS or the Social Security Administration stating that if you do not pay them immediately, you will be subject to late fees, additional taxes, or even jail.

The easiest way to protect yourself from an imposter scam is to verify what the caller is saying. Someone who is legitimate will be willing to allow you to confirm their identity. Take a few minutes to confirm the information.

Why should you be cautious when clicking hyperlinks while using social media and email?

Online Shopping Fraud

The second most common type of fraud is online shopping fraud. **Online shopping fraud** is when cybercriminals create fake retail websites or use fake ads, either on legitimate websites or via social media. Online shopping fraud often uses fake reviews.

Another tactic with online shopping and shopping in person is the bait and switch scam. **Bait and switch** is an illegal sales technique in which a seller advertises a product to persuade consumers to buy a more expensive product. The bait is a bargain product that gets customers to

Why should you use caution when considering products you see demonstrated by a social media influencer?

visit the store, either in person or online. However, when they attempt to purchase the advertised product, the product is not available, and a more expensive product is offered.

Protecting yourself from shopping fraud can be as simple as checking for return policies, reading the reviews for complaints, verifying that the website is secure, and paying with a credit card. Also, remember that if something appears to be too good to be true, it probably is.

Infomercials

An **infomercial** is a lengthy paid advertisement with testimonials and product demonstrations. These advertisements generally last 15 to 30 minutes and target people who want to improve their appearance or health. For example, products for weight loss, removing wrinkles, and hair growth are commonly seen on infomercials. While the product may be reputable, there is no guarantee, and the claims about results may be greatly exaggerated. With infomercials, finding out whether the business is reputable, and the product works before you buy is essential. Be cautious about giving credit card numbers over the telephone. Do not assume that because something worked for the paid actors or social media influencers describing the product on social media that you will receive the same results. You must also beware of add-ons, such as high shipping and handling charges and club memberships. Although you may get your initial shipment at a reduced price, you unknowingly may be signing up for some other hidden commitment, such as regular monthly shipments.

Infomercials can also be created by social media influencers who are advertising or demonstrating a product hoping that their followers will order the product. The influencer receives a commission on each product sold and can also make money from each view of their video.

Internet Service Scams

These scams often begin with a text message or email offering tech support because they have identified a virus on your device. They may ask to "take over" your computer to fix the problem, giving them access to your private information or to install malware. **Malware** is short for malicious software that is downloaded to your computer when you click a link provided by the cybercriminals. The malware can damage your electronic device or access our personal data from the device.

Your best form of protection is to keep your virus protection up-to-date and if you need service, you initiate the call. Rarely will a legitimate company contact you, and if they do, they will understand if you wish to disconnect the call so that you can call the company directly to confirm.

Sweepstakes or Lottery Scams

Consumers lose billions of dollars each year to telemarketing or online fraud. One warning sign is the offer of a free prize if you pay shipping and handling. A genuinely free prize never requires that you pay a fee. Foreign lotteries are illegal, and sweepstakes requiring you to pay any money are not legitimate.

Fraudulent marketers will ask you to wire money or give them a credit card number to claim your prize. Unsolicited calls or messages from telemarketers who

know about you should sound an alarm. Promises of big prizes, beautiful vacations, and no-risk investments usually turn out to be fraudulent. The marketers collect the tax, fees, delivery charges, and other "costs" from you, and then you never receive your prize.

Other Types of Online Fraud

Common types of online fraud include:

- Phishing and spoofing. Cybercriminals can send email or messages that appear to be from a legitimate source, asking you to provide private information such as your bank account. These messages are known as phishing messages. Spoofing is when cybercriminals create a website that looks like a business to get you to log in so that they can steal your log in credentials.
- Data breach. A data breach is when a cybercriminal hacks into a legitimate system to steal data.
- Ransomware. This is a type of malware that prevents the user (typically a business) from using their computer systems until they pay a ransom to recover the data. Most ransomware is distributed through a phishing email. You can protect yourself by being aware of online scams. You should never send money to someone you meet online, share personal information with someone you do not know, or click on hyperlinks in email, instant messages, or social media posts. Legitimate businesses will never ask you for your password. Always go directly to the company's website when you are conducting business.

Low-Balling

Repair shops sometimes use a deceptive practice called low-balling. **Low-balling** is a technique where a company advertises a product or service at a low price to lure in customers and then attempts to persuade

How do repair shops use the low-balling strategy?

them that they need additional products or services. For example, an appliance repair person quotes a price, but after dismantling the appliance, they discover other repairs that will cost extra. If the consumer refuses to make the additional repairs, the repairperson may charge extra fees for reassembly.

Another form of low-balling involves applying pressure to convince car owners that their cars need additional work for safe operation. For example, a repair shop may offer a special on brake replacements. But when the mechanics inspect the brakes, they find other repairs that may not be necessary. Customers may wind up with a front-end alignment, wheel balancing, or other repairs that are not as urgent as they believe.

To protect yourself from this type of low-balling, state that you want no repairs other than those agreed upon unless the repair shop informs you of the additional cost ahead of time and you choose to authorize the extra maintenance. You should not pay for unauthorized work. Before having a major job done, get a second opinion. Discuss major car repairs with someone you trust who knows about the mechanical aspects of cars. Find a mechanic you know and can trust. Do not take your vehicle to repair shops you know nothing about.

Pyramid Schemes

A **pyramid scheme** is a multilevel marketing plan that promises members (distributors) commissions from their sales and those of other members they recruit. A cash investment is usually required to become a distributor of the product being sold. The pyramid consists of managers at the top and many middle and lower distributors who arrange parties to sell products to friends and acquaintances and recruit new distributors. The managers at the top make big profits by selling the products to the distributors below them in the pyramid—not to the public. However, most distributors lower in the pyramid never make a profit or recover their initial investment. Instead, they are left with many low-quality products that no one wants to buy and cannot find new members to recruit.

The best defense against pyramid sales schemes is to remember that you cannot expect to make big profits without hard

Why do Ponzi schemes need more and more investors to continue?

work. Before committing to such a plan, investigate it. Talk to people who have purchased the products. Check with local consumer protection agencies. Think it through. What is the company's track record? Does the company have evidence to back up its claims? Who will buy this product? Will your commission depend on recruiting other distributors? Be skeptical if the company requires you to buy a "starter kit" of sales brochures and product inventory.

Ponzi Schemes

A **Ponzi scheme** is a fraudulent investment operation in which money collected from new investors is used to pay off earlier investors. A person represents themself as an expert financial adviser. The "expert" promises solid investment returns, usually much higher than the market in general. For a while, the fraudster maintains the appearance of a legitimate business and pays dividends to the victims. This helps lure in new investors, often through recommendations. But the dividends are being paid with money from new investors, while the fraudster pockets the rest of the money. Eventually, the investment accounts fail, and the investors lose their money.

Source: iStock.com/ipopba

How can you avoid telemarketing and online scams?

The fraudster is prosecuted, but the money is often never recovered.

The local Better Business Bureau is the best protection against this type of swindle. The Bureau is equipped to investigate unsound businesses. Insist upon seeing credentials, annual financial reports, and proof of past dealings. Invest only in established firms with a proven track record.

Telemarketing and Online Marketing Scams

Many companies use telemarketing and online marketing to sell customers products they do not need. You can protect yourself from these calls by saying "No, thank you" and hanging up or by deleting the email or message and reporting it as junk to your internet or cellular provider. You can significantly reduce the number of unwanted telemarketing calls you receive by signing up with the government's National Do Not Call Registry. You can register for free online at www.donotcall.gov.

Around holidays and after disasters, fraudulent telemarketers and online marketers may claim to represent charities and ask for donations. Before giving money to someone claiming to represent a major company or charity, check with the organization to verify the person's claims. The local Better Business Bureau will have a record of solicitors who repeatedly engage in questionable practices.

> ✓ **Checkpoint**
>
> What are different types of scams?

Being a Responsible Consumer

Learning to identify various deceptive marketing tactics is the first step toward being a responsible consumer. Prevention is your best choice. After you have been swindled, it is difficult to undo the financial damage. To protect yourself, be alert for the warning signs of a scam. Educate yourself on products and prices and seek redress when necessary.

Identify Deceptive Practices

When you hear unrealistic claims, be suspicious. Watch for warning signals in claims or offers made through advertising and by salespeople. Below is a list of common warning signals of possible deception that should catch your attention. Protect yourself by knowing these warning signs.

- You are contacted unexpectedly. For example, you receive an email, text, or telephone call telling you that you owe the IRS and if you do not pay immediately, you can be arrested and go to jail.
- You are told that you must act now. If they tell you that you must claim your prize immediately by providing your bank account or credit card information, it is probably a scam.
- They ask for your personal information. If a company contacts you to ask for personal information, tell them you will call them back with the information or provide it the next time you are at the business.
- You need to wire money. Never wire money to anyone you do not know.
- It sounds too good to be true. Then it is probably a scam.

Shop Smart

Our economy produces a large assortment of products from which to choose. The methods used to sell them sometimes need to be more accurate. Although the internet provides helpful shopping tools, it also presents hidden dangers. There are many things you can do to help make wise buying decisions.

- Shop at several stores. Comparison shopping involves comparing the quality, price, and warranties for the same products at several different stores or websites. Online price-comparison search tools are very useful for this.
- Be aware of prices. Know regular or list prices of everyday items. Terms often used in advertising, such as *manufacturer's list price* and *suggested retail price* and phrases such as *$40 value for only $35*, attract your attention. But the prices may not be reduced.
- Understand sale terminology. Sale means that goods are being offered for sale but not necessarily at reduced prices. **Clearance** implies that the merchant wants to clear out all the advertised merchandise. **Liquidation** means the merchant wants to sell the inventory or merchandise immediately to turn it into cash. These terms are often used interchangeably, and no reduction in price is given.
- Avoid impulse buying. When you shop, take a list with you and buy only what is on the list. Avoid displays of products that attract your attention but are unnecessary. Do not let the convenience of online shopping lure you into buying something you do not need.
- Plan your purchases. Thoroughly research major purchases before making your choice. Read online and printed product information and comparative reviews. Do not make major purchases when you are emotionally stressed or have

impaired judgment. Ask questions so you are sure that you understand claims, features, prices, and terms. For example, the product may show the net price after a mail-in rebate. However, you may not qualify for the rebate, or it may have expired.

- Compute unit prices. Unit pricing is the cost for one unit of an item sold in packages of more than one unit. For example, to compare the price of a 15-ounce box with the price of a 24-ounce box, divide the total price of each box by the number of ounces in it. The result is the price per ounce. The lowest unit price for products of comparable quality is the best buy.
- Read labels. Know ingredients and materials and what they mean. For example, a shirt that is 100 percent cotton may shrink, or if it is a dress shirt, it will probably have to be pressed each time you wear it. A product labeled Dry Clean Only will be more expensive to maintain.
- Check containers carefully. Be sure packages have not been opened or damaged. Report any suspicious openings in packages to the store manager.
- Read contracts. Read and understand contracts and agreements before signing them.
- Keep receipts and warranties. Print out warranty statements and sales receipts from online purchases. For all major purchases, keep receipts and warranties, guarantees, or other written promises in case you need to make returns or get replacements later.

Sharpen Your Personal Finance Skills
Computing Unit Prices

Justin has decided to prepare meals for the week to avoid eating out and to save money. While picking up groceries, he remembers that he needs spaghetti sauce and sees two options. He wants to make sure he gets the best value for the money he spends.

Justin's options are to buy 24 ounces for $6.84 or 15 ounces for $4.89. To determine which is better, Justin computes the cost per unit by dividing the total cost by total units:

$$\$6.84 \div 24 \text{ ounces} = \$0.285 \text{ per ounce}$$
$$\$4.89 \div 15 \text{ ounces} = \$0.326 \text{ per ounce}$$

In this case, Justin finds that the 24-ounce container is the better buy.

Try It Out!

Justin is looking to purchase packs of ramen noodles to have available for a quick snack. Based on the previous example, determine which of the following is the better buy: three packages for $0.89 or six packages for $1.99?

- Compute total cost. Check the total cost of an item, including supplementary item, such as batteries, delivery charges, finance charges, and other add-on costs. In some cases, the base price may be lower than for similar products, but once you add up all the related charges, you will find that the total cost exceeds other choices.
- Ask for references. Ask company representatives for references to ensure they represent the company. Call the company to check.
- Be loyal. Patronize online and brick-and-mortar businesses that have good reputations and have served you well in the past. Tell others when you have a good experience and ask others for recommendations for doctors, accountants, repair shops, and other service businesses. Read online reviews and look for verified customers. If all the reviews are good, they may not be true.
- Check up on businesses. Check for valid certifications, licenses, bonding, and endorsements. Use your local Better Business Bureau and your state's business records division to ensure you get service from qualified and reputable professionals.
- Wait a day for major purchases. Try waiting at least 24 hours before making a major purchase to be sure you are not making the purchase on impulse or

How can you protect yourself when shopping online?

Source: iStock.com/vittaya25

being pressured into buying it. Many people change their minds after a cooling-off period. If you still want the product after further consideration, you can be sure you are buying it for the right reasons.

Online Shopping

You are responsible for protecting yourself if you shop online. Here are some tips to follow when shopping over the internet:

- Shop at secure websites. Look for *https* in the web address. This indicates the website is secure.
- Check the website address, called the uniform resource locator (URL). Most business web addresses should be followed by .com; government addresses should be followed by .gov; nonprofit organization addresses often use .org; and college or university addresses use .edu. Research sites that use nonstandard URLs. Most are legitimate businesses, but some may not be trustworthy. Always check to make sure the website is secure before inputting your personal information.
- Read the website's privacy and security policies. These policies are usually listed in a section entitled Privacy and Security. Determine if the site intends to share your information with a third party or another company. If the policies are not posted, do not trust the site.
- Shop safely. The safest way to shop online is with a credit card, a prepaid gift card, or one of the online payment options on a secure site. You can protest the charge through your credit card company if something goes wrong. With a prepaid gift card, you do not have to supply personal information, thus preventing identity theft.
- Share only the essentials when you order. Never provide a Social Security number, date of birth, or other information not relevant to the purchase.

When you explore different websites, be aware that you are not always anonymous. Some sites can immediately determine certain information about you when you visit that site, such as the type of computer system you use, the company you use to access the internet, and the last web page you visited.

At some websites you must log in, register, and/or give information about yourself. This information is saved and often shared with others. These "digital footprints" enable companies to determine whether you are a potential customer and what types of interests you have.

Some businesses electronically record information about your visit to their site by depositing a piece of information called a cookie onto your computer. Once a cookie is saved on your computer, that website can keep track of information about your visit, such as which parts of the site you visit. This helps site operators determine the most popular areas of their site. It also helps them improve the site and its offerings. Cookies also allow for more efficiency when revisiting a site because:

- Your preferences for visiting certain areas of the site are stored in your cookie file. The next time you return, the section you like best may already be displayed for you.
- You may be alerted to new areas of interest based on web pages you have previously visited.
- Your past purchases may be recorded in the cookie file so that the site knows what you like; thus, you may be shown special offers on products and services tailored to your interests.

Some versions of browser software can be set to notify you before a website places a cookie on your computer. Then you can choose to accept or reject the cookie. Some browsers will allow you to deactivate a cookie. You can also delete cookie files, but you will lose the personal customization offered by the sites. Many computer users find it important to systematically remove cookies and other information linking their computer usage to specific sites. This helps protect your privacy.

Think Critically

1. What websites do you visit regularly? What information have you given them about yourself? How might companies use this information?
2. What are the advantages and disadvantages of having cookies stored on your computer?
3. What are ways that you can manage your digital footprint to protect your privacy and personal information?

- Save or print the confirmation order. Keep the copy of what you have ordered as well as the page showing the company name, address, phone number, and legal terms.
- Know shipping and return policies. Check the website for cancellation and return policies.
- Use common sense. If it seems too good to be true, it probably is!

Stay Informed

You are responsible for educating yourself about products and services before you buy. To protect yourself, actively seek consumer information in the following ways:

- Become familiar with sources of information on goods and services, such as *Consumer Reports* and consumer-oriented websites.
- Read warranties and guarantees. Ask questions so that you can fully understand performance claims. Get written guarantees and warranties whenever possible.
- Read and understand care instructions before using a product.
- Analyze advertisements about products before buying. Know why you are interested in the product or service and decide what you want before you buy.

- Know the protections offered by consumer protection laws and know how to seek a remedy to consumer problems. Inform consumer protection agencies of fraudulent or unsafe performance of products and services. Make your dissatisfaction known to help others avoid the same problem and to prompt producers to improve their product or service.
- Post comments (both positive and negative) about products on websites and social media so that others can benefit from your experience. Read through similar postings before you buy or do business with a company.
- Report wants likes, and dislikes, as well as suggested improvements and complaints, to retailers and manufacturers.
- Keep good records of complaints, product defects, actions taken to resolve problems, names of people you have talked to, and so on. You will need these forms of evidence to support your claims.

✓ Checkpoint

Name and describe two ways to shop smarter.

Check Your Understanding

1. Describe the two most common types of consumer fraud. (LO 20.2.1)

2. What is the first step toward being a responsible consumer? (LO 20.2.2)

Apply Your Understanding

1. Watch a social media ad and research the source of the ad. Is this a legitimate business, or could this be considered a type of fraud? Explain your reasoning. *Note:* Include a link to the ad with your answer. (LO 20.2.1)

2. Your grandmother received a call from the IRS telling her that she owed $10,000 in back taxes. Explain to your grandmother why this was a scam attempting to scare her into sending money. (LO 20.2.2)

The Essential Question

What are some major forms of deception in the marketplace, and how can consumers protect themselves?

A: Major forms of deception include imposter scams, online shopping fraud, infomercials, internet service scams, sweepstake or lottery scams, low-balling, pyramid schemes, Ponzi schemes, and telemarketing and online marketing scams. To protect themselves, consumers can shop smart, use precautions when online, and stay informed.

Summary

20.1 Our Market Economy

- An economic system refers to the process used by society to decide what to produce, how to produce it, and for whom to produce it.

- Hands-on economic systems involve government controls over the way decisions are made. Examples are communism and socialism.

- Hands-off economic systems do not involve central authority; individuals make the choices. Traditional and pure capitalism are examples.

- Most economies today are mixed. A free-enterprise system with some governmental controls is today's market economy.

- In market economies, producers and consumers play active roles. Producers are the manufacturers or makers of goods. Consumers are the buyers and users of goods and services.

- All economies face the problem of scarcity because resources are limited but consumer wants and needs are increasing and unlimited.

- In a market economy, the interaction of supply and demand determines what will be produced, in what quantities, and at what prices.

- Consumers have the ultimate power in a market economy. Producers also have power because they can employ various techniques to influence consumer buying decisions.

- To function smoothly, a market economy needs competition, purchasing power, and informed consumers.

- All economic systems use some form of money or medium of exchange. Money must be readily divisible, durable, and recognizable as a store of value.

- Fiat money is backed by faith in the general economy and government of the country.

- Money is subject to the forces of supply and demand. Governments can manage money supply through monetary policy.

- Banks can create more money by lending money they have on deposit from customers. The money multiplier indicates how much more money can be created.

20.2 Consumer Responsibilities

- The marketplace offers fraudsters many opportunities for deceptive practices.

- Fraud can lead to identity theft, which involves stealing personal information to gain access to a person's finances.

- Imposter scams are the most common type of fraud.

- Online shopping fraud is a growing type of fraud.

- Informercials may be a form of online shopping fraud by offering inferior products.

- Internet service scams attempt to steal personal information by taking over a computer or other electronic device.

- Sweepstakes and lottery scams convince people to pay a small handling fee to receive a large prize that does not exist.

- Other types of online fraud can involve phishing or spoofing, data breaches, and ransomware.

- Repair shops use low-balling when they offer a repair at a low price but then suggest other "necessary" services to run up the price.

- Pyramid schemes are a type of multilevel marketing plan that depend on recruiting multiple levels of distributors. Distributors are promised commissions from their own sales and other members they recruit.

- Ponzi schemes lure in potential investors with promises of high returns, but, in fact, dividends are paid from new investors' money.

- Fraudulent representation can occur through telemarketing and online marketing scams.

- To be a responsible consumer, learn to identify deceptive practices, follow wise buying habits, and stay informed.

Check Your Knowledge

1. Who decides what goods and services will be provided in each of the four types of economic systems? (LO 20.1.1)

2. Describe a market economy. (LO 20.1.2)

3. Explain how the Federal Reserve can "grow" or "shrink" money in the economy. (LO 20.1.3)

4. Select two deceptive practices. Define each and explain why they are so common. (LO 20.2.1)

5. Why is it important for a consumer to protect themselves from fraud? (LO 20.2.2)

Apply Your Knowledge

1. What are the implications of a hands-on and a hands-off economic system on innovation and resource allocation? (LO 20.1.1)

2. Is the United States a market economy or a mixed economy? Explain your answer by listing the characteristics of a market economy and identifying how the U.S. economy fits each characteristic. (LO 20.1.2)

3. When would the Federal Reserve want to "shrink" the amount of money in the economy? Explain why they would want to do this. (LO 20.1.3)

4. Have you ever watched a social media influencer demonstrate a product? Did you purchase the product? If so, did it work in the same way that the influencer said it would work? If you did not purchase the product, what was the reason you decided not to make the purchase? (LO 20.2.1)

5. One of the ways you can protect yourself from internet fraud is to only use secure websites. Another way is to only use a secure wi-fi network. What is a secure wi-fi network and how can you determine if you are using a secure network? (LO 20.2.2)

Share Your Knowledge

Work in teams of two to four students to complete the following activities.

1. The supply of products impacts the quantity of goods available for sale while demand impacts the number of products desired by consumers. As a team, create a presentation or other creative product to demonstrate what happens to prices in the following situations. (LO 20.1.2)

    a. A hurricane causes major damage along the coast of the Gulf of Mexico, shutting down the gasoline refineries in the area.

    b. A pandemic forces people to stay home, reducing the need for them to drive to and from work and limiting their ability to travel by air or train.

    c. The weather conditions are perfect for raising corn, creating an increase in the amount of corn products to manufacture food.

    d. A new drug is approved by the U.S. Food and Drug Administration (FDA) for diabetes control. One of the side effects is rapid weight loss.

2. Visit the Federal Trade Commission's website to learn about the latest frauds and schemes being carried out against consumers. Create a video or some other informative product on a new scheme that is not discussed in this chapter. (LO 20.2.1)

3. Create a large-print reference card (include pictures and limited text) that can be distributed at a local retirement community to build awareness and explain how consumers can protect themselves from scams that impact the elderly. (LO 20.2.2)

Connect and Reflect

Base your answers to the following questions on your own personal thoughts, preferences, and experiences.

1. Why is money important in our economy, and how does money help consumers buy the things they need and want? In your opinion, what are ways that money can make the United States stronger and better for everyone? (LO 20.1.3)

2. Some celebrities and social media influencers lend their names to products that later turn out to be ineffective or harmful to consumers. The celebrities are paid to endorse the product by claiming they have used it. But in many cases, the celebrities know very little about it. Some celebrities have been held legally liable because people relied on their claims. When a celebrity—whether an entertainer, athlete, or influencer—endorses a product or service, do you seek to buy it based on their opinion alone? Do you think this marketing tactic is effective? Is it ethical? Explain why or why not. (LO 20.2.1)

3. What steps can you take to be a responsible consumer and protect yourself from fraud? How would these actions help you make smart and safe choices when buying goods and services? (LO 20.2.2)

Chapter Project

Record all purchases you make in a week and then analyze the impact of those purchases on the environment and your personal health. Create a written report or digital presentation summarizing your findings and proposing personal actions for more responsible consumption.

21 Chapter

Consumer Protection and Dispute Resolution

21.1 Consumer Rights and Laws

The Essential Question

What rights do you have as a consumer, and what types of protection are provided by consumer laws?

Learning Objectives

By the end of this lesson, you should be able to:

LO 21.1.1 Describe consumer rights.

LO 21.1.2 Identify protections provided by major federal consumer protection laws.

Key Terms

- time-shifting
- space-shifting
- generic drugs
- flammability
- recall
- childproof
- care labels

Consider This ...

Coy bought a computer using an online auction website. To complete the purchase, he provided his credit card number and expiration date, along with his name and home address for shipping.

"I think you can get a pretty good deal when you buy online," he told his instructor. "But at the same time, I worry about giving personal information to a vendor that I don't know. Before I made the purchase, I checked the Better Business Bureau's website and found that this company meets its criteria and that there are no complaints filed against it. I also checked some other consumer complaint websites and didn't find any complaints posted about the company. That makes me feel a little better, but I know I'm still taking a risk. Do you think there are any other ways I can protect myself when shopping online? What do I do if this was not a legitimate sale?"

Read and Reflect

1. What rights does Coy have as a consumer?

2. What recommendations would you give Coy to ensure that he is protected when shopping online?

3. What options does Coy have if this is not a legitimate sale? What if the product does not meet the description outlined?

LO 21.1.1 Consumer Rights

For many years, the consumer's position in the marketplace was known as buyer beware. Consumers had little protection against unfair business practices. As abuses have become apparent, new rights for citizens and consumers have arisen.

Consumer Bill of Rights

One of the most important advances in consumer protection was the adoption of the Consumer Bill of Rights. This law was proposed by President Kennedy in 1962. It outlines the four basic rights of consumers:

1. The right to safety. This right protects consumers against products that are hazardous to life or health. It implies that products should cause no harm to their users if used for their intended purpose.
2. The right to be informed. This right protects consumers from product information that is fraudulent, deceitful, or misleading and assures them that they will be given the facts needed to make intelligent and informed product choices.
3. The right to choose. This right ensures consumers that they will have access to a variety of quality products and services offered at competitive prices.

What are the basic provisions of the Consumer Bill of Rights?

Source: iStock.com/FangXiaNuo

4. The right to be heard. This right allows consumers to voice complaints and concerns about a product or service. It also gives consumers a voice in formulating government policies related to consumer interests.

In 1985, the United Nations endorsed consumer rights through the United Nations Guidelines for Consumer Protection, and they were expanded to include four more consumer rights, for a total of eight basic rights:

5. The right to the satisfaction of basic needs. This right demands that people have access to basic, essential goods and services, including adequate food, clothing, shelter, health care, education, public utilities, water, and sanitation.
6. The right to redress. This right assures that buyers can receive fair settlement (such as compensation) for valid claims involving misrepresentation, inferior products, or unsatisfactory services.
7. The right to consumer education. This right gives consumers access to information and programs that help them acquire the necessary knowledge and skills to make better marketplace decisions. When educated, consumers are aware of basic consumer rights and responsibilities and know how to act on them.
8. The right to a healthy environment. This right asserts that people should live and work in a clean, safe, healthy environment that is nonthreatening to the well-being of present and future generations.

Airline Passenger Rights

In 1999, it became apparent that airline passengers were being treated unfairly. Thus, many saw the need for a bill of rights for airline passengers. In 2009 and 2011, the U.S. Department of Transportation (DOT) expanded these rights by adding several more rules.

Basic protections for airline passengers now include the following:

- Reservations. Once you have a confirmed reservation, you will be provided a seat on that flight even if there is no reservation record in the airline's computer system. If you have a ticket, electronic or print, an agent cannot deny boarding because there is no reservation "in the computer." (However, if you do not show up for a flight and fail to cancel the reservation, you are considered a no-show, and the airline can cancel any continuing or return reservations.)

- Refunds. If you cancel a ticket for a "nonrefundable fare," you may be able to apply the fare toward a future flight, minus any applicable charges or cancellation fees. If you cancel a refundable ticket, your refund will be issued in the same manner as your purchase (for example, if you used a credit card, the credit card will be credited).

- Delays and cancellations. Airlines are not required to compensate passengers for delayed or canceled flights, but they must promptly notify consumers of delays of over 30 minutes and cancellations and diversions.

- Bumped flights. Compensation is required if you are "bumped" from an oversold flight. The only exception to this requirement is if the airline can claim extraordinary circumstances, such as weather or security issues. If you are voluntarily bumped, you may receive a free ticket or voucher. If you are involuntarily bumped, you have the right to compensation, which can be as much as 200 to 400 percent of the cost of your one-way fare.

- Extended tarmac delays. U.S. airlines operating domestic flights cannot permit an aircraft to remain on the tarmac for more than 3 hours, except for safety, security, and air traffic control-related reasons. The rule also requires U.S. airlines to provide basic services, such

Do you think there is a need for an airline passengers' bill of rights? Why or why not?

as access to working lavatories and food and water. In April 2010, this rule was expanded to include a 4-hour limit on the tarmac for international flights experiencing delays.

- Fee disclosures. Airlines must disclose all potential fees on their websites, including but not limited to fees for baggage, meals, canceling or changing reservations, or advanced or upgraded seating.

Consumer Technology Bill of Rights

As a result of technology and its widespread use by consumers, a Consumer Technology Bill of Rights was introduced by Congress in 2002. It recognizes the reasonable, personal, and noncommercial rights of consumers related to technology. Provisions include the following:

1. Time-shifting. Users can record legally acquired video or audio for later viewing or listening. This is referred to as **time-shifting**. For example, you can record a TV show and watch it later.

2. Space-shifting. Users have the right to use legally acquired content in different places. This is referred to as **space-shifting**. For example, you can download your data from one cloud platform and store it on another.

3. Backup copies. Users can archive or make backup copies of their content for use if the original copies are destroyed.
4. Platform of choice. Users can use legally acquired content on the electronic platform or device of their choice.
5. Translation. Users can translate legally acquired content into comparable formats.
6. Use of technology. Users have the right to use technology to achieve the rights enumerated in the first five rights.

Patients' Bill of Rights

Abuses in managed care and other related institutions created the need for a patients' bill of rights. These policies were adopted by the President's Advisory Commission on Consumer Protection and Quality in the Health Care Industry in 1998. Further rights were proposed in 2008, and in 2010, when the Affordable Care Act was signed, an updated Patient's Bill of Rights was created. Broadly, patients have the following rights:

- Information about quality. Patients must be able to receive accurate, easy-to-understand information about health plans, healthcare professionals, and hospitals and clinics so they can choose wisely.
- Choose a healthcare provider. All health plans must offer a wide enough range of coverage options. Women have the right to choose a gynecological and obstetrical professional. If a health care plan does not provide these basic provisions, a patient has the right to go outside the plan at no additional cost.
- Emergency services. A patient has the right to seek emergency care if a reasonable person would consider the event an emergency.
- Decision making. A patient has the right to be given all necessary information to make their own healthcare decisions. They have the right to refuse treatment. It is recommended that patients create a living will to ensure their wishes are carried out.

- Respect. All patients have the right to be treated with respect and good manners. In turn, patients have the responsibility to treat healthcare professionals with respect.
- Confidentiality. Healthcare professionals cannot discuss your health history with anyone unless you have given permission for them to do so. You have the right to access all your healthcare records.
- Patient responsibilities. As a patient, you have the responsibility to eat healthfully, try to stop bad habits, listen to your doctors' opinions and advice, complete agreed-upon treatments, and tell your healthcare provider what they need to know to treat you properly. In addition, a patient has a responsibility to take care not to spread disease, show respect for healthcare workers, take the time to understand health plans, do their best to pay bills in a timely manner, report fraud, and follow the rules and regulations governing the health plan.

Other Consumer Rights

In addition to the consumer rights mentioned here, there are many other rights and responsibilities of consumers. For example, in 2023, President Joe Biden proposed the Blueprint for an AI Bill of Rights. Although not a law at the time this book was written, the AI Bill of Rights proposal will be a guide that allows society to protect people from the threats posed by the misuse of artificial intelligence. Another example is Europe's AI Act, which was approved in December 2023. The details of the act will be developed in 2024 and include regulation for artificial intelligence.

✓ Checkpoint

What are the consumer rights related to technology, passenger rights, and health care?

LO 21.1.2 Consumer Protection Laws

Over the years, Congress has passed many laws to protect consumers from unsafe products and unfair or deceptive business practices. These laws help ensure that consumers get quality goods and services for their hard-earned dollars. Some of these laws have been updated and amended over time.

Food, Drug, and Cosmetic Laws

In 1937, a Tennessee drug company marketed a new wonder drug that would appeal to pediatric patients. However, the solvent in this untested product was a highly toxic chemical like antifreeze. Over 100 people died, many of whom were children. The public outcry reshaped the drug provisions of a new law proposed that year to prevent such an event from happening again. The Food, Drug, and Cosmetic Act of 1938 requires that foods be safe, pure, and wholesome; drugs and medical devices be safe and effective; and cosmetics be safe. The law also requires truthful labeling on these products, including the name and address of the manufacturer. In addition, the law mandates that the U.S. Food and Drug Administration (FDA) approve drugs before they can be sold.

This law has been amended several times. Some of the amendments and new acts related to food, drugs, and cosmetics include:

- In 1951, the Durham-Humphrey Amendment defined over-the-counter drugs and prescription drugs by adding an amendment that defines prescription medications as those unsafe for self-medication and requiring prescriptions to be dispensed by a licensed pharmacist.

- In 1962, the Kefauver-Harris Amendment was created in response to the thousands of children born with congenital disabilities due to the use of thalidomide to relieve morning sickness. This amendment required drug manufacturers to provide evidence of a drug's safety and for side effects to be disclosed. It also prohibited generic drugs from being marketed using the trade name. **Generic drugs** have the same chemical structure as trade name drugs. Pharmaceutical companies are allowed to replicate trade name drugs once the patent for the drug has expired.

- In 1976, the Medical Device Amendment was created to classify medical devices into three categories of risk and to share that information.

- In 1980, the Infant Formula Act was passed to establish a minimum nutrient requirement for infant formula and put quality measures into place related to infant formula.

- In 1983, the Orphan Drug Act was created to incentivize the development of drugs (called orphan drugs) to treat rare diseases such as cystic fibrosis and Huntington disease.

- In 1983, the Federal Anti-Tampering Act made it a crime to tamper with packaged consumer products.

- In 1984, the Drug Price Competition and Patent Term Restoration Act expanded the number of drugs that could be reviewed under the abbreviated new drug application process. This process made it less costly and time-consuming for generic drugs to reach the market. The Office of Generic Drugs was established in 1989 as a result of the act.

- In 1990, the Nutrition Labeling and Education Act required FDA-regulated foods to include nutrition labels with all nutrient content and health claims.

- In 1994, the Dietary Supplement Health and Education Act defined and established regulations for dietary supplements.

- In 1996, the Food Quality Protection Act regulated the use of pesticides in food cultivation and incentivized the creation of safer pesticides.
- In 2005, the FDA formed the Drug Safety Oversight Board.

More recently, the FDA has worked to make clinical trials more inclusive to help medical experts determine if there are differences in drug responses among different demographic groups in the population. For example, are there differences in drug interactions based on age or gender?

Flammable Fabrics Act

The Flammable Fabrics Act of 1953 enabled the Consumer Product Safety Commission to set flammability standards for clothing, children's sleepwear, carpets, rugs, and mattresses. **Flammability** is the capacity to catch on fire. The law prohibits the selling of wearable apparel made of easily ignited material. The flammability standard for children's sleepwear requires that the garment will not catch fire when exposed to a match or small fire. The flame-retardant finish must last for 50 washings and dryings. In 1967, Congress amended the Flammable Fabrics Act to expand its coverage to include interior furnishings as well as paper, plastic, foam, and other materials used in consumer products.

Meat Inspection Laws

Numerous acts that standardize inspection procedures have been passed to protect consumers who purchase chicken and beef. The Poultry Products Inspection Act of 1957 requires poultry to be inspected for harmful contaminants. These requirements also apply to imported meat and poultry products, which must be inspected under equivalent foreign standards. In 1967, the Wholesome Meat Act, an update to the Meat Inspection Act of 1906, provided for stricter standards for processing facilities of meat products. States are required to have meat inspection programs equal to that of the federal government, which are administered by the U.S. Department of Agriculture (USDA).

Hazardous Substances Act

The Hazardous Substances Act of 1960 requires that warning labels appear on all household products that are potentially dangerous to the consumer. The purpose of the warning labels is to help consumers safely store and use these products and to provide information about first-aid steps to take if an accident happens. In most cases, products found to be unacceptably hazardous must be recalled. A **recall** is a request for consumers to return a defective product to the manufacturer for a refund or repair.

Cigarette Labeling, Tobacco, and Smoking Laws

The Cigarette Labeling and Advertising Act of 1965 requires tobacco companies to place a warning label on cigarette packaging. The warning label advises consumers of

What purpose do warning labels serve?

health hazards from smoking. The original labels read: "Caution: Cigarette Smoking May Be Hazardous to Your Health." Today, these warning labels are even more specific. The current labels read: "Surgeon General's Warning: Smoking Causes Lung Cancer, Heart Disease, Emphysema, and May Complicate Pregnancy."

In 2016, the Family Smoking Prevention and Tobacco Control Act was added. This act regulates electronic nicotine delivery systems (ENDS), enforces federal tobacco laws, and helps prevent youth access to tobacco products. And since 2023, stores that sell tobacco products have been required to display warning signs and information that tobacco companies lied to consumers about the health risks of using tobacco products.

National Traffic and Motor Vehicle Safety Act

The National Traffic and Motor Vehicle Safety Act of 1966 established national safety standards for automobiles. It was enacted to reduce traffic accidents as well as the number of deaths and injuries to people involved in traffic accidents. The National Highway Traffic Safety Administration enforces provisions of the act. Its responsibilities include increasing public awareness of the need for safety devices, testing for safety, and inspecting vehicles for proper safety equipment.

Fair Packaging and Labeling Act

The Fair Packaging and Labeling Act of 1967 requires product labels to contain accurate names, quantities, and weights. These rules apply to all types of products, such as groceries, cosmetics, cleaners, and chemicals.

Amendments to the Fair Packaging and Labeling Act were passed in 1992. These laws require labels to include conversion of quantities into a metric measurement in addition to the U.S. system of weights and measures.

Civil Rights Act

As part of the Civil Rights Act of 1968, the Fair Housing Act prohibits discrimination in the purchase, sale, rental, or financing of housing based on race, skin color, sex, nationality, or religion. It was amended in 1988 to add disability and family status as protected classes.

Toy Safety Laws

The Child Protection and Toy Safety Act of 1969 bans the sale of toys and children's articles that contain hazardous substances or pose electrical, mechanical, or thermal dangers. Such products can be inspected and removed from the marketplace. The act requires special labeling for children's products, along with devices that make potentially dangerous products **childproof**, or resistant to tampering by young children.

Other toy safety laws have been enacted over the years. The Toy Safety Act of 1984 permits quick recall of toys and other articles intended for use by children that might present a substantial risk of injury. In 1994 Congress passed the Child Safety Protection Act, which strengthened earlier standards and imposed strict labeling laws for manufacturers and retailers of children's toys that may present a danger to small children, such as small balls, marbles, and balloons. The Consumer Product Safety Improvement Act of 2008 requires that children's toys and infant products undergo testing before sale.

The legislation further banned use of toxic chemicals, such as lead paint, from toys and other products.

Care Labeling Rule

The Care Labeling Rule of 1971 requires that clothing and fabrics be labeled permanently with laundering and care instructions. **Care labels** give instructions for cleaning, wash and dry temperatures, and other care needed to preserve the product. The labels must stay attached and be easy to read for the life of the garment. This law was amended in 1984 to allow for exceptions to the rule for fabrics that may be damaged as a result of having a permanent label. These fabrics include leather, gloves, hats, and reversible clothing. In 1997, the law was updated to allow for the use of symbols on labels instead of written instructions.

Family and Educational Rights and Privacy Act

The Family and Educational Rights and Privacy Act (FERPA) of 1974 is a federal law that protects the privacy of student education records. Parents and students 18 years of age or older have the right to inspect and review the students' education records maintained by the school. Errors or misleading information may be corrected. Schools must obtain written permission

Connections to Your World
Food Label Regulations

Many people depend on properly labeled foods to maintain their health and to meet dietary restrictions. For example, Coy is gluten-intolerant. This means that he cannot eat foods that contain any amount of wheat protein. If foods are not labeled properly with every ingredient, Coy is at risk. Foods that are produced in other countries and shipped to the United States for consumption do not have to meet the same standards, either in purity or in labeling. Some foods produced in the United States are shipped into Mexico for processing to avoid having to follow these requirements; yet the labels may say things such as "Grown in the USA," leading people to believe that the food products meet U.S. standards. Some people feel that all foods, regardless of where they are grown or processed, should have to meet the same standards to be sold in the United States. Others believe that following these regulations only increases the cost.

Think Critically

1. Which side do you agree with and why?
2. What level of regulation would you recommend for food standards sold in the United States? Explain.
3. How important is it that foods labeled "organic" are really organic? Explain.

from the parent or student before releasing any information from a student's education record. Only directory-type information, such as name, address, phone number, and date of birth, may be disclosed without consent. Parents and students may request that even this information not be disclosed. One important requirement is that Social Security numbers cannot be used as student ID numbers.

Health Insurance Portability and Accountability Act

The Health Insurance Portability and Accountability Act (HIPAA) of 1996 sets rules about who can see your health information. The law applies to, among others, doctors, pharmacies, hospitals, health insurance companies, employer group health plans, and Medicare and Medicaid.

Protected information includes medical records, conversations, information about you stored in a computer system, and billing information. Consumers are allowed to have a copy of their health records, make corrections, know how information is being used, and decide whether to permit to share this information. Also, due to HIPAA, Social Security numbers cannot be used as a personal identifier for patients.

Children's Online Privacy Protection Act

The Children's Online Privacy Protection Act of 1998 applies to the online collection of personal information from children under age 13. The act details what a website must include in a privacy policy, when and how to seek verifiable consent from a parent or guardian, and the responsibilities of

Connections to Your World
Consumer Privacy

In 2012, the Obama administration proposed a Consumer Privacy Bill of Rights as part of a comprehensive blueprint for future legislation to protect consumers' privacy. The intent was to give consumers more control over how their personal information is used on the internet and to set principles for companies that use personal data, which is any data that can be linked to a specific individual. The bill failed to pass in 2015. Since that time, multiple bills have been introduced focusing on consumer and internet privacy. These bills include the CONSENT act, The Internet Bill of Rights, and the 2023 Consumer Data Privacy Act.

Think Critically

1. Do you think there is a need to tighten and enforce consumer privacy rights in the collection of personal data in this country? Why or why not?

2. What types of penalties would you suggest against companies and others who do not adhere to consumer privacy standards? Explain.

the website to protect children's privacy and safety online. Websites that do not comply with the act's provisions are subject to sanctions levied by the Federal Trade Commission (FTC).

Privacy of Consumer Financial Information

The Gramm-Leach-Bliley Act of 1999 regulates how financial institutions may disclose private consumer information and allows consumers to opt out of information sharing. It also requires financial institutions to notify consumers about their privacy policies.

Dodd-Frank Act

In 2010, the Dodd-Frank Wall Street Reform and Consumer Protection Act increased oversight of banks and financial institutions and created the Financial Stability Oversight Council. The act also established the Consumer Financial Protection Bureau, which regulates subprime mortgages and other predatory lending practices.

Other Consumer Protection Acts

There are many other consumer protection acts that you can learn more about through research. Some of these include the Homeowners Protection Act, the Electronic Fund Transfer Act, and the Fair Credit Billing Act.

> ### ✓ Checkpoint
>
> Briefly describe three of the consumer protection acts covered above.

Check Your Understanding

1. What four rights were added to the Consumer Bill of Rights in 1985? (LO 21.1.1)

2. Throughout history, how have consumer protection laws impacted the safety and privacy of consumers? (LO 21.1.2)

Apply Your Understanding

1. How has technology changed the way we view consumer rights and protections? (LO 21.1.1)

2. Which consumer protection law has the most significance for you? Describe how you and other consumers have benefited because this law was passed. (LO 21.1.2)

The Essential Question

What rights do you have as a consumer, and what types of protection are provided by consumer laws?

A: Consumers have basic rights, such as the right to safety, the right to be informed, the right to choose, and the right to be heard. They also have rights when it comes to flying on airlines, using technology, and receiving medical care. Congress has passed many laws to protect consumers from unsafe products and unfair or deceptive business practices. These laws help ensure that consumers get quality goods and services for their hard-earned money.

The Essential Question

What are some government and private sources of consumer assistance, and how can you promote and protect consumer interests through contacting public officials?

Learning Objectives

By the end of this lesson, you should be able to:

LO 21.2.2   Describe the government and private sources of consumer assistance.

LO 21.2.2   Explain consumer advocacy and how to contact public officials to express opinions and file complaints.

Key Terms

- United States Department of Agriculture (USDA)
- National Institute of Standards and Technology (NIST)
- Food and Drug Administration (FDA)
- Consumer Product Safety Commission (CPSC)
- Federal Communications

- Commission (FCC)
- Federal Trade Commission (FTC)
- United States Postal Inspection Service (USPIS)
- Federal Aviation Administration (FAA)
- Securities and Exchange Commission (SEC)
- Consumer Financial Protection

- Bureau (CFPB)
- Better Business Bureau (BBB)
- National Consumers League (NCL)
- Consumer action
- Consumers union
- consumer advocate

LO 21.2.1   Sources of Consumer Protection

When you need assistance with a consumer problem, numerous government organizations are available to help you. These organizations are found at the federal, state, and local levels. There are also private consumer protection organizations.

Federal Agencies

Many federal government agencies provide information of interest to consumers. Some of these agencies handle consumer complaints, and others direct complaints to agencies or sources that address consumer issues. All these agencies maintain websites that offer an abundance of helpful information to consumers.

Department of Agriculture

The **United States Department of Agriculture (USDA)** is responsible for developing and executing federal government policy on farming, agriculture, forestry, and food. It works to support the country's agricultural economy; protect and conserve our natural resources; and provide a safe, sufficient, and nutritious food supply for the American people.

Within the USDA, there are several agencies that exist to meet various consumer needs regarding the food supply in this country. The Food Safety and Inspection Service ensures that the commercial supply of meat, poultry, and processed egg products is safe, wholesome, and correctly labeled and packaged. The Food and Nutrition Service provides food assistance programs, such as the Supplemental Nutrition Assistance Program (SNAP, formerly called the Food Stamp Program) and the National School Lunch Program, and information on diets, nutrition, and menu preparation. The Center for Nutrition Policy and Promotion develops nutrition research, education, and promotion programs for the American public. It developed the MyPlate food guide, which illustrates the five food groups and reminds consumers to eat healthy portions from each group.

National Institute of Standards and Technology

The **National Institute of Standards and Technology (NIST)** is an agency within the U.S. Department of Commerce. One of its missions is to develop standards of business excellence. NIST presents the Malcolm Baldrige National Quality Award each year to U.S. businesses that achieve high quality standards in their business practices.

NIST also sets uniform standards of weights and measures. The NIST is why you do not have to shop with a tape measure or scale to ensure you get what you pay for. NIST sponsors a network of state and local agencies that set performance standards for measuring devices to determine the costs and amounts of products sold to consumers. For example, agencies of the NIST network determine the amount of error acceptable for a gas pump or grocer's scale and establish testing procedures for enforcing standards.

The NIST also runs one of the world's two atomic clocks, which is the source of the nation's official time, and co-invented closed captioning for people with impaired hearing. NIST research has also contributed to a wide variety of technological developments, including image processing, smoke detectors, and pollution control.

Food and Drug Administration

One of the many agencies within the U.S. Department of Health and Human Services is the **Food and Drug Administration (FDA)**. The FDA enforces laws and regulations

How does the FDA protect consumers?

preventing distribution of mislabeled foods, drugs, cosmetics, and medical devices. The FDA does the following:

- Requires testing and approval of all new drugs
- Tests new and existing products for health and safety standards
- Provides standards and guidelines for poisonous substances
- Sets standards for identification, quality, and volume of food containers
- Establishes guidelines for labels and proper identification of product contents, ingredients, nutrients, and directions for use
- Investigates complaints
- Conducts research and issues reports, guidelines, and warnings about substances found to be dangerous or potentially hazardous to health

Consumer Product Safety Commission

The **Consumer Product Safety Commission (CPSC)** protects consumers from unreasonable risk of injury or death from potentially hazardous consumer products. The commission develops and enforces standards for consumer products, bans products that are dangerous, arranges recalls, and conducts research on potential product hazards. In addition, the CPSC offers many publications on safety education.

Federal Communications Commission

The **Federal Communications Commission (FCC)** regulates interstate and international communications by radio, television, wire, satellite, and cable. It is important to understand that the FCC does not control online content. In addition to educating and informing consumers about telecommunications goods, services, and regulations, the

FCC's responsibilities also include issuing operating licenses for radio and TV stations, presiding over legal hearings about matters involving communications, and maintaining decency standards. The Consumer and Governmental Affairs Bureau develops the FCC's consumer policies and handles consumer questions and complaints.

Federal Trade Commission

The **Federal Trade Commission (FTC)** regulates unfair methods of competition, false or deceptive advertising, deceptive product labeling, and the concealment of true credit costs. The FTC is also the federal clearinghouse for complaints of identity theft. The FTC's Bureau of Consumer Protection enforces federal consumer protection laws, helping to enhance consumer confidence. The Bureau also oversees the U.S. National Do Not Call Registry.

United States Postal Inspection Service

The **United States Postal Inspection Service (USPIS)** is a federal law enforcement agency that investigates consumer problems pertaining to illegal use of the mail. The USPIS enforces postal laws, protecting consumers from dangerous articles, fraud, pornography, and identity theft involving the mail.

Federal Aviation Administration

The **Federal Aviation Administration (FAA)** oversees the U.S. commercial aviation industry for the Department of Transportation. It maintains regulations and standards that airline companies, such as United, Delta, and Southwest, must follow to transport passengers. The FAA is also responsible for certifying that all commercial aviation aircraft, pilots, companies, and airports meet the standards set forth by federal regulations. The FAA also oversees the nation's air traffic control system, which directs commercial, private, and military aircraft across the United States.

Securities and Exchange Commission

The main purpose of the **Securities and Exchange Commission (SEC)** is to protect investors and maintain the integrity of the securities markets. The SEC requires companies to disclose certain financial and other information so that investors can make informed decisions about investment options. The SEC also oversees stock exchanges, brokers, and investment advisers to protect investors in their dealings with securities professionals. The SEC's Office of Investor Education and Advocacy serves investors with securities-related questions or complaints about investment fraud or the mishandling of their investments by securities professionals.

Consumer Financial Protection Bureau

The **Consumer Financial Protection Bureau (CFPB)** was created in 2011. Their mission is to create strong guardrails to protect consumers and financial markets against irresponsible mortgage lending. The CFPB provides resources for consumer education, and the office is authorized to investigate violations of law. The bureau also conducts research related to consumer issues. For example, the CFPB found that credit card companies charged consumers more than $130 billion in interest and fees during 2022.

State and Local Assistance

Most states have a consumer protection agency, or the state attorney general may handle consumer complaints. Many county and city governments also have consumer protection offices. Consumer leagues and public-interest research groups are also active at the state and local levels, with newsletters, pamphlets, handbooks, and websites on current consumer issues.

At the local level, consumers have access to legal aid societies, consumer action reporters, and consumer representatives on local utility or licensing boards. Independent consumer groups focusing on specific issues, such as food prices, may operate on the local level as well.

Private Organizations

Not all consumer protection agencies are found at the government level. There are many private organizations for consumers to access when they need to gather information or file complaints.

Better Business Bureau

The **Better Business Bureau (BBB)** is a nonprofit organization focused on creating a more trusting relationship between businesses and consumers. It provides free reports on millions of businesses to help consumers make more informed decisions. The reports contain information about

How can consumers use the services of the BBB?

Source: iStock.com/RainStar

the business, customer reviews, and any complaints filed against the company. These reports are available on the BBB's website.

If consumers are dissatisfied with a business transaction, they can file a complaint with the BBB. Complaints can be filed over the phone, in writing, or by using the BBB's online complaint system. The BBB then acts as an intermediary between consumers and businesses to resolve the dispute in a quick and fair manner.

National Consumers League

The **National Consumers League (NCL)** is the nation's oldest nonprofit consumer organization. Initially formed to improve working conditions for working-class women, today the NCL represents consumers on marketplace and workplace issues such as child labor, privacy, food safety, and medication information. They also operate Fraud.org (formerly the National Fraud Information Center). This website provides consumers with free information they need to avoid becoming victims of fraud and identity theft. It also has an online fraud report form that consumers can fill out to report telemarketing and online fraud attempts.

Consumer Action

Consumer Action is a national nonprofit advocacy and education organization. Formed in 1971, the organization staffed one of the earliest consumer advice and assistance hotlines, and its picket of British Motors in 1972 established the right of aggrieved consumers to picket businesses. Consumer Action is known for its multilingual consumer education and support in the fields of credit, banking, privacy, insurance, and utilities. It is also known for its Credit Card Survey, an annual survey about credit cards, banks, and lending practices.

Consumers Union

Consumers Union is a nonprofit organization best known as the publisher of *Consumer Reports*, a monthly magazine that publishes reviews, comparisons, and ratings of consumer products and services. Consumers Union buys all products it tests and accepts no advertising to ensure that all ratings are unbiased. In addition to its research and publishing activities, Consumers Union has four advocacy offices that attempt to influence consumer policy.

Consumer Advocates

In addition to working with private organizations, consumers may also seek the support of a **consumer advocate**—a person who actively promotes consumer causes. When consumer advocates find, through research and investigation, that an injustice or dangerous condition exists, they pursue them on behalf of all consumers. Consumer advocates may file lawsuits against companies to force them to meet safety standards, correct inequitable situations, or properly inform consumers of dangers in the use of their products.

> ### ✓ Checkpoint
>
> What do consumer protection agencies do to help protect consumers?

LO 21.2.2   Consumer Advocacy

Consumer advocacy is when individuals or groups of people take action to promote and protect the interests of consumers. The ways you can act include letter writing, publicity, and attending public meetings. You can contact public officials for any reason. Some of the ways consumer advocacy has worked

Why is it important to share your views on consumer-related issues with government officials?

in the past have resulted in many of the laws or amendments to the laws discussed earlier in this chapter.

Contacting Public Officials

National elected officials include the president and vice president and members of Congress. State elected officials include the governor, secretary of state, treasurer, attorney general, superintendent of public instruction, labor commissioner, and state senators and representatives.

Each court (federal, state, and local) has at least one judge and several clerks of the court to assist in filing and information gathering. County elected officials may include the county administrator, district attorney, sheriff, and tax assessor, plus several commissioners. Other elected local officials may include the mayor, city council members, and city manager.

In addition, many branches of government now employ communications specialists who are responsible for planning, organizing, and directing public outreach and educational programs. For example, they may develop public service announcements to alert consumers to fraudulent activities.

If you wish to communicate with a public official about a consumer issue, there are several ways to do so.

- In person. You can make an appointment during regular office hours as well as attend meetings of government bodies, which are generally open to the public (except for executive sessions). Almost all hearings offer citizens the opportunity to speak.
- By phone. Brief phone calls at reasonable hours are generally effective. Your state may supply toll-free numbers for contacting public officials.
- By email. Sending an email is usually the most immediate way to reach a public official. Many public officials have email forms on their official websites that allow constituents (people who live in the areas they represent) to contact them with comments, questions, or concerns. You may also find email addresses of public officials on government websites.

- By letter. To be effective, a letter written to the appropriate representative should clearly state the purpose of the letter, identify the proposed legislation or bill with which you have concerns, refer to only one issue, and arrive while the issue is current. Provide reasons for your position on the issue and avoid being emotional. Describe what action you want the public official to take.
- By social media. You can follow and communicate with most public officials via their social media accounts. Many times, you may receive a response to a social media post that is public before you receive a response to other forms of communication.

✓ Checkpoint

Why would you want to contact an elected official about a consumer protection issue?

Check Your Understanding

1. What is the purpose of consumer protection agencies? (LO 21.2.1)
2. What issues have consumer advocacy groups improved? (LO 21.2.2)

Apply Your Understanding

1. Select a federal agency that provides consumer protection. Describe what it does for consumers, and list several more things you would like to see the agency do. (LO 21.2.1)
2. How does a consumer advocate help consumers? What issues do you think are important for advocates to understand and work on today? (LO 21.2.2)

The Essential Question

What are some government and private sources of consumer assistance, and how can you promote and protect consumer interests through contacting public officials?

A: There are many federal agencies that provide consumer assistance. Examples include the U.S. Department of Agriculture (USDA), the Food and Drug Administration (FDA), and the Federal Trade Commission (FTC). Private organizations such as the Better Business Bureau (BBB) and the Consumers Union also provide assistance. You can contact public officials to express opinions and concerns or file complaints in person or by phone, e-mail, letter, or social media.

The Essential Question   What remedies are available for consumers when trying to resolve a dispute, and what dispute resolution strategies should they use?

Learning Objectives

By the end of this lesson, you should be able to:

LO 21.3.1 Define remedies available to consumers other than individual lawsuits.

LO 21.3.2 Outline strategies to resolve consumer complaints.

Key Terms

- redress
- disputing a charge
- mediation
- arbitration
- small claims court

LO 21.3.1 Resolving Consumer Disputes

Lawsuits are lengthy, expensive, and emotionally draining, and usually not the best option for solving consumer complaints. Fortunately, for consumers who buy a defective product or are unhappy with a product or service, they can pursue other redress options. **Redress** is to correct an undesirable or unfair situation.

Informal Discussions

Whenever you have a consumer dispute, you should first try to work with the merchant or manufacturer. Informal discussions that lead to solution are much less expensive and easier to achieve than other remedies.

Contact the retailer, seller, or other party you have a dispute with. Describe the situation and your proposed remedy. Listen carefully to the other side and look for ways to settle the argument so that both sides have their interests met. In many cases, you can resolve the issue without taking further action.

If the informal discussion process does not work, you can proceed to more serious steps, such as withholding payment, returning or refusing merchandise, or disputing a charge.

Withholding Payment

As a consumer, you can withhold payment in a purchase dispute. This assumes you have the merchandise but still need to pay

Why should you resolve a dispute through informal discussions rather than pursue other remedies?

Source: iStock Essentials/Istock

for it. However, you must submit your complaint in writing and explain why you are withholding payment on the disputed amount. You cannot have double remedies, for example, you cannot expect to keep the merchandise and withhold payment.

Returning or Refusing Merchandise

You can refuse delivery or return merchandise to the seller. Even if the seller refuses to accept it back, you can leave it at the store or another business location. In some cases, you can mail it back or have it delivered back to the business. Be sure to get and keep any receipts or other evidence that the goods were returned. This proves that you have yet to benefit from having something you refuse to pay for.

Disputing a Charge

If you used credit or a payment app such as PayPal, Venmo, Apply Pay, or Google Pay for a purchase, you could dispute the charge within 60 days of receiving your credit card statement or making the purchase with a payment app. **Disputing a charge** generally means asking the payment issuer to reverse the charge on your account.

To dispute a charge, you must follow procedures outlined by credit card company or payment app. After gathering information and any documentation from you, the merchant of your dispute. If the merchant responds, the credit card or payment app company will evaluate the information provided by both sides. If the decision is in your favor, a credit is issued to your account from the merchant's account. If the matter is not decided in your favor, you must pay the amount in dispute. If the merchant does not respond, the credit card issuer typically will decide in your favor and issue you a credit from the merchant's account.

By law, disputes must be resolved within two billing cycles or 90 days, whichever comes first. If you used a credit card, during the investigation, making payments for other items you have charged on your credit card is important. Your credit should not be damaged if you follow the proper procedures for disputing credit charges.

Governmental Assistance

You may wish to seek help from a federal government agency to stop some objectionable practices and help you get your money back.

Sharpen Your Employability Skills
Communicating Effectively to Resolve a Consumer Issue

Assume you purchased a new computer from a local retailer, using cash. After a week's use, the battery no longer holds a charge. You want to return it, but unfortunately you did not keep the receipt from the merchant. Role-play this situation with a classmate who acts as the store manager. What will you say to the manager? What are you willing to accept or do to achieve a favorable resolution?

Figure 21.1   Government Assistance for Consumers

Automobiles	National Highway Traffic Safety Administration
Collection, Credit	State Consumer Protection Division (at your state capital)
Drugs/Foods	Food and Drug Administration
Household	Consumer Product Safety Commission
Investment Fraud	Federal Trade Commission Securities and Exchange Commission
Medical/Dental	State Board of Medical Examiners State Department of Commerce State Board of Dental Examiners State Health Division State Board of Pharmacy
Medicare	Social Security Administration
Misrepresentation/Fraud	State Consumer Protection Division Local District Attorney Local or State Better Business Bureau
Transportation	Surface Transportation Board
Warranties	Federal Trade Commission

Many sources of consumer assistance from the federal government were discussed earlier. In addition, most states have attorney general offices with consumer protection services available to consumers. Websites for state attorneys general often have complaint forms that consumers can fill out. The state office will investigate the complaint and take appropriate action. **Figure 21.1** lists many forms of state and federal assistance for consumers.

✓ Checkpoint

What are three ways to resolve consumer disputes?

LO 21.3.2   **Recommended Strategies for Dispute Resolution**

The Federal Trade Commission (FTC) is a government agency with the mission to protect the public from deceptive or unfair business practices and unfair methods of competition. Their job is to protect consumers and promote competition, which impacts the economic life of all Americans. The FTC recommends five strategies a consumer can use when they have an issue with a product or service. Consumers can return to the store or website, write a consumer complaint letter, seek help from an agency, post online reviews, and (as a last resort) seek alternative dispute resolution methods.

Return to the Store or Website

Sometimes, the resolution can be as simple as returning the product to the retailer, either by going to the store in-person or through the online return process outlined on the company's website. If a return request is denied, you may have to take additional steps for the return. Ask to speak to the manager if you are at the store and be prepared to explain the problem with the product or service. If the product is broken, damaged, or faulty, you can usually receive a refund or replacement if you ask politely. If the issue is with poor quality service or repairs, you may need to explain, in detail, what was wrong. Most businesses want to know about any problems with their products or services so that they can take corrective action and avoid future complaints and unfavorable reviews. Bring any receipts, proof of payment, contracts, warranties, or other documents to the business. If you are returning online, send copies (keep the originals) of the documents to the company. Make sure that you are attempting to return the product within the specified return policy for the store.

As part of the process, be prepared to explain what you are asking for. Do you want a refund? Do you want the product replaced? Are you willing to receive store credit? Be ready to explain why you want the remedy you are seeking. Many businesses will offer store credit as it is less expensive for them and gives the business a chance to keep you as a customer.

Send an Email or Letter

If your attempt to return the product or receive a refund for the product or service did not work, your next step is to make your complaint in writing. An effective complaint message will:

- Be clear and concise. Describe the product or service and include important details, for example, the name of the product, a serial or model number, and the date and place of purchase.
- Explain the problem. In *clear* language, explain what was wrong with the product or service. Keep the comments simple and factual.
- Ask for a specific action or remedy. Do you want a refund, replacement, or store credit? State what remedy you want and explain why you want that specific remedy.
- Include copies of documents. Send copies of the receipts for products or services. If you attempted to have the item repaired, include the receipt for the repairs. Include any relevant information and documents to support your request.
- Add a deadline. Tell the company how long you are willing to wait for them to take action. Give them a reasonable time frame, such as 30 days, to respond. Include in your message what you will do if you do not hear from them. This could be reporting the issue to your state's attorney general or the consumer protection office.
- More hints for success. Always be polite in your written correspondence. Provide your name, address, and a phone number so that they can reach you when the company attempts to respond to your message. If you are mailing the letter, send it via certified mail and keep the receipt from the post office. If you send an email or use the company's website, take a screenshot of the message before you submit. This will provide documentation of when you sent your message.

Seek Help from an Outside Agency

If you do not hear back from the business or their solution is not acceptable, you can contact various government agencies

How are consumers protected if they write a negative online review?

for help. The most common ways to get help are through the state attorney general office or consumer protection office. You can also contact a national consumer organization like Call for Action or Consumer Action. Both organizations help consumers with issues. You can also contact the Better Business Bureau for help. If you feel like you are the victim of fraud, you can contact the fraud division of the FTC using their website: https://ReportFraud.ftc.gov. You can also visit https://USA.gov/consumer for more advice on filing consumer complaints.

Post an Online Review

You can post a review of the company and the product online at several different websites. Most online companies allow reviews on their websites. When posting a review, make sure that you state the issue clearly and politely. Like writing a complaint letter, you must be clear and concise when describing the product or service and explaining the problem. Make sure to include essential details, including the date of purchase. Keep your comments simple and factual.

The Consumer Review Fairness Act was created to protect consumers when they post honest opinions about a business or its products and services. The act prohibits companies from threatening you with legal action if you do not remove the review.

Alternative Dispute Resolution

The final action for consumers is to use a more formal dispute resolution option. These options include either mediation or arbitration, small claims court, or a lawsuit.

Mediation and Arbitration

Mediation is when a third party helps you and the other party try to resolve the problem. The mediator is there to help you reach an agreement, but it is up to the two parties of the dispute to reach an agreement. **Arbitration** is a less formal legal action. You and the other party will need to appear at hearings, present evidence, and possibly even call witnesses. Arbitration is legally binding. Both parties are required to follow the order that comes from arbitration.

Small Claims Court

If the disputed amount is relatively small, consider taking the matter to a small claims court. A **small claims court** is a court of limited jurisdiction that resolves cases involving small amounts. Attorneys are typically not allowed; hence, small claims court is often considered the "people's court." There is no jury; a judge decides the matter. Most states set a maximum amount of $2,000 to $5,000 in damages that can be recovered in a small claims court. No formal record is made of the small claims court hearing.

Small claims courts are easy to use. You can file a claim by filling out a form at your county courthouse. The costs of filing a claim are small, typically $50 to $150.

When you buy products online, you are taking a risk. If a product is defective, you often cannot return it to a physical store and talk to the manager. However, you do have avenues for redress when shopping on the internet. Online dispute resolution services include filing a complaint and having an independent online service help you resolve it. There are numerous online dispute resolution services available for e-consumers.

Filing a complaint with the Better Business Bureau (BBB) is the most popular method consumers use for online transaction disputes. At the BBB's website (www.bbb.org), consumers can use its online complaint system to file complaints against businesses. The BBB then acts as a mediator to try to get both sides to come to a fair resolution.

If you decide to file a complaint, go to the appropriate website and complete forms that explain the issue. The online merchant should respond, and both of you can continue a dialog until all issues are covered. This service is sometimes called hosted message board negotiation, and it is a free process for consumers. You post your needs and request for action. The business responds, and a conversation follows. You should have specific information, proof of purchase, and other documentation to support your claims. Merchants are willing to participate in the process because they want to retain you as a customer while being treated fairly themselves.

You also have avenues for redress through agencies such as the Federal Trade Commission (FTC) and your state attorney general's consumer protection division. However, this can be a time-consuming process, and you often receive no financial settlement. Thus, it is wise to shop carefully online and buy only from merchants you know and trust. Doing this will lower your risk of getting into a dispute, and if there is a dispute, it will increase your chances of a successful resolution.

Think Critically

1. Have you purchased something online that was of poor quality or was not what you ordered? How did you resolve the problem?
2. In what ways is online shopping riskier than shopping in a physical store?
3. Some people feel that going through the complaint process is not worth the hassle. In these cases, they take a loss for the low-quality product or service. What are your thoughts on filing complaints for online purchases? Does the product have to hold a certain value before you would file a complaint? Explain.

To file a claim, you must know the name and address of the person or business with whom you have a problem. You must also know the amount in contention and clearly state why you are entitled to the money.

Legal Action

If all else fails, legal action may be necessary. Legal action is when you sue another party for damages. Legal action involves lawyers and courts. You will be required to pay legal fees. If you win the lawsuit, the other party typically covers your legal fees. If you lose the lawsuit, you may be responsible for all legal fees, including those of the other party.

✓ **Checkpoint**

What are some strategies for consumer dispute resolution?

Check Your Understanding

1. Describe informal dispute resolutions. (LO 21.3.1)
2. Explain what each of the five strategies are in consumer dispute resolution. (LO 21.3.2)

Apply Your Understanding

1. Colt runs a small landscaping business. One of his clients was not happy with the job he did removing debris from their yard and made a complaint. What can Colt do to resolve the issue with his customer? (LO 21.3.1)

2. Lane has tried to resolve a consumer complaint related to repairs on his vehicle's transmission. None of his attempts have succeeded and his vehicle is not drivable, so he had the transmission repaired by another repair shop, where the mechanic told him that the first mechanic installed the incorrect parts on his transmission. The new repair shop provided Lane with written documents stating what was done incorrectly and how they corrected the error. What next step can Lane take to receive compensation for the error from the first repair shop? (LO 21.3.2)

The Essential Question

What remedies are available for consumers when trying to resolve a dispute, and what options are available when they do not work?

A: The easiest ways to resolve disputes is through informal discussions, withholding payment, returning the products for replacement or refund, and disputing charges. If these do not work, the FTC recommends five strategies for resolving complaints. As a last resort, consumers can request arbitration or mediation, take the business to small claims court, or begin more formal legal proceedings.

Summary

21.1 Consumer Rights and Laws

- Consumer abuses have led to consumer bills of rights and consumer protection laws.

- The Consumer Bill of Rights outlines basic rights that consumers should expect in the marketplace.

- Airline passenger rights provide protections to paying passengers on commercial airlines.

- The Consumer Technology Bill of Rights outlines permissible reproduction and uses of purchased digital content.

- A patients' bill of rights was enacted in 1998 to give patients more control over medical decisions, treatments, and records. Further rights were ensured with the passage of the Affordable Care Act in 2010.

- Laws around the regulation of artificial intelligence (AI) are being considered and may be adopted in the future.

- Congress has passed many laws to protect consumers from unsafe products and unfair or deceptive business practices.

- Some laws (such as the Food, Drug, and Cosmetic Act and the Flammable Fabrics Act) set standards for product purity and safety.

- Many laws (including the Fair Packaging and Labeling Act, the Nutrition Labeling and Education Act, and the Hazardous Substances Act) set rules for product labeling.

- Several laws (such as toy safety laws and the Children's Online Privacy Protection Act) are designed to protect children from harm.

- Several laws placed limits on access to or the release of consumers' private data.

21.2 Consumer Agencies and Consumer Advocacy

- There are numerous government and private organizations that help protect consumers. Government organizations are found at the federal, state, and local levels.

- The U.S. Department of Agriculture (USDA) works to provide a safe, sufficient, and nutritious food supply for the country.

- The National Institute of Standards and Technology (NIST) rewards standards of excellence in business and sets uniform standards of weights and measures.

- The Federal Drug Administration (FDA) approves new drugs, tests products for safety, and sets labeling guidelines.

- The Consumer Product Safety Commission (CPSC) enforces product standards and bans or recalls hazardous products.

- The Federal Communications Commission (FCC) regulates communications by radio, television, wire, satellite, and cable. It does not control online content.

- The Federal Trade Commission (FTC) regulates methods of unfair competition, deceptive marketing practices, and concealment of the true costs of credit.

- The United States Postal Inspection Service (USPIS) investigates problems pertaining to illegal use of the mail.

- The Federal Aviation Administration (FAA) oversees the U.S. commercial aviation industry.

- The Securities and Exchange Commission (SEC) protects investors and maintains the integrity of the securities markets.

- The Consumer Financial Protection Bureau (CFPB) protects consumers and financial markets against irresponsible mortgage lending.

- Most states and many counties and cities have a consumer protection agency. At the local level, consumers have access to legal aid societies, consumer representatives on licensing boards, and independent consumer groups.

- Private organizations, such as the Better Business Bureau (BBB) and Consumers Union, can assist consumers with incidents of unethical and illegal practices.

- Consumer advocacy is when individuals or groups take action to promote and protect the interests of consumers. Actions can include publicizing issues and attending public meetings.

- If consumers have an issue or a complaint, they can contact public officials in person or by phone, email, letter, or social media.

21.3 Consumer Disputes and Dispute Resolution

- Consumers can resolve most disputes themselves through various redress options. Redress is to correct an undesirable or unfair situation.

- An informal discussion with a merchant or manufacturer is often the best way to resolve a dispute.

- Consumers can withhold payments in a purchase dispute if they have received the product before paying for it.

- Consumers can attempt to return products for a replacement or refund.

- Disputing charges is another remedy for consumers. If the consumer pays for products or services with a credit card or a payment app, they can work with their payment company to dispute the charges. The decision by the credit card or payment app company is binding.

- Government agencies may also be able to help with consumer disputes.

- The Federal Trade Commission (FTC) recommends five strategies for resolving consumer disputes. The strategies include returning to the store or website, sending an email or letter, seeking help from an outside agency, posting an online review, and using an alternative dispute resolution program.

- The Consumer Review Fairness Act protects consumers who post honest reviews about products.

- If other resolutions do not work, consumers can request arbitration or mediation, go to small claims court, or seek legal action.

- Legal action involves lawyers and courts and can be costly.

Check Your Knowledge

1. What is the purpose of the laws that protect consumer rights? (LO 21.1.1)

2. Identify the law that protects consumers from each of the following abuses:
   a. A box states that it contains 12 ounces of product when it contains only 9 ounces.
   b. A doctor tells an employer that an employee has a potentially expensive medical condition. Rather than risk higher health insurance premiums, the employer fires the employee.
   c. A company develops a new "miracle" drug. To get it on the market quickly, the company does not test it sufficiently.
   d. A company develops an effective new cleaning product. However, the chemicals it contains are quite dangerous. To avoid scaring potential customers, the company does not mention the dangers on the label. (LO 21.1.2)

3. List state and local sources that can aid with a consumer complaint. (LO 21.2.1)

4. Select three government or private sources of consumer assistance. Explain the purpose of each. (LO 21.2.1)

5. What is potentially the most effective way to contact a public official? (LO 21.2.2)

6. What should a consumer be prepared to do if they return a defective product to a store? (LO 21.3.1)

7. When writing a complaint letter or email, what should be included in the message? (LO 21.3.2)

Apply Your Knowledge

1. Select a consumer bill of rights described in the chapter that is most important to you and explain why. (LO 21.1.1)

2. Select any garment from your closet. Read the care label. What kinds of information are on the label? How is this information helpful? (LO 21.1.2)

3. Your friend Diego told you about a situation where he thinks he was treated unfairly when trying to find an apartment. Describe the steps Diego should take to file a complaint. (LO 21.2.1)

4. Select one issue that you feel strongly about related to consumer rights. Create a social media post that you could share on the appropriate elected official's social media profile. If your parent(s)/guardian(s) approve, make the post, and share the response you received with your class. (LO 21.2.2)

5. How would you handle a situation where you are eating at a nice restaurant and the server brings you a meal that is not what you ordered? What consumer dispute remedy could you request, and what resolution would be satisfactory for you? (LO 21.3.1)

6. Find a negative online review for a product you are considering purchasing or have purchased in the past that is written poorly or in an angry tone. How would you rewrite the review to be more effective? (LO 21.3.2)

Share Your Knowledge

Work in teams of two to four students to complete the following activities.

1. Write a teenager consumer bill of rights in an area that concerns the members of your group, such as privacy rights, mental health, equality, or financial independence. What rights would you like to have guaranteed to you as a citizen? Create a way for your group to present your bill of rights. Use one of the bills of rights in Lesson 21.1 as an example. (LO 21.1.1)

2. Visit the Securities and Exchange Commission's website (www.sec.gov). Go to the "About" menu on the homepage and select "Securities Laws" from the drop-down menu. As a group, choose a law to research, including its historical background, key provisions, the law's impact on the economy, the criticisms or legal challenges to the law, and how the law compares to similar laws in other countries. Present your findings to the rest of the class. (LO 21.2.1)

3. Select another country and research its consumer protection laws. How are they different from laws in the United States? (LO 21.1.2)

4. Research the Consumer Review Fairness Act (CRFA). As a group, discuss different perspectives on the CRFA's effectiveness and potential areas for future amendment or improvement. Present your conclusions to the class. (LO 21.3.2)

Connect and Reflect

Base your answers to the following questions on your own personal thoughts, preferences, and experiences.

1. What is a real-life situation or experience where you felt your consumer rights were violated? Reflect on how you handled the situation and the impact consumer rights have on your everyday life. (LO 21.1.1)

2. Why are your rights under the Family and Educational Rights and Privacy Act (FERPA) important to you? What could happen if these rights were not protected? (LO 21.1.2)

3. How do you think the decisions and policies made by public officials or the courts can influence and shape consumer rights? Reflect on a specific example from recent current events where government actions had an impact on the rights and protections of individual consumers. (LO 21.2.2)

4. Have you ever returned a product to the store or online website? Describe the experience and what you wish you had done differently. (LO 21.3.1)

Chapter Project

Create a timeline of the various consumer laws, acts, and policies that have been created since 1980. Include the agencies that were involved or created as part of the timeline. Also include a short statement about the purpose of each law and agency.

Reflecting on Your Career of Interest

Once you begin planning for and working toward a career of interest, it is important to periodically reflect on the steps you are taking to prepare yourself and to assess how well the chosen career aligns with your goals.

Reflect and Revisit

Based on the career exploration research and activities you completed in previous units, reflect on your findings to determine how well your chosen careers aligns with your personal interests, skills, and ability to provide your desired standard of living after high school. Write a short reflection essay or create a presentation that addressees, at a minimum, the following questions:

1. What information did you learn about career clusters and career pathways?
2. What are the key takeaways you found while researching your career of interest?
3. Based on your research findings, how may you further develop or revise your career plan?
4. What steps can you take while in high school and after to prepare for the career?
5. Would your chosen career provide you with the standard of living you desire? Explain. How did you determine this?
6. Has your research changed your thoughts on your potential career path? Why or why not?
7. What advice would you give to a friend who is just beginning their career exploration?

Unit 6: Project

Consumer rights and responsibilities can be linked to philanthropy. Philanthropy is the charitable giving by individuals and organizations to worthy societal causes. It is a powerful tool that can make the world a better place for future generations. It is a misconception that only the wealthy can contribute. Regardless of their financial status, every individual can make a significant difference.

Philanthropy takes many forms. While we often hear about the monumental philanthropic gifts—such as those from Bill and Melinda Gates, Warren Buffett, Michael Bloomberg, MacKenzie Scott, Serena Williams, and Oprah Winfrey—to various global charities, it is important to remember that philanthropy is not limited to the wealthy. Each of us has the potential to contribute in some way.

As a high school student, you have a unique opportunity to make a difference in your community. Volunteering at a local food bank, assisting elderly or disabled neighbors with snow shoveling, tutoring younger students, walking dogs at an animal shelter, or collecting books for a children's hospital can all contribute. These acts benefit others and foster personal growth and a sense of fulfillment.

There are several ways you can learn about becoming a volunteer. Your high school may already work with organizations where you can volunteer.

Apply Your Knowledge

Select one or more of the following activities to complete. Get permission from your parent(s) or guardian(s) and/or the appropriate authority at your school.

1. Research how to identify questionable charities by visiting one website that provides information about fake charities, such as those below. Then, create a way to share what you learned.
   - Internal Revenue Service website
   - Federal Trade Commission website
   - Charity Navigator website
   - GuideStar.org website
2. Select one organization in your local community where volunteers are needed. Interview someone at the organization to discover what help they need. If they are interested, work with the organization to create social media posts to help the organization share its needs with the community. Write a summary of the activities you completed to share with your teacher and class.
3. Select one organization where you can volunteer your time. Spend at least 10 hours over the next 2 months volunteering. Share what you learned.
4. Start a drive at your school to collect something that is needed in your community. For example, collect nonperishable foods to donate to the local food pantry, toiletry items for a homeless shelter, toys for an angel tree near the holidays, or something else that interests you. Once you have permission, complete the following tasks:
   - Organize the activity
   - Create promotional materials to advertise the drive
   - Determine where and how the items will be collected
   - Arrange to deliver the items to the organization

Unit 6: Winning Edge

Personal Financial Literacy

The Personal Financial Literacy Event measures your personal finance knowledge. Students must be able to apply reliable information and systematic decision-making to personal financial decisions. The Personal Financial Literacy Event consists of a financial literacy exam and a role-play scenario with a business executive. Finalists will compete in a second role-play event. Participants will have 10 minutes to review the scenario and develop a professional approach to solving the problem. Participants will have 10 minutes to present their action plan to the judge. After the participant's explanation, the judge can ask questions about the scenario.

Go to DECA.org/compete for more detailed information.

Performance Indicators

- Explain how federal and state/provincial regulators help protect consumers.
- Identify the warning signs of fraud.
- List steps that can be taken if a consumer is a victim of fraud.

Try It Out!

You are to assume the role of consumer protection counselor at a nonprofit agency. You will meet with a new client (judge), Paul, who wants to know about an investment opportunity in cryptocurrency. Paul had an investment agent call him to discuss the cryptocurrency investment opportunity. The agent claimed that Paul could earn a 500 percent rate of return in the next 6 months if he invested in their cryptocurrency program, and the agent guaranteed there would be no risk. If Paul was not pleased with the results, he could withdraw from the program at any time and receive his entire investment back.

The agent stressed that this was a once-in-a-lifetime offer and Paul had only 24 hours to decide. Paul is an older adult with enough resources to live comfortably in retirement but would like to be able to leave his children an inheritance, and this seems like the perfect opportunity to do so. Paul is a little skeptical because the agent did not have a license and said one was not needed. Paul is coming to you for advice.

You will need to explain to Paul all the warning signs demonstrated by the agent. You must also explain how regulators protect people from fraud and the steps to be taken if a consumer is the victim of fraud.

You will meet with Paul in your office. The meeting will begin with Paul greeting you and asking about cryptocurrency choices. After you have explained the consumer fraud protections, Paul may ask you questions and conclude the meeting by thanking you for your time.

www.deca.org/compete

Glossary y Glosario

20/10 rule   a plan to limit the use of credit to no more than 20 percent of your yearly take-home pay, with payments of no more than 10 percent of monthly take-home pay

regla 20/10   plan para limitar el uso del crédito a no más del 20 por ciento del salario de bolsillo anual, con pagos no superiores al 10 por ciento del salario de bolsillo mensual

401(k)   a defined-contribution plan for employees of companies that operate for a profit; employees choose the percentage of salary they want to contribute to their account, and the employer deducts this amount from their paychecks and puts it into the employees' accounts

401(k)   plan de aportes definidos para empleados de empresas que operan con fines de lucro; los empleados eligen el porcentaje del salario que desean aportar a su cuenta y el empleador deduce esa cantidad de sus sueldos y lo asigna a las cuentas de sus empleados

403(b) plan   a defined-contribution plan for employees of schools, nonprofit organizations, and government units

plan 403(b)   plan de aportes definidos para empleados de escuelas, organizaciones sin fines de lucro y organismos de gobierno

50-30-20 budget plan   plan to spend 50 percent of your net pay on needs, 30 percent on what you want, and 20 percent on savings and retirement

plan de presupuesto 50-30-20   plan para organizar los gastos de manera que el 50 por ciento del salario neto se destina a pagar necesidades, el 30 por ciento a comprar lo que se desea y el 20 por ciento a reservar como ahorro y fondo de retiro

529 College Savings Plan   a tax-advantaged savings plan to allow families to save for future education costs

Plan de ahorro 529 para la universidad   plan de ahorro con ventajas impositivas que permite a las familias ahorrar para afrontar los costos de la educación

80 percent rule   requires homeowners to have insurance equal to 80 percent of the replacement costs for the house to receive full coverage from the insurance company

regla del 80 por ciento   regla que exige a los propietarios de una vivienda contar con un seguro equivalente al 80 por ciento de los costos de reposición de la vivienda a fin de recibir cobertura total de la compañía de seguros

A

acceleration of benefits   allows people diagnosed with a severe medical condition that will likely lead to their death in 12 or 24 months, or other specified period, to collect a portion of their life insurance benefits before death; typical benefits are between 50 to 90 percent of the face value of the policy

aceleración de los beneficios   la aceleración de los beneficios permite a las personas con una enfermedad grave, que posiblemente les ocasione la muerte en el término de 12 o 24 meses u otro período determinado, cobrar una parte de su seguro de vida antes de morir; los beneficios más comunes van del 50 al 90 por ciento del valor nominal de la póliza

account number   a 5- to 17-digit number used to identify your personal bank account

número de cuenta   número de 5 a 17 dígitos que se usa para identificar una cuenta bancaria personal

adjusted balance method   method by which the finance charge is applied only to the amount owed after you have paid your bill each month

método de saldo ajustado   método por el cual el costo financiero se aplica solo al monto que se adeuda luego de haber pagado la factura cada mes

adjusted gross income   determined as income adjustments subtracted from gross income

ingreso bruto ajustado   se determina como ajustes del ingreso restados del ingreso bruto

adult foster care   personal care and services provided for adults in a facility outside of the home

sistema de acogida para adultos servicios y cuidados personales provistos a personas adultas en un establecimiento que no es su propia casa

Affordable Care Act (ACA) purpose of this law is to increase the availability and affordability of health insurance while controlling rising medical costs for individuals and the government

Ley de Cuidado de la Salud a Bajo Precio (ACA, en inglés) ley cuyo propósito es ampliar la disponibilidad y la asequibilidad de los seguros de salud al tiempo que se controla el incremento de los costos médicos para los individuos y el gobierno

agency bond a bond issued by government agencies or by government-sponsored enterprises (GSEs)

bono emitido por una agencia gubernamental bono que emiten las agencias del gobierno o empresas patrocinadas por el gobierno (GSE, por sus sigla en inglés)

annual percentage rate (APR) the cost of credit expressed as a yearly percentage

tasa de porcentaje anual (TPA) costo del crédito expresado como porcentaje anual

annual percentage yield (APY) the actual interest rate an account pays, stated on a yearly basis with the compounding included

porcentaje de rendimiento anual (PRA) tasa de interés real que paga una cuenta, fijada en forma anual con el interés compuesto incluido.

annual report a summary of a corporation's financial results for the year and its prospects for the future

memoria anual resumen de los resultados financieros de una empresa correspondientes al año y su proyección para el futuro

annuity a contract in which you make a lump-sum payment or series of payments that earn interest in return for regular disbursements, often after retirement

anualidad contrato en el cual se realiza un pago único o una serie de pagos que rinden interés a cambio de desembolsos regulares, comúnmente después de jubilarse

appraised value home value determined by examining the structure, size, features, and quality as compared to similar homes in the same geographic area

valor de tasación valor de una vivienda que se determina examinando sus características, estructura, tamaño y calidad en comparación con viviendas similares en la misma zona geográfica

appreciation an increase in value over time

apreciación aumento del valor a lo largo del tiempo

apprenticeship program an opportunity to learn an art, trade, or skill from an expert

programa de aprendizaje oportunidad de aprender un arte, oficio o habilidad de un experto

arbitration less formal legal action; you and the other party will need to appear at hearings, present evidence, and possibly even call witnesses; arbitration is legally binding

arbitraje acción legal menos formal; una parte y la otra deberán presentarse a distintas audiencias, presentar pruebas y, posiblemente, también presentar testigos; el arbitraje es legalmente vinculante

assessed value home value set annually by the city or county in which you live for purposes of computing property taxes owed against your home

valor fiscal valor de una vivienda determinado anualmente por la ciudad o el condado en el que uno vive con el fin de computar contra la vivienda los impuestos sobre la propiedad que se adeudan

assets items of value that a person owns

activos artículos de valor que posee una persona

assigned risk pool consists of people who cannot obtain auto insurance due to the high risk they present

grupo de riesgo asignado grupo de riesgo compuesto por personas que no pueden acceder a un seguro automotor debido al alto riesgo que presentan

attractive nuisance a dangerous place, condition, or object particularly attractive to children, such as a swimming pool

peligro atrayente lugar, circunstancia y objeto peligroso que es especialmente atractivo para los niños, como una piscina

auction market where buyers enter competitive bids, and sellers enter competitive offers simultaneously

mercado de subastas lugar donde los compradores compiten para obtener las cosas que los vendedores ofrecen para otorgar a quien les presente la mejor oferta

audit an examination of income tax returns

auditoría   evaluación de la declaración del impuesto sobre los ingresos

Automated Clearing House (ACH)   an electronic network used to securely accept deposits and distribute payments

Cámara de Compensación Automatizada (ACH)   red electrónica usada para aceptar depósitos y distribuir pagos de manera segura

automated teller machine (ATM) fee   typically charged by an ATM that does not belong to your bank or credit union

comisión por uso del cajero automático   recargo que comúnmente se cobra por el uso de un cajero automático que no pertenece al banco ni a la cooperativa de crédito de la que uno es cliente

automatic deduction   represents money you have authorized your bank or another organization to move from one account to another regularly

deducción automática   representa el dinero que una persona le autoriza mover regularmente de una cuenta a otra a un banco o cualquier otra organización

average daily balance method   method by which creditors calculate your balance on each day of the billing cycle

método del saldo promedio diario   método por el cual los acreedores calculan el saldo cada día del ciclo de facturación

B

bait and switch   an illegal sales technique in which a seller advertises a product to persuade consumers to buy a more expensive product

táctica de atractivo engañoso   técnica de ventas ilegal por medio de la cual un vendedor publicita un producto para persuadir a los compradores de comprar otro producto más caro

balanced fund   a mutual fund that seeks growth and income but attempts to minimize risk by investing in a mixture of stocks and bonds rather than stocks alone

fondo de inversión diversificado   fondo de inversión mutua que busca ampliarse y obtener ingresos pero se propone minimizar el riesgo invirtiendo en distintas acciones y bonos en lugar de hacerlo solo en acciones

bank fees   cover the operating costs of banks and credit unions; customers pay these fees for using banking services

comisiones bancarias   comisiones que cubren los gastos operativos de los bancos y cooperativas de crédito; los clientes pagan estas comisiones por usar los servicios que prestan los bancos

bank reconciliation   the process of matching your checkbook register with the bank statement

conciliación bancaria   proceso por el cual los registros de la chequera se concilian con el extracto de cuenta

bankruptcy   a legal process that relieves debtors of the responsibility of paying their debts or protects them while they try to repay

quiebra   proceso legal que libera a los deudores de la responsabilidad de pagar sus deudas o que los protege mientras hacen lo posible por cancelarlas

bargaining   the process of negotiating an employment contract for union members

negociación laboral   proceso por el cual se discute un contrato de trabajo para los miembros de los sindicatos

basic health insurance   usually includes medical, hospital, and surgical costs

seguro de salud básico   seguro que comúnmente incluye los costos médicos, hospitalarios y quirúrgicos

bear market   a prolonged period of falling stock prices and a general feeling of investor pessimism

mercado bajista   período prolongado en el que las acciones tienden a bajar de precio y en el que predomina un pesimismo general entre los inversores

beneficiary   someone who will inherit the money after the death of the account holder

beneficiario   persona que heredará el dinero de una cuenta cuando muera su titular

benefits   compensation or perks that are provided to the employee in addition to their salary or wages

beneficios   compensación o prestaciones otorgadas a un empleado además de su salario o paga

Better Business Bureau (BBB)   a nonprofit organization focused on creating a more trusting relationship between businesses and consumers

Better Business Bureau (en español) organización sin fines de lucro cuyo objetivo principal es crear una relación de mayor confianza entre las empresas y los consumidores

billing statement an itemized bill showing charges, credits, and payments posted to your account during the billing period

estado de cuenta resumen detallado que muestra uno por uno los cobros, créditos y pagos asignados a una cuenta durante el período de facturación

blended family brings two separate families together to form a new family unit

familia ensamblada es la que reúne dos familias separadas para formar una familia nueva

blue chip stocks stocks of large, well-established corporations with a solid record of profitability

acciones de primera categoría acciones de grandes empresas, caracterizadas por su excelente reputación y sólida trayectoria de rentabilidad

bond a debt obligation of a corporation or a state or local government; loan that must be repaid at maturity

bono obligación de deuda que contrae una empresa o gobierno estatal o local; préstamo que debe pagarse a su vencimiento

bond default occurs when the issuer cannot meet the interest or principal payments

cesación de pago de los bonos ocurre cuando el emisor no puede cumplir con el pago principal o el pago de los intereses

bond fund a group of bonds that have been bundled together and sold to investors in shares, like stock

fondo de bonos serie de bonos que se agruparon y vendieron a los inversores en acciones, como capital

bond listings extensive tables that contain information about recent trades of bonds

cotización de bonos tablas detalladas que contienen información sobre la compraventa de bonos más reciente

bond rating tells the investor the risk category assigned to a bond

calificación de los bonos indica al inversor la categoría de riesgo asignada a un bono

bond redemption occurs when a bond is paid off at maturity

rescate de bonos se produce cuando un bono se paga llegado su vencimiento

bonus incentive pay based on the quality of work done, years of service, or a company's sales and profits

gratificación incentivo que se paga teniendo en cuenta la calidad del trabajo realizado, los años de servicio o las ventas y ganancias de una empresa

brokerage firm acts as the intermediary to connect buyers and sellers of securities

agencia de valores empresa que actúa como intermediario para conectar a los compradores con los vendedores de títulos

budget a spending and saving plan based on your expected income and expenses

presupuesto plan de gasto y ahorro que se basa en los ingresos y gastos previstos

bull market a prolonged period of rising stock prices and a general feeling of investor optimism

mercado alcista período prolongado en el que las acciones tienden a subir de precio y en el que predomina un optimismo general entre los inversores

business plan an extensive document that outlines the path a business intends to take to earn and grow revenues

plan de negocio documento detallado que describe el camino que una empresa se propone seguir para obtener ganancias e incrementar su renta

C

callable bond a bond that the issuer has the right to pay off (call back) before its maturity date

bono rescatable bono cuyo emisor tiene derecho de pagar (rescatar) antes de su vencimiento

capacity the ability to repay a loan with present income

capacidad aptitud para devolver un préstamo con los ingresos presentes

capital gains an increase in the value of a stock over time

ganancias de capital incremento en el valor de una acción con el paso del tiempo

capital loss results when a stock's price goes below the price the investor initially paid

pérdida de capital   se produce cuando el precio de una acción cae por debajo del valor que había pagado inicialmente el inversor

capital   the value of property you possess (such as bank accounts, investments, real estate, and other assets) after deducting your debts

capital   valor de la propiedad que se posee (como cuentas bancarias, inversiones, inmuebles y otros bienes) luego de deducir las deudas

capitalism   an economic system in which producers and consumers are free to operate and compete in business transactions with minimal, if any, government interference or regulation

capitalismo   sistema económico en el cual productores y consumidores son libres de operar y competir en las transacciones comerciales con mínima o directamente ninguna intervención o regulación del gobierno

car-buying service   allows you to choose the vehicle features you want and have a professional car buyer handle the price negotiation

servicio de compra de automóviles   permite elegir las características del vehículo que uno desea y contar con un comprador de carros profesional para que negocie el precio

car detail   a service provided by specialists who clean and polish the exterior and cleaning and treating the interior

detallado automotriz   servicio provisto por especialistas que lavan y lustran el exterior de un vehículo y limpian y tratan su interior

car registration   license tag fee for a motor vehicle

registro de vehículo   arancel correspondiente a la matrícula de licencia de un vehículo

car title   a legal document that establishes ownership of the vehicle

título de vehículo   documento legal que establece a quién pertenece el vehículo

car warranty   protects the car owner from costly mechanical repairs

garantía de auto   protege al automóvil de las reparaciones mecánicas costosas

care labels   give instructions for cleaning, wash and dry temperatures, and other care needed to preserve a product

etiquetas de cuidado   proporcionan instrucciones de limpieza, lavado y temperaturas de secado así como de otros tipos de cuidado necesarios para preservar un producto

cash deficit   occurs when expenses are greater than estimated income

déficit de caja   ocurre cuando los gastos superan los ingresos estimados

cash surplus   occurs when income exceeds expenses

excedente de caja   ocurre cuando los ingresos superan los gastos

cash value   the savings accumulated in a permanent life insurance policy you would receive if you cancelled your policy

valor en efectivo   ahorros acumulados en una póliza de seguro de vida permanente que la persona asegurada recibiría si cancelara la póliza

cashier's check   also called a bank draft; a check written by a bank on its own funds

cheque de caja   también llamado cheque de tesorero; cheque emitido por un banco sobre sus propios fondos

certificate of deposit (CD)   a deposit that earns a fixed interest rate for a specified length of time

certificado de depósito (CD)   depósito que obtiene una tasa de interés fijo por un determinado plazo de tiempo

certificate of participation (COP)   an investment in a pool of mortgages purchased by a government agency or government-sponsored enterprise

certificado de participación (CDP)   inversión en un fondo común hipotecario comprada por una agencia de gobierno o empresa patrocinada por el gobierno

certified check   a personal check a bank has certified. Certified checks are written from a personal or business account and delivered to the payee

cheque certificado   cheque personal que certificó un banco. Los cheques certificados se emiten desde una cuenta personal o comercial a favor del tenedor

Chapter 11 bankruptcy   a reorganization form of bankruptcy for businesses that allows them to continue operating under court supervision as they repay their restructured debts

Capítulo 11 de la ley de quiebras   forma de reorganización de la quiebra para las empresas que les permite seguir operando bajo la supervisión de un tribunal mientras pagan su deuda restructurada

Chapter 13 bankruptcy   a reorganization form of bankruptcy for individuals; it allows debtors to keep most of their property and use their income to pay a portion of their debts over 3 to 5 years

Capítulo 13 de la ley de quiebras   forma de reorganización de la quiebra para los individuos; permite a los deudores conservar la mayoría de sus bienes y usar sus ingresos para pagar una parte de sus deudas en el plazo de 3 a 5 años

Chapter 7 bankruptcy   a liquidation form of bankruptcy for individuals; wipes out most debts in exchange for giving up most assets; some assets that are considered necessary for survival may be retained

Capítulo 7 de la ley de quiebras   forma de liquidación de la quiebra para los individuos; elimina la mayoría de las deudas a cambio de la entrega de la mayoría de los bienes; pueden conservarse los bienes que se consideren necesarios para la supervivencia

character   a responsible attitude toward honoring obligations, often judged on evidence in the person's credit history

solidez   actitud responsable frente al pago de las obligaciones, comúnmente juzgada sobre la base de la evidencia que consta en el historial crediticio de la persona

checking account   allows you to write checks or transfer money electronically to make payments

cuenta corriente   permite emitir cheques o transferir dinero electrónicamente para efectuar pagos

child support   monthly payments to the custodial parent to help provide food, clothing, and shelter for the children

manutención infantil   cuota mensual que se le paga al padre o madre encargado de la custodia de un niño como ayuda para costear la alimentación, vestimenta y vivienda de los niños

childproof   resistant to tampering by young children

a prueba de niños   resistente a la manipulación de los niños pequeños

claims adjustors   determine the value of the property destroyed or damaged by a covered hazard (also known as insurance adjusters)

liquidadores de siniestros   determinan el valor de la propiedad destruida o dañada por un siniestro cubierto (también conocidos como peritos de seguros)

classic cars   rare cars and older vehicles that are kept in excellent condition

automóviles clásicos   carros poco comunes y vehículos antiguos que se mantienen en excelente estado

clearance   implies that the merchant wants to clear out all the advertised merchandise

liquidación   implica que el comerciante quiere terminar toda la mercadería promocionada

closing costs   the expenses incurred in transferring ownership from buyer to seller in a real estate transaction

costos de cierre   gastos derivados de la transferencia de propiedad de un comprador a un vendedor en una transacción inmobiliaria

COBRA   a federal law enacted in 1986 that allows people who leave their job to continue their health insurance under the company plan for a limited period (usually 18 months)

COBRA   ley federal promulgada en 1986 que permite a las personas que dejan su trabajo conservar su seguro de salud bajo el plan de la empresa por un período limitado (usualmente 18 meses)

codicil   a legal document that modifies parts of a will and reaffirms the rest

codicilio   documento legal que modifica partes de un testamento y reafirma el resto

coinsurance clause   provision requiring policyholders to insure their building for a stated percentage of its replacement value in order to receive full reimbursement for a loss

cláusula de coaseguro   instrumento que requiere a los asegurados que aseguren su inmueble por un porcentaje determinado de su valor de reposición para recibir el reintegro total en caso de pérdida

collateral   property pledged to assure loan repayment, such as a house, car, or furniture being purchased

garantía   bienes tales como un casa, un vehículo o muebles en proceso de compra, que se entrega como prenda para asegurar que el préstamo será devuelto

collectible   any physical asset that appreciates over time because it is rare or desired by many

pieza de colección   cualquier bien físico que se revaloriza con el paso del tiempo porque es inusual o deseado por muchos

collective values ideals and values that are important to society

valores colectivos ideales y valores que son importantes para la sociedad

collision coverage auto insurance that protects your car against damage from accidents

cobertura por colisión seguro automotor que protege al vehículo contra los daños por accidente

commercial property land and buildings that produce income through leasing or renting

propiedad comercial tierra e inmuebles que generan ingresos mediante su alquiler o arredramiento

commodity a raw material or agricultural product

bien primario materia prima o producto agrícola

common stock represents a type of stock that pays a variable dividend and gives the holder voting rights

acción común representa un tipo de acción que paga un dividend variable y otorga al accionista derecho a voto

communist economic system the government owns and controls most, if not all, of the productive resources of a nation (also known as a command system)

sistema económico comunista el gobierno es dueño y controla si no todos, casi todos los recursos productivos de una nación (también conocido como sistema de control)

community colleges offer various degree and certificate options and operate under an open-access admissions policy

colegios comunitarios ofrecen distintas opciones de títulos y certificados y funcionan de acuerdo con una política de ingreso abierto e irrestricto

company advertising advertising intended to promote the image of a store, company, or retail chain

publicidad de empresas publicidad destinada a promocionar la imagen de una tienda, empresa o cadena minorista

company risk associated with owning one company's stock; bad management decisions, other internal missteps, or even external situations can have a negative impact on a company's performance and, therefore, on the value of your investment in that company

riesgo empresario asociado con ser el propietario de las acciones de una empresa; malas decisiones administrativas, otros desaciertos internos o, incluso, situaciones externas, pueden tener un impacto negativo sobre el desempeño de la empresa y, en consecuencia, sobre el valor de la inversión en ella

comparison shopping involves checking several places to be sure you are getting the best price for equal quality

compras comparativas implican verificar distintos lugares para asegurarse de obtener el mejor precio por la misma calidad

competition rivalry among sellers in the same market to win customers

competencia rivalidad entre vendedores de un mismo mercado para ganar consumidores

compound interest interest paid on the original principal plus accumulated interest

interés compuesto interés que se paga sobre el principal original más el interés que se acumula

comprehensive coverage auto insurance that protects you from damage to your car from causes other than a collision

cobertura integral seguro automotor que protege al vehículo de daños por causas distintas de una colisión

compressed workweek a work schedule that fits the standard 40-hour workweek into less than 5 days; the typical compressed workweek is 10 hours a day for 4 days, followed by 3 days off

semana laboral comprimida esquema de trabajo que cubre las 40 horas tradicionales de trabajo semanal en menos de 5 días; la semana laboral comprimida comúnmente incluye 4 días de 10 horas de trabajo por día, seguidos de 3 días libres

compression test for a motor vehicle; can tell you whether to expect serious engine trouble ahead, such as head gaskets about to fail

prueba de compresión realizada en un vehículo automotor; puede indicar si el motor presentará serios problemas en el futuro, como fallas en las juntas de culata

conditions the overall economic climate and external environment (in relation to credit)

condiciones clima económico general y ambiente externo (en relación con el crédito)

condominium (or condo) an individually owned housing unit in a complex with shared ownership of common areas

condominio unidad de vivienda de propiedad individual ubicada en un complejo en el que se comparte la propiedad de las áreas comunes

Consumer Action a national nonprofit advocacy and education organization; known for its multilingual consumer education and support in the fields of credit, banking, privacy, insurance, and utilities

Consumer Action (acción del consumidor) organización nacional sin fines de lucro de defensa y educación del consumidor; conocida por la educación y el apoyo multilingüe que brinda a los consumidores en lo que respecta a cuestiones de crédito, bancos, privacidad, seguros y servicios públicos

consumer advocate a person who actively promotes consumer causes

defensor del consumidor persona que promueve activamente las causas de los consumidores

Consumer Financial Protection Bureau (CFPB) creates strong guardrails to protect consumers and financial markets against irresponsible mortgage lending

Oficina para la Protección Financiera del Consumidor de los Estados Unidos (CFPB, en inglés) crea fuertes barreras de seguridad para proteger a los consumidores y mercados financieros contra los préstamos hipotecarios irresponsables.

Consumer Product Safety Commission (CPSC) protects consumers from unreasonable risk of injury or death from potentially hazardous consumer products

Comisión de Seguridad de Productos del Consumidor (CPSC, en inglés) protege a los consumidores del riesgo injustificado de lesión o muerte por productos de consumo potencialmente peligrosos

consumers the buyers and users of goods and services

consumidores compradores y usuarios de bienes y servicios

Consumers Union a nonprofit organization best known as the publisher of *Consumer Reports*, a monthly magazine that publishes reviews, comparisons, and ratings of consumer products and services

Consumer Union (unión de consumidores) organización sin fines de lucro conocida por publicar *Consumer Reports*, una revista mensual con reseñas, comparaciones y calificaciones de servicios y productos de consumo

contingencies conditions that limit a buyer's liability in case one or more of the conditions are not met

contingencias condiciones que limitan la responsabilidad del comprador en caso de que no se cumplan una o más condiciones

conventional loan a mortgage agreement that does not have government backing and is offered through a commercial bank or mortgage broker

préstamo convencional acuerdo hipotecario que no cuenta con respaldo gubernamental y se ofrece mediante un banco comercial o asesor hipotecario

convertible bond a corporate bond that can be converted to shares of common stock

bono convertible bono de una empresa que puede convertirse en acciones de capital comunes

coordination of benefits a health insurance provision that specifies how the insurers will share the fee when more than one policy covers a claim

coordinación de beneficios disposición de un seguro de salud que especifica de qué manera los aseguradores dividirán el arancel cuando la prestación está cubierta por más de una póliza

copayment the specified amount that the insured must pay for each doctor or hospital visit

copago monto determinado que la persona asegurada debe pagar por cada visita al médico o al hospital

cosigner someone who will take full responsibility for paying back a loan, along with you

cosignatario persona que asumirá la total responsabilidad de devolver el préstamo junto con el prestatario

covenants, conditions, and restrictions (CC&Rs) rules designed to maintain property values and protect the interests of all property owners

convenios, condiciones y restricciones (CCyR) reglas diseñadas para preservar los valores de la propiedad y proteger los intereses de todos los propietarios

cover letter also known as a letter of application and is a one-page formal business letter that describes your interest in and qualifications for the position

carta de presentación también conocida como carta de solicitud de empleo es una carta comercial formal de una página que describe el interés y las calificaciones de una persona para el puesto de trabajo que solicita

credit using someone else's money and agreeing to pay it back later

crédito usar el dinero de otra persona y acordar su devolución a futuro

credit bureau a business that gathers stores, and sells credit information to other businesses

agencia de información crediticia empresa que reúne, almacena y vende información crediticia a otras empresas

credit counseling a service to help consumers manage their debt load and credit more wisely

asesoría en materia crediticia servicio ofrecido para ayudar a los consumidores a administrar sus deudas y créditos de manera más prudente

credit freeze a consumer request that requires the credit bureaus to deny all access to a consumer's credit information or files

congelamiento de la información crediticia solicitud del consumidor para que las oficinas de información crediticia nieguen el acceso a la información o documentos crediticios del consumidor

credit history the complete record of your borrowing and repayment performance

historial crediticio registro completo de la actuación de una persona respecto de sus préstamos y devolución

credit inquiry a request by a business with a permissible purpose to check your credit

consulta sobre el crédito pedido de una empresa para verificar con un propósito atendible el crédito de una persona

credit management following an individual plan for using credit wisely

manejo del crédito consiste en seguir un plan individual para usar el crédito de manera prudente

creditor a person or business that loans money to others

acreedor persona o empresa que presta dinero a otros

credit payment plan records your debts and a strategy for paying them off

plan de pago del crédito registra las deudas y una estrategia para pagarlas

credit repair the process of reestablishing a good credit rating

reparación crediticia proceso por el cual se restablece una buena calificación crediticia

credit report a written statement of a consumer's credit history

informe del crédito resumen escrito del historial crediticio de un consumidor

credit score tells potential creditors the likelihood that you will repay debt as agreed

calificación crediticia indica a los posibles acreedores la probabilidad de que una persona pague la deuda según lo convenido

credit union operates like a bank; however, it is a nonprofit company owned by people with accounts there

cooperativa de crédito opera como un banco; sin embargo, es una empresa sin fines de lucro cuyos dueños tienen cuentas en ella

creditworthy a determination of whether someone is a good risk in terms of credit

capacidad crediticia evaluación para determinar si una persona representa un riesgo positive en términos crediticios

cremation following death, the process of reducing a body to ashes in a high-temperature oven

cremación proceso posterior a la muerte de una persona que consiste someter su cuerpo a un horno de alta temperatura para reducirlo a cenizas

custodial parent the parent with whom the children live

padre encargado de la custodia padre con el que viven los hijos

custom a long-established practice that takes on the force of an unwritten law

costumbre práctica establecida hace muchos años que adquiere la fuerza de ley no escrita

cyclical stocks stocks that are affected by ups and downs in the economy

valores cíclicos acciones afectadas por los vaivenes de la economía

D

dealer add-ons high-priced, high-profit car dealer services that add little or no value

accesorios y complementos servicios altamente costosos y rentables que ofrecen las empresas concesionarias de vehículos que suman prácticamente poco o ningún valor

debenture a corporate bond based on the company's general creditworthiness and reputation

obligación bono corporativo basado en la capacidad crediticia y reputación general de una empresa

debit card a bank card that deducts money from a checking account to pay for purchases

tarjeta de débito tarjeta bancaria que deduce dinero de una cuenta corriente para pagar compras

debt collector a person or company hired by a creditor to collect the overdue balance on an account

cobrador de deudas persona o empresa contratada por un acreedor para cobrar el saldo atrasado de una cuenta

debt consolidation a finance company loans you money to pay off your debt

consolidación de deuda una empresa financiera presta dinero para pagar la deuda

debt management plan enables you to make a single monthly payment to a credit counseling organization that distributes the funds to creditors based on a payment schedule

plan de gestión de deuda permite realizar un único pago mensual a una organización de asesoría crediticia que distribuye los fondos a los acreedores basándose en un cronograma de pagos

debt settlement program a company negotiates with your creditors on your behalf to reduce the amount of debt you owe

plan de liquidación de deuda una empresa negocia con los acreedores en nombre del deudor para reducir el monto que se debe

debtor a person who borrows money from others

deudor persona que pide dinero prestado a otras

deception occurs when false or misleading claims are made about a particular product's quality, price, or purpose

engaño se produce cuando se realizan afirmaciones falsas o confusas sobre la calidad, precio o propósito de un producto

deductible the amount of money you pay toward a covered insurance claim

franquicia monto de dinero que se paga con la perspectiva de reclamar la cobertura contratada en el seguro

deductions amounts subtracted from gross pay

deducciones montos que se restan de la remuneración bruta

deed legal document that transfers title of real property from one party to another

escritura documento legal que transfiere el título de la propiedad de una de las partes a la otra

defensive stocks stocks that remain stable and pay dividends during an economic decline (also called noncyclical stocks)

acciones de defensa acciones que se mantienen estables y pagan dividendos durante una caída económica (también llamadas acciones no cíclicas)

deferred billing a service available to charge customers where purchases are not billed to the customer until much later than the standard billing time

facturación diferida servicio para cobrar a los clientes disponible en los lugares donde las compras no se facture al cliente hasta mucho después del tiempo de facturación estándar

defined-benefit plan a company-sponsored retirement plan in which employees receive a set monthly amount for life beginning at retirement based on wages earned and the number of years of service

plan con beneficios definidos plan de retiro patrocinado por una empresa en el que a partir del momento en que se jubilan, los empleados empiezan a recibir de por vida un monto mensual determinado que se basa en la paga que ganó cada uno y la cantidad de años de servicio

defined-contribution plan a company-sponsored retirement plan in which employees receive a periodic or lump-sum payment based on their account balance and the performance of the investments in their account

plan con aportes definidos plan de retiro patrocinado por una empresa en el que los empleados reciben un pago único o periódico basado en el saldo de su cuenta y el rendimiento de las inversiones que guarda en ella

demand   the willingness and ability of consumers to purchase goods and services at various prices

demanda   voluntad y capacidad de los consumidores para comprar bienes y servicios a diversos precios

demand deposit   an account on which money may be withdrawn at any time—that is, on demand

cuenta a la vista   cuenta en la cual el dinero puede retirarse en cualquier momento, es decir, en cuanto lo solicite el titular de la cuenta

dependent student   student who is younger than age 24, working on an undergraduate degree, unmarried, not a parent, along with a few other situations

estudiante dependiente   estudiante menor de 24 años, que cursa una licenciatura, es soltero, no tiene hijos, entre otras circunstancias

depreciation   decline in property value due to normal wear and tear

depreciación   caída en el valor de la propiedad a causa de su desgaste natural

differentiated tuition   higher postsecondary tuition that may be required for highly technical fields such as engineering, business, and the lab sciences

enseñanza diferenciada   instrucción que posiblemente se requiera luego de la formación secundaria para materias altamente técnicas como la ingeniería, los negocios y las ciencias de laboratorio

direct deposit   allows your net pay to be deposited electronically into your bank account

depósito directo   permite depositar la remuneración neta electrónicamente en la cuenta bancaria

disability insurance   a plan that makes regular payments to replace income lost when illness or injury prevents the insured from working

seguro por discapacidad   plan que efectúa pagos regulares para reemplazar la pérdida de ingresos cuando la persona asegurada no puede trabajar a causa de una enfermedad o lesión

discharged debt   previous debts erased by the court during bankruptcy proceedings

deuda exonerada   deudas previas borradas por el tribunal durante el proceso de quiebra

discount brokers   buy and sell securities for clients for a reduced commission or zero commission fees

asesores financieros de descuento   compran y venden títulos para sus clientes por una comisión reducida o directamente sin cobrar comisión

discrimination   the act of treating people differently based on prejudice rather than individual merit

discriminación   consiste en tratar a las personas de manera diferente por prejucio y no por su mérito individual

disposable income   the money you have left to spend or save after taxes and other required and optional deductions are taken

ingresos disponibles   dinero que queda para gastar o ahorrar luego de descontar los impuestos y otras deducciones requeridas y opcionales

disputing a charge   generally means asking the payment issuer to reverse the charge on your account

impugnar gastos   en general significa solicitar al emisor del pago que revierta el gasto en nuestra cuenta

dissolution of marriage   a legal process in which a judge dissolves the marriage (also called divorce)

disolución del matrimonio   proceso legal en el que un juez disuelve el matrimonio (también llamado divorcio)

diversification   spreads risk among diverse types of investments

diversificación   reparte el riesgo entre diversos tipos de inversión

dividend reinvestment   using dividends previously made on the stock to buy more shares

reinversión de los dividendos   utilización de los dividendos previamente obtenidos con las acciones para comprar más acciones

dividends   money paid to stockholders from the corporation's earnings or profits

dividendos   dinero que se paga a los accionistas proveniente de las utilidades o ganancias de la empresa

divorce decree   a final statement of the dissolution decisions

sentencia de divorcio declaración final de las decisiones de disolución

dollar-cost averaging systematically purchasing an equal dollar amount of the same security at regular intervals, regardless of the share price

inversión regular constante repartida consiste en comprar de manera sistemática la misma cantidad en dólares del mismo título en forma regularmente espaciada, con independencia del precio de la acción

double indemnity means that the beneficiary is paid double the face amount of the insurance policy

doble indemnización significa que al beneficiario se le paga dos veces el valor nominal de la póliza de seguro

down payment part of the purchase price paid in cash at the time of purchase

anticipo parte del precio de compra que se paga en efectivo en el momento de la compra

downsizing an economic event where jobs are eliminated because company revenues are falling while costs are rising

recorte de personal hecho económico en el cual se eliminan empleos porque la renta de la empresa cae mientras los costos suben

driving record includes the number and type of traffic tickets you have received for driving infractions and misdemeanors, along with the number of accidents in which you have been involved

historial de manejo incluye la cantidad y el tipo de multas de tránsito generadas por infracciones y delitos de manejo menores, así como la cantidad de accidentes en las que el conductor estuvo involucrado

dual enrollment allows high school students to earn both college credit and complete requirements for high school graduation simultaneously

doble matriculación permite a los estudiantes secundarios obtener al mismo tiempo créditos universitarios y completar los requisitos para graduarse en la escuela secundaria

duplex a building with two separate living units that share a common central wall

dúplex edificio con dos unidades de vivienda separadas que comparten una pared central

E

early college can be found on college campuses, within traditional high schools, or through community colleges; students who participate in early college programs receive both a high school diploma and an associate degree (up to 2 years of college credit) by taking a combination of high school and college courses

ingreso anticipado puede ocurrir en los campus universitarios, en las escuelas secundarias tradicionales o en los colegios comunitarios; los estudiantes que participan en los programas de ingreso anticipado reciben tanto un diploma de estudios secundarios como un grado de asociado (hasta 2 años de crédito universitario) por tomar una combinación de cursos de la escuela secundaria y de la universidad

early withdrawal penalty occurs when any part of money is taken from a CD before the maturity date

penalidad por retiro anticipado ocurre cuando cualquier parte del dinero se retira de un CD antes de la fecha de vencimiento

earnest money a deposit that accompanies an offer to buy a property

arras depósito que acompaña la oferta para comprar una propiedad

earnings per share (EPS) a corporation's after-tax earnings, called net profit, divided by the number of common stock shares outstanding

utilidades por acción (GPA) ganancia de una empresa luego de deducir los impuestos, denominada ganancia neta, dividida por la cantidad de acciones comunes en circulación

economic risk may result in gain or loss because of changing economic conditions

riesgo económico puede derivar en ganancia o pérdida como resultado de los cambios en las condiciones económicas

economy refers to all activities related to producing and distributing goods and services in a geographic area

economía se refiere a todas las actividades relacionadas con la producción y distribución de bienes y servicios en una zona geográfica

electric cars run on batteries that you charge through a special plug at your home or at charging stations

vehículos eléctricos funcionan con baterías que el usuario puede cargar a través de un enchufe especial en su casa o en estaciones de carga

electronic funds transfer (EFT) uses a computer-based system that enables you to move money from one account to another without writing a check or exchanging cash

transferencia electrónica de fondos (TEF) emplea un sistema informático que permite movilizar dinero de una cuenta a otra sin necesidad de emitir un cheque ni de intercambiar dinero en efectivo

emerging stocks stocks in young, often small, corporations with higher overall risk than those of companies that have been successful for many years

acciones emergentes acciones de empresas jóvenes, comúnmente pequeñas, con un riesgo general más alto que el de las empresas que han sido exitosas durante muchos años

employee assistance plan (EAP) a group benefit that allows employees and their families to seek counseling and other services

programa de asistencia al empleado (EAP) beneficio grupal que permite a los empleados y sus familias obtener asesoramiento y otros servicios

encryption a code that protects your account name, number, and other information by making it unreadable to others

encriptación código que protege información como el nombre de la cuenta, el número y otros datos en general haciéndola ilegible para terceras personas

endorsement in banking is a security step to help the bank verify that you are the proper recipient of the funds and authorizes the bank to deposit the money into your account or to give you cash; endorsement in insurance is a written amendment to an insurance policy that reflects its changes

endoso en cuestiones bancarias, el endoso es un paso de seguridad que ayuda al banco a verificar que somos los destinatarios correctos de los fondos y autoriza al banco a depositar el dinero en nuestra cuenta o a entregarnos efectivo; en cuestiones de seguros, es una enmienda escrita que se introduce en la póliza para reflejar los cambios

entrepreneur a person who takes the risks of being self-employed and owning a business

emprendedor persona que asume los riesgos de trabajar por cuenta propia y como dueño de su negocio

equity the difference between the market value of the property and the amount owed

capital diferencia entre el valor de mercado de la propiedad y el monto adeudado

escrow account used to collect property taxes and insurance on a home

cuenta de plica para utilizada para depositar el dinero de los impuestos sobre la propiedad y los montos del seguro de una vivienda

escrow closer an independent person who gathers and verifies information, prepares the closing statement of what the buyer owes and the credits that have been applied

agente de plica persona independiente que reúne y verifica información, prepara el resumen de cierre con el saldo deudor del comprador y los créditos que se aplicaron

estate all that a person owns, less debts owed, at the time of the person's death

patrimonio todo lo que posee una persona al momento de su muerte, menos las deudas por pagar

estate tax a tax on property transferred from an estate to its heirs

impuesto sobre el patrimonio impuesto sobre la propiedad transferido del patrimonio a sus herederos

estimated tax the amount of tax you estimate you will owe on income received without withholdings

impuesto estimado monto que uno estima que deberá pagar como impuesto sobre el ingreso recibido sin las retenciones

eviction the legal process of removing a tenant from rental property

desalojo proceso legal por el cual se expulsa a un inquilino de la propiedad en alquiler

exchange platforms where securities are traded

plataforma bursátil espacio donde se comercializan títulos

exchange-traded fund (ETF) a pooled investment security like a mutual fund; it tracks an index fund or similar security

fondo de inversión cotizado en bolsa (FCB) título de inversión compartida similar a un fondo mutuo; sigue un fondo indexado o título similar

exempt status   available to those who know they will not earn enough in one year to owe income tax

situación de exención   disponible para las personas que saben que en el transcurso de un año no ganarán lo suficiente como para que se les cobre impuesto sobre los ingresos

exempted property   assets considered necessary for survival

propiedad exenta   bienes que se consideran necesarios para sobrevivir

exemption   when computing taxes, an amount you may subtract from your income for each person who depends on your income to live

exención   cuando se computan impuestos, monto que puede restarse de nuestros ingresos por cada persona que depende de nuestros ingresos para vivir

experience   the knowledge and skills acquired from working in a career field

experiencia   conocimientos y destrezas que se adquieren al trabajar en un campo profesional

extended family   consists of three or more generations living as a family unit (also called multi-generational families)

familia extendida   consta de tres o más generaciones que viven como unidad familiar (también llamada familia generacional)

extended warranty   covers the costs of expensive repairs and defects not covered by the standard warranty or that occur after the standard warranty expires

garantía extendida   cubre los gastos de reparaciones costosas y defectos que no cubre la garantía común o que se presentan una vez que venció la garantía común

F

face value   the amount a bondholder will be repaid at maturity

valor nominal   monto que un bonista debe recibir al vencimiento del bono

FAFSA (Free Application for Federal Student Aid)   part of the Federal Student Aid Office and the Department of Education, which manages student financial assistance programs authorized under Title IV of the Higher Education Act of 1965

Solicitud Gratuita de Asistencia Federal para Estudiantes   (FAFSA, en inglés) parte de la Oficina de Asistencia Federal para Estudiantes y del Departamento de Educación que gestiona los programas de asistencia financiera para estudiantes autorizados en virtud del Título IV de la Ley de Educación Superior de 1965

Family and Medical Leave Act (FMLA)   provides up to 13 weeks of unpaid time from work in any 13-month period

Ley de Licencia Familiar y Médica   (FMLA, en inglés) otorga hasta 13 semanas de licencia sin goce de sueldo dentro de cualquier período de 13 meses

family budget   a plan that allocates spending, saving, borrowing, and investing of the family's pooled resources to meet future goals

presupuesto familiar   planificación que asigna los recursos comunes de la familia a gastos, ahorros, préstamos e inversiones para cumplir metas futuras

Federal Aviation Administration (FAA)   oversees the U.S. commercial aviation industry for the Department of Transportation; it maintains regulations and standards that airline companies must follow to transport passengers

Administración Federal de Aviación   (FAA, en inglés) supervisa la industria de la aviación comercial de los EE. UU. para el Departamento de Transporte; mantiene las normas y los estándares que las aerolíneas deben cumplir para transportar pasajeros

Federal Communications Commission (FCC)   regulates interstate and international communications by radio, television, wire, satellite, and cable

Comisión Federal de Comunicaciones   (FCC, en inglés) regula las comunicaciones interestatales e internacionales por radio, televisión, cable y satélite.

Federal Deposit Insurance Corporation (FDIC) insurance   offers standard insurance amount is $250,000 per depositor, per banking institution, for each account type

Corporación Federal de Seguro de Depósitos   (FDIC, en inglés) ofrece seguro estándar por montos de $250,000 por depositante, por institución bancaria, para cada tipo de cuenta

Federal Reserve   called the Fed, is the economic institution in the Unites States that sets interest rates, manages the money supply, and regulates financial markets

Reserva Federal   llamada la Fed, es la institución económica de los EE. UU. que fija las tasas de interés, administra la oferta de dinero y regula los mercados financieros.

Federal Trade Commission (FTC)   regulates unfair methods of competition, false or deceptive advertising, deceptive product labeling, and the concealment of true credit costs

Comisión Federal de Comercio   (FTC, en inglés) regula los métodos de competencia desleal, la publicidad falsa o engañosa, el etiquetado engañoso de los productos y el encubrimiento de los verdaderos costos del crédito

FHA loan   a government-sponsored loan that carries mortgage insurance

préstamo FHA   préstamo patrocinado por el gobierno que incluye un seguro hipotecario

fiat money   refers to today's money, which is not backed by gold, but by faith in the general economy and government of the country

dinero fíat   se refiere al dinero actual, que no está respaldado por oro, sino por la fe en la economía en general y el gobierno del país

FICO score   most used credit scoring model, used by over 90 percent of creditors; each consumer has three FICO scores—one for each of the three major credit bureaus

Puntaje FICO   es el modelo de puntaje de crédito más utilizado, el que aplican más del 90 por ciento de los acreedores; cada consumidor tiene tres puntajes FICO: uno para cada una de las tres principales agencias de información crediticia

fiduciary financial advisor   is legally required to only make recommendations to the client if it is in the client's best interest; typically works for a registered investment advisor (RIA)an RIA, and most chartered financial analysts (CFAs) act as a fiduciary

asesor financiero fiduciario   por ley, únicamente puede hacer recomendaciones que convengan solo a los intereses del cliente; por lo general, trabaja para un asesor de inversiones registrado y la mayoría de los analistas financieros certificados actúan como fiduciarios

filing status   tax-filing group based on your marital status as of the last day of the tax year

categoría de declaración impositiva   categoría impositiva a la que pertenece el contribuyente según su estado civil a partir del último día del año fiscal

finance charge   the total dollar amount of all interest and fees you pay for the use of credit

costo financiero   monto total en dólares correspondiente a todo el interés y las comisiones que se pagan por el uso del crédito

finance company   an organization that makes high-risk consumer loans

empresa financiera   organización que hace préstamos de alto riesgo a los consumidores

financial plan   a set of goals for spending, saving, and investing the money you receive

plan financiero   conjunto de metas de gasto, ahorro e inversión del dinero que se recibe

financing   when a consumer borrows money from a bank, store, or credit card company to make a purchase today

financiación   se produce cuando un consumidor pide prestado dinero a un banco, tienda o empresa de tarjeta de crédito para hacer una compra en el momento

fixed expenses   costs that do not change from month to month

gastos fijos   costos que no cambian de mes a mes

fixed rate   cost of credit that does not change

tasa fija   costo del crédito que no cambia

fixed-rate investment   an investment such as a bond that pays a specified amount of interest on a regular schedule

inversión a tasa fija   tipo de inversión, como un bono, que paga una determinada cantidad de interés en forma regular

fixed-rate loan   a loan for which the interest rate does not change (go up or down) over the life of the loan

préstamo a tasa fija   préstamo cuya tasa de interés no cambia (no sube ni baja) durante el plazo del préstamo

flammability   the capacity to catch on fire

inflamabilidad   capacidad de prenderse fuego

Flex 125 Plan   an employee benefit program that allows employees to set aside money, pre-tax, to help pay deductibles, copayments, and other health expenses during the year that are not covered by insurance

Plan Flex 125   programa de beneficios para los empleados que les permite reservar una determinada cantidad de dinero, antes de pagar impuestos, para costear franquicias, copagos y otros gastos de salud que se producen durante el año y que no están cubiertos por el seguro

flextime   a work schedule that allows employees to choose their working hours within a defined time limit

horario flexible   esquema laboral que permite a los empleados elegir en qué horarios trabajar dentro de un límite de tiempo definido

follow-up   contact with the employer after the interview but before hiring occurs; it reminds the employer who you are, which could improve your chance of getting the job

seguimiento   contacto con el empleador posterior a la entrevista pero previo a la contratación; le recuerda al entrevistador quién eres, lo cual puede mejorar nuestras posibilidades de obtener el puesto de trabajo

full coverage   when all five types of insurance are purchased together in a single policy

cobertura total   modalidad en la que los cinco tipos de seguro se contrata juntos en una sola póliza

full-service brokers   provide analysis and opinions based on their judgments and experts' opinions at the company they represent; in addition to buying and selling securities for their clients, they research various investments and keep clients up to date on market trends and stock performance while providing investment ideas and recommendations

agentes de servicio completo   proporcionan análisis y opiniones sobre la base de su criterio y juicio de expertos a la empresa que representan; además de comprar y vender títulos para sus clientes, estudian diversas inversiones y mantienen a sus clientes actualizados sobre las tendencias del mercado y el desempeño de las acciones mientras que proponen ideas y hacen recomendaciones de inversión

furnished rental   provides the basics—bed, dresser, sofa, chairs, lamps, dining table and chairs, and essential appliances

alquiler equipado   proporciona el equipamiento básico: cama, tocador, sofá, sillas, lámparas, mesa y sillas de comedor y electrodomésticos esenciales

futures   type of contract that obligates the buyer to purchase, or the seller to sell, stock or a commodity for a specified price at a date in the future

futuros   tipo de contrato que obliga al comprador a comprar, o al vendedor a vender, acciones o bienes primarios por un precio determinado en una fecha futura

G

gap insurance   an optional type of car insurance that will help pay off your loan if the car is totaled or stolen and you are upside-down

seguro de protección garantizada   tipo de seguro automotor opcional que ayuda a devolver el préstamo si el vehículo fue robado o quedó completamente destruido en un siniestro

garnishment   a legal process that allows part of your paycheck to be withheld for debt payment

embargo   proceso legal que permite retener parte del sueldo para pagar deudas

gems   natural, precious stones like diamonds, rubies, sapphires, and emeralds

gemas   piedras preciosas naturales, como los diamantes, rubíes, zafiros y esmeraldas

general obligation (GO) bond   a municipal bond backed by the power of the issuing state or local government to levy taxes to pay back the debt

obligación ordinaria   bono municipal respaldado por el poder del estado emisor o el gobierno local para recaudar impuestos con los cuales pagar la deuda

generic drugs   have the same chemical structure as trade name drugs

medicamentos genéricos   tienen la misma estructura química que los medicamentos con marca comercial

gift tax   a tax applied to a gift of money or property

impuesto sobre donaciones   impuesto aplicado al dinero o propiedad recibido como regalo

gig worker   works a temporary or on-demand job, typically in a service industry

trabajador temporario independiente   trabaja de manera temporaria por pedido, por lo general en la industria de los servicios

global fund   a mutual fund that purchases international stocks and bonds as well as U.S. securities

fondo global   fondo mutuo que compra acciones y bonos internacionales y también títulos de los EE. UU.

goal   a desired end toward which efforts are directed

meta   fin deseado hacia el cual se dirigen los esfuerzos

grace period   as it relates to credit is a timeframe within which you may pay your current credit card balance fully and incur no finance charge; a grace period as it relates to a rental property is specified in the lease and allows 3 to 7 days before late fees are applied

período de gracia   en lo que respecta al crédito, es un margen de tiempo dentro del cual se puede pagar por completo el saldo vigente de la tarjeta de crédito y no incurrir en gastos de financiamiento; en lo que respecta a inmuebles en alquiler, el período de gracia se determina en el contrato y concede de 3 a 7 días de plazo antes de la aplicación de multas por pago con atraso

grants   a form of financial aid that needs to be repaid only if you withdraw from school or do not complete the required service obligation

subvención   tipo de ayuda financiera que debe devolverse solo si el beneficiario deja la escuela o no completa la obligación de servicio requerido

gross income   all the taxable income you receive during the year

ingresos brutos   todos los ingresos imponibles obtenidos durante el año

gross pay   total amount earned before deductions are subtracted

remuneración bruta   monto total que se gana antes de restarle las deducciones

group health insurance   a type of health insurance plan offered by an employer or member organization for their employees (the group)

seguro de salud grupal   tipo de plan de seguro de salud ofrecido por un empleador u organización miembro a sus empleados (el grupo)

growth and income fund   a mutual fund whose investment aims to earn returns from dividends and capital gains

fondo de crecimiento e ingresos   fondo mutuo cuya inversión busca obtener retornos de los dividendos y ganancias de capital

growth fund   a mutual fund whose investment goal is to buy stocks that will increase in value over time

fondo de crecimiento   fondo mutuo cuya meta de inversión es comprar acciones que aumentarán de valor con el tiempo

growth stocks   stocks in corporations that reinvest their profits into the business so that it can grow

acciones de crecimiento   acciones de empresas que reinvierten sus ganancias en el negocio para que crezca

guest   someone you specifically ask to come to your house

invitado   persona a la que le pedimos específicamente que venga a nuestra casa

H

health insurance   a plan for sharing the risk of high medical costs from injury or illness

seguro de salud   plan para compartir el riesgo de altos costos médicos derivados de una lesión o enfermedad

health insurance exchange   provides a set of government-regulated and standardized health care plans from which uninsured and underinsured individuals may purchase health insurance policies

mercado de seguros de salud   ofrece un conjunto de planes de atención de la salud estandarizados y regulados por el gobierno de los cuales las personas no aseguradas o subaseguradas reducido pueden comprar pólizas de seguro de salud

health maintenance organization (HMO)   a group plan offering prepaid medical care to its members

organización de mantenimiento de la salud   (OMS) plan grupal que ofrece atención médica prepaga a sus miembros

health savings account (HSA)   associated with a medical plan with a higher annual deductible than typical health plans; the insured takes the money that would have gone toward the premiums for basic health coverage and deposits it into an HSA to pay qualified medical expenses not covered by insurance, including deductibles and copayments

cuenta de ahorros para la salud   (HSA) asociada a un plan médico con una franquicia anual más alta que la de los planes de salud tradicionales; la persona asegurada toma el dinero que se hubiera destinado a las primas para una cobertura básica de salud y lo deposita en una CAS para pagar gastos de medicina calificada no cubiertos por el seguro, incluidos copagos y franquicias

hedge any investment or action that offsets against loss from another investment

cobertura cualquier inversión o acción que compense o contrarreste las pérdidas causadas por otra inversión

high deductible health plan (HDHP) a plan that combines a Health Savings Account (HAS) or a Health Reimbursement Arrangement (HRA) with a high deductible conventional medical plan

plan de salud de franquicia alta (HDHP, en inglés) plan que combina la modalidad de Cuenta de Ahorro para la Salud (HRA, en inglés) o Acuerdo de Reintegro de Salud (HRA, en inglés) con un plan médico convencional de franquicia alta

homeowners insurance protects property owners from property and liability risks

seguro para la vivienda protege al propietario de una vivienda contra los riesgos que puede correr el inmueble o contra los riesgos derivados de su responsabilidad civil ante terceros

hospice a nonprofit program consisting of medical and support services provided by a team of professionals and volunteers for those who are dying and their families

residencia para enfermos terminales programa sin fines de lucro que brinda apoyo y servicio médico a través de un equipo de profesionales y voluntarios a las personas enfermas, que están a punto de morir, y a sus familias

hybrid a vehicle that combines an internal combustion (gas-powered) engine with an electric motor

híbrido vehículo que combina un motor de combustión interna (alimentado con combustible) con un motor eléctrico

I

identity theft occurs when someone gets enough information about you to assume your identity; one of the largest and fastest-growing crimes in the United States and around the world

robo de identidad se produce cuando alguien obtiene suficiente información sobre otra persona para asumir su identidad; es uno de los delitos más extendidos y de más rápido crecimiento en los EE. UU. y en todo el mundo

imposter scam occurs when fraudsters target people by pretending to be someone else

trampa de impostor ocurre cuando estafadores se dirigen a las personas con una identidad falsa para fingir ser alguien distinto

impulse buying occurs when you buy something without thinking about it and making a conscious decision

compra impulsiva se produce cuando una persona compra algo sin pensar ni tomar decisiones conscientes sobre lo que adquiere

incentive pay a form of compensation that encourages employees to strive for higher performance levels

incentivo salarial forma de compensación que alienta a los empleados a trabajar más esmeradamente para elevar su nivel de desempeño

incentives monetary or nonmonetary rewards used to motivate employees to work harder

incentivos recompensa monetaria y no monetaria usada para motivar a los empleados a que trabajen más duramente

income fund a mutual fund whose investment goal is to produce current income on a steady basis in the form of interest or dividends

fondo de ingresos fondo mutuo cuya meta de inversión es producir ingresos corrientes de manera regular mediante intereses o dividendos

income stocks stocks in corporations with a consistent history of paying high dividends to stockholders

acciones de reparto acciones en empresas con una trayectoria sólida en el pago de dividendos altos a los accionistas

incontestable clause a provision of a life insurance policy stating that once the policy has been in effect for a specified time, usually 2 years, the insurer may no longer question items on the application to deny coverage

cláusula inapelable previsión incluida en una póliza de seguro de vida que establece que una vez que la póliza estuvo vigente durante un determinado período, usualmente 2 años, el asegurador no puede cuestionar los elementos que aplican para negar la cobertura

indemnification an agreement where an insurer helps cover loss, damage, or liability incurred from a covered event

indemnización acuerdo por el cual el asegurador ayuda a cubrir la pérdida, el daño o la responsabilidad relacionados con el suceso cubierto

independent contractors people who work for themselves and contract with businesses; they do not work for an employer

contratistas independientes personas que trabajan por su propia cuenta y hacen contratos con las empresas; no trabajan para un empleador

index fund a mutual fund that tries to match the performance of a particular index by investing in the companies included in that index

fondo índice es un fondo mutuo que busca replicar el rendimiento de un índice en particular invirtiendo en las empresas incluidas en ese índice

individual retirement account (IRA) a retirement savings plan that offers tax advantages and allows individuals to set aside a specified amount each year

cuenta de retiro individual (IRA, en inglés) plan de ahorro de retiro que ofrece ventajas impositivas y permite a las personas reservar un monto determinado cada año

industry advertising advertising intended to promote a general product group without regard to where these products are purchased

publicidad de una industria publicidad destinada a promover en general productos de un sector industrial independientemente del lugar donde se compran esos productos

industry risk affects groups of businesses; for example, if you invest in the candy industry, a nationwide trend toward dieting or the avoidance of sugar may adversely affect your investment

riesgo industrial afecta a grupos de empresas; por ejemplo, si se invierte en la industria de las golosinas, una tendencia nacional a hacer dieta o evitar el consumo de azúcar puede afectar negativamente la inversión en ese sector industrial

inflation a rise in the general level of prices

inflación aumento en el nivel general de los precios

infomercial a lengthy paid advertisement with testimonials and product demonstrations

infomercial aviso publicitario extenso y pago que incluye testimonios y demostraciones de uso de los productos

infraction a minor violation that is punishable by a fine

infracción falta menor que se sanciona con una multa

inheritance tax imposed on an heir who inherits property from an estate

impuesto sobre la herencia se carga sobre el heredero que recibe bienes patrimoniales como herencia

innovations new ideas, products, or services that bring about changes in the way we live

innovaciones ideas, productos o servicios nuevos que introducen cambios en nuestra forma de vida

inspection report a written that details the existing conditions of the house and property

informe de inspección escrito que detalla las condiciones en que se encuentra la vivienda y los bienes

installment credit a loan with fixed payments or installments that must be repaid in full, including all finance charges, by a specified due date; also called *closed-end credit*

crédito a plazos préstamo con pagos fijos o cuotas que debe devolverse en su totalidad, incluidos los gastos financieros, antes de una fecha establecida; llamado también *crédito no renovable*

insurable interest any financial interest in life or property such that the insured would suffer financially if the life or property were lost or harmed

interés asegurable cualquier interés financiero sobre la vida o la propiedad que la persona asegurada podría padecer financieramente si sufriera pérdidas o daños con relación a la vida o la propiedad

insurable risk a pure risk faced by many people for which the amount of the loss can be predicted

riesgo asegurable riesgo puro que enfrentan muchas personas para el cual puede predecirse el monto de la pérdida

insurance a method for spreading individual risk among a large group of people to make losses more affordable for all

seguro método para repartir el riesgo individual entre muchas personas de modo que las pérdidas resulten más fáciles de costear para todos

interest earnings on your deposit in an account

interés ganancias obtenidas por el depósito en una cuenta

intermediate-term goal something you wish to accomplish in the next few months or in the next year

metas a mediano plazo objetivos que uno desea alcanzar en los próximos meses o en el año siguiente

internship programs allow students to earn industry credentials and even college credit while completing their core academic requirements for high school graduation

programas de pasantías permiten a los estudiantes hacerse de referencias en la industria e incluso ganar crédito universitario mientras completa los requisitos académicos obligatorios para graduarse de la escuela secundaria

investing risk the chance that an investment's value will decrease

riesgo de inversión posibilidad de que el valor de una inversión disminuya

investing using long-term savings to grow money over time

invertir usar ahorros de largo plazo para que el dinero crezca con el tiempo

investment-grade bond considered a high-quality, low-risk bond

bono con grado de inversión considerado de alta calidad y bajo riesgo

invoice price the price the dealer paid for a new car

precio de factura precio que la concesionaria de vehículos pagó por un vehículo nuevo

involuntary bankruptcy occurs when creditors petition the court, asking the court to declare the debtor bankrupt

quiebra involuntaria ocurre cuando los acreedores elevan una petición al tribunal para solicitar que declare la quiebra del deudor

itemized deductions expenses you can subtract from adjusted gross income to determine your taxable income

deducciones detalladas gastos que pueden restarse del ingreso bruto ajustado la para determinar ingresos imponibles

J

job application a form that asks questions to be sure you are qualified for a job opening

solicitud de empleo formulario en el que se hacen preguntas para asegurarse de que la persona está calificada para el puesto de trabajo

job creation occurs when the economy grows (consumer demand is increasing) and new workers are hired

creación de empleo ocurre cuando la economía crece (aumenta la demanda de los consumidores) y se contratan nuevos empleados

job interview a face-to-face meeting, which can take place in-person or via an online meeting tool such as Zoom, with a potential employer to discuss a job opening

entrevista laboral reunión frente a frente que puede realizarse en persona o de manera remota en línea, mediante una herramienta como Zoom, con el posible empleador, para hablar sobre la vacante de trabajo

job rotation a job design in which employees are trained to do more than one specialized task; they regularly rotate from one task to another

rotación laboral formato de trabajo en el cual los empleados se capacitan para realizar más de una tarea específica; normalmente rotan de una tarea a otra

job sharing a job design in which two people share one full-time position; they split the salary and benefits according to each person's contributions

trabajo compartido formato de trabajo en el cual dos personas comparten un empleo de tiempo completo; dividen el salario y los beneficios de acuerdo con los aportes que realiza cada persona

judgment a court order allowing creditors to collect the debts you have agreed to pay

fallo orden de un tribunal que permite a los acreedores cobrar las deudas que una persona acordó pagar

junk bond has a low quality rating or no rating at all

bono basura tiene una calificación de baja calidad o directamente ninguna calificación

K

Keogh plan   a tax-deferred retirement savings plan available to self-employed individuals

Plan Keogh   plan de ahorro de retiro con impuestos diferidos disponible para personas que trabajan por cuenta propia

L

landlord   a rental property's owner, or owner's representative

propietario   dueño del inmueble en alquiler o representante del dueño

lease   a written agreement that allows a tenant to use the property for a set period at a set rent payment

contrato de arrendamiento   acuerdo escrito que permite a un inquilino usar la propiedad durante un determinado período de tiempo, como se establece en el pago de la renta

leasing   a type of car financing where you rent a car from the dealership

arrendamiento   tipo de financiación para vehículos en la cual el vehículo se alquila directamente del concesionario o del distribuidor

lemon   a car with substantial defects that the manufacturer has been unable to fix after repeated attempts

limón   en EE. UU., un vehículo con notables defectos que el fabricante no pudo reparar luego de reiterados intentos

lemon laws   exist in many states and protect consumers from the consequences of owning or leasing a defective car; allow you to get a new car or your money back

ley de limón   existen en diversos estados y protegen a los consumidores de las consecuencias de haber comprado o alquilado por arrendamiento un vehículo defectuoso; permiten obtener un vehículo nuevo o recuperar el dinero

lessee   person who takes possession of a rental property

arrendatario   persona que toma posesión de la propiedad en alquiler

lessor   person responsible for a rental property (also called landlord)

arrendador   persona responsable de la propiedad en alquiler (también llamado casero)

letter of recommendation   attests to your character, abilities, and experience; it is written by someone who can be relied upon to give an honest report of your skills and abilities

carta de recomendación   da cuenta del carácter, capacidades y experiencia que tenemos; es escrita por alguien en quien confiamos que hará un informe sincero de nuestras destrezas y capacidades

leverage   using borrowed money to buy securities

apalancamiento   consiste en usar dinero prestado para comprar títulos

liabilities   money or debts owed to others

pasivo   dinero o deudas que debemos pagar a otras personas

liability coverage   insurance to protect against claims for bodily injury to another person or damage to another person's property

cobertura de responsabilidad   seguro de protección contra reclamos por lesiones físicas a otra persona o daños a la propiedad ajena

liability risk   the chance of loss that may occur when your errors or actions result in injuries to others or damage to their property

riesgo de responsabilidad   posibilidad de pérdida que puede ocurrir cuando los errores o acciones de una persona causan lesiones a otras o daños a su propiedad

life insurance   provides funds to the beneficiaries when the insured dies

seguro de vida   proporciona fondos a los beneficiarios cuando muere la persona asegurada

lifelong learning   involves seeking new knowledge, skills, and experiences to add to your professional and personal growth

educación permanente   implica adquirir nuevos conocimientos, destrezas y experiencias para ampliar el crecimiento profesional y personal

lifestyle business   a small business that provides a good income for the owner and allows them more freedom to meet personal needs

negocio de estilo de vida   negocio pequeño que proporciona buenos ingresos al propietario y le da mayor libertad para satisfacer sus necesidades personales

life–work balance   occurs when the employee places as much emphasis on personal life goals as they do on career goals

equilibrio entre vida y trabajo   ocurre cuando el empleado pone tanto énfasis en las metas para su vida personal como en sus metas laborales

line of credit   a pre-established amount that can be borrowed on demand with no collateral

línea de crédito   monto preestablecido que puede solicitarse en préstamo sin necesidad de garantías

liquidation   means the merchant wants to sell the inventory or merchandise immediately to turn it into cash

liquidación   significa que un comerciante desea vender su inventario o mercadería de inmediato para convertirla en efectivo

liquidity   a measure of how quickly you can get your cash from an account without loss of value

liquidez   medida de la velocidad con que una persona puede obtener dinero en efectivo de una cuenta sin que pierda valor

load   a sales fee that is likely to be incurred if you buy a mutual fund through a broker

cargo   gasto de venta en el que se puede incurrir si se compra un fondo mutuo a través de un agente

loan origination fee   the amount a bank or other lender charges to process loan papers

arancel por trámites de iniciación del préstamo   monto que una banco u otro tipo de prestamista cobra para procesar la documentación del préstamo

loan shark   an unlicensed lender who charges illegally high interest rates

prestamista usurero   prestamista no registrado que cobra ilegalmente altas tasas de interés

lobbying   an organized activity by lobbyists (paid activists) to influence public officials to pass laws and make decisions that benefit a profession

cabildeo   (lobby) actividad organizada por cabilderos (activistas remunerados) para influir en los funcionarios públicos que aprueben leyes y tomen decisiones que beneficien a una profesión

long-term care insurance   designed to cover the expenses of long-term services and support such as help with daily living activities or provide payment for staying in a long-term care facility

seguro de cuidados a largo plazo   diseñado para cubrir los gastos a largo plazo de servicios y apoyo, como acompañamiento o ayuda para las actividades de la vida diaria, o para pagar la estadía en una residencia a largo plazo

long-term disability   coverage results when people have a condition that affects their ability to work, and it generally begins when short-term benefits end; the plans usually cover 50 to 70 percent of monthly salary; benefits last until you can return to work or for the number of years stated in the policy

incapacidad a largo plazo   la cobertura corresponde a las personas con una enfermedad que afecta su capacidad para trabajar y, por lo general, comienza a aplicarse cuando terminan los beneficios a corto plazo; el plan comúnmente cubre de 50 a 70 por ciento del salario mensual; los beneficios duran hasta que la persona puede volver a trabajar o la cantidad de años establecida en la póliza

long-term goal   what you wish to achieve in the next year or longer

meta a largo plazo   objetivo que se desea alcanzar el año siguiente o más adelante

loss aversion   implies that losses due to a decision are weighted more in the consumer's mind than gains that may occur from the decision

aversión a la pérdida   implica que las pérdidas ocasionadas por una decisión pesan más en la mente del consumidor que las ganancias que pueden obtenerse por esa decisión

loss leader   an item of merchandise marked down to an unusually low price, sometimes below the retailer's cost

artículo de promoción   mercadería rebajada de precio a un valor inusualmente económico que, a veces es incluso menor que el de costo minorista

low-balling   a technique where a company advertises a product or service at a low price to lure in customers and then attempts to persuade them that they need additional products or services

técnica de la bola baja (técnica de lowball)   consiste en publicitar un producto o servicio a bajo precio para atraer a los consumidores y luego intentar persuadirlos de que necesitan productos o servicios adicionales

M

major medical coverage   protects against the catastrophic expenses of a severe injury or illness

cobertura médica mayor   protege contra los enormes gastos asociados con lesiones o enfermedades graves

malware   malicious software that is downloaded to your computer when you click a link provided by the cybercriminals

malware   programa malicioso que se descarga a una computadora al hacer clic en un enlace provisto por ciberdelincuentes

managed care plans   insurance plans that rely on a network of healthcare providers; to receive maximum reimbursement, participants in a managed care plan must select doctors from the network

planes de atención médica administrada   planes de seguro que dependen de una red de prestadores de servicios de salud; para recibir un máximo reintegro, los beneficiarios de un plan de atención médica administrada deben seleccionar médicos de esa red

market economy   market forces, based on individual freedoms and government decisions, determine which goods and services are produced and how they are distributed

economía de mercado   las fuerzas del mercado, basadas en las libertades individuales y las decisiones del gobierno, determinan qué bienes y servicios producir y cómo distribuirlos

market risk   caused by the business cycle—periods of economic growth or decline; when the economy is doing well, the financial markets usually follow (and vice versa)

riesgo de mercado   dependiente del ciclo económico: períodos de crecimiento o caída de la economía; cuando la economía funciona bien, los mercados financieros generalmente acompañan (y viceversa)

market value   the highest price a property will bring on the market

valor de mercado   precio más alto con el que una propiedad llegará al mercado

market value   the price for which the stock is bought and sold in the marketplace

valor de mercado   precio por el que se compra y se vende una acción en el mercado

maturity amount   how much you will receive (principal plus accrued interest from date of deposit) if you choose to redeem your CD

monto de vencimiento   cantidad que se recibe (principal más interés acumulado desde la fecha de depósito) si se desea reclamar el CD

maturity date   the date on which an investment becomes due for payment

fecha de vencimiento   fecha en la cual una inversión está en condiciones de ser pagada

mediation   occurs when a third party helps you and the other party try to resolve a problem

mediación   se lleva a cabo cuando un tercero ayuda a las otras dos partes a resolver un problema

Medicaid   government-sponsored health insurance for people with low incomes and limited resources

Medicaid   seguro de salud patrocinado por el gobierno para las personas con ingresos bajos y recursos limitados

medical coverage   auto insurance that pays for medical, hospital, and funeral costs of the insured and their family and passengers, regardless of fault (also called personal injury protection)

cobertura médica   seguro automotor que cubre los gastos médicos, hospitalarios y funerarios de la persona asegurada así como los de su familia y pasajeros, independientemente de la infracción (también llamado protección personal contra lesiones)

Medicare   federal government-sponsored health insurance for people aged 65 or older

Medicare   seguro de salud patrocinado por el gobierno federal para las personas de 65 años o mayores

minimum payment   the least amount you may pay that month under your credit agreement, though you may pay more to reduce your debt faster

monto mínimo   monto mínimo que se permite pagar en el mes según el acuerdo crediticio, aunque se puede pagar más para reducir la deuda más rápido

minimum wage   a base-level hourly wage that employers are required to pay for some employees

paga mínima   remuneración básica por hora que los empleadores deben pagar a algunos empleados

money   anything that can be used to settle debt

dinero cualquier recurso que pueda usarse para cancelar una deuda

money market account an interest-bearing checking account that pays a higher interest rate but usually has more restrictions

cuenta del mercado monetario cuenta corriente que devenga intereses y paga una tasa de interés más alta pero que comúnmente tiene más restricciones

money market fund a mutual fund that invests in safe, liquid securities, such as Treasury bills and bonds that mature in less than a year

fondo del mercado monetario fondo mutuo que invierte en títulos seguros y líquidos, como las letras del Tesoro y bonos que vencen en menos de un año

monopoly a market with many buyers but only one seller

monopolio mercado con muchos compradores pero un solo vendedor

mortgage a loan to purchase real estate

hipoteca préstamo para comprar inmuebles

moving violation any violation of the law committed by the driver of a vehicle while it is in motion

infracción en movimiento cualquier violación de la ley cometida por el conductor de un vehículo en circulación

multiline discount discount for having more than one type of policy (such as auto insurance and homeowners insurance) with a company

descuento multilínea descuento por tener más de un tipo de póliza (como seguro automotor y seguro para la vivienda) con una empresa

multipolicy discount discount for insuring more than one vehicle with the same company

descuento multipóliza descuento por asegurar más de un vehículo con la misma empresa

municipal bond a bond issued by state or local government

bono municipal bono emitido por el gobierno estatal o local

mutual fund a professionally managed group of investments bought using a pool of money from many investors

fondo mutuo grupo de inversiones compradas con dinero de un fondo común de muchos inversores administrado profesionalmente

N

National Consumers League (NCL) represents consumers on marketplace and workplace issues such as child labor, privacy, food safety, and medication information

Liga Nacional de Consumidores (NCL, en inglés) representa a los consumidores en cuestiones de mercado y de trabajo, como el trabajo infantil, la seguridad alimentaria y la información sobre la medicación

National Institute of Standards and Technology (NIST) an agency within the U.S. Department of Commerce; one of its missions is to develop standards of business excellence

Instituto Nacional de Estándares y Tecnología (NIST, en inglés) agencia dependiente del Departamento de Comercio, una de sus misiones es desarrollar estándares de excelencia comercial

Food and Drug Administration (FDA) enforces laws and regulations preventing distribution of mislabeled foods, drugs, cosmetics, and medical devices

Administración de Alimentos y Medicamentos (FDA, en inglés) regulan la ley y las normas que previenen la distribución de alimentos, medicamentos, cosméticos y dispositivos médicos rotulados de manera incorrecta

needs the items necessary for maintaining physical life; they include food, water, shelter, clothing, and basic medical care; safety and security could also be added to this list

necesidades elementos necesarios para mantener la vida física; incluyen los alimentos, el agua, la vivienda, la vestimenta y atención médica básica; la seguridad y la sanidad también pueden incluirse en esta lista

net asset value (NAV) tells you the market price for a share of a mutual fund

valor de activo neto (VAN) indica el precio de mercado de una acción de un fondo mutuo

net pay amount of pay left after all deductions are taken

remuneración neta monto de la paga que queda luego de aplicar todas las deducciones

net worth the difference when you subtract your liabilities from your assets

patrimonio neto   diferencia que resulta de restar el pasivo del activo

no-fault insurance   auto insurance in which drivers receive reimbursement for expenses from their insurer, no matter who caused the accident

seguro independiente de la culpabilidad objetiva   seguro automotor en el que el asegurador reintegra a los conductores los gastos sin importar quién causó el accidente

nonmoving violation   any violation of the law involving a car that is not in motion

infracción estacionaria   cualquier violación de la ley que involucre a un vehículo que no está en movimiento

nonsufficient funds (NSF) fee   may be charged by the bank it you attempt to spend more than is available in your account

arancel por fondos insuficientes (MFI)   puede imponerlo el banco si alguien intenta gastar más dinero del que dispone en su cuenta

notary public   verifies a person's identity, witnesses the person's signature on a legal document, and then notarizes the signature as valid

notario público   verifica la identidad de una persona, es testigo de la firma de una persona en un documento legal y luego certifica que la firma es válida

nuclear family   consists of two parents and at least one child

familia nuclear   consiste de dos padres y al menos un hijo

O

odd-number pricing   setting prices at uneven amounts rather than whole dollars to make them seem lower

precios de valor impar   precios establecidos en montos de cifras impares en lugar de valores redondos en dólares para hacer que parezcan más bajos

offer   an invitation to enter into a contract that is made with serious intent by one person to another person

ofrecimiento   invitación para participar de un contrato que una persona realiza con intenciones serias a otra persona

oligopoly   exists when only a few sellers produce a similar product or service

oligopolio   existe cuando solo unos pocos vendedores ofrecen un producto o servicio similar

online shopping fraud   occurs when cybercriminals create fake retail websites or use fake ads, either on legitimate websites or via social media

fraude en el comercio virtual   ocurre cuando ciberdelincuentes crean sitios web falsos o usan publicidad falsa ya en sea en sitios web legítimos o a través de los medios sociales

open access   means anyone with a high school diploma or GED may attend classes at the community college

ingreso irrestricto   significa que cualquier persona con un diploma de estudios secundarios o un certificado GED de aprobación del examen de educación general puede asistir a un colegio comunitario

open-end credit   enables a borrower to use credit up to a stated limit; as payments are made, the limit allows for more use of credit

crédito renovable   permite al prestatario usar el crédito hasta un límite determinado; a medida que realiza los pagos, el límite se extiende para permitir usar más crédito

opportunity cost   the loss of a benefit that could have been derived from the option not chosen; the value of your next best choice—what you are giving up

costo de oportunidad   pérdida de un beneficio que podría haberse obtenido con la opción no elegida; valor de la siguiente mejor opción: lo que se está resignando

opt out   elect not to accept changes to credit card policies

opción de rechazo   posibilidad de no aceptar los cambios a las políticas de uso de la tarjeta de crédito

option   the right, but not the obligation, to buy or sell stock or a commodity for a specified price within a specified period

opción   derecho, pero no obligación, de comprar o vender acciones o bienes primarios por un precio determinado dentro de un período determinado

out-of-pocket maximum   an insurance clause that caps or sets a maximum that the insured must pay out of pocket during any calendar year

máximo de bolsillo cláusula del seguro que pone un tope o fija un máximo que la persona asegurada debe pagar de su bolsillo durante cualquier año del calendario

overdraft a check written for more money than your account contains

sobregiro acción en la que un cheque se emite por una cantidad mayor de la que hay en la cuenta del pagador

overdraft protection allows the bank to pay for transactions even if your checking account does not have enough money to cover transactions

protección contra sobregiro permite al banco pagar transacciones incluso si la cuenta corriente no tiene suficiente dinero para cubrirlas

overinsuring buying more insurance than is necessary

sobreasegurar adquirir más seguro que el necesario

overtime time worked beyond your regular hours

horas extra tiempo adicional que se trabaja fuera de las horas regulares

oxidize occurs when paint permanently loses its color and shine because of a chemical reaction with the air

oxidación ocurre cuando la pintura pierde su color y brillo en forma permanente a causa de una reacción química producida con el aire

P

P/E ratio a stock's price to earnings ratio

relación P/G relación entre el precio de una acción y la ganancia

paintless dent removal a service in which a suction device is attached to your car to remove small dents

reparación de abolladuras sin retirar la pintura servicio para el que se utiliza un aparato de succión que se acopla al vehículo para retirar las pequeñas abolladuras

par value an assigned dollar value given to each share of stock

a la par valor asignado en dólares para cada acción del capital

pawnbroker (or pawnshop) a legal business that makes high-interest loans based on the value of personal possessions pledged as collateral

casa de empeño negocio legal que otorga préstamos a altas tasas de interés basados en el valor de las pertenencias personales ofrecidas como garantía

payee the person who receives a check

tenedor persona que recibe un cheque

payor the person or business writing a check

pagador persona o empresa que emite un cheque

payroll savings plan allows you to authorize your employer to make automatic deductions from your paycheck each pay period

plan de ahorro vía nómina permite autorizar al empleador para que realice deducciones automáticas del sueldo en cada período de pago

peer-to-peer lending allows individuals to obtain loans from other individuals without using a financial institution; also called *social lending*

préstamo entre particulares permite a las personas obtener préstamos individualmente de otras personas sin recurrir a una institución financiera

penny stocks low-priced stocks of small companies that have a limited history of success

acciones de escaso valor, también llamadas *penny stocks*, acciones de bajo precio emitidas por pequeñas empresas que tienen una trayectoria de éxito limitado

permanent investments investment choices that are held for the long run—5 or 10 years, or longer

inversiones permanentes opciones de inversión que se retienen a largo plazo: 5 o 10 años, o más

permanent life insurance remains in effect for the insured's lifetime and builds a cash value

seguro de vida permanente se mantiene vigente durante toda a vida de la persona asegurada y genera valor en efectivo

personal preferences your likes and dislikes

preferencias personales lo que le agrada y desagrada a una persona

personal property floater additional insurance coverage for valuable items not covered by the primary policy

póliza flotante para la propiedad personal cobertura de seguro adicional para los objetos de valor no abarcados por la póliza primaria

personal risk the chance of loss involving your income and standard of living

riesgo personal   posibilidad de perder los ingresos y el estándar de vida

phishing   a scam that uses online pop-up or e-mail messages to deceive you into disclosing personal information

***phising* o ciberestafa**   fraude que consiste en usar mensajes emergentes o de correo electrónico para engañar a una persona con el propósito de que revele información personal

point of service (POS)   plans that combine the features of HMOs and PPOs to provide people with more choices and control over medical benefits

planes adecuados al lugar de servicio (ALS)   combinan las características de los planes OMS y OPP con más opciones y control respecto de los beneficios médicos

policy limits   a cap on the total lifetime benefits you may receive from your insurance company

límites de la póliza   tope a los beneficios de por vida totales que pueden recibirse de la empresa aseguradora

polishing compound   a substance that can smooth out surface scratches, scuffs, and stains

compuesto para pulir   sustancia que puede remover rayones, raspaduras y manchas de una superficie para dejarla pareja

political risk   political changes or instability in the government that may reduce the value of your investment

riesgo político   cambios políticos o inestabilidad en el gobierno que pueden reducir el valor de la inversión

Ponzi scheme   a fraudulent investment operation in which money collected from new investors is used to pay off earlier investors

esquema Ponzi   operación de inversión fraudulenta en la que el dinero recaudado con los nuevos inversores se usa para pagar a los primeros inversores

portability   means that when you leave your employer, you can continue paying the premiums on an insurance policy and convert your group policy into an individual policy

portabilidad   significa que, al dejar a un empleador, se pueden seguir pagando las primas de una póliza de seguro y convertir la póliza grupal en una individual

portfolio   collection of investments

cartera   colección de inversiones

power of attorney   a legal document authorizing someone to act on your behalf

poder notarial   documento legal que autoriza a una persona a actuar en representación de otra

preapproval   the process of completing the mortgage application and providing the documentation required to perform an extensive credit and financial background check; the preapproval process will help the borrower know specific loan details like the interest rate to be charged, the amount of down payment required, and the maximum loan amount

preaprobación   proceso durante el cual se completa la solicitud de una hipoteca y se proporciona la documentación solicitada para llevar a cabo una extensa verificación de los antecedentes crediticios y financieros; el proceso de preaprobación ayudará al prestatario a conocer detalles específicos del préstamo, como la tasa de interés y la cuota inicial requerida como anticipo, así como el monto máximo del préstamo

precious metals   tangible metals with known and universal value worldwide

metales preciosos   metales tangibles con valor universal conocido en todo el mundo

predatory lender   a lender that may take advantage of an emergency

prestamista oportunista   prestamista que saca ventaja abusiva de una emergencia

pre-existing condition   a health problem, such as diabetes or cancer, that a person had before their new health insurance coverage began

condición preexistente   problema de salud, como la diabetes o el cáncer, que una persona padecía antes del inicio de la nueva cobertura del seguro de salud

preferred provider organization (PPO)   a network of healthcare providers that includes doctors and hospitals who band together to provide health services for set fees

organización de prestadores preferidos (OPP)   red de prestadores de servicios de salud que incluye médicos y hospitales que se agrupan para proporcionar servicios de salud a aranceles fijos

preferred stock   a type of stock that pays a fixed dividend, but stockholders have no voting rights

acción preferente   tipo de acción que paga un dividendo determinado pero los accionistas no tienen derecho a voto

premium   fee assumed by an insurer for an identified risk

prima   costo que asume un asegurador por un riesgo identificado

prequalify   the process of determining how much money you are qualified to borrow

precalificar   proceso por el que se determina si una persona está calificada para obtener un determinado monto de dinero en préstamo

previous balance method   method by which the finance charge is imposed on the entire amount owed from the previous month

método del saldo previo   método por el cual un costo financiero se impone sobre el monto total adeudado del mes previo

primary market   a place where corporate, municipal, and agency bonds can be purchased when a company or group first issues them (also called new issue market)

mercado primario   lugar donde pueden comprarse bonos de empresas, municipios y agencias cuando una empresa o grupo pone a la venta la primera emisión (también llamado mercado de emisión)

prime rate   the interest rate that banks offer to their best business customers, such as large corporations, and is based on the Federal Reserve's federal funds overnight rate

tasa preferencial   tasa de interés que los bancos ofrecen a sus mejores clientes comerciales, como las grandes empresas, y se basa en la tasa de interés a un día de los fondos federales de la Reserva Federal

principal   the amount borrowed for a loan, or the unpaid portion of the amount borrowed, on which the borrower pays interest; also the amount of money you deposit into a savings account

principal   monto solicitado como préstamo, o la porción impaga de la cantidad prestada, sobre el cual el prestatario paga interés; también, la cantidad de dinero que se deposita en una cuenta de ahorro

probate   the legal process of proving that a deceased person's will is valid and then administering and distributing that person's estate upon death

validación de un testamento   proceso legal que consiste en probar que el testamento de una persona fallecida es válido para luego administrar y distribuir su patrimonio en virtud de su fallecimiento

producers   the manufacturers or makers of goods and services for sale

productores   fabricantes o creadores de bienes o servicios para vender

product advertising   advertising intended to convince consumers to buy a specific good or service

publicidad de productos   publicidad destinada a convencer a los consumidores de comprar un bien o servicio determinado

production possibility frontier (PPF)   a curve on a graph that shows the possible quantities of two products that can be produced using the same resources; the PPF shows the most efficient use of scarce resources and the tradeoff between the two items (also called a production possibilities curve)

frontera de posibilidades de producción (FPP)   curva en una gráfica que muestra las posibles cantidades de dos productos que pueden producirse usando los mismos recursos; la FPP muestra el uso más eficiente de los recursos escasos y el intercambio entre ambos productos (también llamada curva de posibilidades de producción)

professional development   updating your skills

desarrollo profesional   actualización de las destrezas de una persona

professional jobs   one of the highest-paying career groups; workers in professional jobs are considered knowledge workers

empleo profesional   una de las categorías laborales que paga mejores ingresos; las personas que se desempeñan en puestos de trabajo profesional son consideradas trabajadores del conocimiento

profit sharing   a plan that allows employees to share a portion of the company's profits at the end of the corporate year

participación en las ganancias   plan que permite a los empleados compartir una porción de las ganancias al cierre del año fiscal

progressive tax   takes a larger share of one's income as the amount of income grows

impuesto progresivo   se queda con una porción más grande de los ingresos a medida que estos aumentan

promissory note   a written agreement between two parties, the debtor and the creditor, to pay back a loan

pagaré   acuerdo escrito entre dos partes, el deudor y el acreedor, para devolver un préstamo

property risk   the chance of loss or harm to personal or real property

riesgo de propiedad   posibilidad de pérdida o daño de la propiedad personal o inmueble

proportional tax   also known as a flat tax, is one for which the rate stays the same regardless of income

impuesto proporcional   conocido también como impuesto plano, es un impuesto en el cual la tasa se mantiene igual sin importar el ingreso

prospectus   a legal document issued by an investment company that details the securities it offers for sale

prospecto   documento emitido por una empresa de inversión que detalla los títulos que ofrece en venta

proxy   a stockholder's written authorization to transfer their voting rights to someone else, usually a company manager

poder   autorización escrita de un accionista para transferir sus derechos de voto a otra persona, comúnmente un gerente de la empresa

public corporation   a company whose stock is traded openly on stock markets

empresa de capital abierto   empresa cuyas acciones se comercializan abiertamente en los mercados de capitales

public goods   goods and services provided by the government to its citizens

bienes públicos   bienes y servicios provistos por el gobierno a los ciudadanos

pure risk   a chance of loss with no chance for gain

riesgo puro   posibilidad de pérdida con ninguna posibilidad de ganancia

pyramid scheme   a multilevel marketing plan that promises members (distributors) commissions from their sales and those of other members they recruit

esquema de pirámide   plan de mercadotecnia de múltiples niveles que promete a los miembros (distribuidores) comisiones de sus ventas y de los otros miembros que reclutan

R

rate   the percentage of interest you will pay on a loan

tasa   porcentaje de interés que se paga por un préstamo

rate shopping   involves looking for the best interest rate on an auto or mortgage loan

comparación de tasas   implica buscar la mejor tasa de interés para un préstamo automotor o hipotecario

reaffirmation   an agreement to pay debts that have been legally discharged

reafirmación   acuerdo para pagar deudas que han sido legalmente exoneradas

real estate   buildings and land

inmuebles   edificios y tierras

real estate investment trust (REIT)   a corporation that pools the money of many individuals to invest in a diversified class of properties

grupo de inversión en activos inmobiliarios   (GIAI) empresa que reúne dinero de muchos individuos en un fondo común para invertir en diversas clases de propiedades inmuebles

real estate syndicate   a group of investors who pool their money to purchase high-priced real estate as a short-term investment (often called a limited partnership)

consorcio inmobiliario   grupo de inversores que reúnen su dinero en un fondo común para comprar inmuebles de alto valor como inversión a corto plazo (generalmente llamado sociedad limitada)

rebate program   a credit incentive program through which you get back a portion of what you spent in credit purchases over the year

programa de reembolso   programa de incentivo al crédito mediante el cual se recupera una porción de lo que se gastó en compras a crédito a lo largo del año

recall   a request for consumers to return a defective product to the manufacturer for a refund or repair

devolución   procedimiento por el cual se solicita a los consumidores que regresen un producto defectuoso a su fabricante para que lo repare o restituya el dinero

redress   correct an undesirable or unfair situation

reparación   corrección de una situación indeseable o injusta

references   people who have known you for at least a year and can provide information about your skills, character, and achievements

referencias   personas que conocemos desde hace al menos un año y pueden proporcionar información sobre nuestras destrezas, carácter y logros

regressive tax   takes a smaller share of one's income as the amount of income grows

impuesto regresivo   se queda con una porción más pequeña de los ingresos a medida que estos aumentan

remote work   a working model that allows employees to work offsite and remain in contact with their employers through technology; often these employees can complete work tasks using cloud computing and video conferencing

trabajo remoto   modelo de trabajo que permite a los empleados trabajar fuera del lugar de trabajo y mantener el contacto con los empleados a través de la tecnología; comúnmente, los empleados pueden completar sus tareas laborales mediante servicios de computación en la nube y sistemas de videoconferencia

rent charge   similar to the interest rate you would pay on a vehicle loan; this amount will be written into the lease agreement as a dollar amount you will pay each month

carga sobre la renta   similar a la tasa de interés que se paga sobre un préstamo automotor; este monto se incluirá por escrito en contrato de alquiler como una cantidad en dólares que deberá pagarse mensualmente

rental agreement   a written contract that allows you to leave your rental property any time if you give the required notice (also called a month-to-month agreement)

contrato de arrendamiento   acuerdo escrito que permite abandonar la propiedad rentada en cualquier momento con el debido aviso previo (también llamado contrato de alquiler mensual)

rental inventory   a detailed list of current property conditions

inventario de alquiler   lista detallada de las condiciones en que se encuentra el inmueble

renters insurance   protects renters from property and liability risks

seguro de inquilino   protege a los inquilinos de los riesgos de propiedad y responsabilidad

renting   the process of using another person's property for a fee

alquilar   proceso por el que se paga un monto para usar el inmueble de otra persona

rent-to-own option   you rent furniture with an option to buy

alquiler con opción de compra   posibilidad de alquilar muebles con la alternativa de comprarlos

repayment plans   plans for repaying loans

planes de pago planes para pagar los préstamos

replacement value   the cost of replacing an item regardless of its actual cash (market) value

valor de reposición   costo de reponer un artículo independientemente de su valor en efectivo real (de mercado)

residence hall   (or dormitory) an on-campus building with many small rooms rented to students

residencia estudiantil   edificio dentro del campus universitario integrado por varias habitaciones pequeñas que se alquilan a los estudiantes

residual value   a car's value at the end of the lease period

valor residual   valor de un vehículo al final del período de alquiler

resume   describes your work experience, education, abilities, interests, and other information that may interest an employer; it tells the employer neatly and concisely who you are and what you can do, and it highlights key skills and interests

currículum   describe su experiencia laboral, educación, habilidades, intereses y otra información que puede interesar a un empleador; le informa de manera ordenada y concisa quién es usted y qué puede hacer, y destaca sus habilidades e intereses clave

retraining   involves learning new and different skills so that an employee can retain the same level of employability

recapacitación   implica aprender destrezas nuevas y diferentes para que el empleado mantenga el mismo nivel de empleabilidad

return on investment (ROI)   used to evaluate the efficiency of an investment; calculated as Current Profit on Stock/(Purchase Price + Commission)

retorno de la inversión   (RI) se usa para evaluar la eficiencia de una inversión; se calcula como Ganancia corriente sobre las Acciones/(Precio de compra + Comisión)

revenue   a source of income

renta   fuente de ingresos

revenue bond   a municipal bond issued to raise money for a public-works project

bono pagadero con la renta   bono municipal emitido con el propósito de recaudar dinero projectos de obras públicas

reverse mortgage   a loan available to homeowners aged 62 or older that allows them to convert their home equity into income

hipoteca inversa   préstamo disponible para los propietarios de viviendas de 62 años o más que les permite convertir su patrimonio inmobiliario en ingresos

rewards program   a credit incentive program through which you will earn points, cash back, airline miles, or other special awards that you can redeem later

programa de beneficios   programa de incentivo crediticio mediante el cual una persona gana puntos, recibe dinero en efectivo, acumula millas de vuelos en avión u obtiene otro tipo de beneficio que se puede reclamar para usar en otro momento

right-to-work laws   prohibit unions from requiring employees to become union members; the companies are considered open shops, a place of employment where the workers are not required to join or financially support a union

leyes sobre el derecho a trabajar   prohíbe a los sindicatos exigir a los empleados que se afilien a ellos; las empresas se consideran negocios abiertos, un lugar de trabajo donde a los trabajadores no se les exige unirse ni apoyar financieramente a un sindicato

risk   a state of uncertainty where certain situations may result in loss or another undesirable outcome

riesgo   estado de incertidumbre en el que determinadas situaciones pueden derivar en una pérdida u otro resultado indeseable

risk adverse   refers to an investor who approaches investing with more caution

averso al riesgo   alude al inversor que aborda la inversión con más cautela

risk assessment   a systematic study of the risks that you face

evaluación de riesgo   estudio sistemático de los riesgos que se enfrentan

risk avoidance   lowers the chance for loss by not engaging in the activity that could result in the loss

evasión del riesgo   disminuye la posibilidad de pérdida al no involucrarse en actividades que podrían derivar en pérdida

risk capacity   depends on your personal and financial goals and your timeline to achieve those goals; the greater the risk you are willing to take, the greater the potential returns

capacidad de riesgo   depende de las metas personales y financieras así como del tiempo programado para alcanzarlas; cuanto más riesgo se desea asumir, mayores serán los potenciales retornos

risk management   forecasting and evaluating financial risk then developing a plan to avoid or minimize the impact of the risk

gestión del riesgo   permite anticipar y evaluar el riesgo financiero y luego desarrollar un plan para evitar o minimizar su impacto

risk management plan   lists risks you have identified, your assessment of their financial impacts, and the techniques that you plan to use to manage each risk

plan de gestión del riesgo   enumera los riesgos identificados, la evaluación sobre su impacto financiero y las técnicas que se planea usar para gestionar cada riesgo

risk reduction   lowers the chance of loss by taking measures to lessen the frequency or severity of losses that may occur

reducción del riesgo   disminuye la posibilidad de pérdida tomando medidas para limitar la frecuencia o gravedad de las pérdidas que pueden ocurrir

risk retention   the process of accepting the consequences of risk (also called risk assumption)

aceptación del riesgo   proceso por el cual se asumen las consecuencias del riesgo (también llamado proceso de retención)

risk tolerance   the amount of uncertainty that is acceptable to you

tolerancia al riesgo   cantidad de incertidumbre que una persona es capaz de soportar

risk transfer   passes risk to another party (also called risk sharing)

transferencia de riesgo   traslada el riesgo a un tercero (también llamada riesgo compartido)

robo-advisor   a digital platform that follows an automated long-term passive index strategy based upon algorithms

asesor robótico   plataforma digital que sigue una estrategia automatizada de indexación pasiva a largo plazo basada en algoritmos

Roth IRA   an IRA where contributions are taxed, but earnings are not

Roth IRA   cuenta IRA donde se los aportes se gravan con impuestos pero las ganancias no

routing number   a unique nine-digit number that is the address of your financial institution

número de enrutamiento   número único de nueve dígitos que representa la dirección de una institución financiera

rule of 72   a technique for estimating the years required to double your money at a given rate of return

regla de 72   técnica para estimar los años requeridos para duplicar el dinero a una tasa de retorno dada

S

safe deposit box   box offered by financial institutions to customers to store valuable items or documents

caja de seguridad   caja ofrecida por instituciones financieras a sus clientes para guardar objetos valiosos y documentos

safety of principal   means that you are guaranteed not to lose your savings deposit, even if the bank or other financial institution fails and goes out of business

seguridad del principal   significa que la persona cuenta con la garantía de no perder el depósito de sus ahorros, aun si el banco u otra institución financiera abandona el negocio

salary   a fixed amount of gross pay

salario   monto establecido como remuneración bruta

scarcity   basic economic problem in any economy; consumers' wants are unlimited, while the resources for producing the products to satisfy these wants are limited

escasez   problema económico básico de cualquier economía; los deseos de los consumidores son ilimitados mientras que los recursos para producir los productos que satisfacen esos deseos son limitados

scholarships   gifts of money that you do not need to repay and can be offered through multiple sources, such as the educational institution, nonprofit agencies, professional associations, businesses, and local organizations

becas   dinero otorgado como regalo que no es necesario devolver y puede provenir de distintas fuentes, como una institución educativa, agencias sin fines de lucro, asociaciones profesionales, empresas u organizaciones locales

secondary market   where most bonds are purchased; created when investors buy and sell previously issued stocks and bonds from one another with the help of brokers

mercado secundario   mercado en el que se compran la mayoría de los bonos; se crea cuando los inversores compran y venden acciones y bonos previamente emitidos entre ellos con la ayuda de agentes

Section 125 plans   programs that allow employees to customize benefit plans to meet their specific needs with flexible plan options on a pretax basis

Planes de la Sección 125   programas que permiten a los empleados adaptar los planes de beneficios a sus necesidades específicas con opciones flexibles de planes antes de deducir impuestos

secured bond   a bond backed by specific assets that serve as security to assure debt repayment (also called a mortgage bond)

bono garantizado   bono respaldado por bienes específicos que sirven como garantía para asegurar el pago de la deuda (también llamado bono hipotecario)

secured credit card   like a debit card that allows you to build your credit

tarjeta de crédito garantizada   como una tarjeta de débito que permite construir crédito

securities   a type of financial investment, such as stocks and bonds, with monetary value

títulos   tipo de inversión financiera, como acciones y bonos, con valor monetario

Securities and Exchange Commission (SEC)   protects investors and maintains the integrity of the securities markets

Comisión de Bolsa y Valores   (SEC, en inglés) protege a los inversores y preserva la integridad los mercados de valores

securities exchange   a marketplace where brokers representing investors meet to buy and sell securities

mercado de títulos y valores mercado al que los agentes bursátiles asisten en representación de los inversores para comprar y vender títulos y valores

security deposit a refundable amount paid in advance to protect the owner of a property against damage or nonpayment by a renter

depósito de seguridad monto reembolsable que se paga por adelantado para proteger al dueño de la propiedad contra daños o el incumplimiento de pago del inquilino

self-assessment inventory lists your strong points and areas of needed growth and development; it will also include your plan for improvement

inventario de autoevaluación enumera los puntos fuertes de uno mismo y las áreas con necesidad de crecimiento y desarrollo; también incluirá un plan de mejora

self-employment working for yourself

trabajo por cuenta propia trabajo independiente

seller's acceptance a formal agreement to the terms of the buyer's offer, forming a contract between the parties

aceptación del vendedor acuerdo formal sobre los términos de la oferta del comprador que constituye un contrato entre las partes

seller's counteroffer rejects the original offer with a listing of what terms would be acceptable

contraoferta del vendedor rechaza la oferta original con una lista de los términos que serían aceptables

seniority the length of time a person has held a job; it is used to determine promotions, transfers, and vacation time; generally, more seniority means more job security

antigüedad período de tiempo que una persona ha permanecido en su trabajo; se utiliza para determinar promociones, transferencias y extensión de las vacaciones; generalmente, más antigüedad significa más seguridad laboral

service credit involves providing a service for which you will pay later

servicio a crédito implica proveer un servicio por el que se pagará luego

service jobs jobs in which you perform a task or a service for a person or business; service jobs are a large and increasing sector of the job market

empleos de servicio empleos en los que se realiza una tarea o servicio para una persona o empresa; los empleos de servicio constituyen un sector amplio y creciente en el mercado laboral

share account a savings account representing ownership interest

cuenta compartida cuenta de ahorros que representa interés para los titulares

short selling selling stock borrowed from a broker that must be replaced later

venta al descubierto venta de acciones a préstamo de un agente bursátil que luego deben reponerse

short-term disability replaces a wage earner's salary if they have a condition affecting their ability to work; it pays up to a certain percentage (typically 70 percent or more) and generally lasts between 3 and 6 months

incapacidad a corto plazo reemplaza el sueldo del asalariado si padece alguna enfermedad que afecte su capacidad para trabajar; paga hasta un porcentaje determinado (tradicionalmente 70 por ciento o más) y en general dura entre 3 y 6 meses

short-term goal a goal you expect to reach in a few days or weeks

meta a corto plazo meta que se espera alcanzar en los próximos días o semanas

side business a small business in which the owner pursues their passion, hobby, or secondary occupation, while working full-time for an employer

negocio paralelo negocio pequeño cuyo dueño desarrolla como pasión, pasatiempo o segunda ocupación mientras trabaja a tiempo completo para un empleador

signature form provides an official signature that the financial institution can use to compare to the signature you write on your checks or when signing electronically on debit and credit card transactions; helps the bank verify your identity

formulario de firmas permite contar con una firma oficial que la institución financiera puede usar para comparar la firma que una persona hace en sus cheques o cuando firma electrónicamente las transacciones con tarjeta de débito o crédito; ayuda al banco a verificar la identidad de las personas

simple interest interest computed only on the amount borrowed; assumes one payment at the end of the loan period

interés simple interés que se computa solo sobre el monto que se tomó prestado; supone un pago al final del período de préstamo

Simplified Employee Pension (SEP) plan a tax-deferred retirement plan available to small businesses (also called a SEP-IRA)

Plan de Pensión Simplificada para Empleados (SEP, en inglés) plan de retiro con intereses diferidos disponible para pequeñas empresas (también llamado SEP-IRA en inglés)

single-parent family one parent raising at least one child

familia monoparental un padre cría al menos a un hijo

skipped-generation family consists of at least one child being raised by one or more grandparents

familia de salto generacional consta de al menos un niño criado por uno o más abuelos

small claims court a court of limited jurisdiction that resolves cases involving small amounts

tribunal de instancia tribunal de jurisdicción limitada que resuelve casos asociados con pequeñas cantidades

Social Security a federal insurance program that benefits people who are retired or disabled

Seguro Social programa federal de seguro que beneficia a personas retiradas o discapacitadas

socialist economic system, characterized by a large degree of government control of many of the decisions within the nation (also called a planned system)

sistema económico socialista, caracterizado por un alto grado de control gubernamental en lo que respecta a las decisiones dentro de la nación (también llamado sistema planificado)

space-shifting refers to using legally acquired content in different places

espacio desplazado alude al uso de contenido legalmente adquirido en diferentes lugares

speculative investing happens when you make bold and high-risk investment choices

inversión especulativa ocurre cuando se eligen alternativas de inversión audaces y de alto riesgo

speculative risk may result in either gain or loss

riesgo especulativo puede derivar en ganancia o pérdida

spousal support money one former spouse pays to support the other (also called alimony or maintenance)

pensión alimentaria dinero que un ex cónyuge paga para mantener al otro (también llamado derecho de alimentos o manutención)

standard account a bank account that usually has no or a small monthly service fee; may or may not pay interest

cuenta común cuenta bancaria que generalmente tiene muy bajo o ningún costo de mantenimiento mensual; en algunos caso no da intereses

standard deduction for taxes, determined annually by the federal government; you are eligible if you do not have many deductions

deducción estándar de impuestos, determinada anualmente por el gobierno federal; una persona califica para solicitarla si no tiene muchas deducciones

sticker price manufacturer's suggested retail price (MSRP) for a new car

precio de lista precio minorista oficial sugerido por el fabricante para un vehículo nuevo

stock a unit of ownership in a corporation

acción unidad de participación en la propiedad de una empresa

stock split an increase in the number of outstanding shares of a company's stock

desdoblamiento de acciones incremento del número de acciones en circulación del conjunto de acciones de una empresa

stock symbol a unique series of letters that identify the security for trading purposes

código de cotización serie única de letras que identifican una acción para su comercialización

stop-payment order asks the bank to not honor a specific check

orden de suspensión de pago solicita al banco que no abone un cheque en particular

strategic investing the careful management of investment alternatives to maximize the growth of your portfolio over the next 5 to 10 years

inversión estratégica administración cuidadosa de las alternativas de inversión para maximizar el crecimiento de la cartera de acciones en el transcurso de 5 a 10 años

student loan type of financial aid that must be repaid with interest

préstamo estudiantil tipo de ayuda financiera que debe devolverse con intereses

studio apartment also known as an efficiency apartment; has one large room that serves as the living room, dining area, and bedroom

estudio también llamado monoambiente; tiene un solo ambiente amplio que sirve al mismo tiempo como sala, comedor y dormitorio

subscribers businesses that pay a monthly fee to a credit bureau for access to information about their customers' accounts—names, addresses, credit balances, on-time payment records, and other credit information

suscriptores empresas que pagan una tarifa mensual a una agencia de información crediticia para acceder a información sobre las cuentas de sus clientes: nombre, dirección, saldo del crédito, historial de pagos a tiempo y otros datos crediticios

sunk cost an expense that occurred in the past for which money was spent and cannot be recovered

costo irrecuperable gasto realizado en pasado cuyo dinero no puede recuperarse

supply the quantity of goods and services that producers can provide at various prices

oferta cantidad de bienes y servicios que los productores suministran a distintos precios

T

target market a specific consumer group to which the products are designed to appeal

mercado destinatario grupo específico de consumidores para los cuales se diseñan productos que pretenden atraer su interés

tax a payment imposed on a taxpayer by a governmental unit

impuesto pago que un organismo de gobierno carga sobre un contribuyente

tax bracket an income range to which a tax rate is applied

categoría impositiva rango de ingresos al que se le aplica una tasa de interés

tax credit a reduction of taxes owed

crédito fiscal reducción de los impuestos que se adeudan

tax evasion willful failure to pay taxes

evasión impositiva acción deliberada con la que se elude pagar los impuestos

tax liability the total tax you owe on a year's income

pasivo fiscal total de impuestos que se adeudan sobre los ingresos de un año

taxable income the income on which you will pay tax

ingresos imponibles ingresos sobre los que se pagan impuestos

technical schools provide students with authentic learning experiences and opportunities to develop academic and technical skills that can help prepare them for the next step on their career path through hands-on learning

escuelas técnicas escuelas que brindan a los estudiantes oportunidades y experiencias de aprendizaje auténticas para que desarrollen destrezas académicas y técnicas capaces de ayudarlos a prepararse para el próximo paso en su carrera mediante el aprendizaje práctico de primera mano

temporary investments choices that should be reevaluated within a year or less

inversiones temporarias opciones que deberían volver a evaluarse al cabo de un año o menos

tenant a person who rents property (also called renter)

inquilino persona que alquila una propiedad (también llamado locatario)

term life insurance remains in effect for a specified period, such as 20 years; coverage ceases if the insured survives beyond that time with no remaining value; has no savings component

seguro de vida a término fijo permanece vigente por un período determinado, por ejemplo 20 años; la cobertura termina si la persona asegurada vive más allá de ese plazo sin valor remanente; no incluye ningún componente de ahorro

time the period during which the borrower will repay a loan; it is expressed as a fraction of a year

plazo período durante el cual el prestatario devolverá el préstamo; se expresa como fracción de un año

time-shifting refers to recording legally acquired video or audio for later viewing or listening

cambio de tiempo se refiere a la grabación de material de video o audio legalmente adquirido para mirar o escuchar en otro momento

title insurance protects the buyer from any claims arising from a defective title

seguro de título protege al comprador de cualquier reclamo que surja de un título inmobiliario defectuoso

title proof of ownership

título prueba de propiedad

townhouse a type of apartment that has two or more levels

casa urbana adosada tipo de apartamento con dos o más niveles

trade jobs any job whose duties require advanced training and skills often gained through means other than a bachelor's degree

empleo de oficio empleo cuyas tareas requieren capacitación y destrezas avanzadas, comúnmente distintas de las que se adquieren a través de una licenciatura

trade-off getting something in return for giving up something else

intercambio acción por la que se obtiene una cosa a cambio de resignar otra

trade school allows students to learn specific skills related to a technical career

escuela de oficios permite a los estudiantes aprender destrezas específicas relacionadas con una carrera técnica

traditional economic system the people decide what decisions will be made and how they will be made

sistema económico tradicional sistema en el que las personas eligen qué decisiones tomarán y de qué manera lo harán

traditional IRA retirement plan with which you can deduct your contribution each year from your taxable income

cuenta de retiro individual tradicional, o IRA tradicional, plan de retiro en el cual cada año los aportes se pueden deducir de los ingresos imponibles

trespasser an unlawful intruder

intruso persona ingresa ilegalmente a un lugar

trust a legal document in which an individual, called the trustor, gives someone else, called the trustee, control of property for ultimate distribution to another person who is the beneficiary

fideicomiso documento legal en el que un individuo, llamado fiduciante, le otorga a otro, llamado fideicomisario, control de la propiedad para distribuir en última instancia a otra persona, que es la beneficiaria

Truth in Savings Act (TISA) a federal law passed in 1991 and is part of the FDIC Improvement Act of 1991; the purpose of TISA is to promote competition between banks and credit unions by mandating the disclosure of information related to interest rates, fees, and other items associated with banking accounts

Ley de Veracidad en la Información de Ahorros (TISA, en inglés) ley federal aprobada en 1991 que forma parte de la Ley de Perfeccionamiento de la Empresa Federal de Seguros de Depósito (FDIC, en inglés) de 1991; el objetivo de la ley TISA es promover la competencia entre bancos y cooperativas de crédito exigiendo la publicación de información referida a tasas de interés, aranceles y otros datos asociados con cuentas bancarias

U

U.S. savings bond involves loaning funds to the U.S. government that will be repaid with interest at a later date

Bono de Ahorro de los EE. UU. implica prestar fondos al gobierno de los EE. UU., quien luego los devolverá con interés

U.S. Treasury securities debt obligations issued by the U.S. government and are secured by the full faith and credit of the United States (also called Treasuries)

Títulos del tesoro de los EE. UU. obligaciones de deuda emitidas por el gobierno de los EE. UU. garantizadas por la total confiabilidad y crédito de los EE. UU. (también llamados valores del Tesoro)

umbrella liability insurance supplements your basic auto and home liability coverage by expanding limits and including additional risks (also called personal umbrella policy)

cobertura de responsabilidad global complementa la cobertura básica del vehículo y la vivienda expandiendo sus límites e incluyendo riesgos adicionales (también llamada cobertura suplementaria de responsabilidad civil personal)

undergraduate student a student who has not yet earned a bachelor's degree

estudiante universitario estudiante que aún no obtuvo su título de grado o licenciatura

unemployment insurance state-provided insurance that pays a worker who has lost their job and meets the state eligibility requirements for the funds

seguro de desempleo seguro provisto por el estado que se paga a un trabajador que ha perdido su trabajo y reúne los requisitos de elegibilidad estatal para acceder a los fondos

unfurnished rental usually includes basic kitchen appliances, such as a stove and refrigerator, but little else

alquiler no equipado usualmente incluye electrodomésticos de cocina básicos, como estufa y refrigerador, y nada más

uninsured/underinsured motorist coverage auto insurance that pays for injuries to you and your passengers when the other driver is legally liable but unable to pay

cobertura contra conductor no asegurado o subasegurado seguro automotor que paga por las lesiones que puede sufrir una persona o los pasajeros que lleva en su vehículo cuando otro conductor es legalmente responsable pero no puede asumir los costos

uninvited guest someone who is presumed to have permission to be on your property, such as door-to-door solicitors or delivery people

invitado sin invitación persona que supuestamente dispone de permiso para estar en nuestra vivienda, como un vendedor puerta a puerta o un repartidor de comida

union a group of people who work in the same or similar occupations and who are organized to benefit the employees in those occupations

sindicato grupo de personas que comparten la misma ocupación laboral o una similar y están organizadas para beneficiar a los empleados que también tienen esa ocupación

unit pricing tells you how much an item costs per ounce or other unit of measure

precio por unidad indica cuánto cuesta un artículo por onza u otra unidad de medida

United States Department of Agriculture (USDA) responsible for developing and executing federal government policy on farming, agriculture, forestry, and food

Departamento de Agricultura de los EE. UU. (USDA, en inglés) organismo responsable de desarrollar y llevar a cabo políticas relativas a la ganadería, agricultura, silvicultura y alimentación

United States Postal Inspection Service (USPIS) a federal law enforcement agency that investigates consumer problems pertaining to illegal use of the mail

Servicio de Inspección Postal de Estados Unidos (USPIS, por sus siglas en inglés) agencia federal que regula la ley y realiza investigaciones sobre los problemas que afectan a los consumidores en relación con el uso ilegal del correo

university typically larger institutions that offer undergraduate (bachelor's degrees), and advanced degrees (master's and doctoral degrees); the professors teach and conduct research in specialized fields

universidad comúnmente, institución grande que ofrece títulos de grado (licenciaturas) y títulos avanzados (maestrías y doctorados); los profesores enseñan y realizan trabajos de investigación en campos especializados

unmanaged care plans allow participants to choose any doctor and be reimbursed for a percentage of the expenses incurred after a deductible is met (also called fee-for-service plans)

planes de atención médica no administrada permiten a los beneficiarios elegir cualquier médico y recibir un porcentaje de reintegro por los gastos afrontados al costear una franquicia (también llamado planes de pago por servicios)

unsecured credit a credit account that does not require collateral from the consumer

crédito sin garantía cuenta de crédito que no exige garantías al consumidor

unused credit the remaining credit available to you on current accounts; it is your credit limit minus the amount you already owe

crédito sin usar crédito que queda disponible en las cuentas corrientes; es el límite del crédito menos el monto que se adeuda

upgrading advancing to a higher skill level to increase your usefulness to an employer

actualización avance de una persona a un nivel superior de destreza para que aumente su utilidad frente a su empleador

upside-down when you owe more on a car loan than the vehicle is worth

amortización invertida ocurre cuando la cantidad de dinero que se debe por el préstamo del automóvil supera lo que vale el automóvil en sí

Used Car Rule requires that dealers fully disclose to buyers what is and is not covered under warranty for a used vehicle

Regla del vehículo usado requiere que los vendedores revelen claramente a los compradores qué cubre y qué no cubre la garantía de un vehículo usado

usury law a state law that sets a maximum interest rate that may be charged for consumer loans

ley de usura ley estatal que establece la tasa de interés máxima que puede cobrarse para los préstamos a los consumidores

utility a measurement of something's usefulness

utilidad medida de la practicidad de una cosa

V

values the principles by which a person lives

valores principios según los cuales vive una persona

variable expenses costs that vary in amount and type, depending on your choices

gastos variables costos que varían en cantidad y tipo, según las preferencias de cada persona

variable rate cost of credit that changes in response to economic conditions

tasa variable costo del crédito que cambia según las condiciones económicas

variable-rate loan a loan in which the interest rate goes up and down with inflation and other economic conditions; creditors can raise the rates on variable-rate loans and credit cards

préstamo de tasa variable préstamo en el cual la tasa de interés aumenta y disminuye según la inflación y otras condiciones económicas; los acreedores pueden incrementar las tasas sobre los préstamos de tasa variable y las tarjetas de crédito

vehicle emission test verifies that a vehicle meets the minimum clean-air standards

prueba de emisiones vehiculares verifica que un vehículo cumple los estándares mínimos de aire limpio

vehicle identification number (VIN) an alphanumeric number that identifies each vehicle manufactured or sold in the United States

número de identificación vehicular (NIV) código alfanumérico que identifica cada vehículo fabricado y vendido en los EE. UU.

venture business a small business in which business owners want their businesses to grow into large companies with unlimited growth potential

iniciativa comercial negocio pequeño cuyos dueños desean que se convierta en una empresa grande con potencial de crecimiento ilimitado

vested the point at which employees have full rights to their retirement accounts

cumplimiento pleno punto a partir del cual los empleados tienen derecho absoluto de disponer de sus cuentas de retiro

voluntary bankruptcy the most common kind of bankruptcy; occurs when a debtor files a petition with a federal court asking to be declared bankrupt

quiebra voluntaria tipo de quiebra más común; se produce cuando un deudor solicita a un tribunal federal que lo declare en quiebra

voluntary compliance related to taxes, means all citizens prepare and file tax returns on their own

cumplimiento voluntario en relación con los impuestos significa que todos los ciudadanos preparan y presentan por su cuenta la declaración de impuestos

W

wage a fixed hourly rate earned by employees

paga monto fijado por hora que ganan los empleados

waiting period can range from 30 days to 6 months before disability insurance begins (also known as an elimination period)

período de espera tiempo que puede variar entre 30 días y 6 meses antes de que comience a regir el seguro por discapacidad (también conocido como período de carencia)

wants items beyond basic needs that improve your quality of life; although they may be necessary for your happiness, you do not need them for physical survival

artículos deseables cosas que no están relacionadas con las necesidades básicas pero que igualmente mejoran la calidad de vida; aunque pueden ser necesarias para sentirse satisfecho, no son impre-scindibles para la supervivencia física

wealth the accumulation of assets

riqueza acumulación de bienes

will a legal document that tells how an estate is to be distributed when a person dies (also called a testament)

testamento documento legal que establece cómo debe distribuirse el patrimonio de una persona cuando ella muere (también llamado última voluntad)

withholding allowances reductions in the amount of tax withheld from a paycheck; based on income tax filing status

exención de retenciones reducción en la cantidad de impuestos retenidos de un sueldo; se basa en la categoría de declaración impositiva

worker's compensation a form of insurance that covers an employee who has suffered an injury or illness from job-related duties

indemnización laboral tipo de seguro que brinda cobertura a un empleado que ha sufrido una lesión o enfermedad a causa de su trabajo

work-study a federal program that pays you to work part time while in school

programa trabajar y estudiar o-estudio programa federal que paga a los estudiantes por trabajar medio tiempo mientras asisten a la universidad

Y

yield the percentage of increase in the value of your savings due to earned interest

rendimiento porcentaje de incremento en el valor de los ahorros debido al interés ganado

Z

zero-coupon bond a bond that is sold at a deep discount, makes no interest payments, and is redeemable for its face value at maturity

bono cupón cero bono que se vende con un significativo descuento, no paga interés y puede cobrarse por su valor nominal en el momento del vencimiento

Index